Language in the USA

This textbook provides a comprehensive survey of current language issues in the USA. Through a series of specially commissioned chapters by leading scholars, it explores the nature of language variation in the United States and its social, historical, and political significance.

Part 1, "American English," explores the history and distinctiveness of American English, as well as looking at regional and social varieties, African American Vernacular English, and the *Dictionary of American Regional English*. Part 2, "Other language varieties," looks at Creole and Native American languages, Spanish, American Sign Language, Asian American varieties, multilingualism, linguistic diversity, and English acquisition. Part 3, "The sociolinguistic situation," includes chapters on attitudes to language, ideology and prejudice, language and education, adolescent language, slang, Hip Hop Nation Language, the language of cyberspace, doctor–patient communication, language and identity in literature, and how language relates to gender and sexuality. It also explores recent issues such as the Ebonics controversy, the Bilingual Education debate, and the English-Only movement.

Clear, accessible, and broad in its coverage, *Language in the USA* will be welcomed by students across the disciplines of English, Linguistics, Communication Studies, American Studies and Popular Culture, as well as anyone interested more generally in language and related issues.

EDWARD FINEGAN is Professor of Linguistics and Law at the University of Southern California. He has published articles in a variety of journals, and his previous books include *Attitudes toward English Usage* (1980), *Sociolinguistic Perspectives on Register* (co-edited with Douglas Biber, 1994), and *Language: Its Structure and Use*, 4th edn. (2004). He has contributed two chapters on English grammar and usage to the recently completed *Cambridge History of the English Language*.

JOHN R. RICKFORD is Martin Luther King Jr. Centennial Professor of Linguistics, Stanford University, and Director of Stanford University's program in African and Afro-American Studies. He has published articles in a variety of journals, and his previous books include *Dimensions of a Creole Continuum* (1987), *African American Vernacular English* (1999), and *Spoken Soul: the Story of Black English* (co-authored with his son Russell Rickford, 2000). Most recently, he has co-edited with Penelope Eckert *Style and Sociolinguistic Variation* (Cambridge University Press, 2001).

Language in the USA
Themes for the Twenty-first Century

EDWARD FINEGAN

University of Southern California

JOHN R. RICKFORD

Stanford University

CAMBRIDGE
UNIVERSITY PRESS

CAMBRIDGE UNIVERSITY PRESS
Cambridge, New York, Melbourne, Madrid, Cape Town, Singapore, São Paulo

Cambridge University Press
The Edinburgh Building, Cambridge, CB2 2RU, UK

Published in the United States of America by Cambridge University Press, New York

www.cambridge.org
Information on this title: www.cambridge.org/9780521771757

First published 2004
Fifth printing 2006

Printed in the United Kingdom at the University Press, Cambridge

A catalogue record for this book is available from the British Library

Library of Congress Cataloging in Publication data
Language in the USA: Themes for the Twenty-first Century / [edited by] Edward Finegan,
John R. Rickford.
     p.   cm.
ISBN 0 521 77175 7   ISBN 0 521 77747 X (pbk.)
1. United States–Languages.   I. Title: Language in the USA: II. Title: Language in the United States
of America.   III. Finegan, Edward   IV. Rickford, John R.
P377.L33   2004
409′.73 – dc22   2003055819

ISBN-13   978-0-521-77175-7 hardback
ISBN-10   0-521-77175-7 hardback

ISBN-13   978-0-521-77747-6 paperback
ISBN-10   0-521-77747-X paperback

Contents

Part 3 The sociolinguistic situation

Figures

Tables

Contributors

H. Samy Alim, Duke University
Richard W. Bailey, University of Michigan
John Baugh, Stanford University
Robert Bayley, University of Texas at San Antonio
Mary Bucholtz, University of California, Santa Barbara
Connie Eble, University of North Carolina
Penelope Eckert, Stanford University
Lily Wong Fillmore, University of California, Berkeley
Edward Finegan, University of Southern California
Joshua A. Fishman, Yeshiva University (emeritus)
Lisa Green, University of Texas at Austin
Cynthia Hagstrom, California State University, Northridge
Joan Houston Hall, University of Wisconsin, Madison
Thom Huebner, San José State University
William A. Kretzschmar, Jr. University of Georgia
Rosina Lippi-Green, independent scholar and novelist
Ceil Lucas, Gallaudet University
Denise E. Murray, Macquarie University
Patricia Nichols, San José State University (emeritus)
Geoffrey Nunberg, Stanford University
James Peterson, University of Pennsylvania
Dennis R. Preston, Michigan State University
Carmen Silva-Corvalán, University of Southern California
Linda Uyechi, Stanford University
Clayton Valli, Deceased (formerly Georgetown University)
Terrence G. Wiley, Arizona State University
Walt Wolfram, North Carolina State University
Akira Y. Yamamoto, University of Kansas
Ana Celia Zentella, University of California, San Diego
Ofelia Zepeda, University of Arizona

Acknowledgments

With tremendous gratitude, we acknowledge our indebtedness to the many individuals who contributed to this volume: to Kate Brett of Cambridge University Press, who invited us to undertake the work and solicited and interpreted reviews of the prospectus that helped shape the current contents, and who offered all manner of support, including invigorating hikes through the California mountain ranges, and to Andrew Winnard, Lucille Murby, and Helen Barton who guided the volume through its final production stages. Julie Sweetland at Stanford University helped immeasurably with our final proof reading. We extend our appreciation to Geoffrey Nunberg for his foreword to the volume. Above all, we are grateful to the contributing authors, whose expertise and passion for their subjects are evident in every chapter, and we are thankful to those authors who stepped in to write chapters when ill health or other significant setbacks prevented almost half a dozen initial contributors from completing chapters. We especially express our appreciation for the patience authors showed as the book faced delays of various sorts. On a personal note, we are grateful to Angela Rickford and Julian Smalley for support and encouragement throughout the project.

Finally, we wish to dedicate this book to Charles A. Ferguson, a founding father of modern sociolinguistics, who died in 1998, and to his spouse Shirley Brice Heath, who has made and continues to make significant contributions to sociolinguistics and the ethnography of communication.

Foreword

The French are funny about their language, as everyone knows. But then, so are the Germans, the Italians, the Belgians, the Canadians, the Turks, the Slovakians, the Russians, and the Sri Lankans. And so are we in the United States, for that matter, although we tend to make only an intermittent public fuss about it. In many other nations, "the language question" is a persistent topic for newspaper editorials, television talk shows, and parliamentary debates, and occasionally the source of major political crises. In the USA, discussions of language tend to rumble along in Sunday-supplement features and the usage screeds arrayed in the language shelves at the back of the bookstore.

Every so often, though, controversies over the language erupt into a wider national discussion in America. That has happened perhaps half-a-dozen times in the last half century. In the early 1960s, there was a furor over the publication of the Merriam-Webster's *Third New International Dictionary*, which took what critics regarded as an excessively permissive attitude toward usage – it refused to condemn the use of *ain't* for "am not," and it included the "incorrect" use of *like* as a conjunction, as in "Winston tastes good like a cigarette should." The dictionary's derelictions were front-page news for months – *The New York Times* condemned it as a "bolshevik" document, and the *Chicago Daily News* took it as the symptom of "a general decay in values."

Other recent American language controversies have followed more or less the same pattern – they flare into wide discussion for a relatively brief period, and then, when the point is made, they subside again into the back pages of the national consciousness. From the 1960s onward, for example, there has been a series of debates sparked by efforts to reform the English vocabulary in the interest of social justice, some of them involving the feminist program of eliminating sexist usage, and some involving the introduction of new terms to describe groups defined by race, ethnicity, physical condition, sexual orientation, and the like.

Then there was the English-Only movement, which received a huge amount of national attention from the mid-1980s onward, as several groups tried to have English declared the official language of the country and eliminate bilingual programs and services. The campaign resulted in the adoption of English-Only measures by a number of states, and continues today in the form of state initiatives aimed at ending bilingual education.

In December of 1996, the great "Ebonics" controversy was set off when a local school board in Oakland, California announced it would be adopting a new approach to helping inner-city African American students to master standard English. The program was widely but inaccurately reported as recognizing African American English – or "Ebonics," the term used by the school board – as a legitimate language of instruction, and as rejecting the need for students to master the standard language. The resulting controversy raged for months, as virtually every major newspaper editorialized against the Oakland program, and cartoonists and Internet wags had a field day with Ebonics jokes.

Those affairs remind us that while we Americans like to think of ourselves as easy-going about language, our feelings about it actually run very deep, and it can take only the slightest pretext to arouse our national passions – the appearance of a new dictionary, the adoption of a speech code at a university, or the action of a local school board. In fact, a certain forgetfulness about the importance of language is one of the abiding characteristics of American language attitudes – every language controversy seems unprecedented.

There are historical reasons for this. The United States hasn't had a continuously tumultuous linguistic history in the way many other nations have. We have always had a single dominant language – and a relatively homogeneous one, without the major divisions of dialects that most European nations have had to deal with in the course of their nation-building. American English may have notable regional and class differences, but they are nowhere near as broad as the differences that have separated the regional varieties of nations like France, Germany, or Italy. And while there are some varieties that depart substantially from the standard English pattern, they have been spoken by marginal or disempowered groups, so haven't been deemed worthy of serious consideration by the mainstream media until recently.

True, America has never been without large communities of speakers of languages other than English – indigenous peoples, the language groups absorbed in the course of colonial expansion, like the French-speakers of Louisiana and the Hispanics of the Southwest, and the great flows of immigrants in the period between 1880 and 1920 and over the past thirty years or so. And from the eighteenth century onward there have been energetic efforts to discourage or suppress the use of other languages. But these episodes have generally been local or regional rather than national affairs, and interest in them has generally waned as language minorities became anglicized or as waves of immigration decreased.

It isn't surprising, then, that assimilated English-speaking Americans are apt to take the dominance of standard English for granted – and, often, to become irritated when linguistic diversity obtrudes itself. "This is America – speak English," people complain, with the implication that the identification of English with American national identity was always unproblematic and natural before recent times, and that earlier generations of immigrants eagerly abandoned their native languages for English in the interest of becoming "true Americans." That has become a central element of American linguistic mythology, and it helps to explain why English-speaking Americans tend to think of the mastery of a foreign language not just as a difficult accomplishment, but as a suspicious one. Teaching students a foreign language, the Nebraska Supreme Court opined eighty years ago, must "naturally inculcate in them the ideas and sentiments foreign to the best interests of their country." While few people today would put that point so baldly, a great many people still have the sense that a loyal American can't serve two linguistic masters.

That attitude contributes to many Americans' readiness to support English-only measures and to believe claims that America is faced with a "dangerous drift toward bilingualism." By the same token, Americans become indignant when they believe that a school board is maintaining that a nonstandard variety is "just as good" as the standard language, when everyone has been taught since the seventh grade that features like the "double negative" are illogical forms of speech.

In fact these are just two signs of a chronic American blindness to the complexities of our sociolinguistic history and of the contemporary linguistic situation. As the anthropological linguist Dell Hymes observed more than twenty years ago in his foreword to the 1981 *Language in the USA*, "The United States is a country rich in many things, but poor in knowledge of itself with regard to language."

Since then, to be sure, there has been an enormous amount of scholarship and research that has illumined the variety and richness of the American linguistic scene, much of which is summarized and explained in the chapters of this book. These questions aren't restricted to the role of languages other than English and the status of the minority language varieties like African American English or the ongoing efforts to preserve Native American languages. They also extend to the particular problems faced by the users of American Sign Language, to the efforts of groups to forge linguistic identities for themselves, and to the challenges faced by anyone who speaks English with an accent that happens to be stigmatized.

These questions have become far more urgent over the past twenty years. Courts, legislatures, government agencies, corporations, public officials, college administrators – there's scarcely a sector of American life that hasn't found itself having to make complex decisions about language policies and programs, as the United States tries to come to terms with the challenges of diversity. Too often, people respond to these issues by appealing to "common sense" ideas about language, which usually amount to no more than myths and folklore. Indeed, to linguists who have studied these questions, most of these "everyday common sense" ideas about language sound very much the way an appeal to "everyday common sense" ideas about inflation would sound to an economist – they're hardly the grounds that you would want to rely on for making policy.

But an understanding of language diversity is important for other reasons, as well. As the chapters in this *Language in the USA* make clear, there is virtually no important social issue or cultural development in American life that isn't somehow signaled in language. The changing consciousness of gender roles, the emergence of hip hop culture, the development of new communications media like the Internet, the sociology of adolescence – all of these phenomena have a linguistic side that isn't significant just for its own sake, but sheds a particular light on the social phenomenon it's connected to.

In the end, that's the greatest cost of the conventional ideas and attitudes that people tend to bring to language. If you come to language with the ready-made categories that society prepares for you – "good" and "bad," "correct" and "incorrect," and the like – you will almost certainly be deaf to its complexities and subtleties.

Take the various uses of the word *like* that have become popular among adolescents and, increasingly, among other speakers as well: "I was like standing there and she like came up to me," or "So I was like, Hello?" To listen to a lot of columnists and critics, *like* is no more than a meaningless noise or the sign of an alarming decline in communication skills among adolescents. But charges like that are always self-deceptive – do those critics really mean to claim that they spoke in polished, slang-free sentences when *they* were teenagers? Worse still, they miss the point. As shown in a chapter of this book, *like* is actually doing a subtle kind of conversational work in adolescents' speech, one you can attend to only if you are willing to set your linguistic preconceptions aside.

Language in the USA will unquestionably be an important resource for policy-makers and decision-makers, and it should make us all better citizens, attuned to the sociolinguistic complexities of the contemporary American scene. But perhaps my greatest hope for the book is that it will help to make us all better *listeners*, as well – both to the diverse voices around us and to our own.

Geoffrey Nunberg

Preface

It is almost a quarter of a century since Cambridge University Press published *Language in the USA*, edited by Charles A. Ferguson and Shirley Brice Heath. In his foreword to the 1981 volume, Dell Hymes noted that it was "the first book to address the situation of language in the United States as something to be known comprehensively and constantly to be better known." Since then, *Language in the USA* has come to be widely used and appreciated as a resource for students of language, for teachers, and for a general public seeking a comprehensive, accessible introduction to the linguistic richness and variability of the United States.

While deeply inspired and influenced by *Language in the USA*, the present volume is not intended as a revised edition of the original, and even less as a replacement for it. Several chapters in the original have become classics in their own right. Others are timeless. Even those that seem less relevant now are of historical interest. We plan to draw on both volumes in our classes, and we believe other readers will also want to retain the resources of both. Only four of the original *Language in the USA* authors (Fishman, Nichols, Wolfram, and Zentella) recur in this book, and in each case they do so with new chapters.

The purpose of this new volume is to take a similarly comprehensive, but necessarily selective, look at language in the USA, but through the lenses of today's issues and contemporary developments – ones that characterize the beginning of the twenty-first century. Since 1981, there have been significant changes in the sociolinguistic and political situation in the USA, and we have gained greater understanding about language and language variation in American society. We are certainly more conscious today of multilingualism and dialect variation and their educational and sociopolitical implications, as witnessed by recent public controversies, political campaigns, and state ballot initiatives centered on these issues. And while our nation is an older nation now, it is infused with extraordinary linguistic vitality from the everyday talk of adolescents and the words and music of hip hop artists.

Some of our chapter titles are brand new simply because their subject matter was completely or virtually non-existent a quarter of a century ago, as with the chapters treating the language of cyberspace, rap and hip hop, the Oakland Ebonics controversy, the English-Only movement, and the *Dictionary of American Regional English*. Other phenomena discussed in the present volume but not the 1981 volume did exist earlier (as with American Sign Language, Asian American voices, adolescent language, and the relationships among language and gender and sexuality), but they were not then as salient, not then as well studied, and not then recognized as of such theoretical or social significance as they are today. Still others (such as issues having to do with language and education, especially bilingual education) are discussed in both volumes, but dramatic new developments like the passage of Proposition 227 in California (in 1998) and Proposition 203 in Arizona (in 2000) have become focal points for significant educational, political, and legal debate and warrant the additional focus on them here.

Other changes include the fact that we now treat Spanish in two chapters (instead of one) and that Spanish is highlighted in other chapters, in recognition of its increased prominence throughout the United States. *Language in the USA: Themes for the Twenty-first Century* also has three general chapters on English dialects instead of one, with separate chapters on regional and social variation, and a chapter dealing exclusively with the *Dictionary of American Regional English*. Contrary to the possible perceptions or hopes of some, dialect variation is not disappearing in the USA.

The chapters in this book are grouped into three broad sections: Part 1, dealing with varieties of American English; Part 2, exploring other language varieties in the USA (including creole and Native American varieties, and Spanish on the East Coast and the West); and Part 3, focusing on the sociolinguistic situation (including language ideology, language attitudes, slang, the language of doctors and patients, the representation of ethnic identity in literature). Our introductions appear at the head of each chapter, and it is our hope that this placement will invite more student readers than might be drawn to introductions grouped together at the beginning of the volume or preceding each section.

Language in USA: Themes for the Twenty-first Century is a shorter book than the 1981 volume, despite its having a few more chapters. The marketing constraint on its length meant omitting certain topics we would otherwise have included. Inevitably, some readers will miss topics that were treated in the earlier volume but not here. We hope that all readers will find favorite chapters in the current volume and that its perspectives will launch inquiries into topics of interest among student readers, policy makers, and the educated public. In his foreword, Dell Hymes described the 1981 volume as "a resource to citizens, a spur to scholars, a challenge to those who shape policy and public life." We believe that description has turned out to be accurate, and we believe the content of the current volume is much enriched by the spur the original volume provided.

John R. Rickford   Edward Finegan

PART 1

American English

1

American English: its origins and history

RICHARD W. BAILEY

Editors' introduction

This chapter explores the origins and history of American English, with an underlying focus on its linguistic diversity. *Guaiacum*, taken from the Taino language in the Bahamas in 1533, was the first American word to enter the English language. But, as Richard W. Bailey notes, English speakers migrating to the North American mainland and the Caribbean from the seventeenth century on had many other contacts with Native American languages, and influences from Native American languages on American English vocabulary were extensive. They include words like *chocolate*, *canoe*, and *powwow*, which have survived to the present day, and words like *mangummenauk* (an edible acorn) and *netop* ('a good friend'), which have not survived.

This chapter surveys the population growth and linguistic development of the USA century by century, repeatedly acknowledging the inputs from its various ethnic strands: for example, *bogus* (African), *juke-box* (African American), *cookie* (Dutch), *bayou* (French), *macaroni* (Italian), *geisha* (Japanese), *vigilante* (Spanish), *lutefish* (Swedish), and *bagel* (Yiddish). American English is more than the sum of inheritances from its input languages, of course, and this chapter details its many innovations, including initialisms like *AIDS*, manufactured words like *Kleenex*, derived forms like *antinuclear*, compounds like *rock star*, and shortenings like *bra*.

But at the heart of the story throughout is the relative multilingualism and multidialectalism of the USA and its corresponding linguistic attitudes and ideologies. In the seventeenth century, for instance, pidgin-like varieties of English were exemplified among both Amerindian and African speakers, and there was open respect for linguistic diversity and substantial interest in it. By the late eighteenth century, the USA was highly multilingual, more so than the average European nation then or now, and accommodations were being made in schools and churches for non-English varieties, German and Mohawk among them. But in the immigration-restricted half-century that followed World War I, the USA was more monolingual than ever, and multilingualism became "unpatriotic." Another issue this chapter traces across the centuries is how different American English is – and how different it should be – from British English. The fear that the two varieties would drift away to the point of mutual unintelligibility has proved to be unfounded, and American English combines both vibrant diversity and relative commonality.

"O my America, my new found land" wrote John Donne in the 1590s in a sensuous comparison of his mistress's nakedness with the "late discoveries" made on the far western shore of the Atlantic. English adventurers had penetrated the mystery of the North American continent and had brought back wonders – animals and plants unknown in England, and even people, Manteo and Wanchese, Amerindians brought to Queen Elizabeth's court as part of the bounty of Walter Raleigh's 1585 voyage to Roanoke Island in present-day North Carolina. Those who missed the opportunity of introducing themselves to these visitors could read the whole story in Thomas Harriot's *Briefe and True Report of the New Found Land of Virginia* (1588). Modern enthusiasts for the details of space aliens merely continue the excitement these "new" people and their exotic homeland aroused in Britain four hundred years ago.

America was reflected in the English language half a century before these first-hand contacts, however. The first word of American origin to reach English was *guaiacum*. That word took a roundabout route from the Taino language of the Bahamas where it was used for a tropical plant and the medicine derived from its resin. In 1519, it appeared in a Latin medical treatise by Ulrich von Hutten, who regarded *guaiacum* as a cure for an affliction he suffered himself, a mysterious sickness associated with the siege of Naples that had ended in 1495 but was actually an export from the new world to the old. When the disease reached England, it was known as the *French pox* (the earliest known citation of this phrase is from 1503), and it was a devastating infirmity. By 1510, it had claimed ten million victims, a huge share of the world population at the time. Naturally there was great interest in finding a cure, and von Hutten identified, correctly, that the disease came from Columbus's first voyages to the Caribbean. He even was able to discern the Spanish mispronunciation of the Taino word; the Spanish write *guaiacum*, he said, but "the people of that yland pronounce with open mouthe Huaicum." Thomas Paynell, an advocate of scientific works in English rather than in Latin, translated von Hutten's book, and so, in 1533, *guaiacum* became the first word of American origin to enter the language. (Not until 1686, in a translation from an Italian poem, did English acquire another name for the disease *guaiacum* was supposed to cure, one taken from the name of the shepherd-hero of the work, *syphilis*.)

When speakers of English began to arrive on American shores to create permanent settlements, they found themselves in a very diverse linguistic culture. Historians of the language have interpreted the evidence very selectively and have offered as evidence of cultural contacts among the many languages of early America the borrowings from indigenous languages that have survived into modern usage. *Chocolate, canoe, iguana, tobacco, tomato* and other such words from the Caribbean and known everywhere suggest wonderment at the novelty of the American landscape and the things found in it. As evidence of how early American English reveals the experience of English settlers, however, they give a skewed and misleading picture. Other similarly exotic words were used in English and then disappeared. Thomas Harriot's book about Virginia has seventy-six of them, including *openayk* (a kind of potato) and *sacquenummener* (cranberry). Such words as these were used on an equal footing with *chocolate* and *tomato*, and it was not obvious at the time which would survive and which vanish. If we look at *all* the words used by the colonists, a richer and more varied language community begins to appear.

Language history, then, has tended to select examples that have two qualities: features that reached and were used in a metropolitan center (in our case, London) and those that endured for two or many generations. But this approach is far too selective. For the people living at the time of American settlement, there was no way to foresee that *moccasin* would endure and *mangummenauk* (an edible acorn) would not. The history of the language needs to look not only at the center and the enduring, but also at the edges and at the evanescent. We need, in short, to look at how people used the linguistic resources available to them to interpret their experience and to communicate with others.

When people find themselves in a situation of "mixed languages," they behave in ways that are remarkably the same over time. Some are resolute in their mono-lingualism, refusing to even attempt to communicate with people who speak other dialects or languages. These people breed the linguistic attitude of *purism* and flatly reject any usages that they detect as being "foreign." Thus, in the nineteenth century, one English purist hated the foreign and "obscure" words of learned people and proposed that *witcraft* (which sounds so English) be used instead of the foreign word *logic*, and he thought that *birdlore* sounded far better than *ornithology*. In the twentieth century, a writer with similar views wanted to get rid of *piano* and replace it with *keyed-hammer-string*. (This peculiar preference for native words he called "Blue-Eyed English.") Other people become quite thor-oughly multilingual, and can switch from one language (or dialect) to another with barely a trace to show which language (or dialect) is their "mother tongue." Most people, however, find themselves someplace between these two extremes: they know a "little" of another language (or dialect) and can use it to effect. Sometimes these touches of the "other" kind of speech are used in cruel jokes that assert the superiority of one way of speaking over another; sometimes they show a striving after a "real" command of that language (or dialect) as people attempt to "pass" for members of the community they revere. But even these people whose language reflects vicious hatred or excessive devotion to a culture other than their own are a minority.

Most of us seek to compromise linguistic differences and to tolerate diversity. If one person says *pail* and the other *bucket*, they may get along fine without giving up their preferences. In time, one term may begin to displace another and for many reasons. One may seem more "old-fashioned" and the other more "up-to-date." (Linguistic history often discerns that the apparently new and the actually old may be the same thing.) One may seem "rustic" (however that complex term is valued) and the other "cosmopolitan." One may seem "polite" and the other "rude." One may seem "evasive" and the other "frank." All of these ideas about the meanings of words (or grammatical structures or pronunciations) influence what will happen in the future, and it would be foolish to predict which of the two (or several) alternatives will prevail.

Language variety (which is everywhere) consists of a series of approximations, simplifications, and other negotiated differences. Linguistic historians, unfortunately, have often tried to make more sense of the history entrusted to them than the record allows. Our hindsight blinds us to how the past resembles the present. We demand that people speak to us in our "own language" at the same time we willingly (and even enthusiastically) yearn to communicate in the different and very attractive languages (or dialects) of those whom we admire. Emulation and disdain enter into a complex, and unpredictable, set of forces, and everyone (except the resolute monolinguals) participates. Categories like *koiné*, *contact language*, *lingua franca*, *mixed language*, *pidgin*, and *creole* are offered to make sense of what is quite normal: variety. We all speak "English" but no two of us speak it in the same way.

When English speakers came to America, they encountered a new context, and where there were the most languages there was the greatest mingling of them – in ways that still influence English. Nowhere was this mixture greater than in the Caribbean, and, just as English speakers had acquired *guaiacum* at second hand, so new words from the Caribbean entered English before English mariners had actually been there: *cocos* (later *coconut*), *flamingo*, and *furacane* (later *hurricane*) in the 1550s and 1560s. When they did arrive, they found themselves in *palavers* or conversations involving many languages, and from these talks words of American origin entered English with or without the mediation of the earlier arriving Spanish and Portuguese. Seaports and shipboard were where these conversations took place, and the ports of call were in Europe, in the Caribbean, and in West Africa from Sierra Leone to Benin. This long coast of Africa was called *guinea*, and the things associated with it, whether in Africa or America, sometimes had names involving that word – for instance *guinea pea* and *guinea pepper* (= *cayenne*), both in use before permanent settlements of English people had been established on the North American continent. But it was not just Amerindians and Africans who contributed to American English. Mariners and settlers began to speak with the Dutch in ways they never had before when they were separated from them by only a few miles of saltwater (thus giving the "Americanism" *cookie*) or with the Spanish (giving the "Americanism" *cockroach*) or with the Germans (giving the "Americanism" *cole slaw*).

These words, and others like them, did not arise as isolated examples but as part of a rich and diverse communicative context. Some of them were selected because they named things genuinely new to the colonizing English speakers, particularly names for unfamiliar animals (like the *skunk*) or plants (like the *pecan*). Some of these were drastically adapted from the Amerindian languages at their source – so, for instance, early documents in English refer to a vegetable written down as *isquontersquash*, which was soon reduced to *squash*, and the *wejack* acquired a simplified English spelling that seemed to make a sort of sense, *woodchuck*. Others were new applications of old words (like *robin*, though the English robin is a quite different bird) or of combinations of words (like *bluefish* for a succulent and new kind of seafood abounding in Atlantic waters).

It would be wrong, however, to presume that borrowing and adapting words was based on logic, some need to fill "gaps" with new labels when new experiences arise to conscious attention. In fact, change involving the intersection of two (or many) languages is not logical at all. Many new American English expressions emerged at the very center of speaking. *Netop*, for instance, was a word borrowed from one of the Algonquian languages of New England to express the idea of "a good friend," an idea that hardly needed a new term in English. An author in 1890, when most Native Americans had been exterminated or expelled from New England, recalled: "Fifty years ago, in New England, this word [*netop*] was not very uncommon among the older people. It meant a close friend, a chum, a companion." Early documents show that *netop* was a familiar term in the earliest days of colonization and was used by people with scant knowledge of Native American languages (or none).

European curiosity about the "new world" extended to the languages spoken there. In 1502, a Bristol merchant brought to England the first known Native American visitor (who, as was tragically common, soon succumbed to some European disease), and, after a half century of indifference, yet more were brought across the Atlantic to be inspected and studied. The great flowering of interest in languages, particularly ancient ones, in sixteenth-century England, fed curiosity about these newly encountered ones. (Since the biblical story of Babel was a firm foundation of belief, part of the inquiry was to discover if these North Americans might be a "lost tribe" and to see if their languages might resemble Hebrew, Syriac, or some other language of the biblical era.) Early in the next century, at least two English boys, Tom Savage and Henry Spelman, were sent as hostages to guarantee the return of some Native Americans of Virginia from a visit to England. They soon became bilinguals and were thus positioned to act as intermediaries between the two cultures. Through such persons, Native American influence on American English was much facilitated.

When Thomas Harriot arrived in Virginia in 1586, he already knew something about the language spoken there from many months' study with Manteo and Wanchese, the visitors brought to England the year before. (Wanchese was an unwilling guest, but Manteo was enthusiastic and was eagerly baptized. On their return to Virginia, Wanchese escaped to his tribal group, but Manteo – now known as "John White" – continued to act as an intermediary.) Harriot was a man of remarkable genius, particularly in mathematics, and in preparation for the Roanoke voyage he taught Walter Raleigh the rudiments of celestial navigation so the expedition might find its way in the open ocean. As the principal scientist among the adventurers, he presented a remarkable amount of information in his *Briefe and True Report*, and a page of his phonetic alphabet to represent the sounds of the language has only recently been discovered. Unfortunately most of Harriot's papers were destroyed in the great fire of London in 1666, but it is at least symbolic that the one complete sentence in Algonquian that survives in his hand is *Kecow hit tamen*, which he translated as "What is this?" (see Salmon 1996).

The arrival of the so-called "Pilgrims" in Massachusetts in 1620 brought town-dwellers into harsh contact with the American wilderness. Once again, bilinguals were present to bridge the communication barrier, this time in the persons of Squanto and Samoset. Squanto had been kidnapped from Cape Cod and had spent time in England; Samoset, from Maine, knew "some broken English" from contact with English fisherfolk who had been making seasonal voyages to the rich harvests of fish along the coast. As with Harriot's visit, relatively few of the expressions noticed by the immigrants from England endured (*wigwam* and *powwow* are two that did) but the *Thanksgiving* celebrated at the Plymouth Colony in 1621 eventually (and much later) evolved a special American holiday.

Roger Williams, a colonist who arrived in Massachusetts in 1631, provided the first thorough and published attempt to record Amerindian languages. Williams was expelled from Plymouth in 1635 for "new and dangerous ideas" and estab-lished a colony in modern Rhode Island – as he described it, halfway between the French (in present-day Canada) and the Dutch (in modern New York). In his *Key into the Language of America* (1643: 53), he propounded a radical idea: "*Boast not proud* English, *of thy birth & Blood,/Thy brother* Indian *is by birth as Good*." In the preface, he describes the death-bed conversation he had with a close friend, a Pequot named Wequash. As a seventeenth-century clergyman, Williams had a clear notion of the right way to die, and he exhorted Wequash to repent his misdeeds in life. Wequash replied: "Me so big naughty Heart, me heart all one stone." In these two sentences are revealed some aspects of the interlanguage that developed between Europeans and Native Americans: simplification of the pronoun system (so that *me* covers the territory of *I*, *me*, and *my*), deletion of forms of *be* (so that *is* does not appear in "me heart all one stone"), and general-ization of some words (so that *naughty* covers territory usually discriminated into *sinful*, *wicked*, *evil*, *bad*, and other synonyms). For the most part, these various interlanguages had little long-term effect on American English, though the idea they represent is still current (in, for instance, "Me Tarzan, You Jane").

Barbados, in the Caribbean, offers an illuminating picture of the language mixture found on American shores. Established as an English colony in 1627, the island was a center for tobacco growing, a profitable crop for the newly addicted Britons. By 1642, the population had increased to 37,000, most of them indentured servants from the impoverished regions of England, Scotland, and Ireland, but some of them petty criminals, prostitutes, captured rebels from Ireland, and other persons not wanted at home. In the 1640s, proprietors discerned that sugar cane was a more profitable crop than tobacco, but the indentured servants and the others were unwilling to engage in the harsh work required to cultivate it. The solution was to import African slaves for the cane fields and to drive the white settlers away (many of them going to Jamaica or Virginia and the Carolinas). Departure and disease reduced the European-descended part of the population in Barbados, and the importation of Africans vastly increased.

By the time an English traveler arrived to report on conditions there, Barbados had been transformed so that Africans outnumbered Europeans by two to one.

Richard Ligon, publishing his book in 1657, offered three reasons to explain why a slave revolt had not taken place. The first two involved severity of treatment and public demonstrations of gunfire; the third showed that there was a severe language policy in place.

> Besides these, there is a third reason, which stops all designes of that kind, and that is, They are fetch'd from severall parts of *Africa*, who speak severall languages, and by that means, one of them understands not another: For some of them are fetch'd from *Guinny* and *Binny*, some from *Cutchew*, some from *Angola*, and some from the River of *Gambra*.   (Ligon 1657: 46)

Of course no such policy of mixing people of differing languages could have any long-term effect, and English (in a form soon nearly unrecognizable to new arrivals) was the core language to which all the others contributed. And the model for English was not that of London but the one spoken in the outlying districts of England and of Scotland and Ireland. (Writing in 1655, an English law lord noted, "The prisoners of the Tower shall, 'tis said, be Barbadozz'd" – that is, exiled to Barbados – and these prisoners were unlikely to have spoken the prestige dialect of the day.) Despite the turmoil of exile to and exodus from Barbados, some of these features of English endured. For instance, the word *screel* 'scream' is still found only in three places in the English-speaking world: Scotland, Northern Ireland, and Barbados. Even today, pronouncing the consonant *r* after vowels (as in *fur* and *first*) is typical of Barbados, though not of Jamaica or of the southeastern part of the United States. This feature thus links Barbados to other parts of the Americas settled by Scots and Irish – for instance, eastern Canada and Appalachia.

More deliberate mixture of languages is well illustrated in the 1663 translation of the Bible by John Eliot into Natick, the language he encountered in colonial Massachusetts. This remarkable volume "introduced" to speakers of Algonquian the English word *Biblum* 'Bible' and a host of names like *Abraham*, *Isaac*, *Beersheba*, and other "exotic" terms borrowed into English from Hebrew. In these words, Eliot supplied the community he wanted to make literate (and Christian) with "foreign" words. But he also needed to interpret the pastoral culture of the biblical era to hunter-gatherers of the New England forest. How was he to translate *sheep* for a people who had only seen these animals grazing in their English-speaking neighbors' pastures? He used, of course, the term that the Native Americans had already heard, *sheep*, and from that borrowing he offered *s[h]ephausuonk* 'lamb' and *shepsoh* 'shepherd.' He also embedded English words in Algonquian grammar: 'wut*angel*sumoh God' (an "angel of the Lord") and '*horse*sumoh *Pharoh*' ("horsemen of *Pharaoh*"; italics added). Eliot was a wise and sensitive man, and he recognized that his intended audience did not categorize foreign farm animals as did his immigrant neighbors. So when he came to render the *cattle* that occupied the stable where Jesus was born, he called them what his Natick-speaking hearers (and readers) called them: *horses*.

Efforts like those of Williams and Eliot to place Native Americans and English people on an equal footing were not enduring. About 1674, Daniel Gookin, named

"Superintendent of the Indians in Massachusetts," wrote a proposal to English philanthropists to abandon efforts to make the native peoples literate in their own languages and to pursue "with all industry and diligence" the goal of encouraging them "to speak, read, and write the English tongue." Consequently, borrowings from the languages of the Atlantic seaboard diminished, but new American expressions continued to arise from the existing resources of the language: for instance, *Indian corn* (shortly reduced to *corn* and applied to a plant unknown in Britain), *husk* (the verb to describe removing the outer leaves from the ear), *roasting ears*, *Indian cake* (made from *corn meal*).

At the end of the seventeenth century, language variety was everywhere. Tituba, a central figure in the Salem witch trials in 1691–92, was a Barbadian living as a slave in the household of Samuel Parris in Massachusetts, and her "confession" precipitated the arrest of more than 150 people and the execution of nineteen of them. Her English shows only the slightest trace of her Caribbean origin, but a trace nonetheless.

> Q. "What Covenant did you make w'th that man that Came to you?
>   What did he tell you."
> TITUBA: "he Tell me he god."

> (Breslaw 1996: 195)

Though the first Africans had come to the North American colonies in 1619, there is very little evidence of the languages they used or the English they came to speak. A fleeting example is found in a discussion of smallpox inoculation in a medical work by Cotton Mather and written in 1721. Mather learned about inoculation from an African servant of his, and then enlarged that knowledge by corresponding with medical authorities abroad. But the most persuasive voices were African.

> I have since mett with a Considerable Number of these *Africans*, who all agree in one Story; That in their Countrey *grandy-many* dy of the *Small-Pox*: But now they Learn this Way: People take Juice of *Small-Pox*; and cutty-skin, and putt in a Drop; then by'nd by a little *sicky, sicky*: then very few little things like *Small-Pox*; and no body dy of it; and no body have *Small-Pox* any more. (Mather 1972: 107)

Details of Mather's linguistic mimicry still survive in Caribbean English: *bambye* 'a little later,' *cut i skin* 'cut their skin,' *grandy-many* 'very many' (parallel to present-day *Granman* 'chieftain'), *sicky, sicky* (repetition of words to intensify the meaning as in *stupid-stupid* 'very stupid') (see Allsopp 1966).

In 1600, there had been no English speakers permanently resident in North America; by 1700, there were 250,000 persons of European and African origin. The eighteenth century, however, was one of astonishing growth, and by 1780 (when the Atlantic colonies freed themselves from the British monarchy) there were 2.8 million. (The share of the African American population increased from 10 percent to 20 percent in the same eighty-year period.) As settlements formed into communities and some communities into cities, linguistic variety increased. At the time of the revolution, more than a fifth of European-Americans had some mother tongue other than English. As the century drew to a close, Americans of European origin formed themselves into distinct language communities. Some 17 percent of the population of New York and New Jersey was Dutch; 9 percent of Delaware was Swedish; and a third of the population of Pennsylvania was German. In the Northwest Territories, 57 percent of the European-descended population was French, and in Georgia 30 percent were from Scotland and Ireland.

There was no question that English would be the language of the new republic – despite a persistent myth to the contrary – but these linguistic and ethnic communities were far more diverse than any nation-state in Europe. It is surprising, in fact, that there is not more evidence in present-day English of this diversity. *Fardowns* (people from the north of Ireland) and *Corkonians* (from the south of it) were well-represented in the language community of the early republic, and Dutch and Germans gave some of their customs (and the names for them) to the national culture – for instance, *Santa Claus* from Dutch and *Kriss Kringle* from German. Isolation (self-sought or imposed) to some extent kept these communities apart.

Individual words distinctive of American English in the eighteenth century are not difficult to identify: *banjo* and *bogus* (from African sources), *bayou* and *portage* (from French), *cookie* and *cruller* (from Dutch), *caucus* and *barbecue* (from Amerindian languages). But they are mere remnants of what was once a language community of rich diversity. Few institutions promoted linguistic stability over large areas. Literacy levels were low, books scarce, and newspapers uncommon. Newcomers felt no reluctance about changing the names of the places they inhabited to fit new circumstances. In 1663, English speakers from Connecticut marched into New Amsterdam and, on the very day of their conquest, re-named it *New York*. *Wall Street* in that city conceals its Dutch origin; there was no wall there when it was laid out but a community of Walloons. But Dutch was not swept away. Writing in 1756, one observer of New York reported: "English is the most prevailing Language amongst us, but not a little corrupted by the *Dutch* Dialect, which is still so much used in some Counties, that the Sheriffs find it difficult to obtain Persons sufficiently acquainted with the English Tongue, to serve as Jurors in the Courts of Law" (quoted by Read 1937: 97).

Were readers of this chapter to be transported by time machine to the American colonies at the time of the revolution, they would find themselves in communities with as many languages (if not more) than any modern city in the same region. In 1753, Benjamin Franklin had lambasted the Germans in Pennsylvania: "Those who come hither are generally the most stupid of their own nation . . . ; and as few of the English would understand the German language and so cannot address them either from the press or pulpit, it is almost impossible to remove any prejudices they may entertain" (quoted by Heath 1981: 9–10). Yet Franklin's bigoted views did not prevail, and until the beginning of this century American schools offered instruction in German, recognizing as the US Commissioner of Education had written in 1870, "the German language has actually become the second language of our Republic" (Heath 1981: 13).

German was not the only alternative to English, of course. The Reverend Benjamin Mortimer, a Moravian pastor in New York City, traveled in 1798 to what is now Brantford in southern Ontario where a large Mohawk community had formed after the disruption of the American revolution:

> A church, with a handsome steeple, has lately been erected here by order of the British government. Here the service of the English church is read every Sunday, by an Indian, in the Mohawk language, and an English sermon, interpreted into Mohawk, is preached twice a year, by a minister from Newark, who afterwards administers the sacraments. The Indian church is well attended, both by the Indians and white people, and the greatest order is preserved.   (Doyle 1980: 30)

Translations of service books and biblical passages into Mohawk were approvingly noted by Mortimer.

Even within English-speaking communities, there was diversity to be heard based on origin and social class. Writing in Maryland in 1773, Jonathan Boucher expressed dismay: "What is still less credible is, that at least two-thirds of the little education we receive are derived from instructors, who are either *indented servants*, or *transported felons*" (Read 1938: 70). (Vast numbers of British convicts were routinely transported to America before 1780; Australia was founded as a penal colony since the newly formed United States was no longer willing to admit them.) Advertising for immigrants who ran away from their indentures before completing them routinely mentioned distinctive English dialects: West Country, Yorkshire, Scotland, and Ireland – for instance, "Run away . . . Isaac Baxter . . . a little pock marked, and by his dialect may be known to be a native of the north of Ireland" (quoted with many other examples by Read 1938). Americans of the time took pride in the "uniformity" of their English over great distances, but this comparison was measured against the much greater diversity of the British Isles over a smaller territory.

At the beginning of the nineteenth century, two views emerged about the distinctiveness of American English. For patriots, especially Noah Webster, it was obvious that an independent nation should have an independent language – even if it was only a variety of English. Most intellectuals believed that there was a direct connection between language and "civilization," and for Webster a monarchy would produce one kind of language and a republic another. Hence Americans ought to foster language change and to embrace new terms like *senate* or *White House* as expressive of a distinctive political culture. But Webster's was the radical view, and conservatives worried that English would fall into mutually unintelligible languages (just as Latin, after the collapse of the Roman empire, had disintegrated into French, Spanish, Portuguese, Italian, and other Romance languages). The most influential of these conservatives was John Pickering who, in 1816, published a "collection of words and phrases" that had been identified in

Britain as "Americanisms." His book, he hoped, would assist Americans in avoid-ing them. He was accurate about what had happened: "We have formed some *new* words; and to some *old* ones, that are still used in England, we have affixed *new significations*: while others, which have long been *obsolete* in England, are still retained *in common use* with us" (Mathews 1931: 67). But Pickering defended a few words in his list of 500 usages – for instance, *barbecue* – and many others are now unfamiliar or unknown – for example, *clitchy* 'sticky' and *quackle* 'almost to choke'. Even so, Pickering led the way for a succession of others, often British visitors to North America, in asserting that American English ought not to be a distinctive variety of the language.

Of course arguments between Webster and Pickering had no effect on the language, and British and American English diverged in the nineteenth century because *both* varieties changed. In the prestige dialect of London, words like *dance* and *grass* were pronounced in new ways; the *r*-sound disappeared in some places in a word and was kept in others (the first *r* in *river* stayed the same and the second one changed); and *h* vanished in some places (for instance, in *up high*) and erupted in others (as the first sound of *elegant*, though London observers vigorously criticized it). Americans kept some old speechways – for instance, the first vowel in *almond* was sounded as the *a* in *ham* – and introduced new ones in ways that created new words out of old ones – *curse* and *cuss*, *parcel* and *passel*.

A series of comic sketches published between 1835 and 1840 captured American English in its considerable variety. Sam Slick, a witty traveling sales-man created by Thomas Chandler Haliburton, journeyed through the northeast, and tells his stories in a vivid Yankee dialect:

> I went out a gunnin once when I was a boy, and father went along with
> me to teach me; well, the first flock of plover I seed, I let slip at them and
> missed them – says father, says he, what a blockhead you be, Sam, that's
> your own fault, they were too far off, you hadn't ought to have fired so soon.
> (Haliburton 1995: 125)

In his travels, Sam meets all sorts of characters with distinctive varieties of English: African Americans and Amerindians, speakers of French, Dutch, German, and Irish. It was a heady mixture of English, and, though exaggerated for comic effect, it represented some of the voices commonly heard in early nineteenth-century North America. The comic Yankee became a stock figure of fun; see fig. 1-1.

American readers and writers took a deep interest in the varieties of English, and humorists – Mark Twain is one of the few of this large group whose reputation survives – carried the Sam Slick tradition forward in newspaper columns and books in which American rustics (with absurd names like Petroleum Vesuvius Nasby), rural women (like Semantha Allen), or immigrants (like "Mr. Dooley") wisecracked social criticism. Such American humor was highly regarded abroad, giving an ideology for a parallel development of humorous writing in Scotland.

Figure 1-1 *An Old Curiosity Shop. A recognizably modern American identity began to emerge in the second quarter of the nineteenth century. In this Boston cartoon from 1849, David Claypoole Johnston satirizes the craze for "antiques" to revive (or invent) the past – here including bucklers and broad swords. The Yankee rustic offers the shopkeeper a ladder-back chair with these words: "How d'du. Hearing as how you buy antic furniter, I bro't you a cheer, that my grand-mother sot in: & was made afore I was born. It's the antickest thing you ever did see I guess." Some elements of this stereotype of American speech still endure. Reproduced by permission of the Clements Library, The University of Michigan.*

Vernacular voices were the enemy of genteel respectability, and they contributed to a reputation of American English as slangy, unrestrained, vulgar, and vital.

Social ideas were sometimes given a linguistic character. A feminist writing in *Godey's Lady's Book* in 1865 thought that women would be recognized for their accomplishments if additional expressions were introduced for the purpose: *Americaness, paintress, professoress,* and *presidentess* (see Mencken 1960: 590–91). Ethnic and racial words were discovered to be damaging and hurtful, though this was a relatively new idea in language ideology. In the 1890s, the greatest of American dictionaries, *The Century* (Whitney 1889–91), had this tentative observation about *nigger*: "*Nigger* is more English in form than *negro*, and was formerly and to some extent still is used without opprobrious intent; but its use is now confined to colloquial or illiterate speech, in which it generally conveys more or less of contempt." Ordinary speech was full of similar expressions, most of them treated as if they did no harm to the persons to whom they were applied – *dago*, for instance, was treated in *The Century* as a perfectly ordinary word. (*The Century* declared: "originally, one born of Spanish parents, especially in Louisiana: used as a proper name, and now extended to Spaniards, Portuguese, and Italians in general." Until falling out of use in many parts of the USA, *dago* was an offensive, "fighting word.")

Yet new migrations westward attracted people from the settled areas of the east and invited new immigrants from abroad – almost all of them European in origin. Now linguistic diversity took a new shape. Settled communities, often ones with some primary language other than English, began to disperse – partly because of necessity (overcrowding or worn-out soil) and partly because the Americans no longer felt the intense attachment to place that had rooted Europeans in the tiny patches of land where their ancestors had toiled and were buried. There was a yearning for the *frontier* (itself an Americanism in meaning), defined by the historian Frederick Jackson Turner as "the hither edge of free land" (quoted by Barnhart and Metcalf 1997: 35). The consequent migrations led to new words: *ranch* and *vigilante* (from Spanish), *jazz* and *jukebox* (from African Americans), *macaroni* and *spaghetti* (from Italian), *geisha* and *tycoon* (from Japanese), *lefse* and *lutefisk* (from Swedish), *bagel* and *nosh* (from Yiddish), and thousands of other borrowings from the languages of immigrants. Westward migrations, accelerated by the turmoil of the Civil War and its aftermath, tended to submerge dialect differences found on the eastern seaboard and to contribute to a more uniform variety of American English in the west, but differences remained nonetheless.

Early in the twentieth century, waves of immigrants arrived and populated American cities, particularly in the industrial northeast. Buffalo, Cleveland, Detroit, Chicago, and Milwaukee became centers of vital ethnic communities, many from southern and eastern Europe. Once again, loan words from language contact entered the larger community of English. These can be illustrated through food names: *baloney, chorizo, frankfurter, kielbasa, kishke, pepperoni, piroshki, tamale, wiener*. Following World War I, however, restrictive laws drastically reduced the number of new immigrants, and during the next half century America gradually became more monolingual than it had been for nearly three hundred years. "Americanization" campaigns, given stringent legal force in some parts of the country, made multilingualism seem unpatriotic, and as a consequence borrowings from foreign languages became much less frequent than formerly. English-sounding alternatives were preferred over the borrowed words: *hot dog* rather than *frankfurter*, *cottage cheese* rather than *smearcase*, *polish sausage* rather than *kielbasa*, *brats* rather than *bratwurst*. The distinctiveness of American English remained, of course, but the source of new expressions took new directions – initialisms (like *AIDS*), manufactured words (like *Kleenex*), derivations (like *antinuclear* or *environmentalism*), phrases (like *big top*), compounds (like *rock star*), shortened forms (like *bra* and *phone*) – among other strategies to refresh and renew the word stock.

Almost from the beginnings of American independence, observers have been concerned that it would diverge so far from British English as to approach mutual unintelligibility, and, more recently, some have seen it locked in a global competition with other varieties around the world, competing with them for speakers and conveying a threatening cultural imperialism. Such dire predictions have not yet come true. Nor are they likely to since English exists in the communities that speak it; persons who identify with family, neighborhood, region, and nation will variously express those identities – some more local, some less. As long as people talk to each other, they will come to speak the same language. American English has a distinctive heritage, but it is merely one variety among many, all of which deserve respect and encouragement.

Suggestions for further reading and exploration

Ideological statements about American English – it's a good language or a bad one; it's getting better or worse – are found in Baron (1985) and Bailey (1991). Its history is accessibly and amusingly treated in Read (2002). The most comprehensive treatment of the subject is found in the various editions of H. L. Mencken's *The American Language*, a book that first appeared in 1919 and continued to grow larger and larger until, at the end of the author's life, it had reached three huge volumes. A best-selling history for a mass audience is Bryson (1994). Baron (1990) describes efforts to use laws to force English on reluctant Americans.

References

Allsopp, Richard. 1996. *Dictionary of Caribbean English Usage*. Oxford: Oxford University Press.

Bailey, Richard W. 1991. *Images of English: a Cultural History of the Language*. Ann Arbor: University of Michigan Press.

Barnhart, David K., and Allan A. Metcalf. 1997. *America in so Many Words: Words that Have Shaped America*. Boston: Houghton Mifflin.

Baron, Dennis. 1985. *Grammar and Good Taste: Reforming the American Language*. New Haven: Yale University Press.

 1990. *The English-Only Question: an Official Language for Americans*. New Haven: Yale University Press.

Breslaw, Elaine G. 1996. *Tituba, Reluctant Witch of Salem*. New York: New York University Press.

Bryson, Bill. 1994. *Made in America: an Informal History of the English Language in the United States*. New York: William Morrow.

Doyle, James, ed. 1980. *Yankees in Canada: a Collection of Nineteenth-Century Travel Narratives*. Downsview, Ontario: ECW Press.

Eliot, John. 1663. *Mamvsse Wunneetupanatamwe Up-Biblum God*. Cambridge MA: Samuel Green.

Haliburton, Thomas Chandler. 1995. *The Clockmaker: Series One, Two, and Three*, ed. George L. Parker. Ottawa: Carleton University Press.

Heath, Shirley Brice. 1981. "English in our National Heritage." In *Language in the USA*, eds. Charles A. Ferguson and Shirley Brice Heath. Cambridge: Cambridge University Press. Pp. 6–20.

Johnston, David Claypoole. 1849. *Scraps*. New Series 1, plate 3. Boston: D. C. Johnston.

Ligon, Richard. 1657. *A True & Exact History of the Island of Barbados*. London: Humphrey Moseley.

Mathews, Mitford M. 1931. *The Beginnings of American English*. Chicago: University of Chicago Press.

Mather, Cotton. 1972. *The Angel of Bethesda*, ed. Gordon W. Jones. Barre, MA: American Antiquarian Society.

Mencken, H. L. 1919–48. *The American Language*. New York: Alfred A. Knopf.

  1960. *The American Language: Supplement II* (1948). New York: Alfred A. Knopf.

Read, Allen Walker. 1937. "Bilingualism in the Middle Colonies, 1725–1775," *American Speech* 12: 93–99.

  1938. "The Assimilation of the Speech of British Immigrants in Colonial America," *Journal of English and Germanic Philology* 37: 70–79.

  2002. *Milestones in the History of English in America*. Durham NC: Duke University Press.

Salmon, Vivian. 1996. "Thomas Harriot (1560–1621) and the Origins of Algonkian Linguistics." In Salmon's *Language and Society in Early Modern England: Selected Essays, 1981–1994*, ed. Konrad Koerner. Amsterdam: John Benjamins. Pp. 143–72.

Whitney, William Dwight, ed. 1889–91. *The Century Dictionary: an Encyclopedic Lexicon of the English Language*. New York: The Century Company.

Williams, Roger. 1643. *A Key into the Language of America*. London: Gregory Dexter.

2
American English and its distinctiveness

EDWARD FINEGAN

Editors' introduction

This chapter explores a topic of enduring interest to many Americans (and their counterparts in England): the distinctiveness of American English vis-à-vis British English. After cautioning that we should be careful to consider features in comparable registers or situations (e.g., newspaper writing with newspaper writing and conversation with conversation), Edward Finegan launches into a discussion of vocabulary differences on either side of the Atlantic. Many of the examples he discusses involve automobiles, traffic, and travel (British *motorway* and *roundabout* vs. American *freeway* and *traffic circle*), but other domains – household items and package labels – are rich in contrasts too. A noteworthy source of distinctive American words (some very old) are those borrowed from the languages of Native American and Latino populations, including place names like *Malibu* (from Chumash) and *El Paso* (from Spanish) and foods like *persimmon* and *tortilla*.

Going beyond the stereotypical "tomayto/tomahto" examples, the chapter surveys a number of recurrent pronunciation differences between American and British English, some involving consonants (pronouncing /t/ in words like *auto* as a sound like [d] or as an aspirated [tʰ]), some vowels ("mo-bal" vs. "mo-bile"), and some stress or accent (*garáge* vs. *gárage*). Among other things noted, regional pronunciation is less varied in the USA than in Britain; although Britain is geographically smaller, it has a longer and more complex settlement history.

Contrary to the popular perception that there are few grammatical differences between American English and British English, this chapter draws our attention to a wide range of examples. Many of them come from analyses of computerized corpora of American and British speech and involve quantitative rather than qualitative differences. The list includes agreement rules, mid-sentence ellipsis (*When [are] you coming back?*), relative pronouns (more *that* in American English, more *which* in British English), past participles (*gotten* vs. *got*), and other parts of speech. The chapter also covers spelling differences between the national varieties (e.g., *favor/favour* and *pajamas/pyjamas*) and closes with a discussion of prospects for the future. Whereas the influences of different immigrant and ethnic groups in each country could lead to increasing divergence, increasing use of the Internet could lead to greater convergence in spelling and other conventions, particularly in the written English of the most highly educated sectors of both populations, which already show the least variation.

National varieties of English

When the Harry Potter books are published in the USA and produced as films, not only are expletives like *Cor!* and *Blimey!* replaced by more familiar American ones, but other expressions that Americans would readily understand such as *whilst* and *straight away* are likewise "translated." In another context, even university textbooks are sometimes "translated" from one national variety of English into another: Canadian into US English, US into Australian English, and so on. In textbooks, some translation is cultural (interchanging baseball and cricket terms, for example). In linguistics textbooks, alternative pronunciation codes and illustrations might be needed so as not to perplex readers.

Like all national varieties of any language, American English (AmE) varies across regions and social groups and across the social situations in which it is used. To characterize AmE, this chapter identifies illustrative features that mark it as distinct, and for practical and historical reasons the English of Britain is the point of comparison. British English (BrE) encompasses more than the English of England, but this chapter makes no systematic reference to the English of Northern Ireland, Scotland, or Wales. Of course, AmE and BrE influence one another, and some expressions recognizably American to older Britons seem home-grown to younger ones (Trudgill and Hannah 2002: 55).

Dialect refers to any variety of a language that is characteristic of a particular social group. The term is traditionally associated with regional varieties such as those of New York City or the South, but the characteristic varieties of working-class speakers and middle-class speakers are also sometimes called social dialects or sociolects. African American English and Latino English are prominent ethnic group dialects of AmE. In the speech of any one person, characteristics of several social group memberships come together, including those of sex, age, socioeconomic status, regional origin, and education.

The term *register* refers to language varieties that are characteristic not of social groups but of social situations. Conversations, sermons, lectures, campaign speeches, and sports broadcasting are examples of spoken registers. Written registers include recipes, class notes, personal letters, newspaper headlines, and scientific reporting. Each register has characteristic linguistic features. Salutations in business letters (*Dear Ms. Portillo*, *Dear Sirs*) differ from those in personal letters (*Hey Ashley, Dear Devon*). Every text – every piece of natural language – represents characteristics of both its situation and its speaker or writer; every text is simultaneously register and dialect. Naturally, spoken texts and informal written ones signal more about a person's social group affiliations than do formal written texts, which tend to be "standardized."

Some linguistic features are found in AmE or in BrE but not in both. For example, in talk of motor vehicles, speakers of AmE refer to *trunk*, *hood*, *gas*, *wrench*, and *truck*, speakers of BrE to *boot*, *bonnet*, *petrol*, *spanner*, and *lorry*. Other features occur in both varieties but much more frequently in one or the other. A word, a meaning, a pronunciation – any linguistic feature – may be so much more common in one variety that it serves as a salient marker of identification. As an example, *vacation* and *maybe* are far more common in AmE, *holiday* and *perhaps* far more common in BrE.

Features and frequencies of features differ from register to register, so when making comparisons across dialects it is important to compare equivalent registers – conversation with conversation, news reporting with news reporting. This chapter cannot identify all the types of distinctive features or provide comprehensive lists of the features it does identify. It can only illustrate and, in the suggestions for further reading, point to fuller coverage.

Vocabulary

Probably most words brought to America on the tongues of English colonists still carry the same or closely related meanings on both sides of the Atlantic. But other words have arisen, and some older words have shifted meaning, not always in the same way on both sides of the Atlantic. A conversation between American and British friends today would highlight the effects of a centuries-long separation, as we can illustrate in a domain undeveloped when English settlers first arrived on American shores. Americans use the terms *highway* and *freeway* (not *motorway*), *traffic circle* (not *roundabout*), and we usually *pass* (rather than *overtake*) other motorists. We refer to *traffic jams*, not *jams*, to *detours* instead of *diversions*, and to *construction* or *maintenance* instead of *roadworks*.

BrE terms like *contraflow* (traffic moving in the "wrong" direction), *tailback* (*backup*), and *verge* (*grass strip, boulevard*) are unfamiliar in the USA, and hearing about a new *dual carriageway* or Edinburgh's infamous *Barnton roundabout tailback* would puzzle most Americans. Americans who have passed a *driver's test* and received a *driver's license* can *rent a car*, check the *tires* of the *rental car*, make sure the interior has been *vacuumed* and the *windshield* cleaned, and then, assuming the *line* isn't overly long, drive out of the *parking lot* or *parking structure* to start a *vacation*. Britons, after passing a *driving test* and getting a *driving licence*, would *hire a car*, check the *tyres* of the *hire car*, ensure the *windscreen* was clean and the interior *hoovered*, and then, assuming a short *queue*, drive out of the *car park* to go on *holiday*.

Many differences in the customary vocabulary and idioms of AmE and BrE crop up in intimate domains like the home, where there is relatively little shared communion between Yanks and Brits: *can* for *tin*, *eggplant* for *aubergine* and *zucchini* for *courgettes*, *dessert* for *pudding*, *baked potato* for *jacket potato*, *stove* for *cooker*, even *supper* for *tea* and *dish towel* for *tea towel*. Still, there is not much that speakers of AmE and BrE wouldn't understand in one another's speech, especially in context. Consider labels on packaged goods. Some terms differ in customary expression, where the alternative could occur but doesn't, as with *nutrition facts* (instead of BrE *nutrition information*) and *mixing bowl* (instead of *basin*). An American package might invite customers with *questions* (not *queries*) to phone the company *at* (not *on*) its toll free number. Features more likely to be remarked are those that could *not* be said in the other variety. Instead of *calories*, British food packages list *energy* – but they do so in units of *kilojoules* and *kilocalories*, which are not generally familiar in the USA. In reference to a promotional guide for consumers, a Bostonian would be baffled by the instruction to send *a crossed cheque in the amount of £3.99*. Even a dollar equivalent and the spelling *check* would not clarify the notion.

Some common shorthand terms like *math*, *TV*, and *ad* differ from *maths*, *telly*, and *advert*; in addition, here is a short list of everyday AmE and BrE equivalents:

face cloth/wash cloth = flannel   *band aid = plaster*
diaper = nappy   *sweater = jumper*
pants = trousers   *sneakers/running shoes = trainers*
underpants = pants   *flashlight = torch*
apartment = flat   *realtor = estate agent*
sidewalk = pavement   *zee = zed* ('the letter *z*')
trash can/garbage can = dustbin   *fired = sacked*
busy signal = engaged   *laid off = made redundant*
pay raise = pay rise   *tailor made = bespoke*

Names for dishes in cuisines that are popular in the USA but not in Britain contribute to AmE distinctiveness. British visitors to a Mexican restaurant in El Paso, Los Angeles, or Chicago might need to inquire about such menu items as *albondigas, burrito, ceviche, chili relleno, chorizo, empanada, enchilada, frijoles, guacamole, huevos, rancheros, mariscos, salsa, pescado, taco, tamale, tortilla, chipotle, mole, fajita, tostada, arroz con pollo, salsa roja, salsa verde, salsa de chile rojo*, and *tostadas con carne* – foods enjoyed with a cold *cerveza* 'beer' and the sounds of a *mariachi* band. Comparable lists could be made for Brazilian, Cuban, Japanese, Korean, and Thai cuisines.

Not only in culinary terms have neighboring and faraway cultures exercised a distinctive imprint on American vocabulary. Of these borrowings from Spanish, some are old, others recent: *arroyo, barrio, bronco, corral, canyon, hacienda, hombre, hoosegow, jalapeño*, (beef) *jerky, lariat, mesa, mesquite, pancho, peyote, presidio, pronto, pueblo, rodeo, salsa, serape, tequila, tomatillo*, and *siesta*. (*Macho* and *mucho* are not included because they did not enter English through AmE.) In Arizona, California, Colorado ('red, reddish'), Nevada ('snow, snow covered'), and other southwestern states, and even in Alaska, Florida, Maine, Montana ('mountain'), and elsewhere, thousands of place names bear witness to the influence of earlier Spanish and Mexican culture: *Amarillo* ('yellow'), *Cape Canaveral* ('place of canes'), *El Monte, El Paso* ('the passage'), *Fresno* ('ash tree'), *Las Cruces* ('the crosses'), *Las Vegas* ('the meadows'), *Los Angeles* ('the angels'), *Los Gatos* ('the cats'), *Los Osos* ('the bears'), *Marina del Rey* ('marina of the king'), *Palo* ('tree') *Alto* ('high'), *Rancho Mirage, Sacramento, Santa Fe* ('holy faith'), *San Luis Obispo* ('Saint Luis Bishop'). In many cities, Spanish names grace streets, neighborhoods, rivers, canyons, and mountains, including *Rio* ('river') *Grande, Merced* ('mercy') *River, Sierra Nevada*, as well as social institutions, such as *Alcatraz* ('pelican') *Island, El Toro* ('bull') *Marine Base*, and *El Conquistador* ('conqueror') *Resort*. From San Diego to San Francisco along Route 101, travelers see reminders of California's Hispanic past in the roadside signs shaped like mission bells and proclaiming *El Camino Real* 'the royal road.'

Borrowings from Native Americans are particularly distinctive of AmE, and many cities, states, and rivers bear Indian names: *Arkansas, Kansas, Malibu, Milwaukee, Minnesota, Mississippi, Oklahoma, Penobscot, Texas, Waukesha, Winnipesaukee, Wiscasset, Wisconsin*, and thousands of others. Some words originating in AmE reflect Native American culture: *mocassin, terrapin*, and *tomahawk* (from Algonquian languages), *papoose* and *sachem* (Narragansett), *sagamore* (Penobscot), *squaw* and *powwow* (Narragansett and Massachusett), *tepee* (Dakota), and *wigwam* (Abenaki). Others identify animals or plants unfamiliar to the arriving colonists, who borrowed the names from Native Americans but adapted their pronunciations to English patterns: *chipmunk, raccoon, skunk, woodchuck, opossum, persimmon, sequoia*, and *squash*. In addition, compounds incorporating the word *Indian* were coined, among them *Indian file, Indian giver, Indian summer*, and *Indian wrestling*. Finally, from the often hostile interaction between settlers and Native Americans arose nouns like *warhoop, war dance, snake dance, warpaint*, and *warpath*, as well as verb phrases like *be on the warpath, bury the hatchet* ('make peace'), and *smoke a peace pipe*.

In the early history of the American colonies, contact between English-speaking colonists and the Dutch in New Amsterdam contributed the place names *Brooklyn, Bronx, Staten Island, Bowery, Harlem, Hellgate, Teaneck, Tarrytown*, and many ending in *-kill* 'stream' (*Cobleskill, Catskill, Fish Kill*), along with the everyday words *boss, cole slaw, cookie, cruller, snoop*, and *stoop*. Contact with French brought *prairie, bayou, butte, jambalaya, palisades* ('a line of cliffs along a waterfront'), *pecan, praline*, and such place names as *Louisiana, Maine*, and *Vermont*. Later, Yiddish-speaking immigrants contributed *klutz, schlep, schlemiel, schtick, schmo, schmooze, schmuck*, and *schnook*, which are better known in metropolitan areas than elsewhere. Other languages, including German and Swedish, have contributed as well.

AmE has shown inventiveness in creating colloquial and slang expressions, and of course many have spread to other varieties. The following, identified in *Webster's New World College Dictionary* as having American origins, are listed in *The Concise Oxford Dictionary*, although the highlighted ones are marked North American or chiefly North American: *jamboree, jalopy, widget,* **schoolmarm**, *scofflaw, sidekick, wisecrack, sideburns,* **pencil pusher**, *jack pot, jack hammer, pushover, press conference,* **hope chest**, *jigsaw* and *jigsaw puzzle, pratfall,* **mess hall**, **honky-tonk**, *hoofer, joyride, wolf whistle, whodunit*, and *tip off*, as well as the shortened or combined forms **pen** ('penitentiary'), *wiz, prom, sicko, sickie, psychobabble,* **preemie**, *wino, hoopla, megabuck, jazz, jazzy*, and *honest-to-goodness*. Not listed in the *Concise Oxford* are *square shooter, poop sheet, press agent, press box*, and *jug head*, among others. A British reader of *Time* or *Newsweek* would note distinctly American expressions only a few times on any page, matching the few distinctly British expressions an American reader of *The Economist* would note. In shared domains like science and scholarship, or where economic, financial, and political alliances support frequent analysis in print, vocabulary differences tend to fade.

Pronunciation

Some pronunciation features of AmE are so well known as to be stereotyped. Examples include vowel correspondences, such as the stressed vowel in *tomáto* (ay vs. ah) and *banána* (nan vs. nahn), the first vowel in *leisure* (rhyming with *seizure* but in BrE with *pleasure*), and the miscellany represented in *vitamin* (vite-a vs. vit-a), *schedule* (sked vs. shed), *charade* (raid vs. rahd), and *privacy* (prive vs. privv). Stress patterns may also differ. AmE stresses the first syllable in the words *controversy* and *renaissance* and the compounds *weekend* and *ice cream*, BrE the second syllable. There are also differences of intonation patterns in utterances, especially questions, but we lack space to address intonation here. The most significant pronunciation differences affect sets of sounds and classes of words, as illustrated below.

Consonants

Intervocalic /t/ and /d/

Between vowels and vowel-like sounds, /t/ and /d/ are typically pronounced alike: *metal, bitter*, and *matter* sound like *medal, bidder*, and *madder*. To be more precise, /t/ and /d/ are pronounced alike between vowels when the preceding syllable is stressed, as in *mótto* and *píty*. This *t/d* sound is a flap or tap of the tip of the tongue and is represented by [ɾ] in the International Phonetic Alphabet (the "IPA"). When /t/ precedes a stressed vowel (*tin, ténder, autónomy, petúnia*), it is pronounced with aspiration, as [tʰ]. In the same circumstances in which /t/ and /d/ are pronounced alike within words, they are pronounced alike across words, as in *bet a bit* and *bed 'n' breakfast*. Irrespective of stress patterns, BrE generally aspirates /t/ even between vowels, as in *water* and *later*.

Postvocalic /r/

AmE generally pronounces /r/ when it occurs after a vowel in the same syllable (*car, sure, card, beard, motor, later*). That makes it a "rhotic" variety. By contrast, some British dialects have lost /r/ in such words and are "non-rhotic." In the dialects of metropolitan New York City, eastern New England, and some southern Atlantic coastal areas, /r/ is *variably* dropped. That means some social groups drop it more frequently than others and more so in some registers than others. The catch phrase "Pahk the cah in Hahvad Yahd" lightly captures the *r*-lessness of eastern New England, which in this regard resembles BBC English and some other British dialects.

Initial /h/

Many words spelled with initial *h* are pronounced alike in AmE and BrE – some with /h/ (*history*, *hospital*), others without it (*honor*, *hour*). Possibly all dialects vary the pronunciation of pronouns like *he, him, his, her*, and *hers*, with /h/ dropped more frequently in relaxed speech. But in words like *house, home, here*, and *who*, AmE shows a strong tendency to preserve initial /h/ where dialects of BrE frequently omit it, especially with *have* words (*'ave a safe journey*). With *herb* and *herbal*, AmE usually omits and BrE usually preserves /h/. With *human* and *humor*, only some AmE dialects pronounce /h/.

WH-words – *when, which, where, why*

In southern dialects of AmE, the *when, which, where* words are pronounced as though spelled "hwen," "hwich," etc. This "hw" sound is represented by [ʍ]; thus [ʍɛn], [ʍɪtʃ], and [ʍɛr]. In these dialects, *which* and *witch* are not homonyms. In northern dialects, however, WH-words are pronounced with [w], not [ʍ], so *which* and *witch* are pronounced alike, as are *where/ware*, *whet/wet*, *whether/weather*, and *why* and the name of the letter *y*.

The *Asian, Persian* class

In AmE, the *si* in words such as *Asia* and *Asian*, *Persia* and *Persian*, represents "zh" ([ʒ], or in some American books [ž]) and not the "sh" sound [ʃ] often heard in BrE ([ʃ] is represented in some American books by [š]). In AmE, *glacial* is invariably pronounced with a medial "sh" as [gleʃəl], not as in BBC English sometimes as [glesiəl]. In AmE, *immediately* has five syllables (im-mee-dee-it-lee) and is not pronounced "im-meed-jit-lee."

Vowels

The *half, fast, path* class

The vowel of the *cat, fat, mat* class of words tends to be pronounced alike in AmE and BrE – as [æ], although the vowel shifts discussed below and in chapter 4 create considerable variation in AmE. In AmE, the vowel of *cat* appears in the *half, fast, path* words, where the vowel is followed by a fricative such as /f/, /s/, or /θ/ (θ represents the *th* of *thick* and *thin*). For these words, some dialects of BrE (including BBC English) have the vowel sound of *father* [ɑ]. Some AmE dialects have the vowel of *father* in the word *aunt* (which is more commonly pronounced like *ant* [ænt]), but otherwise the so-called "broad a" is heard in the *half, fast, path* class only in eastern New England.

The *tune, duty* class

Pronounced as though spelled "toon," "doo," "enthoosiastic," "noo," and "lood" are the *tune, dew, enthuse, new,* and *lewd* words (with syllables beginning in /t/, /d/, /θ/, /n/, or /l/ and followed by /u/). Only seldom – and principally from older Americans – would you hear the pronunciations "tyune" and "dyuty" or "choon" and "jewty," as in some varieties of BrE.

The *mobile, missile* class

Adjectives like *mobile, facile, fertile, missile,* and *sterile* are pronounced as though ending in *-al*; thus "fert-al" corresponds to BrE "fer-tile." *Juvenile* is pronounced both ways (the noun usually with *-aisle,* the adjective with *-aisle* or *-al*). *Reptile,* a noun, is pronounced with *-aisle* on both sides of the Atlantic.

Diphthongs

In most AmE dialects, the vowels of words like *pie* and *tie* ([aɪ]), *soy* and *boy* ([ɔɪ]), and *cow* and *now* ([aʊ]) are complex sounds (called *diphthongs*) that move from an onset vowel ([a] or [ɔ]) to an end point vowel ([ɪ] or [ʊ]). (You can experience this movement by slowly saying *pie, soy, now.*) In pronouncing *I'm,* AmE speakers generally monophthongize the diphthong, keeping only the onset vowel [a] and producing "ahm." In dialects of the South, diphthongs are more often monophthongized to pronunciations that can be perceived by outsiders as "tah" [tʰa] for *tie* and "taw" [tʰɔ] for *toy.* Coupled with the pronunciation of [ʍ] in WH-words, this produces "wha" [ʍa] (or [ʍæ]) for *why* and "ha" [ha] (or [hæ]) for *how* in southern dialects, while northerners say [waɪ] and [haʊ].

Vowel mergers

Two sets of vowel mergers are prominent, though they have differerent regional distributions. In much of the South, the vowel sounds of *pit* and *pet* are merged preceding nasals as in *pin ~ pen,* which sound to speakers of other dialects like *pin,* and *him ~ hem* (which sound like *him*). Elsewhere, especially in eastern New England, western Pennsylvania, and much of the West, the vowels of *cot* and *caught* are merged or merging, so that *hock* and *hawk, Don* and *Dawn, wok* and *walk,* and other such pairs are indistinguishable.

Vowel shifts

Underway at the present time are two significant shifts of vowel pronunciations, a relatively recent Northern Cities Shift and an older Southern Shift, both of which are described briefly in the following chapter.

Stress patterns and vowel reduction

Compare the AmE pronunciation of the three-syllable *li-bra-ry* and four-syllable *sec-re-ta-ry* with the BrE "lie-bree" and "sec-re-tree." BrE tends to maintain a more even stress pattern in words and has fewer vowels reduced to schwa (the name given to the first vowel of *above* and the final vowel of *soda* and represented by [ə]). For example, in words like *construction* and *condition*, AmE maintains a full vowel only in the stressed middle syllable and shows a reduced vowel (schwa) in the initial and final syllables: [kən dɪ ʃən] and [kən strʌk ʃən]; by contrast, speakers of BrE tend to say [kɒn dɪ ʃən] and [kɒn strʌk ʃən], with a reduced vowel only in the final syllable. *Laboratory* has four syllables on both sides of the Atlantic, but is pronounced in AmE as "lá-bra-tòr-ee" and BrE as "la-bór-a-tree." Similar differences appear in kindred forms, including *commentary*, *lavatory*, and *dictionary*, invariably with four syllables in AmE but often three in BrE.

In some words borrowed relatively recently from French, the stress pattern of the original is preserved to a greater degree in AmE. *Garage* and *fillet* have primary stress on the final syllable (ga-ráj, fil-láy), while BrE stresses the initial syllable (gá-ridge, fíll-it); note how the stress patterns affect the vowel of the respective final syllables. *Ballet* is pronounced "bal-lay," but AmE stresses the second syllable, BrE the first. Among other borrowings from French, *patois*, *massage*, *debris*, and *beret* are pronounced in AmE with stress on the final syllable, in BrE on the initial syllable.

Pronunciation variation

Across regional groups

Even combined, England, Scotland, Wales, and Northern Ireland are no larger than Oregon, the tenth largest state in the USA, so one might expect more linguistic variation in the USA. Given Britain's longer and more complex pattern of settlement history, however, dialect differences there are greater than in the USA. The relative uniformity of AmE should not suggest, however, that a visitor to Atlanta, Boston, Charleston, Chicago, Dallas, Minneapolis, New York, Seattle, and San Francisco would fail to note characteristic regional pronunciations. (See chapters 3 and 6 of this volume.)

Across socioeconomic groups

At least in urban areas along the eastern seaboard of the USA, variation across socioeconomic status groups appears to follow similar patterns in AmE and BrE. For example, in New York City and in Norwich, England, *-ing* is pronounced with and without "the g." In both cities, middle-class residents pronounce the *g* ([ɪŋ]) more frequently than working-class residents. Said the other way around, *-ing* is pronounced without the *g* ([ɪn]) more frequently by working-class than by middle-class speakers. Some dialects of the American South have such frequent *-in'* pronunciations that *-in'* is said to be used "almost exclusively," and the same is true in the north of England and in some Scots dialects (Labov 2001: 90).

For the sound represented by *th* in *this* and *brother* ([ð]), many speech communities in the USA and Britain have more frequent [d] pronunciations among lower-ranked socioeconomic groups than among higher-ranked groups. Likewise for the pronunciation of *th* as [t] in words like *think* and *with*: lower-ranked groups say [t] more frequently than higher-ranked groups. New York City residents vary their pronunciation of words with *th*, and among some speakers the [d] and [t] pronunciations are so frequent that the Big Apple has been stereotyped as having a "dis, dat, dem, and dose" dialect and its speakers as uniformly saying "toity-toid and toid" (for 33rd Street and 3rd Avenue). (See chapters 4 and 26.)

Across ethnic groups

The dialects of African Americans and Latinos have been studied more than those of other ethnic groups. (African American English is treated in chapter 5, and observations about the English of Latino communities appear in chapters 10 and 11. For a book-length treatment of Chicano English, see Fought 2003.) The English of Asian Americans has been studied less thoroughly (see chapter 13), as has that spoken by Native Americans (see Leap 1993).

On English-language radio and television broadcasts, correspondents generally speak without marked social group accents, although attentive listeners may occasionally identify traces of regional origins. An interesting phenomenon can be observed in the speech of Latino radio and television announcers and reporters. Latino correspondents typically do not exhibit dialect markers in the body of their reports, but some use a marked ethnic pronunciation of their own names when they sign off. CNN's Maria Hinojosa identifies herself as "mah-REE-ah ee-noh-HOH-sah," avoiding typical English vowel reduction and pronouncing the characteristic trill *r* in REE. Likewise, news reports delivered by Latino correspondents often display characteristic pronunciations of Latino names: *de la Cruz* as "deh-lah-CROOS," *Fuentes* as "FWEHN-tehs," and *Hernandez* as "ehr-NAHN-dehs." Such ethnically marked pronunciations highlight a reporter's pride in his or her ethnic identity.

Grammar and sentence structure

While it is commonly said that AmE has few distinctive grammatical features, some are noteworthy.

Agreement rules

Verb agreement with collective nouns

One difference concerns agreement rules between verb and subjects that are collective nouns (*family, staff, team, committee*) or the names of sports teams (*Cleveland, Manchester*), or companies, organizations, and institutions (*Lipton, Ford, CNN, the government*). In AmE, all these require a singular verb (*The federal government is considering, The team has won*), while BrE allows a singular or plural verb (*Manchester is/are ahead by one, Staff was/were invited*). The following clauses (from the British National Corpus) would not normally occur in AmE: *Once ITV **realize** the BBC **are** going ahead*; *CNN never **say** we made a mistake . . .*; *The dead man's family **are** in shock*; *the Government **are** not wholly to blame for this recession.* Neither would this company slogan from a box of tea: *Brooke Bond **don't** make tea bags for anyone else!* The AmE subject–verb agreement pattern is determined by the singular or plural *form* of the noun rather than by its sense. About the Anaheim Angels baseball team, AmE says *Anaheim **has won*** but *The Angels **have won***. British publications increasingly use the AmE pattern.

Ellipsis in conversation

Ellipsis is the technical term for the kind of grammatical shortening that results from omission of certain structures. In sentences like the following, AmE shows twice as much mid-sentence ellipsis of the auxiliary verb as BrE (*Longman Grammar of Spoken and Written English*, hereafter called LG; see Biber et al. 1999):

> *When you coming back?* (compare *When **are** you coming back?*)
> *How you doing?* (compare *How **are** you doing?*)

Generally, however, AmE shows less ellipsis than BrE. It less often omits the combined subject and auxiliary, as in *Want it?* (compare ***Do you** want it?*), *Like it?*, and *Wanna clear a crowded room?* and less often omits the combined subject and main verb, as in *Serious?* (compare ***Are you** serious?*) and *Too early for you?* (compare ***Is it** too early for you?*). It also shows half as much initial ellipsis and final ellipsis as BrE (LG 1108), as in these examples (all taken from a "Judge Judy" television broadcast):

> *Yes, no question about it.* (compare *Yes, **there's** no question about it.*)
> (Don't slur your words.) *Sorry.* (compare ***I'm** sorry.*)
> (Did you press any charges?) *I tried to.* (compare *I tried to **press charges**.*)
> (Now, he didn't hit you first.) *Yes, he did.* (compare *Yes, he did **hit me first**.*)

Auxiliaries in questions and replies

In conversation and fiction, AmE shows an overwhelming preference for question forms with *do* (***Do you have** any novels about horses?*). By contrast, in conversation BrE prefers ***Have you got** any novels about horses?* (which is uncommon in AmE) and in fiction ***Have you** any novels about horses?* (LG 216).

Relative clauses and the relative pronouns *which* and *that*

In certain structures, relative pronouns can be omitted, as you can see by comparing *Are those the books **that** you lost?* with *Are those the books you lost?* Sometimes when the relative pronoun is expressed, either *which* or *that* may be grammatical: *the books **that** you lost* or *the books **which** you lost*. AmE shows a somewhat stronger preference for introducing such relative clauses (called restrictive or defining relative clauses) with *that* rather than *which*, while BrE shows a stronger preference for *which*. In news writing, *that* is 50 percent more frequent in AmE and in conversation twice as frequent as in BrE (LG 616).

But neither, but nor

AmE can begin a conjoined negative clause with *but neither* (or with *neither* or *nor*) + auxiliary verb. *Congress should not be running monetary policy, **but neither** should it . . . let Alan Greenspan decide the country's economic priorities* (AmE, *Newsday*). The BrE equivalent is *but nor* + auxiliary verb, an expression that is uncommon in AmE: *She makes no excuses for Runt or Pig, **but nor** does she judge them* (BrE, *Guardian*).

Parts of speech

Verbal forms

Past tense and past participle of *get*

In AmE, *got* can serve as a simple past tense meaning 'became' (*She got tired*) or 'arrived' (*when she got home*). Both *got* and *gotten* can serve as the past participle of *get*, but they are not used equivalently, and *gotten* is strongly preferred in AmE, as in: *The president's war efforts **have gotten** high marks* (AmE, *Newsweek*). BrE examples may strike American ears as ungrammatical: *No amount of NATO pressure would **have got** it even on to paper* (BrE, *Economist*).

In AmE, *Have you got any?* is a frequent equivalent to BrE *Do you have any?* (which is also familiar in AmE). In a shortened form, it appears in *I got a deadline early Monday*, and it underpins a currently popular *Got milk?* advertising campaign. *Gotten* often means 'received' or 'acquired,' as in *Have you gotten any?* Contrast these uses with those where *have got* means simply 'have': *We've got ID cards now, We've got locked gates* (*Los Angeles Times*).

Omitting the infinitive marker *to*

In some contexts, AmE shows a robust tendency to omit the infinitive marker *to* after *come, go, help*, and certain other verbs (Todd and Hancock 1986: 477), as in 1 and 2 below, or to make them compound verbs as in 3. Compare these three examples with 4, 5, and 6, which are BrE:

1. *You wanna **go get** some water?* (*Los Angeles Times*)
2. *Proceeds will **help establish** a wetlands protection fund.* (*Cleveland Plain Dealer*)
3. *I feel it's only right that I **come and help out**.* (*Boston Globe*)

4. *. . . you'll already know where **to go to buy** your uniform.* (*Daily Telegraph*)

5. *. . . what this study **will help to establish** is what consumers really mean . . .* (*Guardian*)

6. *. . . a friendly wizard who **can help you to find** a red and gold scarf . . .* (*Daily Telegraph*)

Negation

Among distinctive features of AmE is a preference for certain patterns of negation and a marked infrequency of others. According to LG (161), AmE conversation shows a strong preference for *do not have the* (*don't have the time, do not have the information*) and *have no* (*has no plans, have no doubt, has none of your character, has nothing to fear*) as compared with BrE. Curiously, the *have no* form so heavily preferred in AmE conversation is used with equal frequency in AmE and BrE fiction and news registers. AmE conversation shows little or no use of *have got no* (*have got no one to love, have got nothing to hide*), *have not got a/any* (*has not got an easy task*), and *have not the* (*has not the strength*).

Modals

In conversation, the modals *must, will, better*, and *got to* are less frequent than in BrE. By contrast, *going to* (often pronounced "gonna") and *have to* ("hafta") are more common than in BrE (LG 488). Except in legal registers, the use of *shall* has practically vanished (and is diminishing in BrE as well).

Noun phrases

Compound nouns

AmE commonly uses singular forms of nouns in compounds like *rent policy, drug fund, drug enforcement unit, wage ordinance*, and *new fair market rent policy*, whereas BrE shows a preference for plural forms of the first element, as in *drugs policy, drugs fund, drugs enforcement unit, wages ordinance, prisons policy, taxes policy, market rents policy*, and *future rents policy*. In AmE, if the first element of the compound noun phrase is itself a compound already containing a plural form (e.g. *hate crimes* or *war crimes*), then the larger compound incorporates that plural: *hate crimes policy, war crimes punishment*.

Definite articles

In some expressions, AmE and BrE omit the article with relatively general senses of the noun: *in school, to class, in college, to church*. In other expressions, AmE custom calls for the definite article where BrE omits it; those would include: *in the hospital, at the university*, and *of the term* for BrE *in hospital, at university*, and *of term*.

Complex noun phrases in journalistic prose

AmE news writing shows an inclination to place noun phrases or strings of nouns before names of people or events, while BrE prefers the information after the proper noun, as an appositive.

American style	British style
D.C. police chief *Charles Ramsey*	*Diana Krall,* **a Canadian**
Freaks and Geeks *producer* Judd Apatow	*John Lennon,* **the founder Beatle**
Orlando Magic basketball star *Patrick Ewing*	*Josh Bolten,* **the head of the president's domestic policy staff**
Joel and Ethan Coen's tragicomic cardiograph The Man Who Wasn't There	*David Owen,* **a staff writer for the New Yorker**

Pronouns

For '*you* plural,' *you all* or *y'all* occurs in conversation three times as often in AmE as in BrE (LG 330). By contrast, *you two* occurs half as often. Besides the Southern *y'all* are other regional forms, including *yuns* (in Western Pennsylvania and the Ohio Valley) and *yous* (notably in metropolitan New York City). *You guys* is increasingly common as a simple plural for addressing males or females.

AmE and BrE use the indefinite pronouns *anybody* and *anyone*, but at least in fiction AmE shows a stronger preference for the -*body* forms (*anybody, everybody, nobody, somebody*), while BrE prefers *anyone, everyone, no one,* and *someone* (LG 352).

Terms of address

Distinctive terms of address – especially more generic ones – include *buddy* (for BrE *mate*), *miss* (for BrE *madam*, though *madam* is also frequent in AmE and *ma'am* especially in the South). Other address terms include *folks* (always plural) and, especially among younger Americans, *guys* and *you guys* (usually plural), *dude* (typically singular), *bro* and *brotha* (especially among African Americans). British favorites like *lads*, *love*, and *you lot* are very rare in AmE.

After a full name introduces someone (*Alice Burner Gunnerson, Andrew Beckis*), *The New York Times* prefers title plus surname (*Ms. Gunnerson, Mr. Beckis*). Britain's *Economist* has a similar policy (*Mr Bush warned Mr Sharon that Mr Arafat must remain unharmed*). By contrast, after initial mentions, US publications like *Time* and the *Los Angeles Times* prefer bare surnames (*Bush said Cheney would be cleared by the SEC*).

Adverbs

Unmarked adverbs and the amplifier *real*

Characteristic of AmE is the use of the amplifier *real*, as in *real good, real tall, real soon,* and *real fast,* instead of *really good, really tall*. Posted along many roads, signs say *Go slow,* displaying an older historical adverb form.

The amplifiers *pretty, quite* and *rather*

AmE conversation prefers the amplifier *pretty* (*pretty easy*, *pretty funny*, *pretty good*) over the BrE equivalent *quite*, and this use of *pretty* occurs about four times as often as in BrE (LG 567). *Quite* as an amplifier (*quite big*, *quite easy*, *quite good*) is not common, occurring only one-seventh as often as in BrE. While AmE and BrE use *quite* and *pretty* with the adjectives *sure* and *good*, AmE tends to limit *quite sure* to negative contexts (*not quite sure*, *never quite sure*), whereas in BrE it occurs in negative and positive contexts (*She was probably quite sure*). As an amplifier, *rather* seems formal in AmE and is not common.

The adverbs *immediately* and *directly*

Immediately and *directly* are adverbs in AmE and BrE. Unlike BrE, though, AmE does not permit their use as subordinators as in these BrE examples from the British National Corpus, a 100-million word reservoir of written and spoken texts:

- *I could have hauled each fish out of the swim* **immediately** *it was hooked and kept disturbance down to a minimum.* (compare AmE **immediately after**)
- **Directly** *he was in, he jerked impatiently at the reins, called to the horse, and they were off!* (compare AmE **Directly after**)

Prepositions

In AmE in certain environments a preposition may be omitted (*write* **to** *me* or *write me*), where BrE tends strongly to keep it. By contrast, AmE sometimes requires a preposition where BrE can omit it; compare BrE *to save him learning to dislike such politicians* with AmE *to save him* **from** *learning to dislike such politicians*.

The preposition is often omitted from references to days of the week and certain other time references, as well as after certain verbs:

American English only	American and British English
have a doctor's appointment Monday	*have a doctor's appointment* **on** *Monday*
departed **JFK** *on time*	*departed* **from JFK** *on time*

In some phrases, different prepositions are preferred. An American *store* **on** *Main Street* is a British *shop* **in** *the High Street*. In telling time, AmE prefers *a quarter of eleven* or *quarter* **till** *eleven* and *a quarter* **after** *ten* or *twenty* **after** *nine*, but can also use the customary BrE forms *quarter* **to** *eleven* and *twenty* **past** *nine*. There are a few minor differences in the form of prepositions, as with **around** *the house* and **toward** *the light* rather than the more common BrE **round** *the house* and **towards** *the light*. Because *different* is a very common adjective, the AmE preference for *different* **than** rather than BrE *different* **from** or *different* **to** is striking. Given that usage guides criticize *different **than***, some published writing prefers *different **from***, but it appears to be vanishing from AmE conversation. Some phrasal verbs also have different prepositions: Yanks *come **across*** as arrogant, Brits *come **over*** as stiff.

Idioms and slang

Many, although certainly not all, idioms originating in the USA are known in other varieties as well. The older verb *bite the dust* (which appears in the *OED*) and the more recent *be on the same page* (which does not), as well as such noun phrases as *bottom line* and *slam dunk* (both of which make appearances in the OED) are not confined to the USA.

Modern preferences such as AmE *take a look* over BrE *have a look* are numerous and usually not perplexing.

Especially among younger speakers of AmE today, stand-alone *Cool!* (with a distinctive intonation) is exceptionally frequent as an expression of approval or endorsement. It serves, for example, as an apt response to hearing what someone does for a living or for recreation.

> A: *What kind of work do you do?*
> B: *I'm a sewage treatment supervisor.*
> A: *Cool!*

This usage derives from the more familiar use of adjectival *cool*, as in *In Bangkok we took in a temple and had a little riverboat tour, which was real cool.*

Even the briefest discussion of informal styles in AmE must note the use of *way* as an adverb meaning 'very, much/many more, more by far,' as in *way cool* and *way more*. Especially among younger speakers, this *way* is extremely popular: *way more sports*, *way more hits*, *way more mileage*, and *way more than kids*. The absence of an unambiguous instance in the British National Corpus suggests that this usage has not yet caught fire in BrE, although recent Internet examples can be found.

Semantics

Word senses

Some words carry different meanings. As an example, *mad* means 'angry,' as it did for Shakespeare at the time English first arrived in North America, while in BrE it means 'insane' (a sense also familiar in AmE). *Presently* means 'at present, now, currently' and is not understood to mean 'in a short while, shortly,' its usual sense in BrE and the sense represented in AmE *momentarily* 'in a moment.' Above, we saw that *pants, tin, torch, jumper,* and *diversions* carry different meanings in AmE and BrE. There are many other instances besides these, and some can cause at least brief puzzlement in conversation.

Sports metaphors

American culture favors metaphors drawn from business, politics, food, and guns (all of which are illustrated in Tottie 2002). Above all, though, sports metaphors dominate. On the popular television interview program "Hardball," only tough questions are *thrown at* guests, and a *softball* question would be regarded as partisan. Other metaphors from baseball, the national sport, include *stepping up to the plate*, *striking out* and having *two* (or *three*) *strikes against you*, getting to *first base*, being *out in left field*, throwing *a curve* or *a curve ball*, being a *utility infielder*, and *sitting in the bleachers*. By no means, however, do all popular sports metaphors reflect baseball, as illustrated in these examples from golf, basketball, boxing, gaming, and football:

- *Lord Robertson in NATO is hard at work with a resolution . . . that would **tee up** . . . prime Article 5 responsibilities.* (Secretary of State Colin Powell)
- *We are undertaking **a full court press** diplomatically, politically, militarily . . .* (Colin Powell)
- *It's not easy **to get up off the mat after such a blow**.* (New York City Fire Department Chief Daniel Nigro)
- *Anyone who **bets** against America is simply wrong.* (New York Stock Exchange chairman Dick Grasso)
- *The Monday-morning **quarterbacking** on Al Gore's defeat has begun.* (Newspaper columnist Chuck Raasch)

Discourse markers and miscellaneous

Discourse markers

As a discourse marker, *now* (***Now** what I mean is . . .*) is less than half as frequent in AmE as in BrE, while *you see* occurs only an eighth as frequently (LG 1097). The discourse markers *well* (***Well**, I'm not sure*) and *I mean* are somewhat more frequent in AmE than in BrE, while *you know* is more than twice as frequent (LG 1096). As a conversational backchannel, *right* is common in AmE, but as a discourse marker for a conversational transition AmE prefers *all right* and *alright then* (LG 1098), as in ***All right**, let's do it*.

Miscellaneous

Interjections
As a response form, *okay* – the most famous Americanism – is at least ten times more common in AmE than in BrE, while *yeah* is only somewhat more frequent

and *yes* only half as frequent. Much more commonly heard in AmE than in BrE are the interjection *wow* (eight times more frequent) and the attention seeker *hey* (six times more frequent), while the response elicitor *huh* is ten times as frequent in AmE. The interjection *oh* is used about equally in AmE and BrE conversation (LG 1096–97).

Greetings

As a greeting, *hi* is eight times as frequent in AmE as in BrE, *hello* only two-thirds as frequent. *Bye bye* is twice as frequent in AmE, but *bye* alone occurs with about the same frequency on both sides of the Atlantic (LG 1097).

Polite expressions

The expressions *sorry*, *pardon*, and *please* are less common than in BrE, but *thank you* and *thanks* are twice as common (LG 1098). BrE *ta* 'thanks' is all but unknown in the USA.

Hedges

AmE exhibits far more frequent occurrences of the hedges *maybe*, *kind of*, and *like*, while BrE prefers *sort of* (LG 869). Compare *There's **like** no place to put the stuff* with BrE *We **sort of** were joking about it*. Note also AmE *Well, but **maybe** it's good* and *Her bones are **kind of** cracking*.

Expletives

In conversation, expletives are abundant on both sides of the Atlantic – but not necessarily the same ones with the same frequency. In AmE, *my God* occurs twice as often as in BrE, but *God* only half as often. About twice as common are the euphemisms *my goodness*, *my gosh*, *geez*, and *gee*. The common British swear words *bloody*, *bloody hell*, and so on are rarely heard in the USA, and the same is true for the verb *sod* (*sod it!*) and the noun (*you sod*) (LG 1098). Also unfamiliar are *Cor* (a "vulgar corruption" of *God*, the *OED* calls it), *blimey* (a "vulgar corruption" of *blind me!* or *blame me!*), and *bugger*.

Spelling

AmE prefers *-ize* over *-ise* (*subsidize, generalize, liberalize, organize*, but *advertise*); *-or* over *-our* (*favor, rumor, labor, color, succor, savior, harbor, behavior, parlor*). Affecting fewer words are preferences for *-er* over *-re* (*meager, center, theater*) and *-se* over *-ce* (*license, defense, offense*).

Before adding the sufix *-ment* to verbs ending in *e*, AmE drops the *e*: *judgment, abridgment, acknowledgment* instead of BrE (and occasional AmE) *judgement, abridgement, acknowledgement*.

Conventions for consonant doubling distinguish *canceled, dialed, kidnaping, modeled, signaled, traveled* and *traveler* from BrE *cancelled, dialled, kidnapping*, etc. By contrast, AmE doubles *l* in *installment, fulfillment, skillful*, and some others, where BrE usually does not. Miscellaneous spelling differences crop up in words such as *fetal*, *maneuver*, and *encyclopedia*, instead of the sometimes preferred BrE versions *foetal*, *manoeuvre*, and *encyclopaedia*. In addition, the following AmE ~ BrE pairs are familiar, none signaling a pronunciation difference, except that BrE *tsar* is sometimes pronounced with initial [ts] rather than [z] as in AmE. The AmE spellings are apparently spreading.

catalog ~ *catalogue*	*check* ~ *cheque*
curb ~ *kerb*	*program* ~ *programme*
czar ~ *tsar*	*story* ~ *storey*
jail ~ *gaol*	*tire* ~ *tyre*
pajamas ~ *pyjamas*	*ton* ~ *tonne*

Other spelling distinctions represent pronunciation differences: *aluminum* (not *aluminium*), *specialty* (not *speciality*), and *spelled, learned, burned* (not *spelt, learnt, burnt*), although AmE pronunciation varies between [d] and [t] for these last three. AmE *leaned* [liːnd] has neither the alternative British spelling *leant* nor the pronunciation "lent" [lɛnt].

Prospects for the future

No one can confidently predict degrees of divergence or convergence between AmE and BrE in the future. One might expect that shared film and television would lead to greater similarity but, except in some domains of vocabulary, the exposure to language these media represent seems less powerful an agent of change than one might imagine. Further, to the extent that AmE and BrE are influenced by different immigrant groups, they may tend to diverge. The same may be said of the influence of long-standing ethnic groups, in particular African Americans, whose relationship to other varieties of AmE may be in flux. In any case, changes affecting AmE or BrE could spread to the other variety.

For the most part, the features discussed in this chapter reflect standard varieties. But there is less variation across educated speakers than other speakers, and variation from region to region is greater across lower ranked socioeconomic groups than across higher ranked ones. Thus, while there may be greater commonality and increasing understanding in US and UK books, magazines, and newspapers, the everyday conversation of ordinary citizens, enlivened as it is by the independent tides that govern intimate colloquial forms, may increase distinctness. Differences in spelling and other orthographic matters will likely shrink, partly from increased use of the Internet and the widespread use of university textbooks published by international publishing houses and distributed worldwide.

To return to the Harry Potter books and films mentioned at the top of this chapter, critics have claimed a serious loss of cultural exchange in such substitutions as *English muffin* for BrE *crumpet*, *field* for *pitch*, and *two weeks* for *fortnight* (Gleick

2000). For the time being, though, at least younger speakers of AmE and BrE may benefit from the occasional "translation." How far into the future, and to what extent, translation will be needed remains an open question.

Acknowledgments

In identifying features to discuss, I have relied principally on Trudgill and Hannah (2002) and especially for quantitative data on Biber et al. (1999), referred to as LG within the chapter. Some illustrations I have taken from the British National Corpus, Lexis-Nexis, and assorted newspapers and magazines, and sometimes they have been slightly altered. My appreciation also goes to Julian Smalley, originally of Nottinghamshire, for his observations about English in the USA.

Suggestions for further reading and exploration

No one has written more energetically about AmE than H. L. Mencken and Mencken (1963) is a convenient abridgment of his three-volume work. Chapters 3 and 6 of the present volume discuss variation within AmE, while chapter 20 treats slang and chapter 21 hip hop. An excellent source of historical information about slang is Lighter's (1994–) multivolume dictionary, while Chapman's (1995) single-volume dictionary is handy and informative. Craigie and Hulbert (1960) and Mathews (1951) are classic historical dictionaries of AmE. Flexner and Soukhanov (1997) and Flexner (1982) are coffee-table books, rich with informative slices of AmE. Crystal (2003), another big book, treats English more broadly. Barnhart and Metcalf (1997) makes delightful reading about selected Americanisms, one each for most years from 1555 (*canoe*) and 1588 (*skunk*) to 1996 (*soccer mom*), 1997 (*Ebonics*), and 1998 (*millennium bug*). Trudgill (1985) provides an amusing sociolinguistic perspective of a visit to the USA by a British tourist. Showing special sensitivity to nonnative speakers and teachers of English as a Foreign Language, Tottie (2002) is fresh, accessible, and interesting. The quarterly *American Speech* offers cutting-edge discussions of a wide range of topics.

References

Barnhart, David K. and Allan A. Metcalf. 1997. *America in So Many Words: Words that Have Shaped America*. Boston: Houghton Mifflin.
Biber, Douglas, Stig Johansson, Geoffrey Leech, Susan Conrad, and Edward Finegan. 1999. *Longman Grammar of Spoken and Written English*. London: Longman [called LG].
Chapman, Robert L., ed. 1995. *Dictionary of American Slang*, 3rd edn. New York: Harper-Collins.
The Concise Oxford Dictionary, 10th edn. 1999. Oxford: Oxford University Press.
Craigie, William A. and James R. Hulbert, eds. 1960. *Dictionary of American English on Historical Principles*. Chicago: University of Chicago Press.

Crystal, David. 2003. *The Cambridge Encyclopedia of the English Language*, 2nd edn. Cambridge: Cambridge University Press.

Flexner, Stuart Berg. 1982. *Listening to America: an Illustrated History of Words and Phrases from our Lively and Splendid Past*. New York: Simon and Schuster.

Flexner, Stuart Berg and Anne H. Soukhanov. 1997. *Speaking Freely: a Guided Tour of American English from Plymouth Rock to Silicon Valley*. New York: Oxford University Press.

Fought, Carmen. 2003. *Chicano English in Context*. New York: Palgrave Macmillan.

Gleick, Peter H. 2000. "Harry Potter, Minus a Certain Flavour." *New York Times*. July 10. A 19.

Labov, William. 2001. *Principles of Linguistic Change. Vol. 2: Social Factors*. Malden MA: Blackwell.

Leap, William L. 1993. *American Indian English*. Salt Lake City: University of Utah Press.

Lighter, J. E., ed. 1994–. *Random House Historical Dictonary of American Slang*, vols. 1, 2. New York: Random House.

Mathews, Mitford M., ed. 1951. *A Dictionary of Americanisms on Historical Principles*. 2 vols. Chicago: University of Chicago Press.

Mencken, H. L. 1963. *The American Language*, 4th edn. and 2 supps., abridged by Raven I. McDavid, Jr. New York: Knopf.

Todd, Loretta and Ian Hancock. 1986. *International English Usage*. London: Croom Helm.

Tottie, Gunnel. 2002. *An Introduction to American English*. Oxford: Blackwell.

Trudgill, Peter. 1985. *Coping with America*, 2nd edn. Oxford: Blackwell.

Trudgill, Peter and Jean Hannah. 2002. *International English: a Guide to Varieties of Standard English*, 4th edn. London: Edward Arnold.

Webster's New World College Dictionary, 4th edn. 1999. New York: Macmillan.

3 Regional dialects

WILLIAM A. KRETZSCHMAR, JR.

Editors' introduction

This chapter treats *regional* dialects – a topic of tremendous interest to the general public. The first part is introductory, covering, among other things, the fact that no two people speak exactly alike but that regional speech is still a reality, for people from the same region do speak more like each other than like people from other regions. The US regional dialects developed in part from the separateness and isolation of the earliest colonial settlements and in part from the different mixtures of people who populated each region (Native American, German, African, and so on). Although some of the distinctiveness of the speech habits of the earliest settlers has been ironed out, broad regional patterns still remain, although they are constantly in flux, and they are to some extent abstractions.

The chapter draws extensively on maps and tables, and William A. Kretzschmar uses them to outline the boundaries and salient features of the main (Eastern) American English dialects in the mid-twentieth century, based on the work of legendary American dialectologist Hans Kurath. Kretzschmar shows how Kurath established isoglosses that demarcated dialects on the basis of people's familiarity with lexical alternatives like *darning needle* (Northern), *mosquito hawk* (Southern), and *snake feeder* (Midland), all of which refer to the 'dragon fly.' Subsequent analyses of pronunciation patterns essentially confirmed the regional dialect patterns that had been established on the basis of word use.

The chapter closes with a discussion of twenty-first-century regional dialect patterns. More recent studies of the word usage and pronunciation patterns of US dialects confirm the broad regional speech difference identified half a century earlier, but vocabulary and pronunciation changes have occurred, and to quote Labov and Ash (1997) (who are cited at length in this chapter), "the local accents [of major US cities] are more different from each other than at any time in the past." This chapter suggests that something closer to a uniform national dialect is spoken by the well educated, but that regional differentiation and vibrancy are evident among working-class and lower middle-class Americans.

Background

While all Americans know there are regional dialects of American English (see chapter 26), it is actually quite difficult to prove them right. Detailed investigation of what Americans say – their pronunciation, their grammar, the words they use for everyday things and ideas – shows that each of us is an individual in our language use, not quite the same as any other person studied. All English speakers do of course share a great many words, a core grammar, and much the same sound system but, despite all that we share, American English speakers also vary in their speech. Some, for example, know that a *dragonfly* can be called a *snake feeder* or a *mosquito hawk*, others that it can be called a *darning needle*. Some rhyme the word pairs *cot* and *caught* and *Don* and *dawn*, but others do not rhyme them. To say how they got into the swimming pool last summer, some would say *dived*, others *dove*. There are various possible pronunciations and word choices and grammatical constructions for almost anything that any American would ever want to say – and thus the number of possible combinations of the choices that anyone could make is practically infinite. Surveys carried out in the middle of the twentieth century for the American Linguistic Atlas Project (ALAP) demonstrated that no two speakers in the extensive survey gave exactly the same set of responses to its questionnaire about everyday speech (cf. Houck 1969). It is simply not true that all Americans from a particular region share exactly the same choices of words, pronunciations, and grammar, or that a complete set of choices from one region (say, the North) is different from the set chosen by speakers from another region (say, the South). Moreover, speakers from different social groups within the same locality, and even the same speaker in different situations and at different times, will make different linguistic choices (see part 3 of this volume, "The Sociolinguistic Situation").

Yet we are not wrong to notice that people from different regions of the USA do seem to speak English differently. In large terms, the speech of people from one region is generally more similar to the speech of people from the same region and less similar to the speech of people from other regions. Americans can often (though not always) recognize the speech of a fellow American as coming from a different part of the country from our own, just as we can recognize an American speaker as talking differently from, say, a speaker of British English or Australian English – though we often cannot recognize a Canadian speaker so readily. What we are recognizing in any of these cases is a tendency for people from a particular place to make some of the same choices of words, pronunciations, and grammar as other people from the same place. Analysis of data from the American Linguistic Atlas Project shows that among a wide range of linguistic features tested, any particular feature tends to be used by people who live relatively close to each other (Kretzschmar 1996a, Lee and Kretzschmar 1993). Words that are not known by very many people in the ALAP survey tend to be known by people who live near each other; and words known by larger numbers of speakers tend to be found in geographical clusters, rather than distributed evenly across the survey area. Other studies also suggest that geography is one of the most important factors for sharing variant linguistic features (e.g., LePage and Tabouret-Keller 1985, Johnson 1996). Such tendencies for any given linguistic feature to be used in specific places can be described statistically for the ALAP survey data. In real life, when we hear relatively unfamiliar words or pronunciations or grammar in someone's speech, we have to guess where those features might be used according to our own sense of probability.

The relative association of particular features of English with Americans from some particular part of the country has its roots in American history. Unlike England, where the English language has a history stretching back to the fifth century AD, North America has a history of settlement by English speakers of only about 400 years. The relatively short period of settlement has not allowed time for dialect differences as sharp as those found in Britain (e.g., between Scottish English and the English of the Thames Valley) to develop in North America – and it is not likely that such sharp regional differences will emerge in future, given mass public education and other social conditions that do not favor the development of sharp dialect differences. Yet regional differences have in fact emerged in North America and they show no sign of disappearing.

Two factors led to the development of dialects in America. First, and by far the most important, settlements in the American colonies began as separate isolated communities, and each developed somewhat different speech habits during the early colonial period. As settlement proceeded inland from the coastal outposts, the speech habits of the coastal communities were carried to the interior by sons and daughters of the established colonists and by new immigrants who landed at the coast and acquired speech habits as they made their way to the frontier (which for some immigrants took years). Settlement proceeded generally westward in three large geographical bands as far as the Mississippi River, corresponding to what is now the Northern tier of states, a Midland region, and the Southern region. In the North the speech habits that became established in Upstate New York (which differed from the speech of New York City and its environs, originally Dutch in settlement, and from the speech of New England, which was separated from the Inland North by mountains) were carried westward by means of water travel on the Erie Canal and Great Lakes as far as northern Illinois, Wisconsin, and Minnesota. The South had no convenient waterway to facilitate travel, and the varied topography of the land – mountains, the piney woods, wiregrass – was not all well suited to the pattern of plantation agriculture that dominated the colonial economies of Virginia and the Carolinas. Southern settlement thus proceeded more slowly, and in a patchwork of communities across Georgia and Alabama until settlers reached more generally suitable plantation lands in the plains and Mississippi Basin areas of Tennessee, Mississippi, Louisiana, and East Texas. Philadelphia was the focal city for settlement in the Midland region, which proceeded west in two broad streams. The National Road was built through Pennsylvania, eventually as far as central Illinois, close to the present-day route of Interstate 80. Settlement took place along the road, and settlers could also reach the Ohio River valley and then use the waterway to settle farther inland. This more northerly stream of Midland settlement carried Midland speech habits, which mixed to some degree with the speech habits of the Northern region. The more southerly stream of Midland settlement followed the course of the Shenandoah River south through Virginia towards the Cumberland Gap in Tennessee. Mostly these South Midland settlers were subsistence farmers, and they occupied whatever land could support them throughout the Appalachian Mountain region and the uplands as far west as Arkansas, and also in the lowlands of the Southern states where the land was not suitable for plantations. In addition to Midland speech habits, these settlers also acquired speech habits characteristic of the Southern region, especially those Midlanders who found their way to marginally productive land near plantation country. These historical patterns of settlement – North, Midland, and South – created the basic framework of regional American dialects that we still see – and hear – today. (See figure 3-1 [Kurath 1949: fig. 3], which we will discuss further below.)

The second historical factor that influenced regional varieties was the people who originally settled the separate colonies. Each colony had its own particular mix of colonists who spoke dialects from different areas of England, or who did not speak English at all. Undoubtedly, some traces of these immigrant speech habits have survived. Lists are available that highlight the contributions to the American English vocabulary of Native Americans, Germans, the Spanish, and other non-English-speaking groups (Marckwardt 1958: 22–58). A list of the contribution of words from African languages to Gullah, a Creole variety still spoken in the Sea Islands off the southern coast is also available (Turner 1949), along with a list of words of African origin still used in the southeast (McDavid and McDavid 1951). As for British dialect influences, special studies of the relationship between Scottish English and Appalachian English have been made (e.g., Montgomery 1989, 1997, Montgomery and Nagle 1993). However, so-called "colonial leveling" resulted from a tendency not to preserve any more than occasional distinctive habits of regional English dialects or isolated words or usages from immigrant languages other than English. Speculative accounts (e.g., Trudgill 1986) of a colonial American koiné (a regional dialect used as the common language of a larger area) perhaps overstate the case, since we see that different settlement patterns have created different and long-lasting dialect regions, but there were indeed reasons for settlers not to maintain the sets of speech habits that marked British dialects of English (Kretzschmar 1997). Whole communities of speakers of a dialect or language did not usually settle together, and most communities that began as homogeneous settlements in time blended into the surrounding culture. The strict religious communities of the Pennsylvania Dutch that still preserve their (now archaic) German language are the exception that proves the rule. Thus it is not true that any American regional variety of speech derives particularly from one British dialect source. Appalachian English, for instance, is not particularly descended from Scottish English, although it does show some Scottish influence. Because of population mixture, each colony had a range of speech habits out of which its own regional characteristics could eventually emerge (see, e.g., Miller 1999). ALAP evidence shows that dialect areas in the eastern USA share essentially the same original word stock, but have preserved it differently (Kretzschmar 1996b). While we cannot discount influences from British dialects and the non-English-speaking population, these influences were secondary to the formation of their own speech habits by the early populations of the different colonies.

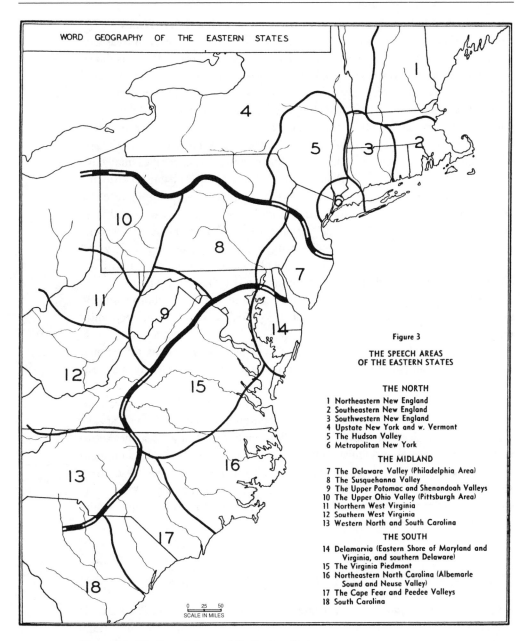

Figure 3

THE SPEECH AREAS
OF THE EASTERN STATES

THE NORTH

1 Northeastern New England
2 Southeastern New England
3 Southwestern New England
4 Upstate New York and w. Vermont
5 The Hudson Valley
6 Metropolitan New York

THE MIDLAND

7 The Delaware Valley (Philadelphia Area)
8 The Susquehanna Valley
9 The Upper Potomac and Shenandoah Valleys
10 The Upper Ohio Valley (Pittsburgh Area)
11 Northern West Virginia
12 Southern West Virginia
13 Western North and South Carolina

THE SOUTH

14 Delamarvia (Eastern Shore of Maryland and
   Virginia, and southern Delaware)
15 The Virginia Piedmont
16 Northeastern North Carolina (Albemarle
   Sound and Neuse Valley)
17 The Cape Fear and Peedee Valleys
18 South Carolina

0   25   50
SCALE IN MILES

Figure 3-1 *The Speech Areas of the Eastern States*
Source *From Kurath 1949*

Finally, it is unwise to assume that speech habits that we associate with a particular region have been used there for a long time. Among features most commonly associated with Southern American English, the pronunciation of the vowel in *fire* as a near rhyme with *far*, the pronunciation of *pin* and *pen* as words that rhyme, and the vocabulary item *fixin' to* 'preparing to, about to' were rare or non-existent before the last quarter of the nineteenth century (Bailey 1997). Likewise, other features commonly associated with Southern speech such as lack of pronunciation of -r after vowels (as in words like *four* pronounced as *foa* or *foe*) and *a*-prefix on verbs with *-ing* endings (like *a-running*) are also in rapid decline. Similarly, the relatively infrequent variant terms for *chest of drawers* in ALAP data from the eastern USA actually recapitulate terms found in old furniture pattern books (Burkette 2001). The most common American term for this piece of bedroom furniture is now *dresser*, but in the ALAP data of the 1930s and 1940s the most common term was *bureau*, and other terms, now relics, may have been prominent still earlier (Burkette 2001). While individual habits of speech – whether words or pronunciations or grammatical usages – are likely to come and go, the tendency to use different habits in different regions will nonetheless continue. As a consequence, regional variation may well persist in much the same geographical patterns even after such changes in speech habits (cf. Bailey and Tillery 1996). It is thus fair to say that regional dialects of American English are continuously rebuilding themselves, simultaneously dying away with the loss of some speech habits that formerly characterized them and being reborn with new speech habits that speakers might recognize as probably coming from a particular region.

The remainder of this chapter presents evidence for the status of regional dialects in the mid-twentieth century and the beginning of the twenty-first century. First, evidence collected for the ALAP project is used to characterize mid-twentieth century regional varieties; then, more recent evidence is given for regional variation. For both periods it is important to remember that "speaking a regional dialect" is really nothing more than a tendency for a speaker to make some of the same linguistic choices as other people from the same location. A "dialect" is thus a generalization, an abstraction that seizes upon a few selected linguistic features to characterize a variety of the language. A dialect is not a social contract or a comprehensive set of linguistic rules by which all the residents of an area must abide.

Regional dialects at mid-twentieth century

Figure 3-1, a 1949 map of dialect areas in the eastern USA based on ALAP evidence, is an example of a dialect generalization. In order to make the map, Hans Kurath, one of the most accomplished dialect geographers, began with individual words, like those used to designate the *dragonfly*, and he plotted where ALAP speakers used them, as in figure 3-2 (Kurath 1949: Map 141). You can see that *darning needle* mostly occurs in the North, *mosquito hawk* and *snake doctor* in the South, and *snake feeder* in Pennsylvania and areas of the Appalachian Mountains as far south as western North Carolina. Such a neat pattern, where each different variant seems to occupy its own part of the map, is extremely unusual in the ALAP evidence; most patterns of distribution for words (or for pronunciations

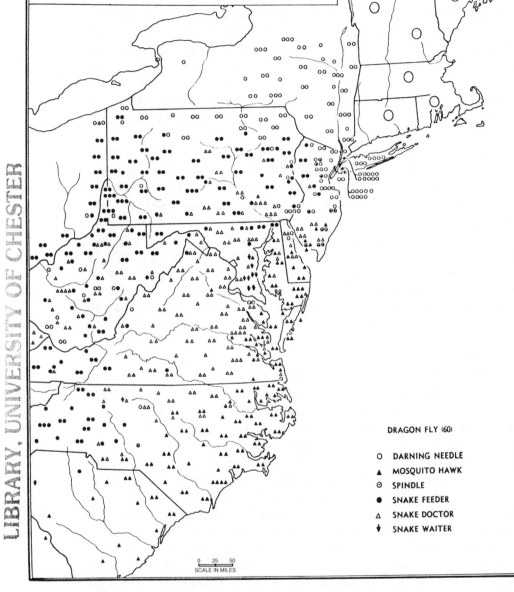

Figure 3-2 *Dragon fly*
Source *From Kurath 1949*

or grammatical features) show a rather spotty areal distribution, with more than one alternative in use in any given area. The *dragonfly* variants, however, show only a relatively small number of words out of their own areas, for example, occurrences of *snake doctor* too far north in Pennsylvania or *darning needle* too far south in West Virginia. From maps like these, the dialect geographer carefully selected features from which to make a different kind of map such as is shown in figure 3-3 (Kurath 1949: figure 5a). He drew best-fit lines, called "isoglosses," to indicate the boundary of the majority usage of his carefully chosen words. Here, the dotted line shows the Southern boundary for *darning needle*, which matches where *darning needle* occurred most of the time in figure 3-2, except for the stray occurrences in West Virginia. To speak in terms of tendencies, if someone heard an American from the time of the ALAP survey say the word *darning needle* in reference to an insect, it would be a very good guess to say that the speaker came from north of the isogloss – but the guess might be wrong because *darning needle* was also used occasionally elsewhere.

Figure 3-3 also shows the next stage of that older process for making a dialect generalization. In this case, the researcher tried to find words whose isoglosses would run in about the same place. Here *darning needle* is combined with isoglosses for *whiffletree* (a variant term for part of the equipment for hitching horses to a wagon – still an everyday rural practice in the 1930s and 1940s) and *pail* (as opposed to *bucket*), all terms used in the North. Such a combination of isoglosses is called a "bundle," and bundles of isoglosses are represented by the boundaries of dialect areas shown in figure 3-1. The heavy black lines in Pennsylvania and Maryland/Virginia represent the thickest bundles of isoglosses. At each end of the heavy black lines, their continuation has been represented with a double line to indicate less agreement in the path of the bundled isoglosses. For instance, in figure 3-3 the isoglosses diverge in eastern Pennsylvania and New Jersey, just where the double lines appear in figure 3-1. All of the thinner lines separating the subsidiary dialect areas of the region also represent bundles of isoglosses, but the bundles have fewer constituents than the ones represented by the heavy black or double lines. There was no fixed rule for how many isoglosses had to be present to make a bundle, but the numbers were quite small in relative terms. Out of the thousands available in the ALAP data, only about 400 words were plotted for Kurath's (1949) *Word Geography*, and only a very small number of the mapped words yielded clear isoglosses at all, much less isoglosses that ran together to form bundles that could mark major and subsidiary dialect boundaries. This earlier technique allowed Kurath to confirm judgments he had made about American dialect areas on the basis of his experience and his study of historical settlement patterns: all he needed was a small number of representative isoglosses for that purpose (see Kretzschmar 1992, 1996a). A later study showed that patterns of American pronunciation in the ALAP data largely matched the patterns derived from the vocabulary variants (Kurath and McDavid 1961). The dialect boundaries of figure 3-1 are thus more suggestive of tendencies rather than being sharp boundaries where, if speakers crossed them while traveling, they could hear sharply different dialects in the speech of the local population on each side. Travelers who go long distances before stopping are apt to hear greater differences in speech habits between stops than they would have heard if they had stopped more frequently along the way.

In addition to these famous maps, Kurath also produced tables indicating whether a word was used regularly (marked by X), fairly commonly (marked

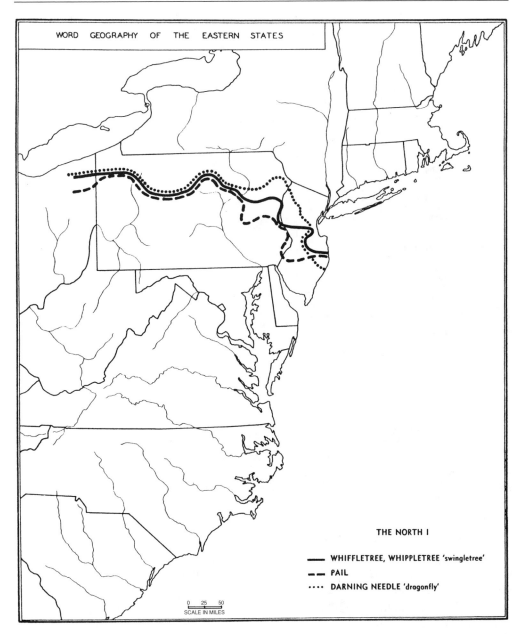

WORD GEOGRAPHY OF THE EASTERN STATES

THE NORTH I

—— WHIFFLETREE, WHIPPLETREE 'swingletree'
— — PAIL
···· DARNING NEEDLE 'dragonfly'

0   25   50
SCALE IN MILES

Figure 3-3 *The North I*
Source *From Kurath 1949*

by —), rarely (marked by · or a blank space), or not at all in the subsidiary dialect
areas of a major dialect region. Figure 3-4 is the table for the Northern region
(Kurath 1949: table I). Only a few terms such as *pail* and *darning needle* are shown
as being used throughout the North, and a few more occur in most of the North
but are lacking in one of the subsidiary dialect areas. (The numbers in parenthesis
after each word – e.g., pail (17) – refer to discussion elsewhere in Kurath's book

THE NORTHERN AREA

	Ohio	New York State		New England	
× regular — fairly common rare		Upstate	Hudson Valley	Western	Eastern
(1) The North					
pail (17)	×	×	×	×	×
whiffletree (21)	×	×	×	×	×
boss! (37)	×	×	×	×	×
johnny cake (44)	×	×	×	×	×
darning needle (60)	×	×	×	×	×
angle worm (60)	×	×	—	×	×
stone wall (16)		—	×	×	×
nigh-horse (39)	—	—	—	—	×
(2) The North without Eastern New England					
stoop (10)	×	×	×	×	
stone boat (21)	×	×	×	×	
fried-cakes (45)	×	×	—	—	
lobbered milk, loppered milk (47)	×	×	×	×	
sugar bush (61)	×	×	×	—	
button ball (61)		×	×	—	
belly-gut(ter) (95)	×	×	—	—	
(3) The North without the Hudson Valley					
buttry (10)	—	—		—	—
spider (17)	×	×		×	×
fills, thills (20)	×	×		×	×
teeter board (22)	×	×		×	×
coal hod (23)	—	—		×	×
hasty-pudding, Indian pudding (50)	×	×		×	×
Dutch cheese (47)	×	×		×	—
horning (82)	×	×			

Figure 3-4 *The Northern Area*
Source *From Kurath 1949*

and are not germane to our discussion here.) The tables also show that some words are used in only two of the major dialect regions, but not in all three. For example, figure 3-5 shows words that were used in the Midland and the South, but not as much in the North (Kurath 1949: table V). Figure 3-6 shows words used in the North and the South, but not throughout the Midland (Kurath 1949: table VI). The table for the Southern region (figure 3-7; Kurath 1949: table III), which includes a column for the South Midland, indicates clearly the complexity of speech habits in different areas of this most recognizable of American regional dialects. These tables show us again that Kurath's major American dialect regions are generalizations that, while not wrong, are based on a small number of representative words and that the dialect regions contain large degrees of internal variation within them.

In addition to the plotting of separate pronunciations as they occurred throughout the ALAP survey area, mid-twentieth-century dialect geographers also wished

THE MIDLAND AND THE SOUTH

X regular — fairly common . rare	South				Midland				North
	South Carolina	North Carolina	Virginia Piedmont	Eastern Shore	South Midland	Western Pennsylvania	Eastern Pennsylvania	West Jersey	
dog irons, fire dogs (8)	X	X	X	.	X	—	.	.	.
paling fence (16)	X	X	X	X	X	X	X	—	.
bucket (17)	X	X	X	X	X	X	X	X	
spicket (18)	—	X	X	X	X	X	X	X	
singletree (21)	X	X	X	X	X	X	X	X	—
seesaw (22)	X	X	X	X	—	—	X	—	—
comfort (29)	X	X	X	X	X	—	X	X	X
pully-bone (37)	X	X	X	X	X	—	.	X	
corn pone (44)	X	X	X	X	X	X	X	—	
roasting ears (56)	X	X	X	X	X	X	X	—	
pole cat (59)	X	X	X	X	X	X	X	.	.
ground squirrel (59)	X	X	X	X	X	X	X	.	
granny (woman) (65)	X	X	X	X	X	—	—	X	.
right smart (74)	X	X	X	X	X	X	X	X	.
agin I get there (89)	—	—	—	—	X	—			
Christmas gift! (93)	X	X	X	X	X	—	—		

Figure 3-5 *The Midland and the South*
Source *From Kurath 1949*

THE NORTH AND THE SOUTH

X regular — fairly common . rare	South				Midland		North			
	South Carolina	North Carolina	Virginia Piedmont	Eastern Shore	South Midland	North Midland	Hudson Valley	Upstate New York	Western New England	Eastern New England
quarter to (4)	—	—	X	—		.	—	—	—	—
curtains (9)	.	.	—	—	—		.	.	X	X
piazza (10)	X	X	.	—			—	.	X	X
gutters (11)	X	X	X	—		—	X	.	—	X
corn house (14)	—	.	X	—			—	X	X	X
spider (17)	—	—	.	—			—	X	X	X
low, loo (36)	X	X	X	X	.		—	—	—	X
harslet (37)	X	X	X	X	—		—		—	X
nanniel (38)	—	—	—	X	.		—		—	—

Figure 3-6 *The North and the South*
Source *From Kurath 1949*

to construct vowel systems that showed the relationship between vowel sounds within dialect regions. They isolated four types of vowel systems in the eastern USA, as shown in figure 3-8 (Kurath and McDavid 1961: 6–7).

Differences between the systems are subtle and still noticeable in the speech of Americans from the regions specified. The vowels found in the words *crib*, *three*,

THE SOUTHERN AREA

	South Midland			South					
				Virginia Maryland			The Carolinas		
× regular — fairly common · rare	Western N. C.	West Virginia	Valley of Virginia	Piedmont	Tidewater	Eastern Shore	Albemarle Sound	Cape Fear	South Carolina
(1) The South and the South Midland									
light-bread (44)	×	×	×	×	×	×	×	×	×
clabber (47)	×	×	×	×	×	×	×	×	×
snack (48)	×	–	–	×	×	×	×	×	–
middlins (46)	×	×		×	×	×	–	×	
ash cakes (44)	–	·	–	×	×	–	–	–	–
(hay) shocks (14)	×	×	×	×	×	·	×	×	·
(corn) shucks (56)	×	×	×	×	×	×	×	×	×
you-all (43)	–	–	×	×	×	–	×	×	×
waiter (82)	–	–	–	–	–	–	–	–	–
pallet (29)	×	–	×	×	×	·	×	×	×
gutters (11)	×	·	×	×	×	·	×	×	×
(barn) lot (15)	×	–	·	×	·		×	×	
roll the baby (64)	–		·	×	–	·	–	×	·
salad (55)	–		·	×	×	·	×	×	
rock fence (16)	×	×	×	×	–	·			
(2) The South									
low (36)	–	·		×	×	×	×	×	×
hasslet (37)	–			×	×	×	×	×	×
lightwood (8)			–	×	×	×	×	×	×
turn of wood (19)				×	×	×	×	×	–
co-wench! (37)				×	×	×	×	×	×
(3) Virginia and the South Midland									
garden house (12)				–	×	·	×		
wesket (27)			·	–	–	–			
lumber room (10)	·		–	×	–	·	·		
soft peach (54)	·		·	×	–	·			
nicker (36)	–	×	–	×	–	–	·		
snake doctor (60)	·	–	×	×	·	·			
come up! (38)	–	–	–	×	·	·			
batter bread (44)			·	×	×				
(4) The Carolinas and the South Midland									
whicker (36)	–				–	×	×	×	×
johnny cake, a griddle cake (44)	–		·		·	×	–	–	–
clabber cheese (47)	×	–			·	·	×	×	–
breakfast strip (46)	–				·	·			
kerosene (24)	×					–	×	×	×
woods colt (65)	×	×	–				–	×	×
goop! (38)	–				·			×	×
(5) The Southern Coast									
curtains (9)		·	·		·	×	–	×	·
spider (17)					–	·	×	×	×
mosquito hawk (60)					–	×	×	×	×
press peach (54)					–		×	×	×
piazza (10)					–		×	×	×
earthworm (60)					–		×	×	×

Figure 3-7 *The Southern Area*
Source *From Kurath 1949*

Type I: *Upstate New York, Eastern Pennsylvania, and the South Midland*

crib:three	ɪ	i		ʊ	u	wood:tooth
ten:eight	ɛ	e	ɜ	ʌ	o	sun:road
bag	æ		ɑ		ɔ	law
five		ai	au		ɔi	boil
			thirty			
			crop			
			down			

Type II: *Metropolitan New York, the Upper South, and the Lower South*

crib:three	ɪ	i		ʊ	u	wood:tooth
ten:eight	ɛ	e	ɜ	ʌ	o	sun:road
bag	æ				ɔ	law
			ɑ		ɒ	crop:car
five		ai	au		ɔi	boil
			thirty			
			down			

Type III: *Eastern New England*

crib:three	ɪ	i		ʊ	u	wood:tooth
ten:eight	ɛ	e	ɜ	θ	o	road:rode
bag:car	æ	a		ʌ	ɒ	sun:law, crop
five		ai	au		ɒi	boil
			thirty			
			down			

Type IV: *Western Pennsylvania*

crib:three	ɪ	i		ʊ	u	wood:tooth
ten:eight	ɛ	e	ɜ	ʌ	o	sun:road
bag	æ				ɒ	law, crop
five		ai	au		ɒi	boil
			thirty			
			down			

Figure 3-8 *Vowels systems in the Eastern USA*
Source *From Kurath and McDavid 1961*

ten, *eight*, and *bag* are shared by all four regional pronunciation systems, as are those in the words *thirty* and *down* and those in the words *wood* and *tooth*. By contrast, the other vowels vary in the relationships within the four systems of figure 3-8, and the variation increases in the separate subareas included in the four systems (Kurath and McDavid 1961). In type III for Eastern New England, for instance, the vowel of *car* (and other words like it) is fronted so that it is close in pronunciation to the vowel of *bag* (this is the "Boston" pronunciation often imitated in the phrase "pahk the cah"). Eastern New England also shows a merger of two vowel sounds kept separate in types I and II, the vowels of *crop* and *law*. The vowel system of Western Pennsylvania also has merged these two vowel sounds, but does not have the (fronted) Boston vowel in *car*. The type II system (Metropolitan New York, the Upper South, and the Lower South) does not merge the vowels of *crop* and *law,* but those vowels are more retracted into the low-back vowel range. Metropolitan New York does not share one of the features strongly associated with Southern and South Midland pronunciation, namely, the "slow diphthong" that makes speakers from other regions hear the word *fire* as *far*. It is one of the "phonic and incidental features" that color the pronunciation of every subarea (Kurath and McDavid 1961).

American regional dialects for the twentieth-first century

The ALAP researchers described regional American dialects as they existed in the middle of the twentieth century. We now consider what has happened to the regional patterns during the rapid technological and cultural change that has swept America along since World War II, and we consider future prospects for regional dialects.

A more recent treatment by Carver (1987) has mapped American vocabulary with reference to the *Dictionary of American Regional English* (*DARE*) for which field work was carried out in the 1960s and 1970s (Cassidy et al. 1985–). He found essentially the same dialect areas that Kurath and McDavid had found, although he used a different method to create his maps and preferred different names for some areas. He often noted that some of the words earlier selected for the mid-twentieth century ALAP isoglosses were rare at the time of the *DARE* field work, or no longer found at all. This does not mean that the earlier regional dialect areas had disappeared. Quite the opposite: since the later dialect areas are much the same as the earlier ones, the more recent lists of words from the different areas are successors of the earlier ones. The speakers of the regional dialects changed their habits, but the basic regional patterning of American speech remained in place.

An index of entries in the first two *DARE* volumes provides lists of the words for which all of the different regional labels were used (*An Index* 1993). For instance, there are 1,540 words labeled as "South" and 1,318 as "South Midland," although 851 of these words actually carried both labels (Metcalf 1997: 267). These counts give an indication of the extent to which words can be associated with American dialect regions. The figure for the label "Northern" is smaller (624), but still substantial. Hawaii had the most words (133), followed by Texas (125), California (123), Pennsylvania (113), and Louisiana (110); New York is also prominent if labels for New York City are added to those for the state ($87 + 35 = 122$) (Metcalf 1997: 273–74). It is not unreasonable to talk about the speech of a state, although state boundaries are political and not usually defined by isoglosses or other linguistic means. As the counts show, however, a smaller number of words associates with any state than with labels for dialect areas. From Kurath's earlier maps, it is evident that a state often has more than one major dialect region within its borders. Only 56 words in the first two volumes of *DARE* were associated with cities, and more than half of those were associated with New York City (Metcalf 1997). *DARE* evidence thus confirms the persistence of large American regional dialect patterns into the second half of the twentieth century, even if some words have become obsolete and others have emerged to take their place. *DARE* suggests that these large regional patterns may be more salient, at least according to word counts, than states or cities as ways to describe and recognize American dialect patterns.

Extensive work in urban areas, particularly in Philadelphia and New York City, has confirmed the vitality of regional dialects. William Labov and his associates found "increasing diversity" in the pronunciation of US English and sought to highlight

> the main finding of our research, one that violates the most commonsense expectation of how language works and is supposed to work. In spite of the intense exposure of the American population to a national media with a convergent network standard of pronunciation, sound change continues actively in all urban dialects that have been studied, so that the local accents of Boston, New York, Philadelphia, Atlanta, Buffalo, Detroit, Chicago, and San Francisco are more different from each other than at any time in the past . . . Though the first findings dealt with sound change in Eastern cities, it is now clear that it is equally true of Northern, Western and Southern dialects. (Labov and Ash 1997: 508)

Three large patterns of sound change have been identified, and they are called the Northern Cities Shift, the Southern Shift, and Low Back Merger (Labov 1991). The term *sound change* refers to the fact that the pronunciation of both vowel and consonant sounds is not eternally fixed but may change over time. For discussion of regional dialects, such changes are important because they are not uniform for all speakers. Different changes occur within different groups of speakers. The term *shift* refers to the apparent tendency of English vowels to change not one at a time but according to larger characteristic patterns. The Low Back Merger is best characterized by the fact that the words *cot* and *caught*, and the names *Don* and *Dawn*, are homophones in the area of the merger, while people elsewhere pronounce them differently. One ongoing change of the Southern Shift is the seeming reversal (the facts are actually somewhat more complicated) of the pronunciation of what in the USA are traditionally called the *long e* (IPA [i])

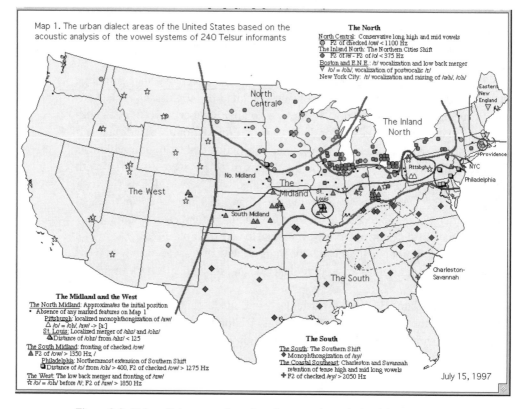

Figure 3-9 *Urban dialect areas based on the acoustic analysis of the vowel
systems of 240 Telsur informants*
Source *http://www.ling.upenn.edu/phono_atlas/NationalMap/NatMapl.html*

and *short i* (IPA [ɪ]) sounds. Among Southern Shift speakers, the name *Bill* is
pronounced much like the name *Beale* would be pronounced in other parts of the
country, and vice versa, and *steel mill* is pronounced close to what most people
in the rest of the country would recognize as *still meal*. The Northern Cities Shift
involves a sequence of changes so that each of the following words might be
heard and interpreted as something else by speakers from outside the area: *Ann* as
Ian, bit as *bet, bet* as *bat* or *but, lunch* as *launch, talk* as *tuck, locks* as *lax* (Labov
1991: 19).

The resulting patterns of sound change have specific geographic extension, as
shown in figure 3-9 from the Atlas of North American English.

As Labov explains the map,

> A remarkable finding of [figure 3-9] is that the major phonological boundaries
> of the U.S. as determined by new and vigorous sound changes which arose
> in the twentieth century coincide with the major lexical boundaries based on
> vocabulary.

In other words, the Northern Cities Shift occurs in the region occupied by what Kurath had called the Northern dialect area. Like the ALAP data, the Atlas of North American English also describes subsidiary areas. Thus, Eastern New England and the Inland North correspond to areas that Kurath also suggested (Labov's North Central region is farther west than Kurath's surveys). Kurath's Midland dialect region is recapitulated in Labov's Midland and West, which is characterized by the Low Back Merger pattern. As figure 3-8 shows, Western Pennsylvania shows a merger of *crop* and *law*, and it is this merger that serves as the centerpiece of Labov's description of the western part of Kurath's Midland and Far West. (The Low Back Merger pattern also applies in Canada.) Finally, the region for the Southern Shift corresponds to the Coastal and Upper South areas identified in the mid-twentieth century, and the Southern Shift has urban extensions in Philadelphia and New York City (Labov 1991: 36–37). As figure 3-8 shows, Kurath and McDavid had previously associated the vowel pattern of New York City with that of the South.

Observation of ongoing sound change confirms the one constant we expect for all languages: they will continue to change as long as people speak them. We are perhaps surprised that changes in American English seem to be occurring *within* the dialect regions described on mid-century evidence, in regions that have their foundations in the history of American primary settlement patterns. American regional dialects show no signs of disappearing; they are simply showing natural internal changes in the habits of their speakers.

What should we think of Labov's surprise, probably shared by many readers of this chapter, that "intense exposure of the American population to a national media with a convergent network standard of pronunciation" has not broken down regional dialects? This paradox – the strong continued existence of regional dialects when most educated Americans think that dialect variation is fading – is the topic for another essay (Kretzschmar 1997), but it is possible to say here that American English has developed a national dialect for the usually well-educated participants in a national marketplace for goods, services, and jobs. The well-educated share a national speech pattern within their own social stratum, unlike earlier periods in the history of American English when they shared regional dialects with working-class and lower-middle-class speakers. The solution to the paradox of the rise of national speech habits and the continuing existence of regional ones as set forth by Labov is that regional dialects are not separate from the social factors that influence the language habits of speakers – which should not surprise us at all once we come to think about it.

Suggestions for further reading and exploration

For information about the different regional surveys and for examples of complete lists of what people said in response to particular survey questions for the American Linguistic Atlas Project (ALAP), go to *http://www.us.english.uga.edu*.

The most recent handbook describing the methods used is Kretzschmar et al. (1993). For early summaries of findings, see Kurath (1949), Atwood (1953), McDavid (1958), and Kurath and McDavid (1961). For dialect developments toward the end of the twentieth century, see Carver (1987). One of the best informed and most entertaining writers on regional American English was Raven McDavid, some of whose essays have been republished in McDavid (1979; see especially "Postvocalic -r in South Carolina," "The Position of the Charleston Dialect," and "Sense and Nonsense about American Dialects") and McDavid (1980; see especially "New Directions in American Dialectology"). Other collections of articles that treat regional American variation include Glowka and Lance (1993), Frazer (1993), and Schneider (1996). Evidence about early regional variation may be found in Mathews (1931). A synthesis of ideas on colonial development of varieties is Kretzschmar (2002). For Southern American English, Pederson's monumental *Linguistic Atlas of the Gulf States* (1986–92) is complemented by Bernstein et al. (1997) and Johnson (1996). The *Oxford Dictionary of Pronunciation for Current English* (2001) offers side-by-side American and British pronunciations, and its discussion of American English points out many differences in regional pronunciations. For lots of linguistic fun, browse in any volume of *DARE* (Cassidy and Hall 1985–2002) or visit the website for the Atlas of North American English at *http://www.ling.upenn.edu/phono_atlas*.

References

An Index by Region, Usage, and Etymology to the Dictionary of American Regional English, vols. I and II. 1993. *Publication of the American Dialect Society* 77.

Atwood, E. Bagby. 1953. *A Survey of Verb Forms in the Eastern United States*. Ann Arbor: University of Michigan Press.

Bailey, Guy. 1997. "When Did Southern American English Begin?" In *Englishes Around the World: Studies in Honor of Manfred Görlach*. Vol. 1, ed. Edgar Schneider. Amsterdam: John Benjamins. Pp. 255–76.

Bailey, Guy and Jan Tillery. 1996. "The Persistence of Southern American English," *Journal of English Linguistics* 24: 308–21.

Bernstein, Cynthia, Thomas Nunnally, and Robin Sabino, eds. 1997. *Language Variety in the South Revisited*. Tuscaloosa: University of Alabama Press.

Burkette, Allison. 2001. "The Story of Chester Drawers," *American Speech* 76: 139–57.

Carver, Craig. 1987. *American Regional English: a Word Geography*. Ann Arbor: University of Michigan Press.

Cassidy, Frederic G. and Joan Houston Hall, eds. 1985–2002. *Dictionary of American Regional English*. Cambridge: Belknap/Harvard University Press.

Frazer, Timothy, ed. 1993. *Heartland English*. Tuscaloosa: University of Alabama Press.

Glowka, Wayne and Donald Lance, eds. 1993. *Language Variation in North American English*. New York: Modern Language Association.

Houck, Charles. 1969. "A Statistical and Computerized Methodology for Analyzing Dialect Materials." Unpublished Ph.D. dissertation, University of Iowa.

Johnson, Ellen. 1996. *Lexical Change and Variation in the Southeastern United States 1930–1990*. Tuscaloosa: University of Alabama Press.

Kretzschmar, William A., Jr. 1992. "Isoglosses and Predictive Modeling," *American Speech* 67: 227–49.

    1996a. "Quantitative Areal Analysis of Dialect Features," *Language Variation and Change* 8:13–39.

    1996b. "Foundations of American English." In Schneider. Pp. 25–50.

1997. "American English for the Twenty-first Century." In *Englishes Around the World: Studies in Honor of Manfred Görlach*, vol. 1, ed. Edgar Schneider. Amsterdam: John Benjamins. Pp. 307–23.

2002. "American English: Melting Pot or Mixing Bowl?" In *Of Dyuersitie and Change of Language: Essays Presented to Manfred Görlach on the Occasion of his Sixty-fifth Birthday*, eds. Katja Lenz and Ruth Möhlig. Heidelberg: C. Winter. Pp. 224–39.

Kretzschmar, William A., Jr., Virginia G. McDavid, Theodore K. Lerud, and Ellen Johnson, eds. 1993. *Handbook of the Linguistic Atlas of the Middle and South Atlantic States*. Chicago: University of Chicago Press.

Kurath, Hans. 1949. *A Word Geography of the Eastern United States*. Ann Arbor: University of Michigan Press.

Kurath, Hans and Raven I. McDavid, Jr. 1961. *The Pronunciation of English in the Atlantic States*. Ann Arbor: University of Michigan Press. [rpt. 1982, Tuscaloosa: University of Alabama Press].

Labov, William. 1991. "The Three Dialects of English." In *New Ways of Analyzing Sound Change*, ed. Penelope Eckert. Orlando: Academic Press. Pp. 1–44.

Labov, William and Sharon Ash. 1997. "Understanding Birmingham." In Bernstein, Nunnally, and Sabino, eds. Pp. 508–73.

Lee, Jay and William A. Kretzschmar, Jr. 1993. "Spatial Analysis of Linguistic Data with GIS Functions," *International Journal of Geographical Information Systems* 7: 541–60.

LePage, Robert and Andrée Tabouret-Keller. 1985. *Acts of Identity*. Cambridge: Cambridge University Press.

Marckwardt, Albert H. 1958. *American English*. New York: Oxford University Press.

Mathews, Mitford. 1931. *The Beginnings of American English*. Chicago: University of Chicago Press.

McDavid, Raven I., Jr. 1958. "The Dialects of American English." In W. Nelson Francis, *The Structure of American English*. New York: Ronald Press. Pp. 480–543.

1979. *Dialects in Culture*. Ed. William A. Kretzschmar, Jr., with the assistance of James McMillan, Lee Pederson, Roger Shuy, and Gerald Udell. Tuscaloosa: University of Alabama Press.

1980. *Varieties of American English*. Ed. Anwar Dil. Stanford: Stanford University Press.

McDavid, Raven I., Jr. and Virginia G. McDavid. 1951. "The Relationship of the Speech of American Negroes to the Speech of Whites," *American Speech* 26: 3–17.

Metcalf, Allan. 1997. "The South in *DARE*." In Bernstein, Nunnally, and Sabino, eds. Pp. 266–76.

Miller, Michael. 1999. *Dynamics of a Sociolinguistic System: Plural Formation in Augusta, Georgia*. Eds. Ronald Butters and William A. Kretzschmar, Jr., *Journal of English Linguistics* 27, Number 3.

Montgomery, Michael. 1989. "Exploring the Roots of Appalachian English," *English World Wide* 10: 227–78.

1997. "Making Transatlantic Connections between Varieties of English: the Case of Plural Verbal -s," *Journal of English Linguistics* 25: 122–41.

Montgomery, Michael and Stephen Nagle. 1993. "Double Modals in Scotland and the Southern United States: Trans-Atlantic Inheritance or Independent Development?" *Folia Linguistica Historica* 14: 91–107.

Oxford Dictionary of Pronunciation for Current English. 2001. Eds. Clive Upton, William A. Kretzschmar, Jr., and Rafal Konopka. Oxford: Oxford University Press.

Pederson, Lee. 1986–92. *Linguistic Atlas of the Gulf States*. 7 vols. Athens: University of Georgia Press.

Schneider, Edgar, ed. 1996. *Focus on the USA*. Philadelphia: John Benjamins.

Trudgill, Peter. 1986. *Dialects in Contact*. Oxford: Blackwell.

Turner, Lorenzo D. 1949. *Africanisms in the Gullah Dialect*. Chicago: University of Chicago Press.

4

Social varieties of American English

WALT WOLFRAM

Editors' introduction

This chapter explores the nature of social dialects within American English – in relation to which the stakes are much higher than they are for regional dialects. Your employability, intelligence, sincerity (even guilt) may be judged solely on the basis of the status-, ethnicity-, age- or gender-based variety you speak. These dimensions can interact with each other as well as with region, so that a linguistic feature that is socially distinctive in one city or ethnic group may not be distinctive in another. Vernacular varieties tend to have negatively valued or stigmatized features (like double negatives), while so-called "standard" varieties are negatively defined as lacking them.

Contrary to popular perception, as Walt Wolfram observes, "group exclusive" usages (e.g., "All women and no men say X") are rarer than "group preferential" usages (e.g., "Women are more likely than men to say X"), at least in the USA. Thus it is important to use quantitative methods to study socially conditioned linguistic variation, and to follow the accountability principle, which entails reporting the percentages of each variant observed out of the total number of cases in which it could have been used. Using an example involving variation between -ing and -in, in words like *walking* and *swimming*, Wolfram shows us how to do the requisite quantitative analysis and how to look for the linguistic and social or psychological factors that constrain linguistic variation. Linguistic variation is almost never haphazard.

In exploring social status (or class) differences, Wolfram distinguishes between the method of using "objective" multi-index scales and the method of eliciting the subjective views of community members. Whether investigators use consensus models of society or conflict models can also affect the analysis, and the extent to which social networks and local identity are taken into account can also make a significant difference. The chapter closes with a discussion of the social evaluation of language features, noting that the classification of these features as prestigious or stigmatized is often directly related to similar classifications of the people who use or avoid them. Wolfram also explains a long-standing sociolinguistic distinction among socially marked features that function as stereotypes, markers, or indicators, depending on whether they elicit overt comment and involve stylistic variation as well as variation across social groups.

The job interview was going smoothly. And then the applicant wrapped a double negative around the use of *seen* as a past tense in the sentence *Nobody never seen nothing*. At that point, the interviewers formed an indelible impression of the candidate's social background and unsuitability for the job. Incidents like that point to the severe judgments that often are made in our society based upon perception of language as it relates to social position (Lippi-Green 1997 and this volume). People may be judged on capabilities ranging from innate intelligence to employability and on personal attributes ranging from sincerity to morality based solely on the perception of social differences in language. It is quite shocking to realize how quickly and categorically we may judge a person's background and character based simply upon a few utterances or, in some instances, the choice of a single word. Dialect differences related to region may be interpreted by the American public as matters of quaint curiosity and may even hold a certain amount of aesthetic charm but the stakes are different – and much higher – when it comes to differences in American English related to social status.

Although people often think of social varieties of language as if they were distinctive, unidimensional entities, it is not quite that simple. Even though we use the term "social dialect" or "sociolect" as a label for the alignment of a set of language structures with the social position of a group in a status hierarchy, the social demarcation of language does not exist in a vacuum. Speakers are simultaneously affiliated with a number of different groups that include region, age, gender, and ethnicity, and some of these other factors may weigh heavily in the determination of the social stratification of language variation. For example, among older European-American speakers in Charleston, South Carolina, the absence of *r* in words such as *bear* and *court* is associated with aristocratic, high-status groups (McDavid 1948) whereas in New York City the same pattern of *r*-lessness is associated with working-class, low-status groups (Labov 1966). Such opposite social interpretations of the same linguistic trait over time and space point to the arbitrariness of the linguistic symbols that carry social meaning. In other words, it is not really the meaning of what you say that counts socially, but who you are when you say it.

Generally speaking, the term social dialect is used to refer to differences that are associated with groups that are unequal in status and power. When language differences represent groups that are unequal in their power relations, it is quite common for society at large to interpret the differences in terms of the *principle of linguistic inferiority*. According to this principle, the speech of a socially subordinate group will be interpreted as linguistically inadequate by comparison with that of the socially dominant group. Thus, in popular culture, dialects associated with socially disfavored groups are thought to be nothing more than unworthy and corrupted versions of the varieties spoken by their socially favored counterparts. This interpretation is altogether contrary to the linguistic facts, which demonstrate the intricate patterning of language apart from its social evaluation and the arbitrary link between linguistic form and social meaning. Therefore, linguists take a united stand against any definition of dialect as a corrupt version of the standard variety. For example, a resolution adopted unanimously by the Linguistic Society of America at its annual meeting in 1997 asserts that "all human language systems – spoken, signed, and written – are fundamentally regular" and that characterizations of socially disfavored varieties as "slang, mutant, defective, ungrammatical, or broken English are incorrect and demeaning."

In American society, the notion of social dialect tends to be strongly associated with the varieties of English spoken by socially subordinate groups even though, technically speaking, the varieties spoken by socially dominant groups are certainly social varieties as well. The varieties of English associated with these socially subordinate groups are often referred to as *vernacular dialects*. The term vernacular dialect is used in a way analogous to the way that the term vernacular language is used to refer to local or native languages of common communication that contrast with the official standard language of a multilingual country.

Part of the reason that the term social dialect is so strongly associated with vernacular varieties is related to the fact that the speech of low-status groups in American society tends to be much more socially marked than that of high-status groups. To a large extent, vernacular varieties are characterized by the presence of socially conspicuous and negatively valued structures – so-called "nonstandard dialect structures." By the same token, socially favored varieties of English tend to be characterized by the absence of negatively valued, or socially stigmatized, features rather than by the presence of socially prestigious features. In fact, one possible definition of so-called "standard English" characterizes it as a variety of English that does *not* exhibit socially stigmatized structures of English – a negative definition – rather than a variety typified by any particular set of positively valued structures (Wolfram and Schilling-Estes 1998). Americans seem to be more concerned that speakers avoid negatively valued features of speech than adopt positively valued ones. Accordingly, the notion of social dialects in American society has come to be associated with the vernacular varieties spoken by low-status groups.

The patterning of social differences in language

A popular perception of social dialects holds that all members of a given social group use certain structures and that members of other social groups never use these forms. But the reality of social dialect differentiation is much more complicated than that. Different linguistic variables may correlate with social-status groupings in a variety of ways, given varying histories of dialect contact, dialect diffusion, and changes in group relations. The pattern of dialect distribution that most closely matches the popular perception of dialect differences is referred to as "group-exclusive usage," where one group of speakers uses a form but another one never does (Smith 1985). In its ideal interpretation, group-exclusive usage means that *all* members of a particular community of speakers would use the dialect form whereas *no* members of other groups would ever use it. This ideal pattern is rarely, if ever, maintained in dialects. The kinds of social groupings and intersecting web of social factors that typify group affiliations in society are just too complex for this pattern to work out so neatly. In the first place, the definition of any social group usually involves a constellation of characteristics rather than a single dimension, thus making the simple correlation of a linguistic form with social position intricate and multidimensional. Furthermore, in many cases, actual social distinctions between groups exist on a continuum, and linguistic differences accordingly show a continuous rather than discrete correlation with social traits.

Notwithstanding the qualifications that have to be made when talking about group-exclusive dialect features, there certainly are forms of American English that are not shared across groups defined on the basis of relative social status. The essential aspect of these dialect forms, however, seems to be that speakers from other groups do *not* use them rather than that all the members of a particular group do use them. Group-exclusive usage is therefore easier to define negatively than positively. Viewed in this way, there are many dialect features on all levels of language organization that show group-exclusive social distribution. For example, grammatical structures such as subject–verb agreement in sentences such as *We was down there* or the use of regularized past tense verb forms such as *We growed tomatoes last year* may show group-exclusive usage in that only speakers of some low-status groups use these forms while speakers of high status groups do not.

In contrast to group-exclusive forms, *group-preferential* forms are distributed across different groups or communities of speakers, but members of one group simply are more likely to use a given form than members of another group. For example, empirical studies of the use of *-in'* [ɪn] versus *-ing* [ɪŋ] in forms such as *swimmin'* for *swimming* or *doin'* for *doing* show that speakers of all social ranks actually use the *in* variant some of the time, but that speakers from low-status groups use *in'* at a much higher frequency level than their high-status counterparts. Thus, we can say that the use of *-in'* for *-ing* is a group-preferential pattern rather than a group-exclusive one. Group-preferential patterns may derive from the nature of the dialect variable or the nature of the social reality that underlies the social variable. For example, as we noted earlier, there are dimensions of group affiliation, interactional relationship, and ideological perspective that make social position far more complex than the simple designation of group membership based exclusively on socioeconomic status. We would not expect the symbolic effect of a group-preferential pattern to be as socially significant as a group-exclusive marking, although popular stereotypes of group-preferential dialect patterns sometimes treat them symbolically as if they were group-exclusive. The popular characterization of vernacular dialects of English in their use of *dese*, *dem*, and *dose* for *these*, *them*, and *those* is such an instance where the stereotype of group-exclusive behavior actually betrays a fairly complex pattern that is really group-preferential and also highly variable. Studies of community populations within particular regions of the United States have shown that, on the whole, socially diagnostic pronunciations are more likely to show group-preferential patterns than grammatical features do. For example, in a given Southern community, a phonological pattern such as the loss of the glide of the /ay/ vowel of *time* /taym/ or *side* /sayd/ as *tahm* [taːm] or *sahd* [saːd] respectively, or the deletion of the *r* in words like *bear* and *court* will show a group-preferential pattern in which all status groups use these features to some extent, with differences in relative frequency rather than absolute usage differentiating social-status groups. On the other hand, grammatical features such as the use of the completive *done* in *They done messed up* or the use of a regularized verb in *We growed beans* would show a group-exclusive pattern in that low-status groups use these features to some extent while high-status speakers avoid them completely.

The social dimension of dialect differences

In almost every society, some people have social prestige, power, and money, while others have little of these commodities. Few people would disagree about the social status classification of individuals who possess these attributes to an extremely high or extremely low degree. We would hardly mistake a chief executive officer of a major corporation who resides in a spacious house in an "exclusive" part of town for an uneducated, unskilled laborer from the "wrong side of the tracks." The reality of social stratification seems obvious, but identifying the unique set of traits that correlates with social-status differences in a reliable and reductive way is not always so simple. Ultimately, social-class distinctions seem to be based upon status and power, where status refers to the amount of respect and deference accorded to a person and power refers to the social and material resources a person can command, as well as the ability to make decisions and influence events. The challenge is to reduce these abstract notions to objective, measurable units that can be correlated in meaningful ways with linguistic variation. Different kinds of procedures have been used with varying degrees of success in attempts to capture the construct of social class.

The traditional sociological approach to social-status differences isolates a set of objectified socioeconomic characteristics that are used to rank individuals in some way. Typical variables include occupation, level of education, income, and type of residential dwelling, with ranked levels within each variable. For example, occupations may be scaled based on categories ranging from "major professionals" to "unskilled laborers"; education scales may range from professional and graduate school to less than three years of schooling, and residency scales may range from housing with more than two rooms per person and with a bathroom per each person to housing with three persons or more per room and with no indoor plumbing. Different weightings may then be assigned to variables if one trait is considered more significant than another. For example, occupation may be weighted more heavily than education or residency in computing a socioeconomic status score. The overall ranking obtained from combining scores for the variables is the *socioeconomic status*, usually abbreviated SES. Although this kind of ranking system yields a continuous scale, it is possible to divide the distribution of scores into separate social-status groupings, with labels such as upper-class, middle-class, working-class, and so forth.

In recent years, SES scales have been subject to considerable scrutiny, as social scientists began to realize that most of these scales are grounded in the values of mainstream middle-class and higher-class populations (Rickford 1986). For example, researchers investigating language and gender have pointed out that females traditionally have been grouped into socioeconomic categories based on the characteristics of husbands, fathers, or other male "heads of household," often with wildly misleading results (McConnell-Ginet 1988).

As an alternative to the strict objectification of social-status differences assigned by an outside social scientist, it is possible to rely upon community members to make judgments about status differences. Ultimately, the real discriminators of social class are the members of the community themselves. From one perspective, social classes are constituted by the community, and they have no independent status outside the attitudes and perceptions of the group. Thus, members of a community are rated by other community members in terms of certain imputed status traits. Is a person "upper crust" or from the "wrong side of the tracks"? Typically, communities have their own designations for particular subgroups in terms of the social status hierarchy, and these can be tapped to determine class distinctions. As with externally assigned objective measures, however, there are problems in relying upon community members for the assignment of social-status differences. Different pictures of social class may emerge from representatives of different segments of the community, both on an individual and class level. For example, the lower classes may perceive social-class structure very differently from the upper classes. So even if we rely on subjective, community-based divisions, we are not assured consistency in determining social divisions.

Furthermore, the view of class presented here, which is based on analyses of Western society, emphasizes social agreement on the evaluation of prestige and behavioral norms. That is, it is believed that all social groups share certain expectations for appropriate and desirable behavior and also view increases in social status as positive and desirable. In this view, sometimes referred to as the "consensus model" of social class, individual competition is emphasized over conflicts between classes (Rickford 1986, Guy 1988). But it is also possible to view class differences as conflicts between those who control resources and means of production and can live off of the profits of the workers on the one hand and the workers who earn the profits for those in power on the other hand. Under such a "conflict model," class differences are viewed as the consequences of divisions and conflicts between the classes, and linguistic differences, in turn, are seen as a reflection of the interests of different classes and conflicts between classes. Accordingly, the dichotomy between standard and vernacular may be viewed as the symbolic token of a class struggle. In other words, those who speak less standardly do not value standard speech as they do under the consensus model; rather, they use vernacular speech forms as a symbolic expression of separation from the upper classes with whom they conflict.

Ideally, a valid assessment of social-class differences should combine both objective and subjective measurements of many types of behavioral roles and values, but this is often easier said than done. Even to the extent that this is possible, such a perspective does not assure a neat fit between social status or class differences and language variation. We have already noted that there are other social variables that intersect with social class, but there are also additional factors pertaining to community life and relationships that may set apart linguistic variation from other social status considerations. For example, one of the important correlates of linguistic differences relates to the so-called *linguistic marketplace*, in which a person's economic activity, broadly defined, is associated with language variation. People in certain occupations tend to use more standard varieties of the language than members of the same social class who hold other occupations. Thus, teachers or salespeople, who have to confront public expectations of language usage, may be more standard in their language than their social status peers in other occupations where they are not expected to use standard language forms. A person's "linguistic market index," a ranking assigned to speakers based upon descriptions of their socioeconomic life histories, may correlate with language differences more closely than traditional social-status designations, according to some researchers (see, e.g., Sankoff and Laberge 1978).

Another parameter intersecting with strict social class relates to the "social network." There may be important differences in interactional activity that correlate with language differences. For example, social networks characterized by repeated interactions with the same people in several spheres of activity (e.g., work, leisure, church) tend to correlate with a greater concentration of the dialect features associated with that group (Milroy 1987) than those with looser affiliations. Problems in the neatness of fit between social class and language, then, are not simply problems in the definition of social class, although these problems certainly exist. Instead, many of the difficulties in the straightforward correlation of social status with language variation relate to the ways in which social factors interact with each other in their effect on linguistic variation.

Also, in small, isolated communities where "everybody knows everybody," the correlation of language differences and socioeconomic differences may not be nearly as significant as in large, urban communities characterized by a high degree of social distance among different groups of speakers. For example, on the island of Ocracoke, an Outer Banks island off the coast of North Carolina, some of the most vernacular speakers are men who went to college off the island and later returned to the island (Wolfram and Schilling-Estes 1997). These men are among the most influential and powerful people on the island, owning considerable property and making considerable amounts of money from the tourism industry, yet they maintain a strong vernacular dialect. They also interact on a regular basis with outsiders, conducting business and socializing with them more than some other islanders. They maintain the vernacular because they wish to project a "traditional islander" identity rather than to identify with the middle-class or upper-class mainlanders, who typically are associated with standard speech forms. Thus, matters of identity and personal presentation have to be considered along with conventional status measures and factors pertaining to interactional networks in considering the relationship between language variation and social-status differences.

Systematic variability in social dialect differentiation

As noted previously, the careful examination of dialect forms shows that social varieties of American English are sometimes differentiated on the basis of how frequently particular forms are used rather than whether or not a variant is used. Individual speakers may fluctuate in their use of variants, sometimes using one form and sometimes using an alternate, only the relative frequencies of usage serving to differentiate social varieties. Consider the following excerpt showing the fluctuation of -*ing* and -*in'* within the speech of an individual during a single speech event.

> We were walk*in'* down the street and we saw this car go*ing* out of control. The driver looked like he was sleep*ing* at the wheel or someth*in'*. The next thing I knew the car was turn*in'* around and just spinn*ing* around. I thought the car was com*in'* right at me and I started runn*in'* like crazy. I was so scared, think*ing* the car was gonna hit me or someth*in'*. . . .

In the ten examples of the form -*ing* in this passage, four end in -*ing* and six in -*in'*. This kind of variation, where a speaker sometimes produces one variant and sometimes an alternate one, is referred to as "inherent variability." The term inherent variability reflects the fact that this fluctuation is an internal part of a single linguistic system, or dialect, and should not be considered to be the result of importations from another dialect or of speech errors. In other words, there is no evidence that the speaker fluctuating between -*ing* and *in'* is switching between two dialects, one exclusively using -*ing* and another exclusively using -*in'*. Instead, the speaker is using a single dialect system – with two pronunciation variants of this ending – and the speaker sometimes uses one form and sometimes the other.

Over the past several decades, one of the important discoveries to emerge from the detailed study of social varieties of English is that dialects are sometimes differentiated not by the absolute presence or absence of particular forms, but by the relative frequency with which the variants occur. In fact, for a number of phonological and grammatical features, dialects are more typically differentiated by the extent to which a particular feature occurs (its relative frequency) rather than by its complete absence or categorical presence.

For four social-status groups of Detroit speakers, table 4-1 displays the frequency levels of the phonological variable *in'* for -*ing* and the syntactic variable called pronominal apposition (e.g., *My mother,* **she's** *coming to school* as opposed to *My mother's coming to school*). Although the counts represent the mean scores for each social group, each of the individual speakers in the groups also exhibits variability between -*ing* and -*in'*, as well as between *my mother, she* . . . and *my mother* . . . Frequency levels were computed for individual speakers by first noting all those cases where a form like -*in'* might have occurred – namely, in unstressed syllables ending in -*ing*. Then the number of cases in which -*in'* actually occurred was counted. For example, in the sample passage given earlier, there are ten cases

Table 4-1 *Relative frequency of variable phonological and grammatical structures in four social groups in Detroit, Michigan*

	Upper-middle	Lower-middle	Upper-working	Lower-working
Mean percentage of –*in'* forms	19.1	39.1	50.5	78.9
Mean % of pronominal apposition	4.5	13.6	25.4	23.8

Source: Adapted from Shuy, Wolfram and Riley 1967

where -*in'* could have occurred, but only six of them, or 60 percent, were actually produced with the -*in'* form. This tabulation procedure follows a fairly standard format for determining frequency levels of dialect forms.

The fact that there is fluctuation between forms such as -*ing* and -*in'* does not mean that the fluctuation is random or haphazard. Although we cannot predict which variant might be used in a given instance, there are factors that can increase or decrease the likelihood that certain variants will occur. These factors, known technically as "constraints on variability," are of two major types. First, various social factors such as social affiliation correlate systematically with an increase or decrease in the likelihood that a particular variant will occur. In other words, looking at table 4-1, we can say that a speaker from the lower-working class is more likely than speakers from other classes to use both -*in'* for -*ing* and pronominal apposition. But that is only one social factor that correlates with the relative incidence of -*in'* and -*ing*. Dividing the speakers on the basis of age, sex, ethnicity, or a division of the conversation from which these forms were taken on the basis of topic and interlocutor, would show that all of these factors intersect with social status. This is one of the reasons that we noted earlier that social status intersects with other social factors in its correlation with language variation. In fact, social status is not always the primary factor in the constellation of social factors that correlates with linguistic variation. In cases of rapid language change, for example, age may show a stronger correlation with language variation than status, and, in another instance, region may be a primary variable and status a secondary or moderating factor. Though status is often an important factor, its relative effect in relation to other social factors may vary considerably.

Even with microscopic attention to social details, not all of the systematic influences on variation can be accounted for simply by appealing to various social factors. There are also aspects of the linguistic system itself that may affect the variability of particular forms. Particular kinds of linguistic contexts, such as the kinds of surrounding forms or the type of construction in which the form occurs, may also influence the relative frequency with which these forms occur. Because the linguistic influences on variation operate apart from the social factors that correlate with variability, these are sometimes referred to as "independent

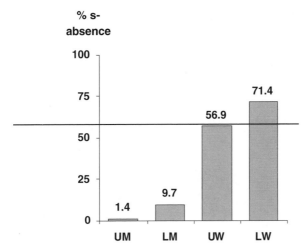

Figure 4-1 *Example of sharp stratification: third-person singular s-absence among upper-middle (UM), lower-middle (LM), upper-working (UW), and lower-working (LW) class speakers in the African American community of Detroit, Michigan*
Source *After Wolfram 1969*

linguistic constraints" on variability. For example, the occurrence of *-ing* in a verb (*She was swimming in the river*) versus a noun (*Swimming is fun*) affects the relative incidence of *-in'* apart from the consideration of any social variables. Similarly, speakers of particular social groups who use *was* with plural subjects (e.g., *We was there*) typically do so more frequently with subjects that are noun phrases (such as *The dogs was here*) than with subjects that are pronouns (such as *They was here*). This pattern emerges when all social factors are controlled. So constraints on the variability of socially diagnostic items show complex sensitivity to a set of system-internal, structural factors as well as of social and psychological factors external to the linguistic system.

As mentioned, linguistic variables may align with given social-status groupings in a variety of ways. For example, consider the ways in which two linguistic variables are distributed across four social strata within the African American community of Detroit, Michigan (Wolfram 1969). The variables are third-person singular suffix absence as in *She go to the store* for *She goes to the store*, given in figure 4-1, and *r*-lessness after a vowel such as *bea'* for *bear* or *cou't* for *court*, given in figure 4-2. The sample for these two variables is the same population of speakers representing the African American community in Detroit. Notice that here the social-status differences are restricted to a particular ethnic group and region. As it turns out, in a Northern, Midwestern region such as Detroit, these diagnostic variables are pertinent only to social-status differences within the African American community, thus showing how social varieties are embedded within broader cultural and regional contexts. In fact, neither of the linguistic structures differentiated in figure 4-1 and figure 4-2 is pertinent to the social

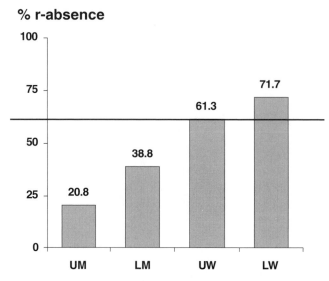

Figure 4-2 *Example of gradient stratification: postvocalic r-absence among*
upper-middle (UM), lower-middle (LM), upper-working (UW), and
lower-working (LW) class speakers in the African American community of
Detroit, Michigan
Source *After Wolfram 1969*

varieties of European Americans in Detroit. The social differentiation of language
among African Americans in Detroit obviously reflects both the roots of this
community as a Southern transplant community and the segregation patterns that
have served to maintain somewhat different patterns of social differentiation for
African Americans and European Americans in this metropolitan area.

In figure 4-1, the linguistic variation correlates with certain discrete social
layers. The groups designated "middle class" (UM = upper-middle class and
LM = lower-middle class) according to conventional socioeconomic indices
such as level of occupation, education, and residency show very little -*s* absence
whereas working-class (UW = upper-working class and LW = lower-working
class) speakers show significant levels of -*s* absence. The distribution of -*s* use
shows a wide separation between middle-class and working-class groups and is
therefore referred to as a case of "sharp stratification." On the other hand, the
distribution of *r*-lessness in figure 4-2 indicates a pattern of "gradient stratification" or "fine stratification," in which the relative frequency of *r*-lessness changes
gradually from one social class to the adjacent one.

In the examples given in figure 4-1 and figure 4-2, sharp stratification is illustrated by a grammatical variable and gradient stratification by a phonological
one. Although there are exceptions, grammatical variables are more likely to
show sharp stratification than phonological variables. This underscores the fact
that grammatical features are typically more diagnostic of social differences than
phonological ones in American society. In other societies, for example England

and New Zealand, phonological variables may carry an equal or greater burden of social differentiation than grammatical features.

Since there are different patterns of correlation between social stratification and linguistic variation, it is sometimes difficult to answer the question of how many social dialects there are in English. On one level, this question is best answered by examining the social stratification of particular linguistic structures. From this perspective, the answer may range from two, for a sharply stratified variable that shows a basic dichotomy between two broadly defined social groups, through six or seven varieties for finely stratified features. For linguistic variation showing a correlation with two basic social groups, the popular perception that there are two social dialects – the socially acceptable and unacceptable implied in the popular designation of "standard" and "nonstandard" dialects – may be matched by the reality of social stratification. For other variables, however, multi-layered social dialect differentiation is clearly indicated. It is important to understand that both continuous and discrete patterns of sociolinguistic variation may simultaneously exist within the same population and community. The kind of correlation that exists between social factors and linguistic variation may thus be a function of both social and linguistic considerations; there is no single pattern that can be applied to this co-variation.

The social evaluation of linguistic features

Although there is no inherent social valuation associated with the variants of a linguistic structure, it is not surprising that the social values assigned to certain groups will be attached to the linguistic forms used by the members of those groups. It is thus no accident that so-called standard varieties of a language typically are associated with socially favored and dominant groups and that "nonstandard" dialects are associated with socially disfavored, low-status groups. The selection of particular linguistic structures for social evaluation may be arbitrary, but their evaluation tends to correlate with the social evaluation of the groups who use them. *Socially prestigious* variants are those forms that are positively valued through their association with high-status groups as linguistic markers of status, whereas *socially stigmatized* variants carry negative connotations through their association with low-status groups. In grammar, most prestige forms are related to prescriptive norms of standardness or even literary norms. For example, the use of *whom* in *Whom did you see?* or the placement of *never* at the front of the sentence in *Never have I seen a more gruesome sight* might be considered prestige variants in some social contexts. Apart from these somewhat special cases, it is difficult to find clear-cut cases of prestige variants on the grammatical level of language, particularly in the grammar of ordinary informal conversation.

In American English, examples of prestige variants are also relatively rare in phonology. The use of an "unflapped" /t/ in words like *better* or *latter* (e.g., [bɛtɚ] as opposed to [bɛɾɚ]) as used by a select group of "Brahmin" dialect speakers found in the Boston metropolitan area may be an example of a prestige variant, as would some other phonological characteristics of this dialect, but this is a fairly isolated, somewhat unusual situation. The pronunciations of this restricted prestige dialect are modeled more on standard British English, or Received Pronunciation, than on American English. The fact that an external norm serves as a model for prestige in this instance is actually a commentary on the relative absence of authentic prestige variants in American English dialects. In some regions, the pronunciation of *either* as [aɪðɚ] instead of [iðɚ] or the pronunciation of *vase* as [vɑz] versus [veɪz] may be associated with high status, but these relate to the pronunciation of single lexical items rather than phonological systems and are therefore more properly considered lexical than pronunciation variants.

For present-day American English, it is clear that the vast majority of socially diagnostic structures exist on the axis of stigmatization rather than the axis of prestige. Classic illustrations involving grammatical features include the familiar cases of multiple negation (e.g., *They **didn't** do **nothing***), regularized verb forms (e.g., *He **knowed** they were right*), and different subject–verb agreement patterns (e.g., *We **was** there*). Stigmatized phonological features include *-in'* for *-ing* (e.g., *stoppin'*, *swimmin'*), [d] or [t] for *th* (e.g., [deɪ] or [de] *they*, [tɪŋk] *think*). There are also lexical shibboleths such as *ain't*. It is relatively easy to come up with examples of stigmatized variants for different levels of linguistic organization as compared with prestigious variants. This observation is part of the rationale which may lead to the conclusion that standard English is more adequately characterized by the absence of negatively valued, stigmatized items than by the presence of positively valued, prestige items as suggested earlier.

Stigmatized and prestigious variants do not exist on a single dimension in which the alternative to a socially stigmatized variant is a socially prestigious one, or vice versa. The absence of multiple negation, for example, is not particularly prestigious; it is simply not stigmatized. Thus, it is not prestigious to say *She didn't do anything* for *She didn't do nothing*; it is just not stigmatized. Similarly, the non-prestigious variant for *either* [iðɚ] is not necessarily stigmatized; it is simply not prestigious. In fact, there are very few cases in English in which there exists a socially prestigious alternate for a socially stigmatized variant.

The discussion of the social evaluation of linguistic features up to this point has been undertaken from the vantage point of those who place high value on the widespread, institutional language norms established by higher-status groups. These norms are overtly perpetuated by the agents of standardization in our society – teachers, the media, and other authorities responsible for setting the standards of linguistic behavior. These norms are usually acknowledged across a full range of social classes on a community-wide basis. Linguistic forms that are assigned their social evaluation on the basis of this widespread recognition of social significance are said to carry *overt prestige*. At the same time, however, there may exist another set of norms that relates primarily to solidarity with more locally defined social groups, irrespective of the social status of these groups. When forms are positively valued apart from, or even in opposition to, their social significance for the wider society, they are said to carry *covert prestige*. In the case of overt prestige, the social valuation lies in a unified, widely accepted set of social norms, whereas with covert prestige the positive social significance lies in the local culture of social relations. It is therefore possible for a socially stigmatized variant in one setting to have covert prestige in another. A local youth who adopts vernacular forms in order to maintain solidarity with a group of friends clearly indicates the covert prestige of these features on a local level even if the same features stigmatize the speaker in a wider, mainstream context such as school. The notion of covert prestige is important in understanding why vernacular speakers may not aspire to speak socially favored dialects, even when these speakers may evaluate the social significance of linguistic variation in a way that superficially matches that of their high-status counterparts. Thus, widely recognized stigmatized features such as multiple negation, nonstandard subject–verb agreement, and different irregular verb paradigms may function at the same time as positive, covertly prestigious features in terms of local norms.

In recent years, the maintenance or even heightening of vernacular language features among non-mainstream speakers has been viewed in terms of power as well as prestige. For example, working-class men may use vernacular variants as a means of projecting power rather than covert prestige, since working-class men traditionally have held occupations associated with physical toughness and manliness (and hence vernacular language features) rather than with advanced education.

The social significance of language forms may change over time, just as linguistic structures themselves change. It may be difficult for present-day speakers of English to believe that linguistic shibboleths such as *ain't* and multiple negation were once socially insignificant, but the historical study of the English language certainly supports this conclusion. Furthermore, shifts in social significance may take place from generation to generation. For example, in New York City (Labov 1966) and in some regions of the South (Feagin 1990), the social significance of postvocalic /r/ (as in *cart* or *farm*) has shifted during the past fifty years. For the older generation, there is very little social-class stratification for the use of postvocalic *r*, but younger speakers show a well-defined pattern of social stratification in which the presence of /r/ (e.g., *cart*) is more highly valued than its absence (e.g., *caht*). And, as noted earlier, postvocalic *r*-lessness in Southern speech was once a prestigious pronunciation, following the prestige model for British English. However, the valuation of *r*-less speech has changed over the decades, and today it is working-class rural groups in the South who are most characteristically *r*-less rather than urban upper-class speakers. Because *r*-lessness used to carry prestige, older upper-class groups in some regions of the South retain a high incidence of *r*-lessness; by contrast, younger upper-class speakers tend to pronounce *r* in this context. At the same time, younger, rural working-class speakers may be relatively *r*-less, thus uniting older metropolitan and younger rural speakers in *r*-lessness but with quite different social meanings associated with the *r*-lessness.

The social significance of linguistic variables may also vary from region to region. Growing up as a native Philadelphian, I pronounced *aunt* and *ant* the same [ænt]; furthermore, I associated the pronunciation of *aunt* [ɑnt] differently from *ant* [ænt] with high-status groups. In later life, I was quite surprised to discover that the pronunciation of *aunt* I considered prestigious and even "uppity" was characteristic of some Southern dialects regardless of social status, including highly stigmatized vernacular varieties such as African American Vernacular English.

Although some socially diagnostic variables have regionally restricted social significance, other variables may have general social significance for American English, in that a particular social evaluation holds across regional boundaries. Many grammatical variables have this type of broad-based significance. Virtually every population in the USA that has been studied by social dialectologists shows social stratification for structures like multiple negation, irregular verb forms, and subject–verb agreement patterns. On the whole, phonological variables are more apt to show regionally restricted social significance than are grammatical variables. No doubt, this is due to the fact that grammatical variables have been ascribed the major symbolic role in differentiating socially differentiated dialects in American society. Phonological variables show greater flexibility, as they are more likely to be viewed as a normal manifestation of regional diversity in English. This is particularly true in the case of vowel differences.

There are several ways in which speakers within the sociolinguistic community may react to socially diagnostic variables. Speakers may treat some features as *social stereotypes*, where they comment on their use. Items such as *ain't*, "double negatives," and *dese, dem,* and *dose* are classic features of this type. Stereotypes can be regionally specific or generalized and may carry either positive or negative connotations. *Ain't* and "dese, dem, and dose" are widely recognized as "bad grammar," while features like the pronunciation of *high tide* as something like "hoi toid" (as in the speech of coastal North Carolina) are strongly stereotyped but only locally. Further, the latter feature carries positive associations in that it is often associated with "British English" or even "Shakespearean English." It qualifies as a stereotype because it is the subject of commentary.

As with other kinds of behavioral stereotyping, we have to be careful to differentiate the actual sociolinguistic patterning of linguistic stereotypes from popular beliefs about their patterning. These beliefs are often linguistically naive, although they may derive from a basic sociolinguistic reality. For example, people tend to believe that working-class speakers always use the stereotypical *dese, dem,* and *dose* forms and middle-class speakers never do. This belief is not supported empirically, although there is a correlation between the relative frequency of the nonstandard variant and social stratification. Similarly, the Outer Banks "hoi toid" vowel is a defining dialect trait of the region, but it is in flux and its rate of usage is highly variable. Furthermore, stereotypes tend to focus on single vocabulary items or selective subsets of items rather than more general phonological and grammatical patterns. For example, speakers may focus on a single lexical item like *ain't* or the restricted pronunciation pattern involving *tomatoes* in which *'maters* is stigmatized and *tomahtoes* is prestigious. Finally, we have to understand that popular explanations for sociolinguistic differences are often rooted in the same type of folk mythology that characterizes other behavioral stereotyping and therefore must be viewed with great caution.

Another role that a socially diagnostic feature may fill is that of a *social marker*. In the case of social markers, variants show clear-cut social stratification, but they do not show the level of conscious awareness found for the social stereotype. Various vowel shifts seem to function as social markers. There is clear-cut social stratification of the linguistic variants, and participants in the community may even recognize this distribution, but the structure does not evoke the kind of commentary and strong value judgments that the social stereotype does. Even if people don't talk about these features in any direct manner, there are still indications that they are aware of their existence at an unconscious level. This awareness is often indicated by shifts in the use of variants across different styles of speaking. The incidence of prestigious variants tends to increase and the use of stigmatized variants to decrease as we use more formal speech styles. For example, a speaker who is conversing with an employer during a business meeting will use more *-ing* [ɪŋ] for *-ing* but will use more *-in'* [ɪn] when talking with friends over lunch.

The third possible sociolinguistic role that a socially diagnostic feature may fill is that of a *social indicator*. Social indicators are linguistic structures that correlate with social stratification without having an effect on listeners' judgment of the social status of speakers who use them. Whereas social stereotypes and social markers are sensitive to stylistic variation, social indicators do not show such sensitivity, as shown by the fact that levels of usage remain constant across formal and informal styles. This suggests that the correlation of socially diagnostic variables with social-status differences operates on a more unconscious level than it does for social markers or stereotypes. Although social indicators have been identified for some communities of English speakers, practically all of the socially diagnostic variables in American English qualify as social markers or stereotypes rather than indicators.

Conclusion

The differentiation of language on the basis of relative social status constitutes one of the most marked dimensions of variation in American English. Many forms are socially stigmatized because of their association with socially disfavored groups whereas few structures are considered prestigious because of their association with high-status groups. Accordingly, most studies of social dialectology have focused on vernacular dialect communities excluded from the mainstream by their vernacular dialect rather than elitist groups who set themselves apart from other groups by their prestigious language. As we have seen, the co-variation of social position and linguistic variation is neither simple nor unidimensional. In the determination of language use, social rank invariably intersects with other social and psychological dimensions of people's position in society and with internal dimensions of the linguistic system itself. Thus, the assessment of the precise role of social status per se in the establishment of social varieties of English can often be a significant descriptive challenge. Nonetheless, no aspect of language variation is of more consequence in American society than that related to the linguistic demarcation of social rank.

Suggestions for further reading and exploration

Social aspects of diversity in American English were highlighted in several large-scale studies of Northern metropolitan areas in the 1960s, including Labov's (1966) study of English in New York City and Wolfram's (1969) analysis of Detroit, though earlier treatments such as McDavid's (1948) analysis of postvocalic /r/ in South Carolina set the stage for examining social varieties of American English. Labov (1966) is a classic example of the correlation of linguistic variation with traditional socioeconomic status indices. Rickford's (1986) article on the need for new approaches to social class analysis and Guy's (1988) chapter on language and social class address limitations of traditional sociolinguistic approaches to social class. Milroy (1987) offers an alternative method for correlating language variation and social division by indicating how interactional relationships may influence dialect maintenance and change. Sankoff and Laberge (1978) provide a different alternative based on the construct of the linguistic marketplace. A more detailed discussion of social dialects in American English can be found in Wolfram and Schilling-Estes (1998).

References

Feagin, Crawford. 1990. "The Dynamics of Sound Change in Southern States English: from R-less to R-full in Three Generations." In *Development and Diversity: Linguistic Variation Across Time and Space*, eds. Jerold A. Edmonson, Crawford Feagin, and Peter Mühlhäusler. Dallas: Summer Institute of Linguistics/University of Texas at Arlington. Pp. 29–146.

Guy, Gregory R. 1988. "Language and Social Class." In *Linguistics: the Cambridge Survey, IV*, ed. Frederick J. Newmeyer. New York: Cambridge University Press. Pp. 37–63.

Labov, William A. 1966. *The Social Stratification of English in New York City*. Washington DC: Center for Applied Linguistics.

Lippi-Green, Rosina. 1997. *English with an Accent: Language, Ideology, and Discrimination in the United States*. London/New York: Routledge.

McConnell-Ginet, Sally. 1988. "Language and Gender." In *Linguistics: The Cambridge Survey, IV*, ed. Frederick J. Newmeyer. New York: Cambridge University Press. Pp. 75–99.

McDavid, Raven I. 1948. "Postvocalic /-r/ in South Carolina: a Social Analysis," *American Speech* 23: 194–203.

Milroy, Lesley. 1987. *Language and Social Networks*. 2nd edn. Baltimore: University Park Press.

Rickford, John R. 1986. "The Need for New Approaches to Social Class Analysis in Sociolinguistics," *Language and Communication* 6: 215–21.

Sankoff, David and Suzanne Laberge. 1978. "The Linguistic Market and the Statistical Expla-
    nation of Variability." In *Linguistic Variation: Models and Methods*, ed. David Sankoff.
    New York: Academic Press. Pp. 239–50.
Shuy, Roger W., Walt Wolfram, and William K. Riley. 1967. *Linguistic Correlates of Social
    Stratification in Detroit Speech*. USOE Final Report No. 6-1347.
Smith, Philip M. 1985. *Language, the Sexes and Society*. New York: Blackwell.
Trudgill, Peter. 1972. "Sex, Covert Prestige, and Linguistic Change in the Urban British English
    of Norwich," *Language in Society* 1: 179–95.
Wolfram, Walt. 1969. *A Linguistic Description of Detroit Negro Speech*. Washington DC:
    Center for Applied Linguistics.
Wolfram, Walt and Natalie Schilling-Estes. 1997. *Hoi Toide on the Outer Banks: the Story of
    the Ocracoke Brogue*. Chapel Hill: University of North Carolina Press.
    1998. *American English: Dialects and Variation*. Malden, MA: Basil Blackwell.

5

African American English

LISA GREEN

Editors' introduction

This chapter explores the nature of African American English, the single-most studied American English variety over the past three decades, and one that has also been at the center of public controversies involving education. Lisa Green begins by commenting on the profusion of labels this variety has attracted over the years, including "Negro Dialect," "Black Communications," and "African American Language" in addition to the "African American English" designation (AAE) she favors. While these terms vary to some extent according to changing social climates and ideologies, the point she emphasizes is that AAE is a linguistic system, with well-defined rules.

After a brief overview of alternative views about the origins of AAE (including the Substratist, Creolist, Anglicist, Founder principle, and Settler principle views), the chapter focuses on its present-day characteristics. While its vocabulary does include current slang (e.g., *off the chain* 'good, exciting, outstanding'), familiar mainly to preadolescents and young adults, it also includes general vocabulary known by AAE speakers of all age groups (e.g., *saditty* 'conceited, uppity'), and verbal markers like invariant *be* for a habitual or recurrent activity. Using a single complex sentence, *Didn't nobody ask me do I be late for class* ('Nobody asked me if I am usually late for class'), the chapter illustrates characteristic AAE syntactic features like negative inversion, multiple negation, and the formation of embedded yes/no questions.

Under "Sound patterns," this chapter discusses the restrictions on the occurrences of consonant clusters like *-ld* and *-st* (as in *wild west*) and the alternative realizations of English "th" as /t/, /d/, /f/, or /v/ in AAE. In each case, the processes are not haphazard but systematic and rule-governed. The author also refers to the rhythmic intonation that many believe is a key element in "sounding black," a potential source as well of negative "linguistic profiling." The chapter closes with a discussion of the representations of AAE in film, with examples and descriptions of some of its key grammatical features, like remote past BIN (*Dey BIN practicing for one hour*) and existential *it's* (*It's a fly messing with me*). You can learn more about these topics in chapters 15, 16, 21, and 23.

African American English, the linguistic variety spoken by many African Americans in the USA, is a system with specific rules for combining sounds to form words and words to form phrases and sentences. Although words in this linguistic system are identical in spelling to words in other varieties of English, some of them may have different meanings.

Among the many labels used to refer to this variety over the past forty years are "Negro dialect," "American Negro speech," "Black communications," "Black dialect," "Black street speech," "Black English," "Black Vernacular English," "African American language," "African American English," and "African American Vernacular English." One observation about these labels is that they coincide with the social climate, so the periods during which *Negro*, *Black*, or *African American* appeared in the label coincide with the periods during which the speakers were referred to as "Negro," "Black," or "African American." A second observation is that the names sometimes indicate something about the features used to characterize the variety, as with "Black communications" referring to communication patterns and features in the speech of black people. Along these same lines, "Black street speech" was first used by John Baugh as a label for "the nonstandard dialect that thrives within the black street culture," a variety "constantly fluctuating, as new terminology flows in and out of colloquial vogue" (Baugh 1983: 5–6). It is important to note that "street speech" was used to capture the speech of some groups of African Americans who participated in the street culture in urban areas, not necessarily the speech of those engaged in rackets and other types of illegal activities. (See chapter 21 of this volume.)

A number of terms in the list are compounds in which the first elements are adjectives referring to the speakers (e.g., Black, African American) and the second are nouns referring to the language – English – from which the general vocabulary of the variety is taken. These terms indicate that the characterizing features of the variety are uniquely related to the history, culture, and experiences of Blacks although the variety shares many features with mainstream and other varieties of English. Also, while some researchers have chosen to use "African American English," others agree on "African American Vernacular English." "Vernacular" is often used to underscore the point that what is being referred to is a spoken language with socially stigmatized linguistic patterns. As is clear from characterizations such as "African American language" and "Black communications," "English" is not always used in the label. Another case in point is "Ebonics," which is not on the list because that term was created to refer specifically to the language of people of African descent that had its roots in West African languages, and not as a reference to any dialect of English (Williams 1975: vi; see also chapter 16 of this volume). During the highly publicized Oakland, California school board case in 1996–97, Ebonics was used synonymously with the labels on the list. The general public and the media have latched onto the term, not always using it in accordance with its intended original meaning. It is clear that today the term "Ebonics" has been extended and is used interchangeably with the labels given at the beginning of this paragraph.

In this chapter and elsewhere in this book, African American English refers to a linguistic system of communication governed by well defined rules and used by some African Americans (though not all) across different geographical regions of the USA and across a full range of age groups. While AAE shares many features with mainstream varieties and other varieties of English, it also differs from them in systematic ways. Because languages and dialects alike are rule governed and because there are differing views about the relationships between dialects and languages, this chapter does not take up the question whether AAE should be regarded as a language or as a dialect of English. Still, it is useful to note two other sociolinguistic situations in which the question has arisen. Consider that Mandarin and Cantonese share a common writing system and are considered to be dialects of Chinese despite the fact that they are not mutually intelligible. Monolingual speakers of Cantonese cannot understand spoken Mandarin, and monolingual speakers of Mandarin cannot understand Cantonese. By contrast, Serbo-Croat has separated into three *languages* (not dialects) called Serbian, Croatian, and Bosnian. Addressing the question as to whether AAE is a dialect or a language would require analysis of definitions of language and dialect and of complex social situations that lie beyond the scope of this chapter. Suffice it to say that, like all languages and like all dialects, AAE is a systematic means of communication (see chapter 16 of this volume.)

Views of the origins of AAE

A frequently asked question among professional linguists and others concerns the origins of AAE. How did it begin, and what are its historical relations? To answer such questions, historians of AAE must consult various kinds of information sources. They must compare data from other varieties of English (early American English, for example, and varieties in the African diaspora) and Caribbean creoles. A narrow definition of creole is a language that develops from a pidgin, and a pidgin is a simplified means of communication among speakers who do not share a common language. Unlike pidgins, creoles have native speakers and, as a consequence, a more extensive vocabulary and grammar than a pidgin (see chapter 7 of this volume). As a further means of determining characteristics of early AAE, linguistic historians analyze language data from the recorded speech of ex-slaves and investigate the sociohistorical conditions of slave life on plantations in the South to draw conclusions about factors and linguistic situations that may have affected the development of language among the slaves. Researchers do not always agree on the extent of the contribution to AAE made by African languages, creoles, and English, nor even on the structure of earlier varieties of AAE, and several hypotheses have been suggested about the origin of AAE:

- **Substratist view**: AAE is structurally similar to West African languages brought by slaves to the colonies, and it is only superficially similar to English. These West African languages are referred to as substrate languages because of the subordinate social status of their speakers with respect to social status of English speakers.
- **Creolist view**: AAE is related to and shares features with creoles such as Jamaican Creole and Gullah (spoken on coastal Carolinas and in Georgia). AAE may have started off as a creole given that slaves from

Africa and the West Indies brought creoles with them to the colonies (see chapter 8 of this volume).

- **Anglicist or dialectologist view**: AAE developed from an English base, which accounts for the characteristic patterns it shares with English varieties. AAE is thus more closely related to English than to creoles or West African languages.
- **Founder principle view**: The language of the founders of colonial America impacted the language of Africans who came to America and their offspring. These Africans and their descendants had the goal of adapting to the norms of the colonies.
- **Settler principle view**: AAE was created by African slaves but did not begin as a creole. Instead it developed from contact between Europeans and Africans in the seventeenth century.

As more documents such as ex-slave narratives and other texts are analyzed, the origin of AAE continues to be addressed.

The system of African American English

Whatever the earlier history of AAE, speakers today adhere to specific rules for putting sounds together to form words and for combining those words and phrases into sentences.

Words and phrases

In the minds of some Americans, the mention of AAE or of any other label listed above conjures up notions of bad grammar or slang. Slang of course makes up a part of AAE, as it makes up part of other varieties, but it is only a small part of the vocabulary of AAE. As is true of other varieties, AAE slang is limited largely to pre-adolescents and younger adults, for whom it serves particular social functions (see chapter 20 of this volume). Besides thousands and thousands of words that are shared with mainstream and other varieties of English, AAE contains unique vocabulary of its own. The mental dictionary of AAE speakers includes the information needed to use words and expressions grammatically: their pronunciation, part of speech, possible positions in a sentence, and meaning. The vocabulary of AAE can be viewed in three parts: words and phrases used by speakers in a range of age groups that cross generational boundaries; special verbal markers; and slang.

In the thumbnail sketch below, only incidental comments are given about the pronunciation of vocabulary items. Information about where in a sentence a word or phrase may occur is not given although a word's part of speech is noted.

General words and phrases
- *ashy* Adjective. Dry appearance of the skin. *That lotion is good for ashy skin.*

- *call _self* Verb. An observation that a person is not meeting perceived standards. *He call hisself cooking.*
- *get over* Verb. Take advantage of, succeed by using wit but little effort. *The students tried to get over on the teacher.*
- *saditty* Adjective. Conceited, uppity. *Having confidence is one thing, but she is downright saditty.*
- *mannish* Adjective. (1) Said of boys who are behaving inappropriately for their ages. (2) Mature. (1) *Those three boys try to hang with those older guys; they are so mannish.* (2) *Look at the way that little two year old holds his pencil and thinks about what to draw. He's just mannish.*
- *womanish* Adjective. (1) Said of girls who are behaving inappropriately for their ages. (2) Mature. (1) *She stays out much later than a twelve-year-old should. That's just womanish.* (2) *Your little niece is so womanish. Yesterday, I watched her while she entertained all the guests at her tea party.*

Verbal markers

- *be* Indicates a recurring activity or state. *Sometimes they be sitting in the conference room in the library.*
- *BIN* (pronounced with stress) Situates an activity or state in the remote past. *They BIN sitting in the conference room; they didn't just get there.*
- *dən* (pronounced without stress) Indicates a completed activity whose resultant state holds now. *He dən read all the* Little Bill *books.*

Current slang

- *already* (with stress on first syllable) Adverb. Expresses agreement.
  A: We should'a told the truth, not lied.
  B: AL-ready.
- *get my praise on* Verb. To praise or worship. *I'm going to early morning service where I can get my praise on.*
- *off the chain* Adjective. Good, exciting, outstanding. *That party was off the chain.*
- *whoadie* Noun. Comrade (New Orleans, Louisiana, usage). *What's up, whoadie?*

The first group of lexical items is included under "General words and phrases" because speakers of all age groups in different geographical areas use them. One of the items is *call _self*, in which pronouns such as *my*, *her*, *his* and *they* are attached to *_self*, depending on the subject. As in the example above, the subject is *he*, so the pronoun *his-* (an AAE variant of *him-* in *himself*) must be used with *_self*. Besides occurring before an *–ing* verb, *call _self* can occur before a noun or an adjective, as in *He call hisself a Louisiana chef and can't even make gumbo* and *She call herself friendly and won't even speak to people.* In the opinion of the observers, the persons do not meet the standards of a Louisiana chef or a friendly person.

The verbal markers *be* and *BIN* can precede verbs, adjectives, nouns, prepositions, and adverbs, but *dən* can precede only verbs. These verbal markers are similar in pronunciation to auxiliaries and verbs in other varieties of English, but they have meanings unique to AAE. Current slang is included in the final category. Note that information about the particular geographical area in which the lexical item is used is also given, as indicated in the entry for *whoadie*.

Sentence patterns

Many characteristic features of AAE are from that part of the linguistic system that puts words together to form sentences (technically called "syntax"). Speakers of AAE form sentences according to the rules of its syntax. The point can be illustrated with the negative sentence, *Didn't nobody ask me do I be late for class* ('Nobody asked me if I am usually late for class').

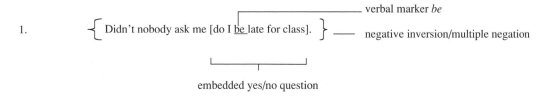

1.

                  { Didn't nobody ask me [do I be late for class]. }   verbal marker *be*

                                      negative inversion/multiple negation

                          embedded yes/no question

For explanatory purposes, this sentence can be analyzed as having three AAE features: inversion/multiple negation; embedded yes/no question; and habitual *be*. Speakers, of course, do not think in terms of features when they speak; they simply – and automatically – form sentences according to the rules of whatever variety they are speaking. Negative inversion/multiple negation involves a sentence that begins with more than one negative word – in this case, the auxiliary *didn't* and the indefinite pronoun *nobody*. This sentence type is labeled "negative inversion" because the two initial elements carry negative markers and occur in an inverted order – that is *didn't nobody ask* instead of *nobody didn't ask* (the auxiliary verb usually follows instead of precedes the subject). This is characteristic of AAE and of certain other varieties of English. In the sentence *They didn't leave*, the auxiliary *didn't* follows the subject *they*, but in sentence 1 the auxiliary and the subject appear in the reverse order – not *nobody didn't* but *didn't nobody*.

A second AAE feature of sentence 1 is the verbal marker *be*, which serves to give the part of the sentence enclosed in square brackets a habitual meaning, something like '*usually* late for class.' Habitual *be*, as it is called, always occurs in its bare form, never as *is*, *am*, or *are*. Habitual *be* is a major characteristic of AAE and helps distinguish it from other varieties of English. Sentences containing habitual *be* are often mistaken by speakers of other varieties of English as incorrect English; such speakers take habitual *be* as an incorrect form used instead of *is*, *am*, or *are*. Actually, however, the grammar of AAE does not permit habitual *be* in place of *is, am*, or *are* but allows speakers to use it only to indicate habitual meaning. To indicate present time, speakers of AAE must use a form of *is* or *are* (*She is running*) or no auxiliary verb at all (*She running*). With first-person singular subjects, AAE grammar requires *am* (*I am running*), and **I running* would be ungrammatical. (The asterisk * indicates that the construction violates the rules of the variety in question.) It is interesting to note that hip hop artists use this habitual *be* in their lyrics. For example, it occurs in Black Star's "Thieves in the Night":

> A lot of cats who buy records are straight broke
> But my language universal they be reciting my quotes.

Also, as Alim explains in chapter 21, another *be* (he calls it *be₃*), which is used differently than habitual *be*, occurs in hip hop nation language contexts. The extent to which this other *be* is used in regular conversation in AAE, that is, in contexts other than hip hop nation language, is not clear.

The third feature, embedded inversion, occurs in the part of the sentence set off by square brackets. *Do I be late for class* looks like a question because the auxiliary *do* precedes the subject *I*, as it would in yes–no questions (*Do I tell lies?*). In AAE, this question can be set ("embedded" is the technical term) within a larger declarative sentence. By contrast, in mainstream and other varieties of English, speakers use *if* or *whether* when embedding such a sentence within a larger one and do not invert the auxiliary and subject: *Nobody asked me **if I am** usually late for class*. The information that a speaker must know in order to form a sentence like example 1 can be summarized as follows:

- An inverted negated auxiliary and negated subject can introduce a negative declarative sentence.
- The verbal marker *be* indicates habitual meaning.
- A yes–no question set within a larger declarative sentence is not a request for a yes–no response and not a direct quote.

In AAE, *BIN* indicates that some activity or state started or happened in the remote past. Depending on context, remote past may mean fifteen years ago or a mere fifteen minutes ago.

2. a.   Bruce BIN running.   'Bruce has been running for a long time'
   b.   Bruce BIN a teacher.   'Bruce has been a teacher for a long time'
   c.   Bruce BIN quiet.   'Bruce has been quiet for a long time'
   d.   Bruce BIN in the house.   'Bruce has been in the house for a long time'
   e.   Bruce BIN there.   'Bruce has been there for a long time'
   f.   Bruce BIN ran.   'Bruce ran a long time ago'

In 2a–2e, Bruce has been involved in an activity (running), or been a professional (a teacher), or had some attribute (quiet), or been in a place (the house, there) for a long time. In 2f, he is in the state of having run. Although the time period (how long the activity has been in progress or been completed) is not explicitly stated, listeners have an idea about the length of time the speaker has in mind. Perhaps Bruce has been a teacher for fifteen years, but perhaps he's been quiet for only fifteen minutes, which would be a long time for a good talkative teacher like Bruce. It is ungrammatical in AAE to use time phrases (e.g., *two hours ago*) with *BIN* to indicate how long an activity has been completed, so speakers cannot say **Bruce BIN ran two hours ago* to mean 'Bruce ran two hours ago'; instead, speakers would have to say *Bruce ran two hours ago*.

In AAE, *dən* indicates that an event is completed or finished and in its resultant state.

3.   Bruce dən ran.   'Bruce has already run'

Dən is similar to the *done* in Southern varieties of English, but these forms differ in a number of ways. For instance, *dən* precedes only verbs (and *already*, as in *He dən already left*), but in at least one Southern White variety (that of Anniston, Alabama; see Feagin 1979: 132), 'done' precedes the adjective *dead*.

The verbal markers *be*, *BIN*, and *dən* pattern similarly in several ways. As an example, they share the characteristic of not allowing the contracted *not* (*n't*) to attach to them, as shown by the ungrammatical examples: **ben't*, **BIN't*, **dən't*. As a result, there must be another way of negating sentences with these markers, such as *They be putting too much gumbo in that pot*. The corresponding negative construction cannot be **They ben't putting too much gumbo in that pot* because *n't* cannot attach to *be*. The grammatical negative sentence is *They don't be putting too much gumbo in that pot*, in which *don't* is the negated form. Likewise the corresponding negative sentences for *Bruce BIN eating too much gumbo* and *Bruce dən ate that gumbo* must be *Bruce ain't BIN eating too much gumbo* and *Bruce ain't dən ate that gumbo*. Because these markers cannot be negated by attaching *n't* to them, elements such as *don't* and *ain't* must be used in the corresponding negative constructions. Speakers use these markers correctly in positive and negative sentences, evidence that they understand the rules for using them. For example, speakers know that if they use *be*, *BIN*, and *dən* in negative contexts, they cannot simply add *n't* to them. They follow the rule that says it is necessary to negate them by using separate auxiliaries *don't* and *ain't*.

Many of these distinctive features are presented in table 5-1.

Table 5-1 *Examples of AAE linguistic patterns*

AAE sentence	General description	Mainstream English gloss
I never be looking for that.	grammatical verbal marker *be* construction	'I usually never look for that'
*I be never looking for that.	ungrammatical because verbal marker *be* precedes the adverb *never*	
When I change the oil, I like to see how much it be dən burned.	verbal marker consisting of habitual *be* and resultant state *dən* (habitual resultant state)	Literally: 'When I change the oil, I like to see how much oil the truck has burned'
They'a be dən got older.	verbal marker consisting of *be* and *dən* (future resultant state)	'They will have gotten older'

(cont.)

Table 5-1 *(cont.)*

AAE sentence	General description	Mainstream English gloss
They BIN practicing for one hour.	Remote past *BIN* can occur with a time phrase if the phrase (e.g., *one hour*) indicates how long the practices usually last. This sentence cannot mean that they started practicing one hour ago. *BIN* refers to a long time, NOT to one hour, the length of time the practices usually last.	'They have been practicing for one hour stretches for a long time'
Dey got a fly messing with me.	*Dey got* can introduce a sentence meaning something exists.	'There is a fly bothering me/A fly is bothering me'
It's a fly messing with me.	*It's* can introduce a sentence saying something exists.	'There is a fly bothering me/A fly is bothering me'
I had got strep throat on the last day of school.	*Had* in some contexts (often when relaying an account of an event) can indicate past tense.	'I got strep throat on the last day of school'
I can show you some of the stuff we tesses them on.	*Tes* (vs. 'test') occurs in AAE due to the restrictions on final *st*. Once *tes* is produced, when *s* is added to it, it behaves like the plural *mess*. The form *s* (or *es*, depending on how the word ends) can indicate a habitual meaning, as in 'usually test them on.' In mainstream English, this would be similar to saying, *He <u>tests</u> them on reading comprehension.* In AAE, the *s* form is not used only with singular subjects (as *we* in the example is plural).	'I can show you some of the stuff we usually test them on'
She steady talking.	The form of *is* does not have to occur after the subject *she*. But if speakers stress the sentence as in *She IS steady talking*, *is* would probably be pronounced. This *is* differs from verbal marker *be*, as in *She be steady talking*, which must be present to indicate the habitual meaning associated with it. *Steady* means doing something nonstop or consistently.	'She is talking nonstop'
She come telling me it was hot.	*Come*, a marker that precedes verbs ending in *–ing*, is used to indicate speaker indignation.	'She had the nerve/audacity to tell me it was hot'

Sound patterns

One well-known characteristic of the AAE pronunciation system is the restriction on the occurrence of certain combinations of consonant sounds, especially at the ends of words. The restriction is placed on the following:

pt (as in *kept*)   st (as in *best*)   ld (as in *cold*)
ct (as in *act*)   ft (as in *left*)   nd (as in *spend*)

As a result, words that in other varieties of English end in *st* or *nd*, for example, may be produced in AAE as though they ended in *s* or *n*, respectively. In AAE, *spend* would be pronounced *spen*, *left* as *lef*, and *mask* as *mass*. The restriction AAE places on consonant combinations such as *nd*, *ft*, and *sk* is not placed on *nt* or *nk*. That means that a word like *mint*, which ends in *nt* is not pronounced as *min*, nor is *think*, which ends in *nk* (but sounds more like *ngk*), pronounced as *thin* or *thing*. They are pronounced as *mint* and *think*, respectively, with final consonant clusters. Auxiliaries like *can't*, *won't*, and *ain't* that end in *n't* behave slightly differently than main verbs and nouns that end in *nt* (e.g., *went* and *mint*). They are often pronounced without the full *n't*, and the vowels in the words are nasalized. This means that instead of producing the final *n't*, speakers end the words by beginning to produce the nasal sound *n*. This results in the production of a nasalized vowel as opposed to the full final *n't*, for example [dõ] for *don't*.

AAE also imposes restrictions on some consonant combinations in the middle of words. The combination *nd* occurs at the end of *spend* but in the middle of *spending* and *kindness*. When the combination occurs in the middle of the word and precedes a suffix that begins with a consonant (as with *-ness* in *kindness*), only the first consonant of the *nd* combination is usually pronounced. *Kindness* is more likely to be pronounced *kiness* (without the *d*), a pronunciation also used in some speech situations and environments by speakers of other varieties of English, including mainstream English. When the consonant combination is in the middle of the word and precedes a suffix that begins with a vowel (as with *-able* in *acceptable*), both consonants are usually pronounced. When the consonant combination precedes other suffixes that begin with a vowel, however, it may not be pronounced, as with the verbs *spening* ('spending') and *builing* ('building'). Although the *nd* and *ld* combinations precede the *–ing* suffix, which begins with a vowel, only the first consonant (*n* or *l*) in the combination may be pronounced. The vowel-initial suffix *–ing* is a special case because the clusters preceding it may be pronounced (as in *spending*), or only the first consonant in the cluster may be pronounced (as in *spening*). This does not seem to be the case with the vowel-initial suffix *–able*, in that the clusters preceding it are generally always pronounced (*acceptable*, not **accepable*). Speakers of AAE follow regular established patterns in producing and combining sounds; the grammar of AAE – like the grammar of every other language variety – does not permit sounds to be left off words haphazardly.

In general, when speakers produce and hear speech sounds, they do not think of the processes used to make them or the descriptive properties of the sounds.

When they produce the sounds represented as *t*, *d*, *f*, and *v*, they do not realize the similarities to the sounds represented by *th*. In some instances, speakers of AAE produce a *t*, *d*, *f*, or *v* sound in words in which the *th* sound occurs in mainstream varieties of English. For instance, the pronunciations *dese*, *wit/wif*, *birfday*, *baf*, and *smoov* occur often in AAE, while **these**, **with**, **birthday**, **bath**, and **smooth** occur in mainstream varieties. As with the sound patterns in all language varieties, the patterns in AAE are completely systematic. The *d* sound occurs at the beginning of a word (as in *dese* 'these') and the *t* sound at the end (as in *wit* 'with'). The *f* sound occurs in the middle (as in *birfday* 'birthday') and at the end (as in *baf* 'bath'), and the *v* sound occurs at the end (as in *smoov* 'smooth'). The *v* sound can also be pronounced in the middle of words in environments in which *th* occurs between vowels, as in *muver* 'mother' and *bruver* 'brother.' The grammar of AAE does not permit haphazard substitution of the sounds *t*, *d*, *f*, or *v* for the *th* sound. Whether speakers of AAE pronounce *t*, *d*, *f*, or *v* depends on the special properties of the corresponding *th* sound and its position in the word.

In mainstream varieties of English and in AAE, the *th* spelling represents two different pronunciations – the one in *thigh* and *bath* and the one in *thy* and *bathe*. Both *th* sounds are produced with the tongue between the teeth, but to produce the one in *these* and *bathe* the vocal cords vibrate and cause what is technically called "voicing." By contrast, to produce the *th* sound of *bath* or *birthday* the vocal cords do not vibrate – the sound is not voiced. The *th* sound in *these* and *smooth* is said to be voiced. The *th* sound in *bath* and *birthday* is said to be voiceless.

The *t* and *f* sounds are similar to the voiceless *th* sound (*with*, *birthday*) in that they too are made without vibration of the vocal cords – *t* and *f* are not voiced sounds. On the other hand, the *d* and *v* sounds are similar to the voiced *th* sound (*these*, *bathe*) in that they are made with vibration of the vocal cords – *d* and *v* are voiced sounds. The generalization is this: AAE speakers produce *t* and *f* (voiceless sounds) in environments where voiceless *th* occurs in other varieties of English but produce *d* and *v* (voiced sounds) in environments where voiced *th* occurs in other varieties of English. Also, AAE speakers often produce the *d* sound at the beginning of a word where voiced *th* occurs in other varieties of English (cf. *dese* and *these*), but they usually produce voiceless *th* sounds at the beginning of all words in which it occurs in other varieties of English. That is, along with speakers of most other varieties of English, AAE speakers produce the *th* sound in words like *thistle*, *think*, and *thirty*. Unlike speakers of varieties of Irish English and some speakers of New York City English, AAE speakers generally do not say *tistle*, *tink*, and *tirty*.

The preceding examples illustrate some of the sound patterns of AAE that affect individual consonants, but some patterns also affect syllables, words, phrases, and sentences. When listeners observe that African Americans have a rhythmic way of speaking, they may be commenting indirectly about sounds and rhythms affecting syllables, words, phrases, and sentences. A phrase commonly used to characterize the speech of some African Americans is "sounding Black." It is not quite clear which features lead listeners to conclude that a speaker "sounds black," but some listeners feel that they can make this determination. This is not a new issue. In 1972 in a paper entitled "'Sounding' Black or 'Sounding' White," Rickford raised the question of what specific features were used to identify black and white speech and found the more varied intonation of black speech most significant. More recently, the issue of identifying a person's race on the basis of voice quality or speech patterns has been addressed in the media. In 1995, during a widely publicized court case, one of the attorneys was accused of suggesting that race could be determined by one's voice. The following excerpt (Margolick 1995) is from *The New York Times* article reporting the relevant portion of the trial:

> But on cross examination, Christopher A. Darden, a prosecutor, contended that in statements to friends, Mr. Heidstra had identified the two people as a young white man and an older black one, and even identified Mr. Simpson as one of the speakers. "I know it was O.J. It had to be him," Mr. Darden said Mr. Heidstra told a friend.
>
> Mr. Heidstra dismissed the suggestion that he had identified the speakers by their age or race as "absurd," insisting he could not have told whether they were "white or brown or yellow." When Mr. Darden pushed him, Mr. Cochran rose angrily to object . . .
>
> Simply by suggesting that someone's race can be gleaned from the sound and timbre of his voice, Mr. Darden opened up once more the volcanic issue of race . . .

John Baugh is conducting research on linguistic profiling and has found that listeners respond unfavorably to him when he uses his "black voice" (see Baugh 1999). In a National Public Radio (NPR) interview (Smith 2001), Baugh explained that he had conducted a series of experiments that involved making telephone calls to inquire about the availability of apartments. As he produced the following introductory statement, he modified the sound of his voice and manner of speaking: "Hello, I'm calling about the apartment you have advertised in the paper." Tovia Smith, the NPR reporter, expanded on Baugh's comments about his experiment:

> After more than a hundred calls, Baugh found that his black voice got less than half as many calls back as his white voice. His more recent study suggests that more than 80 percent of people correctly infer a person's race just from hearing them count to 20. In real conversation, it's even easier to tell. Shawna Smith, of the National Fair Housing Alliance, says she sees linguistic profiling all the time in housing, insurance, mortgages and employment.

More and more research is being conducted on rhythmic and intonational patterns of AAE to determine the extent to which speakers use such patterns uniquely as well as the role they play in identifying a person's race.

Representations of AAE in film

While questions about the validity of AAE, that is, whether it follows set rules or exists at all, are addressed frequently in educational and linguistic research, there is no question that certain linguistic patterns are associated with the speech of African Americans. In this section, we consider the representation of language used by African American characters in film. (For discussion of the representation of African American language in fiction and other literary genres, see chapter 23 of this volume.)

One strategy filmmakers employ to represent blackness could be called "figurative blackface," which differs from literal blackface in minstrelsy. In minstrel shows, actors literally went through a process of making up their faces with black paint and their lips with red lipstick. They also used exaggerated language and body features such as bulging lips and eyes that matched the blackened faces to create grotesque characters.

Figurative blackface and minstrel devices are used in the 1998 film *Bulworth*, starring Warren Beatty and Halle Berry. The film is the story of Bulworth, a white senator, who is transformed into a politician concerned about the plight of people in inner cities. After being introduced to inner city life by a streetwise African American girl named Nina, Bulworth is taken in by the "culture." He enjoys the nightclub environment with Nina, dancing, smoking marijuana, eating barbecued ribs, and acting as a disc jockey. It appears that the denouement of the experience is his rhyming. In searching for Nina in the many rooms of the nightclub, he chants:

> What I really want to know is where did little Nina go
> I'm looking here, I'm looking there, but I can't find her anywhere
> Nina, Nina, has anybody seen her?

At the point when he sees her, he sings, "Nina, Nina, where you bina?" In this scene, Bulworth puts on figurative blackface as a means of simulating "black culture." The film appears to be a modern day minstrel show in which Bulworth uses minstrel devices such as cool talk, rhyming, body language, and types of clothing that are intended to mirror the image of black males in the inner city.

Figurative blackface is used in *Bulworth*, but figurative blackface and literal blacking up occur in Spike Lee's *Bamboozled*, a 2000 film about racism in television. Throughout the film, the white senior vice president of the entertainment division of a television network puts on figurative blackface as he uses current slang and "keeps it real" in other ways. The literal blacking up occurs in *Mantan: the New Millennium Minstrel Show*, the minstrel television show within *Bamboozled*. The stars of *Mantan* are Mantan and his dumb-witted sidekick Sleep n Eat. (See Green 2002 for more discussion of blackface in *Bamboozled*.)

Sentence patterns can also be used as markers of black images in film. The verbal marker *be* that indicates habitual recurrences is used in the 1994 film *Fresh*, about the coming of age of a streetwise African American adolescent and his struggles in the inner city. In addition to drugs and violence, language is used to create images of the urban ghetto. In the film, African American characters of all age groups use features associated with AAE. The verbal marker *be* seems to be strongly associated with the language of adolescent males, and it occurs often in the speech of African American and Latino characters (especially adolescent and teenage males), as in these examples:

4.   Why you come home so late? You know Aunt Frances **be** getting
         worried when you come home so late.
      All his phones **be** tapped, man.
      My grandma **be** cooking at home.
      But I know she still **be** going back there sometime for like her
         clothes and stuff she **be** keeping over there.

These *bè* constructions communicate that an activity (getting worried, cooking at home, keeping stuff over there) happens from time to time or that something is in a certain state (phones are tapped) from time to time. They are used in line with the meaning and rules specified for the marker in AAE. Other uses of this *be* are ungrammatical, however, as with these examples from *Fresh*:

5. a.   **Michael**: I don't want nobody **be** touching this board.
          Michael's female cousin: You don't own this house. You ain't
          hardly ever be here, so you don't tell us what to do.
   b.   Nikki say James tired of he **be** so small time, wanna be moving
          bigger.

The line spoken by Michael in 5a would be a grammatical sentence of AAE if *to* were inserted before *be* (*I don't want nobody **to be** touching this board*), and 5b would be grammatical with *being* instead of *he be* (*James say he tired of **being** so small time*). Film viewers have an idea of the meaning intended by these lines, but the actual utterances are ungrammatical: they do not follow the syntactic rules of AAE. The recurrence of *be* in the film suggests how strongly the marker is associated with the inner city life and language the film depicts, although ungrammatical uses like those in (5) perhaps indicate that the screenwriter is not fully aware of AAE's regularities and restrictions.

Habitual *be* and other AAE patterns are used by characters in *The Best Man*. The representation of AAE in this 1999 film is interesting, especially compared to the representation in *Fresh*, in which habitual *be* is closely connected to inner city life. In *The Best Man*, habitual *be* is not used by all the African American male young adult characters. Lance and Quentin, the more skilled language users, who also happen to be college educated, use the marker.

Over the past forty years, research on AAE has been addressed from a number of angles, including historical origins, rules of use, expressive language use, and education. Researchers are continuing to study this linguistic variety by considering its representation in literature, film, and hip hop. One important point is that AAE is characterized by well-defined rules. (See Green 2002 for further commentary on the rules of use of AAE.) The sentences and general descriptions in the table 5-1 are examples of the linguistic patterns that occur in AAE.

Acknowledgments

This chapter is based on Green (2002), a book-length treatment of topics discussed here.

Suggestions for further reading and exploration

Wolfram and Thomas (2002) provide a general history of African American English. Rickford (1998), Rickford and Rickford (2000), and Edwards and Winford (1991) discuss the creolist view. Dunn (1976) and DeBose and Faraclas (1993) are good sources for the substratist view. For the Anglicist or dialectologist view, see Poplack (2000); for the founder principle view Mufwene (2000); for the settler principle view Winford (1997, 1998). Good sources of information about intonation in AAE are Foreman (1999), Green (2002), and Tarone (1973). Note also the representation of AAE in films such as *The Brothers*, *Do the Right Thing*, *Imitation of Life*, and *Set it Off*, some of which have explicit content.

References

Bamboozled. 2000. New Line Productions, Inc.

Baugh, John. 1983. *Black Street Speech: its History, Structure, and Survival*. Austin: University of Texas Press.

Baugh, John. 1999. "Linguistic Perceptions in Black and White: Racial Identification Based on Speech." In Baugh's *Out of the Mouths of Slaves: African American Language and Educational Malpractice*. Austin: University of Texas Press. Pp. 135–47.

The Best Man. 1999. Universal Pictures.

Bulworth. 1998. Twentieth Century Fox.

DeBose, Charles and Nicholas Faraclas. 1993. "An Africanist Approach to the Linguistic Study of Black English: Getting to the Roots of the Tense–Aspect–Modality and Copula Systems in Afro-American." In *Africanisms in Afro-American Language Varieties*, ed. Salikoko S. Mufwene. Athens: University of Georgia Press. Pp. 364–87.

Dunn, Ernest F. 1976. "Black-Southern White Dialect Controversy." In *Black English: a Seminar*, eds. Deborah S. Harrison and Tom Trabasso. Hillsdale NJ: Lawrence Erlbaum. Pp. 105–22.

Edwards, Walter and Donald Winford, eds. 1991. *Verb Phrase Patterns in Black English and Creole*. Detroit: Wayne State University Press.

Feagin, Crawford. 1979. *Variation and Change in Alabama English: a Sociolinguistic Study of the White Community*. Washington DC: Georgetown University Press.

Foreman, Christina G. 1999. "Identification of African American English Dialect from Prosodic Cues." In *Salsa VII, Proceedings of the Seventh Annual Symposium about Language and Society*, eds. Nisha Merchant Goss, Amanda Doran, and Anastasia Coles. *Texas Linguistic Forum* 43: 57–66.

Fresh. 1994. Miramax Films.

Green, Lisa. 2002. *African American English: a Linguistic Introduction*. Cambridge: Cambridge University Press.

Margolick, David. 1995. "Simpson Witness Saw a White Car," *The New York Times*, July 13.

Mufwene, Salikoko S. 2000. "Some Sociohistorical Inferences about the Development of African American English." In Poplack, ed. Pp. 233–63.

Poplack, Shana, ed. 2000. *The English History of African American English*. New York: Blackwell.

Rickford, John R. 1972. "'Sounding' Black or 'Sounding' White: a Preliminary Acoustic Investigation of a Folk-Hypothesis," ms., University of Pennsylvania.

    1998. "The Creole Origin of African American Vernacular English: Evidence from Copula Absence." In *African American English: Structure, History and Use*, eds. Salikoko S. Mufwene, John R. Rickford, Guy Bailey, and John Baugh. New York: Routledge. Pp. 154–200.

Rickford, John R. and Russell J. Rickford. 2000. *Spoken Soul: the Story of Black English*. New York: John Wiley and Sons.

Smith, Tovia. 2001. "Scientific Research that's Being Used to Support Claims of Linguistic Profiling." National Public Radio, Morning Edition. September 5, 2001.

Tarone, Elaine. 1973. "Aspects of Intonation in Black English," *American Speech* 48: 29–36.

Williams, Robert, ed. 1975. *Ebonics: the True Language of Black Folks*. St. Louis: Institute of Black Studies.

Winford, Donald. 1997. "On the Origins of African American English – a Creolist Perspective Part I: The Sociohistorical Background," *Diachronica* 14: 305–44.

    1998. "On the Origins of African American English – a Creolist Perspective Part II: Linguistic Features," *Diachronica* 15: 99–154.

Wolfram, Walt and Erik Thomas. 2002. *The Development of African American English: Evidence from an Isolated Community*. Malden MA: Blackwell.

Discography

Black Star. 1997. "Thieves in the Night." Rawkus.

6

The *Dictionary of American Regional English*

JOAN HOUSTON HALL

Editors' introduction

This chapter provides an introduction to the *Dictionary of American Regional English* (*DARE*) by its Chief Editor, who has been associated with the project since 1975. Associate Editor for many years, Joan Houston Hall became Chief Editor of *DARE* in 2000, when Frederic G. Cassidy, the founding Director and Chief Editor, died. *DARE* is one of the most comprehensive and accessible public resources on variation in American dialects, drawing on fieldwork conducted between 1965 and 1970 in more than 1,000 communities across the USA, and supplemented by the evidence of thousands of literary and other sources. Four of a projected six volumes have appeared to date, with completed entries running through Sk-.

The chapter describes several aspects of the fieldwork for *DARE*, including its extensive questionnaire (with 1,687 to 1,847 questions), and the way in which responses were electronically tabulated and analyzed, with the results indicated on *DARE* maps whose dimensions were proportional to the population density in each state. This chapter complements chapter 3 on regional dialects in that it shows how the 1940s distribution of variant words (like *darning needle* and other words for 'dragonfly' discussed in chapter 3) had spread west and otherwise changed (or not) in the intervening years. One of the conclusions of this chapter is similar to that of William Labov (cited in chapter 3): despite greater mobility and the influence of mass media, American English has not become homogenized, but shows striking regional variation.

Drawing on *DARE* entries and its companion indexes, this chapter also discusses the social dialects for which the dictionary shows clear evidence, based on age, gender, race/ethnicity, and education. In this respect it also complements chapter 4 on social dialects. The chapter closes with a brief discussion of what *DARE* tells us about the creativity of American folk language (note *belly-washer*, *goose-drownder*, and many other expressions for a 'heavy rain') and its colorful variant terms for plants and animals. It also notes the rich uses to which *DARE* can be put in the classroom, and the ways in which its resources (including audiotapes currently available, and a CD-ROM yet to be released) might be mined by other researchers.

The *Dictionary of American Regional English* – usually called *DARE* – is a long-term project dedicated to recording the differences in our language as they occur in various parts of the country and among speakers of different social groups. Most Americans have a general awareness of the differences in pronunciation from New England to the South and to the West, and know that people in various parts of the country have different names for such things as a *submarine sandwich* (it's usually a *hero* in New York City, a *grinder* in New England, and a *hoagie* in Pennsylvania and New Jersey, among other names). But many people have also been surprised, on occasion, to discover that one of their own words, phrases, or pronunciations is unfamiliar to others. We tend to think of "dialects" as belonging to other folks but not to us. *DARE* illustrates the tremendous variety of regional patterns found throughout the country, showing that all of us have linguistic features characteristic of regional speech; we are *all* speakers of dialects.

In southern Wisconsin, for instance, where *DARE* is being produced, people like to think of themselves as not having "an accent." But we say 'crick' for *creek* and have what some people think of as "funny" vowels in words like *boat*. We tend to use many words that are characteristic of a broad dialect region designated as "North," but we also share features with people in a smaller region designated as "North Central" (made up of the states of Illinois, Indiana, Kentucky, Michigan, Ohio, and Wisconsin). Sometimes we use words commonly found in the region called "Upper Midwest" (Iowa, Minnesota, Nebraska, North Dakota, and South Dakota). And sometimes the terms we use are found almost solely in Wisconsin (e.g., *Berliner* 'a jelly doughnut' or *flowage* 'a lake formed by the damming of a river'). So, like it or not, we speak a dialect in Wisconsin. And of course the same is true of people in every other part of the country as well.

While it has become popular in recent years to claim that American English is being "homogenized" because of our increasingly mobile society and our love affair with radio, television, and the Internet, the findings in *DARE* demonstrate that there are still thousands of words, phrases, pronunciations, and even grammatical constructions that vary from one place to another. Such variant terms may be restricted to a region as small as a city or as large as most of the country; they may be used by one generation but not another; they may characterize the speech of rural people but not urbanites; or they may represent the usage of a particular ethnic group: as long as they are *not* found throughout the country, in standard use by people of all social groups, they are legitimate terms for treatment in *DARE*.

One of the unique features of *DARE* is that it is based in part on a survey of lifelong residents of more than a thousand communities across the country – from Anchorage, Alaska, to Key West, Florida, and from Hauula, Hawaii, to Allagash, Maine. These people answered an extensive questionnaire, providing comparable responses for more than 1,600 questions and allowing us to map their responses to see which ones are regionally distributed. In addition to the oral data, *DARE* also draws on the evidence gathered through a massive reading program. The *DARE* bibliography currently has nearly 10,000 entries, with sources as diverse as government documents, newspapers, diaries, histories, regional novels, poems, plays, and collections of dialect materials, as well as ephemeral sources such as posters, billboards, newsletters, restaurant menus, and conversations.

To date, four of the projected five volumes of *DARE* entries have been published. Volume I, including extensive introductory materials and the letters A–C, appeared in 1985; Volume II, including D–H, in 1991; Volume III, with the letters I–O, in 1996; and Volume IV, including P through the middle of S, in 2002.

The planning for Volume V calls for publication about five or six years after Volume IV. A sixth volume will follow, containing the bibliography, the *Data Summary* (all of the responses to the fieldwork questions), contrastive maps, and a cumulative *Index* of the regional, social, and usage labels in all five volumes of entries.

The fieldwork for *DARE*

The fieldwork for the *DARE* project was undertaken between 1965 and 1970. At that time many Americans could look back on childhoods when automobiles, radios, and telephones were brand new (or non-existent). Most Americans had some familiarity with rural life, from their parents and grandparents if not from direct experience, and they remembered a time before widespread mechanization. The late 1960s was an ideal time to conduct a language survey: the oldest participants, born in the 1880s and 1890s, could remember hearing stories about the Civil War and themselves knew American life from the dawn of the twentieth century onward; they had seen tremendous changes in their culture and were storehouses of words and expressions for artifacts and practices that had gone out of use. In an attempt to collect and preserve as many of these terms as possible, the selection of informants was deliberately biased towards those over sixty years old. At the same time, care was taken to provide comparison groups by interviewing people between forty and sixty years of age, and others who were younger than forty, to determine which words were going out of use, which were stable, and which were newly entering the language.

The data that were collected, and the maps we can make from the data (see below), present thousands of snapshots of the language of mid-twentieth-century America. But what of the differences in our society between then and now? Are those earlier data really relevant today? It is certainly true that extraordinary changes have taken place in American society in the last thirty-five years, and people are generally better acquainted with other parts of the country than our parents and grandparents were. Yet, in broad terms, most of the regional language patterns that emerge from the fieldwork of 1965–70 are still recognizable today. The boundaries may not be as well defined as they were then, but the basic patterns persist. (It is possible, for instance, to find *hoagies* advertised on the billboard for a tiny café in northern Idaho, as I did in the summer of 1998. But if you were to ask people across the country what they called that kind of sandwich, the large majority of those who said *hoagie* would still live in the region with Pennsylvania and New Jersey at its center.)

The desire to know about the regional patterns in American English was not one that suddenly emerged in mid-twentieth century. Creation of an American dialect dictionary comparable to Joseph Wright's *English Dialect Dictionary* had been one of the reasons for the founding of the American Dialect Society in 1889. Collection of adequate data in this vast nation, however, was rightly recognized as the *sine qua non* of such an ambitious project. Although scholars collected and published word lists from various parts of the country in the decades after the founding of the American Dialect Society, it was not until 1963 that the timing and staffing were right for a full nationwide survey. At that time Frederic G. Cassidy, Professor of English at the University of Wisconsin–Madison, proposed a plan that was accepted by the Society. He was appointed Editor and charged with carrying out the project.

Details of the planning and organization are spelled out in the introductory matter to the first volume of *DARE* (Cassidy and Hall 1985: xi–xxii). For our purposes, it is enough to explain that 1,002 American communities were selected for interviews. The places ranged in size from metropolitan areas to sparsely populated rural communities, chosen both to reflect population density in the country at large and to sample places that had had significant historic impact on a region (for example, the Pennsylvania German communities in southeastern and south central Pennsylvania).

Trained fieldworkers – mostly graduate students, but also faculty members from colleges across the country – were then sent to those places to find and interview people who had been born there and who had spent all, or at least most, of their lives there. In many instances, this in itself was a huge challenge. Fieldworkers had to find a key community member who could point them in the direction of appropriate informants (as the interviewees were called), gain the trust of the informants, and schedule the time for the lengthy interview. It usually took a full week to complete one questionnaire, with the fieldworker fitting sections of it into whatever blocks of time the informants could spare. Because the socio-political climate of the late 1960s was volatile, some fieldworkers found themselves having to convince local authorities that they were not "outside agitators" and that their work was part of a legitimate, scholarly investigation. In most cases, the local people were extremely helpful and proved to be interested in the project and interesting sources of information.

The questionnaire used by the fieldworkers was based on materials gathered over the decades by members of the American Dialect Society in anticipation of this nationwide survey. The questions had been arranged by Frederic G. Cassidy and Audrey R. Duckert at the University of Wisconsin–Madison, and the questionnaire had been field-tested in Wisconsin. After the first seventy-five interviews, about 200 of the original 1,847 questions were dropped as not worthwhile, and a few others added. In order to allay any suspicions on the part of the informants, the questions were organized so that neutral and unthreatening topics such as weather, furniture, and foods came first, with questions of a more abstract or personal nature, such as religion, health, and relationships among people coming later. In all, there were forty-one different categories of questions. Because some informants did not have time to answer the whole questionnaire and others felt unable to answer questions in certain sections (such as hunting, fishing, wildflowers, farm buildings, or farm animals), in many communities the fieldworkers divided the questionnaire among several informants, resulting in a total pool of 2,777 participants. In each case, careful records were kept of the age, sex, race, level of education, and community type for each person so that accurate correlations could be made between the answers to the questions and the social variables of the informants providing those answers. The Appendix to this chapter contains sample questions from the questionnaire.

The *DARE* Maps

As soon as the fieldworkers completed their questionnaires they sent them back to project headquarters, where each informant was given a unique code – such as AL1, for the first informant in Alabama – and all of that person's responses were entered into a database with that code. When all the responses from the 1,002 communities had been entered, the corpus included approximately two and a half million items. The goal was to be able to map each response electronically to see whether it displayed any kind of regional pattern. (While this use of computer methods is common enough today, in 1965 it was a radical innovation.) In order to accomplish that, a unique map had to be devised that would take into account the differences in population density from one part of the country to another so as to give each informant an equal amount of space. The top map shown in figure 6-1 and those in figures 6-2 through 6-4 are the result. Note that while the general outline of the USA seems distorted, the basic shapes and positions of the states have been retained.

A comparison of the states of Connecticut and New Mexico on the *DARE* map and the conventional map in figure 6-1 will help to explain the reasoning behind the "distorted" map. Connecticut is a small but densely populated state, and in order to have the number of interviews proportionate to the population, we needed to interview people in seventeen Connecticut communities. New Mexico, on the other hand, is geographically large but sparsely populated, calling for interviews in only four communities for proportional representation. If we represented our findings on a conventional map, and four people in each state had responded with the same answer, the mapped results would be highly misleading: in Connecticut, the four informants would take up much of the state's allotted space; in New Mexico the four would take up very little space. Yet in Connecticut they represent only 24 percent of the pool, where in New Mexico they are 100 percent of the pool. So with the *DARE* map each informant takes up the same amount of space on the map, and when there are gaps between dots on the map we know they represent places where informants did not use the term rather than places where no one lives. Although *DARE* maps may be confusing at first, with a little practice they are actually easier to "read" than a conventional map.

Earlier Work in American Dialect Geography

Prior to the *DARE* project, research in American linguistic geography had uncovered four *major* dialect areas in the eastern part of the USA – North, North

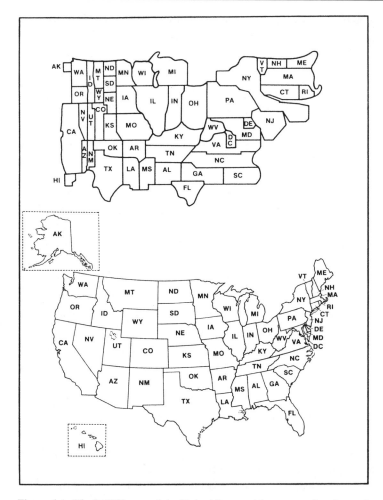

Figure 6-1 *The* DARE *map of the United States with a conventional map for comparison*

Midland, South Midland, and South – as well as numerous smaller ones (see chapter 3 in this volume, particularly figure 3-1 on page 43). The data to support the existence of these speech areas came largely from two major projects: the Linguistic Atlas of New England (for which the fieldwork was conducted in the 1930s) and the Linguistic Atlas of the Middle and South Atlantic States (with most of the fieldwork being conducted in the 1930s and 1940s). *A Word Geography of the Eastern United States* (Kurath 1949) contains maps showing the distributions of hundreds of the words that Hans Kurath and his fieldworkers investigated and providing the basis for his delineations of dialect boundaries. *DARE* researchers expected to corroborate (and sometimes contradict) many of those findings in the eastern states. But since *DARE* was a nationwide survey, and the Atlas projects had covered only the eastern states, the *DARE* maps could also show how these words had spread in the westward movement of American settlers. The following comparison of a few of the maps in the *Word Geography* with those from *DARE*'s fieldwork illustrates not only how eastern distributions had changed (or not) between the 1930s and the 1960s, but also how some words thrived as our population moved further west, and others simply died out.

The map in figure 3-2 (on page 45 of this volume) comes from Kurath's *Word Geography* and shows the east coast distributions of six terms for the insect most widely known as the *dragonfly*. The symbols on the map indicate that each term had a relatively well-defined region of use in the 1930s and 1940s, with some (e.g., *darning needle*, *mosquito hawk*, *snake feeder*, and *snake doctor*) covering relatively large geographic areas, and others (*spindle* and *snake waiter*) being quite restricted. The *DARE* maps for the first four of those words (shown in figure 6-2) show remarkably similar distributions in the eastern states, and describe the westward movements of those words: *darning needle* retains its concentration in New England, New York, New Jersey, and northern Pennsylvania, while spreading across the Inland North (the northern tier of states west of New England) and into much of the West; *mosquito hawk* has its east coast concentration in the Middle and South Atlantic states, while moving west through the Gulf States and into Texas; *snake feeder*, found throughout the Midland area, shows clear westward movement across the central portion of the country, stopping (largely) short of the west coast; *snake doctor*, still common in eastern Pennsylvania, Maryland, Delaware, and the Virginia Piedmont, has spread in both southerly and westerly directions, with scattered occurrences throughout the country. In each of the preceding cases, the westward movement of the lexical item parallels – as would be expected – basic migration patterns of our population.

Spindle and *snake waiter*, on the other hand, do not have corresponding maps in *DARE* for the simple reason that by the time our fieldworkers asked the question the words had practically died out. No informant offered the term *snake waiter*, and only two volunteered *spindle*. The two that offered *spindle* were both in New Jersey, precisely where the term had been found decades earlier. Such cases are graphic illustrations of the relatively quick loss of vocabulary items – words that, rather than expanding with westward movement, succumbed to the dominant terms of surrounding areas. When such terms do manage to hang on in the speech of a small number of older speakers, they become what are known as "relics."

Tight regional patterns of the kind illustrated by *spindle* in the *Word Geography* also occur in *DARE*, as can be seen by the maps in figure 6-3.

The maps illustrate these senses of the headwords: *blue norther* 'a cold wind from the north that brings rapidly falling temperatures'; *gum band* 'a rubber band'; *jam cake* 'spice cake flavored with jam'; *lawyer* 'a freshwater fish more widely known as *burbot*'; *leader* 'a downspout or roof gutter'; and *money cat* 'a calico cat, especially one with at least three colors.' Whether terms like these will become relics or will retain their strong regional focus is difficult to say with certainty. It seems likely, though, that a word like *leader*, for which twenty-six

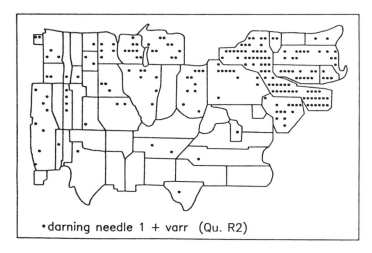

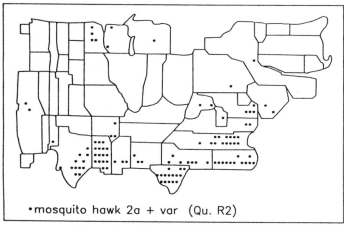

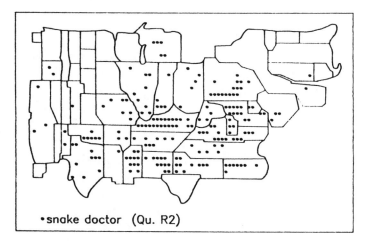

Figure 6-2 *Darning needle, mosquito hawk, snake doctor, snake feeder*

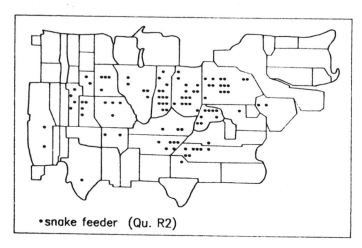

•snake feeder (Qu. R2)

Figure 6-2 (*cont.*)

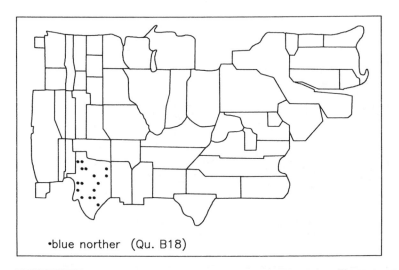

•blue norther (Qu. B18)

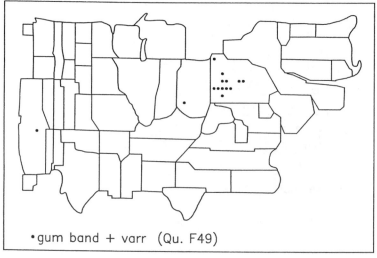

•gum band + varr (Qu. F49)

Figure 6-3 *Blue norther, gum band, jam cake, lawyer, leader, money cat*

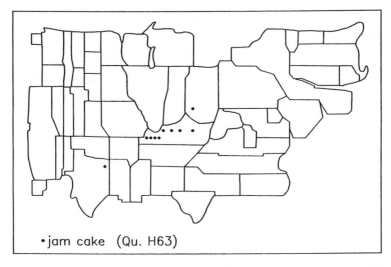

•jam cake   (Qu. H63)

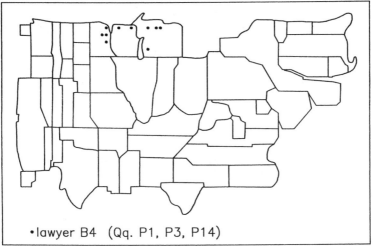

•lawyer B4   (Qq. P1, P3, P14)

Figure 6-3 (*cont.*)

of thirty informants were old between 1965 and 1970, will survive neither the effects of time nor those of the nationalization of the American retail system. Once an item is known by an industry standard, its synonyms tend to fall out of use. *Blue norther*, on the other hand, seems much more likely to persist. Not only were there slightly fewer old informants than would have been expected in proportion to the total informant pool, but we were also able to find citations that are more recent than the *DARE* survey. *Blue norther* also has a better chance for survival than *leader* simply because there is no commercial or other folk term that precisely describes the phenomenon.

More often than they show such small, well-defined patterns, however, the *DARE* maps show that our regional words have much wider distributions, while still not occurring nationwide. Typical patterns are those shown in figure 6-4 in

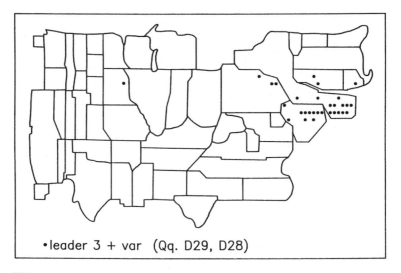

•leader 3 + var (Qq. D29, D28)

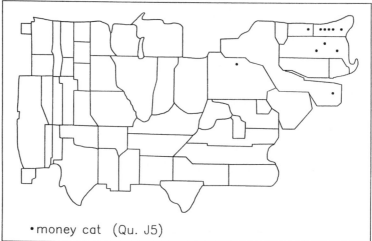

•money cat (Qu. J5)

Figure 6-3 (*cont.*)

which a word occurs, for example, **chiefly in New England** (as illustrated by
the map for *Indian pudding* 'a dessert of sweetened cornmeal'); **chiefly in the
South** (*bank* 'a heap of vegetables covered with mulch for protection in winter');
chiefly in the South and the South Midland (*draw* v C3 illustrating *draw up* 'to
shrink'); and **chiefly in the North, North Midland, and West** (*kaput* 'ruined,
useless, exhausted'). In almost every case, the regional labels are prefaced with
"chiefly" or "especially," to account for the seemingly inevitable "outliers" on
the maps. (The legends to the *DARE* maps include the word as it is entered in
the *Dictionary*; part of speech, section, and sense number when necessary to
distinguish the word from another entry; "+ varr" for entries that include variant
forms of the headword; the *DARE* questions that elicited the response(s) being
mapped.)

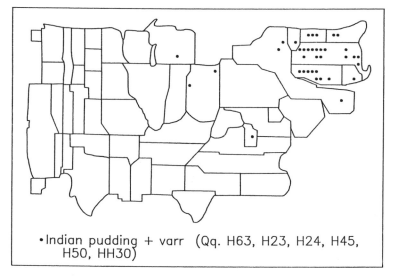

• Indian pudding + varr   (Qq. H63, H23, H24, H45, H50, HH30)

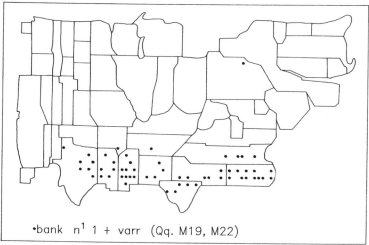

• bank   n[1] 1 + varr   (Qq. M19, M22)

Figure 6-4 *Indian pudding, bank, draw, kaput*

The reasons for these distinctive patterns are more fully described in chapter 3 of the present volume but basically reflect early settlement patterns in the USA, as well as subsequent patterns of migration. The fact that people's travel routes fanned out as they moved further and further west means that the rather well-defined dialect areas of the eastern seaboard lose much of their distinctiveness in the central and western parts of the country. This does not mean that the speech of the west is a complete mishmash, with no distinctive features; but most of the words characteristic of the west are also found elsewhere. So the *DARE* maps often label words as being "**chiefly North, North Midland, West**" or "**chiefly South, South Midland, West**," reflecting the multiple sources of immigrants. Those entries that show words found predominantly in the west usually illustrate

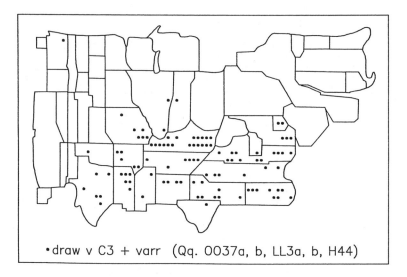

•draw v C3 + varr (Qq. 0037a, b, LL3a, b, H44)

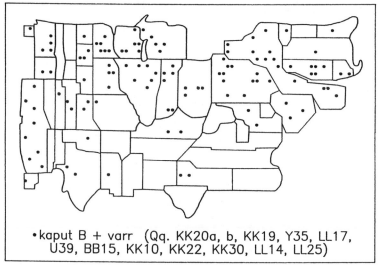

•kaput B + varr (Qq. KK20a, b, KK19, Y35, LL17,
U39, BB15, KK10, KK22, KK30, LL14, LL25)

Figure 6-4 (*cont.*)

such factors as Spanish language influence (such as *adobe, buckaroo, lariat, loco*), local names of plants, animals, and topographic features (e.g., *butte, dust devil, manzanita, mesa, mesquite grass*), or regional economic activities such as ranching and cattle herding (*broomtail, chuck wagon, ditch rider, longhorn*).

Social dialects

In addition to determining the geographic spread of our vocabulary, *DARE* has as one of its goals the analysis of words according to their use by particular social groups. Simply by observing the speakers around us, you know there are some differences in the speech of older and younger people, men and women, Blacks and Whites (these terms were the preferred ethnonyms at the time the *DARE* project was started, and we continue to use them for continuity of terminology), urban and rural dwellers, and those with little formal education and those with advanced degrees. To try to quantify such differences, a computer program was devised that would tally the social statistics (age, sex, race, community type, and level of education) for each informant who gave a particular response, and compare those to the overall statistics for all the informants who answered that same question. This program allows *DARE* editors to determine whether a word is disproportionately frequent in any social category and thus to apply an appropriate social or usage label.

Age distinctions

Not surprisingly, age is the most distinctive social variable. Many of the words labeled "old-fashioned" are expectedly so, since they reflect basic changes in our culture. There is little reason that young people even in the 1960s would be familiar with such words as *barshare plow*, *basket sleigh*, *buttery*, *hod*, or *logrolling*. But other words reflect inexplicable shifts in preferences over time. There is no particular reason, for instance, that the verb *spark* meaning 'to court, woo' (which goes back at least to the early nineteenth century, so is not ephemeral slang) ought to have gone out of use, but the statistics show that it was receding in the 1960s, and observation shows that it is distinctly archaic if not obsolete now. Similarly, *cipher* 'zero,' *dropped egg* 'poached egg,' *emmet* 'ant,' *hindside-before* 'backward,' and *notional* 'opinionated, temperamental' are going out of use even though the items or attitudes to which they refer are solidly entrenched in our culture. Because of the care with which all of the responses from the fieldwork were recorded, and the project's large collection of written citations, *DARE* is in a unique position to be able to trace these kinds of inevitable but unpredictable changes in a living language.

Gender differences

The kinds of gender differences in language that earlier linguistic geographers had discovered tended to correlate closely with women's traditional roles in society. Women tended to use more euphemisms than men (though well-bred men, in the company of women, also shied away from terms like *bull* that were presumed offensive); and women tended to use more nearly standard grammatical forms than men, reflecting both their better opportunities for at least elementary education and their presumed desire to speak "properly." The *DARE* research has found that while some euphemisms (e.g., the exclamations *drat*, *fudge*, *law*, and veiled terms such as *brat* 'an illegitimate child,' and *the curse* 'menstruation') are more common among women than men, there are now few vocabulary distinctions that can be shown to be based on the sex of the speaker. (One striking exception is that the term *pee ant* for a common ant seems to be primarily a women's word, while *piss ant* is strongly biased toward use by men.) As with many other gender barriers, most of those in American English also fell in the last half of the twentieth century.

Racial differences

If the fieldwork for *DARE* were being planned today, the numbers of minority informants would be significantly greater and the informant pool much more diverse than it was, reflecting significant changes in the American populace over the last four decades. But based on the 1960 census figures and reflecting the more homogeneous population at that time, the *DARE* survey included 92.7 percent White informants (including Spanish-speaking Americans), 6.7 percent Blacks, 0.3 percent Asian Americans, and 0.3 percent American Indians (most of these terms were current for ethnic groups in 1965 and are retained for consistency within the project). As a consequence, the kinds of ethnic language differences we found were almost solely between Black and White speakers.

While general glossaries of slang as well as those of jazz, rap, and hip hop have popularized many words associated with the Black community, *DARE*'s aim was to discover the common, everyday words – terms for foods, clothing, games, religion, relationships, and so on – that varied by race of the speaker. The result was more than 400 terms in the first three volumes that are labeled as being used solely or disproportionately by Black speakers. They range from words and phrases that have their origins in African languages (e.g., *buckra* 'a boss, master' or 'a White person in general,' *crack one's sides* 'to laugh hard,' *dayclean* 'daybreak') to those that are well documented in the Scots and English dialects that would have been used by plantation overseers (e.g., *call hogs* 'to snore,' *heard* pronounced as *yeard*), as well as those that originated in America. A few examples, representing many facets of life, are these:

airish 'inclined to put on airs'
beau dollar 'a silver dollar'
bid whist 'a card game'
brad 'a metal piece on a shoe bottom'
catface 'a wrinkle in ironing'
dead cat on the line 'something causing suspicion or concern'
dicty 'stylish, haughty'
dirty hearts 'a card game'
dry drought 'a long drought'
fall out 'to burst out laughing; to faint'
gospel bird 'a chicken'
hickey 'a bump resulting from a sharp blow'

igg 'to ignore'
jump salty 'to get angry'
keen 'sharp, pointed'
kitchen 'hair at the nape of the neck'
little Sally Walker 'a children's singing game'
love bone 'a wishbone' *main man* 'a favorite male friend'
main man 'a favorite male friend'
mercy seat 'the front row in a church'
ofay 'a White person'
outside child 'an illegitimate child'
parrot-toed 'pigeon-toed'
ticky 'fussy, particular'

Distinctions based on education

Variation in American English based on the amount of education of the speaker is most evident in the use of non-standard verb forms and other grammatical constructions as well as in particular stigmatized pronunciations. Such past tense verbs as *clumb*, *drownded*, and *knowed*, and such uses as *badder* and *baddest* for *worse* and *worst*, *borrow* for *lend* ("Will you borrow me five dollars?") and *learn* for *teach* ("I'll learn him a lesson") are characteristic of speakers with little formal education. Similarly, pronunciations such as ['ɔlə(r)z] for *always*, [brɑnəkəl] for *bronchial*, [gɑr'din] for *guardian*, and [lum] for *loam* are found especially frequently among those with little education. Some educational statistics have been surprising, however. It is not clear why such words and phrases as *boob* 'breast,' *down* 'depressed,' *drink like a fish* 'drink excessively,' and *druthers* 'preferences, desires,' should be especially frequent among well-educated speakers, but in the *DARE* survey that was distinctly true.

Urban/rural differences

Aside from such expectable differences as greater familiarity among rural people with farming practices and machinery, animals, and plants, mirrored by city dwellers' greater knowledge of uniquely urban artifacts, the *DARE* survey discovered few language differences between those who live in different kinds of communities. On first realizing that the phrase *not to know one's ass from one's elbow* 'to be ignorant' was used chiefly by urban speakers, I was tempted to speculate that this might be so because *ass* was a rural taboo. That speculation faded quickly, however, when it became clear that to put on a shirt *ass-end-to* 'backwards' was used chiefly by rural speakers. Relatively equal access to education and the media in all community types has apparently contributed to a leveling of urban and rural differences, though it is also true that regional differences often reflect some basic demographic differences (e.g., the Northeast has a higher concentration of urban dwellers than does the South), and the regional differences may take precedence over those based on community type.

Folk language

Because the *DARE* questionnaire was very wide-ranging and the oral interview encouraged informal conversation, many of the responses offered by our informants were those that we frequently hear in speech but rarely find in standard dictionaries. They are excellent examples of "folk" speech – the kind of language we learn from family and friends rather than from our teachers at school. Some of these words and phrases show regional or social patterning, others have scattered distributions, and for others we may have only a single piece of evidence (from the *DARE* fieldwork or elsewhere). But because these entries are less than nationally distributed and not a part of our standard American English vocabulary, they are all "regional" in a broad sense of the word. In many cases they illustrate the creativity of our speakers and the ways in which people have fun with their language. For example, the questions about names for a heavy rain elicited such terms as *belly-washer*, *cob-floater*, *duck-drownder*, *frog-strangler*, *goose drownder*, *gully-washer*, *lightwood-knot floater*, *sod-soaker*, *toad-strangler*, and *trash-mover*. The question asking for names for the rump of a cooked chicken yielded such fanciful terms as *the pope's* (or *bishop's, parson's, preacher's*) *nose*, *the part that went over the fence last*, and *the north end of a chicken flying south*. Phrases used to describe a person who seems very stupid were both plentiful and colorful. In reply to the question "He hasn't enough sense to __," informants supplied such provocative answers as *bell a buzzard*, *grease a gimlet*, *lead a goose to water*, and *pour piss out of a boot (with a hole in the toe and directions on the heel)*, among many others. Additional entries that illustrate the variety of folk terms included in *DARE* are *Adam's housecat* (in the phrase "I wouldn't know him from Adam's housecat"), *bobbasheely* 'a very close friend,' *cahoot* 'to consort, connive,' *dominicker* 'to show cowardice or lack of perseverance,' *even-handed* 'ambidextrous,' *fall off the roof* 'to begin a menstrual period,' *gospel bird* 'a chicken,' *hook jack* 'to play hookey,' *idiot stick* 'a shovel,' *jumbo* 'bologna,' *keskydee* 'a French-speaking person,' *long sugar* 'molasses,' *mixmux* 'confusion,' *noodle* 'to catch fish with the bare hands,' and *Old Huldy* 'the sun.'

Natural science entries

One aspect of American English that is particularly carefully treated in *DARE*, but which is not well documented in most studies of language, is the kind of variation found in the names of plants and animals. Although regional and folk names for angleworms, chipmunks, dragonflies, fireflies, grasshoppers, menhaden, screech owls, and turtles, among others, had been investigated for earlier projects, *DARE* devoted entire sections (with a total of more than 150 questions) to terms used in fishing and hunting and to names for birds, insects, wildflowers, bushes, and trees. In addition, the *DARE* editors who specialize in the natural science entries consult hundreds of scientific reference books in an attempt to determine precisely which genus and species is intended by a particular common name. The result is the most comprehensive treatment available of the regional and folk names for plants and animals. In *DARE*, for instance, one can discover that the bittern, a marsh bird noted for the booming noise it makes before a rain, goes by at least fifty-four names, among them the descriptive and fanciful *barrel-maker*, *belcher-squelcher*, *bog bull*, *bottle-kachunk*, *butter bump*, *dunkadoo*, *fly-up-the-creek*, *night hen*, *plum puddin'*, *postdriver*, *skygazer*, *slough-pumper*, *stake-driver*, *thunder pumper*, and *wollerkertoot*. One can also discover that the term *gopher* applies to at least two different turtles, any of ten different burrowing rodents, a mole, a shrew, either of two crickets, a snake, a rockfish, or a frog. No wonder we can have misunderstandings.

DARE in the classroom

With the entire questionnaire included in the front matter to the first volume of *DARE* (Cassidy and Hall 1985: lxii–lxxxv), other researchers (or teachers and their students) can replicate parts of the fieldwork and compare their findings with those published in *DARE*. Such exercises not only provide students with opportunities for fieldwork, but also provide a diachronic dimension to the whole project, showing how vocabulary use may have changed since the mid-1960s. Quizzes based on the entries in *DARE* can also be used to promote discussion of "the ethnic, racial, or regional prejudice that is also a part of American life," and to "play with language and in the process to learn something about variation, with its social and psychological concomitants" (Algeo 1993: 142).

Uses of *DARE* materials

The published volumes of *DARE* obviously provide tremendous amounts of information about the language we use, the various meanings we intend, the different places words are found, the histories of their forms, and the social nuances of their use. But the published volumes do not come close to exhausting the resources gathered by the *DARE* project. Thousands of the words collected for *DARE* that will not be entered in the *Dictionary* may nevertheless be of use to other researchers; the raw materials from the fieldwork could provide the data for lexical, morphological, phonological, and syntactic studies of many kinds. The data will be published in the final volume of *DARE*; until then they are available for consultation at the *Dictionary* headquarters, where staff members are pleased to assist researchers.

A further invaluable resource gathered during the fieldwork is an extensive collection of audiotapes made by more than 1,800 *DARE* informants. Ranging in length from about half an hour to several hours, the tapes usually include a reading of "Arthur the Rat" (a fairly nonsensical story contrived to elicit words demonstrating crucial sound contrasts) and a period of free conversation in which the informants talked about whatever interested them. The collection was recently re-mastered both for preservation and for duplication purposes, and all of the tapes are now available on cassette at minimal cost. Primary users of the tapes thus far have been actors and drama coaches who want to be able to accurately represent the dialect of a particular geographic region. But the tapes have also been used to study regional and social differences in pronunciation, as well as conversational interactions. The wide variety of topics covered in the conversations also gives the tapes great potential value for oral historians. A project to index the tapes by subject matter, now underway, will significantly facilitate their use for such purposes.

Ultimately the subject index for the tapes will be posted on *DARE*'s web site, where readers can also find additional information about the project and a list (updated quarterly) of words about which the *Dictionary's* editors need additional information. Readers are encouraged to participate in the *DARE* project by responding to the queries posted on the web site *http://www.polyglot.lss.wisc.edu/dare/dare.html*.

Appendix

Sample questions from the *DARE* Questionnaire (letters before the numerals refer to a category of question: e.g., B for weather, E for furniture, H for foods, X for parts of the body):

B26 When it's raining very heavily, you say, "It's raining __."
E20 Soft rolls of dust that collect on the floor under beds or other furniture:
H29 A round cake, cooked in deep fat, with jelly inside:
H42 The kind of sandwich in a much larger, longer bun, that's a meal in itself:
N17 What do you call the separating area in the middle of a four-lane road?
R2 What other names do you have around here for the dragonfly?
X9 Joking or uncomplimentary words for a person's mouth – for example, you might say, "I wish he'd shut his __."
X58 When you are cold, and little points of skin begin to come on your arms and legs, you have __.
DD13 When a drinker is just beginning to show the effects of the liquor, you say he's __.
EE29 When swimmers are diving and one comes down flat onto the water, that's a __.
HH7a Someone who talks too much, or too loud: "He's an awful __."
JJ6 To stay away from school without an excuse:
JJ42 To make an error in judgment and get something quite wrong: "He usually handles things well, but this time he certainly __."

Acknowledgments

Suppport for the *DARE* project has come from many sources. We are particularly indebted to the National Endowment for the Humanities (an independent federal agency), the Andrew W. Mellon Foundation, and the National Science Foundation. Additional assistance has come from numerous other foundations and many generous individuals. To all, we express our deep appreciation.

We also gratefully acknowledge Harvard University Press for their generous permission to reprint the maps included in this chapter. The maps are from the *Dictionary of American Regional English*, eds. Frederic G. Cassidy and Joan Houston Hall, © 1985, 1991, 1996, 2002 by the President and Fellows of Harvard College.

Suggestions for further reading and exploration

Even though it was written more than four decades ago, McDavid (1958) is still an excellent introduction to the field of dialectology, providing both a theoretical framework and an overview of the work done by that time on the projects that were expected to comprise the Linguistic Atlas of the United States and Canada. Although that grand project was not completed, results of some of the area surveys can be found in Kurath (1939–43, 1949); Atwood (1953); Kurath and McDavid (1961); Bright (1971); Allen (1973–76); Pederson et al. (1986–92); Kretzschmar et al. (1993). Cassidy (1982) also provides good introductory material.

For a thorough explanation of the history and methods of the *DARE* project, see the introductory matter to Cassidy and Hall (1985). Cassidy (1973) provides a discussion of how the term "regional" is interpreted in *DARE*; more details on how the regional and social labels are actually applied in the *DARE* are found in Goebel (1997) and Von Schneidemesser (1997). One particular set of regionalisms that elicits frequent queries – *soda*, *pop*, *tonic*, etc. – is discussed in Von Schneidemesser (1996). For a history of the development of computer use by the *DARE* project, see Von Schneidemesser (1990, 1993).

The tool that makes it possible to find specific words used by members of various social groups is an extremely valuable companion to *DARE*'s published volumes: *An Index by Region, Usage, and Etymology to The* Dictionary of American Regional English, *Volumes I and II* (1993); the index to Volume III appeared in 1999. While it may seem counterintuitive to need an index to a dictionary, such a tool is uniquely appropriate for *DARE*. Because the entries are arranged alphabetically rather than being grouped by regional or social categories, the words described by any particular label are scattered throughout the text. The *Index* makes it possible to determine exactly which entries are reported to occur, for example, in New England, Texas, or California; or which ones are found most often among Black speakers, or women, or old speakers; or which come into American English from German, or Norwegian, or Yiddish, or Algonquian; which words are archaisms, euphemisms, or relics; and which items illustrate various linguistic processes such as back-formation (e.g., the creation of the verb *book-keep* from the noun *bookkeeper*), folk-etymology (making understandable forms from unfamiliar ones, such as *brown kitties* for *bronchitis*, or *old-timer's disease* for *Alzheimer's disease*), or metanalysis (false juncture, creating *an eye horse* from *a nigh horse*).

DARE's publisher (Belknap Press of Harvard University Press) intends to make the *Dictionary* available electronically once it is completed; until then, the *Index* makes it possible to do systematic studies of language categories without needing to scan the pages of *DARE* text for examples.

References

Algeo, John. 1993. "*DARE* in the Classroom." In *Language Variation in North American English: Research and Teaching*, eds. A. Wayne Glowka and Donald M. Lance. New York: Modern Language Association of America. Pp. 140–43.

Allen, Harold B. 1973–76. *Linguistic Atlas of the Upper Midwest.* 3 vols. Minneapolis: University of Minnesota Press.

An Index by Region, Usage, and Etymology to the Dictionary of American Regional English, Volumes I and II. 1993. Publication of the American Dialect Society 77.

An Index by Region, Usage, and Etymology to the Dictionary of American Regional English, Volume III. 1999.Publication of the American Dialect Society 82.

Atwood, E. Bagby. 1953. *A Survey of Verb Forms in the Eastern United States.* Ann Arbor: University of Michigan Press.

Bright, Elizabeth S. 1971. *A Word Geography of California and Nevada.* Berkeley/Los Angeles: University of California Press.

Cassidy, Frederic G. 1973. "The Meaning of 'Regional' in *DARE,*" *American Speech* 48: 282–89.

1982. "Geographical Variation of English in the United States." In *English as a World Language*, eds. Richard W. Bailey and Manfred Görlach. Ann Arbor: University of Michigan Press.

Cassidy, Frederic G. and Joan Houston Hall, eds. 1985–2002. *Dictionary of American Regional English.* 4 vols. Cambridge MA: Belknap Press of Harvard University Press.

Goebel, George. 1997. "Social Labels in the *Dictionary of American Regional English,*" *Dictionaries* 18: 178–89.

Kretzschmar, William A., Jr., Virginia G. McDavid, Theodore K. Lerud and Ellen Johnson, eds. 1993. *Handbook of the Linguistic Atlas of the Middle and South Atlantic States.* Chicago: University of Chicago Press.

Kurath, Hans. 1939–43. *Linguistic Atlas of New England.* 3 vols. bound as 6. Reprinted 3 vols. New York: AMS (1972).

1949. *A Word Geography of the Eastern United States.* Ann Arbor: University of Michigan Press.

Kurath, Hans and Raven I. McDavid, Jr. 1961. *The Pronunciation of English in the Atlantic States.* Ann Arbor: University of Michigan Press.

McDavid, Raven I., Jr. 1958. "American English Dialects." In W. N. Francis's *The Structure of American English.* New York: Ronald Press.

Pederson, Lee, et al. 1986–92. *Linguistic Atlas of the Gulf States.* 7 vols. Athens: University of Georgia Press.

Von Schneidemesser, Luanne. 1990. "Computer Usage Changes at the *Dictionary of American Regional English* in the 1980s," *Literary and Linguistic Computing* 5: 270–78.

1993. "*DARE*'s Completion: A Beginning?" *Zeitschrift für Dialektologie und Linguistik: Beihefte* 2: 529–41.

1996. "Soda or Pop?" *Journal of English Linguistics* 24: 270–87.

1997. "Regional Labels in the *Dictionary of American Regional English,*" *Dictionaries* 18: 166–77.

Wright, Joseph. 1895–1906. *English Dialect Dictionary.* 6 vols. London: H. Frowde; New York: G. P. Putnam's Sons.

PART 2

Other language varieties

7

Multilingualism and non-English mother tongues

JOSHUA A. FISHMAN

Editors' introduction

Using the metaphors *spendthrift* and *gravedigger*, Joshua A. Fishman raises important questions about the USA's lavish disregard of one of its great resources, and he suggests an image of the USA as digging the grave of so many languages and compromising its own well being by doing so. Some of the questions posed in this chapter are rhetorical: asking them is sufficient to suggest their answers.

The USA is constantly recomposing itself as "a nation of immigrants." While English is widely regarded as *the* language of mainstream USA, the relegating of other languages spoken by immigrants and their native-born offspring, those languages even of world communities such as Arabic, French, German, Mandarin, Spanish, and Portuguese, to name only a few, are not recognized as great natural and national resources (as they would be viewed in many other parts of the world). In most cases, immigrant languages and those of Native Americans endure not even benign neglect but aggressive discouragement and disparagement. After the terrible events of 9/11, the USA found itself scrambling for citizens fluent in languages that had been long neglected.

As pointed out in this chapter and others (e.g., 9, 10, 11, 13, 14, 17, and 18), immigrant languages in the USA have traditionally experienced an extremely tough time being transmitted into the linguistic repertoires of the grandchildren of immigrants. Except in those very few situations where highly concentrated immigrant communities remained relatively isolated from the English-speaking majority (other than for financial transactions), the USA must be viewed socially as poor soil in its support of language maintenance and transmission. Despite the obvious advantages of cultivating multilingualism in an increasingly global economy, Fishman (like many others) speaks eloquently to the potential costs of linguistic parochialism on our understanding and appreciation of the cultural and ethnolinguistic diversity that is so richly represented among America's immigrant and indigenous populations.

In the end, Fishman expresses hope that, at the very least, school districts may implement two-way bilingual programs, as Palo Alto, California, has done with Spanish–English and Mandarin–English schools, thereby enriching the lives not only of students and teachers in the schools that mount such programs but eventually of all who live in the ethnically and linguistically diverse nation that is the USA.

America, America: spendthrift and gravedigger on the multilingualism front

The sociolinguistic profile of speakers of non-English languages in the USA is a direct reflection of the country's constantly ongoing recomposition as a nation of immigrants. Overwhelmingly, speakers of languages other than English are immigrants themselves or the children of immigrants. This is an important point at which to begin our examination of multilingualism in the USA because, unlike most other countries in which societal multilingualism exists, there are in the USA also few speakers of sidestream languages who are removed from their family's immigrant origins by more than two generations. (I use the term "sidestream" to refer to languages and varieties that are frequently regarded as lying outside the "mainstream.") This is tantamount to saying three things:

(1) the grandchildren and great-grandchildren of American immigrants are overwhelmingly English monolinguals, who have lost direct contact with speakers of the language brought to the USA by their grandparents and great-grandparents;
(2) very few indigenous (or "Native") Americans still speak their traditional aboriginal languages, and those remaining speakers are becoming fewer and fewer;
(3) travel, work, and education do not succeed in imparting daily speaking facility in any non-English language except to a very small number of Americans.

The USA is a country largely established and built by voluntary and involuntary immigrants, and its social dynamics have been such that to this very day any multilingualism among its inhabitants generally marks fairly recent immigrant status. Since, during the course of the past three centuries, millions upon millions of immigrants have arrived on American shores, whereas the total number of monolingual non-English speakers (NES) is now only approximately 2 to 5 million, and the total number of non-English mother tongue (NEMT) speakers (that is, non-school-based) multilinguals in the USA is only about 25 to 30 million, it becomes inescapably self-evident that the process of language shift (or loss of non-English mother tongue) has been a dominant and perhaps even *the* dominant "American experience" almost since the founding of the country. Thus, if we examine multilingualism in the USA today, we are examining an interesting but somewhat "exotic" phenomenon as soon as we leave the immigrant generations themselves behind.

Of course, "leaving the immigrant generations behind" is easier said than done in the USA. During the past two hundred and twenty-five years or so, there has never been a hiatus of more than two generations between the impact of one mass-immigrational period and the impact of the next such period. Beginning with the relatively large French and German "presences" at the end of the eighteenth century (starting before our nation was created), along our border with Canada (giving rise to hundreds of French churches, parochial schools, and periodical publications) and in the concentrated German settlements of Pennsylvania and Ohio (with their hundreds of churches and closed communities), the story has gone on and on for over 200 years. After the Revolution came the Irish mass immigration of the early 1800s (when most of these newcomers were Irish speakers and when Boston and New York became the capitals of the vibrant and extensive Irish press, church, and book-publication culture). Then came the second German mass immigration of the mid-nineteenth century (when hundreds of German schools, churches, newspapers, books, and even colleges populated the American Mid-West). No sooner were these beginning to be digested when the arrival of the millions of Southern Europeans and Eastern Europeans began. It continued from the 1880s to the early 1920s, bringing Italians, Jews, Poles, Ukrainians, and Southern Slavs more generally. Less than fifty years later the Hispanic and Asian/Pacific immigrations began – and have continued apace.

There has never been much time to fully cultivate and clinch the illusion of an indigenous monolingual, monocultural, monoethnic mainstream American society. However, no fully legitimated multilingual/multiethnic society has developed either. It seems that two generations are enough to wipe out non-English language proficiency but by no means enough to wipe out the cultural memories, nor to counteract the grievances derived from discrimination, marginalization, and disappointed aspirations for cultural democracy upon which ethnic identities and movements for revernacularization are both based.

And yet the newest (actual and potential) linguistic resources of the USA have always been so monstrously squandered and destroyed (at worst) or neglected and ignored (at best) that – except for the very most recent immigrants, some of their atypical children, and some rare and "exotic" other exceptions – we have become an overwhelmingly monolingual English-speaking country. *Why has this happened, and is this past history destined to repeat itself ad infinitum?* During the twentieth century, several world languages were caused or allowed to atrophy in the USA. The "big six" throughout the entire twentieth century were German (about half its speakers having been Protestant and half Catholic), Italian, French, Spanish, Polish (all overwhelmingly Catholic), and Yiddish (all Eastern European Jews, called Ashkenazim). Nevertheless, neither the prestige of most of these tongues, nor the number of speakers of them, nor their worldwide utility in commerce, travel, contact with "the old country," industry, academic research, and governmentally conducted international relations have spared them from the same fate as that which has overtaken their much smaller, culturally more distant (from Western experience), and far less practically useful counterparts on the world scene. That being the case, the future even of Spanish, the "macho" language on the non-English language scene for the past two decades, must be viewed with concern and even alarm (see chapters 10 and 11).

God shed his grace on thee: local and periodic ups and downs versus straight-line theories

If we consider mother tongue transmission as being socioculturally constructed (that is, as the result of specific social, economic, and political experiences throughout history), we can see that the unrelenting tendency to monolingualism in a nation of immigrants was not automatic and it was not inevitable. Each one of the non-mainstream languages mentioned above can point to other places in the world where their resettled speakers have successfully pursued and attained a far greater measure of intergenerational mother tongue transmission. Contrasts with Canada for French, Australia for Macedonian and Arabic, Latin America for German and Yiddish, and Israel for English, Yiddish, and perhaps Russian could be particularly instructive. *Why did American soil prove to be so inhospitable by contrast? "Der shteynerner amerikaner bodn!"* ('the stone-hard American soil') my father would whisper under his breath when faced with yet another reversal in connection with his constant efforts to maintain the Yiddish language in the USA.

The first thing to recognize in this connection is that the attrition of American multilingualism has not proceeded uniformly throughout the past two centuries; it cannot be represented by a single, monotonic downward line. Instead, the recurring rise and fall of non-English languages in the USA reveal substantial variation over time in both degree and rate. There are often years, even decades, of upswing, when the arrival of young immigrants of a particular mother tongue continues for a long time, and they settle in close proximity to one another so that they are both absolutely and relatively concentrated with respect to other residents, particularly English-speaking ones. Even some relatively small language groups such as the Pennsylvania Dutch (all of whom are also English speakers and readers, as well as being speakers of Pensylfawnish – and knowledgeable listeners to sermons in "Luther German") have succeeded relatively well in multiplying and retaining their mother tongues by establishing themselves in rural areas *of their own* where they can distance themselves from most kinds of social interaction with outsiders to their own sheltered communities. The same is true for Yiddish-speaking ultra-Orthodox Jews, although they are overwhelmingly urban dwelling. Likewise, French speakers in northern Vermont, New Hampshire, and Maine (three states that border the Canadian province of Quebec) have retained their language more successfully in comparison to their counterparts in Massachusetts and Rhode Island (which are more distant from the Canadian border and closer to English-dominated urban centers).

Spanish speakers in long-established rural communities of Texas, New Mexico, and Arizona have been notably successful in maintaining their mother tongue during six to eight generations, in contrast with newcomers to secondary settlement areas in the mid-west. Hamtramick is an example of a Polish town, in Illinois, that has steadfastly retained its Polish character in language, religion, and culture, while also participating substantially in American life. Amerindian groups (such as various parts of the Navajo Nation) that are sufficiently independent economically and sufficiently isolated spatially have succeeded in making most of their young people bilingual during most periods of their punishing exposure to mainstream America. There are other similar examples scattered throughout the length and breadth of the USA.

All these examples lead us to understand and appreciate the demographic, geographic, economic, and cultural bases of maintaining and controlling the boundaries of social interaction that are a prerequisite if we are to provide non-English languages with functions and statuses that will be able to compete longer and more successfully with those of the mainstream. In addition to the objective factors mentioned above, there are also undeniably subjective factors as well – for example, when anti-multilingualism attitudes or pro-multilingualism attitudes become important operative considerations as well. Anti-German legislation and popular sentiment during and after World War I finally resulted in 1923 in the US Supreme Court decision *Meyer v. Nebraska*, which prohibited states from usurping parental authority to decide which languages their children should learn and in which languages they should be taught (see chapter 18). But by 1923 much damage to German had already been done, only to be followed two generations later by similar damage during the period surrounding World War II.

Then, during the American "ethnic revival" of the mid-1960s to mid-1970s, an upturn in attitudes favoring languages other than English and in language-transmission efforts occurred. At that time a mighty youth-involving, anti-mainstream upsurge coursed through the country, partly co-occurring with and partly related to the war in Vietnam. It resulted in a more visible display of ethnic pride and in elevated rates of non-English mother-tongue claiming (abbreviated NEMTC) on the 1970 census. This was particularly notable among so called "third generation" individuals and is clearly revealed through comparisons to the mother-tongue claims made in the censuses of 1940 or 1960, even among non-English mother-tongue groups that had experienced no (or next to no) immigration in the interim and were, on average, already far beyond child-bearing age. In Table 7-1, note for example that between 1940 and 1970 mother-tongue claiming of Norwegian increased by 152 percent, of Swedish by 236 percent, of French by 181 percent, of German by 169 percent, and of Portuguese by 447 percent. But for these same languages, the percent of increase in the final decade of that period – namely from 1960 to 1970 – was greater: for Norwegian the increase was 412 percent, for Swedish 565 percent, for French 281 percent, for German 324 percent, and for Portuguese 789 percent.

These increases might easily be poo-pooed as mere artifacts resulting from slight inconsistencies in the wording of the mother-tongue questions in 1960 and 1970, except for the fact that other related increases also cropped up in 1970, increases whose interpretation was not clouded by changes in the wording of the census questions. For example, ethnic community broadcasts on radio and television, community schools, local religious units that included traditional

Table 7-1 *Mother tongue of the native-of-native parentage for twenty languages (1940–70), with percent increase 1940–70 and 1960–70*

Mother tongue	1940	(Estimated) 1960	1970	Change 1940–1970	% Increase 1940–1970	Change 1960–1970	% Increase
Total	84,124,840	145,275,265	169,634,926	85,110,086	102	24,359,661	17
English	78,352,180	–	149,312,435	70,960,255	91	–	–
Norwegian	81,160	40,000	204,822	123,662	152	164,822	412
Swedish	33,660	17,000	113,119	79,459	236	96,119	565
Danish	9,100	6,000	29,089	19,989	220	23,089	385
French	518,780	383,000	1,460,130	941,350	181	1,677,130	281
German	925,040	588,000	2,488,394	1,563,354	169	1,900,394	324
Polish	185,820	87,000	670,335	484,515	261	583,335	671
Czech	81,760	34,000	148,944	67,184	82	114,944	338
Slovak	29,260	10,000	86,950	57,690	197	76,950	770
Hungarian	13,180	16,000	52,156	38,976	296	36,156	226
Serbo-Croatian	5,200	7,000	24,095	18,895	363	17,095	244
Russian	13,980	18,000	30,665	16,685	119	12,665	70
Lithuanian	9,400	8,000	34,744	25,344	270	16,744	334
Finnish	14,880	4,000	58,124	43,244	291	54,124	353
Yiddish	52,980	39,000	170,174	117,194	221	131,174	336
Greek	6,160	12,000	56,839	50,679	823	44,839	374
Italian	125,040	147,000	605,625	480,585	384	458,625	312
Spanish	718,980	1,291,000	4,171,050	3,412,070	480	2,880,050	233
Portuguese	11,380	7,000	62,252	50,872	447	55,252	789
Arabic	3,720	4,000	25,765	22,045	593	21,765	544
Total non-English	2,917,780	2,807,000	10,646,702	7,728,922	265	7,826,017	279
Total non-English minus Spanish	2,198,800	1,516,000	6,475,652	4,276,852	195	4,945,867	328

Sources: 1940 and 1960 data from Fishman (1966). 1970 data from *PC (2)-,1A, 1973.*

non-English-language efforts in their programming, and periodicals offering all or part of their contents in languages other than English had also multiplied dramatically between 1960 and 1970. When examined on a state-by-state basis, the correlation between such ethnic community institutional resources and the incidence of 1970 non-English mother-tongue claiming was very high – for example, .90 between non-English broadcasting time for a particular language and "native of native" non-English mother-tongue claiming of that language.

Then, after 1979, when concerns grew about America's slower economic growth relative to Southeast Asia and when the "English-Only" movement found it easy to exploit these concerns (focused as they were on "illegal" Hispanics said to be "flooding" into the USA to escape poverty and warfare in their homelands "south of the border"), new laws and state constitutional amendments were enacted against using languages other than English. It should be noted that in every case the prohibitions applied only to the state governments themselves, and many of the more egregious prohibitions have been judged unconstitutional by the courts. By design in most cases, these laws and ordinances are purely symbolic and annoying because they are, in reality, unenforced and unenforceable. Nevertheless, such English-Only laws foster suspicions, divisiveness, and recriminations that discourage individuals and businesses from public use of languages other than English, and they have, doubtless, again helped undercut non-English mother-tongue transmission in the USA as a whole.

No *federal* law or constitutional amendment along English-Only lines has thus far succeeded in being passed (though not for want of trying), but should such a dark, dark day ever transpire (and should such legislation or amendments be upheld on appeal by the US Supreme Court), it would amount to yet another ideological and attitudinal blow to the language resources of the USA. Given the nearly complete absence of language-*supportive* legislation of the "English-plus" variety, as opposed to the purely *permissive* stance of the 1923 *Meyer v. Nebraska* ruling (which outlawed the anti-German legislation of the Nebraska legislature but stopped short even of suggesting authoritative assistance to maintaining instruction in languages other than English), the negative impact of legislation that *restricts* non-English mother tongues easily carries the day as a sociolinguistic mood-setter in most of American life. The objective demographic, interactive, and economic factors, which have been mentioned above and which in modern urban settings overwhelmingly favor language shift toward English, then rule doubly supreme. Under such circumstances, parents and communities must constantly justify themselves, in the face of a wall of doubt and disbelief, for simply doing what is normal all over the world, namely, making sure their children follow in the ethnolinguistic and ethnocultural footsteps of their parents and grandparents. Still, as the 1970 census data showed, the process of language retention is not simply a uniformly downward trend. Instead, periods of upswing can occur, and particular localities may be well above the general curve of language maintenance. Those data should remind us that people who advocate multilingualism as a general resource for their communities and for the USA as a whole are not sentenced to inevitable failure and that local circumstances and efforts are frequently the ultimate determiners of local success or failure.

And crown thy good: intergenerational non-English mother-tongue transmission

Among the success stories of immigrational non-English mother-tongue retention in the USA are the Pennsylvania German Old Order Amish and Mennonites, as well as the Khasidic Yiddish-speaking Jews. Their successes hinge primarily on their non-participation in American secular or religious life and on their limited interaction with English-speaking Americans outside the economic realm. This particular "old order" pattern has not kept either group from acquiring English early and well. Its self-isolating rejection of modernization, however, does not represent a pattern that is acceptable or available to most other Americans of non-English background. Thus, while self-isolation needs to be understood and some of its lessons tailored for local use in other ethnolinguistic settings, there is neither any chance nor any danger that it will be adopted en masse. Perhaps the main generally applicable lesson is the importance of residential concentration in neighborhoods (as with the Khasidim) or in settlement areas (as with the Old Order Amish and Mennonites). This residential concentration would seem to be a necessary (although, ultimately, not self-sufficient) prerequisite for transmitting non-English mother tongues, whether immigrant or indigenous, across generations. It provides for at least *internal* concentration, so that the bulk of the informal and intimate interactions that children and young folk will encounter in the domain of the home–family–neighborhood–community will be in the traditional ethnic mother tongue

But this obvious initial desideratum is not enough. The rationale for an "own language" (a "lengua propia," as the Catalans are accustomed to say about Catalan in Catalonia, vis-à-vis Castilian throughout all of Spain) must be fully developed. It need not necessarily be anchored in non-participation, as is the case among the Khasidim and the Old Order Amish and Mennonites. It may be anchored in religion itself, or in ethnocultural affiliation, or in the expectation of ethnocognitive enrichment, or even in the conviction that multilingualism enables one to contribute a special service on behalf of the nation (sharing the "wealth" derived from multilingualism with the nation as a whole). Whatever the rationale for multilinguals in the midst of an English-speaking sea, it must be fully and consensually verbalized, strikingly ideologized, organizationally implemented, and frequently reiterated, so that most Americans will foster it and be readier than heretofore to bear both its costs and its benefits.

Both the Khasidim and the Old Order Amish and Mennonites support their own institutions (schools, local religious units, and neighborhood organizations), and they receive only a modicum of support, at best, from either "outsider" agencies or "outsider" individuals. These groups have learned a lesson that only some

Amerindian groups have learned, namely, that unless a culture supports its own major institutions it becomes dependent upon "outsiders" (federal government, city council, state legislature, foundations, and other foreign charities) for the continuation, stabilization, and growth of its own ethnolinguistic lifelines. In turn, that dependence fosters interactive dependencies of other kinds, all in all *not an enviable position for a culture to be in and not one well calculated to guarantee intergenerational continuity of the culture's most valued customs, traditions, and outlooks*. Of course, there is a world of difference between accepting (or even competing for) outside support and being dependent upon such support. Depending on such support is inadvisable for any self-respecting culture concerned with its own cultural reproduction in the context of the USA.

Perhaps local religious units (the term *churches* is not appropriate for other than Christian cultures) are the best examples of what is involved. We Americans do not depend on others – particularly not the government – to basically support our places of worship; yet we are a highly religious nation and, owing to our predominant Protestantism, a fantastically diversified one. True to its Protestant mainstream nature, the number of religious bodies (often called "sects" by the mainstream) continues to expand decade by decade, both by "fission" and by "spontaneous generation," far outstripping any tendencies to unify or discontinue that are also operating. Nevertheless, notwithstanding the "wall of separation between church and state," religious bodies in the USA do accept tax-exempt status for their real estate, for their charitable receipts, and for that portion of their clergy's salary that is expended for parsonage purposes; in addition, their schools receive lunch funds, book funds, student health care and health examination funds, and busing funds or services. This same general principle of "primarily self-supporting operation" is fully applicable to ethnic community-based schools and neighborhood institutions that are *not* religiously affiliated. These too – like the Navajo Contract Schools (and Charter Schools more generally) – must place the main burden of support on the community itself rather than on public or other outside sources. A culture and its language cannot live on an externally dependent life-support system, and nothing promotes good cultural health more than collective efforts to stay alive and healthy on one's own.

Without such self-supported, self-protected, and self-initiated islands of demographically concentrated local non-English language-and-culture transmission, non-English mother tongues lack "safe harbors" wherein the young can be socialized according to the languages, values, and traditions of sidestream cultures; this is particularly true given the social mobility, modernization, and urban interaction so typical of American life. These non-English mother tongues also increasingly lack a protected intimate space for adults and older folks during their after-work and out-of-work lives. The work sphere, the mass media, and the common political system will all guarantee that cultural "safe harbors" do not become foreign, isolated, or hostile enclaves. Indeed, the brunt of American historical experience as a whole has provided ample evidence – even among avowedly separatist language-and-culture groups – that the major language maintenance problem is one of engulfment by the mainstream rather than one of excessive separation from it. The "state into nation" process continues along in its own inexorable way and, thereby, "Americans" continue slowly becoming a "state nationality," just as so many others have done in the past whenever the stability of polity fosters culture, and culture fosters ethnicity.

With brotherhood: non-English languages in the national interest

A dispassionate analysis must lead to the conclusion that although the immigrant and cultural-enclave sectors have a powerful contribution to make toward the goal of fostering multilingualism in the USA, these sectors are weak and too situationally disadvantaged to attain this goal by themselves. Nor is there any rational need for them to do so, if one seriously evaluates the benefits to the USA of greater non-English language resources.

There are other streams already involved in contributing toward these resources, although not necessarily on an intergenerational basis. Federal and, to a lesser extent, state agencies are variously involved in funding the preparation and utilization of the talents of advanced non-English-speaking expertise for the better pursuit of their normal activities. Whether for the innumerable purposes of *internal* services (in such areas as health, welfare, civil rights, voting rights, job training and retraining, immigration and naturalization services, flood relief and other disaster relief, and social security advisement) or for the equally ubiquitous purposes of *external* services (to foster military security, foreign-policy goals, commercial advancements, scientific progress, consular presence and consular services, and so on), there is a huge governmental reliance upon and involvement in fostering functional and high-level multilingualism in the USA. It is reprehensibly wasteful and utterly self defeating of some of our most important national and local goals and processes to vitiate and plow under our immigrant-based language resources (with one hand, so to speak), while attempting to foster very similar resources on the basis of government-initiated language courses, language fellowships, and even language schools (with the other hand). Some coordination is urgently required here (see Fishman 1967). It is as scandalous and injurious to waste "native" language resources as to waste our air, water, mineral, animal, and non-linguistic human resources. *How long must languages and cultures be trivialized when they are learned at home, in infancy and childhood, and respected only when they are acquired during adulthood, where they are usually learned less well and at much greater cost in time and money?*

In connection with respecting, utilizing, and fostering our natural non-English mother-tongue resources, another major culprit is the world of American industry and commerce. Once again we note a frenzied, "off again, on again" scramble for intensive (and expensive) adult courses, on the one hand, and, on the other hand, a deaf ear turned to native language resources that, were they recognized and cultivated on a stable basis, would be of great benefit to all. Nor, finally, can American higher education be pardoned for its continuing deafness, blindness, and general ineptness relative to the languages in its own backyard, not to mention its front yard. Not only do our universities inadequately recognize, utilize, and reward the non-English multilingual talents of faculty members and students, but they also commonly denigrate these talents and plow them under. Of course, it will require special methods, special texts, and special classes (with judicious use of materials that our ethnolinguistic minorities themselves have created for educational purposes) if these largely unrecognized language resources within American higher education are to be constructively tapped and cultivated. This is now finally being done in a few places, for a few languages, and by a few sensitively skilled academics and pedagogues (as, for example, with the "Secular Yiddish Schools of America Collection" at Stanford University). On the whole, though, this arena is another example of waste, ignorance, and hostility toward our own natural multilingual resources.

From sea to shining sea: making the USA safe (or at least safer) for cultural democracy

The attrition visited by the American mainstream upon homegrown multilingualism has come full-circle to bite the very hands of the mainstream-dominated governmental, industrial, educational, and recreational establishments that have so studiously abetted and ignored this attrition for most of America's brief history. *Can our miserable record so far be improved?* Unfortunately, a country as rich and as powerful as the USA, smugly speaking what many regard as "the language that rules the world," can long afford to disregard the problem.

A problem that is disregarded, though, does not thereby cease to be a problem. Instead of quick fixes, a program of "cultural democracy" (ethnolinguistic democracy) is needed in order to "make our country safe for home-grown multilingualism." It is a misrepresentation to claim that in our Anglo-Saxon legal tradition we recognize only individual rights and turn a deaf ear to group rights. We recognize the old as a group that requires special financial and physical support. We recognize women as a group that requires special health, welfare, and "gender"-abuse protection. Children, too, are recognized separately under the law. Handicapped groups are also specially recognized by specific laws, while billions of dollars have been expended to make our sidewalks, public buildings, and public housing "user friendly" for them. These are all groups (in large part self-organized groups) that have been recognized for particularistic treatment because, from the point of view of both justice and equity, it is their due. Furthermore, the distinction between individual rights and group rights is neither hard and fast nor clear-cut (Kymlicka 1995).

Nevertheless, even group rights have been recognized in the "affirmative action" cases of African Americans, Hispanics, and Native Americans, as well as in the cases of Old Order Amish and Mennonites. Laws have been repealed and others passed so that, for example, Khasidim would not be disadvantaged as Saturday Sabbath observers or as requiring (as do the Old Order folk) different schools for their young, particularly their learning-disabled young. The overriding American constitutional need for separation between church and state has been modified in these instances by the recognition that entire religious *groups* (not merely a class of unrelated *individuals*) would be severely aggrieved unless they were separately recognized in constructive ways. *Has not the entire affirmative action effort been made on behalf of group rights where a group injustice is recognized? Why should Americans extend group rights only reluctantly and in confrontational contexts, rather than willingly and creatively, in a constructive context of maximizing human resources? And what is the moral distinction between such rights and the rights already granted to ethnic and religious minorities?*

Are not our internal language resources primarily preserved and fostered by separate cultural groups? As we have done throughout our history, must the USA again merely anglicize the Hispanics, Asians, Pacific islanders, Alaskan natives, Amerindians from south and north of the Rio Grande (we overlook the fact that many whom we view as Hispanics are in their own hearts and minds primarily speakers of Mayan languages, or Nahuatl or Quechua or Aymara, etc.), the Africans, Asia-Indians, Russians, Ukrainians, Iranians, Iraqis (the five last-mentioned group names also being "catch all" designations that reveal our ignorance of ethnolinguistic identities), only to find that we lack speakers of these languages when national interest needs arise? Would group rights to foster their languages for the national good be inherently balkanizing and inherently conducive to civil strife? Certainly not, if their speakers' material progress and political participation in the national arena were also forthcoming, as they have been for most Americans since the disadvantages once suffered by women, blacks, and Catholics (all of whom have benefited from "group rights") have been increasingly overcome. Yes, we need group rights along language lines in order to foster "more stable multilingualism for the general good" in the USA. This has long been recognized by such pioneers of the evolving American dream as Horace Kallen, Michael Walzer, and Lani Guinier. If we intend to make the USA safe for homegrown multilingualism as a national and natural resource, we must become serious about genuine cultural democracy and about group rights for this purpose. Genuine cultural democracy has not harmed Switzerland, nor Finland, nor post-Franco Spain, nor even such favorite whipping boys of the American press as Belgium and Canada. Indeed, there is ample evidence that multilingualism does not lead to increased social strife nor to lowered per-capita gross national product, namely, the European Union's increased protection of lesser used languages in pursuit of its impressive economic progress in the last two decades of the twentieth century. How odd that the continent that has suffered longest from linguistic violence in the past is most willing to forgive and forget such past violence in the hope of future benefits from supportive policies on behalf of more and more state and non-state languages. By contrast, the USA – where language wars have never been waged – is excessively timid, even paranoid, about more productively utilizing the extraordinary language resources it still possesses.

Can the USA be persuaded that it really needs languages other than English? That's the rub! If its government, commerce and industry, and academic "forces" can ever be persuaded of this need, they will have to act more inventively and forcefully on behalf of the speakers of those languages that are already resident in the USA. If they can't be persuaded, then, in a world that is becoming increasingly multilingual, Americans will be consigned to being linguistically retarded or (to use a currently more fashionable and euphemistic term) "linguistically challenged." Particularly in the USA, one cannot platonically proclaim one's love for "multilingualism" while neglecting to provide everything that multilingualism would need to prosper. "Language defense" is a possible focus within the status planning (or sociofunctional) half and the corpus planning (or language-per-se) half of any successful enterprise that genuinely aims to assist contextually weaker or threatened languages. Here my comments apply largely to language defenses having to do with status planning (see also Skutnabb-Kangas 1994, 1995), although in most cases linguistic standardization, elaboration, and cultivation efforts would also be necessary. Various types of language defense activities have been reported by investigators. Along more global lines, some work (Fishman 1991, 1997) has sought to derive general principles of language defense from a multitude of cases throughout the world and throughout history. Individual country or regional cases of language defense have been provided for Latin America (Hamel 1997), France and India (Schiffman 1996), and Macedonia (Topolinjska 1998). A multitude of studies shows that, although they all devote attention to one type or another of language status defenses, these types differ substantially from one another and should not be lumped together. A systematization of the types of language status defenses might bring greater order into the frequent bewilderment of scholars, students, and policymakers as to what could possibly be done to foster the multilingualism that recurringly and currently exists on a communal basis in the USA.

Permissive language defense

The most modest and elementary type of language defense is to foster a "permissive" stance on the part of the majority authorities. Such a stance does not obligate the authorities overtly or constructively to do anything on behalf of disadvantaged languages but simply to abstain from oppositional or deleterious actions toward any languages. The "freedom of speech" provision in the Bill of Rights amendments to the US Constitution does not directly assist those who would like to foster non-English language use, in addition to English. On the other hand, if that provision were enforced, it would prohibit the most obvious legislation against the use of languages other than English. Permissive legislation that promotes language defense would not render the English-Only Movement inoperative nor necessarily prohibit declaring English to be the only language of government. It might merely be an expression of good vibes vis-à-vis languages other than English in the home, family, neighborhood, and community.

Note, however, that even the *Meyer v. Nebraska* decision of the US Supreme Court, which in 1923 invalidated Nebraska's prohibition of using any modern spoken language as a medium for teaching children below the age of twelve led neither to any requirement nor to any explicit encouragement of government *support* for such efforts, even along strictly instructional lines. (Incidentally, this invalidation was subsequently designated the "Magna Carta of language freedom in the USA" [Kloss 1977].) Actually, such permissiveness is merely a hands-off decision and leaves functionally and contextually disadvantaged languages just as disadvantaged as they were before. These languages remain exposed to the Darwinian law of the linguistic jungle: the strong survive and, in competition with the strong, the weak die off.

Basically, permissive rulings and legislation are decorative or "purely symbolic" gestures. They imply more than they deliver. At best they may prepare the ground for future meaningful support, but in and of themselves they do not provide any such support. For far too long, non-English languages in the USA have been trifled with by what amounts to no more than "Fourth of July oratory." When such languages are more than a generation away from their immigrational origins, they are usually not sufficiently robust to be trifled with further, particularly because time is of the essence insofar as their intergenerational continuity is concerned. Most serious non-linguistic matters that require immediate attention are not given merely permissive nods. If education is assumed to be important, laws are passed requiring it, supporting it, fostering it. If language defense (and therefore a more multilingual / multicultural society in the USA) is really considered to be in the public interest (rather than merely a private hobby or private passion), then it too cannot merely be permissively tolerated. Alone, a permissive policy falls short even of a symbolic treatment (see below) and, as such, does not begin to rise to the level of either active or preventive language defense on behalf of multilingualism and the non-English mother tongues of the USA.

Active language defenses

Active language defenses attempt to be therapeutic vis-à-vis disadvantaged languages. They are undertaken when danger is not only *recognized* but when ameliorative steps are *implemented* in order to counteract language endangerment. If we were to follow a medical metaphor, we might say that active language defenses treat the patient in order to overcome a diagnosed illness. But therapy – no matter how restorative – is never as optimal a defense as the prevention of illness. To make matters worse, most of the active language defense on record is more symbolic than substantive. Aggrieved language communities are mollified by having their languages declared "co-official," as with Hawaiian in the Hawaiian Islands and Navajo on the ballots in New Mexico. Activists for endangered languages are often mollified by having their languages utilized on official letterheads or by having a song of theirs sung on an important public occasion (such as happens at Lutheran churches in Minnesota on "Norwegian Language Day"). Even if such public occasions are frequent (like the daily opening of the school day), such remedial steps are frequently too late and commonly too little (as in the case of transitional bilingual education involving recessive languages). Effective language defenses require more than window dressing. Symbolic decorations are not what either daily life or language life are all about, not even for the healthy, let alone for those in ill health. In the absence of serious empirical supervision, experimentation, evaluation, and follow-up relative to specifically defined achievements (such as "overt language use in this or that specified function"), it is very likely that even so called "action research" will be only small scale and symbolic rather than curative. Research may be informative but by itself it is not curative. Many a sick language has been researched to death, and many another is still being researched to death. An honorable burial is not an effective language defense. An effective theory of remedial language defense must fit all ameliorations to the nature and degree of the illness. Subsidizing the televised viewing of adult films that are available in a particular threatened language (e.g., broadcasts of more foreign language films selected for linguistic rather than solely artistic reasons) will probably be totally ineffective in assisting languages with increasingly diminishing rates of intergenerational transmission from Xish-speaking child-bearing adults to Xish-speaking offspring who could ultimately become Xish-speaking child-bearing adults themselves. For such intergenerational transmission really to be reinforced, assistance is needed much closer to the juncture of transmission, for example, in connection with language-infused nursery centers, child-care centers, parenting courses, and so on.

Preventive ("proactive") defenses of threatened multilingualism

The most effective assurance of continued physical health is *preventive* medicine. Similarly, demographically and functionally minoritized languages – which is what all non-English languages in the USA really are – require preventive defenses prior to reaching stages of advanced difficulty. This view is recognized constitutionally in Belgium, where, in small pockets assigned to one or another of the two stronger languages Walloon and Flemish, yet another language (say, German) is nevertheless recognized as meriting particular facilitation. Proactive language defense requires constant evaluation to catch possible difficulties before they reach the galloping contagion or threatening stage. The "sign inspectors" of the Office de la langue française in Quebec might, most charitably, be said to be engaged in proactive francophone language defense efforts in a province in which more than 90 percent of the population is of francophone origin. In fact, the entire francophone movement in Quebec is proactive in the sense that it functions on behalf of a locally dominant but nationally minoritized language. A similar type of assistance in the USA would foster making Spanish official in many election districts and would actively support the native American language Yakima in other districts. Most of those who shed crocodile tears on discovering the sad conditions within the USA of our own outposts of world community languages like French, German, Russian, Chinese, and Arabic are protesting their ignorance too vehemently. *Can it be that they preferred not to know about the "language killing fields" in their own backyards?* It goes without saying, of course, that the rights of English speakers, as individuals or as groups, must not be harmed in any way by co-recognizing or assisting other languages. In addition, such languages will be all the more readily and realistically available, from then on, for the cultural enrichment and for the greater functional versatility of Anglo children as well. Let us learn from world experience that proactive efforts undertaken in the context of and on behalf of local multilingualism, via expanding cultural democracy and multiplying positive contacts between groups, are not the "beginning of the end" for the mainstream but the beginning of new advantages for everyone. Multilingualism is a valid and even urgent goal for multicultural citizenship in the USA, and it is a goal that must not elude the American imagination.

In 1999, the Palo Alto (California) School District, near Stanford University, renewed its long-term support for two-way bilingual education (Spanish–English) in two of its elementary schools and approved the opening of a new elementary school bilingual in Mandarin and English. Palo Alto is an affluent school district and one in which the high standard of living effectively limits the numbers of resident and incoming minorities speaking languages other than English. All of the children involved in these two-way programs have always learned to achieve simultaneously at very high levels of English and Spanish competence, and more and more of them will now be able to do so in another language as well. The Palo Alto School District also enables Korean and Japanese to be taught in its school buildings after school hours and on weekends so that interested students can attain fluency or retain it in these languages, thereby getting high-school foreign language credit for studying them, offering their test scores in these languages among their College Entrance Examination Board credentials, and obtaining advanced placement in these languages at the college level upon graduating from high school. All in all, this promises to be a successful proactive way of rewarding and fostering childhood and adolescent societal multilinguals in the USA.

I am proud of "my" school district's efforts to foster native-born or other early childhood multilingualism and, at the same time, to disprove "gloom and doom" prognostications in that connection. Relative to what the USA needs, it is only a drop in the bucket. Still, it may also be a straw in the wind, indicating that perhaps the tide of fear and suspicion may be turning again and that many Americans now feel sufficiently secure to foster multilingualism at least among those who are already among our more fortunate sons and daughters of elementary-school age. It is a beginning, but it is important to bear in mind that proactive schools alone cannot maintain multilingualism across generations. Other forces in society must also contribute: the family–home–neighborhood–community, first and foremost among them, but also mass media, the workplace, higher education, and major agencies of government. Hopefully, there will be no turning back! Hopefully, a true language-fostering alliance between governmental programs, ethnic community programs, industrial/commercial sector programs, and higher educational programs will come into being, in place of the traditional wasteful and morally sad approach of "too little and too late" on the societal multilingualism front.

Suggestions for further reading and exploration

Schiffman (1996) contains chapters that treat language policy in the USA and other countries, as well as a separate chapter on language policy in California; it is a good introduction to some of the important issues raised in this chapter. You can learn about the Old Order Amish at *http://www.holycrosslivonia.org/amish/origin.htm* and about the Khasidim (also commonly spelt Chasidim) at *http://www.kabbalaonline.org/chasidism*. You may wish to learn more about the three pioneers of the evolving American dream mentioned in this chapter. For Horace M. Kallen, often credited with the notion of "cultural pluralism," see the books in which he promoted the concept, for example, *Cultural Pluralism and the American Idea* (1956) and *Liberty, Laughter and Tears* (1968). For Michael Walzer's views, see Walzer 1997; for Lani Guinier's views, see Guinier and Torres 2002. Chapters 9, 10, 11, 14, 17, and 18 of this book also discuss multilingualism or language maintenance.

References

Fishman, Joshua A. 1967. *Language Loyalty in the United States*. The Hague: Mouton.

Fishman, Joshua A. 1991. *Reversing Language Shift: Theory and Method of Assistance to Threatened Languages*. Clevedon: Multilingual Matters.

   1997. *In Praise of the Beloved Language: a Comparative View of Positive Ethnolinguistic Consciousness*. Berlin: Mouton de Gruyter.

Guinier, Lani and Gerald Torres. 2002. *The Miner's Canary: Enlisting Race, Resisting Power*. Cambridge: Harvard University Press.

Hamel, Ranier Enrique, ed. 1997. "Linguistic Human Rights from a Sociolinguistic Perspective." *International Journal of the Sociology of Language*. No. 127, entire issue.

Kallen, Horace M. 1998. *Culture and Democracy in the United States*. New Brunswick NJ: Transaction.

Kloss, Heinz. 1977. *The American Bilingual Tradition*. Rowley MA: Newbury House. [Repr. 1998. Washington DC and McHenry IL: Center for Applied Linguistics and Delta Systems.]

Kymlicka, Will. 1995. *Multicultural Citizenship: a Liberal Theory of Minority Rights*. Oxford: Clarendon Press.

Schiffman, Harold F. 1996. *Linguistic Culture and Language Policy*. New York: Routledge.

Skutnabb-Kangas, Tove and Robert Phillipson, eds. 1995. *Linguistic Human Rights: Overcoming Linguistic Discrimination*. Berlin: Mouton de Gruyter.

Topolinjska, Zuzanna, ed. 1998. *The Sociolinguistic Situation of the Macedonian Language*. *International Journal of the Sociology of Language*, Issue 131, entire issue.

Walzer, Michael. 1997. *Pluralism and Democracy*. Paris: Esprit.

8

Creole languages: forging new identities

PATRICIA NICHOLS

Editors' introduction

A question of great interest for students and professional linguists alike is, "How and why do new languages arise?" In this chapter Patricia Nichols describes three examples that illustrate how in extraordinary circumstances creole languages arise. Besides examining the social circumstances supporting the formation of Gullah in South Carolina and of Louisiana Creole and Hawaiian Creole, she illustrates these creole languages and describes creole characteristics more generally. The chapter also explores how creoles help forge new social identities.

Creole languages arise in periods of rapid social change in situations where people speaking different languages have extensive contact. Under the right circumstances, speakers incorporate vocabulary from the languages of other groups (usually dominating groups) into a scaffolding of their own ancestral language. Because the languages of the dominating groups are languages of wider communication such as English (for Gullah and for Hawaiian Creole) or French (for Louisiana Creole), outsiders may wrongly judge the creoles to be bastardized versions of the world languages. The particular circumstances surrounding formation of the US creoles differed, but in each case the essential ingredients needed to form a creole existed. In South Carolina, for instance, the slave population represented speakers of many languages of Central and West Africa, and slaves speaking different languages were sometimes deliberately grouped together to prevent a shared or common language to communicate with. If most slaves had no opportunity to learn the language of their masters, it is easy to see how a pidgin arose that would enable communication among them. When speakers of pidgin raised children whose first language was that pidgin, a process of creolization started that led to Gullah, a creole that remains the vital home language in several South Carolina communities to this day.

Creoles around the globe share characteristic linguistic features that reflect universal tendencies in language formation and the particular circumstances in which creoles arise. Those unique circumstances also represent the unique identity of creole-speaking groups, and the principal mark of identity and history for speakers of creole is their language – their Gullah or Louisiana Creole or Hawaiian Creole. Following the lead of other researchers, Nichols calls the formation and use of creoles "acts of identity," and she notes that creoles "demonstrate the creative powers of human beings in desperate times and the power of language to strengthen social bonds over time."

In three different parts of the USA – South Carolina, Louisiana, and Hawai'i – new languages have evolved. These new languages are Creoles, with scaffolding from older, ancestral languages and exterior finishing from a language previously unknown to the ancestral groups. In South Carolina and in Hawai'i, these new languages adopted an English vocabulary, and in Louisiana a French vocabulary. The building blocks, or *substratum*, of the South Carolina and the Louisiana creoles are African, while the primary building blocks of the Hawai'i creole are Asian, Micronesian, and Portuguese. The contributing languages to the creoles reflect the multiple identities of their early speakers. Today these creoles – *Gullah* in South Carolina, *Louisiana Creole* in Louisiana, and *Hawaiian Creole* in Hawai'i – help to define and project social identities of contemporary speakers. Like the new languages, these identities have been forged in an American setting.

Because most speakers of the US creoles are bilingual in the creole and another language of wider communication, outsiders may not realize how widely the creole is spoken within a particular social group. Many creole speakers use it only in the domains of family and friends and speak another language variety elsewhere. None of the US creoles is used as the medium of instruction in schools or as the language of legal documents. Thus, all three have low status in the eyes of the wider public and even for many who speak them. With a vocabulary similar to that of English or French, the creoles are mistakenly thought to be corrupt versions of these world languages.

Nothing could be further from the truth. The US creoles represent classic cases of how, given the right conditions, new languages can come into being in times of rapid social change and extensive language contact (Thomason and Kaufman 1988). In colonial South Carolina and Louisiana, these conditions were plantation slavery on a massive scale when speakers of many different African languages were forcibly brought to work in rice and indigo fields in the early and mid-eighteenth centuries. In Hawai'i, the conditions were those of servitude by large groups of Asians, Portuguese, and Micronesians, who came to work on sugarcane plantations in the early nineteenth century. Living together in slave or servant quarters, these newcomers were effectively cut off from former speech communities and, in a great many cases, even from speakers of their own native languages. As slaves and servants, they were subject to the control of owners and overseers whose language permeated their world of work and commerce. Outnumbering their masters and interacting seldom, if ever, with native speakers from the master class, many of these slaves and servants spoke primarily to each other – developing three new common languages from a combination of grammatical patterns from the ancestral languages and vocabulary from the language of trade and commerce.

Definitions

The word *creole* reflects how words take on new meanings in new circumstances. It originates from a Portuguese verb *criar*, meaning 'to raise (a child).' The past participle *criado* 'a person who is raised,' refers to a child or servant who is born into one's household. By extension, the diminutive *crioulo* came to mean an African slave born in the new Portuguese colony of Brazil and, by further extension, Europeans born in the western hemisphere – which it still means in Portugal. The Spanish borrowed the word as *criollo*, the French as *créole*, the Dutch as *creol*, and the English as *creole* – and extended its meaning to embrace the customs as well as the speech of both Africans and Europeans born in the new colonies (Holm 1988). Its most well-known meaning today in the USA is for the food, music, and customs associated with Louisiana's blend of African, French, and Spanish cultures.

When applied to language, *creole* carries the overtones of something nurtured in a new geographic setting, but linguists use the term to refer specifically to new languages that are the product of intensive contact between two or more very different languages over a short period of time. Creole languages typically develop from *pidgin* languages, which no one speaks as a native language (Sebba 1997). Pidgins are grammatically simple languages used in the marketplace, on ships, or in migratory communities – all places where speakers of many different languages are gathered together in situations that demand intense interaction but afford no opportunity to learn any one language fully. Pidgins take their vocabulary from the language of the social elite in a given situation (superstratum) but use the grammatical structures of the less prestigious but more frequently spoken languages (substratum). As children are born into this dynamic, multilingual society where their parents often speak the pidgin to each other and all their playmates speak it, a more complex grammar begins to evolve – one that meets the needs of native speakers – and a creole is born. In a sense, our US creoles are languages raised by the children of immigrants in a new land.

A creole language is usually characterized as the elaboration of a pidgin language that has acquired native speakers. Most pidgins do not do so. For a creole to develop from a pidgin, access to the original native languages must be cut off – as happens when large numbers of people are transported against their will and kept in subservient conditions for several generations, without opportunities for learning the language of the master class. We can see why these languages are so often disparaged: their speakers are looked down upon because of where they are in the social fabric of the larger speech community.

We can also understand why not all immigrant communities *do* develop pidgins or creoles. Provided they have access to the prestige language through education, work, or other social interaction, children in most immigrant communities become bilingual within a generation, speaking one language at home and another in public. For example, in Florida and the Southwest and in Puerto Rico and some neighborhoods of New York City where Spanish and English exist side by side, a pidgin based on both languages has not evolved although codeswitching between the two languages is common. For a pidgin language to develop, there must be a lack of effective bilingualism, a strong need to communicate, and restricted access to a target language (Harris 1986). (See Nichols 1996 for a fuller discussion of how pidgins and creoles are defined and Holm 1988, 1989 for discussions of specific creole languages throughout the world. See chapter 10 of this volume on the prevalence of codeswitching among bilinguals and Myers-Scotton 2001 on how bilingual speech can lead to the development of a creole.)

Gullah

In the USA, the creole known as Gullah or Geechee originated among African slaves brought to coastal South Carolina in the eighteenth century. Initially, American Indians were enslaved as domestic workers in colonial homes, and European immigrants to South Carolina had a thriving business selling Indian slaves to the New England colonies and the Caribbean. Then an Easter Sunday uprising in 1715 – coordinated by all the Southeastern tribes trading with the Carolina colonials – nearly wiped out the fragile English settlement at Charleston. After this "Yemasee War," the number of native peoples declined sharply, while importation of African slaves to work the new rice fields along the coastal tidewaters increased dramatically. (See figure 8-1.) As the rice economy began to expand, the Europeans showed a preference for slaves from West Africa, particularly the regions of Senegal and Gambia, because, unlike the Europeans, these Africans were familiar with the cultivation of rice (Littlefield 1981). At certain time periods, however, slaves from the Angola region of Central Africa were more readily available, and large numbers of Angolans entered the colony speaking very different languages from the West Africans. Women from the Igbo-speaking region of the Niger basin were represented in disproportionate numbers in the runaway slave records (Littlefield 1981). Coming from a region in Africa where indigo flourished, these women would have made substantial contributions to the success of indigo cultivation and the processed dye cakes that the Carolina planters and farmers exported as a secondary product to rice in the second half of the eighteenth century. Even after being banned in the late eighteenth century, illegal importation of African slaves continued, with estimates of over 90,000 entering the Charleston area directly from Africa in the first decade after 1800 (McMillan 1999). Because so many of these late illegal entries were not recorded, we know little about their ethnic origins. The mix appears to have been similar to that of the earlier period, but Africans from Angola and from the Bights of Benin and from Biafra were more available in the later period. The on-going arrival of many speakers of different African languages throughout the eighteenth century and spilling over into the nineteenth made for a dynamic language situation. The 90,000 new speakers arriving in the very last decade of contact makes it virtually impossible to say with certainty that specific grammatical constructions of Gullah derive from one specific language or language family of West or Central Africa.

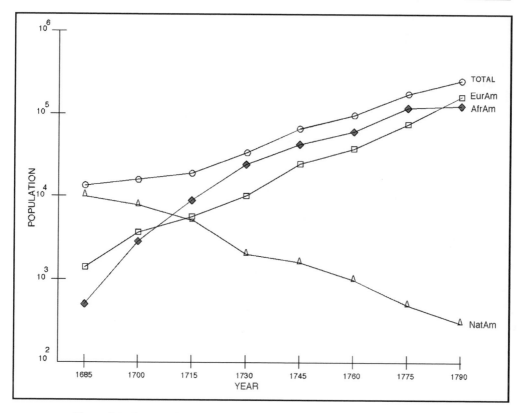

Figure 8-1 *Estimated population by race in South Carolina (east of the mountains) Based on Wood (1989: 38)*
In this logarithmic graph, $10^6 = 1,000,000$; $10^5 = 100,000$; $10^4 = 10,000$; $10^3 = 1,000$; $10^2 = 100$; EurAm = European Americans; AfrAm = African Americans; NatAm = Native Americans

What seems clear is that Africans and Afro Carolinians spoke a wide variety of languages from the beginning of contact and continued to do so until the Civil War and after. In every case where language is mentioned, the runaway slave records indicate that slaves born in the colony spoke a variety of English more intelligible to their masters than newly arrived slaves.

The creole that developed from this mix of peoples speaking together in a new land was concentrated in coastal areas where Africans lived on large plantations. The neck of land formed by the Waccamaw River, where it parallels the Atlantic (figure 8-2), was one of the earliest and longest lived such areas.

There the rice plantations extended between the river and the ocean, with access to both bodies of water (Joyner 1984). These swampy areas were largely abandoned by the Europeans during warm weather because of the malaria transmitted by the *Anopheles* mosquito, which thrived in the tideland waters where the rice grew. Many Africans were less susceptible to the ravages of this disease because

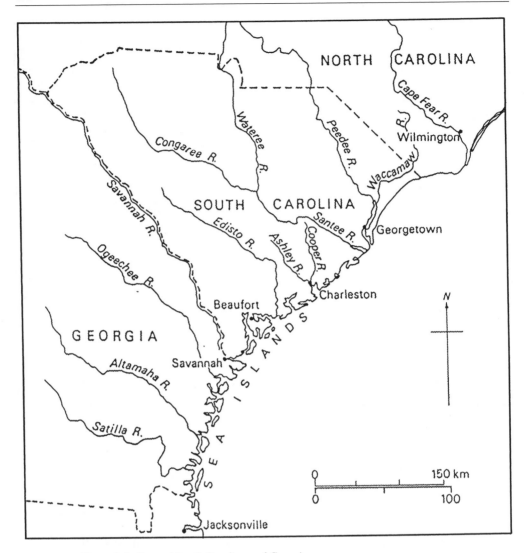

Figure 8-2 *Coastal South Carolina and Georgia*

of an inherited genetic trait (the same trait that causes sickle-cell anemia). Thus, for long periods of time each year, groups of African slaves worked the rice plantations in circumstances where they seldom saw, much less interacted with, a European. Speaking many different, though often related, African languages and having a great need to communicate with each other, they could neither become bilingual in another African language nor learn the English they seldom heard. Instead, they forged a new language out of their many, with grammatical structures that seem clearly to reflect a number of African substratum languages (Turner 1949/2001) and a vocabulary that is now overwhelmingly English – though it may have contained many more African words in early stages. On the larger plantation, the young children of the field slaves were typically cared for during the daylight hours in a "nurse-house" managed by older women whose laboring days in the fields were over. In such settings, children born in the new colony grew up speaking the language of their peers – as children do all over the world. The common language in these nursery settings would have been the evolving creole.

Although many South Carolinians today will claim that Gullah has disappeared, it can still be heard in rural areas where Gullah-speaking communities have had a long history. Coastal South Carolina (Nichols 1976, Weldon 1998) and the Sea Islands of both South Carolina and Georgia (Cunningham 1970, Jones-Jackson 1987, Hopkins 1992) have been studied most, but Gullah can be heard throughout the Coastal Plain in South Carolina in old communities, especially those untouched by the tourist industry. Today it is most often heard among the very old and the very young because it is learned as a language of the home. Many speakers learn and use it as children, move away from their communities for education and jobs where they use a variety of African American English or a regional Standard English, and then return to their communities in retirement when they "re-creolize" their speech. Others never leave their communities of birth and continue to speak the creole within the home and with longtime friends, although they may have public jobs where they speak one or more varieties of English. Important for language transmission and maintenance, many middle-aged adults take jobs in urban centers but leave their young children with older members of their home communities for long periods of time as a solution to child-care problems – reshaping the "nurse-houses" of slavery time to meet contemporary needs for nurture and socialization. Some young adults join the military, traveling and working all over the world but often returning to their home communities when their active service is over. Other adults return sporadically on holidays or for family gatherings but sometimes leave young children with relatives there for extended vacations. Thus, in coastal South Carolina, Gullah continues to have speakers even though it is impossible to estimate their numbers with any degree of accuracy because of the variable patterns of language learning and use over a lifespan.

Many children from Gullah-speaking communities enter school speaking only Gullah. Those teachers in Waccamaw Neck elementary schools who have not grown up in the area report spending as long as a year using some children as "interpreters" between themselves and Gullah-speaking children (personal communication). By about the age of eight or nine, children become bilingual in Gullah and English and can often be observed switching between the two when it is clear that the teacher has not understood a Gullah utterance (Nichols 1996). This process of codeswitching within African American communities has not been systematically studied, but an understanding of it is crucial to teasing out the links between the creole and African American English (AAE). Pre-adolescent children on the Waccamaw Neck use many creole features along with ones that have been identified as characteristic of AAE, as illustrated in this nine-year-old girl's narrative about what she did on Christmas:

A. When Christmas come, I had gone to my Aunt May house. Then my aunt say have to beat my little sister cause she had, she had broke a glass with the cocoa in um.

When Christmas came, I went to my Aunt May's house. Then my aunt said that she had to beat my little sister because she [the sister] had broken a glass with cocoa in it.

B. And then we had gone up to we other cousin house name Neecie. And then we had see, then we, then that night we had gone up to Jerome. Then when we come from there, the dog had come and bite my little sister, and my little sister say, "Owww, Ooooo."

And then we went up to our other cousin's house named Neecie. And then we saw, then we, then that night we went up to Jerome's. Then when we came from there, the dog came and bit my little sister, and my little sister said, "Owww, Ooooo."

C. And then ee say, "Unnnn."

And then she said, "Unnnn."

D. And then she, and then after that – Monday – we, I had gone to my aunt house fuh see my baby sister. And then we had gone and play. And then I had ride her bicycle. And she bicycle had broke.

And then she, and then after that – Monday – we, I went to my aunt's house in order to see my baby sister. And then we went and played. And then I rode her bicycle. And her bicycle broke.

E. And Neecie say, "Oh, Rhetta, see what you done do: broke that girl bicycle!"

And Neecie said, "Oh, Rhetta, see what you have done: broken that girl's bicycle!"

F. I say, "I ain't do um. You do um cause you want me fuh tote you!"

I said, "I didn't do it. You did it because you wanted me to tote [carry] you [on the back of the bicycle]."

An older woman in her eighties uses similar features in an excerpt from a narrative about a drowning in the Waccamaw:

G. And my father and my sister right here over there drown out there in the Waccamaw Bay. They was coming from Georgetown in a row boat. And a boat been coming from this side, name the ___. . . . A big boat. And ee was foggy, and they couldn't see. And when the boat strike the little boat, my brother, he jump on this big boat fuh let the people know what happen. And

And my [god] father and my sister right here over there drowned out there in the Waccamaw Bay. They were coming from Georgetown in a rowboat. And a boat was coming from this side, named the ___. . . . A big boat. And it was foggy, and they couldn't see. And when the boat struck the little boat, my brother – he jumped on this big boat in order to let the people know what had

then they had to go a long ways before they turn round. And when they turn round, my sister and my godfather-dem was done sweep away.	*happened. And then they had to go a long way before they turned around. And when they turned around, my sister and my godfather and all the other people had already been swept away.*
H. And my daddy stand up in Waccamaw River with ee pipe in ee mouth. . . . With his pipe in ee mouth, he was so tall!	*And my daddy stood up in the Waccamaw River with his pipe in his mouth. . . . With his pipe in his mouth, he was so tall!*

These two short narratives exhibit several grammatical constructions that can be identified as creole in origin:

(1) *ee* and *um* as distinguishing subject/possessive *it* from object *it* (A, F, G, H)

(2) no tense marking inflections for simple past on many verbs (A, B, C, G, H)

(3) *done* marking completed action for past perfect verbs (E)

(4) *fuh* introducing a clause of purpose or reason, or one expressing uncertain/unaccomplished events (D, F, G)

(5) no possessive marking for nouns (A, B, E)

(6) no copula (BE-verb) for some clauses containing predicate nominatives, adjectives, or locatives (no examples)

The child has begun to use *had* as a past-tense marker, which she clearly distinguishes from the present-tense *have*. She also uses an African vocabulary item, *tote*, which has passed into general American English to describe a bag used to carry something: *tote bag*.

A Gullah feature that neither speaker uses – but which can still be heard among the very young and very old – is a marker for reiterative or habitual aspect: *duh*, as in "Gregg duh hide." This particular example of *duh* was used to describe a playmate who was ducking down behind an automobile repeatedly, his head disappearing and reappearing over the top of the vehicle.

Children and adults of the Waccamaw Neck can be heard codeswitching between Gullah and a regional variety of AAVE, depending on the social situation. Similar switching between language varieties probably occurred at earlier stages and probably accounts for the grammatical "mix" that can be found in Gullah and other creoles, as waves of different language speakers entered the community over time. For creole development generally, Myers-Scotton (1997, 2001) makes a convincing case that codeswitching between varieties results in the process of "turnover," whereby the grammatical structures used by one generation are at least partially replaced by another set of grammatical structures in subsequent generations – as the proportions of incoming speakers shift the balance between native languages in a dynamic creole society. Such a "turnover" process may have occurred more than once for Gullah, as speakers from different areas of West and Central Africa joined Carolina speech communities.

Hawaiian Creole

Recent socio-historical research on the other US creole with an English vocabulary reveals how important different waves of speakers can be to the development and eventual shape of a stable creole language. Hawaiian Creole (still called *Pidgin* by the islanders themselves) is unique among creoles in that documentation exists for how it has changed with successive language contact between different groups of speakers. The development of Hawaiian Creole can be divided into six phases, beginning with the initial phase of contact between native Hawaiians and small numbers of European American missionaries (1778–1829) and ending with the present phase that began in 1950 when large numbers of mainland European Americans became island residents (Roberts 1998). For language contact, the second through fifth phases are important. The second phase (whaling era of 1830–59) included Chinese and more European Americans than the previous one. The third phase (plantation era of 1860–99) included massive numbers of Chinese, Portuguese, and Japanese laborers. The fourth phase (beginning of territorial era from 1900–19) included large numbers of children born to Chinese and to Portuguese laborers. The fifth phase (middle and end of territorial era from 1920 to 1949) included many native-born descendants of Chinese, Portuguese, and Japanese immigrants. A number of Filipinos also entered the islands during the fourth and fifth phases, but most of these were bachelors or men who had left their wives and families in the Philippines.

Hawaiian Pidgin was the initial contact language to emerge in the islands. This pidgin with a native Hawaiian vocabulary emerged between 1790 and 1820 between native Hawaiians and Europeans of different language backgrounds who visited the islands (Roberts 1995). During the subsequent whaling period, sailors used Hawaiian Pidgin as a trade language, as did early immigrants to the sugar plantations. Linguists have argued at length about the relationship between this early pidgin with its Hawaiian vocabulary and the subsequent one that emerged nearly a century later with an English vocabulary. When English speakers became a presence in the islands during the mid and late 1800s, many native Hawaiians appear to have first learned English as a foreign language under the tutelage of the missionaries, while continuing to use Pidgin Hawaiian for trade with seamen stopping in the islands. The Hawaiian Pidgin English that preceded Hawaiian Creole did not begin to emerge until the period of massive immigration of plantation laborers accompanying European American commercial influence. By the late nineteenth century, this pidgin with an English vocabulary was being widely used as a plantation language (Roberts 1998), owing in large measure to overwhelming numbers of immigrants: by 1890 immigrants and their descendants outnumbered the native Hawaiian and part-Hawaiian population, and by 1934 indigenous Hawaiians represented less than 10 percent of the total population (Reinecke 1969).

One factor that seems very important for development of the creole was the increasing use of English as a medium of instruction for school children. During the decade 1878–88, English began to replace the native Hawaiian language as a medium of instruction in the public schools of Hawai'i (Siegel 2000). English was the preferred language of education for the large population of Portuguese immigrants, many of whom served as overseers on island plantations, and they actively demanded its use in the schools. Because a massive increase in the numbers of children born to Portuguese and Chinese immigrants occurred after 1890, many island-born children thus heard English in the classroom from their teachers and learned Pidgin English on the playground from other children. Island-born children of immigrant parents tended to be bilingual for the first generation, using a home language with parents and the pidgin with their peers. The English of the schools would have represented yet a third language, one that had stiff competition from the other two. Subsequent generations of Chinese and Portuguese children used the creole as their primary language. Japanese immigrants did not come to the islands in large numbers until 1888, and thus their island-born children did not have an initial impact on the common language that evolved (Reinecke 1969). Japanese island-born children, moreover, tended to be more loyal to their home language than did immigrant children of other ethnic groups (Roberts 1998).

The Portuguese seem to have been a significant social link between plantation owners or managers and the plantation laborers, acting as they often did in the role of plantation overseers. Sharing cultural and religious ties with the European Americans, Portuguese children were the largest immigrant group in the schools for the quarter of a century when the creole was stabilizing at the end of the third and beginning of the fourth phase (Siegel 2000). A 1939 study offers a tabulation of "errors" made by children according to ethnic group (Hawaiian, Chinese, Portuguese, and Japanese) and notes specific structures – which we would now recognize as creole grammatical structures – that characterize the speech of children from different ethnic groups (M. E. Smith, cited in Roberts 1998). The frequency of these "errors" for each ethnic group can be linked to the substratum languages spoken at home (Siegel 2000). Portuguese and Chinese immigrant speech of the plantation phase had a strong influence on the grammatical structures of Hawaiian Creole during its formative stages.

The text below appears in a contemporary literary quarterly published by Hawaiian writers (Lum 1990: 72–73). Translation is provided by Kent Sakoda and his colleagues (Diana Eades, Teri Menacker, Ermile Hargrove, and Suzie Jacobs):

A. Anyway, I no can tell if da Bag Man is happy or sad or piss off or anyting l'dat cause he get one moosetash and skinny kine beard wit only little bit strands, stay hide his mout. But his eyes, da Bag Man's eyes, stay always busy . . . looking, lookin, looking.

Anyway, I can't tell if the Bag Man is happy or sad or pissed off or anything like that because he has a mustache and a thin kind of beard with just a few strands hiding his mouth. But his eyes, the Bag Man's eyes are always busy . . . looking, looking, looking.

B. I look back at him, and to me, he ack like he little bit shame. We stay da only small kids sitting down at da tables, me and Russo, but da Bag Man ack like he no like know us.

I look back at him, and it seems to me that he's acting like he's a little embarrassed. Me and Russell, we're the only little kids sitting at the tables, but the Bag Man acts like he doesn't want to know us.

C. Had one nudda guy in one tee-shirt was sitting at da table next to us was watching da Bag Man too. He was eating one plate lunch and afterwards, he wen take his plate ovah to da Bag Man. Still had little bit everyting on top, even had bar-ba-que meat left.

There was another guy in a tee-shirt who was sitting at the table next to us and he was watching the Bag Man too. He was eating a plate lunch and after he was done, he took his plate over to the Bag Man. There was still a little bit of everything on it, it even had some teriyaki meat.

D. "Bra," da guy tell, "you like help me finish? I stay full awready."

"Hey man," the guy says, "do you wanna help me finish this? I'm stuffed."

E. Da Bag Man no tell nutting, only nod his head and take da plate. I thought he would eat um real fast . . . gobble um up, you know. But was funny, he went put um down and go to da counter fo get one napkin and make um nice by his place . . . da fork on tap da napkin. Even he took da plate out of da box, made um j'like one real restaurant. I wanted fo give him sometin too, but I only had my cup wit little bit ice left. I awready went drink up all da Coke and was chewing da ice. Da Bag Man was looking at me now, not at me but at my cup. I nevah know what fo do

The Bag Man didn't say a word, just nodded his head and took the plate. I thought he'd eat it real fast, gobble it up, you know. But the funny thing was that he put it down and went to the counter to get a napkin and set it up nicely at his place . . . with the fork on the napkin. He even took the plate out of its container, made it just like a real restaurant. I wanted to give him something too, but I only had my cup with a little bit of ice left. I had already drunk all of the Coke and was chewing on the ice. The Bag Man was looking at me now, not at me but at my cup. I didn't know what to do though, because it would be

| cause j'like I selfish if I keep my cup but, nevah have nutting inside awready, so shame eh, if you give somebody someting but stay empty. But I nevah know what fo do cause I had to go awready. I thought I could jes leave da cup on da table or be like da tee-shirt guy and tell, "Brah, hea." | *like I was selfish if I kept my cup although it already had nothing in it, so it's embarrassing isn't it, if you give someone something but it's empty. I didn't know what to do because I had to go then. I thought I could just leave the cup on the table or be like the tee-shirt guy and say, "Hey man, here."* |

Several grammatical constructions can be identified as characteristic of Hawai'ian Creole:

(1) the article *da*, used to mark a noun phrase with known referent (A, B, C, D, E)

(2) the pre-verbal stay (*stei*), used to mark non-punctual aspect (B, D, E)

(3) the pre-verbal *bin* (been) or *wen* (went) used to mark simple past (C, E)

(4) no tense marking inflections for past on many verbs (A, B, D, E)

(5) the verb *have/had* used to mark existentials [*there is/there are*] (C)

(6) no copula (B E -verb) for some clauses containing predicate nominatives, adjectives, or locatives (no examples)

(7) *fo* introducing a clause of purpose/reason or a clause expressing uncertain/unaccomplished events (E)

Because Hawaiian Creole is relatively young and relatively well-documented, it is a rich source of material for better understanding creole languages. Today it is reported to be spoken in its most basilectal or conservative form on the islands of Kaua'i and Hawai'i (figure 8-3). Both it and Gullah, whose development has not been as well documented over time, meet the typological criteria for creoles proposed in a recent analysis of the creole prototype: (1) little or no use of inflectional affixes; (2) little or no use of tone for word contrasts or grammatical meaning; (3) use of regular derivational affixes (McWhorter 1998).

Louisiana Creole

Louisiana Creole arose from the early language contact between French colonialists and the African slaves they imported during the period between 1699 and 1750, approximately the same time period in which Gullah was developing in South Carolina. The numbers of Africans in Louisiana during the colonial period, however, never approached the numbers in South Carolina. Moreover, Africans and Europeans were more equal in number after the early period, when Europeans were outnumbered by two to one. Only 20,000 settlers, evenly divided between

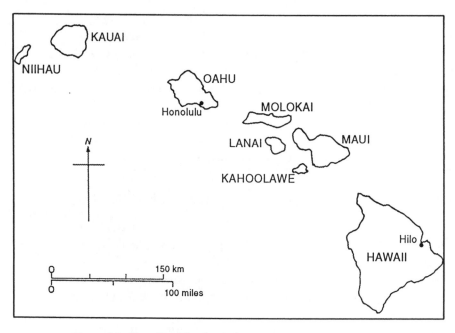

Figure 8-3 *Hawaiian Islands*

whites and blacks, inhabited the territory by the end of the eighteenth century (Valdman et al. 1998). The ratio was tipped in favor of African Louisianans in certain areas, with a two to one ratio in New Orleans and a three to one ratio in Coupée. Today the creole survives in four focal areas of southern Louisiana: (1) the Bayou Teche region, which includes Breaux Bridge and St. Martinville; (2) Pointe Coupée Parish between the Atchafalaya and Mississippi Rivers north of Baton Rouge; (3) the German Coast along the Mississippi River between Baton Rouge and New Orleans; and (4) Bayou Lacombe and Bayou Liberty in St. Tammany Parish between Lake Pontchartrain and the Pearl River (figure 8-4).

Complicating any description of the creole in Louisiana are the three distinct language varieties with French vocabulary that have been spoken there (Louisiana Creole, Cajun French, and Colonial French), as well as the strong presence of English since the mid-nineteenth century. There is little information available about language contact between speakers of indigenous (Indian) languages over time or about their possible contributions to the creole. The brief period of Spanish rule (1763–1800) appears to have had little effect on the languages spoken, except for the fact that the Spanish government welcomed the displaced Acadians from Nova Scotia (speakers of Cajun French), and simultaneously doubled the number of African slaves in the colony. The arrival of the Cajuns tipped the population balance from a majority of Afro Louisianans to a more equal balance of whites and blacks in the overall population (Marshall 1997). Then after Louisiana became a US territory in 1803, large numbers of English-speaking immigrants began arriving. The existing language varieties today can be ranked according to the

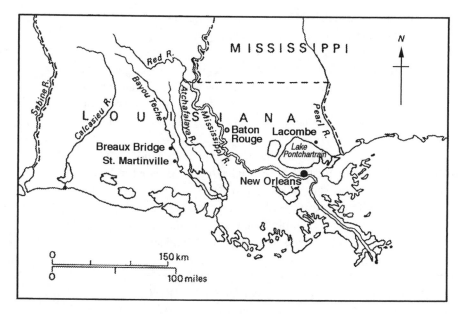

Figure 8-4 *Southern Louisiana*

following hierarchy: English as dominant, Standard French next (promoted in recent years by the Council for the Development of French in Louisiana), then Cajun French, and finally Louisiana Creole (Valdman 1997). The colonial French spoken by the original settlers and their descendants has virtually disappeared (Klingler 1992), and all Louisiana Creole speakers use at least one additional language variety outside the home (Valdman et al. 1998). Many speakers are multilingual, able to use Louisiana Creole and some variety of French, along with English.

It is this pervasive multilingualism over the centuries that provided conditions for the original emergence and continued maintenance of the creole. Initially, African and Caribbean slaves from many different backgrounds were brought to work the farms and plantations along the rivers, with those from the Senegambia region predominating in the early stages. By the second generation some variety of French was being used as a common language. As slaves continued to arrive in the colony from the Caribbean, West Africa, and Central Africa, the newcomers learned the common language from other slaves. In those areas where Africans and their descendants once outnumbered the French colonialists, a creole with a French vocabulary evolved. After 1800, South Carolina planters sometimes moved their entire plantations to Louisiana (Hall 1992), often taking over established French plantations along the rivers and buying French-speaking slaves to join their South Carolina slaves. Louisiana blacks would have learned English from fellow slaves in such settings, well before their masters did so (Klingler 1992). In addition, many poor white immigrants in creole-speaking areas like the German Coast, Pointe Coupée, and St. Martin parishes worked side by side with slaves on the plantations (Marshall 1997). Especially along the German Coast, such immigrants heard more Louisiana Creole than any other language variety and learned it as the common language. Whites today may constitute as much as 25 percent of all Louisiana Creole speakers. The shift toward English as a common language was given a strong push in the 1860s when Louisiana united with other states of the Confederacy in the doomed effort to sustain slavery as a legal institution and promoted English to the state's language of government, commerce, and education.

Throughout its history Louisiana Creole has shown much variation, with the variety spoken in the New Orleans area probably having widespread influence throughout the early years. The variety spoken in the Teche area reflects the influence of Cajun French because of the social interaction between blacks and whites there (Klingler 2000). The example below from Pointe Coupée parish (Valdman and Klingler 1997: 111) reflects the influence of English:

je te kɔ̃ nɛ̃ prã ɛ̃ bari,	*They used to take a barrel*
aveɛk ɛ̃ but lapo, e	*with a piece of skin, and*
je te gɛ̃ ʃofe lapo	*they used to heat the skin*
pu li vini stiff.	*until it became stiff.*
kã li vini stiff,	*When it had become stiff,*
then je bang li.	*then they banged on it.*
mo pãs se de zafɛ	*I think these are things*
je mɛ̃nɛ̃ isi dã slavery	*that were brought over here [from Africa] with slavery.*

Grammatical characteristics of this creole include the following (as noted in Valdman and Klinger's overview 1997):

(1) no gender distinction for the definite article, *la*:
    ʃɛ̃ la trape lɔ̃ dɛ lapɛ̃ la (The dog picked up the scent of the rabbit)
    Note: French, unlike English, marks all nouns, adjectives, and articles as either masculine or feminine; like other creoles, Louisiana Creole does not make these gender distinctions.

(2) the definite article *la* and the plural marker *je* placed after the noun:
    mo sukuje dibwa je (I shook the trees)

(3) the indefinite article ɛ̃ precedes the noun:
    ɛ̃ tas kafe (a cup of coffee)

(4) adjectives usually placed after nouns, showing no gender distinctions

(5) no tense or aspect-marking inflections on the verbs
    Note: In French, tense markers indicating time and aspect markers indicating on-going/habitual or completed action consist of a combination of verb inflections and function words. In the creole, only the separate function words are used.

(6) the pre-verbal *ape* (also *ap* or *e*) used to mark progressive:
     m ap repɔ̃n (I'm answering)

(7) the pre-verbal *te* used to mark anteriority:
     je te ka lir ave ekri (They could read and write)

(8) the pre-verbal *va*, *ale*, and *sa* used to mark future:
     nu va fe la rekɔl, mwɛ̃ e twa (We'll do the harvest, you and I)
     no p ale gɛ̃ ɛ̃ bal (We won't have a dance)
     mo swat mo sa la. (I hope to be there)

(9) the pre-verbal *se* used as a conditional marker:
     mo se kɥ̃ tɥ̃ kɥ nɛ sa (I would like to know that)

(10) no copula (BE-verb) for some clauses containing predicate adjectives
     or locatives:
     li fɛb (She/he is weak)
     je deɔr (They're outside)
     mo swaf (I'm thirsty)

(11) the copula *det* (or *ɛt*) used with verbs of obligation, with passives, and
     with imperatives:
     le piti sipoze ɛt dɥr (The children are supposed to be outside)
     sa gɛ dɛt fe (That has to be done)
     dɛt la a siz ɛr (Be there at six o'clock!)

Louisiana Creole is the only French-vocabulary creole to have the *det* copula.

Acts of identity

How best to sum up what these uniquely American languages have to teach us? They demonstrate the creative powers of human beings in desperate times and the power of language to strengthen social bonds over time.

The formation of these creole languages, as well as their use today, is an example of "acts of identity" (described by Le Page and Tabouret-Keller 1985 for a similar colonial setting). In a new land, peoples speaking many different languages came together to forge new lives and new identities. In South Carolina, use of Gullah correlates with an ethnic identity as a special kind of African American and forms the most important part of that identity. In Louisiana, the correlation between Louisiana Creole and African American identity has also been strong, even though some European Americans also speak it in their homes. Today, in Louisiana, African Americans most fluent in speaking the creole are most apt to identify themselves as "Creole" (Dubois and Melançon 2000). In Hawai'i, the correlation with ethnic identity disappears because Hawaiian Creole actually has helped form a new Hawaiian identity for descendants of native Hawaiians, Portuguese, Chinese, Japanese, and those who came later. All three creoles have united groups of people whose ancestors would not have spoken to each other in their native lands. Carrying reminders of shared experiences in this land, these languages initially met a need to communicate and later a need to identify with members of a community sharing both language and culture.

For adults, speaking creole in the USA today is almost always a choice, one that signals social identity. How long will these creoles remain vital languages? As long as children within the communities can hear and use them.

Acknowledgments

The maps for this chapter were drawn by Frank H. Nichols, Jr. I am grateful to Diana Eades, Jeff Siegel, and Kent Sakoda for help with Hawaiian Creole and to Albert Valdman for material on Louisiana Creole.

Suggestions for further reading and exploration

The *Creolist Archives http://www.ling.su.se/Creole/* contains a wealth of information about past, as well as more recent, scholarship on this language type. An excellent brief overview of pidgins and creoles is provided by Holms (2000); his earlier two-volume work (Holm 1988, 1989) gives an in-depth treatment of both the language type and of individual creoles. Romaine (1988) contains a good discussion of language acquisition factors and of the life cycles of these languages. Thomason and Kaufman (1988) address the challenges such languages present to traditional historical linguistics. For the individual US creoles, Turner (1949/2001) remains the classic study of Gullah and contains phonetically transcribed texts, while Jones-Jackson (1987) offers valuable insights about cultural traditions transmitted through the language. For Hawaiian Creole, Reinecke (1935/1969) provides a sociolinguistic history, and more recent work by Roberts (1998) updates this history with important implications for the origins and development of the creole. Valdman (1997) and his colleagues have been examining the complex language situation in contemporary Louisiana. A dictionary of Louisiana Creole (Valdman et al. 1998) provides a grammatical sketch of the creole, as well as a brief account of its origins. Hall (1992) offers valuable insights about cultural traditions, and Ancelet (1994) has examples of folktales told in the creole.

References

Ancelet, Barry Jean. 1994. *Cajun and Creole Folktales*. New York: Garland.
Cunningham, Irma. 1970. "A Syntactic Analysis of Sea Island Creole (Gullah)." Unpub. Ph.D. dissertation, University of Michigan.
Dubois, Sylvie and Megan Melançon. 2000. "Creole Is, Creole Ain't: Diachronic and Synchronic Attitudes toward Creole Identity in Southern Louisiana," *Language in Society* 29: 237–58.
Hall, Gwendolyn M. 1992. *Africans in Colonial Louisiana: the Development of Afro-Creole Culture in the Eighteenth Century*. Baton Rouge: Louisiana State University Press.

Harris, John W. 1986. *Northern Territory Pidgins and the Origin of Kriol*. Canberra: Department of Linguistics, Research School of Pacific Studies, Australian National University.

Holm, John. 1988. *Pidgins and Creoles, vol. 1: Theory and Structure*. Cambridge: Cambridge University Press.

1989. *Pidgins and Creoles, vol. 2: Reference Survey*. Cambridge: Cambridge University Press.

2000. *An Introduction to Pidgins and Creoles*. Cambridge: Cambridge University Press.

Hopkins, Tometro. 1992. "Issues in the Study of Afro-Creoles: Afro-Cuban and Gullah." Unpub. Ph.D. dissertation, Indiana University.

Jones-Jackson, Patricia. 1987. *When Roots Die: Endangered Traditions on the Sea Islands*. Athens: University of Georgia Press.

Joyner, Charles. 1984. *Down by the Riverside: a South Carolina Slave Community*. Urbana: University of Illinois Press.

Klingler, Thomas A. 1992. "A Descriptive Study of the Creole Speech of Pointe Parish, Louisiana with Focus on the Lexicon." Unpub. Ph.D. dissertation, Indiana University.

2000. "Louisiana Creole: the Multiple-Geneses Hypothesis Reconsidered," *Journal of Pidgin and Creole Languages* 15: 1–35.

Le Page, Robert B. and Andrée Tabouret-Keller. 1985. *Acts of Identity: Creole-Based Approaches to Language and Ethnicity*. Cambridge: Cambridge University Press.

Littlefield, Daniel C. 1981. *Rice and Slaves: Ethnicity and the Slave Trade in Colonial South Carolina*. Baton Rouge: Louisiana State University Press.

Lum, Darrel H. Y. 1990. *Pass On, No Pass Back!* Special issue of *Bamboo Ridge, The Hawaii Writers' Quarterly*, issues 48–49.

Marshall, Margaret M. 1997. "The Origin and Development of Louisiana Creole French." In *French and Creole in Louisiana*, ed. Albert Valdman. New York: Plenum.

McMillan, James A. 1999. "Post-Revolutionary Charleston: African Americans' Ellis Island." Paper presented at symposium on *Early Slavery in Early South Carolina*, Institute for Southern Studies, University of South Carolina, Columbia. February.

McWhorter, John H. 1998. "Identifying the Creole Prototype: Vindicating a Typological Class," *Language* 74: 788–818.

Myers-Scotton, Carol. 1997. "'Matrix Language Recognition' and 'Morpheme Sorting' as Possible Structural Strategies in Pidgin/Creole Formation." In *The Structure and Status of Pidgins and Creoles*, eds. Arthur K. Spears and Donald Winford. Amsterdam: John Benjamins. Pp. 151–74.

2001. "Implications of Abstract Grammatical Structure: Two Targets in Creole Formation." *Journal of Pidgin and Creole Languages* 16: 217–73.

Nichols, Patricia C. 1976. "Linguistic Change in Gullah: Sex, Age, and Mobility." Unpub. Ph.D. dissertation, Stanford University.

Nichols, Patricia C. 1996. Pidgins and Creoles. In *Sociolinguistics and Language Teaching*, eds. S. L. McKay and N. H. Hornberger. Cambridge: Cambridge University Press. Pp. 195–217.

Reinecke, John E. 1935/1969. *Language and Dialect in Hawai'i: a Sociolinguistic History to 1935*. Honolulu: University of Hawai'i Press.

Roberts, Julian M. 1995. "Pidgin Hawaiian: a Sociohistorical Study," *Journal of Pidgin and Creole Languages* 10: 1–56.

Roberts, Sarah Julianne. 1998. "The Role of Diffusion in the Genesis of Hawaiian Creole," *Language* 74: 1–38.

Romaine, Suzanne. 1988. *Pidgin and Creole Languages*. London: Longman.

Sebba, Mark. 1997. *Contact Languages: Pidgins and Creoles*. New York: St. Martin's Press.

Siegel, Jeff. 2000. "Substrate Influence in Hawai'i Creole English," *Language in Society* 29: 197–236.

Thomason, Sarah G. and Terrence Kaufman. 1988. *Language Contact, Creolization, and Genetic Linguistics*. Berkeley: University of California Press.

Turner, Lorenzo Dow. 1949/2001. *Africanisms in the Gullah Dialect, with a New Introduction by K. W. Mille and M. B. Montgomery*. Columbia: University of South Carolina Press.

Valdman, Albert. 1997. Introduction. In *French and Creole in Louisiana*, ed. Albert Valdman. New York: Plenum. Pp. 1–24.

Valdman, Albert and Thomas A. Klingler. 1997. "The Structure of Louisiana Creole." In *French and Creole in Louisiana*, ed. Albert Valdman. New York: Plenum. Pp. 109–44.

Valdman, Albert, Thomas A. Klingler, Margaret M. Marshall, and Kevin J. Rottet. 1998. *Dictionary of Louisiana Creole*. Bloomington: Indiana University Press.

Weldon, Tracey L. 1998. "Exploring the AAVE–Gullah Connection." Unpub. Ph.D. dissertation, The Ohio State University.

Wood, Peter H. 1989. "The Changing Population of the Colonial South: an Overview by Race and Region, 1685–1790." In *Powhatan's Mantle: Indians in the Colonial Southeast*, eds. Peter H. Wood, Gregory A. Waselkov, and M. Thomas Hatley. Lincoln: University of Nebraska Press. Pp. 35–103.

9

Native American languages

AKIRA Y. YAMAMOTO AND OFELIA ZEPEDA

Editors' introduction

Some chapters of this book discuss one or several languages imported into the USA and one chapter describes a set of creoles originating in the new world. This chapter focuses on languages that Native Americans were speaking when Europeans first arrived on these shores. Some Native American languages are still spoken, though they are now in imminent danger of dying out. As Akira Y. Yamamoto and Ofelia Zepeda explain, many Native American languages are known today only by aging speakers, but children are no longer acquiring them. Some Native American languages are no longer spoken by anyone. With the Native American Languages Act of 1990 and of 1992, federal laws enabled organizations to be established to train native language teachers, carry out research on these languages, and develop teaching materials and other critical resources for documenting and revitalizing these endangered tongues.

In terms that can be understood with a little effort and are well worth the time, this chapter illustrates ways in which Native American languages differ so dramatically in structure from more familiar European languages. For example, basic word order in English is SVO; that's shorthand for Subject before Verb and Verb before Object, as in *The governor* (S) *vetoed* (V) *the bill* (O). Besides SVO, Native American languages also display other orders, including SOV, VOS, VSO, and OVS. They are able to utilize these word orders partly because certain information that is carried in English utterances by word order (e.g., which noun is the subject and which noun is the object) is carried in Native American languages by affixes on the words themselves.

Native American languages also differ in the structure of words themselves. Mohawk and some other Native American languages are "polysynthetic," a term that characterizes languages whose words may contain a large number of meaningful parts, more than are typical of Spanish or English words, even complex ones like *un-re-train-able* or *dis-in-cline-d*. A word of Yup'ik illustrates the point: *qayarpaliyugaqa* is a single word whose six meaningful parts (*qayar-pa-li-yug-a-qa*) combine to carry the meaning, 'I want to make a big kayak for him.'

From an ethnolinguistic viewpoint (a viewpoint that attends to the links between a culture and its language), the kinds of information encoded in words can identify categories that speakers of that language find salient in their perception of persons, things, and events, and in their social interactions. Thus, the wealth of Native American languages represents an intellectual heritage and a cultural goldmine. But we are in danger of losing this heritage if Native American languages continue to fade from use and from memory.

Diversity in Native American Languages

By one estimate, there are more than 6,000 languages in the world (Grimes 2000). They share many characteristics, often referred to as *language universals*, and yet they differ from one another. Such differences are referred to as *language diversity*, and Native American languages show tremendous diversity. They reveal how different groups of people relate to the world around them, and it is precisely this diversity that makes it exciting to study them. Native American languages enable us to see amazing human intellectual capacity for creativity and ingenuity. Unfortunately, though, this rich diversity in Native American languages is disappearing at an alarming rate, as we will discuss later in the chapter.

All languages utilize vowels and consonants. Among Native American languages, many have a relatively small number of vowels, but consonant inventories vary greatly. Cree in Montana has three short vowels /i a o/ and four long vowels /i: e: a: o:/. It has eight consonants /p t c (or ts) k s h m n/ and two semi-consonants /w y/ (Wolfart 1996: 428–30). Eastern Pomo in northern California has five short and five long vowels, and 38 consonants (McLendon 1996: 509–15). Although sound systems of Native American languages are complex and fascinating to students of languages, we will direct our attention to sampling other ways in which Native American languages differ. Each language presented in this chapter may have sounds that are quite different from those in English, and the pronunciation guide is described in footnotes.

Language and worldviews: Kickapoo people's animate and inanimate categories

Let's look at one of the Algonquian languages, Kickapoo or, as the Kickapoo people call their language, *Kiikaapoatowaachiki*. The Kickapoo people live in four communities: about 500 people in Kansas, 1,800 in Oklahoma, 600 in Texas, and 700 in Nacimiento, Mexico. Below we have listed eight words from Kickapoo. Examine the words (a) through (d) in Group A and compare them with words (e) through (h) in Group B.[1] What seems different between the two groups? (*Hint*: How do the words end?)

1. Kiikaapoatowaachiki classification (Murdock et al. 1987)

Group A		Group B	
a. aamowa	bee	e. kahchoochohi	baseball cap
b. aanikwa	ant	f. kesiikahpiyehikani	fork
c. methiikwa	corn	g. mehthooni	boat
d. othekwithema'a	(one's) aunt	h. pokiihi	book

---

[1] The vowel [a] is like *a* in *father*, [o] like *o* in *poke*, [i] like *ey* in *honey*, [e] like *e* in *deck*, and [a] like *a* in *bag*. When the same vowel symbol is repeated, it is simply longer.

You may have concluded that all the words in Group A end with the vowel sound [a] and those in Group B with the vowel sound [i]. Of what importance might this difference be? In fact, [a] and [i] are suffixes that indicate specific meanings. You may have theorized that the [a]-ending indicates a word representing some kind of animal, insect, plant, human, or anything "alive." This characterization is technically called the "animate," and the words in Group B are "inanimate." Thus, at this point, you can state that the Kickapoo people separate things into two categories – "animate" (indicated by the suffix -*a*) and "inanimate" (with the suffix -*i*).

Now here's a challenge. Which of the two suffixes would you attach to the following words?

i.	koohkoos_	pig	l. teetepithaah_	wagon
j.	kiyaasiih_	airplane	m. kwitapithoon_	elevator
k.	meechipahooh_	car		

Answers: i. -a, j. -a, k. -a, l. -i, m. -i.

Did any of these endings surprise you? How do you explain why 'airplane' and 'car' are animate, but 'wagon' and 'elevator' are inanimate? One explanation is that a wagon must be pulled by a horse, while a car appears to move by itself. The elevator indeed looks as if it moves by itself, but it doesn't go anywhere, so it does not quite qualify as "self-moving." How about the following?

n.	ohpeni_	(wild) potato	q. tomaat_	tomato
o.	mahskochiith_	bean	r. manoomin_	rice
p.	aathaicheepihkeeh_	carrot		

Answers: n. -a, o. -a, p. -i, q. -i, r. -i

What distinguishes 'carrot,' 'tomato,' and 'rice' from 'potato' and 'bean'? You may have hypothesized that the first group includes non-traditional food items, relatively new to the Kickapoo people and fairly easy to obtain. Newness, easy access, and easy disposal may have led the Kickapoo people to group them in the inanimate category. On the other hand, those in the second group may have been scarcer, strictly seasonal, and thus required special care in harvesting and processing.

In Kickapoo, then, nouns are categorized into animate and inanimate ones. Additionally, in the Kickapoo people's worldview, animate nouns are characterized as having potential for spirituality.

Language and worldviews: Navajo people's perspective on the world

Another way to categorize things in the world is presented by Navajo, an Athabascan language, spoken by about 130,000 people in the four-corners area (Utah, Colorado, Arizona, and New Mexico). The Navajo people call themselves *Diné*, 'the people.'[2] There are four sets of similar sentences below. Navajo people feel that sentences (a) and (b) are natural. While sentence (c) is natural, sentence (d) is not. Similarly, (e) and (g) are fine, but (f) and (h) are not. Those that are not acceptable are marked with an asterisk.

2.   Navajo classification

a. Hastiin ashkii yinoołchééł.
man   boy   yi-is.chasing   'The man is chasing the boy.'

b. Ashkii hastiin binoołchééł.
boy   man   bi-is.chasing   'The boy is getting chased by the man.'

c. Ashkii łééchąą'í yinoołchééł.
boy   dog   yi-is.chasing   'The boy is chasing the dog.'

d. *Łéécąą'í ashkii binoochééł.
dog   boy   bi-is.chasing   'The dog is getting chased by the boy.'

e. Łéécąą'í na'azísí yinoołchééł.
dog   gopher yi-is.chasing   'The dog is chasing the gopher.'

f. *Na'azísí łéécąą'í binoołchééł.
gopher   dog   bi-is.chasing   'The gopher is getting chased by the dog.'

g. Na'azísí na'ashjé'ii yinoołchééł.
gopher spider   yi-is.chasing   'The gopher is chasing the spider.'

h. *Na'ashjé'ii na'azísí binoołchééł.
spider   gopher bi-is.chasing   'The spider is getting chased by the gopher.'

In the above examples, we find the following: (1) *hastiin* 'man' and *ashkii* 'boy' seem equal in their relationship because either one can be placed before the other; (2) *łééchąą'í* 'dog' does not seem to belong to the same category with *hastiin* 'man' and *ashkii* 'boy'; (3) *łééchąą'í* 'dog' and *na'azísí* 'gopher' seem to belong to different categories because *łééchąą'í* 'dog' can chase *na'azísí* 'gopher,' but the gopher cannot be chased by the dog; and again (4) *na'azísí* 'gopher' and *na'ashjé'ii* 'spider' belong to different categories. Then, we may hypothesize that Navajo people see different relationships among the things and beings in the world. After testing the hypothesis with more example sentences, we come to understand that there may be at least eight hierarchically ordered categories of animacy. Briefly, the Navajo animacy hierarchy looks like the following:

Group 1: persons (except babies), lightning
Group 2: baby, horse, donkey, mule, bull, bear, wolf, wild cat
Group 3: sheep, goat, turkey, eagle, cat, dog, chicken, coyote
Group 4: squirrel, gopher, mouse, rabbit, snake, frog, turtle
Group 5: spider, worm, centipede, scorpion

---

[2] The symbol [ł] represents an l-like sound except that no voicing occurs. Prepare your mouth as if you are going to produce [l] as in *leak*. Flatten your mouth a bit and blow the air out from the sides of your tongue. You hear a lot of friction and produce what is technically called a voiceless lateral fricative. Some vowels are pronounced with the passage to the nasal cavity open, thus producing nasalized vowels, and these are indicated by a hook under them (e.g., ą ę į). The ['] mark on a vowel indicates a high tone.

Group 6: windstorm, flood, sunshine, range fire, and other natural
   forces except lightning
Group 7: plants, inanimate objects
Group 8: abstractions such as old age, hunger, disease, germs, emotions

The classification represents the Diné worldview in which things are seen in terms of their inherent qualities such as: (1) capacity for having intent or purpose, (2) intelligence, (3) strength, vigor, aggressiveness, special potency, (4) usefulness to humans or relatedness to humans, and (5) capacity for movement.

Possession relationships

A language may reflect how its speakers view the world in the way it expresses the relationship between an object and its owner, generally called the possession relationship. In this context, we examine a dialect of the Keres language spoken by approximately 1,900 (half the total population of) Acoma Pueblo people in New Mexico. Dialects of the Keres language are spoken also by Pueblo peoples in Cochiti (525 speakers, or half the population), Laguna (2,060 speakers, 30 percent of the population), Santo Domingo (2,965 speakers, 95 percent of the population), San Felipe (1985 speakers, 90 percent of the total population), Santa Ana (384 speakers, 60 percent of the population), and Zia (504 speakers, 70 percent of the total population), all in New Mexico (Hilaire Valiquette in Endangered Languages Survey 1996).[3]

3. Acoma Keres possession expression (Silver and Miller 1997: 20–23)

dʸñuuni	'pottery'
s'adʸñuuni	'my pottery'
kɨçadʸñuuni	'your pottery'
k'adʸñuuni	'his or her pottery'
sk'adʸñuuni	'someone's pottery'

The word for 'pottery' can occur by itself or in the possession expression. You will notice that *dʸñuuni* 'pottery' can be easily identified in the examples above. The possession relationship seems to be indicated by *s'a-* 'my,' *kɨça-* 'your,' *k'a-* 'his or her,' and *sk'a-* 'someone's.' Compare them with the following:

*édí	'foot'	(The asterisk indicates this form is not appropriate.)
sédí	'my foot'	
ṣasdí	'your foot'	
kasdí	'his or her foot'	
skasdí	'someone's foot'	

---

[3] The symbol ['] represents a "catch-in-the-throat," technically called a glottal stop and represented in IPA as [ʔ]. The symbol [ç] with a dot underneath represents *ts* as in *cats*, with the tongue curled back so that the back side of the tip of the tongue touches the gum (alveolar) area. This is called the alveolar retroflex. Other retroflex sounds are also marked with a dot underneath. When [n] (as in *noon*) has the symbol [~] over it ([ñ]), it represents the sound found in *news* [nyu:z], technically called the palatal nasal.

The possession relationship here is indicated by *s-* 'my,' *ṣ-* 'your,' *k-* 'his or her,' and *sk-* 'someone's.' The term for 'foot' cannot occur by itself, as indicated by the asterisk on **édí*. Our observations, then, are something like the following:

a. Acoma Keres seems to show two ways of expressing possession relationships.

b. Some nouns, namely, those for objects and things, can occur with or without possession-indicating prefixes. These are technically called alienable possession, meaning that the relationship between the possessor and the possessed is not a necessary one and that the one can exist without the other.

c. Some nouns such as body parts cannot exist apart from the one to whom they belong. Unlike English, Acoma Keres cannot refer to a foot or any body part as if it is lying on the ground. By definition, body parts must be a part of someone. This relationship is called inalienable possession. Typically, inalienable possession indicates a close relationship between a part and a whole and most often includes body parts and kin relations (see also Pomo examples below).

Kinship terms

In the language of the Eastern Pomo people, the kinship relationship must be expressed with whom the relation exists, the inalienable relationship. Pomo people spoke seven distinct languages and Eastern Pomo was one of them. In 1959, no Eastern Pomo children were acquiring the language (McLendon 1996: 509). Our guess is that of the 4,766 people who identified themselves as Pomo in the 1990 census, there are perhaps only a few speakers in different rancherias (reservations). Let's examine their kinship words.[4]

4. Eastern Pomo kinship words (McLendon 1996: 522–26)

	my __	your __	his/her __
mother's mother (and sisters)	qá:c'	mi:qá:	ha:mi:qá:
mother's father (and brothers)	ká:c'	mi:ká:	ha:mi:ká:
father's mother (and sisters)	má:c'	mi:má:	ha:mi:má:

In Eastern Pomo, when a speaker expresses the second person's relationship to a relative, it is indicated by the prefix [mi:] (e.g., *mi:qá:* '<u>your</u> mother's mother'),

---

[4] Eastern Pomo has a Spanish-like dental [t] and another t-sound, pronounced farther back at the alveolar ridge and symbolized with a dot underneath [ṭ]. Remember that Keres has a retroflexed *ts* [ç] – where the dot underneath [c] indicates retroflex. Most voiceless sounds [p t t c č k q] may also accompany the glottal stop. Note that [c] is like English *ts* as in *cats*, the sound [č] is like *ch* as in *church*, and [q] is somewhat similar to the *qwaq qwaq* sound that a duck makes. The [q] sound is like [k] but produced farther back in the mouth closer to the throat. When these sounds [p t ṭ c č k q] accompany the glottal stop, as the breath is released, it produces a popped sound called the glottalized stop sounds. We symbolize these as [p' t' ṭ' c' č' k' q']. The colon (:) marks a long vowel, as in Hualapai *a:* or Kickapoo *aa*.

and the third person's relationship by [ha:mi:] (e.g., *ha:mi:qá:* 'his/her mother's mother'). The basic "unmarked" form is used to indicate the speaker's relationship to the relative (e.g., *qá:c'* 'my mother's mother').

In addition to the notion of inalienable relationship among relatives, Eastern Pomo shows a fascinating fact about how kinship terms represent the nature of their social organization. In English, what do we call our father's brother? *Uncle.* How about our mother's brother? Also *uncle.* What do we call our father's sister? *Aunt.* Mother's sister? Also *aunt.* Mother's father? *Grandfather.* Father's father? Also *grandfather.* What then, seems to be the way we distinguish among our relatives? We pay attention to the generational difference: my children's generation, my own generation, my parents' generation, my parents' parents' generation, and so on. In Eastern Pomo, speakers distinguish {father's brothers, his sisters, and his parents} from {mother's brothers, her sisters, and her parents}.

b.

	my __	your __	his/her __
mother	ník'	mi:tʰé	ha:mi: tʰé
mother's older sister	tʰú:c'	mi: tʰú:c'	ha:mi: tʰú:c'
mother's younger sister	šé:x	mi: šé:x	ha:mi: šé:x
mother's brother	cʰé:c'	mi:cʰé:	ha:mi:cʰé:
father	hárik'	me:ʔé	ha:me:ʔé
father's sister	wé:x	mi:wé:x	ha:mi:wé:x
father's brother	ké:x	mi:ké:x	ha:mi:ké:x

What is the term in English for my mother's sister's children? My mother's brother's children? They are all *cousins.* Look at the Eastern Pomo examples in (c) below. What do you observe? My mother's sister's children are referred to with the same terms used for my brothers and sisters (dé:x, méx, dú:xac'). Also, my mother's brother's sons are referred to with the same terms as my mother's brothers (cʰé:c') and my mother's brother's daughters are referred to with the same terms as my mother's younger sisters (šé:x).

c.

	my __	your __	his __
older sister	dé:x	mi:dé:x	ha:mi:dé:x
older brother	méx	mi:méx	ha:mi:méx
younger sibling	dú:xac'	mi:dú:xac'	ha:mi:dú:xac'
mother's sister's daughters who are older than oneself	dé:x	mi:dé:x	ha:mi:dé:x
mother's sister's sons who are older than oneself	méx	mi:méx	ha:mi:méx
mother's sister's children who are younger than oneself	dú:xac'	mi:dú:xac'	ha:mi:dú:xac'
mother's brother's daughters	šé:x	mi:šé:x	ha:mi:šé:x
mother's brother's sons	cʰé:c'	mi:cʰé:	ha:mi:cʰé:

Complicated as the kinship terms of the Eastern Pomo may look, they indicate attention paid not so much to generational differences as to the male's or female's relatives and the age differences within the same generation. What, then, is so important about this? We may hypothesize that the kinship terms guide who should take care of whom (e.g., paternal uncles will look after their sisters and their children, and the sons of one's paternal uncles will also do the same). It also guides who can marry whom (e.g., one cannot marry one's mother's sister's child, one's cousin, because s/he is one's sister or brother).

Beyond kinship terms: animals and things

In some languages, there may be more categories distinguished in expressing the possession relationship. In Acoma Keres, possession of animals is expressed with the help not of prefixes, as with kinship words and body parts, but of the word $d^y\acute{a}$ for 'pet':

5. Owning animals in Acoma

> kawaayu s'ad^{y}á   'my horse'
> díya k'ad^{y}á   'his dog'

Review the Acoma Keres possession examples in 3 above (p. 157). Since *s'a-* is 'my' and *k'a-* is 'his/her,' then the expression *kawaayu s'ad^{y}á* means 'horse my-pet' and *díya k'ad^{y}á* 'dog his/her-pet.' Thus, we find that Acoma Keres distinguishes at least three kinds of entities: body parts and kinship words as one group, domesticated animals as another, and all other things as still another group.

In English, we talk about *having* a grandson, *having* a wife, or *having* a brother. In many Native American languages, expressions of having someone as kin may come as a surprise. Let's examine how such relations are expressed in Hualapai, an Upland Yuman language spoken by approximately 1,000 people (including some children) in the northwestern part of Arizona.

6. Hualapai relationship expression (Watahomigie et al. 2001: 141–56)

> a. ko: 'one's daughter's child/grandchild'
>
> Mach mako:vngyu?
> ma-ch   ma-ko:-v-ng-yu
> you-Subject you-grandchild-State-SS.2-Aux/do/Q[5]
> 'Are you grandchilded? = Do you have a grandchild?'
> – E'e, 'ko:vyu.

---

[5] The term State is used to indicate stativity, that is, the suffix *-v* tells us that there exists a state resulting from the action of the verb. The abbreviation SS (same subject) means that the subject of the first verbal element (here 'to be grandchilded, have a grandchild') and the subject of the second verbal element (here the auxiliary verb *-yu*) are the same ('you' in this example). Q stands for question marker. The numbers 1, 2, and 3 represent first person ('I'), second person ('you'), and third person ('she' or 'he'), respectively. When one segment is translated into two or more words in English, English words will be separated by a period. For example, Hualapai *va* means 'this right here,' and the morpheme-by-morpheme translation of *nya 'sálva* is indicated as *nya'-sal-va* (1 1-hand-this.right.here) 'my hand.' The glottal stop ['] in *'-sal-va* is the first person matter 'I.' This literally means 'I I-hand-this.right.here' = 'my hand.'

e'e   '-ko:-v-yu
yes   I-grandchild-State-Aux/be
'Yes, I am grandchilded. = Yes, I have a grandchild.'

b. nyahmí'   'husband'

Nyach John 'nyahmi:wi.
nya-ch   John '-nyahmi:-wi
I-Subject John I/him-husband-Aux/do
'I husbanded John. → I am married to John.'

Does Hualapai use the verb equivalent to the English *have*? What we find instead
are kinship words used as verbs. Thus, Hualapai people say "I am grandchilded"
instead of "I have a grandchild." If one is married, then she is "husbanded" or
he is "wifed." We know these kinship words are verbs because the regular verbal
prefixes[6] and verb endings occur with them.

How are sentences put together?

Many languages of the world place the verb (V) at the end of a sentence, preceded by subject (S) and object (O). Many Native American languages, including
Eastern Pomo, Hualapai, and Navajo exhibit this SOV word order. Another common order is SVO, as in English. SOV and SVO orders characterize probably
90 percent of the world's languages. Other languages utilize still other word
orders, such as VSO and VOS.

Tohono O'odham: flexible word order

The language of Tohono O'odham, 'the people of the desert,' is spoken in southern
Arizona and northern Sonora, Mexico. The majority of the tribe's approximately
20,000 people live in Arizona. One estimate says that there are about 10,000
speakers. They have language classes in public schools, and in the community
they have a radio program in the language. The Tohono O'odham Nation is one
of the first tribes to establish a language policy of its own.

7.   Tohono O'odham word order (Akmajian et al. 1995: 208–09; see also Zepeda
     1983)

Huan 'o wakon g ma:gina.
Huan 'o   wakon   g   ma:gina
John Auxiliary is/was.washing Determiner car
'John is/was washing the car.'

All the sentences below are equally good:

a. Huan 'o g ma:gina wakon.   (John the car is/was washing)
b. Wakon 'o g ma:gina g Huan.   (is/was washing the car John)

---

[6] The prefixes are the glottal stop ['] for 'the first person,' *m-* or *ma-* for 'the second person,' and no
   prefix (sometimes called the zero prefix) for 'the third person.'

c. Wakon 'o g Huan g ma:gina.   (is/was washing John the car)
d. Ma:gina 'o wakon g Huan.   (the car is/was washing John)
e. Ma:gina 'o g Huan wakon.   (the car John is/was washing)

Tohono O'odham has a flexible word order, and the interpretation of what is being done to whom relies heavily on context. The only requirement in all these sentences is that the auxiliary *'o* be placed in second position and that the determiner *g* occur with the noun unless the noun sits at the beginning of the sentence.

Hualapai: relatively fixed word order with case-marked nouns

Some languages such as Hualapai utilize strategies that clearly mark the subject, object, and other roles of nouns in a sentence. The nouns may have suffixes that tell us about their roles such as *subject*, *object*, *instrument* (with), *locative* (at, in), *benefactive* (for), *comitative* (together with someone), etc.

8. Hualapai[7]

> Ba:h**ch** aha**đ** i'v<u>m</u> a:vkwiny.
> ba:-h-ch   ahađ   i'-v-m   a:vk-wi-ny
> man-the-**Subject** dog. *Object* stick-<u>Instrument/with</u> he/it.hit-Auxiliary/do-Past
> 'The man hit the dog with a stick.'

In Hualapai, the suffix *-ch* marks the noun as subject, a lack of suffix marks the object, and the suffix *-m* identifies the noun as an instrument. When a language uses such a system to indicate the roles of nouns (generally called a case system), word order may become more flexible and sentence elements may be changed around relatively freely. If it is an SOV language like Hualapai, however, the verb remains as the last element of the sentence. We will see below that some languages may not even have such a concern.

Kickapoo: an SVO language with flexible word order

Kickapoo shows several interesting characteristics that are shared by many other Native American languages (Murdock et al. 1987). First is its relative flexibility in ordering elements within a sentence. As noted above, the order VOS is rare in the languages of the world, yet the Kickapoo people would tell us they could use such an order, as in 9(e) below. The Kickapoo examples in 9 are very similar to those in 7 from Tohono O'odham.

9. a.   Nehchiimeeha wachaaho'a manoomini.

> ne-hchiimeeh-a   wachaaho-'a manoomin-i
> I-little.sister-Animate/Singular cook-she/it rice-Inanimate
> 'My little sister is cooking rice.'

b.   Nehchiimeeha manoomini wachaaho'a.   (my little sister rice is cooking)
c.   Manoomini nehchiimeeha wachaaho'a.   (rice my little sister is cooking)

---

[7] The symbol [đ] represents the dental [t̪], except that it sounds somewhat between the voiced [d̪] and voiceless [t̪].

d.   Manoomini wachaaho'a nehchiimeeha.   (rice is cooking my little sister)
e.   Wachaaho'a manoomini nehchiimeeha.   (is cooking rice my little sister)

Second, the Kickapoo people are especially careful when there are two animate third persons in a sentence: an animate subject acting on an animate object. The subject of the sentence is marked one way (technically called the proximate), the animate object a different way (technically called obviative). Thus the Kickapoo people will know which third person is acting on which other third person.

10. Kickapoo obviation

   a. Newachaaho pahkahaakwaha.
       ne-wachaaho   pahkahaakwah-a
       I-be.cooking.it/Animate chicken-Animate
       'I am cooking chicken.'

   b. Kewachaaho pahkahaakwaha.
       ke-wachaaho   pahkahaakwah-a
       you-be.cooking.it/Animate chicken-Animate
       'You are cooking chicken.'

   c. Nekiya   wachaaho'a   pahkahaakwahani.
       ne-kiya   wachaaho-a   pahkahaakwah-ani
       my-mother-Proximate she.be.cooking-her/him/it.Animate chicken-Obviative
       'My mother is cooking chicken.'

Example (c) shows that the object *pahkahaakwah-* 'chicken' and subject *nekiy-* 'mother' are marked differently. When both subject and object are animate third person, the subject (*nekiy-* 'my mother') is marked with *-a* and the object (*pahkahaakwah-* 'chicken') with *-ani*. This system is called obviation.[8]

Words are made up of many parts

You may have noticed that Native American languages often present complex verb forms. In fact, a verb itself may include all the information that is usually expressed as a whole sentence in English. This is related to a striking structural characteristic of many Native American languages, termed polysynthesis. Mohawk words, for example, consist of many meaningful parts (Mithun 1996: 138). The Mohawk people live on both sides of the Canadian–US border. On the US side, 5,638 Mohawks live just south of the St. Lawrence River, New York, and perhaps a half of them speak the language. On the Canadian side, 7,671 Canadian Mohawks live

[8] This system is also involved in the noun form when there are two third persons involved: a. *nékiya* 'my mother'; b. *kékiya* 'your mother'; c. *ókiyani* 'his/her mother.' When the possessor (my, your, his, her) and the relative are both third person, the ending of the noun must follow the rule of obviation. Thus, '(his or her) mother' *okiy-* must have the obviative suffix *-ani*. Try with *sitheeh-* 'maternal uncle.' What will be 'my maternal uncle'? How about 'your maternal uncle' and 'his/her maternal uncle'? d. *nesítheeha* 'my uncle'; e. *kesítheeha* 'your uncle'; f. *osithééhani* 'his/her uncle.'

along the southern bank of the St. Lawrence River and on Cornwall Island. The following are two examples of Mohawk words with many meaningful parts.

11. Mohawk: one word with many meaningful parts (see Mithun 1996: 138–9)

    a. sahųwanhotúkwahse'
        s-a-hųwa-nho-tú-kw-ahs-e'
        again-past-she/him-door-close-un-for-punctual
        'she opened the door for him again'

    b. yųterihwayʌstáhkwha'
        yų-te-rihw-yʌ-hst-áhkw-ha'
        she-self-word-learn-cause-use.for-habitual
        'one uses it to cause oneself to learn words' = school

Another example of polysynthesis comes from an Alaskan Eskimo group that makes its home in the Yukon and Kuskokwim deltas. They call themselves *Yup'ik* 'Real People.' In the 1990s, Central Alaskan Yup'ik was spoken by approximately half of the estimated 22,000 people in the traditional area and perhaps a few thousand people in the urban areas. In Yup'ik, we also find single words expressing complex thoughts:

12. Yup'ik: one word with many meaningful parts (see Miyaoka 1996: 330)

        qayarpaliyugaqa
        qayar-pa-li-yug-a-qa
        kayak-big-make-want.to-Direct.Transitive-1st.person.Subject/for.3rd.person
        'I want to make a big kayak for him.'

There are other Native American languages that show relatively shorter forms of verbs, but they, too, typically include meanings expressing **person** (who is acting on whom, that is, first person subject, second person subject, third person subject, first person subject acting on second person object, and so on), **number** (how many are involved), **gender** (masculine or feminine; animate or inanimate), and other important information. These pieces of information may be encoded in verbs and also, as we will see below, in nouns, articles, and other places in the grammar.

Person and number

The concepts of person, number, and gender may be expressed in verbs, nouns, articles, and other grammatical categories. Tohono O'odham shows some of the most fascinating ways to express the concept of number.

13. Tohono O'odham singular and plural nouns (see Akmajian et al. 1995:19)

    a. kawyu   'horse'
        <u>ka</u>kawyu   'horses'
    b. gogs   'dog'
        <u>go</u>gogs   'dogs'

    c. daikuḍ   'chair'
        dadaikuḍ   'chairs'

Given a word *hu'u* 'star,' what will 'stars' be? It will be *hu'hu'u*. The first syllable of the base (singular) form is repeated in a process called reduplication. This same principle works with the verbs.

14. Tohono O'odham singular and plural verb forms (Farmer and Demers 1996: 27; see also Zepeda 1983)

    a. ñeok   '(I/you/he/she) speak'
        ñeñeok   '(we/y'all/they) speak'

    b. him   '(I/you/he/she) walk'
        hihim   '(we/y'all/they) walk'

    c. dagkon   '(I/you/he/she) wipe (something)'
        dadagkon   '(we/y'all/they) wipe (something)'

Reduplication here indicates how many are doing the action.

    The Cree, an Algonquian language-speaking people, reside mostly in Canada, but also in the foothills of the Bearpaw Mountains in Montana. According to the 1990 census, there were approximately 4,255 Cree people, 54 percent of whom resided off the reservations. Many of those on reservations still speak the language. Cree shows one of the most complex person systems as expressed in its verbs:

15. Cree verb paradigm (Wolfart 1996: 412–13)

    a. Niwa:pama:w.   'I see him.'
    b. Niwa:pama:wak.   'I see them.'
    c. Niwa:pama:na:n.   'We see him.' (the hearer not included, exclusive 'we')
    d. Kiwa:pama:naw.   'We see him.' (the hearer included, inclusive 'we')
    d. Niwa:pama:na:nak. 'We see them.' (the hearer not included, exclusive 'we')
    e. Kiwa:pama:nawak. 'We see them.' (the hearer included, inclusive 'we')
    f. Kiwa:pama:w.   'You see him.'
    f. Kiwa:pama:wak.   'You see them.'
    g. Kiwa:pama:wa:w.   'Y'all see him.'
    h. Kiwa:pama:wa:wak. 'Y'all see them.'
    i. Kiwa:pamin.   'You see me.'
    j. Kiwa:pamina:n.   'You see us.'
    k. Kiwa:pamina:wa:w. 'Y'all see me.'
    l. Kiwa:pamina:wa:wak. 'Y'all see us.'
    m. Wa:pamime:w.   'He sees her.'
    n. Wa:pamime:wak.   'They see him.'

What seem to be the parts indicating the first person subject 'I'? What about the second person subject 'you'? How about the third person subject 'he/she'? The prefix *ni-* indicates 'I,' *ki-* 'you,' and there is no marking for 'he/she.' The endings indicate not only the person of the object but also the number of the subject and the number of the object. Thus, *-a:w* says 'a singular subject is acting on the third person singular object'; *-a:wak* that 'a singular subject is acting on the third person plural object.' When the subject is the second person and the object the first person, the Cree verbs show a different paradigm, and this also applies to the third person subject and third person object.

Many languages have three-way number distinctions: singular, dual (for two), and plural (for three or more). In Hualapai some verbs demonstrate more than three-way distinctions:

16. Hualapai verbs

    a. to stand

skwi:	'(one person) to stand'	
Marych skwi:kyu.		'Mary is standing.'
đaskwi:k	'(two persons) to stand'	
Marych Johnam đaskwi:kyu.		'Mary and John are standing.'
gige:vk	'(a few or more) to stand'	
Marych Johnam Billam gige:vkyu.		'Mary, John and Bill are standing.'
gigæyvk	'(several or many) to stand'	
Marych Johnam Billam Caseym Joanam gigæyvkyu.		'Mary, John, Bill, Casey, and Joan are standing.'
gijgæyvk	'(many) to stand'	
Ba:jach bay gijgæyvkyu.		'People are all standing.'

    b. to sit, to live

wa'k or wa:k	'(one) to sit'
ba:yk	'(two) to sit (together)'
wayó'k	'(a few or more) to sit (together)'
wayo:k	'(many) to sit (together)'

    c. to go

ya:mk	'(one) to go'
be:mk	'(two) to go'
ya:mjk	'(a few or more) to go'
ya:jmk	'(many) to go'

Mithun (1998: 165) shows examples from Central Pomo in which 'sit' is expressed by five verbs, depending on the type and number of the subject and on where the sitting is taking place. Central Pomo is spoken approximately 100 miles north of San Francisco in three communities: Point Arena–Manchester Rancheria on the Pacific Coast, and the Hopland and Yokaya Rancherias forty miles inland. Only a few speakers survive.

17. Central Pomo verb distinction for 'sit'

čʰmáw	'one person sits alone on a chair, a bird perched on a branch'
bamáw	'a group of people sit on a bench, a row of birds perched on a wire'

čóm   'a container of liquid sitting on a table'
ʔčʰaːw   'a person sitting on the ground'
napʰów   'a group of people sitting on the ground'

Gender

Gender is another category that shows up in different ways among Native American languages. Some languages show sex-based distinctions. These languages include Tunica. Tunica people are now with Biloxi people forming the Tunica–Biloxi tribe on their 130-acre reservation in Louisiana. These two groups together have about 430 people but no speakers. Other languages demonstrating sex-based distinctions include Chinook (approximately 1,200 people live in Oregon and Washington, but they have never been recognized as an Indian tribe by the Bureau of Indian Affairs; there are no speakers), Quileute (about 874 people live around the mouth of the Quillayute River and near the Pacific Ocean coastline of the western Olympic Peninsula of Washington State; there are a few speakers), Seneca (6,241 people reside on the Tonawanda, Cattaraugus, and Allegany reservations in western New York State, and in Canada; there are at most 200 speakers), and other Northern Iroquoian languages (Mohawk, Oneida, Onondaga).

18. Sex-based gender distinctions (Mithun 1996: 142–43)

In Tunica, nouns referring to male persons are generally marked as masculine and those referring to female persons as feminine.

> táčɔha-ku (chief-MASCULINE)
> tánisara-hči (girl-FEMININE)

Most count nouns for inanimate things are masculine, but mass nouns are feminine:

> tášihkali-ku (rock-MASCULINE)
> táwiši-hči (water-FEMININE)

Collective animate entities are masculine:

> táčahta-ku (Choctaw-MASCULINE)

In Mohawk, the masculine marker -ha- is used for male persons and personified animals or characters, while the feminine indefinite pronoun-ʔ-meaning 'one, someone, people' is used for some female persons.

> wahahnekíːra'   'he drank it'
> wa'ehnekíːra'   'someone or she drank it'

In other languages (such as the Algonquian languages Kickapoo and Cree), gender is based on the animate–inanimate distinction. In Plains Cree, spoken in central Canada, nouns referring to humans, animals, spirits, trees, and plants are typically animate. It is an interesting fact that the singular forms of Cree nouns do not have any distinct way to mark their being animate or inanimate. It is only with plural nouns that we can tell which are animate and which are inanimate. Noun modifiers and also verbs, however, must be distinguished for animate or inanimate (Silver and Miller 1997: 24–25).

19. Cree animate/inanimate-based gender distinctions

Animate nouns

na:pe:w	'man'	na:pe:w-<u>ak</u>	'men'
iskwe:sis	'girl'	iskwe:sis-<u>ak</u>	'girls'
si:si:p	'duck'	si:si:p-<u>ak</u>	'ducks'
aspwa:kan	'pipe'	aspwa:kan-<u>ak</u>	'pipes'
<u>awa</u> na:pe:w	'this man'	<u>o:ki</u> na:pe:w-<u>ak</u>	'these men'
<u>awa</u> si:si:p	'this duck'	<u>o:ki</u> si:si:p-<u>ak</u>	'these ducks'

Inanimate nouns

mo:hkoma:n	'knife'	mo:hkoma:n-<u>a</u>	'knives'
astotin	'cap'	astotin-<u>a</u>	'caps'
mi:nis	'berry'	mi:nis-<u>a</u>	'berries'
<u>o:ma</u> astotin	'this cap'	<u>o:hi</u> astotin-<u>a</u>	'these caps'
<u>o:ma</u> mi:nis	'this berry'	<u>o:hi</u> mi:nis-<u>a</u>	'these berries'

Shape, substance, and manner

Young and Morgan (1987) list eleven Navajo verbs for 'handling'; each one specifies the *size*, *shape*, *number*, *texture*, or *animacy* of the thing handled. Some languages may use one root with different affixes.

20. Navajo Verbs of 'handling' in the Perfective Form

a. -ą́   b. -lá   c. -tą́   d. -łtsooz   e. -łtį́   f. -tłéé'
g. -nil   h. -jaa'   i. -łjool   j. -ką́   k. -yį́

All eleven forms given above mean 'handling' some object. What then differentiates them? The following is a brief list of things that can be used with each of the above:

a. handling a solid, roundish, compact object (apple, barrel, inflated balloon, basket, chair, chunk of cheese, hat, boot, glove)
b. handling a slender, flexible object (a strip of bacon, uninflated balloon, belt, cornhusk, flower, blade of grass, a pair of objects such as gloves or boots)
c. handling a thin, stiff object (an antler, arrow, banana, flat basket, string bean, bow, broom)
d. handling a flat, flexible object (an empty bag, blanket, coat, cobweb, dollar bill, newspaper, quiver)

e. handling an animate object (baby, fly, kitten, snake, man)
f. handling a mushy object (butter, melted cheese, cornmeal mush, scrambled egg, a gob of grease, ice cream, mud, pitch, mashed potatoes)
g. handling multiple separable objects (acorns, beads, beans, dishes)
h. handling profuse, multiple objects (grapes, berries, cookies)
i. handling non-compact matter (a wad of down, horsetail, tangled pile of intestine, shredded lettuce, moss, snarled wad of thread or string, bunched up towel, loose wool)
j. handling an open container (acorns in a basket, ashes, beer in a mug or open bottle, ice-cream cone)
k. Handling a load or large, bulky object (a big bag, bed, rolled blanket, Christmas tree, firewood, a man on a stretcher)

Examples of sentences

a. Jooł naa ní'ą́, ya'?   'I gave a ball to you, right?'
    Aoo', shaa yíní' ą́.   'Yes, you gave it to me.'
d. Naaltsoos shaa yíníłtsooz, ya'?   'You gave paper to me, right?'
    Aoo', naa níłtsooz.   'Yes, I gave it to you.'
e. Bisóodi baa yíníłtį, ya'?   'You gave a pig to him/her, right?'
    Aoo', baa níłtį.   'Yes, I gave it to him/her.'
g. Paul, Mary béeso ła' yinínil, ya'? 'Paul gave some money to Mary, right?'
    Aoo', Paul, Mary béeso ła' yeinínil. 'Yes, Paul gave some money to Mary.'
j. Jélii nihaa yíníką́, ya'?   'You gave jello to us, right?'
    Aoo', nihaa níką́.   'Yes, I gave it to you.'

Besides 'give,' these categories are also applied to verbs such as 'set down,' 'pick up,' 'carry,' 'haul,' and 'put.' In Navajo and also Apache, speakers must consider the shape and substance of items they handle.

Navajo and Apache belong to the Athabascan language family. About 30,000 Apache people form several tribal communities, including the Fort Sill Apache Tribe in Oklahoma (103 members in 1992), the Mescalero Apache Tribe in New Mexico (3,511), the Jicarilla Apache Tribe in New Mexico (3,100), the San Carlos Apache Tribe in Arizona (7,562), and the White Mountain Apache Tribe in Arizona (12,503). Perhaps one-third of the total population of Apache people speak the language.

21. Hualapai verbs of 'carrying'
    a. đabek   'to carry on horseback'
    b. gavnawk   'to carry a baby, child'
    c. hu:h'k jiwo:k   'to carry on one's head'
    d. ke:k   'to carry on one's back'
    e. vawalk   'to carry a large container'
    f. vine:k   'to carry firewood or objects'
    g. yigok   'to carry something or someone light'

Let us examine another verb. Many languages differentiate eating in general from eating meat. Navajo again demonstrates more categories for verbs of eating.

22. Navajo verbs of eating

By surveying the types of food involved with each of the verbs, try to construct your explanation of the way Navajo people might see the differences among these verbs.

a.	yiyáá'	muskmelon, plant, weed, corn, ice, grass, turkey, bread, fried bread, apple, egg, dumpling, fat, berry, blue-jay, cornmeal
b.	yí'aal	corn, ice, herb, cookie, cake, bean, onion, grape
c.	yiłchozh	corn, grass, cabbage, leaf, intestines, stomach
d.	yishghal	turkey, sheep, meat, elk, blue-jay, sheep's head, liver, kidney, chicken, rabbit, intestines, stomach
e.	yishkid	muskmelon, bread, fried bread, apple, egg, sheep's head, liver, kidney, cabbage, cookie, cake, candy, potato, orange, tomato, watermelon
f.	yiłts'ee'	fat, marrow, chili, squash, butter, jello, oatmeal, syrup
g.	yishdééł	muskmelon, turkey, sheep, herb, elk, bread, fried bread, apple, egg, dumpling, berry, sheep's head, liver, kidney, cabbage, cookie, candy, orange, peach, tomato, watermelon, grape

Answers: a. eating in general; b. eating 'hard or chewy object'; c. eating a 'long stringy object'; d. eating 'meat'; e. eating 'one round object'; f. eating 'mushy matter'; g. eating 'separable objects.' What the Navajo verb tells us is not the mere act of eating, but the appreciation for food and the intimate and complex relationships between the act and the object acted on (Landar 1964).

Position

In some languages, when speakers report that there are humans, animals, or any other things, the report must include a characterization of the objects with different existential verbs (sitting, standing, lying). We cannot just express something being there, but we must specify that it is sitting, standing, or lying (Mithun 1996: 144).

23. Tunica position 'sitting,' 'lying,' 'standing' (Haas 1941, cited in Mithun 1996: 144)

In the examples below, the underlined parts tell us about the position of the object.

a.	tasaku <u>ʔuná</u>	'There is the dog (in a sitting position).'
b.	tasaku <u>kalʔurá</u>	'There is the dog (in a standing position).'
c.	tasaku <u>ʔurá</u>	'There is the dog (in a lying position).'

How about the most typical position of the following? Fill in the blank with *ʔuná, ka'lʔurá*, or *ʔurá*.

d.	turunatʔɛku __	'There is the bullfrog.'
e.	tehkunaku __	'There is the mosquito.'
f.	taniniku __	'There is the fish.'
g.	tɔmahkaku __	'There is the alligator.'
h.	ʔekša __	'There is a pine tree.'

Answers: d. ʔuná   e. ʔuná   f. ʔurá   g. ʔurá   h. kalʔurá

Languages like Omaha, Ponca, Kansa, Osage, and Quapaw, the Dhegiha branch of the Siouan language family, have a large set of definite articles suffixed on nouns. The articles distinguish animacy, number, shape or position, and movement (Mithun 1996: 144). These suffixes are given below in 24. Approximately half of the 6,000 Omaha people live on the reservation in Nebraska and it was estimated in the 1980s that about half the population spoke the language. There are two groups of Ponca people: the Northern Ponca Tribe of Nebraska, with about 900 members in the late 1980s, and only a few elders speaking the language; and the Ponca Tribe of Oklahoma (Southern Ponca), with 2,360 members in 1993, but only a few elders speaking the language. The Kansa people now live in Oklahoma and are officially known as the Kaw Nation of Oklahoma. Among 1,678 members in 1993, there were only about a dozen elders who spoke the language. Osage people also reside in Oklahoma. The population in 1993 was 11,000, among whom fewer than 300, it was estimated, spoke the language. Quapaw people are another Dhegiha member of the Siouan language family in Oklahoma. Of approximately 2,000 members in the 1980s, only a handful spoke the language.

24. Ponca definite articles indicating animacy, number, position, and movement

a.	-kʰe	for inanimate horizontal object
	-tʰe	for inanimate standing object
	-ðą	for inanimate round object
	-akʰá	for singular animate agent[9]
	-amá	for singular animate agent in motion or plural
	-tʰą	for animate singular patient[10] in standing position
	-ðį	for animate singular patient in motion
	-ma	for animate plural patient in motion
	-ðįkʰé	for animate singular patient in sitting position
	-ðąkʰá	for animate plural patient in sitting position

The following sentences show how these are actually used (Dorsey 1890, cited in Mithun 1996: 144).

---

[9] The term agent refers to the "doer" of an action. The agent often appears as the subject in a sentence.

[10] The term patient refers to the "recipient" of an action, the person who is affected by the action. The patient often appears as the object in a sentence.

   b. Maščįge ak^há   páðį   ðạk^há weðai t^he.
      Rabbit the   Pawnee the   found them
      'Maščįge (the Rabbit) detected the Pawnee.'

   c. Mį ðạ hídexči   t^hédi, . . .
      sun the at the very bottom when
      'When the sun was at the very bottom of the sky, . . .'

In (b), Rabbit is marked as a singular animate agent, that is, the one who acts on something. The Pawnee were characterized as a group of people sitting around. In (c), the sun is categorized as an inanimate object.

Instrument

Many Native American languages have instrumental affixes (i.e., prefixes and suffixes) that indicate how a particular action may be performed. In the following examples, *ba-*, *s-* and *š-* are prefixes.

25. Central Pomo instrumental prefixes (Mithun 1998: 169–70)

      Prefixes: ba- 'orally'   s- 'by sucking'   š- 'by handle'
      Verb root: yól 'mix'

And thus we have:

   a. bayól   'while humming a song, suddenly put in words'
     syól   'wash down cookies/doughnuts with coffee or tea'
     šyól   'stir with a spoon'

Now let's add more prefixes:

   b. ča-   'by sawing or slicing'
     h-   'by poking, jabbing, thrusting'
     m-   'by heat'
     ma-   'by stepping or twisting wrist'
     ša-   'by shaking, moving long object lengthwise'
     ʔ-   'by fine hand action, especially fingers'

In the following examples, how do the prefixes in (b) above contribute to the meaning of the words?

   c. čayól   'chop several things together, as onions and celery for stew'
     hyól   'add salt or pepper'
     myól   'throw various ingredients together into a pot'
     mayól   'mix, as shortening with flour to make pie crust'
     šayól   'sift dry ingredients'
     ʔyól   'throw various ingredients into a bowl with fingers'

In the preceding sections, whenever we introduced a Native American language, we provided information about the speakers. Now let us turn to the situation of Native American languages.

Language situations in Native American communities

General questions

What do we know about the situations of the languages of the world? How do you answer the following questions?

Question 1: How many languages are there in the world?

500 1,000 2,000 4,000 over 6,000

Answer: The *Ethnologue* (Grimes 2000) reports 6,818 languages in the world.

Question 2: How many of these languages have more than a million speakers?

100 300 500 700 1,000 over 1,000

Answer: Three hundred and thirty (4.8 percent of the total) have one million or more speakers (totaling 5,089,528,969).

Question 3: How many have fewer than 10,000 speakers?

100 300 500 700 1,000 over 1,500

Answer: There are 3,248 languages (48 percent of the total) that have fewer than 10,000 speakers (altogether 7,981,128 people). The average number of speakers of the languages of the world is about 6,000.

Question 4: Which are the top five languages with the most mother-tongue speakers? How would you rank the rest of the languages? (Place 1–5 in front of the top five languages.)

English	Russian	French	German	Mandarin Chinese
Spanish	Hindi	Bengali	Cherokee	Japanese
Swahili	Portuguese	Navajo	Ainu	Tohono O'odham
Arabic				

Answer: The following are very rough figures. (1) Mandarin Chinese (885 million); (2) English (450 million); (3) Spanish (266 million); (4) Hindi (182 million); (5) Arabic (181 million).[11]

Question 5: What percentage of the languages of the world (Question 1) will be still spoken at the end of this century?

10% 30% 50% 70% close to 100%

---

[11] 6: Portuguese (175 million); 7: Bengali (162 million); 8: Russian (160 million); 9: Japanese (126 million); 10: French (122 million); 11: Standard German (118 million); 12: Swahili (30 million or more); 13: Navajo (approximately 130,000); 14: Cherokee (the Eastern Band of Cherokee Indians in western North Carolina, approximately 9,800 of whom 1,000 speak the language; and the Cherokee Nation of Oklahoma: over 122,000, of whom 13,000 speak the language); 15: Tohono O'odham (the majority, approximately 20,000, live in Arizona; one estimate says there are about 10,000 speakers); 16: Ainu (the majority of these indigenous people live in the northernmost island of Hokkaidō, Japan, and a smaller population reside in Sakhalin Island, Russia; of the estimated 25,000 Ainu people, only about fifty are said to speak the language).

Answer: Approximately 30 to 50 percent may be lost during the twenty-first century. In one estimate, close to 90 percent of the languages spoken now will be lost.

Question 6: How many native American languages were there in the USA and Canada at the time of European contact?

50   100   200   300   600   over 1,000

Answer: In one estimate (Krauss 1998: 9), there were well over 300 languages, and in another 250 (Silver and Miller 1997: 7). In yet another estimate (Goddard 1996: 3), there were well over 400, perhaps close to around 600. These languages are grouped into sixty-two families. For the classification of the Native languages of North America, see Goddard (1996: 4–8; 1996: 290–323).

Question 7: How many Native American languages are there now in the USA and Canada?

50   100   200   300   600   over 1,000

Answer: In 1997, there were about 211 languages, of which 175 were in the USA (although not necessarily as a major means of communication). Krauss (1998: 11–12) groups these 175 languages into four classes according to their vitality:

- Class A: languages still spoken by all generations including young children; 20 languages (11%).
- Class B: spoken only by the parental generation and up; 30 languages (17%)
- Class C: spoken only by the grandparental generation and up; 70 languages (40%)
- Class D: spoken only by the very oldest, over 70 years of age, usually fewer than ten persons and almost extinct; 55 languages (31%)

This means that only twenty languages (thirty-two when we include Canada) are being acquired by children. These languages will be relatively safe. Over 70 percent (Classes C and D) of the Native American languages in the USA, however, are in an extreme danger of extinction.

Why did it happen?

The history of the indigenous peoples in the USA has been a history of suppression and deprivation of rights. In 1887, for example, J. D. C. Atkins, Commissioner of Indian Affairs, reported:

> [Our nation] approaches nearer than any other nationality to the perfect pro-
> tection of its people. *True Americans all feel that the Constitution, laws,
> and institutions of the United States . . . are superior to those of any other
> country; and they should understand that by the spread of the English lan-
> guage will these laws and institutions be more firmly established and widely
> disseminated*. Nothing so surely and perfectly stamps upon an individual a

national characteristic as language . . . No unity or community of feeling can be established among different peoples unless they are brought to speak the same language, and thus become imbued with like ideas of duty . . .

The instruction of the Indians in the vernacular is not only of no use to them, but is detrimental to the cause of their education and civilization and no school will be permitted on the reservation in which the English language is not exclusively taught.   (Atkins 1887: xxi–xxiii; italics added)

At the opening of the twenty-first century, we still see a similar attitude toward Native American peoples and their languages. For example, an argument not unlike the one invoked by J. D. C. Atkins has been used to establish English-Only policies, and twenty-four states have already passed such legislation (see chapters 17 and 18).[12]

Issues of language choice, of majority and minority conflicts, of identity crises, and of numerous other concerns result when two or more cultures come into contact. This is especially true when the contact situation is imbalanced – one is more powerful politically, militarily, economically, or demographically. This is also true when the contact situation is a relatively long lasting one. Native American peoples had to face the Europeans in exactly this permanent and power-imbalanced encounter situation. Children were educated in boarding schools where the language of instruction and of communication was English. People as young as in their forties still remember their boarding-school days when one word of their ancestral language out of their mouth resulted in their mouth being rinsed with Ivory soap to wash out their "bad" language. When they became parents, they certainly did not want their children to go through the same hardship. So they encouraged their children to learn English, not their ancestral languages. What a powerful and effective method of replacing ancestral languages with English this was!

Native American Languages Acts

In response to the language decline among Native American communities and also responding to English-Only attempts, a powerful grassroots movement was initiated in 1988 at the International Conference of Native Language Issues Institute. The conference produced a resolution that found its way to Senator Daniel K. Inouye, chair of the Senate Select Committee on Indian Affairs, and two years later it became the Native American Languages Act, which officially addresses the fundamental rights of Native American peoples. From the ten-part statement in Section 102 of the Act, we read:

---

[12] In the year 2000, another important US Senate Bill 2688 (The Native American Languages Act Amendments Act of 2000) was formulated, and a number of Native American language teachers, community language advocates, and scholars presented testimonials before the Senate Special Committee on Indian Affairs. The bill aims at supporting the development of Native American language survival schools.

The Congress finds that –

(1) the status of the cultures and languages of Native Americans is unique and the United States has the responsibility to act together with Native Americans to ensure the survival of these unique cultures and languages;

(2) special status is accorded Native Americans in the United States, a status that recognizes distinct cultural and political rights, including the right to continue separate identities;

(3) the traditional languages of Native Americans are an integral part of their cultures and identities and form the basic medium for the transmission, and thus survival, of Native American cultures, literatures, histories, religions, political institutions, and values;

(5) there is a lack of clear, comprehensive, and consistent Federal policy on treatment of Native American languages which has often resulted in acts of suppression and extermination of Native American languages and cultures;

(8) acts of suppression and extermination directed against Native American languages and cultures are in conflict with the United States policy of self-determination for Native Americans;

(9) languages are the means of communication for the full range of human experiences and are critical to the survival of cultural and political integrity of any people;

Section 104 declares:

It is the policy of the United States to –
preserve, protect, and promote the rights and freedom of Native Americans to use, practice, and develop Native American languages.

October of 1992 saw the birth of the Native American Languages Act of 1992, which authorized funds for community-based language programs.

Along with the grass-roots movement, these two laws have done several things: (1) Native American communities have become more aware of the alarmingly rapid decline of their ancestral languages; (2) Native American communities began to search for ways to revitalize their languages; (3) linguists and other professionals began to re-evaluate their own work with Native American languages; (4) that re-evaluation by professionals has led to a critical assessment of their roles vis-à-vis language-endangered communities; (5) Native American communities and academic professionals rediscovered each other; and (6) more and more cooperative language revitalization projects began to form.

One good example of such cooperation is the American Indian Language Development Institute (AILDI), a teacher-training institute conceived and developed by Lucille Watahomigie and Leanne Hinton (see McCarty et al. 1997; Watahomigie and Yamamoto 1987; Zepeda and Hill 1991). AILDI continues to train Native American language teachers, English as a Second Language (ESL) teachers, multicultural teachers, curriculum developers, and materials developers and has attracted teachers of Native American languages throughout the USA and Canada, as well as from Brazil and Venezuela. Its co-directors, Ofelia Zepeda and Teresa McCarty, persuaded the University of Arizona of the important role of the institute to the State of Arizona and the rest of the country, and in 1996 the university committed permanent funding for the institute. In Alaska, a similar teacher-training institute (Athabaskan Language Development Institute) has been implemented by linguists and educators of the University of Alaska at Fairbanks and the Tanana Chiefs Conference.

In California, linguists and educators such as Leanne Hinton and Nancy Richardson are working with community people using an innovative language revitalization approach known as the "master–apprentice" program. A speaker in the community, an elder, forms a partnership with an aspiring young language learner, and the two spend time together doing things *in* the language. In many communities, this is the only viable way to transmit knowledge of the language to the young, one at a time in a real life context. With its ninety-eight languages, California is one of the most linguistically diverse places in the world. Of the ninety-eight, forty-five have no fluent speakers, seventeen have only between one and five speakers, and thirty-six have only elderly speakers (Hinton 1998: 83). In Oklahoma, a team of linguists from the University of Kansas (Marcellino Berardo, Tracy Hirata-Edds, Mary Linn, Lizette Peter, Nathan Poell, Tracy Williams, Akira Yamamoto), language teachers, and elders are working together in linguistic training, documentation of languages, development of language materials, and teacher training (see Linn et al. 1998). In Hawai'i, Nā'ilima Gaison, Carole Ishimaru, Kauanoe Kamanā, Keiki Kawai'ae'a, Larry Kimura, Hau'oli Motta, Nāmaka Rawlins, Kalena Silva, William (Pila) Wilson, and their team of 'Aha Pūnana Leo continue their Hawaiian teacher training and immersion programs. In Alaska, Angayuqaq Kawagley and the team at the Alaska Native Language Center provide a wide range of services. In New Mexico, Christine Sims of the Linguistic Institute for Native Americans works with Pueblo communities. In Oregon, the University of Oregon offers a summer institute for Native American language teachers.[13]

Why consider Native American languages and their diversity?

As we have seen, Native American languages present diversity at all levels of the linguistic system. When we lose a language, it means a "tremendous loss to the cultural richness and distinctness of the native communities" (Goddard 1996: 3). Because "the scientific study of the mind is a venerable pursuit in human intellectual history, and the human capacity for language is the human mind's most prominent feature" (Hale 1998: 192), the loss of linguistic diversity is a loss to scholarship and science. In language revitalization projects, "it is crucial to record how good speakers use their language, what they choose to say in the multitude of settings that constitute their daily lives, how they describe their own experiences, how they provide explanations, and especially how they interact with

---

[13] The Indigenous Language Institute (Inée Yang Slaughter, Executive Director) is an active resource center for indigenous language revitalization programs.

each other" (Mithun 1998: 191). Even when there are no more speakers, "such a record will lay a foundation for their descendants to discover the intricate beauty of a system unlike any other, and a chance for us all to appreciate some of the capacities of the human spirit" (Mithun 1998: 191). When we lose a language, we lose a segment of beauty, richness, intellectual history, and the human mind. That is why we cannot afford to let any language disappear.

Acknowledgments

We are grateful to Tracy Hirata-Edds, Kimiko Yasaka, and the late Kenneth Hale, who carefully and critically read an earlier version of this chapter and provided insightful comments and valuable suggestions. Very special thanks are due to Dr. Mary Willie for her help with Navajo data. The section on Diversity in Native American Languages is inspired by the writings of Marianne Mithun, and we gratefully acknowledge our indebtedness to her.

Suggestions for further reading and exploration

Cantoni (1996) includes articles that discuss the state of Native American languages, the importance of language diversity, and how indigenous languages are taught; it also includes the text of the Native American Languages Act of 1990. Mithun (1999) provides an excellent overview of Native American languages. The articles in Grenoble and Whaley (1998) sample the situations of languages from different continents, with excellent discussions about why we must try to preserve the diversity of languages. Now also available at the Summer Institute of Linguistics Website *http://www.sil.org/ethnolog/*, Grimes (2000) covers over 6,818 languages spoken in 228 countries and includes a brief description of the status of each language. Hale et al. (1992) describes why language diversity is important for humanity, what is happening to the indigenous languages of the Americas, and what some indigenous communities are doing to reverse language shift. Hinton (1994/5) explains how effectively a severely endangered language can be learned by pairing a teacher (master) and a student (apprentice). Hinton (1994), a delightful book on the California Indian languages, shows how languages demonstrate different ways of looking at the world. The articles in Hornberger (1996) describe how language policies and people's attitudes affect whether languages decline or are maintained; the book focuses on the role of literacy in revitalization of languages. Matsumura (1998) samples the language situations in South America, India, the Arctic region, China, Southeast Asia, Africa, Russia, Japan, and Thailand, and it discusses methods of language maintenance. McCarty and Zepeda (1998) is an excellent collection that demonstrates how indigenous language groups in the Americas are revitalizing their ancestral languages. The articles in Reyhner (1997) cover a wide range of issues on teaching indigenous languages, from theory to practice. Robins and Uhlenbeck (1991) is a comprehensive treatment of the situations of languages in different regions of the world. Skutnabb-Kangas and Phillipson (1995) presents an excellent discussion of language policies and how they may infringe on or enhance linguistic human rights.

Selected websites

The most comprehensive coverage of languages of the world is found in "Ethnologue" http://www.ethnologue.com that includes maps and information on the status of a language.

American Indian language links *http://www.members.dandy.net/~orocobix/langlinks.htm*, hosted by the Jatibonicu Taino Tribal Nation of Boriken, includes links to dictionaries, fonts, grammars, and an impressive array of source material on Native American languages.

The UNESCO Red Book on endangered languages *http://www.tooyoo.L.u-tokyo.ac.jp/ichel/ichel.html* has descriptions and samples of endangered languages from Asia and the Pacific, Africa, South America, Europe, Northeast Asia, and elsewhere. The "Linguistic Olympics" *http://www.darkwing.uoregon.edu/~tpayne/lingolym/loreport.htm* provides a fun and educational problem-solving activity designed for secondary school students (ages eleven through eighteen).

Three organizations are worth special mention: Indigenous Language Institute *http://www.indigenouslanguage.org*; Linguistic Society of America *http://www.lsadc.org*; Society for the Study of the Indigenous Languages of the Americas *http://www.ssila.org*.

References

Akmajian, Adrian, Richard A. Demers, Ann K. Farmer, and Robert M. Harnish. 1995. *Linguistics: an Introduction to Language and Communication*, 4th edn. Cambridge: MIT Press.

Atkins, J. D. C. 1887. *Annual Report of the Commissioner of Indian Affairs to the Secretary of the Interior for the Year 1887*. Washington DC: Government Printing Office.

Cantoni, Gina, ed. 1996. *Stabilizing Indigenous Languages*. Flagstaff: Center for Excellence in Education, Northern Arizona University.

Endangered Languages Survey. 1996. Committee on Endangered Languages and their Preservation, Linguistic Society of America. Available online at *http://www.indigenous-language.org/endangered/index.html*.

Farmer, Ann K. and Richard A. Demers. 1996. *A Linguistics Workbook*, 3rd edn. Cambridge: MIT Press.

Goddard, Ives, ed. 1996. *Languages* (*Handbook of North American Indians*, vol. 17). Washington DC: Smithsonian Institution.

Grenoble, Lenore A. and Lindsay J. Whaley, eds. 1998. *Endangered Languages: Current Issues and Future Prospects*. Cambridge: Cambridge University Press.

Grimes, Barbara, ed. 2000. *Ethnologue*, 14th edn. Dallas: Summer Institute of Linguistics.

Haas, Mary. 1941. "Tunica." Extract from *Handbook of American Indian Languages*, Pt. 4: 1–143. New York: J. J. Augustin.

Hale, Ken. 1998. "On Endangered Languages and the Importance of Linguistic Diversity." In Grenoble and Whaley. Pp. 192–216.

Hale, Ken, Michael Krauss, Lucille Watahomigie, Akira Yamamoto, Colette Craig, LaVerne Masayesva Jeanne, and Nora England. 1992. "Endangered Languages." *Language* 68: 1–42.

Hinton, Leanne. 1994. *Flutes of Fire: Essays on California Indian Languages*. Berkeley: Heyday Press.

  1994/5. "Preserving the Future: a Progress Report on the Master–Apprentice Language Learning Program" and "Ten Points for Successful Language Learning." *News From Native California* 8(3): 14–20.

  1998. "Language Loss and Revitalization in California: Overview." In McCarty and Zepeda. Pp. 83–93.

Hornberger, Nancy H., ed. 1996. *Indigenous Literacies in the Americas*. Berlin: Mouton de Gruyter.

Krauss, Michael. 1998. "The Condition of Native North American Languages: the Need for Realistic Assessment and Action." In McCarty and Zepeda. Pp. 9–21.

Landar, Herbert. 1964. "Seven Navaho Verbs of Eating." *International Journal of American Linguistics* 30(1): 94–96.

Linn, Mary, Marcellino Berardo, and Akira Y. Yamamoto. 1998. "Creating Language Teams in Oklahoma Native American Communities." In McCarty and Zepeda. Pp. 61–78.

Matsumura, Kazuto, ed. 1998. *Studies in Endangered Languages. Papers from the International Symposium on Endangered Languages, Tokyo, November 18–20, 1995*. Tokyo: Hituzi Shobo.

McCarty, Teresa L. and Ofelia Zepeda, eds. 1998. *Indigenous Language Use and Change in the Americas. International Journal of the Sociology of Language* 132.

McCarty, Teresa L., Akira Y. Yamamoto, Lucille J. Watahomigie, and Ofelia Zepeda. 1997. "School–Community–University Collaborations: the American Indian Language Development Institute." In Reyhner. Pp. 85–104.

McLendon, Sally. 1996. "Sketch of Eastern Pomo, a Pomoan Language." In Goddard. Pp. 507–50.

Mithun, Marianne. 1996. "Overview of General Characteristics." In Goddard. Pp. 137–57.

  1998. "The Significance of Diversity in Language Endangerment and Preservation." In Grenoble and Whaley. Pp. 163–91.

  1999. *The Languages of Native North America*. Cambridge: Cambridge University Press.

Miyaoka, Osahito. 1996. "Sketch of Central Alaskan Yupik, an Eskimoan Language." In Goddard. Pp. 325–63.

Murdock, Anita, Pauline Wahpepah, Zelma Garza, and Akira Y. Yamamoto. 1987. *Kiikaapoa-towaachiki: Kickapoo Reference Grammar*. Choctaw OK: Kickapoo Bilingual/ Bicultural Education Materials Development Program.

Reyhner, Jon, ed. 1997. *Teaching Indigenous Languages*. Flagstaff: Center for Excellence in Education, Northern Arizona University.

Robins, Robert H. and Eugenius M. Uhlenbeck, eds. 1991. *Endangered Languages*. Oxford: Berg.

Silver, Shirley and Wick R. Miller. 1997. *American Indian Languages: Cultural and Social Contexts*. Tucson: University of Arizona Press.

Skutnabb-Kangas, Tove and Robert Phillipson, eds. 1995. *Linguistic Human Rights: Overcoming Linguistic Discrimination*. Berlin: Mouton de Gruyter.

Watahomigie, Lucille J. and Akira Y. Yamamoto. 1987. "Linguistics in Action: the Hualapai Bilingual/Bicultural Education Program." In *Collaborative Research and Social Change: Applied Anthropology in Action*, eds. Donald D. Stull and Jean J. Schensul. Boulder CO: Westview Press. Pp. 77–98.

Watahomigie, Lucille J., Jorigine Bender, Philbert Watahomigie, Sr., and Akira Y. Yamamoto, with Elnora Mapatis, Malinda Powskey, and Josie Steele. 2001. *Hualapai Reference*

Grammar, rev. and expanded edn. ELPR Publications A2-003. Kyoto: Endangered Languages of the Pacific Rim Project.

Wolfart, H. C. 1996. "Sketch of Cree, an Algonquian Language." In Goddard. Pp. 390–439.

Young, Robert W. and William Morgan. 1987. *The Navajo Language: a Grammar and Colloquial Dictionary*, rev. edn. Albuquerque: University of New Mexico Press.

Zepeda, Ofelia. 1983. *A Papago Grammar*. Tucson: University of Arizona Press.

Zepeda, Ofelia and Jane H. Hill. 1991. "The Condition of Native American Languages in the United States." In Robins and Uhlenbeck. Pp. 135–55.

10

Spanish in the Northeast

ANA CELIA ZENTELLA

Editors' introduction

Spanish has more speakers and more prominence in the USA than any language except English, and it is also the most popular "foreign" language studied in American secondary schools. This chapter describes Spanish in the Northeast – the character, origins, and speakers of Spanish in the New England states and New York, New Jersey, and Pennsylvania. The Spanish of the Northeast is spoken by immigrants and their children from the Caribbean and from Central America and South America, not chiefly by Mexican immigrants, as in the Southwestern USA. Ana Celia Zentella, herself the daughter of a Mexican father and a Puerto Rican mother, has studied Spanish speakers in New York City and elsewhere.

With fascinating detail, this chapter describes the patterns that characterize immigration into the Northeast from Spanish-speaking areas – Puerto Rico (long a protectorate of the USA and peopled by residents who are US citizens), the Dominican Republic, and South America's Colombia, to name some. This chapter documents the loss of Spanish language fluency in the children and grandchildren of these immigrants, striking notes that are also struck in other chapters that touch on the challenges of maintaining languages other than English in the USA (see especially chapters 7, 9, 11, 13, 14, and 17).

About the character of Spanish as it is spoken in the Northeast, the chapter provides documentation of its special features as influenced by the diverse origins of its speakers and its contact with English in spheres inside and outside the home and workplace. It also documents the contributions Spanish has made to English and illustrates the increased richness that vitalizes languages that borrow vocabulary from one another. It documents *indigenismos* (words borrowed by Spanish speakers from the indigenous Indian groups of the Caribbean and Latin America) such as *canoa* 'canoe' and *huracán* 'hurricane' (both of which have found their way into English) and *africanismos* (words of African origins borrowed from the slaves) including *banana*. Most of the words borrowed into Spanish have not been borrowed into English, but you can see them arrayed here. Besides the vocabulary, the chapter provides details about what distinguishes the accents of various groups of Spanish speakers in the Northeast. The vitality that belongs to Spanish and its speakers in the Northeast is palpable in this chapter.

Note that in this chapter, "Hispanic" appears in references to government statistics. Otherwise, the generic term "Latino," which is customary in Spanish, is used as a convenience, even though "Latino/a" would make the inclusion of males and females more obvious.

In the summer of 1998, when Sammy Sosa and Mark McGuire battled to be the first to break Babe Ruth's home-run record, the most excited fans were in the Dominican Republic, where Sosa was born, and in New York City, Providence,

Rhode Island, Lawrence, Massachusetts, and other cities in the Northeast where Dominicans have settled in large numbers. Similarly, when the New York Yankees won what my baseball-loving husband refers to as the "World Serious," Puerto Ricans on the island and throughout the Northeast celebrated the feats of native sons Bernie Williams, Jorge Posada, and Ricky Ledée. US Americans may know which athletes, singers, or movie stars are Hispanic, but few can pinpoint each one's homeland as accurately as Latinos (the term preferred in the Northeast). No surprise there, since everyone tends to root for the "home team," but US Latinos do not always define their "home team" in the same way. Often, they cross national boundaries to unite with each other – as they do in their proud support of Sosa, Williams, and other Latino personalities, or to unite with US American society as a whole – as in their love of US sports, movies, and demo-cratic institutions. Similarly, the distinct varieties of Spanish spoken by the largest groups of Latinos in the Northeast sometimes serve as nationalist flags that stress each group's unique identity, but at other times Latinos consider the Spanish language a common linguistic denominator that embraces all Spanish speakers. From an anthro-political linguistic perspective, this chapter introduces you to the Spanish speakers in the Northeast and to the varieties of Spanish they speak. By an anthro-political linguistic perspective, I mean that a language cannot be divorced from the demographic, socioeconomic, racial, and political realities of its speak-ers. An explanation of those realities reveals the extent of Latino diversity, and it challenges blanket references to "a Hispanic community," or "Spanish speakers," as if a monolithic group existed. Most important, I hope this chapter contributes to your enthusiasm for linguistic and cultural diversity, and to an understanding of the changes we must work for in order to reap the benefits that await a multilingual and multicultural USA.

Spanish speakers in the Northeast

Who are the principal groups of Spanish speakers in the Northeast, and where are they concentrated? Consisting of the six New England states (Connecticut, Maine, Massachusetts, New Hampshire, Rhode Island, Vermont), plus New Jersey, New York, and Pennsylvania, the Northeast was home to 5.2 million Hispanics, or 15 percent, of the 35 million Hispanics in the USA in 2000. The Midwest saw the greatest increase (81%), but the West continued to be the region with the largest number, over 15 million (Centro 2000). While the numerical and historical pres-ence of Spanish speakers is greatest in the West, the diversity of Spanish speakers in contact with each other and with speakers of English and other languages is greatest in the Northeast. This diversity, and the concentrated pockets of Spanish speakers that exist in specific sections of the region, hold significant implications for linguistic and cultural change.

One state (New York), one city (New York), and one group (Puerto Ricans) have dominated the Northeast since the turn of the twentieth century but, as the new century proceeds, more cities are attracting Latinos, and other groups of Latinos are increasing at a faster pace than Puerto Ricans. In particular, Dominicans represent more than 20 percent of New York's Latinos, despite being significantly undercounted in the 2000 Census. They have changed the composition of in-migrant enclaves in the city (for example, in Washington Heights) and in other states (for example, Providence and Lawrence). (Note that the term "in-migrant" includes immigrants from separate nations and new arrivals from colonies or territories of the receiving nation (Baker 1996).) Every state in the Northeast has at least one town that is identified with Spanish speakers from one country primarily. The largest Cuban community outside of Florida lives in Union City, New Jersey, and Colombians have expanded beyond their principal base in Jackson Heights (in Queens, a borough of the City of New York) to Long Island, and to several other states. The most surprising change to occur in the Northeast in the 1990s is the arrival of large numbers of Mexicans. Long the dominant group in the Southwest, West, and Midwest, Mexicans were insignificant in the Northeast until the Immigration Reform and Control Act was passed in 1986. There were fewer than 13,000 Mexicans in New York City in 1980, but the amnesty provided by the Act contributed to a 173 percent increase in the city and put New York State in tenth place nation-wide in terms of Mexican-origin population (Valdés de Montano and Smith 1994). The most telling evidence of a growing Mexican presence is the proliferation of *taquerías* 'taco stands,' replacing pizzerias and *cuchifrito* (typical Puerto Rican food) restaurants. Similar growth has occurred in the surrounding states, to such an extent that in the 1990 census Mexicans emerged, surprisingly, as the second largest group of Hispanics (after Puerto Ricans) in three northeastern states (Pennsylvania, Connecticut, New Hampshire) and as the leading group in two states (Vermont and Maine).

Unfortunately, Census data do not provide an exact portrait because, as the Census Bureau has admitted, Latinos have been undercounted consistently, and because the number of undocumented Latinos is unknown. The undercount for Mexicans alone in the state of New York was estimated at over 6,000 (Valdés de Montano and Smith 1994), and Dominican leaders in several states believe that the true number of Dominicans may be twice as high as the official count. Table 10-1 lists the six northeastern states with the largest proportion of Latino residents, and the percentage increase in Latino population in each state between 1990–2000. The number of Hispanics in every state except New York grew by half or more than half. The number in Rhode Island, home to a growing Dominican immigration, almost doubled.

Puerto Ricans still outnumber other residents of Hispanic origin in seven of the region's nine states. Representatives of two other Caribbean nations, the Dominican Republic and Cuba, contribute to the strong Caribbean flavor of the Northeast; this explains why *salsa* in this region usually refers to a Caribbean dance rhythm, not a condiment. But Caribbean Spanish speakers increasingly are in contact with diverse Latin American in-migrants. For example, the Caribbean share of the Latino population in the region's largest city, New York, declined from 72 percent in 1990 to 57 percent in 2000 (Centro 2000). The groups that are

Table 10-1 *Hispanics in six northeast states: state population in millions, percent of state population that is Hispanic, percent of Hispanic population growth from 1990–2000*

State	State population	% Hispanic	Hispanic Population Growth 1990–2000 (%)
New York	19.0	15.1	29.5
Pennsylvania	2.2	3.2	69.7
New Jersey	8.4	13.3	51.10
Massachusetts	6.3	6.7	49.1
Connecticut	3.4	9.4	50.3
Rhode Island	1.0	8.7	98.5

Source: Based on tables and information in Centro (2000)

displacing Caribbeans include, but are not limited to, Ecuadorians and Argentines in New Jersey; Salvadorans, Guatemalans, and Hondurans in Massachusetts; and Peruvians in Connecticut. Mexicans lead in two of the four smallest and most northern states (Maine and Vermont), and Guatemalans occupy third place in Rhode Island. However, in those four states (Maine, Vermont, Rhode Island, New Hampshire), speakers of French or Portuguese swamp Spanish speakers. The Northeast constitutes an extraordinary laboratory for the study of languages in contact, dialects in contact, and the interaction of multilingual and multidialectal contacts.

New York City deserves special mention because (as described in detail in Zentella 1997b) it includes the most diverse mix of Latinos in the region, if not the country. More than 2 million Latinos constitute 27 percent of the city's 8 million residents. It might surprise you to know there are more Spanish speakers in New York City than in thirteen Latin American capitals (García 1997: 6). At least 10,000 representatives from each of fourteen Caribbean, Central and South American nations – and Spain – were recorded in 1990. In 2000, the largest Latino groups in New York City were Puerto Ricans (36.5% of Latinos in NYC) and Dominicans (18%). Cubans have been reduced to 1.9 percent, but South America, principally Colombia, Ecuador, and Peru, with smaller numbers from Argentina, Chile, Bolivia, Venezuela, and Uruguay, contributed 10.9 percent to the Latino population. Central America, principally El Salvador, Panama, and Honduras, with smaller numbers from Guatemala, Nicaragua, and Costa Rica, contributed 4.6 percent. The category of Other Latinos (18.6%) was inflated by miscategorized Dominicans and Colombians. By 2010, immigrants from Central and South America will outnumber Caribbeans in New York City for the first time. The Puerto Rican proportion of the city has been declining steadily (from 61 percent in 1980 to 36.5 percent in 2000), as Puerto Ricans move out of the Northeast (Florida and Puerto Rico are popular destination choices) and as new arrivals outpace them. The most dramatic growth among Latinos in New York City occurred among Salvadorans, whose numbers multiplied 280 percent between 1980 and 1990. Most significantly, the new century has witnessed the Mexicanization of Puerto Rican neighborhoods.

Given this statistical portrait, you can see why it would be unwise to assume that any Latinos you met in the Northeast would be Puerto Rican. It is always best to ask. Most non-Puerto Ricans make a point of distinguishing themselves from Puerto Ricans because they are proud of their homeland, which is to be expected, but many also try to avoid the stigma that is unfairly attached to Puerto Ricans. Puerto Ricans were the first non-European, Spanish-speaking, and racially mixed population to arrive in great numbers a generation after the massive European immigrations of the early twentieth century had become assimilated. They confronted discrimination in housing, education, health, and the legal system, and the scars from those battles are still visible. Latinos who are anxious to disassociate themselves from the poverty, drop-out rates, and crime that plague lower-working-class Puerto Rican ghettoes often do not realize how much of what they are able to achieve is due to the early efforts of Puerto Ricans. They also ignore the extent to which each group's progress is shaped by factors beyond its control. The most important factors not only affect a group's overall success, they determine the English and Spanish skills that its members maintain, develop, or lose. Principally, they involve the historical and political relationship between the USA and each group's homeland; when, why, and how each group came to the USA; the skills, education, and racial features of the émigrés; and the socioeconomic conditions of the areas where they ended up. Also crucial are the prevailing attitudes towards immigrants in general and toward specific groups of Latinos and dialects of Spanish in particular. Within a few years after arriving, most newcomers learn hard lessons about the tyranny of the black versus white dichotomy in the USA, which may assign brother to one race and sister to another, while it ignores the culture of both.

A comparison of the distinct in-migration experiences of the Latinos in the Northeast is beyond the scope of this chapter, but some crucial contrasts must be noted. The situation of Puerto Ricans is unique because those born on the island, which has been a territory of the USA since 1898, as well as those born on the US mainland, are all US citizens. They were the first Latin Americans to come to the east coast in large waves, and they did so because of the social and economic upheavals caused by direct US control of their homeland. In contrast, other Caribbean, Central and South American in-migrants come from independent nations, where US responsibility for the impoverished conditions is less direct and uninterrupted. In Puerto Rico, the US government imposed English-Only policies in the schools and the courts for fifty years (from 1898 to 1948), and it still controls the island's commerce, banking, education, and legal system. When US control was threatened by a growing nationalist fervor for independence, officials attempted to de-populate the island by persecuting its leaders, sterilizing its women, drafting its men, and exporting its workers (Maldonado-Denis 1972). The high point of Puerto Rican in-migration occurred after World War II, between

1945 and 1955, almost two decades before civil rights legislation tackled the unfair practices to which Blacks and Latinos were subjected. A direct flight from San Juan to New York City helped transport cheap labor to the farms and sweat shops of the Northeast. Puerto Ricans faced many of the problems that earlier non-English speaking in-migrants faced, but they carried the additional burden of being "racialized" (Urciuoli 1996), which means that they were viewed as a racial group instead of as an ethnic group. Moreover, gatekeepers in the schools, hospitals, social service agencies, and courts favored the Americanization model that they believed had worked for their grandparents, and "English-Only" was central to that model. The inapplicability of that model to people who were born US citizens in a Spanish-speaking territory of the USA, and who move back and forth between that territory and the mainland depending on economic conditions created by the USA, caused problems that remain unsolved. Since 1980, the majority of Puerto Ricans living in the continental USA were born and raised on the mainland and not in Puerto Rico, making them unique among Latinos in the Northeast. The education and employment figures of the second generation are better than those of the first, but Puerto Ricans remain among the poorest of all groups in the USA.

The circumstances of Puerto Ricans differ significantly from those of Cubans, Dominicans, and Colombians, the majority of whom were born and raised in Latin America and began emigrating in large numbers during the 1960s. The first of three major Cuban migrations followed Fidel Castro's victory in Cuba in 1959. With substantial assistance from the US government, most of its middle-class members settled in Florida, but a good number went to New York, where the majority of Cubans in the USA lived before the revolution, and to New Jersey. In the Dominican Republic, the death of its long-standing dictator in 1961, a subsequent civil war and US invasion in 1965, and the Immigration Act of 1965 – which abolished the national origin quota system – triggered the beginning of a huge exodus. In its wake, New York City has become "the capital of Dominicans abroad," hosting "the largest concentration of Dominicans outside of their home island" (Pessar 1995: 22). The Upper West Side of Manhattan, especially Washington Heights, is their primary enclave. In contrast, Colombians, who began to arrive in large numbers in the 1970s because jobs at home were scarce and drug wars and terrorism had escalated, did not establish a community in Manhattan. They headed for Jackson Heights, Queens, which became, and remains, the home of more than half of the Colombians in New York.

Much has been made of the willingness of Americans to welcome those who fled dictatorships or political persecution. The Cuban exodus, for example, "pulled at the very heart of American patriotism and sense of justice and compassion" (Boswell and Curtis 1983: 58). But the cool reception given to other persecuted groups, Dominicans and Haitians in particular, suggests that racial prejudices played a role. Cuba's population is approximately one fourth black or mulatto, and Colombia's Chocó region is almost all black, but the overwhelming majority of those who left Cuba and Colombia beginning in the 1960s were white and middle class, which facilitated their adjustment. The dark skin and lower-working-class background of most Dominicans made their adjustment more similar to that of Puerto Ricans. And the 125,000 Cubans who came in the 1980 flotillas, 20 percent of whom were black, were received with hostility, even by previous Cuban migrants (Boswell and Curtis 1984).

In any case, Latinos who arrived in and after the 1960s found that cities in the Northeast were used to Spanish speakers, and could provide some appropriate services. Also, they were able to count on the Puerto Rican community, including its *bodegas* ('grocery stores' that specialize in Latin American foodstuffs), to make their transition easier. One Dominican who moved to New York City in 1962 recalls: "In those early years, we Dominicans were helped a lot by Puerto Ricans who already knew the ropes. I and most of my friends started out by living as boarders with Puerto Rican families. Puerto Ricans also helped us when we needed our own apartment or a job" (Pessar 1995: 23). As varied national-origin communities established themselves in specific neighborhoods, they attracted more arrivals from their homelands as well as members of newer Spanish-speaking exoduses, particularly Mexicans, Ecuadorians, Guatemalans, Salvadorans. Eventually, those who found jobs away from the big cities encouraged new migrant trends. They revitalized communities like Providence, RI, where Dominicans lead the growth rate, and Poughkeepsie, NY, where émigrés from Oaxaca, Mexico became one tenth of the town's population in the 1990s (Berger 1999: A29). In the twenty-first century, it is likely that Latin Americans fleeing economic crises, civil wars, hurricanes, earthquakes, and political repression will continue to believe that moving to the Northeast will make their dreams come true.

The dreams of some have been realized more than the dreams of others. Due to the demographic, political, racial, and socioeconomic factors outlined above, Cuban, Colombian and other South American immigrants have the highest income and education levels among US Latinos, while Mexicans, Puerto Ricans, and Dominicans have the lowest (Institute for Puerto Rican Policy 1995). Compare the rates of those who lived below the poverty level in 1996: 36 percent of Puerto Ricans, 31 percent of Mexicans, 21 percent of Central and South Americans (high rates of Dominican poverty included), 17 percent of Cubans, and 9 percent of non-Hispanic Whites (US Bureau of the Census 1998). Surprisingly, proficiency in English is not as important a determinant of income as most advocates of "English-Only" laws would claim. The great majority of Latinos (circa 90 percent) in the USA speak English, and Spanish is being lost faster than other languages were lost in early twentieth-century America (Crawford 1999). Yet Latinos who are monolingual in English do not necessarily earn more than Spanish monolinguals. The per-capita income of Latinos who lived in Jackson Heights and Elmhurst (both in Queens), where 36 percent of the Latinos were monolingual in Spanish, was almost double that of Latinos in Mott Haven (the Bronx, a borough of the City of New York), where 27 percent of the Latinos were monolingual in English (García 1995). Sadly, the loss of Spanish does not guarantee economic advantages, while it causes intergenerational and identity conflicts. Increasingly, the second generation cannot speak Spanish and two-thirds of the first, or immigrant, generation also shift to English as their primary language within fifteen years of arrival (NCLR 1992). The middle class that learned to read and write Spanish at school in their native country, and then found it advantageous for employment or education in their new country, have the best chance of holding on to Spanish. The global economy of the twenty-first century will require more bilinguals, but unless language and educational policies change, working-class Latinos will be left behind because they will be increasingly monolingual, in English.

The factors that affect each national-origin community's chances of making money and keeping its language also play a vital role in the identity or identities that its members adopt. Traditionally, US history books have promoted the "melting pot" view of America that levels all differences and produces similarly assimilated Americans. Other images, that of the "salad bowl" or "mosaic," convey the idea that groups maintain their distinctive features but work together for the greater good. All of these interpretations of US society presume that the most desirable goal is the wholesale integration of different cultures that have severed all other ties. In contrast, contemporary analyses of international migration reject the popular "bimodal framework that assumed one of two outcomes – either permanent settlement or permanent return . . . ," and the "decoupling of, and discontinuity between, the two locales" that such a framework implies (Pessar 1997: 1). Based primarily on the experiences of Caribbean migrants and other Latin Americans who do not fit the "settler–sojourner model," researchers call for "a more dynamic approach that affirms transnational identities, processes, and structures. . . ." (Pessar 1997: 3). Language plays a critical role in the formation of transnational identities. Speakers who continue to speak like their compatriots demonstrate that they have not severed connections to their native country. In every Latino *barrio* 'neighborhood,' the vitality of those connections is apparent in the proliferation of goods and services that tie family members in the States to those in Latin America. Check cashing and money transfer agencies are at the top of the list. The money Latinos send home, which is estimated at hundreds of millions of dollars per year in New York City alone, is a major source of income for entire Latin American nations, and of lucrative profits for the business owners in the USA (Lin 1991).

A walk down any *barrio* main street will take you past restaurants that serve *comida típica* 'native food,' long distance telephone calling booths, travel agencies, international shippers and movers, and newspaper stands that sell some of the twenty-five Spanish-language dailies that are flown into the Northeast each day. Unlike generations of earlier immigrants who had to wait days before they received word when an emergency occurred, many of today's new Americans keep in frequent touch with families thousands of miles away. The accessibility of global telecommunications and the ease of pre-paid phone cards, for those who can afford them, make calls more likely than letters. The telephone keeps them abreast of news on the home front, and it also keeps them in touch with the local ways of speaking. Native pronunciations, vocabulary, intonation, greetings, leave takings, jokes, narratives, and so forth, are all instantiations of the home culture, which sustain transnational identities abroad. Part of the satisfaction in calling home is re-connecting with particular individuals, and with the words, sounds, and uses of language that you were raised with, and that you identify with "being an X" for example, a Dominican from el Cibao, a Mexican from Puebla, and so on. In many Northeast cities, people from the same Latin American country or region congregate in churches, social clubs, soccer teams, and so on to share those feelings of mutual understanding. But frequent interaction with Spanish speakers from other countries, and the dominant role of English, change some of the ways in which Spanish is spoken and used. In particular, because Latinos from different countries face similar obstacles in adapting to life in the USA – and discuss them using the words and ways of speaking that reflect those experiences – they contribute to the formation of a pan-Latino identity that crosses national boundaries.

Transnational identities and pan-Latino identities are not necessarily in competition. Sometimes individuals stress their national origin, particularly when asked, "What are you?," but at other times they identify themselves as part of the larger Latino or Hispanic population in the USA. This is particularly true for those of the second generation, like me, with parents from two different Latino backgrounds – in my case, Puerto Rican and Mexican. And those of us who live, study, and work with African Americans often incorporate them in our "we" or *nosotros*, in recognition of our mutual minority status. The multiple identities that Latinos in the Northeast can adopt are reflected in and communicated by the bilingual and multidialectal repertoires that many command. One Puerto Rican *bloque* 'block' in New York City's East Harlem was home to five varieties of Spanish (Popular Puerto Rican, Cuban, and Dominican Spanish, Standard Puerto Rican Spanish, English-dominant Spanish), and four varieties of English (Puerto Rican English, African American Vernacular English, "Spanish-ized" English, Standard New York City English) (Zentella 1997a). Not every community member could speak all the dialects, but all community members heard them on a daily basis (except that the Cubans lived there for only three years). Specific gender and age networks were linked to specific dialects. For example, the primary code of the young US-born mothers was Puerto Rican English, but they also communicated in African American Vernacular English (AAVE), Popular Puerto Rican Spanish, and Standard New York City English. In addition, the daily purchases they made at the Dominican *bodega* and the assistance they provided Cuban immigrants helped them understand two more Spanish dialects.

Other communities provide other mixes, but the results are the same: Latinos in working-class *barrios* learn to negotiate linguistic and cultural diversity with an ease that most middle-class Anglos do not have. Young Latino writers put their multi-dialectal skills to good use in their English novels, poetry, and short stories, but readers who are stumped by AAVE expressions, sentence-long switches to Spanish, one-word insertions from various dialects of Spanish, or imitations of Spanish-influenced (Hispanicized) English cannot appreciate their work fully. The author of *Drown* (Díaz 1996) conveys a Dominican teenager's adventures in New Jersey by seamlessly merging many ways of speaking. Readers who don't understand "a dope idea," "*vaina*," "mad paper," "the same *flaca*," "dis," "a *pendejo* cop," "*yo ando más que un perro*," "tagged," "*Quisqueya*," "an expression of *askho* on his face," and "jewel luv it" can still follow the story, but they will miss a lot of the "flava."

Spanish language in the Northeast

Few Latinos can identify the national origin of every Spanish speaker because there are almost two dozen Spanish-speaking nations, and within each nation there are regional and class dialects. Nearly everyone thinks they know a Mexican accent when they hear one, but not every Mexican speaks like Cantinflas or the great Mexican singers whose movies made them famous throughout Latin America; Mexico is a big country with many regional varieties and class and ethnic distinctions. Usually, Latinos are able to recognize their own compatriots by their Spanish, and sometimes they know what people from neighboring countries sound like. In the Northeast, however, they meet Spanish speakers who were born far from their homeland, including representatives from each of the five major dialect regions of Latin American Spanish: the Caribbean, Mexico, the Andes, Río Plata, and Chile (Henríquez Ureña 1970). The more they interact with Spanish speakers from other countries, the more they learn to associate particular vocabulary items, intonation patterns, and variations in pronunciation with specific countries, and sometimes they adopt them.

How different are the dialects of Spanish that Latinos in the Northeast speak, and exactly how do they differ? In fact, the Spanish dialects of Latin America are more similar to each other than are the Spanish dialects of Spain, or the English dialects of the world. That's because they are younger than the dialects of Spain and more geographically united than the dialects of English, so they have undergone comparatively fewer changes. Also, the Royal Academy of the Spanish Language attempts to regulate the language via its dictionaries and grammatical pronouncements. As a result, all Spanish speakers can understand each other after they get used to the words and pronunciations that make each dialect unique. In the Northeast, the most frequently heard dialects are those of the Caribbean – Puerto Rico, the Dominican Republic, and Cuba.

The Caribbean was the cradle of the Spanish language in the Americas. Columbus claimed the islands of the Taíno Indians, known today as the Spanish Antilles, on his first and second trips (1492, 1493), more than two decades before Cortés landed in Mexico. Within a few years, Santo Domingo, DR (1496), San Juan, PR (1508), and Havana, Cuba (1514) were bustling ports where the galleons from Spain unloaded settlers and slaves and replenished their supplies before embarking for the South American mainland. Santo Domingo was the first seat of government for Spain's administrators, and it established the first Spanish institutions in the conquered lands – a cathedral, hospital, and university. As the Spaniards encountered new flora, fauna, and ways of life, they adapted, created, or borrowed new words, which spread to the other colonies and were adopted in Spain also. The Taíno and African vocabulary that took hold in the Caribbean includes words that are part of the world's Spanish today, some of which have made their way into English and other languages. Others are known only in the Caribbean, and still others are unique to Cuba, Puerto Rico, or the Dominican Republic, where they originated. The following list has a few examples of popular words in each category:

Indigenismos 'words of Indian origin'   *Africanismos* 'words of African origin'

In world-wide Spanish, and borrowed by other languages

huracán	'hurricane'	*banana*	'banana'
canoa	'canoe'	*ñame*	'yam'

Caribbean Spanish

caimito	'a tropical fruit'	*bemba/bembe*	'large lips'
batey	'front yard'	*guineo*	'banana'

Cuba

jimaguas	'twins'	*cumbancha*	'fiesta'
guajiro	'peasant'	*ñampiarse*	'to die'

Dominican Republic

Quisqueya	'mother of all lands' (the DR)	*furufa*	'ugly'
curí	'rabbit'	*mangú*	'dish of boiled mashed plantains'

Puerto Rico

guares	'twins'	*guingambó*	'okra'
jíbaro	'peasant'	*jurutungo*	'distant place'

The few hundred words of Indian and African origin that pepper Caribbean Spanish are overshadowed by the *criollo* vocabulary, that is, words that were invented or changed by the islanders (*criollos*) who came to identify themselves as Dominicans, Cubans, or Puerto Ricans in contrast to the *peninsulares*, settlers born in Spain. Much of the *criollo* vocabulary in the Caribbean is shared, for example, *guayo* 'grater,' *buchipluma* 'falsifier,' *tosta'o* 'crazy' (see the dictionaries of each country's regionalisms: Malaret 1955, Ortiz 1975, Pichardo 1976, Santiestéban 1997). Additionally, each island has unique items that serve as national identifiers, including laments (*Ay bendito* 'Oh, goodness,' PR), terms of address (*Oye, chico* 'Listen, fella,' Cuba), and exclamations (*Anda al diablo* 'damn,' DR). Popular Puerto Rican words are *nene/nena* 'little boy/girl,' *pantallas* 'earrings,' *chiringa* 'kite.' Dominicans say *chele* 'penny,' *aguaita* 'look,' *chichigua* 'kite'; and Cubans say *buró* 'desk,' *tonga* 'pile,' *papalote* 'kite.' The great bulk of the vocabulary of the Caribbean, however, is shared with the entire Spanish-speaking world.

The frequency with which Caribbean vocabulary items are heard throughout the Northeast has led to some lexical leveling. In New York City, for example, Puerto Ricans, Dominicans, Cubans, and Colombians maintain their regional dialect, especially for in-group conversations, but almost everyone has picked up words from one or more of the other dialects (Zentella 1990a). Those that are not easily forgotten are learned the hard way, as a result of embarrassing moments caused when a common term, like the words for "insect" or "papaya," turn out to have a taboo meaning in another dialect. Words that are not taboo, but are very common, become popular in almost everyone's Spanish. If you want to find a local bus or grocery, ask about *la guagua* and *la bodega*; if you are offered a *china*, expect an orange – not a Chinese female; and if you hear *chévere*, something is 'terrific.' A few Caribbean words become generalized, but Caribbean Spanish speakers often make an effort to avoid or translate regionalisms that Latinos from other regions may not understand, and the same courtesy is extended to them. Ultimately, the Spanish vocabulary that is heard in the Northeast descends from the Taíno–African–Spanish mix that took place five hundred years ago in the Caribbean, which is now mixing with dialects from other parts of the Spanish-speaking world. This inter-dialectal mix is further enriched by words that are borrowed from English, as when the competing ways of saying "kite" in at least four dialects of Spanish are neutralized by the widespread adoption of *kite* (Zentella 1990).

The regional origin of Spanish speakers is given away by intonation patterns and pronunciation, even before they are identified by lexical items. The way each group *canta* 'sings' – referring to the customary rise and fall of voices in declarative sentences, or questions, or exclamations, and so on – is distinctive. Both the specific "songs," or intonation contours, and the consonants and vowels of the Spanish of an area, are rooted in the indigenous languages of the original inhabitants, the dialect(s) from Spain spoken by those who settled the area, and the slaves' African languages. Little is known about Taíno and other Indian languages of the Caribbean because the native peoples of that region were virtually exterminated by the middle of the sixteenth century. As a result, scholars believe that the impact of Indian languages on the Spanish of the area was limited. To replace the Indians, Africans were enslaved in large numbers to carry on with the work, especially in the cane fields of lowland areas. Reportedly, the Africans learned Spanish and accommodated quickly to their European masters' culture (Rosario 1970: 13), but stigmatized pronunciations are often falsely assumed to have originated with them. Lipski (1994: 96) maintains that speakers of west African languages, particularly KiKongo, Kimbundu/Umbundu, Yoruba, Efik, Igbo, Ewe/Fon, and Akan, accelerated or reinforced Spanish pronunciations that corresponded to their own, but they originated very few features, which are now rare. As for the origin of the Spaniards who settled the Caribbean colonies, immigration figures point to southern Spain (Andalusia), as do the characteristics of present day Andalusian Spanish. The colonists and sailors who came from Andalusia had a greater impact on Spanish in the Caribbean and ports all along the coasts of Central and South America than did speakers of Castilian, the principal dialect of north central Spain (Canfield 1981, Cotton and Sharp 1988). The Castilian-speaking clerics and administrators sent by the crown to the predominantly inland seats of power left their mark on the Spanish of those cities – Mexico, Lima, and Cuzco, for example – as did the principal Indian languages and cultures that were not exterminated. In any case, as is true of the dialects of Latin America and Spain today, Andalusian and Castilian varieties of Spanish were enough alike during colonization that "few Castilians or Andalusians had to significantly modify their speech in order to communicate with one another" (Lipski 1994: 46).

The regular and extended contact of Andalusian Spanish with African languages and with the remnants of Indian languages and cultures in Latin America's ports during the colonial era explains why dialects in very distant countries, for example, Guayaquil, Ecuador and the Dominican Republic, resemble each other today. "Coastal/lowland dialects show a homogeneity over vast geographical expanses . . . ," and "the phonetic similarities between coastal Latin American Spanish and Andalusian Spanish are striking . . ." (Lipski 1994: 8). The expanse referred to includes Cuba, the Dominican Republic, Puerto Rico, the Atlantic and Pacific coasts of Mexico, Central America's Pacific coast, Venezuela, and the Pacific coast of South America from Colombia to northern Chile. The phonetic similarities that speakers from this region share in their informal, popular Spanish, and that distinguish them from speakers raised in the interior highlands of Mexico, Central and South America, are few and primarily affect consonants. The principal phonetic markers, which are heard every day in the Northeast, are the following:

(1) /s/ (which may be written with an <s> or <z>) may be aspirated (pronounced like the /h/ in *her*) or deleted altogether when it is at the end of a syllable or a word:
andaluz /andaluh/ or /andalu/   'Andalusian'
estos costeños   /ehtoh kohteñoh/ or /eto koteño/   'these coastal people'

(2) the letters <g> (before <e>, <i>), and <j> are aspirated, not pronounced as a fricative, as in the German pronunciation of "Bach":
gente joven   /hente hoven/   'young people'

(3) /-n/ at the end of words sounds like the final sound in "sing" /sɪŋ/. It may be deleted and the vowel that remains becomes nasalized:
sin ton ni son   /siŋ toŋ ni soŋ/ or /sĩ tõ ni sõ/   'without rhyme or reason'

(4) syllable-final and word-final /l/ and /r/ are often difficult to distinguish, particularly in the speech of the least educated. (Many Asians who speak English as a second language also neutralize /l/ and /r/, but

in Spanish this occurs in final position only.) Sometimes final /l/ is realized as [r] but, more frequently, syllable final /r/ is realized as [l], for example:

delantal /delantar/ 'apron'; *reportar* /repoltal/ 'to report'

(5) /d/ between vowels is deleted: *almidonado* /almionao/ 'starched'.

Of these variations, the deletion or aspiration of syllable-final or word-final /-s/ (see (1), hereafter referred to as "final /s/") is most commented on, and the debate reveals contrasting cultural attitudes toward the pronunciation of /s/. Spanish speakers who are not from the coastal areas of Latin America criticize the aspiration or loss of /s/ so mercilessly that I refer to the phenomenon as "the tyranny of –s." Their insistence that "the best Spanish" is one that pronounces every word as it is written is their basis for arguing that Colombia deserves that honor. Ignorant of the Andalusian origin and African strengthening of the aspirated or deleted final /s/ in Caribbean Spanish – or perhaps because of it – and of the Castilian and Indian roots of its maintenance in Bogotá and other highland dialects, they view deletion or aspiration as the sloppy habits of low-status speakers. In fact, the widespread instability of final /s/ throughout the coastal areas and, in particular, the high rates of aspiration among Cubans and Puerto Ricans and of deletion among Dominicans (Terrell 1982a, b) are maintained as a consequence of negative attitudes towards the stressing of final /s/, especially in informal speech.

In formal settings, like judicial proceedings or poetry readings, educated speakers in the Caribbean tend to pronounce final /s/. But otherwise, rapid fire pronunciations of final /s/ communicate vanity, self-importance, or – in males – effeminacy (Rosario 1970: 81, Nuñez Cedeño 1980). Dominicans, in particular, ridicule compatriots who emphasize final /-s/, accusing them of "*hablando fiSno*," ('talking fine,' with an intrusive /s/ in *fino*) or of "*comiendo eSpaguettiS*" ('eating spaghetti,' said stressing each /s/). In the Northeast, then, the Caribbean preference for the aspiration or deletion of final /s/, which has meaningful cultural implications for them, is stigmatized by speakers from Colombia and the interior regions of South America. Since many of the critics enjoy higher academic, racial, and socioeconomic status than those they criticize, speakers of Caribbean Spanish suffer heightened feelings of linguistic insecurity, which encourage the loss of Spanish and exacerbate their social and educational problems (Zentella 1990a). The irony is that while the aspiration or deletion of final /s/ is discredited, the aspiration of /s/ at the beginning of a syllable or between vowels (hereafter referred to as "initial /s/"), which occurs in the central highlands of Colombia but not in the Caribbean, is ignored. Even highly educated *cachacos* (Colombians from the central highlands) say /pahamos/ instead of /pasamos/ for *pasamos* 'we pass,' and aspirate the first /s/ in words with more than one, for example, *asesino* /ahesino/ 'assassin.' In fact, ". . . central Colombia is unique in the Spanish-speaking world in reducing /s/ more frequently in syllable-initial than in syllable-final position" (Lipski 1994: 209). Nor is Colombia free of final /s/ aspiration or deletion, both of which are common in the *costeño* 'coastal' Spanish spoken in Cartagena and Barranquilla on the Caribbean coast, and along the Pacific coast.

The details about consonants and vowels in Spanish dialects are important because they prove that judgments concerning linguistic correctness are actually social judgments, that is, they are not based on linguistic facts but on group fears, involving class and racial prejudices. An educated Latino elite can attack pronunciations of the poor that deviate from the written standard, but ignore their own deviations conveniently. It is not the aspiration or deletion of /s/ in itself that is "good" or "bad," but the way it is evaluated by those in authority. The /r/ after vowels suffers a similar fate in Northeast English. Pronouncing *hunter* or *New York* without the /r/, for example, is stereotyped as working-class "New Yawkese" and looked down upon. But /r/ after vowels is also deleted in the "King's English" in England, which enjoys high prestige, and in New England the Kennedys and other wealthy families are proud to be alumni of Ha:vad. The fact that the same feature can be a source of humiliation in one community and a source of pride in another proves that rules about how to speak "correctly" always favor the more powerful.

When Latinos are asked to imitate members of their own or other Spanish-speaking groups, they produce the same few items consistently. The stereotypical markers that identify Puerto Ricans, Dominicans, Cubans, and Mexicans sometimes incite feelings of linguistic incompetence, but most continue to be popular because they communicate the uniqueness of each group.

The velar R in Puerto Rican Spanish (PRS): *arrastrar la doble rr*

In PRS, the pairs *corro* 'I run' and *cojo* 'I take,' *Ramón* (man's name) and *jamón* 'ham' can sound similar. The Spanish trilled r, which is written as a single <r> at the beginning of words and as a double <rr> in the middle of words, sounds like a drum roll in most varieties of Spanish. Speakers of PRS sometimes have a velar R instead, akin to the raspy German ch in Bach, which some refer to as *arrastrar la doble rr* 'to drag the double <rr>.' Sometimes it can be less raspy and sound closer to the English <h> as in 'her,' in which case the distinction between <rr> or initial <r> and <j> may be lost, as in *corro* and *cojo*, *Ramón* and *jamón*. At the beginning of the twentieth century, the velar R was more prevalent in the northwest and southeast of the island, and among the lower working class. By the 1960s it had spread to about half the population in all municipalities and social classes (Navarro Tomás 1948, Rosario 1970); urban sprawl since then has undoubtedly extended its domain. Velar R is often regarded as unique to PRS, but Canfield (1981: 44) cites it for the extreme southeast of the Dominican Republic, and Varela (1992: 54) assures us that it is "*un hábito lingüístico general*" 'a general linguistic habit' in Cuban Spanish. Negative attitudes toward velar R in Spanish run high and contribute to its users' feelings of linguistic insecurity, but that is not the case in other languages that have a similar R, for example, French and Brazilian Portuguese. It may be that the trilled /r/ in Spanish is in the process of becoming more like the velar R of other Romance languages, with Puerto Ricans and other Caribbean Spanish speakers in the vanguard of that change.

Syllable final /r/ and /1/ in Dominican Spanish: *hablar con la i*

El Cibao, the impoverished agricultural region of the Dominican Republic that was home to the bulk of Dominicans now in the USA, is stereotyped as replacing the /r/ in syllable final position with /i/, for example, *cantar> cantai* 'to sing,' *cuarto> cuaito* 'room,' 'money' (this is called "vocalization"). Because, as explained earlier, final /r/ and /l/ can be neutralized in Caribbean Spanish – or /r/ can be realized as /l/ – some working-class speakers extend the vocalization of /r/ to words with an /l/ at the end of a syllable, for example, *maldito > maidito* 'damned,' *capital > capitai* 'capital city.' These pronunciations, which were heard throughout the Caribbean up to the nineteenth century, are archaisms that remain in the north central Cibao region, particularly in the speech of its older, less educated, and more rural inhabitants (Jorge Morel 1974). Since many poor immigrants came from that economically hard hit area, *hablar con la i* 'to talk with the i' is an expression mistakenly used to stereotype all Dominicans. Syllable-final /r/ and /l/ are unstable in much of the Caribbean, but they undergo different changes in different regions of the Dominican Republic. The word *carne* 'meat,' for example, can be pronounced four different ways in the Dominican Republic: North /kaine/, Capital area in South /kalne/, Southeast /kanne/, Southwest /karne/ (Canfield 1981: 44). Educated speakers in all areas maintain the traditional Spanish pronunciation, the one favored in the Southwest.

Cuban Spanish gemination

Cubans are known for dropping syllable final /l/ and /r/ and doubling the following consonant (a process called gemination), for example, *porque* > /poːkke/ (where ː indicates a long vowel), *Alberto* > /aːbbeːtto/. The island's regional and class variations are not represented fully in the USA because the early post-revolution immigrants were predominantly middle class, and because Cubans have not had regular contact with the dialects of their island for forty years as a result of hostile US–Cuba relations. No communities in the Northeast can match Dade County – where Miami is – in size, power, or the viability of its Spanish. But many of the darker skinned Cubans who left Cuba beginning in 1980 did not feel welcome in Miami, and some chose to join the Cubans in New Jersey and New York. As a result, "the majority of Cuban nonwhites live in the northeastern Unites States, where the reputation for racial tolerance is better than in the South" (Boswell and Curtis 1984: 103). The Spanish of the late twentieth-century arrivals revealed recent innovations in Cuban Spanish, especially in the speech of males of "low socioeconomic extraction." Guitart (1992) claims that these *Cheos* (a nickname like "Mac"), round the front vowels /i/ and /e/ and lower their pitch, and that these features represent a "defiant Macho talk" that separates its speakers from middle-class Cubans. In contrast, Varela (1992) maintains that exiles from all regions of Cuba and all three immigration waves do not differ markedly in their pronunciation, except for the influence of English on those born in the USA. But Varela's study is limited to residents of Miami and New Orleans, and it does not specify the socioeconomic strata included. Varela believes that Miami Cuban Spanish in general differs in fluency, pronunciation, and vocabulary from that spoken by Cubans in New York and other states, but those differences have yet to be studied.

Mixtecan Mexican Spanish vowels

The majority of Mexicans who live in the Northeast come from the Mixteca region of Mexico, specifically the states of Puebla, Oaxaca, and Guerrero (Valdés de Montano and Smith 1994). Whereas coastal Mexican Spanish deletes final /–s/, as occurs in the Caribbean, the Mixteca conserves final consonants. Instead, all of central Mexico is known for frequently reducing unstressed vowels, so that *pues* 'well then' is rendered as /ps/, and I have heard /skrets/ for *secretos* 'secrets.' The reduction of vowels before /–s/ serves to make their /–s/ even more prominent. Another feature that distinguishes the Mixtecans in the Northeast are the lexical items that come from Nahuatl, for example, *chamaco* 'young boy,' *cacahuate* 'peanut.'

The migration consists primarily of young men under twenty-five – so many in fact that their hometowns have become "nurseries and nursing homes" that survive on remittances from workers in the Northeast (Valdés de Montano and Smith 1994: 4). In order to help their families back home as much as possible, they may work long hours and share crowded living spaces with compatriots, which affords them few opportunities to learn formal English and little time to socialize with other Spanish speakers. Those who work in the northern New England states have contact with fewer varieties of Spanish than those in New York or New Jersey, and are more likely to be influenced by the Portuguese or French of co-workers. Isolation from families, compatriots, other Spanish speakers, or English speakers has an impact on immigrants' social well being and acclimation to the USA, as well as on their language development. Linguistically, much depends on whether this predominantly young population marries Mexicans, Anglos, Spanish speakers from the Caribbean or other countries, or members of non-Latino ethnic and racial groups who share their workplaces and neighborhoods. When my Mexican father married my Puerto Rican mother in 1929, the Latino community in New York City was so small that its members were compelled to learn about, and from, each other. Nowadays it is easier to stay in communication with your family in Latin America, and to remain insulated within your group in the USA. On the other hand, the sheer numbers of, and proximity to, speakers of diverse varieties of Spanish in the populous cities of the Northeast occasion a great deal of inter-dialectal communication and accommodation. Nowhere are the repercussions of this inter-Latino contact more evident than in the Spanish of members of the second generation.

"Nuyoricans," "Dominican Yorks," and "Spanglish"

The expression "hyphenated Americans" refers to members of ethnic groups who identify themselves as Americans with roots in another country, such as German-Americans and Italian-Americans. Often, they are monolingual in English, socially assimilated, and structurally incorporated. Some Latinos who know English identify themselves in similar ways, for example as Mexican-Americans or Cuban-Americans, but most prefer to be identified as "Mexicans," "Cubans," and so on (de la Garza et al. 1992). In communities with significant numbers of US-born or US-raised youth, however, new terms that reflect a more integrated dual identity have appeared, such as Nuyoricans, Rochestericans, Dominican Yorks. These young people usually are English-dominant, and the Spanish they speak reflects that reality. Despite having been made to feel ashamed of their Spanish by critics who deride it as "Spanglish," many are rehabilitating the labels that "diss" their languages and identities. Engaging in a process of semantic inversion that recalls African Americans' success in turning "Black" from a negative to a positive description in the 1960s, some Latino youth embrace "Spanglish," "Nuyorican," "Dominican York," and so on, as proud emblems of their hybrid identities and ways of speaking.

While poets formed the vanguard of this affirmative movement (see Algarín and Piñero 1975), linguists contributed by analyzing the complex grammatical rules that bilinguals must know in order to be effective code-switchers – the linguistic term for talking in two languages or dialects, sometimes in the same sentence. Many studies have proven that Spanish–English code-switchers usually switch complete sentences, or insert nouns or short phrases from one language into another (details in chapters 5 and 6 of Zentella 1997a). Bilinguals code switch to accomplish meaningful communicative strategies with other bilinguals, and to express their participation in two worlds graphically. But the stereotypical view is that only people who don't know Spanish or English well speak Spanglish, and that they have created a new pidgin or creole (see chapter 8). Words that Spanish speakers have borrowed from English (anglicisms) are offered as proof of the new language, although the latest compilation of (Miami) Spanglish words includes fewer than 100 loans (Cruz and Teck 1998). Most of the Spanglish vocabulary in the Northeast reflects life in urban centers, and even Spanish monolinguals pick up words like *bildin* 'building,' *par-taim* 'part-time,' *frizando* 'freezing,' *boila* 'boiler,' *biper* 'beeper,' *trobol* 'trouble.' They have become part of the region's Spanish vocabulary.

The English origin of these loans is obvious and direct, but it is less direct in words like *librería*, *aplicación*, *soportar*, *papel*, *regresar* – Spanish words that have taken on new meanings because they sound similar to, or overlap semantically with, words in English (cf. Otheguy 1993). In addition to their original meanings ('book store,' 'application' as in 'a coat of paint,' 'to bear,' 'paper/stationery,' 'to return/go back'), they are acquiring definitions that are influenced by English. *Librería* is used for 'library' instead of *biblioteca*, *aplicación* for a job application instead of *solicitud*, *soportar* for 'to support someone financially' instead of *mantener*, *papel* for newspaper instead of *periódico*, and *regresar* for 'return an item' instead of *devolver*. The loans and calques of US Latinos constitute an additional inventory in the Spanish vocabulary that newcomers learn, along with the unfamiliar words of other Spanish-speaking countries. Newcomers follow the principle that all speakers use when they encounter new words in new settings: "I guess that's the way they say it here."

Earlier I explained that most working-class Latinos are undergoing language loss; the process of attrition is most obvious in the limited range of Spanish tenses and moods commanded by the US born. Tenses beyond the present, preterit, and imperfect are the last to be learned and the first to be lost, as documented by Silva-Corvalán (1994) in Los Angeles and reaffirmed (except for the West Coast changes in *ser/estar* 'to be') by Zentella (1997a) for East Harlem. Communication among generations is still possible because speakers have learned to accommodate to each other, but a grasp of formal oral and written Spanish eludes most of the poor in every generation. Loss is accelerated for those who have little contact with Spanish speakers, while those who work or live with newcomers may reinvigorate their language skills. The process is rarely predictable on an individual level because changes in relationships, schools, jobs, residence, language policies and general attitudes cause changes in language skills. But the overall shift to English is accelerating among those born in the USA, and they constitute the majority of Latinos in the country. Even "younger immigrants anglicize [switch to English] very rapidly and subsequently give birth to children of English mother tongue" (Veltman 1990: 120). Sadly, the loss of Spanish does not translate into academic success. In 1996, US-born Latinos of US-born parents, a generation that is overwhelmingly monolingual in English, had higher drop out rates than US-born Latinos with immigrant parents (Waggoner 1999).

The Latino century?

The 1980s and the 1990s were both hailed as the "decade of the Hispanics" because of increased Latino immigration, but Latino concerns never became a vital part of the national agenda. As we enter a new century, analyses of domestic problems continue to be polarized along black/white lines, with little room for class, ethnic, multiracial or multilingual views. Many Latinos support Black civil rights struggles because they themselves are viewed as non-whites and have experienced similar oppression. As evidence, young Latinos in the Northeast – of dark and light complexions – often speak English like African Americans, and a (very) few African Americans have learned some Spanish. But the diversity of Latinos is seldom acknowledged, and little is known about the issues that separate specific groups, like abortion or the death penalty, or positions that are defended by the majority, like support for bilingual education and the repudiation of English-Only laws (Zentella 1990b). When Latinos are portrayed as a monolithic horde of "illegal aliens" that threatens the future of English and the American way of life (see also Crawford 1992, Zentella 1997b), it fuels fears that erupt into anti-Latino, anti-Spanish violence, even murder. The Latino Coalition of Racial Justice was formed to denounce the escalation of bias incidents in New York City, including the 1994 murder of an Ecuadorian immigrant who was beaten to death by a gang that was "yelling obscene epithets about Mexicans" (Steinhauer 1994).

Respect for new Americans of diverse Latino backgrounds must be rooted in respect for their distinct ways of speaking Spanish, which symbolize their connection to their homeland, and for the pan-Latino varieties of English and Spanish that reflect their new allegiances. But notions of linguistic correctness that are based on class, regional, and racial prejudices foster invidious inter-group and intra-group comparisons by, for example, imposing the tyranny of syllable final –s, dismissing loans as "barbarisms," and accusing "Spanglish" speakers of linguicide. The resulting feelings of insecurity and inferiority contribute to educational failure and social alienation. Moreover, the imposition of a standard English-Only ideology (see chapters 15 and 17) creates a cruel no-win situation, because Latinos who abandon Spanish in the hope of being accepted unconditionally are largely unaware that any vestiges of Spanish in their English are interpreted as being lower class and disorderly (Urciuoli 1996). Unfortunately, so many Americans fear that English is in danger from Spanish that analysts attempt to allay those fears by emphasizing the projected demise of Spanish (Veltman 1990), instead of educating the public about the benefits – for all – of bilingualism. Finally, the fervor and success of the English-Only movement make it difficult for proponents of multilingualism to be heard, and vocal defenders of Spanish are branded as opponents of a lingua franca, or proponents of separatism. It is time for a "language conscious" citizenry that appreciates the complexity of our linguistic heritage and welcomes its new configurations by learning other languages and dialects, to help the USA become linguistically competent and culturally sensitive. Latinos in the Northeast are doing their part by learning the varieties of English and Spanish spoken by their co-workers, just as they are learning to dance to *cumbia*, *merengue*, *son*, *plena*, *corridos*, hip hop, swing; and to eat *arepas*, *mangú*, *boliche*, *pasteles*, *tacos*, pizza, hot dogs, and bagels. What is not clear is whether they will continue to cross racial, cultural, and linguistic boundaries alone, and be forced to relinquish their native language in the process. That is up to many of you.

Suggestions for further reading and exploration

The continued arrival of diverse groups of Latinos to the Northeast is documented in the 2000 Census *http://www.census.gov/main/www/cen2000.html*. Hispanics accounted for 27 percent of the population of New York City (approximately

2 million out of 8 million), and Dominicans will soon outnumber Puerto Ricans there and in other cities. But the study of language in the Northeast is in its infancy, and to date most of it focuses on Puerto Ricans. The Language Policy Task Force of the Centro de Estudios Puertorriqueños, at Hunter College (City University of New York), conducted the earliest research in El Barrio beginning in the 1970s, and their reports are available in the Centro library. Those efforts resulted in significant publications by Pedraza, Attinasi, and Hoffman (1980), Poplack (1980), and Pousada and Poplack (1982), challenging the applicability of diglossia, and negative views of Puerto Rican Spanish grammar and bilingual code switching. Alvarez (1991) analyzes the code switching in Spanish and English narratives of the same community. Beyond the city, the discourse of Puerto Ricans living on Long Island is the subject of a book by Torres (1997), while Ramírez (2000) compares the language attitudes of Puerto Ricans in the Bronx and upstate New York with those of Cubans and Mexicans in other states. Little attention has been paid to the distinctive English dialect of Puerto Ricans, but Urciuoli (1996) includes many samples and analyzes the role of accent in the construction of identities.

Research on language in Dominican and other Spanish-speaking communities is limited. Toribio (2000) explores the language and race links that Dominicans forge in their homeland and adapt to US circumstances, and Bailey (2000) investigates language, race, and identity among bilingual and multidialectal Dominican high school students in Providence, Rhode Island. Some comparative studies include Dominican Spanish. Zentella (1990a) is among the first to compare several Spanish-speaking communities in New York City; the emphasis is on lexical leveling among Cubans, Colombians, Dominicans, and Puerto Ricans. García et al. (1988) reports on language attitudes in two communities, the Dominican upper West Side of Manhattan and a neighborhood in Queens that is home to Dominicans and Colombians. Otheguy, García, and Fernández (1989), an intergenerational study of loans and calques, is devoted to Cuban Spanish in the Northeast. Research currently underway by Otheguy and Zentella on subject pronouns in Colombian, Cuban, Dominican, Ecuadorian, Mexican, and Puerto Rican Spanish in New York promises further insight into Spanish in the Northeast.

References

Algarín, Miguel and Miguel Piñero, eds. 1975. *Nuyorican Poetry*. New York: William Morrow.

Alvarez, Celia. 1991. "Code Switching in Narrative Performance: Social, Structural and Pragmatic Functions in the Puerto Rican Speech Community of East Harlem." In *Sociolinguistics of the Spanish-Speaking World: Iberia, Latin America, the United States*, eds. Carol Klee and Leticia Ramos-García. Tempe AZ: Bilingual Press. Pp. 271–98.

Bailey, Benjamin. 2000. "Language and negotiation of ethnic/racial identity among Dominican Americans." *Language and Society* 29: 555–82.

Baker, Colin. 1996. *Foundations of Bilingual Education and Bilingualism*. Clevedon: Multilingual Matters.

Berger, Joseph. 1999. "Detective's Kindness Helps Awaken a City." *New York Times*, Jan. 7.

Boswell, Thomas D. and James R. Curtis. 1984. *The Cuban-American Experience: Culture, Images, and Perspectives*. Totowa NJ: Rowman and Littlefield.

Canfield, D. Lincoln. 1981. *Spanish Pronunciation in the Americas*. Chicago: University of Chicago Press.

Cotton, Eleanor and John Sharp. 1988. *Spanish in the Americas*. Washington DC: Georgetown University Press.

Cruz, Bill, Bill Teck, and editors of Generation ñ Magazine. 1998. *The Official Spanglish Dictionary: Un user's guía to more than 300 words and phrases that aren't exactly español or inglés*. New York: Simon and Schuster.

de la Garza, Rodolfo, Angelo Falcón, Chris García, and John García. 1992. *Latino National Political Survey: Summary of Findings*. New York: Institute for Puerto Rican Policy.

García, Ofelia. 1995. "Spanish Language Loss as a Determinant of Income among Latinos in the Unites States: Implications for Language Policy in Schools." In *Power and Inequality in Language Education*, ed. James W. Tollefson. Cambridge: Cambridge University Press. Pp. 142–60.

1997. "New York's Multilingualism: World Languages and their Role in a US City." In *The Multilingual Apple: Languages in New York City*, eds. Ofelia García and Joshua Fishman. Berlin: Mouton de Gruyter. Pp. 3–50.

García, Ofelia, Isabel Evangelista, Mabel Martínez, Carmen Disla, and Bonifacio Paulino. 1988. "Spanish Language Use and Attitudes: a Study of Two New York City Communities," *Language in Society* 17: 475–511.

Guitart, Jorge. 1992. "Front Vowel Rounding Among Male Speakers in Cuban Spanish." Paper delivered at Spanish in the US Conference, University of Minnesota, Minneapolis, October 23.

Henríquez Ureña, Pedro. 1970 [1940]. *El español en Santo Domingo*. Buenos Aires: Universidad de Buenos Aires.

Institute for Puerto Rican Policy. 1995. *Institute for Puerto Rican Policy Datanote*, 17, August. New York: IPR.

Jorge Morel, Elercia. 1974. *Estudio lingüístico de Santo Domingo*. Santo Domingo: Editorial Taller.

Lin, W. 1991. "The Money Tie that Binds." *New York Times*, October 18, p. 23.

Lipski, John M. 1994. *Latin American Spanish*. London: Longman.

Malaret, Augusto. 1955. *Vocabulario de Puerto Rico*. New York: Las Américas.

Maldonado-Denis, Manuel. 1972. *Puerto Rico: a Socio-historic Interpretation*. New York: Random House.

National Council of La Raza (NCLR). 1992. *Hispanic Education: a Statistical Portrait 1990*. National Council of La Raza Policy Analysis Center.

Navarro Tomás, Tomás. 1948. *El español en Puerto Rico*. Rio Piedras: Universidad de Puerto Rico.

Nuñez Cedeño, Rafael. 1980. *La fonología moderna y el español de Santo Domingo*. Santo Domingo: El Taller.

Ortiz, Fernando, F. 1975. *Nuevo cataura de cubanismos*. La Habana: Editorial de Ciencias Sociales.

Otheguy, Ricardo. 1993. "A Reconsideration of the Notion of Loan Translation in the Analysis of US Spanish." In *Spanish in the United States: Linguistic Contact and Diversity*, eds. Ana Roca and John M. Lipski. Berlin: Mouton de Gruyter. Pp. 135–54.

Otheguy, Ricardo, Ofelia García, and Mariela Fernández. 1989. "Transferring, Switching, and Modeling in West New York Spanish: an Intergenerational Study," *International Journal of the Sociology of Language* 79: 41–52.

Pedraza, Pedro, John Attinasi, and Gerald Hoffman. 1980. *Rethinking Diglossia* (Language Policy Task Force Working Paper No. 9). New York: Centro de Estudios Puertorriqueños.

Pessar, Patricia R. 1995. *Visa for a Dream*. Needham Heights MA: Allyn and Bacon.

Pessar, Patricia R., ed. 1997. *Caribbean Circuits: New Directions in the Study of Caribbean Migration*. New York: Center for Migration Studies.

Pichardo, Estéban and E. Tapia. 1976. *Diccionario provincial casi-razonado de voces y frases cubanas*, 5th edn. La Habana: Editorial de Ciencias Sociales.

Poplack, Shana. 1980. "Sometimes I'll start a sentence in Spanish *y termino en español*: Toward a Typology of Code-switching," *Linguistics* 18: 581–616.

Pousada, Alicia and Shana Poplack. 1982. "No Case for Convergence: the Puerto Rican Spanish Verb System in a Language Contact Situation." In *Bilingual Education for Hispanic Students in the United States*, eds. Joshua A. Fishman and Gary Keller. New York: Teachers College Press, Columbia University. Pp. 207–40.

Ramírez, Arnulfo G. 2000. "Linguistic Notions of Spanish among Youths from Different Hispanic Groups." In *Research on Spanish in the US: Linguistic Issues and Challenges*, ed. Ana Roca. Somerville MA: Cascadilla Press. Pp. 284–95.

Rosario, Rubén del. 1970. *El español de América*. Sharon CT: Troutman Press.

Santiestéban, Argelio. 1997. *El habla popular cubana de hoy: una tonga de cubichismos que le oí a mi pueblo*, 2nd edn. La Habana: Editorial de Ciencias Sociales.

Silva-Corvalán, Carmen. 1994. *Language Contact and Change: Spanish in Los Angeles*. New York: Oxford University Press.

Steinhauer, Jennifer. 1994. "Killing of Immigrant Stuns a Brooklyn Area." *New York Times*, October 16, Sec. 1, p. 39.

Terrell, Tracy D. 1982a. "Current Trends in the Investigation of Cuban and Puerto Rican Phonology." In *Spanish in the United States: Sociolinguistic Aspects*, eds. Jon Amastae and Lucía Elías-Olivares. Cambridge: Cambridge University Press. Pp. 47–70.

1982b. "Relexificación en el español dominicano: Implicaciones para la educación." In *El español del Caribe: Ponencias del VI simposio de dialectología*, ed. Orlando Alba. Santiago, RD: Universidad Católica Madre y Maestra. Pp. 301–18.

Toribio, Almeida J. 2000. "'Nosotros somos dominicanos.': Language and Self-Definition among Dominicans." In *Research on Spanish in the US: Linguistic Issues and Challenges*, ed. Ana Roca. Somerville MA: Cascadilla Press. Pp. 252–70.

Torres, Lourdes. 1997. *Puerto Rican Discourse: a Sociolinguistic Study of a New York Suburb*. Mahwah NJ: Erlbaum.

Urciuoli, Bonnie. 1996. *Exposing Prejudice: Puerto Rican Experiences of Language, Race, and Class*. Boulder CO: Westview.

US Bureau of the Census 1998. *Selected Economic Characteristics of All Persons and Hispanic Persons, by Type of Origin: March 1997*.

Valdés de Montano, L. M. and R. Smith. 1994. *Mexican Migration to the New York City Metropolitan Area: an Analysis of Selected Socio-Demographic Traits and the Links Being Formed between a Mexican Sending Region and New York*. New York: Tinker Foundation.

Varela, Beatriz. 1992. *El español cubano-americano*. New York: Senda Nueva de Ediciones.

Veltman, Calvin. 1990. "The Status of the Spanish Language in the United States at the Beginning of the Twenty-First Century." *International Migration Review* XXIV (1): 108–23.

Waggoner, Dorothy, ed. 1994. *Numbers and Needs*. Washington DC. July.

1997. *Numbers and Needs*. Washington DC.

Zentella, Ana Celia. 1990a. "Lexical Leveling in Four New York City Spanish Dialects: Linguistic and Social Factors." *Hispania* 73: 1094–105.

1990b. "Who Supports Official English, and Why?: The Influence of Social Variables and Questionnaire Methodology." In *Perspectives on Official English: the Campaign for English as the Official Language of the USA*, eds. Karen L. Adams and Daniel T. Brink. Berlin/New York: Mouton de Gruyter. Pp. 161–77.

1997a. *Growing up Bilingual: Puerto Rican Children in New York*. Malden MA: Blackwell.

1997b. "Spanish in New York City." In *The Multilingual Apple: Languages in New York City*, eds. Ofelia García and Joshua Fishman. Berlin: Mouton de Gruyter. Pp. 167–202.

1997c. "The Hispanophobia of the Official English Movement in the US." *International Journal of the Sociology of Language* 127: 71–76.

11

Spanish in the Southwest

CARMEN SILVA-CORVALÁN

Editors' introduction

Spanish has a long history in the Southwest. States such as *California* and *Colorado* take their names from Spanish, as do state capitals including *Sacramento* and *Santa Fe* (New Mexico), as well as hundreds and hundreds of cities and towns and the nearby rivers and mountain ranges. Spanish has contributed many words for everyday phenomena as well. Beginning with its earliest arrival in Florida on the ships of Ponce de León, Spanish has played a central role in American culture, as Carmen Silva-Corvalán describes in this chapter. More than 18 percent of the population of the combined Southwest states (Arizona, California, Colorado, New Mexico, Texas) claim Spanish as a spoken language. Contrary to the misleading view propagated in the mass media, Hispanic-origin Spanish speakers in the Southwest carry strongly positive attitudes toward English. In the 1990 Census, 73 percent of those who identified themselves as speaking Spanish at home also said they spoke English *well*, leaving only 27 percent who did not.

The contribution of Spanish to the English vocabulary (e.g., *adobe, burro, mustang, patio, ranch*) is but one indication of an intimate relationship between Spanish speakers and English speakers. During the twentieth century, English contributed more vocabulary items to Spanish than the other way around, but through the first half of the nineteenth century Spanish was the prestige language of the Southwest and the greater contributor. Unlike the Spanish of the Northeast, which echoes Spanish varieties of several nationalities (see chapter 10), the Spanish of the Southwest is basically a variety of Mexican Spanish, though with noticeable English influence on its vocabulary. As with other non-English languages spoken in the USA, the maintenance of Spanish in the Southwest depends largely on in-migration rather than on its being transmitted from one generation to the next. In-migration is fundamental despite the presence of strong independent contributions that help sustain the language, including Spanish-language newspapers published in many cities, Spanish-language television and radio broadcasts, and several Spanish-language channels and networks, and substantial amounts of advertising budgets for Spanish-language promotion of sales and services within Hispanic communities in the Southwest.

This chapter uses the term "Hispanic" because the US Census Bureau uses it to refer to US citizens or residents of Spanish American or Spanish ancestry. Note, though, that perhaps the majority of those for whom the term is intended seem to prefer the term "Latino."

Census data

> There is no more heterogeneous ethnic group in the United States than the Spanish-speaking.
>
> Carey McWilliams (1990: Foreword)

About 60 percent of the Hispanic (or Latino) population of the USA resides in the five states referred to as the Southwest: New Mexico, Texas, California, Arizona, and Colorado (see table 11-1). The Hispanic population of the Southwest, unlike that of the Northeast, dates back to the sixteenth century, when the earliest expeditions of Spaniards from Mexico came to the region. Since then the Spanish language and Hispanic cultures have been an important component of life in the Southwest.

The 2000 Census showed that 12.5 percent of the population of the USA is of Hispanic origin. Estimates are that by the year 2010 Hispanics will be the nation's largest minority ethnic group and by 2050 will make up 25 percent of an estimated total population of almost 400 million (Day 1996). The Hispanic race/ethnic group would add the largest number of people to the population of the USA because of higher fertility rates and net immigration levels. The predicted growth in the size of the Hispanic population does not necessarily project a corresponding percentage growth in the number of speakers of Spanish, however, since the shift to English is massive once Spanish speakers settle in the USA. Indeed, between 1980 and 1990, the percentage of Spanish speakers did not increase at the same rate as the Hispanic population (Hernández et al. 1996). Still, the expanding Hispanic population's ties with family, friends, and business associates in Latin

Table 11-1 *For the USA and Southwest states: total population; number and percentage of Hispanic population; number of persons five years of age and older who claim Spanish at home*

	Total population	Hispanic	%	Spanish speakers	% Spanish speakers in total population
USA	248,709,873	22,354,059	8.9	11,117,606	4.5
New Mexico	1,515,069	579,224	38.2	398,186	26.3
Texas	16,986,510	4,339,905	25.5	3,443,106	20.3
California	29,760,021	7,557,550	25.4	5,478,712	18.4
Arizona	3,665,228	688,338	18.8	478,234	13.0
Colorado	3,294,394	424,302	12.8	203,896	6.2
TOTAL	55,221,222	13,589,319	24.6	10,002,134	18.1

Note: The 2000 Census shows that the total US population has increased to 281,421,906, of whom 35,305,818 are Hispanics. Among those five years of age or older the USA has 28,101,052 Spanish claimants; New Mexico 485,681; Texas 5,195,182; California 8,105,505; Arizona 927,395; Colorado 421,670

Source: 1990 Census, US Bureau of the Census 1993; percentage of Spanish claimants in total population

America bode well for the maintenance of Spanish as a language of importance to American society because it is spoken by large numbers of residents.

Colonial Spanish

The Spanish language has had a long history in what is now the United States. It was brought first to Florida, in 1513, by Juan Ponce de León. Gradually, Spanish conquerors took over the "Spanish borderlands," including Florida, Louisiana and the Southwest (Craddock 1992), where from the mid-1600s until the first half of the nineteenth century Spanish became the language of prestige.

The period of colonial Spanish was longest in Texas and New Mexico, the territories explored by Spaniards starting as early as 1536. Spanish extended to the new lands as the Southwest became part of the Spanish colonies, and many native Indians became bilingual in their tribal language and the language of the conquerors. The first permanent settlements were established in New Mexico in 1598 (near Santa Fe) and in Texas in 1659 (near El Paso), followed by the establishment of a mission and presidio (a military fortification) at San Antonio in 1718. In Colorado, the first permanent settlement was established as late as 1851 by New Mexican farmers to whom Mexico had granted lands in the San Luis (later Arkansas) River valleys. Spaniards had started exploring Arizona in the 1530s but it was only in 1700 that Jesuit missionaries laboring in the southern part of the region founded the first mission, San Xavier del Bac. The first permanent presidio was founded in 1752 in San Ignacio de Tubac, and twenty-three years later moved to Tucson. California appeared to be too far away from the center of present-day Mexico for the development of a Spanish colony. Furthermore, when the first Spanish settlers came to the region in the second half of the eighteenth century, Spain was starting to lose its economic, military, and political power and lacked the population and resources to colonize Alta 'Upper' California. The first mission in Alta California was founded in San Diego in 1769. By the 1840s there were twenty-one missions from San Diego to Sonoma, as well as four presidios and three pueblos 'villages,' but the non-Indian population reached 7,000 people at most.

The colonial Southwest depended politically on the Spanish Viceroyalty of Nueva España 'New Spain,' which included what is now Mexico. Mexico declared its independence from Spain in 1810 and secured it in 1821, but the "Mexican Southwest" was short lived: Texas declared its independence in 1836, and an ensuing war between the USA and Mexico (1846–48) ended with the Treaty of Guadalupe Hidalgo in 1848, which ceded nearly all the territory now included in the states of New Mexico, Utah, Nevada, Arizona, California, Texas, and western Colorado to the USA. Texas in 1845 and California in 1850 were welcomed as states of the Union, followed by Colorado in 1876. English was immediately declared the only language of instruction in public schools, the language to be used in the courts and in public administration in the newly constituted states. Arizona and New Mexico had to wait until 1912 to be admitted into the Union, perhaps because the majority of the population was Hispanic and the Spanish-speaking population substantial enough to make it difficult to impose English as the sole language of instruction and in public offices.

There were approximately 75,000 Spanish-speaking people in the Southwest by 1848 and immigration was sparse during the second half of the nineteenth century (McWilliams 1990: 57). By the end of the century, then, Hispanics presumably reached about 100,000 in number and were concentrated mostly in Texas (McWilliams 1990: 152). This situation changed in the twentieth century: two massive waves of immigration from Mexico, one following the start of the Mexican Revolution in 1910, the other following World War II, and substantial immigration from Central and South America since then have re-Hispanized the Southwest and spread Hispanic language and culture throughout the Southwest and beyond.

Traditional Southwest Spanish is still spoken in a few enclaves in northern New Mexico and southern Colorado (Bills 1997). This colonial dialect is giving way to the varieties brought in by the twentieth-century newcomers, but it will leave an imprint on Native American languages of the Southwest, especially in the form of numerous loanwords, and on English, including a broad range of words from geographical terms to politics. In turn, Spanish borrowed abundantly from Indian languages, especially Nahuatl, the language of the Aztecs (e.g., *coyote, chocolate, mesquite, aguacate* 'avocado,' *tomate* 'tomato,' *guajolote* 'turkey,' *elote* 'fresh corn'). The influence of the Spanish and English languages on each other in the Southwest, on the other hand, is a continuous reality, although the direction of the influence has changed: in the early period of contact, English borrowed more from Spanish, while the twentieth century saw far more borrowing by Spanish from English, as is usual when one language is politically and socially subordinate to another.

The Anglo settlers could not escape the influence of the language and culture of those who had colonized the Southwest. In the eighteenth century, life in the Southwest had a rural flavor, developed mainly in small villages (pueblos) and in ranches where cattle raising was pivotal. The Spaniards and Mexicans were by then familiar with the flora and fauna of the region and with the *vaquero* 'cowboy' practices that Hollywood would later turn into legend. The newcomers soon learned many of the Spanish words characteristic of the new environment and adapted them to the pronunciation and word formation rules of English, as with *adobe, patio, sombrero, vigilante, desperado, burro, mustang,* and *bronco,* as well as *ranch (rancho), buckaroo (vaquero), vamoose (vamos)*. Numerous cities, towns, rivers, and mountains also have Spanish names today. (See chapter 2 for examples of Spanish borrowings and place names in the USA.)

Southwest Spanish in the twentieth century

During the twentieth century, immigration has re-Hispanized the "Spanish borderlands," and Traditional Southwest Spanish is giving way to other varieties. Persistent economic impoverishment has sent millions of Mexican citizens, mainly

Table 11-2 *Hispanic population in California by place of origin*

Origin	Number	Percentage
Mexico	6,070,637	80.0
Puerto Rico	131,998	1.7
Cuba	75,034	0.9
El Salvador	338,769	4.5
Other Central America	298,887	3.9
South America (mostly Argentina, Colombia, Peru)	182,384	2.4
Other origin (including Spain)	459,841	6.1
TOTAL	7,557,550	100.0

Source: 1990 Census, US Bureau of the Census (1993)

from rural areas, north of the border. Political and economic factors have also motivated thousands from Central and South America and from Spain to emigrate to the USA. California is the preferred destination of political refugees from Central America. These immigrants have brought with them many Spanish dialects, but the dominant ones continue to be the Mexican varieties.

Until the first half of the twentieth century, there were mainly two dialects of Spanish in the Southwest: Traditional Southwest Spanish and a northern Mexico type that shared many features with it. The second half of the century made this picture more complex, adding considerable numbers of speakers from other dialect areas. For instance, at least in California, the significant influx of Central Americans with their characteristic *voseo* (the use of *vos* for singular 'you' instead of *tú*), aspiration of syllable-final *s* (as in *costa* 'coast' pronounced as *cohta*) and frequently also of syllable-initial *s* (as in *sopa* 'soup' pronounced as *hopa*), features unknown in most Mexican dialects, plus differences of vocabulary, may need to be reckoned with in identifying their dialect as an important variety of Spanish in the Southwest. The 1990 Census reported over 300,000 Salvadorans in California and another 300,000 individuals with roots in other Central American countries. Table 11-2 displays the numbers for Hispanic origin individuals in California. With the exception of Central Americans, highly concentrated in California, the relative percentages by place of origin are expected to be similar in the rest of the Southwest.

Because of the overwhelming majority of Mexicans, the Spanish of the Southwest is basically a Mexican variety with heavy influence from English. Alongside the preferred term *Southwest Spanish*, a number of pejorative terms have been coined for this anglicized dialect of Spanish: *Tex-Mex*, *border lingo*, *pocho*, *Spanglish*. Given its own heterogeneity and the diverse levels of proficiency of its speakers, the question arises whether it is possible to characterize this variety, but the endeavor is essential to provide needed information to educators, translators, and interpreters.

Among first-generation immigrants, it is possible that the confluence of dialects leads to the formation of a *koine* (a language variety that emerges when diverse dialects in contact lose some of their differentiating features and become more similar). One study of thirteen Hondurans in El Paso (Amastae and Satcher 1993) shows phonetic convergence in the direction of Northern Mexican pronunciation. For instance, Hondurans pronounce word-final -*n* as -*ng* [ŋ] (*en agua* is pronounced *eng agua* 'in water'), while Northern Mexicans do not. After twenty months of contact with the Northern Mexican variety, Hondurans show a much lower frequency of their native -*ng* in their speech. There is also anecdotal evidence of accommodation to Mexican vocabulary, especially on the part of southern South American individuals (e.g., using *elote* 'fresh corn,' *aguacate* 'avocado,' *yarda* 'yard,' *zacate* 'lawn,' *pelo chino* 'curly hair' instead of *choclo, palta, patio/jardín, césped, pelo crespo*). It is not clear whether Mexicans converge in any way toward Central American dialects, the second most widely spoken in the Southwest, or all "immigrant dialects" move in the direction of an anglicized Spanish variety even among first-generation immigrants.

Another noteworthy aspect of Southwest Spanish has been the influence of Pachuco, originally a form of *caló* or argot associated with the "Pachucos" or "Zoot-Suiters," the gangs of Mexican workers thought to have originated in El Paso at the beginning of the 1930s (*Pachuco* is slang for El Paso), and who later spread to other Southwestern cities. Pachuco contains elements from non-standard Spanish of Spain and Mexico, from American English, and also from the language of gypsies side by side with newly invented words and expressions in an essentially Spanish grammatical structure (Barker 1950). For about thirty years Pachuco was used as a more or less secret language by Mexican-American or Chicano youth gangs, but the gangs of today are said to use less Spanish and to identify less with Mexico (Peñalosa 1980: 85), so the name *Pachuco* has fallen out of use, replaced by *cholo, vato loco*, and other terms for the people, and by *caló* for the argot they speak. Much Pachuco vocabulary has become respectable enough to be incorporated in vernacular (mostly male) discourse. Such words as *vato* 'guy,' *carnal* 'pal,' *ése* 'you-vocative,' *güisa* 'girl,' *ramfla* 'car,' *cantón* 'house,' *placa* 'police' are commonly used in informal speech of the younger generation.

In the Southwest, there is diversity by speaker and by situational use: Spanish ranges from educated standard forms to colloquial standard and non-standard varieties to *caló* and to forms of drastically reduced Spanish among US-born Hispanics.

After English, Spanish is the most spoken language in the USA. In the 1980 Census, slightly over 8 million individuals five years of age and older claimed speaking Spanish at home (5 percent of the total population). By 1990 (see table 11-1) the number had increased to slightly over 11 million (4.5 percent of the total population). A comparison of the figures from 1980 and 1990 displayed in table 11-3 shows significant increases in the percentage of Hispanics and in the percentage of Spanish-speaking claimants in the Southwest. Note that only in California does the percentage of Spanish-speaking Hispanics increase more than the percentage increase of the Hispanic population (75 percent

Table 11-3 *Percentage increase of the Hispanic population and of the Spanish speaking claimants five years of age and older in the Southwest, 1980 to 1990*

	Hispanic population			Spanish speakers		
	1980	1990	%	1980	1990	%
New Mexico	477,222	579,224	21	352,488	398,186	13
Texas	2,985,824	4,339,905	45	2,484,188	3,443,106	39
California	4,554,331	7,557,550	66	3,132,690	5,478,712	75
Arizona	440,701	688,338	56	331,038	478,234	44
Colorado	339,717	424,302	25	179,607	203,896	14
TOTAL	8,787,795	13,589,319	55	6,668,011	10,002,134	50

Source: Based on 1980 and 1990 Census data, US Bureau of the Census (1982, 1993)

versus 66 percent). Texas and Arizona do not show a much lower increase in the percentage of Spanish-speaking claimants, but New Mexico and Colorado do. These differences are most likely linked to different rates of immigration from Spanish-speaking countries into the five states.

The increase in the number of Spanish speakers is due mainly to the continuous and massive influx of immigrants from Spanish-speaking countries in the past ten to fifteen years rather than to the transmission of the language to new generations of Hispanic Americans (Bills 1997, Bills et al. 1995, Hernández-Chávez et al. 1996, Hudson et al. 1995). If immigration is what ensures the growing presence of Spanish in the Southwest, one must wonder whether it is possible to make predictions about the future of Spanish in the USA, and four measures have been proposed (Hudson et al. 1995) to estimate the possibility of maintenance or shift of a minority language: (1) variation in the total number of individuals who claim speaking the minority language at home ("raw count"); (2) variation in the proportion of these individuals in the total population ("density"); (3) variation in their proportion in the corresponding ethnic group ("language loyalty"); (4) variation in the rate of transmission of the minority language across generations ("retention"). Calculated from census data, these measures are also importantly associated with income, education, occupation, and degree of integration into the mainstream culture.

The greatest numbers of individuals who claim speaking Spanish at home are to be found in California and Texas. On the other hand, the proportion of Spanish speakers in the total population (18 percent in the combined five states, see table 11-1) is greatest in New Mexico, followed by Texas and California, although it is likely that Los Angeles and other counties south of Los Angeles in California may have the largest proportion of Spanish speakers in the Southwest. Los Angeles County shows a density of 29 percent, with over 2.5 million individuals claiming the use of Spanish at home in a total population of nearly 9 million (1990 Census). Interestingly, while density correlates strongly with distance from the Mexican border, distance has only a moderate effect on language loyalty and retention (Hudson et al. 1995: 172). With respect to language loyalty (the percentage of Hispanics claiming Spanish as a home language) the 1990 census data may indicate an important decrease in comparison with 1980 in all states except California, a result that may be explained by the much larger number of Spanish-speaking immigrants that California has received since 1980 (Hernández 1997, Hernández et al. 1996).

Language transmission from one generation to another cannot be calculated directly from census data. Thus, the four retention measures mentioned above are based on a comparison of language loyalty in two age groups: 5–17 and 18+ years of age. In 1990, California, Arizona, and Texas show the highest indices for retention across generations, New Mexico and Colorado the lowest. As compared with 1980, however, only California and Colorado have increased the retention measure from the older to the younger generation (Hernández et al. 1996 suggest that unexpected patterns of immigration into Colorado may account for the surprising result there). In every state, loyalty is lower in the younger group of Spanish speakers, a fact that clearly reflects the rapid process of shift to English typical in the Southwest.

The correlations among the four maintenance measures of count, density, loyalty, and retention and a number of demographic factors indicate that the size of the total population, the size of the Spanish origin population, and the number of persons born in Mexico are the strongest predictors for Spanish language use at home. It is not surprising, then, that as immigration from Mexico increased in the 1980s so did the number of individuals declaring Spanish as a home language in the 1990 Census. The poorer and less well-educated counties include higher densities of Spanish speakers and higher retention (Hudson et al. 1995), while the higher the educational and income status, the lower the index of language loyalty. These results support the proposition that, in the Southwest at least, "to the extent that they [Spanish-claiming communities] gain more open access to quality education, to political power, and to economic prosperity, they will do so . . . at the price of the maintenance of Spanish, even in the home domain" (Hudson et al. 1995: 182).

Maintenance of Spanish in the Southwest is substantially dependent upon the steady influx of Spanish-speaking immigrants. Without this constant flow of new immigrants, the outcome would be the demise of Spanish as a societal language in the Southwest. Clearly, however, permanent and seasonal migration are not about to end, nor will opportunities for interaction with family and friends in Mexico diminish so dramatically as to prevent an ever invigorating renewal of Spanish.

Furthermore, Hispanics in the Southwest have become an attractive huge market for all types of businesses which, despite political efforts to suppress the use of Spanish (and other immigrant languages) in public contexts, support advertising in Spanish in the written and audio-visual media, publish instructional manuals and fliers in Spanish, and offer services in Spanish. The importance of the "Latino market" and of the Spanish language is stressed in a *Los Angeles Times* article,

Table 11-4 *Los Angeles County, ability to speak English by those who report speaking Spanish at home*

		Speak English		
	Speak Spanish	Very well	Well	Not well or not at all
5 to 17 years		364,001	167,992	122,060
18 to 64 years		658,725	392,988	743,699
65 years and over		45,588	22,412	47,310
TOTAL NUMBER	2,564,775	1,068,314	583,392	913,069
TOTAL PERCENTAGE		42	23	35

Source: 1990 Census, US Bureau of the Census (1993)

"L. A. County is Hub of Nation's Largest Latino Market by Far, Survey Finds" (August 3, 1998), which reports results of a nationwide study of the spending habits of Hispanics. Almost 80 percent report using media in both languages, but in dense immigrant enclaves such as Los Angeles, 55 to 60 percent of the adults say they prefer advertising in Spanish and comprehend Spanish ads better than English ads. These results induce businesses, politicians, and government offices to reach the millions of less-anglicized Hispanics through the thriving Spanish-language media.

The picture may be less rosy, however. To illustrate, Los Angeles County has the largest concentration of Hispanics in the Southwest. Of about 9 million people there, 37 percent are of Hispanic origin. By far the largest group (2,519,514) is Mexican-American, followed by Salvadorans (about 250,000). Indeed, the concentration of Mexican population in Los Angeles County is second in size only to Mexico City. The density of Hispanic population in the eastern area of Los Angeles, for instance, ranges from 30 percent to 80 percent. Two and a half million Hispanics five years old and older, or 78 percent of the total Hispanic population in the county, declare speaking Spanish at home. This impressive figure might suggest that Spanish is being strongly maintained and that the stereotype ("Hispanics don't want to learn English") might be correct. These assumptions are wrong, however. Constant immigration is the fundamental factor that keeps Spanish thriving in the Southwest. The figures from the 1990 Census support this observation: 53.3 percent of Hispanics in Los Angeles County are foreign born. Only about 30 percent of those who declare speaking Spanish at home are US born. Furthermore, the census does not ask individuals how frequently they speak their heritage language at home nor about their proficiency.

By contrast, the census does give information about English proficiency. For Los Angeles County, with the largest concentration of Hispanics in the Southwest, a high proportion of them foreign born, and only 146 miles from the Mexican border, three factors that would predict strong allegiance to Spanish and poor knowledge of English, the 1990 Census offers the information in table 11-4.

Table 11-5 *Southwest states, ability to speak English by those who are five years of age or older who report speaking Spanish at home*

	Speak Spanish	Speak English			
		"Very well/Well"	%	"Not well/Not at all"	%
Arizona	478,234	384,094	80	94,140	20
California	5,478,712	3,696,545	67	1,782,167	33
Colorado	203,896	174,893	86	29,003	14
New Mexico	398,186	342,776	88	45,410	12
Texas	3,443,106	2,695,476	78	747,630	22
TOTAL	10,002,134	7,293,784	73	2,698,350	27

Source: 1990 Census, US Bureau of the Census (1993)

Sixty-five percent of the Hispanics who report speaking Spanish at home in Los Angeles County also speak English well or very well, and only 35 percent don't speak it well (which does not necessarily mean that they cannot communicate in English within certain restricted domains) or don't speak it at all. This is evidence that a substantial percentage of those who were born outside the USA (recall that only about 30 percent of Spanish speakers are US born) do learn English well enough to participate adequately in American society and probably will not pass a fully functional variety of Spanish to their offspring.

Knowledge of English among the Hispanic population is widespread in the Southwest, as indicated in table 11-5. In the most heavily Hispanic region of the nation, with a high rate of immigration, only 27 percent of those who claim speaking Spanish at home don't know English well or at all. Based on my direct experience of twenty years' studying Spanish in California, I am confident that the 27 percent includes only very few (and exceptional) US-born Hispanics. (See chapters 7, 14, 17, and 18 for more on the maintenance of Spanish and other heritage languages.)

In sharp contrast to Spanish as a first language, Spanish is the most studied as a "foreign language" throughout the USA. In the fall of 1994, 67 percent of all foreign language enrollments in grades 9 to 12 in public secondary schools were in Spanish classes (National Center for Education Statistics 1997: 69). The number of bachelors' degrees awarded is also much higher in Spanish than in any other language: 38 percent of 14,378 B.A. degrees in Foreign Languages and Literatures awarded in the academic year 1993–94 (French is second with 22%) (National Center for Education Statistics 1997: 281). Furthermore, Spanish has acquired some prestige as a symbol of ethnic and cultural roots, and this has led to a renewed interest in learning or reviving the heritage language, and for native speakers of Spanish numerous colleges have instituted courses that emphasize the development of advanced reading and writing skills, which tend to be weak in a home-only language.

Linguistic aspects of Southwest Spanish

The continuous arrival of numerous people from other Spanish-speaking countries has resulted in a considerable increase in the use of different dialects of Spanish in the Southwest. If to these demographic changes we add the absence of a process of standardization of Spanish in the USA, the heterogeneity found among immigrants is not surprising. By contrast, US-born Hispanics speak a relatively homogeneous variety of Spanish in the sense that it is characterized by similar phenomena typical of a situation of intensive and extensive bilingualism: simplification of grammar and vocabulary, intensive borrowing from English, and code-switching between Spanish and English in the same conversational turn.

While the maintenance of Spanish is unquestionable at the societal level, shift to English is common at the individual or family level. The children of first-generation immigrants may acquire Spanish at home, but most of them gradually become dominant in English as they go through a transitional bilingual education program or an English immersion program. (In what follows, first-generation foreign-born immigrants who have come to the USA after age twelve are called "group 1," their offspring [born in the USA or having come to the USA before age twelve] are "group 2," and those with at least one parent qualifying as a member of group 2 are "group 3"). No clear-cut linguistic differences exist between these groups, but only trends that characterize each group in general.

In these situations of societal bilingualism an oral proficiency continuum may develop in the two languages. This *continuum* ranges from standard or unrestricted Spanish to a merely *emblematic* use of Spanish and, on the other hand, from unrestricted to emblematic English. At the individual level, the continuum reveals *dynamic* levels of proficiency in the subordinate language. Speakers can be located at various points along this continuum depending on their level of dominance in one or another language, but in principle individuals can move or be moving toward (hence "dynamic" level) one or the other end of the continuum at any given stage of life. These continua and their characteristic linguistic features have been identified in Mexican-American communities in the Southwest, but no systematic studies have been conducted of other Hispanic communities there.

In the typical family situation, the older child acquires only Spanish at home and maintains a good level of communicative competence in it throughout life, with more loss or less loss depending on a number of factors, while the younger children acquire both Spanish and English at home. These younger children are more likely to develop and maintain a contact variety that is characterized by greater differences from the norms of group 1. Children who are close to their grandparents may acquire Spanish at home, but frequently their proficiency is limited, as illustrated in (1), a conversation between a researcher and José, aged 17. It is obvious that José, third generation in the USA, is making an effort to speak in Spanish:

(1)   R = Researcher; J = José (J, No. 44, group 3)

R: ..... ¿Pero con quién hablas en español tú, a veces, digamos?

J: Hable yo – yo, a ver – yo hable con mi a, abue, abuela – más de mi
     a, abuelo, porque cuando yo hable con mi abuelo él no entende,
     él tiene uno problema – eso – *ears. So whenever I have a chance
     to speak, I speak to my grandparents. So, I don't speak, I just –
     listen to what they're saying, and then I, I – hear it in my brain
     and, and – and try to understand instead of speaking back at them
     because I, – they understand English as much.*

R: ..... Who do you speak Spanish with, sometimes?

J: I speak – I, let's see – I speak with my gr, grand, grandma – more
     than with my gr, grandpa, because when I speak with my grandpa
     he doesn't understand, he has one problem – that – . . .

Example (2), by contrast, reflects a more spontaneous use of Spanish on the
part of Robert, aged 24, from group 2:

(2)   H = Researcher; R = Robert (No. 24)

H: ¿Y tu tortuga cómo la conseguiste?

R: Un día yo y mi papá estábamos regresando de, de, de un parque
    con, con un troque de mi tío. Y estábamos cruzando la calle. Y nos
    paramos porque estaba un *stop sign*. Y mi papá dijo, "Ey, Roberto.
    Quita esa tortuga que está en la calle." Y no le creí, *you know*. Y
    miré. Y creí que era **un piedra**, pero grande. Y no le hice caso.
    Entonces me dijo, "Apúrele. Quita esa tortuga," *you know*. Y me
    asomé otra vez. Y sí era tortuga. ¡Estaba caminando **ese piedra**
    grande! [risa] Pues me salí del carro, del troque. Y fui y conseguí
    el tortuga. Y me **lo** llevé pa' mi casa.

H: And your turtle, how did you get it?

R: One day my dad and I were coming back from, from, from a park
    in my uncle's truck. And we were crossing the street. And we
    stopped because there was a *stop sign*. And my dad said, "Hey,
    Roberto. Remove that turtle from the street." And I didn't believe
    him, *you know*. And I looked. And I thought it was **a stone**, but
    big. And I didn't pay attention to it. So he said, "Hurry up. Remove
    that turtle," *you know*. And I looked again. And yes, it was a turtle.
    That big stone was walking! [laughter] So I got out of the car,
    the truck. And I went and got **the turtle**. And I took **it** home.

In (2), the US-born Robert uses the expressions *you know* and *stop sign*, does not
establish feminine gender agreement in a few noun phrases and one unstressed
pronoun, *lo* 'it' (all represented in boldface; cf. García 1998), and uses only *estar*

'to be' as an auxiliary in progressive constructions (that is, *-ndo* '-ing' sentences like *Juan está leyendo* 'John is reading'), where Mexico-born speakers would likely use other auxiliary verbs (e.g. *venir* 'to come': *Juanito va creciendo rápido* 'Johnny's growing fast,' *ir* 'to go': *Juan iba entrando a la biblioteca* 'John was going into the library'). Even so, Robert's Spanish appears only slightly non-native; it contains the expected agreement of the verb with various subjects; the marking of plurals and gender; subordinate clauses, appropriately used prepositions and conjunctions; and it is perfectly understandable.

Finally, (3) illustrates *emblematic Spanish* – the use of fixed expressions within a conversation conducted in English, a style characteristic of speakers beyond group 2:

(3) C = Researcher; N = Nora (No. 40)

    C: ¿Y cómo lo haces para poder entender todo en español y hablar en inglés? ¿Cómo lo haces?

    N: *Ay, ya no sé*, I don't know. I'm surprised to be able to do that.

    C: And how do you manage to understand everything in Spanish, and to speak in English? How do you manage?

    N: *Ay, I no longer know*, []

Nora's use of Spanish in the utterance *Ay, ya no sé* is mainly emblematic of her ethnicity and of her cultural ties with the Hispanic community. She is indeed at the very bottom of the Spanish proficiency continuum.

The most critical factors that seem to account for the amount of language loss shown at the lowest levels of the proficiency continuum include the highly infrequent use of Spanish; its restriction to use with family and close friends; and neutral subjective attitudes toward its maintenance. But there are exceptions to this scenario. One may occasionally come across a group 2 speaker who never acquired Spanish, or acquired it and lost it altogether, or stopped using it for years and is in the process of reactivating it. Likewise, but exceptionally, a group 3 speaker may have acquired Spanish from birth and maintained it.

Example (4) comes from a speaker in group 3 who stopped using Spanish during her adolescence and had reactivated it about two years before the recorded conversation, after marrying a man from group 1. This is a fairly frequent type of intergenerational marriage that favors the maintenance of Spanish. In this passage, the speaker refers to the time when her husband was laid off and they decided to move to another city.

(4) They were laying off. So, I didn't get laid off. Ramón, Ramón got laid off. And I quit because he got laid off. Because I was working, and he was working at nights . . . *Dije, "No,* <u>si lo van a descansar a él</u> (lit.: if him are-3pl gonna rest him), *¿pa' qué me quedo yo, especial yo?" Yo, de aquí, como, 'onde puedo agarrar trabajo. El, es más difícil, porque* he's not *reglado para 'garrar trabajo.*   (D39, f28,3,ELA42)

I said, "No, if they're going to lay him off, why should I stay, especially me?" I'm from here, so I can get a job anywhere. As for him, it's more difficult, because *he's not* 'fixed' (legalized) to get a job.

Spanish in the Southwest dies "with its morphological boots on" (to borrow a phrase from Dorian 1981). Speakers with the lowest levels of Spanish proficiency are most fluent in English and do not need to use Spanish for any pressing purposes. As a result, the Spanish they use, usually contained in passages of English discourse, retains some verbal inflections, and gender, number, and case markers, as illustrated in (4). No foreign (i.e. English) elements penetrate the grammar of Spanish, but the speaker's Spanish grammar undergoes simplification and loss. On the other hand, bilinguals display the same type of linguistic creativity that characterizes innovations in unreduced monolingual varieties – for instance, they adopt loanwords and make semantic extensions. In this respect, observe the skillful extension of the meaning of *descansar* 'to rest' in (4). As a transitive verb (one that takes an object), *descansar* meaning 'to rest/to lean/to lay' takes an *inanimate* direct object (for instance, *descansa tu cabeza en mi hombro* 'rest/lean/lay your head on my shoulder'). (It may take an *animate* direct object with the meaning 'help/give someone a hand at work.') Perhaps based on the connection between *descansar* and *lay* with the meaning of 'rest/lean,' speakers establish the further link with *lay off*. This has grammatical consequences because the meaning of *lay off* is transferred to *descansar*, which now incorporates the meaning 'to fire (an employee)' and allows an *animate* direct object; linguists call this process a loan translation.

In addition to simplifying grammatical categories and transferring forms or meanings from English, bilinguals develop other strategies aimed at easing the challenge of having to remember and use two different linguistic systems. In the use of Spanish, they regularize forms, develop phrasal constructions to replace complicated words with inflectional endings and, as (4) illustrates, frequently switch between the two languages. Code-switching follows well-defined patterns, it is governed by constraints that are recognized by the bilingual community, and it fulfills a number of communicative functions (Myers-Scotton 1993a, b).

Applying these strategies creates only minor changes in English but more or less massive changes in Spanish. Transfer from English into Spanish is clear in single-word and multiple-word loans (*Cúidate* and *'ai te guacho* (vernacular) / *'ai te veo* (colloquial), from 'Take care!' and 'See you,' become farewell formulas in Spanish), and in the loss of semantic and pragmatic constraints that might be spurred on by English (e.g. certain word-order patterns).

The verbal system is simplified across generations, ranging from a fully standard system to a highly reduced one that retains only three simple indicative tenses (present, preterite, imperfect) and one phrasal tense (future: *Voy a cantar* 'I'm gonna sing'). Between these two extremes are speakers, even in group 3, who use subjunctive and compound forms. Also noteworthy is the preference for imperfect verb forms, when the preterite is required, with stative verbs (e.g. *era* '(it) was,' *estaba* '(it) was,' *tenía* 'he had,' *había* 'there was,' *podía* 'he could,' *quería* 'he wanted' for *fue, estuvo, tuvo, hubo, pudo, quiso*); conversely, with many dynamic verbs, the preterite form of the verb is used instead of the imperfect form (*fue* 'he went,' *corrió* 'he ran,' *habló* 'he spoke,' for *iba, corría, hablaba*) (Silva-Corvalán 1994). Examples (5) to (10) illustrate uses of the verbal system that differ from the norms of group 1 immigrants but may be considered the norm in Southwest Spanish.

(5)   Esta fue la primera casa que compramos. Estamos (for 'hemos estado') como *fifteen years* aquí.

        This was the first house we bought. We've been (lit.: are) for about fifteen years here.

(6)   Iba a ser profesional, pero creo que tenía (for 'tuvo') un accidente.

        He was going to become professional, but I think he had an accident.

(7)   Y estábamos esperando a mi 'amá – porque ella fue a llevar (for 'había llevado') mi hermano a la dentista.

        And we were waiting for my mom – because she went to take my brother to the dentist.

(8)   A: ¿Y qué me dices de tu educación si tus padres se hubieran quedado en México?

        B: No estudiaba (for 'habría/hubiera estudiado') mucho, yo creo.

        A: So what can you tell me about your education if your parents had stayed in Mexico?

        B: I didn't study much, I think.

(9)   Era antes que compraron (for 'compraran') el trailer.

        It was before they bought the trailer.

(10)   A: Ahm no sé – no he hablado con ellos – no más leí un papelito y, la Ana puso en un papelito en la hielera "Gloria is having twins." [se ríen] . . . todavía tiene allí el papel, ¿verdad?

       AM: Yeah, porque no lo he quitado yo porque como está tan bonito. Ahí ['ai] lo voy a dejar hasta que se cae (for caiga).

       A: Uhm, I don't know – I haven't spoken with them – I just read a little note and, Ana put on a little piece of paper on the refrigerator "Gloria's having twins." [they laugh] . . . she still has the note there, right?

       AM: Yeah, because I haven't removed it because it's so cute . . . I'll leave it there until it falls down.'

Numerous pronunciation processes sporadically affect verbal forms as well. For instance, variable absence of complex vowels (called diphthongs) in such forms as *tenen* for *tienen* 'they have,' *moven* for *mueven* 'they move'; use of diphthongs instead of simple vowels, as in *sientí* for *sentí*; regularization of preterite inflexions, as in *pudió* (following the more general model of *comió*, *movió*, etc.) for *pudo* 'he could.' Speakers also omit agreement between subject and verb or within a noun phrase (e.g. between noun and adjective). Other phenomena are characteristic of popular varieties of Spanish but not specific to Southwest Spanish: a few archaisms are retained (*truje* for *traje* 'I brought' and *haiga* for *haya* 'there is'), regularization of *haber* (*ha*, *hamos* for *he* 'I have,' *hemos* 'we have'), addition or elision (a technical term for omission) of *s* in the second person singular of the preterite tense (*comites/comistes* for *comiste* 'you ate'), accent shift and substitution of /n/ for /m/ in certain verb forms – for example, *váyanos* for *vayamos* 'that we go,' *vuélvanos* for *volvamos* 'that we return,' *íbanos* 'we went,' *vivíanos* for *vivíamos* 'we lived' (Hidalgo 1990, Sánchez 1983).

Some features of Southwest Spanish represent more advanced stages of changes that are also taking place in countries where Spanish is the official language. Examples would include extensions in the use of *estar* 'to be/to look' with adjectives at the expense of *ser* 'to be' and the strong preference for the phrasal future over the synthetic one (Gutiérrez 1995), illustrated in (11) and (12).

(11)   Una de esas recá-, recámaras es el *master bedroom*, el más grande. Y el otro está (for 'es') pequeñito.

One of those ro-, rooms is the master bedroom, the largest one. And the other one is small.

(12)   Nosotros vamos a ir (alternative: iremos) en diciembre.

We're gonna go (alternative: 'll go) in December.

Many uses of unstressed pronouns also occur in fully functional varieties in Spain and Latin America, such as uses involving the loss of case marking, gender, number, and even the omission of the pronoun (cf. Urrutia 1995). One important difference is that these phenomena do not all occur in a single fully functional dialect or do not affect all grammatical persons, as they do in some reduced varieties of Southwest Spanish.

One question that arises in this connection is the justification for the commonly heard claim that the Spanish of the Southwest is very different from the Spanish of those in group 1 – or even that it is an aberration. Keep in mind that there are many "Spanishes" in the Southwest, and the statement might apply to the lowest levels of the proficiency continuum, but speakers at these levels use Spanish very rarely and only if forced by special circumstances. In regard to the Spanish used more regularly and with some degree of fluency by US-born Hispanics, what seems to create the negative impression is the simplification of tenses and of gender agreement, and confusions in the use of prepositions. The fact that almost every sentence contains one or more of these phenomena and is thus a possible site for deviation from the norms of group 1, appears to be a strong factor in creating stereotypes of widespread incorrectness and lack of systematicity.

Intensive vocabulary borrowings further promote the harsh evaluation of Spanish as a "mixed language." Spanish has indeed borrowed freely from

English, especially expressions that represent cultural differences and do not have exact correspondences in Spanish:

Southwest Spanish	Possible correspondence in standard Spanish
cama king 'king-size bed'	*cama muy ancha* 'very wide bed'
master bedroom	*dormitorio principal* 'main bedroom'
lonche 'lunch'	*almuerzo ligero* 'light lunch'
esnak 'snack'	*refrigerio* (not widely used) 'snack'
dompe 'dump'	(no word for a place where yard refuse is dumped)

In addition, there is borrowing of technical or special vocabulary associated with occupations or activities, and some of these have stretched beyond the USA to displace the Spanish term: in sports: *jit* 'hit'; *juego* 'game'; *jonrón* 'home run'; in gardening: *graftear* 'to graft'; *espreyar* 'to spray'; *nersería* 'nursery'; in comput-erese: *formatear* 'to format'; *imeil* 'e-mail'; *cliquear* 'to click'; in telecommunications: *biper* 'beeper'; *espíker* 'speaker'; *intercom* 'intercom'; in auto mechanics: *brecas* 'brakes'; *mofle* 'muffler'; *cloche* 'clutch.'

There are also hundreds of other words referring to objects or actions in daily life, adapted from English and then perhaps remembered more easily:

Southwest Spanish	Standard Spanish
puchar 'to push'	*empujar*
mapear 'to mop'	*pasar la fregona*
dostear 'to dust'	*sacudir el polvo*
cuitear 'to quit'	*darse por vencido*
liquear 'to leak'	*gotear*
fensa 'fence'	*reja*
pipa 'pipe'	*cañería*
traques 'tracks'	*rieles*
suiche 'switch'	*interruptor*
biles 'bills'	*cuentas*

Numerous Spanish words have changed their meaning and now incorporate the meaning of an English word that looks or sounds alike:

Southwest Spanish	Standard Spanish
moverse 'to move (to another house)'	*mudarse* (de casa)
papel 'paper'	*ensayo académico*
atender 'to attend'	*asistir*
aplicación 'application'	*solicitud*
colectar 'to collect'	*coleccionar*
grados 'grades'	*calificaciones/notas*

A few other borrowings arguably alter grammatical features of Spanish. Examples include uses of *cómo* 'how,' *tiempo* 'time,' *quebrar* 'to break up,' and sentences related to measurements (of weight, age, etc.), as illustrated in (13) to (18), with a standard Mexican version in each case.

(13)   Y tu carro que compraste, **¿cómo** te gusta?
         and the car you bought, **how** do you like it?'
         Mexican: Y tu carro que compraste, ¿te gusta? (or: ¿Qué tal te gusta?)

(14)   Ahora es el tiempo de refinanciar su casa.
         Now is the time to refinance your home loan.
         Mexican: Ahora es el momento de refinanciar su casa.

(15)   porque otro tiempo – ando en el carro – y empecé a notar que no
         estaba bien
         because another time – I was driving the car – and I started to notice
         that it wasn't working well
         Mexican: porque otra vez/en otra ocasión – . . .

(16)   Mi padre es seis pies [de altura].
         My dad is six feet [tall].
         Mexican: Mi padre mide seis pies.

(17)   [la casa] ahora es cien mil o ciento veinte mil dólares
         Now it [the house] is one hundred or one hundred and twenty thousand
         dollars
         Mexican: Ahora [la casa] cuesta cien mil . . .

(18)   Ya ha tratado ella de quebrar con él.
         She's already tried to break up with him.
         Mexican: Ya ha tratado ella de terminar /romper con él.

Research on Southwest Spanish can no longer afford to ignore linguistic phenomena across speakers who represent varying lengths of residence in the USA, different degrees of proficiency, and the diverse functions of the varieties of the heritage language. Otherwise, statements about Southwest Spanish will risk being inappropriate to characterize the complex sociolinguistic situation. The gradual distancing of the linguistic norms of speakers in group 2 and beyond from those in group 1, for instance, correlates with a sharp reduction of Spanish language use from group 1 to 2 and 3, a slight descent in the strength of positive attitudes toward Spanish, and a significant decline in the degree of commitment to do something concrete in order to maintain the Spanish culture and language (Silva-Corvalán 1994).

Attitudes toward Spanish and English

Obviously the maintenance of Spanish depends not only on individual or group attitudes but also on political attitudes, which determine government and educational policies. In the past ten years or so, political attitudes have not been positive. By contrast, most Hispanics express positive attitudes toward Spanish and willingness to maintain it and pass it on to their descendants (cf. Mejías and Anderson 1988). But these acts of loyalty are in conflict with uncommitted behavior, that is, lack of commitment to turn positive attitudes into action.

In a study I conducted in Los Angeles, attitudes in group 1 appeared slightly more favorable to Spanish than those of groups 2 and 3. Groups 2 and 3 showed a slight favorable trend among the youth, who reject negative statements about Spanish more strongly than their elders. This may be due to societal changes of attitude toward bilingualism in general, and to bilingual education in the past thirty years. Indeed, younger bilinguals have not felt the same degree of pressure against using Spanish in school as their elders had. Some of the younger bilinguals have attended schools that endorsed some form of bilingual education. Thus, despite the recent reaction against linguistic diversity in the USA, Hispanics of all ages now seem to feel freer to speak Spanish and to defend this right, as illustrated in (19).

(19)   C = researcher; R = 50, m46, 3, ELA36

   C: Fíjate. Tú poco a poco has ido viendo que ha llegado más y más gente a la policía que son latinos.

   R: Latinos. Como ahora, estaba en el *catering wagon* y, y, y estaba hablando – Un mecánico mexicano le dijo una a la – al que está cocinando en el *catering wagon*, le dijo una de doble sentido, una palabra de doble sentido nomás. *Nothing serious, nothing serious, you know, just a-* No me acuerdo qué era ni nada. So le hablé yo p'atrás en español. "Ya te agarré la movida," le dije, "Ya te, ya te estoy escuchando." Y luego este gringo estaba a un lado y luego "*Eh*," dice, "*don't speak that foreign language around here.*" Es lo que me dice a mí, *you know. "What do you mean 'foreign language'? That sucker was around here before the English were!"* [R laughs.] *And he says, "Man, you're right!" he says, "You're right!,"* OK? [R and C laugh.]

   C: *He had to accept it, uh?*

   R: *Yeah, he had to accept it. Two reasons: I'm right, and two, I'm the boss.* [R and C laugh.]

   C: There you are. Little by little you've been seeing that more and more people have joined the police who are Latinos.

   R: Latinos. Like now, I was at the catering wagon and, and, and was speaking – A Mexican mechanic said one to the – to the one who's cooking in the catering wagon, he told him a double sense one, just one double sense word. Nothing serious, nothing serious, you know, just a – I don't remember what it was. So I talked to him in Spanish. "I got what you said," I said, "I'm, I'm listening to you." And then this gringo was to one side and then "Eh," he says, "don't speak that foreign language around here!" That's what he says to me, you know. "What do you mean 'foreign language'? That sucker was around here before the English were!" [R laughs.] And he says, "Man, you're right!" he says, "You're right! OK?" [R and C laugh.]

C: He had to accept it, uh?

R: Yeah, he had to accept it. Two reasons: I'm right, and two, I'm the boss.! [R and C laugh.]

Despite positive attitudes, the use of Spanish evidently declines across groups. This situation seems to apply not only at work, in church, and in other public domains, but also within the family. While group 1 speakers report almost exclusive use of Spanish with parents, grandparents, and siblings, some in groups 2 and 3 speak Spanish only frequently, sometimes or even never to their parents and siblings. Parents frequently fail in their goal to maintain Spanish at home. Example (20), a segment of a conversation between Ali (group 1) and her son Eno (group 2), illustrates appropriately.

(20)   A = Ali; E = Eno (Ali's son)

E: If I talked Spanish to my mom, she'd probably think I'm sick. [laughter]

A: I wish you would.

E: I'd shock her. I'd shock her. I, I really would.

A: I wish you would, porque mira. Hay una cosa, m'hijito, muy importante, ¿verdad? Yo todo el tiempo he querido que ustedes hablen, hablen bien los dos idiomas. Siempre. Por eso yo siempre les he hablado en español. Y ahora, es tu responsabilidad, muy grande tu responsabilidad, de que tú hables español para que el niño [E's son] aprenda a hablar – el español.

. . . , because look. There's one thing, my son, that's very important, right? I've always wanted that you speak, you speak both languages well. Always. This is why I've always talked to you in Spanish. And now, it's your responsibility, a big responsibility, to speak Spanish so that the boy [E's son] may learn to speak – Spanish.

It is also frequently the case that where parents have established that only Spanish is to be spoken at home, the "rule" is frequently disregarded by the time younger brothers and sisters are born. Consequently, the youngest do not learn enough Spanish to interact comfortably in this language, and siblings use English among themselves. Example (21) is illustrative.

(21)   . . . y mi hermanita chiquita sí habla español, pero no creo que tiene la voca, el voca, ¿el vocabulario? /Researcher: Sí, el vocabulario./ Sí, no tiene mucha vocabulario para, para estar en una conversación. Y, y yo estaba diciendo, 'Pos otra vez necesitamos de esa regla.'

'. . . and my little sister does speak Spanish, but I don't think she has the voc, the voc, the vocabulary? /Researcher: Yes, the vocabulary./ Yes, she doesn't have much vocabulary to, to be in a conversation. And, and I was saying, 'Well, we need that rule again.'

In the workplace, Spanish tends to be used more with fellow workers than with supervisors. This may be because there are fewer bilinguals in supervisory positions. It may also be the case, however, that the large numbers of recent Spanish-speaking immigrants may stimulate the revival of lost linguistic skills, even if the English-dominant bilingual is in the supervisory position. This situation is represented in the spontaneous description volunteered by Lola (group 2) of her husband's (group 3) proficiency in Spanish. The husband is the son of the owner of the printing company mentioned in (22).

(22)   Y digo yo que este señor [her husband] su español era horrible, ¿verdad?, porque lo había perdido cuando se mudaron a ese (sic) vecindad. Sí, pero cuando nos casamos entonces ya no era el estudiante, ya se puso a trabajar en la planta. Y en la planta, los hombres que trabajan las imprentas casi todos son hispanoamericanos. Vienen de distintos países, pero todos hablan español. Entonces por su amistad, en la imprenta él pudo aprender español.

'And I say that this man his Spanish was horrible, right?, because he had lost it when they moved to that neighborhood. Yeah, but when we got married then he was no longer a student, he started working in the company. And in the company, the men who work at the printing presses are almost all Hispanoamericans. They come from different countries, but they all speak Spanish. So then because of their friendship, in the company he learnt Spanish.'

In addition to the negative effect that the different neighborhood (mostly non-Hispanic) had on the man's Spanish, his wife surmises that he had also stopped using it because his grandparents had passed away at that time.

Writing and reading in Spanish are also infrequent in the community, much more infrequent than listening activities, but some degree of literacy is maintained even in group 3 Hispanics.

As a group, US-born bilinguals do not consider that the preservation or protection of tradition and group integration is the most important motive to maintain their ancestors' language. Indeed, the most important reasons in the three groups do not pertain specifically to Spanish, but to the more general notion of "another language"; for instance, "it's broadening to have more than one language," a purely intellectual reason. This attitude concurs with the opinion expressed by a speaker in group 2, as shown in (23).

(23)   *Insisten que se – claro, las* (sic) *dos [idiomas]. Somos así. Es una cosa – bonito hablar dos idiomas.* [[They insist that – of course, the two [languages]. We're like that. It's – nice to speak two languages.]]

It's something that enriches the person. It's something that enriches the society. It's, it's education, it's culture. It gives you two systems of thinking, you know.

On the whole, then, attitudes toward Spanish language and Mexican culture remain very positive. The loyalty implicit in these positive attitudes, however, seems to be in conflict with a significant decline in the degree of commitment to do something concrete to maintain Mexican culture and language in group 2 and especially in group 3.

Attitudes toward English are positive in every group: "I want my children to learn correct English," "English is the language of this country," "I prefer to speak English with my friends" (groups 2 and 3). Hispanics understand that upward social and economic mobility and full participation in American society require good proficiency in English.

Outside Hispanic communities, attitudes toward Spanish and its speakers are not always positive. The stereotypical image of the Hispanic as racially impure, lazy (the words *siesta* 'nap' and *mañana* 'tomorrow' are frequently incorporated into English discourse to connote slothfulness), and even contemptible has been strengthened in some recent borrowings from Spanish (Hill 1993). Used by speakers of Anglo ethnicity, these borrowings correspond to "Mock Spanish" – "adaptations of Spanish-language expressions to registers of jocularity, irony and parody" (Hill 1993: 147). Consider some of these "Mock Spanish" expressions (from Hill 1995):

- *Hasta la vista, baby* is a derogated Spanish farewell, popularized in the movie "Terminator 2," used to say goodbye to or dismiss someone despised or disliked.
- *El cheapo* uses a Spanish article and a noun formed by adding the Spanish ending *-o* to an English adjective, thus associating the idea of 'cheapness' and low value with Spanish.
- *Enchilada* with an extended meaning to refer to a messy set of things or to a complex problem, as in *the big enchilada* and *the whole enchilada*. Spanish words, then, acquire negative connotations.

Mock Spanish has flourished, argues Hill (1995: 18), because it is not direct and vulgar racist discourse. Rather, to most Anglos it seems innocent and clever. But it is precisely because it is seemingly innocent that it can be used by the educated and uneducated alike, while relentlessly reproducing "a highly negative stereotype of speakers of Spanish" in the USA.

It is important to mention that the English language media has also published positive pieces about Hispanics. Editorials have praised the fact that relatively large numbers of Hispanics exert their right to vote, that Hispanics contribute positively to the economy of the Southwest, that Hispanics are hard working and loyal, family oriented and religious, and that even those in group 1 are achieving the American dream of owning their own home. By contrast, though, I have not found editorials praising the enormous language asset that bilingual Hispanics possess.

The impact of the Spanish-language media in creating a more positive image and in promoting the Spanish language should not be disregarded either. The 1990s have seen the growth of Spanish-language communications, most notably represented by three national television networks. The first Spanish-language television station in the USA began broadcasting in San Antonio in 1955. Galavisión began broadcasting in 1979. Two more networks were established in 1987, Univisión Television and Telemundo Group. These three networks are affiliated with about one thousand cable systems in the USA and own and operate over-the-air stations in many states (Kanellos 1995). Spanish music, movies, soap operas, talk shows, and news programs enter the Southwest through television and strengthen cultural and language ties with nearly 400 million people who speak Spanish around the world today. In addition, Spanish newspapers are published in every large city, and magazines written in "Latino Spanish" may be found on newsstands in and outside communities with a high density of Hispanic population. Spanish radio stations are also numerous.

At the beginning of the twenty-first century, we may affirm that Spanish and Spanish–English bilingualism are not dying out in the Southwest. Rather, Hispanic communities throughout the region give evidence of the complex sociolinguistic phenomenon of societal bilingualism: Spanish illustrates a continuum of levels of proficiency along which speakers move, up or down, either in their lifetime or across generations, intimately interlaced with Anglo language and culture. Given favorable socio-political conditions this dynamic situation may well last for centuries to come.

Suggestions for further reading and exploration

Written in Spanish, Ramírez (1992) offers general information about the main dialects of Spanish in the USA, their sociohistorical context, and their literary production. For the history and culture of Hispanics in the Southwest, McWilliams 1990 (originally published in 1948) is an excellent study. Meier and Rivera (1972) is a readable history of Mexican-Americans. Duignan and Gann (1998) on the history of Spanish-speaking immigrants in the USA includes chapters on Puerto Ricans, Cubans, and other Hispanics, including observations about Spanish language use. A detailed history of Mexican immigrants to Los Angeles from 1900 to 1945 appears in Sánchez (1993), which explores the process of becoming Mexican-American and developing a new Mexican-American culture.

A linguistic overview of Southwest Spanish is yet to be written. Espinosa's (1909–13) classic study of the pronunciation, morphology, and vocabulary of New Mexico Spanish has not been replicated for other regions, although Southwest Spanish is treated in Bills (1974), Hernández-Chávez et al. (1975), and Bowen and Ornstein (1976). Elías-Olivares (1979), a study of language use in a Chicano community of Texas, highlights the importance of considering the existence in bilingual communities of a range of Spanish and English varieties associated with different degrees of formality and levels of proficiency.

Just as Spanish extended to other regions of the USA, so did the studies included in the many anthologies published in the 1980s and 1990s: Durán (1981), Amastae and Elías-Olivares (1982), Elías-Olivares (1983), Wherritt and García (1989), Bergen (1990), Roca and Lipski (1993), Silva-Corvalán (1995), Colombi and Alarcón (1997). Contributions in these volumes have also extended their areas of interest to include more general concerns about the linguistic and cognitive processes characteristic of bilingualism, the role of Spanish in public life and education, and the acquisition of Spanish as a first or second language.

References

Amastae, Jon and Lucía Elías-Olivares, eds. 1982. *Spanish in the United States: Sociolinguistic Aspects.* New York: Cambridge University Press.

Amastae, Jon and David Satcher. 1993. "Linguistic Assimilation in Two Variables," *Language Variation and Change* 5: 77–90.

Barker, George C. 1950. *Pachuco: an American Spanish Argot and its Social Functions in Tucson, Arizona.* Tucson: University of Arizona Press.

Bergen, John, ed. 1990. *Spanish in the United States: Sociolinguistic Issues.* Washington DC: Georgetown University Press.

Bills, Garland. 1997. "New Mexican Spanish: Demise of the Earliest European Variety in the United States," *American Speech* 72: 154–71.

Bills, Garland, ed. 1974. *Southwest Areal Linguistics.* San Diego: Institute for Cultural Pluralism, San Diego State University.

Bills, Garland, E. Hernández Chávez, and Alan Hudson. 1995. "The Geography of Language Shift: Distance from the Mexican Border and Spanish Language Claiming in the Southwestern US," *International Journal of the Sociology of Language* 114: 9–27.

Colombi, M. Cecilia and Francisco X. Alarcón, eds. 1997. *La enseñanza del español a hispanohablantes: praxis y teoría.* Boston: Houghton Mifflin.

Craddock, Jerry R. 1992. "Historia del español en los Estados Unidos." In *Historia del español de América*, ed. César Hernández Alonso. Valladolid: Junta de Castilla y León. Pp. 803–26.

Day, Jennifer Cheeseman. 1996. *Population Projections of the United States by Age, Sex, Race, and Hispanic Origin: 1995 to 2050.* US Bureau of the Census, Current Population Reports, P25-1130. Washington DC: US Government Printing Office.

Dorian, Nancy. 1981. *Language Death.* Philadelphia: University of Pennsylvania Press.

Duignan, Peter J. and L. H. Gann. 1998. *The Spanish Speakers in the United States.* Lanham MD: University Press of America.

Durán, Richard P., ed. 1981. *Latino Language and Communicative Behavior.* Norwood NJ: Ablex.

Elías-Olivares, Lucía. 1979. "Language Use in a Chicano Community: a Sociolinguistic Approach." In *Sociolinguistic Aspects of Language Learning and Teaching*, ed. J. B. Pride. Oxford: Oxford University Press. Pp. 120–34.

Elías-Olivares, Lucía, ed. 1983. *Spanish in the United States: Beyond the Southwest.* Washington DC: National Center for Bilingual Education.

Espinosa, Aurelio M., Jr. 1909–13. "Studies in New Mexican Spanish," *Revue de Dialectologie Romane* 1: 157–239, 269–300; 3: 251–86; 4: 241–56; 5: 142–72.

García, MaryEllen. 1998. "Gender Marking in a Dialect of Southwest Spanish," *Southwest Journal of Linguistics* 17: 49–58.

Gutiérrez, Manuel. 1995. "On the Future of the Future Tense in the Spanish of the Southwest." In Silva-Corvalán, ed. Pp. 214–26.

Hernández Chávez, E. 1997. "Imperativo para la sobrevivencia cultural: la cuestión de la lengua para la estatividad en Nuevo México y en Puerto Rico." Trabajo presentado en el Seminario Internacional sobre la Lengua Española en los Estados Unidos, Universidad Interamericana de Puerto Rico, San Juan, Puerto Rico.

Hernández Chávez, E., Garland Bills and Alan Hudson. 1996. "El desplazamiento del español en el suroeste de EEUU según el censo de 1990." In *Actas del X Congreso Internacional de la Asociación de Lingüística y Filología de la América Latina*, ed. M. Arjona Iglesias, J. López Chávez, A. Enríquez Ovando, G. López Lara and M. A. Novella Gómez. México: Universidad Nacional Autónoma de México. Pp. 664–72.

Hernández Chávez, E., A. D. Cohen and A. F. Beltramo, eds. 1975. *El lenguaje de los chicanos*. Washington DC: Center for Applied Linguistics.

Hidalgo, Margarita. 1990. "On the Question of 'Standard' versus 'Dialect': Implications for Teaching Hispanic College Students." In *Spanish in the United States: Sociolinguistic Issues*, ed. John J. Bergen. Washington DC: Georgetown University Press. Pp. 110–26.

Hill, Jane H. 1993. "Hasta la vista, baby. Anglo Spanish in the American Southwest," *Critique of Anthropology* 13: 145–76.

  1995. Mock Spanish: A site for the indexical reproduction of racism in American English. *http://www.language-culture.org/colloquia/symposia/hill-jane/*

Hudson, Alan, E. Hernández Chávez and Garland Bills. 1995. "The Many Faces of Language Maintenance: Spanish Language Claiming in Five Southwestern States." In Silva-Corvalán, ed. Pp. 165–83.

Kanellos, Nicolás. 1995. *Chronology of Hispanic-American History*. Detroit: Gale Research.

McWilliams, Carey. 1990. *North from Mexico*. New edn., updated by Matt S. Meier. New York: Greenwood.

Meier, Matt S. and Feliciano Rivera. 1972. *The Chicanos: a History of Mexican-Americans*. New York: Hill and Wang.

Mejías, H. A. and P. L. Anderson. 1988. "Attitudes toward use of Spanish on the South Texas Border," *Hispania* 71: 401–07.

Myers-Scotton, Carol. 1993a. *Duelling Languages: Grammatical Structure in Codeswitching*. Oxford: Clarendon.

  1993b. *Social Motivations for Codeswitching*. Oxford: Clarendon.

National Center for Education Statistics. 1997. *Digest of Education Statistics, 1997*, NCES 98-015. Washington DC: National Center for Education Statistics.

Peñalosa, Fernando. 1980. *Chicano Sociolinguistics*. Rowley MA: Newbury House.

Ramírez, Arnulfo G. 1992. *El español de los Estados Unidos: El lenguaje de los hispanos*. Madrid: Mapfre.

Roca, Ana and John Lipski, eds. 1993. *Spanish in the United States: Linguistic Contact and Diversity*. Berlin: Mouton.

Sánchez, George J. 1993. *Becoming Mexican-American*. New York: Oxford University Press.

Sánchez, Rosaura. 1983. *Chicano Discourse*. Rowley MA: Newbury House.

Silva-Corvalán, Carmen. 1994. *Language Contact and Change: Spanish in Los Angeles*. Oxford: Clarendon.

Silva-Corvalán, Carmen, ed. 1995. *Spanish in Four Continents: Studies in Language Contact and Bilingualism*. Washington DC: Georgetown University Press.

Urrutia, Hernán. 1995. "Morphosyntactic Features in the Spanish of the Basque Country." In Silva-Corvalán, ed. Pp. 243–59.

US Bureau of the Census. 1982. *1980 census of population*. Vol. 1. *Characteristics of the Population*. Washington DC: US Government Printing Office.

  1993. *1990 census of population*. Vol. 1. *Characteristics of the Population*. Washington DC: US Government Printing Office.

Wherritt, Irene and Ofelia García, eds. 1989. *US Spanish: the Language of Latinos. International Journal of the Sociology of Language*, special issue No. 79.

12

American Sign Language

CEIL LUCAS AND CLAYTON VALLI

Editors' introduction

Possibly no aspect of language use is more misunderstood than sign language. Probably, too, not many readers will know that American Sign Language – ASL, as it's commonly called – is used in the USA by at least half a million people and perhaps by as many as two million. Among its users are hearing members and deaf members of the American Deaf community. In this chapter, Ceil Lucas and Clayton Valli combine their perspectives to present a description of ASL and its use; many readers will be surprised at how much about ASL and sign languages more generally you have misunderstood. You may also be surprised at how much you know already.

American Sign Language is an autonomous linguistic system whose elements are visual rather than aural. It is a fully formed language, fundamentally like all other languages but differing from most of them in the vehicle used for expression. ASL is not dependent on American English (or on any other language); instead, it has its own system of signs. Some signs are iconic (an iconic sign is one that mimics or directly reflects the referent or meaning) but most signs are arbitrary. In spoken language, too, most signs (in this case, spoken words) are arbitrary, with little or no direct or inherent reference to what they signify.

Like US varieties of English and Spanish, ASL varies geographically (it has dialects) and across social groups. The ASL of men and the ASL of women may differ, as may the ASL of black and white user groups or of older and younger ASL users. Unlike English, whose American variety stems from British English and therefore closely resembles British English, ASL does not derive from American English or British English. ASL cannot be understood by users of British Sign Language (BSL), and vice versa. ASL, like other sign languages (and like spoken languages), changes, especially in response to contact with other languages. Of course, in the US many users of ASL command two languages. Besides signing ASL, they read and write – and some speak – English or some other language. Very little of a fundamental nature that is said of spoken languages in the other chapters of this book could not be said equally of ASL, and as a reader of this chapter you may be surprised at how much you therefore knew about ASL without realizing you knew it.

What is American Sign Language?

American Sign Language, or ASL as it is frequently called, is the language used by members of the American Deaf community.[1] Estimates of the number of users of ASL range from 500,000 to two million in the United States (Schein 1989), and ASL is used in Canada as well. The term "ASL user" includes many different kinds of people. It may refer to the deaf member of a Deaf family in which the primary language is ASL; it may refer to the hearing member of the same Deaf family who acquires ASL as a first language (such individuals are often referred to as "codas," that is, children of deaf adults); it may refer to the deaf members of hearing families who acquire ASL from their Deaf peers in residential school settings; it may refer to late-deafened individuals who learn ASL as adults; and, finally, it may refer to hearing people who have English as their native language and learn ASL as a second language. So the American Deaf community is very diverse. ASL is an autonomous linguistic system that is independent from the system of English or Spanish or other languages used in the USA. It has all of the characteristics of systems that we recognize as languages (Valli and Lucas 2001). In what follows, some of the main characteristics of languages will be discussed in terms of ASL.

For example, ASL is composed of symbols that are organized and used systematically. The symbols in a sign language include manual signs produced with the hands and non-manual signals produced with the face, head, and body. Manual signs have parts, including the handshape (which fingers are open or closed, whether the thumb is open or closed, and so forth), the location of the hand or hands (on the body, on the head, in the space in front of the body), the movement of the hand or hands (up and down, side to side, in an arc), and the orientation of the palm (facing the signer or facing away from the signer). Many signs also have an obligatory facial expression that accompanies them, and eye gaze, head position, and body position all play an important role in ASL. Many signs differ in only one part, as can be seen in figure 12-1: the signs SUMMER, UGLY, and DRY share the same handshape, palm orientation, and movement, but differ in location. To help distinguish signs from English words, note that upper-case letters are conventionally used to represent lexical signs.

The structure of signs is analogous to the structure of spoken language words (Liddell and Johnson 1989). Spoken language words consist of a sequence of consonants and vowels, and signs consist of a sequence of holds and movements. A hold is when the hand is stationary and not changing in any way; a movement is when some part of the sign – the handshape, the palm orientation, the location, the facial expression – is in the process of changing. This structure is illustrated in figure 12-2, where we see the sign DEAF.

[1] Upper-case D is used to denote communities and language users who are culturally deaf, that is, who share values, beliefs, and behaviors about deafness. Lower-case d is used to denote audiological deafness, that is, the physiological condition of not being able to hear. Individuals who are deaf may not necessarily be Deaf.

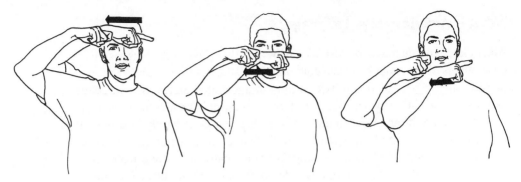

Figure 12-1 *SUMMER, UGLY, DRY*

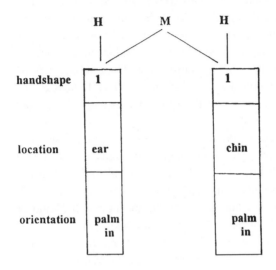

DEAF, citation form

Figure 12-2 *DEAF in the Hold–Movement–Hold model*

It has a 1 handshape (all fingers and thumb closed except for the index), the palm is generally oriented out away from the signer, and the sign moves down from just below the ear to the lower cheek area. The structure of this sign is hold–movement–hold. Other signs consist of movement–hold, or just a hold, just a movement, and so forth.

The form of ASL signs may be arbitrary or iconic. Iconic signs are those where the form of the sign reflects some aspect of the thing or event being represented. Examples can be seen in the signs for TREE (representing the trunk and branches) and CAT (representing a cat's whiskers), as given in figure 12-3a.

Sometimes the form of the sign is arbitrary and does not reflect the form of the thing or activity being represented, as in figure 12-3b, the signs for WRONG and LOUSY. The fact that many signs are iconic, however, does not mean that

Figure 12-3a *The ASL signs TREE and CAT, to illustrate iconicity*

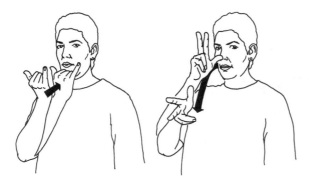

Figure 12-3b *The ASL signs WRONG and LOUSY, to illustrate arbitrariness*

ASL is basically mime or simply a collection of "pictures in the air." ASL has a complex linguistic structure, as do all sign languages.

As mentioned above, ASL is shared by a community of its users, and within the larger ASL community smaller communities may be defined. There is a lot of regional variation in ASL, with different signs in existence for the same concept. There is some evidence that African American signers may sign differently from white signers (Aramburo 1989, Lewis 1998), and researchers have demonstrated that ASL exhibits sociolinguistic variation correlated chiefly with age and region and to some extent gender and parents' language background, that is, Deaf ASL users vs. hearing non-signers (Lucas, Bayley, and Valli 2001). Furthermore, sign language is not universal. The sign language used by the American Deaf community is completely distinct from the sign language used in the British Deaf community and known as BSL, and from the sign language used in the Italian Deaf community (known as Lingua Italiana dei Segni or LIS). Deaf people who know one sign language do not automatically understand another sign language. Natural sign language is not universal.

Like any language, ASL is productive. That is, from a finite set of rules, an infinite number of sentences can be produced, and new messages on any topic can be produced at any time. ASL can be used to discuss any topic, from the

Figure 12-4a *The ASL sign MICROWAVE*

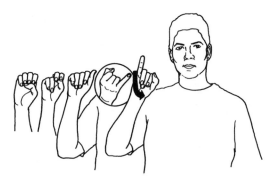

Figure 12-4b *Full fingerspelling J-A-N-E*

concrete to the abstract, from basic survival to philosophy and physics. It can be used to discuss the past and the future and non-immediate situations; it is not restricted in use to the present and the immediate. ASL is used in classrooms from the elementary level through college and graduate school as the medium of instruction for any subject from math and chemistry to literature and linguistics. In addition, ASL is used for creative purposes such as storytelling, word games, and poetry. The creative uses of sign languages have led to a reconsideration of the meaning of literature, as a body of ASL literature clearly exists in the form of videotaped poems and stories (Valli 1993).

Like other languages, ASL has ways to introduce new items into the system. Sometimes this involves using the parts of signs already available and creating a new sign, illustrated in figure 12-4a for MICROWAVE. Sometimes a new concept is represented by fingerspelling, that is, by the use of the manual alphabet to represent written words. The ASL manual alphabet consists of 26 signs for the written symbols of the English alphabet.

Sometimes these signs are produced individually in sequence, such as when someone is introducing himself and fingerspelling his name, for example, J-A-N-E, as seen in figure 12-4b. Very often, however, when fingerspelling is used to represent a new concept, the transition between the separate signs becomes

Figure 12-4c *Reduced fingerspelling #FAX*

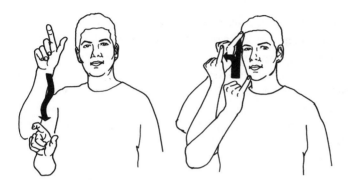

Figure 12-4d *The ASL sign ITALY and the LIS sign ITALY*

very fluid and some signs are even omitted. In these cases, fingerspelling becomes more like signing and is marked with the # symbol. Old examples of this kind of fingerspelling include #BANK and #JOB. As seen in figure 12-4c, #FAX is a more recent addition to the language. Finally, sometimes sign languages add new signs by borrowing from other sign languages. For example, with the ever-growing contact among Deaf people from all over the world, ASL has recently replaced its signs for several countries with the signs used by the Deaf people in those countries. Figure 12-4d shows the ASL sign for ITALY, which is slowly being replaced by the Italian Sign Language (LIS) sign for ITALY.

As in every other language, signs can be broken down into smaller parts. The sign for CAT seen in figure 12-4a has a handshape in which the tip of the index finger contacts the tip of the thumb, with the middle, ring, and pinky finger extended. In this particular sign the handshape has no independent meaning, but sometimes the parts of signs do carry independent meaning. This particular handshape is also the sign for the number 9 and is used in the signs for WEEK, MONTH, and other numeral signs, as illustrated in figure 12-5, with the meaning of 9 weeks, 9 months, and so forth.

As in all other languages, the same group of linguistic symbols that make a sentence may have a variety of meanings, depending both on the non-manual

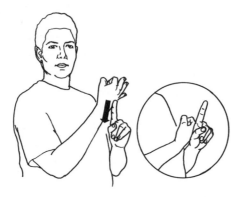

Figure 12-5 *The ASL sign 9 MONTHS*

signals that accompany the sentence and the social context in which the sentence occurs. For example, the sequence of signs HOME YOU can have the meaning of declarative sentence ("You are home"), a yes/no question ("Are you at home?" or "Are you going home?"), an imperative ("Go home!"), or an indirect request ("Can I get a ride home with you?"), all depending on context and the facial expression of the signer. For the yes/no question, for example, the eyebrows would be raised and the head forward, a facial expression quite distinct from the one occurring with the declarative sentence or the imperative one.

Like all other languages, ASL has changed across time and change affects all of the parts of the language: handshapes change, sign locations change, the orientation of the palm changes, two-handed signs become one-handed, one-handed signs become two-handed, and whole signs change as a result of new technologies in society. For example, the old sign for TELEPHONE consisted of two S handshapes (a closed fist), one at the signer's ear and one at the mouth, reflecting early telephone technology. One current sign is a Y handshape (thumb and pinky extended, all other fingers bent into the palm) held at the signer's ear, palm in. Another reflects the TTY (teletypewriter) used in the Deaf community, produced with the tip of the crooked index finger of the right hand moving down the extended index finger of the left hand. And as in all languages, change in ASL is often seen first as variation, that is, as different ways for saying the same thing. Often this variation can be correlated to social factors such as region, age, ethnicity, socioeconomic status, and gender; it is sociolinguistic variation. By way of example, we return to the sign DEAF. In its citation form (the form of a sign that appears in sign language dictionaries and is taught in sign language classes), the sign begins just below the signer's ear and moves down to the lower cheek. In practice, though, this sign is very commonly produced with the movement from the lower cheek to below the ear (that is, the very opposite of the citation form) or simply as a contact of the index finger on the lower cheek. This variation correlates with region, such that signers from Boston are more likely to produce the ear to chin version, while signers from Kansas tend to produce the chin to ear version (Lucas, Bayley, and Valli 2001). Younger and older signers tend to produce the chin to ear version, while middle-aged signers tend to produce the ear to chin one.

Humans are born with an innate capacity to acquire and use language, but children must have coherent and predictable input from adult users of the language, in order to completely acquire their language. This is as true for deaf children acquiring ASL as it is of hearing children acquiring a spoken language. Children who are born deaf into Deaf families easily and naturally acquire ASL as their first language. However, less than ten percent of deaf children are born into Deaf families and the exposure to ASL needed for the unfettered and natural acquisition of the language is frequently problematic. Very often, the hearing parents of deaf infants have no knowledge of or experience with ASL or the Deaf world and are frequently assured by doctors and audiologists that their deaf child can and will learn to speak English. A lot of time and energy is frequently expended teaching the child to speak during the "critical period," that is, the period between birth and age five, when conditions are optimal for acquiring language. Often deaf children do not begin to receive input in ASL until well after age five, and this has an impact on their subsequent acquisition of the language and on their English literacy skills. This contrasts sharply with deaf children who acquire ASL in Deaf families and who tend by and large to have excellent English literacy skills. Free access to a language that a deaf child can easily understand – ASL – seems to have a positive effect in the child's second language as well (Lane, Hoffmeister, and Bahan 1996). Fortunately, research on language acquisition in deaf children (see e.g. Petitto 1993, Petitto and Marentette 1991) that demonstrates the advantages of early exposure to a sign language is beginning to have an impact on early intervention and educational programs for deaf children.

As do the users of other languages, users of ASL monitor their use of language and correct themselves if they think that their production is faulty. And like the users of spoken languages, sign language users write dictionaries, grammars, and linguistic textbooks. That is, they reflect on their language and its use and display what linguists refer to as metalinguistic knowledge. Formal and widespread acceptance of ASL as a real language, however, did not really begin until the early 1960s, with the work of William C. Stokoe, a professor at Gallaudet University, the world's only liberal arts university for the Deaf. It was Stokoe who first recognized that ASL has a linguistic structure that is independent from that of the English he was teaching his students. He outlined the first linguistic description of signs (Stokoe 1960) and, with Dorothy Casterline and Carl Croneberg, published the first dictionary of signs based on linguistic principles in Stokoe, Casterline, and Croneberg (1965). With Stokoe's work, both hearing and deaf people began to recognize ASL as a language in its own right. Prior to his work, while there were many fluent users of the language, ASL was most usually considered to be simply a collection of gestures, a form of mime, or a kind of broken English. Many fluent signers had negative attitudes about their native language, feeling that the use of ASL would make them seem stupid and that "smart" people were people who had good English skills. In addition, many fluent signers did not have a name or a label for their language, referring to it simply as "sign." While a lot has changed since Stokoe's pioneering work in the 1960s, some ASL users still harbor these attitudes. In this way, ASL users are no different from the users of other minority languages. It is common for the users of minority languages to undervalue their language, to underestimate their skills in the language, and view the majority language of the community as being more prestigious than their own language. These are all attitudes still found not only in the American Deaf community, but in Deaf communities around the world.

A historical sketch of ASL

Not much is known about the deaf people who lived in North America before 1817, but some probably came from Great Britain or Europe and some were born here. There were some established Deaf communities such as the well-known one on Martha's Vineyard in which both deaf and hearing people signed (Groce 1985, Lane 1984). Because there was little contact between different communities, several kinds of sign language were probably used in America before 1817, including the so-called *home sign* systems that often develop in hearing families that have a deaf child. As some researchers put it, "The functional use of home gestures can range from simple pointing at objects and acting out messages, to a repertoire of agreed-upon gestures that convey a much more extensive range of information, sometimes even affective information" (Lane et al. 1996: 39–40).

The year 1817 is significant in the history of ASL, as it is the year in which the first school for deaf children was established in the United States. In 1815, Thomas Hopkins Gallaudet, a Protestant minister from Hartford, Connecticut, had traveled to Europe in search of a method for educating Alice Cogswell, the deaf daughter of his neighbor Dr. Mason Cogswell. He had first gone to Great Britain to learn about the oral method used by the Braidwood Schools in Scotland and near London, but the directors of these schools refused to share their methods. While in London, Gallaudet met the Abbé Sicard, who was the director of the Royal Institution for the Deaf in Paris. Sicard was in London with two of his students, Jean Massieu and Laurent Clerc, demonstrating the success of his teaching methods. The method used at the Royal Institution involved the use of French Sign Language along with a set of signs invented to represent parts of written and spoken French not found in French Sign Language. These so-called methodical signs were originally developed by Sicard's mentor, Abbé de l'Epée, the founder and first director of the school in Paris. Sicard invited Gallaudet to the Royal Institution to learn French Sign Language and their teaching methods, and Gallaudet spent several months in Paris. When he returned to the United States, he was accompanied by Laurent Clerc. In April of 1817, Gallaudet and Clerc opened the Connecticut Asylum for the Education and Instruction of Deaf and Dumb Persons – now called the American School for the Deaf. On the ocean crossing to America, Clerc taught Gallaudet French Sign Language and Gallaudet taught Clerc English. Many deaf people and some hearing people came to Hartford to learn the method being used at the newly established school. Some of the deaf students, including some from Martha's Vineyard, brought their own sign language with them. They also learned the sign language being used at the school, which no doubt included many French signs. In fact, a comparison of dictionaries on modern French Sign Language (LSF) and ASL has found 58 percent cognates in a sample of eighty-seven signs (Woodward 1978). Cognates in this case refers to the same or very similar signs for the same concept, and 58 percent represents a high degree of overlap between the two languages.

It seems, then, that several language systems were in contact at the inception of the school, giving rise to a contact language, which "would have then been passed on as a native language to the next generation by Deaf teachers and by Deaf pupils if, when adults, they had Deaf children of their own" (Lucas, Bayley, and Valli 1996: 57). As contact languages are passed down across generations, they typically undergo structural expansion through nativization, so the language used at the school during the first years of its existence was no doubt quite different from modern ASL, which has all the features of a full-fledged language, as we saw above. Furthermore, many graduates of the Hartford school went out and founded schools for the deaf in other parts of the country. "As early as 1834, a single signed dialect was recognized in the schools for Deaf students in the USA. By the time of Clerc's death in 1869, over fifteen hundred pupils had graduated from the Hartford school, and there were some thirty residential schools in the United States with 3,246 pupils and 187 teachers, 42 percent of them Deaf. Most such pupils and teachers married other Deaf persons and had children. This . . . helped to disseminate ASL" (Lane et al. 1996: 58).

So ASL was used as the medium of instruction at the American School for the Deaf. The signs invented to represent parts of English fell into disuse by the 1830s, as had the signs invented to represent French. As early as the 1840s, however, the movement for the oral education of deaf children – that is, using spoken English as the medium of instruction and teaching them to speak English, to the exclusion of ASL – was rapidly gaining momentum, partly due to a cultural change in the USA involving views on creationism and evolution. As Baynton states, "Most of the former [teachers of the deaf] came of age before the publication of Charles Darwin's *Origin of the Species* in 1859, and had constructed their understanding of the world around the theory of immediate creation. Most of those opposed to the use of sign language belonged to a younger generation whose worldview was built upon an evolutionary understanding of the world" (1996: 36–37). And in this view, the use of the spoken language was considered to be more "evolved" than the use of sign language. One of the leaders of the oralist movement was Alexander Graham Bell. In the 1860s, an oral school – now the Clarke School – was established in Massachusetts and at a famous meeting of educators of the deaf in Milan, Italy, in 1880, it was resolved that speech should have preference over signs in the teaching of deaf children and that, in fact, the use of signs would interfere with the learning of speech and lip-reading. These resolutions had a drastic effect on deaf education in the USA. Most deaf teachers lost their jobs and ASL was banned as the medium of instruction: "In 1867 there were 26 US institutions for the education of Deaf children, and all taught in ASL as far as we know; by 1907 there were 139, and none did" (Lane, Hoffmeister, and Bahan 1996: 62). Despite its being banned in educational settings, however, ASL certainly did not disappear from the lives of Deaf people. It continued to be used in their homes and in social interactions with other Deaf people, and it was also maintained in a clandestine fashion at the residential schools. Although it was forbidden in classrooms and although students were routinely punished for using it, ASL flourished in the dormitories. Since most deaf children are born into hearing families and have no automatic access to ASL, the access provided by deaf children from Deaf families in residential schools became crucial for the socialization of deaf children into the Deaf world. To this day, residential schools have very special status in the Deaf community as the sites where Deaf culture is transmitted to deaf children. In fact, recent demographic research (Padden and Tractenberg 1996) indicates that the majority of students who have deaf parents attend residential schools for the deaf. This is in contrast to the vast majority of deaf children who are mainstreamed into programs with hearing children (Ramsey 1997).

What ASL is not

Oralism is the use of the spoken language as the medium of instruction for deaf children, to the exclusion of signing. Oralism dominated the educational scene until the late 1960s, when educators finally began to realize that the achievement levels for Deaf children were well below those of both hearing children and deaf children from Deaf families. This led to the idea that perhaps signs should accompany spoken English, so that Deaf children could see English represented with the hands. The hypothesis was that visual access to English would enhance deaf children's skills in the language. This in turn led to the invention of systems to manually represent English. Such systems are known collectively as Manually Coded English (MCE). An example of MCE is Signing Exact English or SEE. SEE was invented in 1969 by Gerilee Gustason, a deaf Gallaudet University professor of education.[2] SEE uses ASL signs along with signs invented to represent parts of English not found in ASL such as suffixes (*-ly*, *-ness*, *-ment*), verb endings (*-s*, *-ed*, *-ing*), the plural marker (*-s*), and articles such as *the*. The signs are produced in English word order and SEE uses none of the non-manual signals that are an integral part of ASL. SEE became very popular as a medium of

[2] Gallaudet University is the only liberal arts university in the world for deaf and hard-of-hearing people. Located in Washington DC, it was established in 1864 by an act of Congress, and its charter was signed by Abraham Lincoln. During the fall of 2000, Gallaudet had an enrollment of 1,321 undergraduates, 625 graduates, and 93 sign language and professional studies students. Of the 1,011 employees, including faculty and staff, more than one-third are deaf. Located on Gallaudet campus are the Kendall Demonstration Elementary School (with 143 students) and the Model Secondary School for the Deaf (with 214 students). Gallaudet's alumni association was established in 1889 and its sixty-five chapters serve more than 14,000 US and international alumni.

instruction and is still used today in many settings. In many situations, it is used in conjunction with spoken English, in what is commonly known as Total Communication. Total Communication originated as a teaching *philosophy*, that is teachers were encouraged to use any means available to communicate with deaf children – signing, fingerspelling, talking (Denton 1976). It eventually evolved into Simultaneous Communication (Sim-Com) – the simultaneous use of signing and talking – and is accurately described as Sign-Supported Speech since the aural signal takes precedence, and signs tend to be omitted or misarticulated (Johnson et al. 1989). Despite being popular in many educational settings, the usual result of Sign-Supported Speech is a reduced and incomprehensible form of both English and ASL that does not provide deaf students adequate access to academic content.

ASL is not a kind of manual code for English. It is a visual–gestural language with a structure independent of and very different from spoken English. Users of ASL do not speak English while they produce signs, and the word order of ASL is sometimes very different from the word order used in spoken English. ASL exploits the face and body of the signer and the space around the signer to convey grammatical information. Manual codes for English like Signing Exact English are precisely that – *codes* for a spoken language. ASL is not a code for a language; it is a full-fledged language in its own right.

Fortunately, many educators of the deaf now realize that the best way to educate deaf children is simply to provide them access to academic content through a language (as opposed to a *code* for a language) that they can readily understand. Sign languages are being implemented as the medium of instruction not only in the USA but also in many other countries. In an address to the XII World Congress of the World Federation of the Deaf in 1995, then-Secretary General of the United Nations Boutros Boutros-Ghali affirmed that "Deaf people should have the right to use Sign Language as the medium of communication" (as cited in Lane et al. 1996:421). Deaf people around the world are becoming more aware of their sign languages and more empowered every day.

ASL and its users

As we said at the beginning of this chapter, the American Deaf community is very diverse. In the USA, almost all Deaf users of ASL are bilingual: they read and write English and if they come from hearing homes in which another spoken language is used, such as Spanish, Vietnamese, or Chinese, they may also have some familiarity with those languages. The term *bilingual* requires special consideration when it is used in reference to the Deaf community because, while most Deaf people read and write English, they may choose not to *speak* it. This may be because they are profoundly deaf, and having no auditory feedback makes it very difficult to learn to use a spoken language. It may also be for political reasons, that is, they may have been forced during the course of their educational career to learn to speak, to the exclusion of ASL, and, as a consequence, as adults they make the conscious choice not to use their voices. There are other members of the Deaf community who are either hard-of-hearing or late-deafened (that is, they are native English speakers but became deaf as teenagers or as adults), who in some situations speak English and in others sign ASL. The situation in the Deaf community seems to be one of maintained bilingualism, meaning that both ASL and English will continue to have functions in the lives of Deaf people, unlike in some spoken language communities in which one language is being replaced by another. This is mainly because, given its fundamentally visual nature, ASL will continue to be the language that is most accessible and comfortable for Deaf people.

The recent advent of cochlear implants and the idea of finding a prevention or cure for deafness have been a source of concern and alarm within the Deaf community, as they threaten the continuity of the Deaf community and of sign language. In addition, cochlear implants raise ethical issues concerning surgery in children who are not able to choose freely (Lane, Hoffmeister, and Bahan 1996: 389).

The American Deaf community, then, is fundamentally a bilingual one and when languages are in contact, a number of outcomes can be predicted. A distinction must be made between the outcomes of contact between two sign languages and the outcomes of contact between a sign language and a spoken/written language. The former case would be, for example, contact between an ASL user and a user of another sign language such as Italian Sign Language or Thai Sign Language. One outcome of this contact might be lexical borrowing, as seen earlier with the example of the sign for ITALY. If the signers are bilingual in two sign languages, they might on occasion code-switch between the two languages, as do the bilingual users of spoken languages. While signing one sign language, they might experience interference from another sign language.

In the case of contact between a spoken/written language and a sign language, hearing signers may be speaking English and momentarily switch to ASL; Deaf signers may be signing ASL and then stop signing and mouth an English word or phrase. Lexical borrowing occurs between English and ASL, as seen in the ASL compound signs BOY^FRIEND, HOME^WORK, and HOME^SICK, all borrowed from English. Finally, the contact between a sign language and a spoken/written language yields some unique phenomena, such as fingerspelling and combinations of fingerspelling and signs. For example, in the compound sign LIFE^#STYLE, the ASL sign LIFE is followed by the fingerspelling for 'style' (Kelly 1991). Signers may also code-switch between ASL and some form of Manually Coded English (MCE). Many ASL users have been exposed to Signing Exact English (SEE) and other MCEs in school and may use their knowledge of SEE in everyday conversation, to quote an English sentence exactly, for example. Finally, there is a kind of signing that occurs in the American Deaf community known as contact signing (Lucas and Valli 1992), whose structure combines elements of both languages in a kind of code-mixing. Contact signing is produced with ASL signs in English word order and frequently with continuous mouthing but without voice.[3] It incorporates the ASL use of space, body shifting, pointing (indexing) and eye gaze for the setting up of topics and subsequent referral to them throughout the discourse. Contact signing is not codified and is not something that can be formally taught; rather, it occurs quite naturally as a result of contact among bilinguals. Like spoken-language bilinguals, individuals who are bilingual in a signed language and a spoken/written language borrow, code-switch, code-mix, and fingerspell for a very simple reason: because they can. That is, human beings in language contact situations will exploit to the fullest whatever linguistic resources are available to them, and given the availability of two modalities (a spoken language and a signed language) and competence in them, they will use both of them. So, in some ways, there is nothing unique about language contact in the Deaf community. It is simply another instance of human beings going about the business of exploiting the linguistic resources available to them, resources that for obvious physiological reasons include two modalities. There are two unique things about it, however. First, given two modalities, how they will be used cannot necessarily be predicted. Deaf people may mouth to other Deaf people and not use their hands at all; hearing bilinguals may sign to each other when no Deaf people are around; a Deaf person may speak to a hearing person and the hearing person may answer in ASL with no voice; a Deaf and a hearing person may produce contact signing with each other, and so forth. Second, because two modalities are involved, there may be some unique outcomes such as fingerspelling. What *is* predictable and very clear is the existence of ASL and other sign languages as viable and autonomous linguistic systems that are highly valued by the members of Deaf communities all over the world.

Acknowledgments

We are grateful to Lois Lehman-Lenderman for the sign drawings and to M. J. Bienvenu for serving as the sign model.

Suggestions for further reading and exploration

Two excellent sources for further reading are Lane, Hoffmeister, and Bahan (1996) and Padden and Humphries (1988). Both provide a comprehensive overview of the linguistic and sociolinguistic realities and issues. Sociolinguistic issues in both ASL and a number of other sign languages are also explored in the *Sociolinguistics in Deaf Communities* series, edited by Ceil Lucas.

---

[3] Isolated mouthing does occur in ASL, some of the mouthing directly traceable to related English words and some of it completely unrelated to spoken English. This mouthing is, however, quite distinct from the continuous mouthing that occurs in Contact Signing, and both are distinct from simultaneously speaking and signing.

References

Aramburo, Anthony. 1989. "Sociolinguistics of the Black Deaf Community." In *The Socio-linguistics of the Deaf Community*, ed. Ceil Lucas. San Diego CA: Academic Press. Pp. 103–19.

Baynton, Douglas. 1996. *Forbidden Signs. American Culture and the Campaign Against Sign Language*. Chicago: University of Chicago Press.

Denton, David M. 1976. "The Philosophy of Total Communication." Supplement to the British Deaf News. Carlisle: British Deaf Association.

Groce, Nora. 1985. *Everyone Here Spoke Sign Language*. Cambridge: Harvard University Press.

Johnson, Robert E., Scott K. Liddell, and Carol J. Erting. 1989. *Unlocking the Curriculum: Principles for Achieving Access in Deaf Education*. Gallaudet Research Institute Working Paper 89–83. Washington DC: Gallaudet University.

Kelly, Arlene B. 1991. "Fingerspelling Use among the Deaf Senior Citizens of Baltimore." In *School of Communication Student Forum*, ed. E. A. Winston. Washington DC: Gallaudet University School of Communication. Pp. 90–98.

Lane, Harlan. 1984. *When the Mind Hears: a History of the Deaf*. New York: Random House.

Lane, Harlan, Robert Hoffmeister, and Ben Bahan. 1996. *A Journey into the DEAF-WORLD*. San Diego CA: DawnSign Press.

Lewis, John. 1998. "Ebonics in American Sign Language: Stylistic Variation in African American Signers." In *Deaf Studies V: Toward 2000 – Unity and Diversity*. Conference Proceedings. Washington DC: Gallaudet University, College for Continuing Education.

Liddell, Scott and Robert E. Johnson. 1989. "ASL: the Phonological Base," *Sign Language Studies* 64: 195–277.

Lucas, Ceil and Clayton Valli. 1992. *Language Contact in the American Deaf Community*. San Diego CA: Academic Press

Lucas, Ceil, Robert Bayley, and Clayton Valli. 2001. *Sociolinguistic Variation in ASL* . Sociolinguistics in Deaf Communities, Vol. 7. Washington DC: Gallaudet University Press.

Padden, Carol and Tom Humphries. 1988. *Deaf in America: Voices from a Culture*. Cambridge MA: Harvard University Press.

Padden, Carol and R. Tractenberg. 1996. "Intended and Unintended Consequences of Educational Policy for Deaf Children." Unpublished manuscript, University of California at San Diego: Research Program in Language and Literacy.

Petitto, Laura A. 1993. "On the Ontogenetic Requirements for Early Language Acquisition." In *Developmental Neurocognition: Speech and Face Processing in the First Year of Life*, eds. Benedicte de Boysson-Bardies, Scania de Schonen, Peter Jusczyk, Peter MacNeilage, and John Morton. New York: Kluwer Academic Press. Pp. 365–83.

Petitto, Laura A. and Paula F. Marentette. 1991. "Babbling in the Manual Mode: Evidence for the Ontogeny of Language," *Science* 251: 1493–96.

Ramsey, Claire. 1997. *Deaf Children in Public Schools – Placement, Context, and Consequences. Sociolinguistics in Deaf Communities*, Vol. 3. Washington DC: Gallaudet University Press.

Schein, Jerome D. 1989. *At Home among Strangers*. Washington DC: Gallaudet University Press.

Stokoe, William C. 1960. *Sign Language Structure*. In *Studies in Linguistics*, ed. George L. Trager. Occasional Paper 8. Buffalo NY: University of Buffalo.

Stokoe, William C., Dorothy Casterline, and Carl Croneberg. 1965 [rev. 1976]. *A Dictionary of American Sign Language on Linguistic Principles*. Silver Spring MD: Linstok Press.

Valli, Clayton. 1993. "Poetics of American Sign Language." Unpub. PhD dissertation, Union Institute.

Valli, Clayton and Ceil Lucas. 2001. *Linguistics of American Sign Language: an Introduction*, 3rd edn. Washington DC: Gallaudet University Press.

Woodward, James. 1978. "Historical Bases of American Sign Language." In *Understanding Language through Sign Language Research*, ed. Patricia Siple. New York: Academic Press. Pp. 333–48.

13

Asian American voices: language in the Asian American community

THOM HUEBNER AND LINDA UYECHI

Editors' introduction

The USA is a nation of immigrants and the children of immigrants, most of whom did not speak English when they arrived and whose adopted English will always show traces of their ancestry. Among notable groups of recent immigrants are speakers of Asian languages, with numbers large enough to sustain ancestral languages alongside English in some American communities. Asian immigrants are not new to the USA, and in this chapter Thom Huebner and Linda Uyechi describe the struggle many have faced in learning English, including "the role of language in negotiating multiple identities across cultures and generations" and "the emotion-laden burden of coping with racism and language discrimination" in the new land of promise.

The chapter relates the history of Asian contact and immigration, from its beginnings perhaps well before Columbus to its present-day compass across the Pacific and throughout Asia. Though the term "Asian American" has become familiar, this chapter underscores the fact that "Asian American" encompasses members of a community that is "split along several dimensions: first and second waves of immigration, immigrants and refugees, Asians in Hawai'i and Asians on the mainland, different countries of origin, different generations, and different languages." The term covers an enormously diverse "community" whose home languages are members of many language families – Sino-Tibetan, Austro-Asiatic, Austronesian, Indo-European, and Tai, in addition to Japanese and Korean, languages that are generally not recognized as having related family members. For the hugely diverse Asian American community, the authors note, "the glue that binds" is English.

The chapter also addresses major social and linguistic issues among Asian Americans, including language shift to English and language maintenance of ancestral or heritage languages, language discrimination against accented or "yellow" English, and cultural and interpersonal style.

> My mother, because she did not speak any English, found work in Chinatown in a sewing factory. But both [my mother and father] were pursuing ways of supporting a family that were not in line with their original interests. They were both college-educated people who had to essentially give up careers in their fields of interest to come to the States . . .   (Lee 1991: 41–44)
>
> *Sue Jean Lee Suettinger, born in Canton, China, immigrated to the USA with her family in 1952 at age four, graduated from Princeton University in 1970*

There were forty of us Hmong and none of us knew a word of English. My boss used to joke with me. He asked me, "Why do you never speak? If you just say coffee, then I will get you some coffee." I did not want to talk, but he kept bothering me. I finally asked my boss for some coffee, but he told me, "All you have to do is pour it in a cup. You do it yourself."   [Chan 1994: 58]

Jou Yee Xiong, a Hmong refugee, describing her job in a California pharmaceutical company

No matter how many years I am here – even till I die – I will always speak English with an accent. That is a fact that I cannot deny. That is a fact that I cannot escape from. And people would never see me as an American because the conventional wisdom is that if you are American, you should speak with no accent.   [Lee 1991: viii]

Cao O, Chinese from Vietnam, in his mid-thirties

There are people   Lodi   They persist and
who admire   Minneapolis   ask again.
the aesthetics   Chicago
of our traditions   Gilroy   Compliment
                          South Bend   our command of the
And ask politely,   Tule Lake   English language.
Where are you from?   San Francisco
                          New York Los Angeles
                          (excerpt from "American Geisha," Mirikitani 1987)

Janice Mirikitani, a Japanese American poet

Vignettes such as these illustrate the diversity of people covered by the term "Asian American" – recent immigrants and descendants of immigrants – multiple generations representing a range of languages and cultures. These stories focus on experiences with language that are familiar to many immigrants to America: the struggle to learn a new language, the role of language in negotiating multiple identities across cultures and generations, and the emotion-laden burden of coping with racism and language discrimination. To what extent are these experiences unique to the emerging community of Asian Americans? To what extent are they comparable across the spectrum of immigrant communities to which Asian Americans trace their roots? How do those communities differ with respect to their language experiences? Surprisingly, scholars have paid scant attention to the rich and diverse language situations in the Asian American community.

This chapter focuses on the language of those voices: to report the findings of existing studies and to suggest topics that we still know too little about. It starts with a brief history of Asians in America and continues with a discussion of some contemporary language issues in the Asian American community. Although the focus is on the language situations of East Asians, Southeast Asians, South Asians, and Filipinos, readers should bear in mind that similar inquiries need to be made for the growing Pacific Islander communities in the USA, as well as for mixed-race members of the Asian American community.

Asian American voices: history of immigration

While the identification of "Asian Americans" as a politically and socially significant group is a product of community activism in the 1960s and 1970s (Espiritu 1992, Wei 1993), Asians in America have a long and rich history, probably predating Columbus. The discovery of ancient Chinese artifacts along the Pacific coast supports Chinese records reporting their arrival on the North American continent in the fifth century CE. By the period of the Manila Galleon Trade (1593–1815), Filipino and Chinese craftsmen and sailors were employed in Mexico, California, and the Pacific Northwest. On the East coast, the US Immigration Commission first recorded the arrival of Chinese in 1820. In the South, Filipino seamen settled in Louisiana in the 1830s and 1840s. Chinese were reported to be working in 1835 on the island of Kaua'i in the Kingdom of Hawai'i.

Early Asian presence in North America was modest, though. Large-scale immigration occurred later, in two waves. The first wave began in the mid-nineteenth century in Hawai'i, an independent kingdom until its annexation to the USA in 1898, and in California, annexed to the USA in 1848 after the war with Mexico. It ebbed with the passage of the Immigration Act of 1924 and concluded with the Tydings–McDuffie Act of 1934. The second wave of Asian immigration began in 1965 after legislative reform expanded quotas for immigrants from Asia. The impact of this wave continues to be felt today.

Both waves of immigration are jointly characterized by the pull of perceived opportunity for higher wages and standards of living in the USA and by the push of unstable political, economic, or social conditions in the emigrants' home countries. Both also resulted from an aggressive US international stance, the first a direct result of American expansionism and colonialization, the second the result of American military, economic, and cultural penetration in Asia. There are also important differences between these waves of immigration – particularly among the various immigrant groups.

The first wave: entry, exploitation, and exclusion

> We would beg to remind you that when your nation was a wilderness, and the nation from which you sprung Barbarous, we exercised most of the arts and virtues of civilized life; that we are possessed of a language and a literature, and that men skilled in science and the arts are numerous among us; that the productions of our manufactories, our sail, and workshops, form no small commerce of the world . . . We are not the degraded race you would make us.   [Takaki 1989: 112]
>
> *Norman Asing, a Chinese immigrant, in an open letter to Governor*
> *John Bigler, published in the* Daily Alta California *in 1852*

Still unaccustomed
To the language of this land,
I often guess wrong.
(Hosui, in Ito 1973: 619)

I'm writing letters
To my children in English
It is something like
Scratching at an itchy place
Through your shoes.
(Yukari Tomita, in Ito 1973: 626)

Japanese American Issei (first generation) poetry

Then at supper Tosh brought it up again. He spoke in pidgin Japanese (we spoke four languages: good English in school, pidgin English among ourselves, good or pidgin Japanese to our parents and the other old folks), "Mama, you better tell Kyo not to go outside the breakers. By-'n'-by he drown. By-'n'-by the shark eat um up."   [Murayama, 1959]

Milton Murayama, capturing the linguistic diversity in many Japanese American families in Hawai'i during the 1930s and 1940s through Kyo, a young plantation boy

The first wave of immigrants from Asia came largely as unskilled laborers. Many from impoverished rural backgrounds came as sojourners and returned to their homelands. Some elected to settle in their new homes; others found themselves forced to stay for economic or political reasons. In both Hawai'i and California, immigration was initially promoted as a source of cheap labor. In Hawai'i in 1850, an association of mainly American sugar cane planters called the Royal Hawaiian Agricultural Society began to import laborers to supplement the native Hawaiian labor force. Meanwhile, on the North American continent, with US annexation of California in 1848, the rush to clear and settle the new territory, establish an economic presence on the West coast, and open markets in Asia led American capitalists and congressmen to support the importation of Asian laborers. In both cases the first source of labor was China. Spurred by political and economic unrest at home, lured by contracts promising work and wages, enchanted by the discovery of gold in California, and financed by loans from family and labor agents, the number of Chinese living in the USA grew to 63,000 by 1870. Of this number, 77 percent resided in California, but there were also concentrations in the Southwest, New England, and the South. Chinese constituted 29 percent of the population in Idaho, 10 percent in Montana, and 9 percent in California. In Hawai'i, by the turn of the century, some 46,000 Chinese were laboring in the sugar fields.

In both locations, subsequent immigration from other parts of Asia – Japan, Korea, the Philippines, and, on the mainland, South Asia – resulted from racist attempts to check the growth of the Chinese population and confound any attempts at labor organization. In Hawai'i, sugar planters in the 1880s, fearful that Chinese workers would organize, began looking elsewhere for labor. In the USA, the Chinese Exclusion Act of 1882 essentially barred immigration from China, forcing employers to recruit cheap labor from other parts of Asia.

The Chinese Exclusion Act was renewed in 1892 and extended indefinitely in 1902. It became the cornerstone of increasingly restrictive legislation aimed at

Asians in both Hawai'i and the continental USA. From 1790 until 1952 Asian immigrants could not become naturalized citizens, a privilege reserved for whites only (and, by a decision of the US Supreme Court, the ban applied to Asian Indians as well). In 1907, President Theodore Roosevelt signed an executive order prohibiting the remigration of Japanese and Korean laborers from Hawai'i to the continental USA. That same year, workers began arriving on the West coast from India; a total of 6,400 arrived before Congress prohibited immigration from India ten years later. And the next year, the 1908 Gentleman's Agreement restricted immigration from Japan. Finally, the Immigration Act of 1924, aimed specifically at Asians, banned immigration by anyone who was not eligible for naturalization. Discriminatory laws were passed at the state level as well. In California, for example, a 1913 alien land law forbade the ownership of land by anyone not eligible for US citizenship; it was aimed particularly at Japanese immigrants.

In spite of these restrictions, the number of Asians in the USA continued to rise. By the 1920s, some 200,000 Japanese went to Hawai'i and 120,000 to the USA mainland. Motivated in part by the colonialization of Korea by Japan, 8,000 Koreans immigrated to Hawai'i between 1903 and 1920. In 1924 the Immigration Act curtailed Asian immigration, but as citizens of a US territory, Filipinos were technically "American nationals" and were heavily recruited to backfill the need for laborers. By 1930, 110,000 Filipinos had gone to Hawai'i and more than 40,000 to the continental USA. But even Filipino immigration came to a virtual halt, as the Tydings–McDuffie Act (1934) signaled the start of proceedings to sever territorial claims to the Philippines and restrict subsequent immigration from those islands.

From the beginning, both in Hawai'i and on the continent, Asian American immigrant groups were split along national lines as they brought ethnic antagonisms and cultural stereotypes with them from their homelands. In the new land, competition for employment and anti-Asian public policies further encouraged Asian immigrants to dissociate themselves from one another. Japanese and Korean immigrants, for example, did not want to be associated with Chinese.

In contrast, ties within individual Asian ethnic communities were strong. Whether created voluntarily or as a result of segregationist policies and racist pressures, ethnic enclaves contributed to the maintenance of culture and language through temples and churches, community associations and schools, shops, banks, theaters, and newspapers. There were differences, though, between Asian communities in Hawai'i and those on the continent, and those differences impacted language in important ways.

In Hawai'i, plantations were initially dominated by unmarried men who composed a cheap labor force. Pressured by missionaries and noting better output by married men, planters in Hawai'i began to favor and encourage laborers to establish families (Takaki 1983: 119–26). As a result, many Chinese laborers married Hawaiian women and, in addition to their native Chinese, may have spoken a Pidgin Hawaiian (Bickerton and Wilson 1987). Later immigrants, especially from

Japan and Korea, brought families with them or sent for picture brides. Although ethnically segregated camps provided some support for maintaining immigrant languages, the dominance of English in public domains (cf. Huebner 1985), the use of a Pidgin English as the lingua franca of the fields (Reinecke 1969), and the presence of a generation of Hawai'i-born Asians intermingling across ethnic lines in school and playgrounds led to rapid development of a predominantly Asian American form of every day speech – a vernacular called Hawai'i Creole English (HCE). Further reinforced through a system of language-segregated public education, HCE contributed to the development of a "local" identity that continues today (Sato 1985, 1989).

On the continent, the first wave was more diverse and dispersed. Although most settled in California, many also made their ways to other parts of the West, to the South, and the Northeast, including New York. Groups also differed in their gender balance. Chinese, Korean, Filipino and Asian Indian immigrants were predominantly male, forming "bachelor societies" in America. Although discouraged by anti-miscegenation laws, Filipinos and Asian Indians often married Mexican, Native American, and African American women. In contrast, Japanese immigrants included significantly more women, and the greater gender balance contributed to a more ethnically homogeneous community.

Work and settlement patterns were also more varied. Asian immigrants mined for gold in the Sierras, copper in Utah, and coal in Colorado and Wyoming; they built the intercontinental railroad; they labored in the fisheries and canneries of the Pacific Northwest and Alaska; they cultivated fruit and vegetable farms; they worked as hotel keepers and domestic servants; and they provided migrant agricultural labor throughout the West. By the turn of the century they even provided services to other Asians in the growing Asian enclaves in San Francisco, Seattle, Sacramento, Los Angeles, and other cities.

These diverse patterns among Asian immigrants were naturally reflected in their language situations. Those Chinese living in urban enclaves could meet most everyday needs in Chinese. Japanese, too, formed ethnic enclaves. Like other immigrant groups, both the Chinese and Japanese established language schools to transmit the heritage language to the second generation. Koreans, while more geographically dispersed, formed communities around church and nationalist organizations. They maintained the highest literacy rate among the first wave of Asian immigrants and also established Korean language schools for the second generation. In contrast, Asian Indians and Filipinos had no self-sufficient communities. Overwhelmingly male and relatively small in number, Asian Indians often worked in labor gangs and dealt with the larger society through an interpreter. Filipinos could often speak English, and as a consequence were perhaps not driven to ethnic enterprise to the same extent as other Asian groups (Takaki 1989: 336). Those Asian Indians and Filipinos who had married Mexicans often spoke English and Spanish at home and, presumably, retained their native language with friends (Takaki 1989: 311–14). Our understanding of language use for these first wave immigrants is somewhat limited, however, and more in-depth investigations would be useful to our understanding of those circumstances.

Unlike Asians in Hawai'i, Asians on the continent never formed a majority, even in cities with large Chinatowns. Instead, divided by national and cultural differences, and lacking any incentive to break down language barriers, the first wave of Asian groups on the continent remained socially, politically, and linguistically distinct – developing neither a distinctively Asian American language nor a common "local" identity.

The second wave: diversity and pan-ethnic Asian American identity

> My family arrived in America in 1975 when I was four years old. In subsequent years, as my parents were busy chasing the "American Dream," I occupied myself by learning to love America. My Vietnamese language was one of the things I lost in the process . . . Without my Vietnamese language, everything I had accomplished in American society was worthless in Vietnamese society . . . As many immigrants articulate in their own language become reticent in America, so I became reticent within my own community. (Nguyen 1990: 24)
>
> *Viet Nguyen, who lives in Berkeley, California*

With Asian immigration at a trickle, the Chinese, Japanese, and Korean communities in the USA remained generally stable from 1924 until 1965. Fueled by nationalistic animosities and discrimination in the USA, Asian immigrant communities continued to maintain social distance from each other. Ethnic separation peaked in 1942 when President Franklin Roosevelt signed Executive Order 9066 and the American military summarily escorted 120,000 Japanese Americans to concentration camps until the end of World War II. Eager to distance themselves from Japanese Americans, other Asian Americans wore buttons and posted signs in store windows proclaiming they were not Japanese. While their community was imprisoned behind barbed wire, young Japanese American soldiers fought heroically for US victory, thereby highlighting the injustice and hypocrisy of the camps.

World War II and its aftermath resulted in significant policy changes for Asian Americans. Unable to immigrate since before the war, Filipinos served in the US military during the war and became eligible for US citizenship. Chinese American soldiers were allowed to bring home Chinese war brides, and the US alliance with China against Japan led to the repeal of the Chinese Exclusion Act in 1943. In 1948, a US Supreme Court decision ruled California's alien land law unconstitutional, allowing Japanese to own land legally for the first time, and in 1952 the McCarran–Walter Act nullified racial restrictions on nationalization and approved immigration from South Asia and East Asia, though with strict quotas. The ultimate policy change, however, was the passage of the 1965 Immigration

Table 13-1 *Immigrants by country, 1965 and 1970*

Year	China	India	Japan	Korea	Philippines	Other Asia
1965	1,611	467	3,294	2,139	2,963	9,201
1970	6,427	8,795	4,731	8,888	30,507	30,372

Source: Taken from US Department of Commerce, 1975. *Historical Statistics of the United States: Colonial Times to 1970, Part 1.* Washington, DC: US Government Printing Office, p. 107.

Reform Act, which significantly relaxed quotas on Asian immigrants. Five years after the passage of the law, annual immigration from Asia increased dramatically (table 13-1), signaling the second wave of Asian immigrants to the USA.

In the 1970s, the American defeat in Southeast Asia brought refugees from Vietnam, Laos, and Cambodia. Together with other second-wave immigrants and descendants of first wave immigrants, they constitute a more diverse Asian American population than had previously existed – a diversity displayed not only in ethnic and geographical distribution, but also in education and average income (table 13-2). In contrast to the first wave of Asian immigrants, this population is young, mainly urbanized, and fairly well balanced between the sexes.

The changes in demographics were accompanied by political and social changes leading to the emergence of a pan-ethnic Asian American identity. In the post-World War II era, a growing awareness of race-based discrimination helped forge links between formerly distinct communities of Asians. In 1946, for example, a strike to organize plantation workers in Hawai'i included a mix of Asian American ethnicities. But the civil rights movement and American involvement in the Vietnam War were the most significant catalysts in pan-ethnic Asian American struggles on college campuses in the USA during the late 1960s and early 1970s.

Though those struggles have led to an increased recognition of a history of shared experiences among Asians in America, the term "Asian American" continues to refer to a tenuously built "community" that is split along several dimensions: first and second waves of immigration, immigrants and refugees, Asians in Hawai'i and Asians on the mainland, different countries of origin, different generations, and different languages. The remainder of this chapter focuses on the diversity of the Asian American community around language-related issues.

Language in the Asian American community: contemporary issues

From the perspective of language use in the diverse Asian American community, English may be viewed as the "glue that binds." While their elders may have

Table 13-2 *Demographic data on Asian Americans, 1990*

Ethnicity	Chinese	Filipino	Japanese	Indian	Korean	Vietnamese	Cambodian	Hmong	Lao	Thai	Other Asian[1]
Total population	1,645,472	1,406,770	847,562	815,447	798,849	614,547	147,411	90,082	149,014	91,275	302,209
By region: Northeast	445,089	142,958	74,202	285,103	182,061	60,509	30,176	1,731	15,928	11,801	75,307
Midwest	133,336	113,354	63,210	146,211	109,087	51,932	12,921	37,166	27,775	12,981	47,430
South	204,430	159,378	67,193	195,525	153,163	168,501	19,279	1,621	29,262	23,747	72,080
West	862,617	991,080	642,957	188,608	354,538	333,605	85,035	49,564	76,049	42,746	107,392
% Male	49.9	46.2	45.9	53.7	42.3	52.9	48.6	50.9	51.7	41.2	54.3
Mean age	32.1	31.1	36.3	28.9	29.1	25.2	19.4	12.5	20.4	31.8	24.5
% Living in urban area[2]	94.7	88.2	84.7	90.7	89.9	94.3	95.9	91.5	87.1	86.7	87.8
% 18–25 w/ h-s diploma[3]	84.6	83.8	91.4	86.6	82.6	68.4	53.8	48.9	50.7	80.5	84.6
% 25+ w/ BA or more[4]	40.7	39.3	34.5	58.1	34.5	17.4	5.7	4.9	5.4	32.8	41.7
Average household income	46,780	50,713	50,367	59,777	41,311	36,177	24,952	17,198	26,304	40,342	39,795

Source: US Census Bureau, 1990.

[1] Includes Bangladeshi, Burmese, Indonesian, Malayan, Okinawan, Pakistani, Sri Lankan, and others.

[2] Urban areas are defined as having a population of 10,000 or more, including both central and urban fringe.

[3] Percentage of those ages 18–25 who hold a high school diploma, including a general education diploma.

[4] Percentage of those over 25 years old who hold at least a four-year bachelor's degree.

struggled to acquire the language of their chosen country, the second and third generation Asian Americans had native English abilities that allowed them to start dialogues across their parents' persistent national boundaries and to access American college campuses, where the evolution of Asian American consciousness began in the late 1960s and early 1970s (Espiritu 1992, Wei 1993). But acquisition of English is only one of many language issues that shape the Asian American experience. Among them, the ones discussed here are language maintenance and language shift, language discrimination, language as a marker of ethnicity, and language as conventionalized behavior.

Linguistic diversity, language maintenance, and language shift

> My first encounter with a Chinese restaurant was in Cleveland, Ohio. There just weren't any near where I was growing up. I can't speak the language, and you feel intimidated by it when you go into restaurants. Like you keep ordering the same dishes because those are the only dishes you can order. You feel that since you are Chinese, you should be able to speak to other people that look like you. Sometimes they have mistaken me for a Juk-kok (foreign-born Chinese) and started talking to me; I can't understand a word. [Lee 1991: 8–9]
>
> *Sam Sue, a Chinese American born and raised in Mississippi in the 1950s*

> I speak Japanese to my mother. She can read and listen in English, but she can't really speak well . . . Learning Japanese is important, because my grandmother doesn't speak any English, so I have to know Japanese to talk to her. And knowing two languages is nice. Some of my friends can only speak one, so it is kind of neat . . . I don't think of going back to Japan to live when I grow up. I like it here.   [Lee 1991: 19–21]
>
> *Mari, an eleven-year-old Japanese American from New Jersey, whose father works for a Japanese firm in the USA*

> I try to speak Khmer to [my daughter and her cousins], because I think in another five years they're going to forget their own language . . . I love to keep my own language because this is where I came from.   [Crawford 1992: 146]
>
> *Ravuth Yin, a young Cambodian refugee who lost his family during the turmoil of the Pol Pot regime and settled in Lowell, Massachusetts*

The language backgrounds of Asian immigrants represent a virtual tower of Babel – they include languages from most major language families. Chinese includes several related but mutually unintelligible "dialects" that share a common writing system; it is the largest of the Sino-Tibetan languages. Within this family some linguists also include Hmong, the language of highland refugees from Laos. Khmer (the language of Cambodia) and Vietnamese are usually considered Austro-Asiatic (sometimes called Mundo-Mon-Khmer) languages. Hindi and Urdu are Indo-European. Tagalog, Illocano, and other languages of the Philippines are Austronesian. Lao, the language of lowland Laos, is a Tai language. Japanese and Korean show little or no structural or historical relationship to any other language; the relationship between these so-called "isolates" and other languages is not known. While genetic relationships for these two languages are a matter of dispute, some linguists maintain that they are related to each other and some place one or both within the Altaic family.

Typologically, some languages, such as Lao, Hmong, Chinese, and Vietnamese, place the subject before the verb and the object after the verb (SVO), as English does. Korean and Japanese place the verb after subject and object (SOV), and languages from the Philippines put the verb at the beginning of the sentence (VSO). Pilipino, Japanese, and Korean use affixes (attached at the beginning or end of a word stem) or infixes (inserted within a word stem) to indicate grammatical categories like subject and object; they are inflectional languages. In contrast, Chinese, Vietnamese, Lao, and Hmong have few inflections or none, but are tonal languages in which the meaning of a word changes depending on the tone it carries when pronounced. (For descriptions and examples of these languages, see Comrie 1987.)

The writing systems (called "orthographies") are also diverse in form and history. Chinese and Japanese use ideographs (characters or symbols akin to Western symbols like % and & that directly represent ideas), and in addition Japanese simultaneously uses two syllabaries (where each symbol represents a syllable). Left-to-right alphabets are used for Hindi, Lao, and Khmer, while Korean uses an alphabetic script (each symbol represents a sound) within syllable clusters. Latin script is a legacy of Western colonialization in Vietnam and the Philippines. During the twentieth century a number of Hmong writing systems evolved, most from Christian missionaries, but one is believed to be regarded as revealed by a messianic prophet (Smalley et al. 1990).

The functions for writing also vary widely. For example, Korean, Vietnamese, Khmer, and Japanese enjoy the status of being official national languages. The languages of many Filipino and Chinese immigrants, while not national languages in their home countries, are important regional languages with limited official functions in the Philippines and China. By way of contrast, Hmong is neither the national language nor an official language of Laos.

In spite of their diversity, many Asian languages incorporate into their grammar a system of honorifics that mark social relationships among speaker, listener, and topic. Because they define, identify, and reinforce these relationships, they are important aspects of socialization, and they have an important impact on interactions within some parts of the Asian American community. For example, when second generation Japanese Americans failed to use honorifics, their first generation parents thought they were rude and disrespectful (Tamura 1994: 149). For some Cambodian parents in Massachusetts the correct use of honorifics is an important motivation for the maintenance of Khmer among their children (Smith-Hefner 1990: 257). On the other hand, a study of Vietnamese young adults who arrived in the USA before completion of their formal schooling (sometimes called the "1.5 generation") reported that they had no problem using Vietnamese honorifics with their parents but found using them with their own generation problematic. Rather than struggle, they report using English with Vietnamese younger than themselves (Yost 1985).

As with other immigrant groups, the Asian American experience reflects a shift from ancestral language to English by the third generation (see chapters 7 and 14 of this volume), and there appears to be no evidence that this linguistic assimilation is slowing down (Crawford 1992: 127). Indeed, until 1980 the majority of Asian Americans were American born and English speaking (Tajima 1996: 263). There are, however, differences in rates of shifting to English: among immigrants arriving from Asia during the 1960s, Filipinos, Japanese, and Koreans were among those most likely to have adopted English as their usual language by 1976, while Chinese speakers were least likely (Crawford 1992: 127).

As the largest and longest standing of Asian American communities, the Chinese American community presents an interesting focal point to study language shift and language maintenance. One researcher argues that sociocultural factors such as increased immigration rate, concentrated settlement patterns, increased socio-political and socio-economic status, the cultural value of collectivity, a pattern of intra-ethnic marriage, desire for cultural maintenance, and support from the mass media contribute to maintaining Chinese in the Chinese American community (Xia 1992). The emergence of new Chinatowns in communities like Flushing and Sunset Park in New York, and Monterey Park and Cupertino in California would seem to support that conclusion (cf. Fong 1994).

Other researchers maintain that institutions using Chinese language primarily serve recent immigrants, who are better educated, more international in perspective, politically more conservative, and economically more secure than first-wave immigrants. A review of several studies (e.g., Kuo 1974, Li 1982, Veltman 1983, Fishman 1985) concluded that continued immigration from China may make Chinese the most likely of Asian languages to maintain a continued presence in the USA. At the same time, the author of that review found that "the evidence points to rapid shift to English between the second and third generations, resulting in loss of Chinese from the third generation on" (Wong 1988: 217–18). This finding is consistent with the observation that immigration is the paramount reason for linguistic diversity in the USA – and not, as is commonly assumed, the maintenance of the heritage languages from one generation to the next (Crawford 1992).

Two institutions, the church and the language schools, illustrate the changing patterns of language use in the Asian American community. In both Chinese and Korean Christian churches, which are attended principally by first generation immigrants and their second generation children, separate weekly religious services in the heritage language and in English raise questions about any long-term influence that the churches may exercise in maintaining the heritage language across generations (Wong 1988, Kim 1981). The use of English for conducting weekly worship services in Japanese American Buddhist congregations, which are now composed primarily of second, third, fourth, and even fifth generation members, reflects the weak role that religious institutions may play in maintaining heritage languages in the Asian American community. Indeed, other Japanese American Buddhist practices such as Sunday services, Dharma school (the equivalent of Sunday school classes for children), and the use of pews in the worship hall mirror the practices of American Christian churches but do not exist in Japanese Buddhism (Horinouchi 1973, Kashima 1977). Such cultural "adjustments" suggest that these religious institutions are cultural brokers or agents in the establishment of a new Asian American identity, rather than guardians of the heritage language and culture.

Early in the first wave of Chinese and Japanese immigration, religious institutions and benevolent societies established language schools primarily to perpetuate the heritage language and culture. But among second generation Asian Americans, as enthusiasm waned for attending language schools after regular school hours and on weekends, the language schools were generally unsuccessful in contributing to long-term maintenance of heritage languages (Jung 1972, Wong 1988, Tamura 1994). Though many language schools continue even today, they primarily serve the children of recent immigrants.

By contrast, increased enrollment in Japanese, Korean, Vietnamese, and especially Chinese foreign language courses in high schools and colleges across the USA suggests a renewed interest among American-born Asian Americans in their heritage languages. One study reports a stunning 1,140 percent increase in Japanese language classes and a 350 percent increase in Chinese and Korean language classes in American primary, secondary, and college classes between 1982 and 1996 (Sung and Padilla 1998). The increase is due in part to the growing number of Asian Americans who find it more meaningful to learn an Asian language than an Indo-European one (Sung and Padilla 1998: 205), and harkens to a generalization noted in other language communities (Fishman 1967) that "what the son wishes to forget, the grandson wishes to remember" (Hansen 1938). The impact of this trend on retention of heritage languages in the Asian American community remains to be seen.

"Yellow English" and accent discrimination

> When salespersons failed to understand me, they often asked me if I spoke English. Or, conversely, when I failed to comprehend their point, they often chose to speak really slowly and simplistically, enunciate extra clearly, and engage in tiresome repetition . . .   [Chen 1990: 19]
>
> *Wilson Chen, a Chinese American who grew up in the suburbs of*
> *Philadelphia*

> [My] father . . . is truly one of the most brilliant people I know . . . However, he does not speak English well at all. He has a very strong Korean accent. Ever since I was a little girl, I have seen how people treated him because of that. They treat him as if he is an idiot. They would raise their voices, thinking that

would help him understand them better . . . that was always very painful to me. I resolved that I did not want to sound like my father . . . I think that had a very strong influence on why my sisters would never consider someone who is Asian as attractive. My father would embody a lot of unattractive things about Asians to them, he had this accent, he had strange ideas, and he just wasn't American.   [Lee 1991: 28–29]

Andrea Kim born in Hawai'i of a Korean-born father and a mother whose mother was born in Korea

Another thing that reminded me of how different I was was going to speech impediment class. Several of us would be taken to the attic of the school . . . I went because of my accent . . . Today, I still recall this vividly. I couldn't pronounce the r's. I grew up in an environment where my parents have strong Filipino accents . . . I would have to crow like a rooster to make the "er" sound . . . Looking back, my resentment went beyond having a physical impediment. They were telling me the way I pronounced things[,] which was exactly the way my parents pronounced words, was wrong.   [Lee 1991: 45–46]

Victor Merina, a Filipino American who works as a reporter for the Los Angeles Times

My father, for want of a better job, tried to correct his Vietnamese-accented English. In the shower he often bellowed "Shinatown . . . Shinatown." [Lam 1990]

Andrew Lam, born and raised in Vietnam, a writer and a regular commentator for National Public Radio's "All Things Considered"

For Asian Americans – whether they are native or non-native speakers of English – language is problematical. American-born third- and fourth-generation native speakers of English must face other Americans who compliment them on their mastery of English. Within the American stereotype of Asians, this phenomenon stems from an unwillingness to accept the image of a native-English-speaking Asian American. Non-native English speakers are plagued by "yellow English," the negative images of Asian English perpetuated by popular culture (Kim 1975). The images fall into two equally uncomplimentary stereotypes – the verbose and overly flowery fortune cookie speech of Charlie Chan and the monosyllabic primitive grunts and sighs of the Asian house boy muttering "aah-so"!

Indeed, Asian Americans who are non-native English speakers may be more susceptible than other non-native English-speaking Americans to discrimination that is language focused (Lippi-Green 1997). For example, Manuel Fragante, a Filipino-American, was denied a civil service job at the Honolulu Department of Motor Vehicles because he was reported to have a "pronounced" Filipino accent (Matsuda 1991). Similarly, because James Kahakua, a speaker of Standard Hawaiian English, did not speak with a standard (mainland) pronunciation, he was passed over for a job at the National Weather Service in favor of a less qualified white applicant from the mainland (Matsuda 1991). A search of legal databases from 1972 to 1994 reveals twenty-five instances of language-focused discrimination cases, eleven of which involved speakers from Asia (three each from the Philippines and India, two from China, one each from Vietnam, Cambodia, and Korea) but none of which involved speakers from western Europe (Lippi-Green 1997: 156). In each case the Asian speaker was the plaintiff who brought suit against an employer, and in the majority of cases, including the Fragante and Kahakua cases, the employer prevailed.

Distressing as those numbers are, they reflect only those incidents that made it into the courts. At the beginning of this section, Wilson Chen, Andrea Kim, Victor Merina, and Andrew Lam tell their stories. Amy Tan, noted author of *The Joy Luck Club*, also writes of incidents in which, by intervening with her "perfect English," she was able to get results with institutions like a stockbrokerage and hospital that her mother, a Chinese immigrant speaking "broken English," was unable to obtain (Tan 1995). Many other stories go unwritten. A student once reported a story about a Vietnamese American woman whose supervisor told her that she would not advance in the company because of her accent. When she reported the incident to the supervisor's superior, the supervisor denied he had made the comment. As it happened, a co-worker corroborated her story, and the supervisor was forced to apologize.

Clearly, negative images associated with "yellow English" continue to plague the Asian American community. Understanding the full extent of its impact on members of the community and identifying remedies for all forms of language-based discrimination remain a challenge.

Language variation and the influence of African American English

> For us American-born, both the Asian languages and the English language are foreign. We are a people without a native tongue . . . We have no street tongue to flaunt and strut the way the blacks and Chicanos do. They have a positive, self-defined linguistic identity that can be offended and wronged. We don't.   (Chin 1976: 557)
>
> *Frank Chin, a writer and playwright*

> Oh, we claim Asian pri', you know, we kickin' wi' da Asian. Cause I'm down wi' my country, you know . . . dere's a lot a shootin' goin' on arou' here . . . little kids be gettin' all dat bad influence . . . And dat ain' cool, man. Especially da Asian kids.   (transcribed from *Letter Back Home*, Lacroix 1994)
>
> *An anonymous Southeast Asian from the south of Market district in San Francisco*

Struggles with accent aside, what do Asian Americans speak? Controversial media images of Asian Americans as a "model minority group," attaining educational and economic success where other minority groups have failed, would lead Americans to a stereotype of an Asian newscaster (such as Connie Chung or Joie Chen) speaking standard English – a stark contradiction to the "yellow English" stereotype. The truth is that language variation in the Asian American community is not yet well understood. As noted earlier, Hawai'i Creole English serves as a vernacular for Asian Americans in Hawai'i (Sato 1985, 1989), but the situation is less clear cut on the continental USA. Despite research that would predict linguistic differences along racial boundaries, preliminary investigation suggests a largely unexplored diversity of language variety in the Asian American community. One small study (Mendoza-Denton and Iwai 1993), for example, found distinctive phonological characteristics in the English of Nisei (second generation Japanese Americans), a fact that had earlier been reported only impressionistically (Spencer 1950).

Some recent unpublished studies suggest that African American English (AAE) is influential in some parts of the Asian American community. For example, a longitudinal ethnographic study of a group of nine Asian Americans (four Cambodian, two Mien, one Thai-Cambodian, one Vietnamese, one Chinese) and one Mexican immigrant student in a low-income inner-city neighborhood in California found some of their English marked with AAE characteristics, including copula deletion, multiple negation, and invariant BE (Kuwahara 1998). The finding is somewhat surprising because research suggests that shared language characteristics are correlated with a speaker's strong links to a social network that uses a specific language variety. In this study the youths shared only weak links to the African American community. A second study, an analysis of a videotape of young Asian Americans primarily in their early twenties in a low-income area of San Francisco, identified vocabulary, pronunciations, and a cluster of grammatical features characteristic of AAE (copula deletion, habitual form of BE, absence of third person singular -s, and multiple negation) (Uyechi and Pampuch 1997). For both studies, one possible explanation for finding AAE features in these young speakers' speech patterns is that the speakers are not native English speakers and, consequently, that characteristics of their native language are interwoven with English, creating only an impression that they are using AAE. At least for some speakers in Kuwahara's study, however, this explanation does not hold because they first acquired features of standard English and only later shifted to AAE features.

Although the use of AAE features outside the African American community is not unheard of (cf. Wolfram 1974), the finding dispels both the "model minority" and the "yellow English" stereotypes of Asian Americans, while at the same time it raises intriguing new research questions. Is Asian American AAE use identical to that of African American AAE speakers, or do specific AAE features serve as part of a distinct Asian American vernacular? To what extent are AAE features in use in the Asian American community? What is the function of AAE among Asian Americans? Researchers have started to respond to the last question. Positive associations of masculinity and toughness have been linked to the use of AAE, with the hypothesis that the integration of AAE features in their speech provides a symbolic means to reflect the evolving identities of Asian Americans (Kuwahara 1998). A study of Samoan American high school students in Los Angeles demonstrated use of AAE features in their speech, and the investigator hypothesized that those Asian Pacific Islander students use AAE features to establish an urban identity and to maintain social distance from other groups (Sete 1994: 16).

Future research will lead to greater understanding of the role of AAE in the Asian American community, but meanwhile current policymaking should consider the implications of identifying AAE features in parts of this growing community. For example, in the 1997 furor over Ebonics in the schools of Oakland, California, the number of AAE speakers was assumed to be roughly equivalent to the African American student population (see chapter 16 of this volume). In fact, the Oakland schools include a large Asian American population, and if the English of a significant portion of those students includes AAE features, the impact on the school district is even greater than originally thought. Educators and policymakers concerned with AAE will need to consider its origins, forms, and particularly its significance in all communities in which it is used – including parts of the Asian American community.

Interpersonal style: Eastern vs. Western?

> It was painful for a stereotypically academically successful Vietnamese kid like myself to be considered a moron by my parents' friends. Of course, they never said that, but their little smiles at my stumbling attempts at Vietnamese etiquette only made me convinced that my paranoia was founded in reality. (Nguyen 1990: 24)
>
> *Viet Nguyen, who lives in Berkeley, California*

Beyond pronunciation, vocabulary, and grammar, Asian Americans, whether native English speaking or not, face another linguistic challenge – the challenge of reconciling the differences between heritage and mainstream American discourse styles and registers. For example, because of the greater gap in status between overseas-born Chinese children and parents, the parents use a more direct style with their children in exchanges such as commands and requests, while the children use a more indirect style (Lau 1988). Among American-born Chinese parents and children, the distinction is less clear cut.

Even among some second-generation Asian Americans who speak English and can mingle freely among other English-speaking Americans, the conflict between the discourse style of the parents and the American style found outside the home can be problematic. For example, Nisei (second-generation Japanese Americans) are likely to seek the company of other Nisei because of compatible interpersonal styles of discourse (Miyamoto 1986–87). The question of what might constitute a culture-specific discourse style among Asian Americans remains to be explored.

A comparative study of the organizational behavior of second- and third-generation Chinese American and Japanese American women (Okimoto 1998) identifies differences between Chinese and Japanese on the one hand and Western cultures on the other that can affect discourse styles: for example, indirectness versus directness; attention to saving face and giving face versus concern with self-face (Goffman 1955); and the desire to avoid conflict versus the desire to resolve conflict head on. The researcher not only posits a "hybrid" style for her Chinese American and Japanese American interviewees, but also notes differences between Chinese American women and Japanese American women (Okimoto 1998).

An analysis of taped interactions of Chinese speakers of English at academic conferences and business meetings has identified a discourse style in which old information is followed by new information (Young 1982). In the presentation of information by Chinese speakers of English, the pattern is to present reasons before making the main point, so that the shared context presented first should lead to a natural acceptance of the main point. Chinese speakers felt that if the point were stated first, it might sound rude, demanding, or unnecessarily aggressive. In contrast, mainstream American English speakers reacted negatively to the absence of a preview or thesis statement because they expected a request followed by arguments to support it. Often discourse strategies effective in Chinese are transferred to interactions when the speaker is using English, and those strategies are likely to be interpreted as behavioral differences, which are subject to misperceptions, misinterpretations, and misunderstandings. Over time such miscues can lead to stereotypes that are reinforced with every such interaction (Young 1982: 83–84).

Conclusion

At the beginning of the twenty-first century, the term *Asian American* encompasses a group of diverse peoples – sometimes with little more in common than rice. Indeed, the emergence of an Asian American identity challenges commonly held assumptions of ethnicity based on shared national origin, culture, or language. It is particularly odd for an "ethnic" group to lack a distinctive common language. The emergence of the Asian American movement in the 1960s suggests that the common language of Asian America is English. Yet a closer look at language in the Asian American community reveals a cluster of issues that are not well understood. Recent immigrants wish that their children would retain their native language, but the trend is toward its loss. Negative images of "yellow English" plague Asian immigrants as they suffer various degrees of language-based discrimination. Some Asian youths, searching for a distinctive way to express themselves and to define their experience, turn to African American English. And even when non-native and native English speakers use English, vestiges of contrasting discourse styles may contribute to negative stereotypes about Asians and Asian Americans.

This chapter has only touched the proverbial tip of the iceberg in terms of both the history of Asian America and the language of Asian Americans.

Several studies cited here are exploratory, posing more questions than they answer. Ethnographic studies and surveys of Asian American institutions such as churches and language schools are still needed in order to assess language shift and language maintenance. Further study is also needed to understand the extent and impact of language-based discrimination against Asian Americans. More thorough examination of the vernacular of Asian American youth is required not only to determine the extent of African American English use but also to explore the possibility that in some parts of the community a unique Asian American vernacular or vernaculars exist. And more work is required to understand the transfer of Asian discourse styles into American discourse and its impact on the image of Asians and Asian Americans in the USA.

The study of language in the Asian American community is in its infancy. The diverse language heritage and the individual ethnic communities of Asian America provide a particularly rich area for comparative study that will not only shed light on linguistic issues but may also lead to increased understanding of what has been called "the coercively imposed nature of ethnicity, its multiple layers, and the continual creation and re-creation of culture" (Espiritu 1992: 5).

Acknowledgments

The authors would like to thank Rudy Busto and the editors of this volume for their insight and comments on this chapter.

Suggestions for further reading and exploration

An understanding of Asian American history and issues of Asian American identity are prerequisites to the investigation of language in the Asian American community. Informed by contemporary Asian American scholarship, Takaki (1989) and Chan (1991) present insightful histories of Asians in America (and we have relied on them for the historical data in our section, "Asian American voices: history of immigration"). Takaki (1989) draws on life histories, published documents, and personal correspondences to make the story of Asian America come alive. Chan (1991) presents "an interpretive history" that weaves the various strands of Asian American experience into a valuable source book. Encyclopedic works such as Ng (1995) and Natividad (1995) provide rich historical information about Asian Americans.

Of equal significance to the history of Asians in America is understanding of the evolution of a collective Asian American identity. Wei (1993) chronicles the history of the Asian American movement. Espiritu (1992) outlines the emerging Asian American consciousness from the 1960s to the 1990s, providing in-depth discussion of the "panethnicity" and complexity of multiple identities that are engendered when people of diverse origins unite politically and socially to protect and promote a collective interest.

Sources treating language issues in the Asian American community are sparse. McKay and Wong (1988) offer separate chapters on the language situation of Chinese Americans, Filipino Americans, Korean Americans, and Vietnamese Americans, each authored by a scholar-member of the community able to provide well-researched insight into it.

Lippi-Green (1997) explores language discrimination in the USA, implicating the education system, the media, the workplace, and the judicial system for their roles in supporting an ideology that promotes language-based stereotypes and prejudices. Matsuda (1991) reinforces Lippi-Green's conclusions with two striking cases of speakers who took their language discrimination complaints to the courts – and lost. Based on extensive research of sociolinguistic literature, Matsuda argues for remedies to the judicial system.

Although not specifically about language, oral histories, autobiographies, and autobiographical fiction are valuable sources for understanding the context of language and specific language experiences in the Asian American community. Espiritu (1995), Lee (1991), and Chan (1994) are collections of oral histories; Bulosan (1943) and Wong (1945) are autobiographies and part of the Asian American literary canon; Murayama (1959) is a classic novel that captures plantation life and language in Hawai'i during the 1930s, and Lee (1995) is a fictional account of a contemporary second generation Korean American. Critical scholarly works providing further contextualization for Asian American stories include Kim (1982), which examines Japanese American and Chinese American literature, and Sumida (1991), which focuses on Hawai'i's literary tradition.

Actively working to end language-based discrimination, the Language Rights Project is a joint undertaking of the American Civil Liberties Union Foundation of Northern California and the Employment Law Center of the Legal Aid Society of San Francisco; it maintains phone lines in Cantonese, Mandarin, Spanish, and English (1–800–864–1664). Ni (1999) describes one case in which the Language Rights Project aided a Chinese American employee, who prevailed in an accent discrimination case.

References

Bickerton, Derek and W. H. Wilson. 1987. "Pidgin Hawaiian." In *Pidgin and Creole Languages: Essays in Memory of John E. Reinecke*, ed. G. G. Gilbert. Honolulu: University of Hawai'i Press. Pp. 61–76.

Bulosan, Carlos. 1943 [repr. 1990]. *America is in the Heart*. Seattle: University of Washington Press.

Chan, Sucheng. 1991. *Asian Americans: an Interpretive History*. Boston: Twayne.
    1994. "Hmong Life Stories." In Ng et al., eds. Pp. 43–62.

Chen, Wilson. 1990. "Growing up in White America," *Asian Week* (June 15): 19.

Chin, Frank. 1976. "Backtalk." In *Counterpoint: Perspectives on Asian America*, ed. Emma Gee. Los Angeles: UCLA Asian American Studies Center.

Comrie, Bernard, ed. 1987. *The World's Major Languages*. New York: Oxford University Press.

Crawford, James. 1992. *Hold Your Tongue: Bilingualism and the Politics of "English Only."* Reading MA: Addison-Wesley.

Espiritu, Yen Le. 1992. *Asian American Panethnicity: Bridging Institutions and Identities.* Philadelphia: Temple University Press.

1995. *Filipino American Lives.* Philadelphia: Temple University Press.

Fishman, Joshua A. 1967. *Language Loyalty in the United States.* The Hague: Mouton.

1985. "The Community Resources of Ethnic Languages in the USA." In *The Rise and Fall of the Ethnic Revival: Perspectives on Language and Ethnicity*, ed. J. A. Fishman. Berlin: Mouton.

Fong, T. P. 1994. "Economic and Ethnic Politics in Monterey Park." In Ng et al. Pp. 15–42.

Goffman, Erving. 1955. "On Face-work: an Analysis of Ritual Elements in Social Interaction," *Psychiatry* 18: 213–31.

Hansen, Marcus L. 1938. *The Problem of the Third Generation Immigrant.* Rock Island IL: Augustana Historical Society.

Horinouchi, Isao. 1973. "Americanized Buddhism: a Sociological Analysis of a Protestantized Japanese Religion." Unpub. Ph.D. dissertation, University of California, Davis.

Huebner, Thom. 1985. "Language Education Policy in Hawai'i: Two Case Studies and Some Current Issues," *International Journal of the Sociology of Language* 56: 29–50.

Ito, Kazuo. 1973. *Issei: a History of Japanese Immigrants in North America*, trans. Shinichiro Nakamura and Jean S. Girard. Seattle: Executive Committee for Publication of Issei.

Jung, R. 1972. "The Chinese Language School in the US," *School & Society* 100: 309–12.

Kashima, Tetsuden. 1977. *Buddhism in America: the Social Organization of an Ethnic Religious Institution.* Westport CT: Greenwood.

Kim, Elaine H. 1975. "Yellow English," *Asian American Review* 2(1): 44–63.

1982. *Asian American Literature.* Philadelphia: Temple University Press.

Kim, Illsoo. 1981. "The Church as a Basis for the Community." In *New Urban Immigrants: the Korean Community in New York.* Princeton: Princeton University Press. Pp. 187–207.

Kuo, E. C. Y. 1974. "Bilingual Pattern of a Chinese Immigrant Group in the United States," *Anthropological Linguistics* 16(3): 128–40.

Kuwahara, Yuri Lea. 1998. "Interactions of Identity: Inner-City Immigrant and Refugee Youths, Language Use, and Schooling." Unpub. Ph.D. dissertation, Stanford University.

Lacroix, Nith, producer and director. 1994. "Letter Back Home." Video distributed by the National Asian American Telecommunications Association. San Francisco.

Lam, Andrew. 1990. "America Interprets Newcomer Accents with Suspicion." *San Jose Mercury News* Commentary Section. July 10.

Lau, Genevieve Man-Hing. 1988. "Chinese American Early Childhood Socialization in Communication." Unpub. Ph.D. dissertation, Stanford University.

Lee, Chang-Rae. 1995. *Native Speaker.* New York: Riverhead Books.

Lee, Joann Faung Jean. 1991. *Asian Americans: Oral Histories of First to Fourth Generation Americans from China, the Philippines, Japan, India, the Pacific Islands, Vietnam and Cambodia.* New York: New Press.

Li, Wen Lang. 1982. "The Language Shift of Chinese-Americans," *International Journal of the Sociology of Language* 38: 109–24.

Lippi-Green, Rosina. 1997. *English with an Accent: Language, Ideology, and Discrimination in the United States.* New York: Routledge.

Matsuda, M. 1991. "Voices of America: Accent, Anti-discrimination Law, and a Jurisprudence for the Last Reconstruction," *Yale Law Journal* 100: 1329–68.

McKay, Sandra Lee, and Sau-ling Cynthia Wong, eds. 1988. *Language Diversity: Problem or Resource?* Boston: Heinle and Heinle.

Mendoza-Denton, Norma and Melissa Iwai. 1993. "'They speak more Caucasian': Generational Differences in the Speech of Japanese-Americans." *Proceedings of the First Annual Symposium About Language and Society.* (SALSA I). Austin: University of Texas, Department of Linguistics. Pp. 58–67.

Mirikitani, Janice. 1987. "American Geisha." In *Shedding Silence.* Berkeley: Celestial Arts. P. 8.

Miyamoto, S. Frank. 1986–87. "Problems of Interpersonal Style among the Nisei," *Amerasia* 13(2): 29–45.

Murayama, Milton. 1959 [repr. 1988]. *All I asking for is my body*. Honolulu: University of Hawai'i Press.

Natividad, Irene, ed. 1995. *Reference Library of Asian America*. Detroit: Gale Research.

Ng, Franklin. 1995. *The Asian American Encyclopedia*. New York: Marshall Cavendish.

Ng, Franklin, Judy Yung, Stephen S. Fugita, and Elaine H. Kim, eds. 1994. *New Visions in Asian American Studies*. Pullman: Washington State University Press.

Nguyen, Viet. 1990. "Growing up in White America," *Asian Week* 7(16) December 7. Pp. 23, 26.

Ni, Perla. 1999. "Accent Discrimination Claim Costs Company $55,000," *Asian Week* 20(42). June 17–23. *http://www.asianweek.com/061799/news_settlement.html*

Okimoto, Ruth. 1998. "Chinese American and Japanese American Women Professionals: a Comparative Study of their Organizational Communication Behavior and Underlying Cultural Values and Attitudes in the Workplace." Unpub. Ph.D. dissertation, California School of Professional Psychology at Alameda.

Reinecke, John E. 1969. *Language and Dialect in Hawai'i: a Sociolinguistic History to 1935*. Honolulu: University of Hawai'i Press.

Sato, Charlene. 1985. "Linguistic Inequality in Hawai'i: the Postcreole Dilemma." In *Language of Inequality*, ed. Nessa Wolfson and J. Manes. Berlin: Mouton. Pp. 255–72.

    1989. "Language Attitudes and Sociolinguistic Variation in Hawai'i," *University of Hawai'i Working Papers in ESL* 8(1): 191–216.

Sete, A. P. 1994. "'Black English? Hamos don't front like we black!' Language, Identity and Representation among Urban Samoan Adolescents." Unpub. paper, prepared for Anthropology 596, UCLA.

Smalley, William A., Chia Koua Vang, and Gnia Yee Yang. 1990. *Mother of Writing: the Origin and Development of a Hmong Messianic Script*. Chicago: University of Chicago Press.

Smith-Hefner, Nancy J. 1990. "Language and Identity in the Education of Boston-Area Khmer," *Anthropology and Education Quarterly* 21(3): 250–68.

Spencer, Robert F. 1950. "Japanese-American Language Behavior," *American Speech* 25: 241–52.

Sumida, Stephen H. 1991. *And the View from the Shore: Literary Traditions of Hawai'i*. Seattle: University of Washington Press.

Sung, H. and A. M. Padilla. 1998. "Student Motivation, Parental Attitudes, and Involvement in the Learning of Asian Languages in Elementary and Secondary Schools," *Modern Language Journal* 82(2): 205–16.

Tajima, R. 1996. "Site-seeing through Asian America: on the Making of Fortune Cookies." In *Mapping Multiculturalism*, ed. A. F. Gordon and C. Newfield. Minneapolis: University of Minnesota Press. Pp. 263–94.

Takaki, Ronald. 1983. *Pau Hana: Plantation Life and Labor in Hawai'i 1835–1920*. Honolulu: University of Hawai'i Press.

    1989. *Strangers from a Different Shore: a History of Asian Americans*. Boston: Little, Brown.

Tamura, E. H. 1994. "Nisei Attitudes toward Japanese Language Schools: Personal Accounts Shed Light on the Controversy." In Ng et al. Pp. 141–57.

Tan, Amy. 1995. "Mother Tongue." In *Under Western Eyes: Personal Essays from Asian Americans*, ed. Garrett Hongo. New York: Anchor Books/Doubleday.

Uyechi, Linda and Lisa Pampuch. 1997. "Language in the Tenderloin: Traces of the African American Vernacular in the Asian American Community." Unpub. paper, Stanford University.

Veltman, Calvin. 1983. *Language Shift in the United States*. Berlin: Mouton.

Wei, William. 1993. *The Asian American Movement*. Philadelphia: Temple University Press.

Wolfram, Walt. 1974. *Sociolinguistic Aspects of Assimilation: Puerto Rican English in New York City*. Urban Language Series, 9. Arlington VA: Center for Applied Linguistics.

Wolfram, Walt, Donna Christian, and Deborah Hatfield. 1986. "The English of Adolescent and Young Adult Vietnamese Refugees in the United States," *World Englishes* 5(1): 47–60.

Wong, Jade Snow. 1945 [repr. 1989]. *Fifth Chinese Daughter*. Seattle: University of Washington Press.

Wong, Sau Ling. 1988. "The Language Situation of Chinese Americans." In McKay and Wong, eds. Pp. 193–228.

Xia, Ningsheng. 1992. "Maintenance of the Chinese Language in the United States," *The Bilingual Review* 17(3): 195–209.

Yost, M. E. 1985. "Symbols and Meanings of Ethnic Identity among Young Adult Vietnamese Refugees." Unpub. Ph.D. dissertation, Catholic University of America.

Young, Linda Wai Ling. 1982. "Inscrutability Revisited." In *Language and Social Identity*, ed. John J. Gumperz. Cambridge: Cambridge University Press. Pp. 72–84.

14

Linguistic diversity and English language acquisition

ROBERT BAYLEY

Editors' introduction

It is a notable and surprising fact that among residents of the USA nearly one in five persons aged five or above reports speaking a language other than English at home. Equally notable and possibly more surprising is the fact that more than half of those reporting that they use a language other than English at home also report that they know English and speak it very well. In this chapter, Robert Bayley provides a wealth of information about the range of languages spoken in the USA and the growing linguistic diversity prompted by immigration, about the difficulties of learning English in some communities and in some situations, about the continuing strong pattern of language shift from immigrant languages to English, and about the challenge that immigrant communities face in maintaining their heritage languages. You will find surprises on nearly every page of this chapter because much of what residents of the USA know – or think we know – about the use of English and other languages in the USA is partly or entirely wrong.

In this chapter you will discover how many residents of the USA who speak languages other than English have enrolled in ESL classes in recent years and what age groups they come from. You will note historical patterns about the use of English among US immigrants and their children, and you will see that among the barriers that keep eager potential students of English from enrolling in ESL classes are a shortage of such classes and of qualified teachers for them, a lack of time or financial resources, the demands of child care, and a lack of transportation. You will also meet a number of US residents, parents and children of various ages, and hear their stories about learning English and maintaining their heritage languages.

In recent decades the USA has experienced increasing levels of immigration. During the period 1991–2000, the USA received more immigrants than in any decade since 1901–10 (Lollock 2000), and immigration continued to increase in the first years of the new century. Unlike the massive immigration that characterized the last decades of the nineteenth century and the first decades of the twentieth century, however, recent immigrants have come not from Europe but primarily from Latin America and Asia. In 2000 the total foreign-born population of the USA numbered 28.4 million, of whom 51 percent were from Latin America and the Caribbean, 25.5 percent from Asia, 15.3 percent from Europe, and 8.1 percent from other regions (Lollock 2000). 34 percent, or nearly 10 million people, were born in Mexico or Central America. Although immigrants have tended to settle in California, New York, Florida, Illinois, New Jersey, and Texas, they have dispersed to virtually all areas of the country in recent years. To take just one example, the labor force of a meat-packing plant in Maine now consists primarily of Mexican immigrants (Wortham 1997).

The increase in immigration has had political, economic, and educational consequences. From the point of view of language use, the most striking consequences are the increased numbers of people who use a language other than English for a variety of purposes, the ever-growing number of speakers who are acquiring English as a second language, and the continuing shift to English by children and grandchildren of immigrants. This chapter focuses on these developments. First, it provides an overview of the non-native English-speaking population and the increasing linguistic diversity of the USA. Section two focuses on immigrant bilingualism and minority language maintenance and shift. The final section provides an overview of the acquisition of English as a second language by adults in both formal and informal settings (for overviews of educational opportunities for language minority children, see August and Hakuta 1997 and Wong Fillmore's chapter in this volume).

Language diversity

The USA has been home to more speakers of immigrant languages than any other country in the developed world. Moreover, despite the widespread perception that the USA is essentially a monolingual English-speaking country, language diversity has been part of the American tradition since colonial times (Heath 1981, Wiley 1996). In the 2000 census more than one in six people five years of age and older reported speaking a language other than English at home (US Bureau of the Census 2000b). (Census statistics provide the best view of overall trends in the population, even though they must be interpreted cautiously owing to the self-report nature of census data and the widely reported undercount of minority populations.) Table 14-1 shows the most commonly spoken languages other than English in 1990 and 2000, and the increase or decrease in the number of speakers of each language.

With fourteen times the number of speakers of its nearest rival, Spanish was by far the most commonly spoken language other than English. In the 1990s the number of Spanish speakers in the USA expanded at a rapid rate, with an increase of 10,238,575 people, or 57.3 percent. Other languages also showed robust increases, although in absolute numbers their increases were much less than those of Spanish. The number of Russian speakers increased by 192 percent and Vietnamese speakers by 99 percent. Arabic, at 77.4 percent, and Chinese, at 61.8 percent, also showed substantial increases.

While the number of Spanish speakers and speakers of Asian languages and Russian gained ground in the 1990s, the number of speakers of most of the European languages that had been brought to the USA by earlier generations of

Table 14-1 *Most commonly spoken languages other than English, 1990 and 2000*

Language	1990	2000	Change 1990–2000
Spanish	17,862,477	28,101,052	+10,238,575
Chinese*	1,249,213	2,022,143	+772,930
French, incl. Patois, Cajun	1,702,176	1,643,838	−58,338
German	1,547,099	1,383,442	−163,657
Tagalog	843,251	1,224,241	+380,990
Vietnamese	507,069	1,009,627	+502,558
Italian	1,308,648	1,008,370	−300,278
Korean	626,478	894,063	+267,585
Russian	241,798	706,242	+464,444
Polish	723,483	667,414	−56,069
Arabic	355,150	614,582	+259,432
Hindi and Urdu	331,484	579,957	+248,473
Portuguese or Portuguese Creole	429,860	564,630	+134,770
Japanese	427,657	477,997	+50,340
French Creole	187,658	435,368	+247,710
Greek	388,260	365,436	−22,824

* "Chinese" includes speakers of a variety of Chinese dialects, many of which are mutually unintelligible
Source: US Bureau of the Census (1993, 2003a)

immigrants declined. Speakers of Italian decreased by 22.9 percent and speakers of German by 10.6 percent. The 31.3 percent increase in Portuguese is a reflection not only of increased immigration from Portugal, but also from other Portuguese-speaking countries, primarily Brazil.

The national statistics for the main languages other than English provide a convenient illustration of the increasing linguistic diversity of the USA. A closer examination by state and language provides a clearer picture of the changes that have occurred in recent years. In 2000, 17.9 percent of the population five years of age and older claimed to speak a language other than English at home. Table 14-2 shows the states with the highest percentages of speakers of languages other than English, as well as the number of speakers of the most commonly spoken language. Not surprisingly, considering recent immigration patterns, the three states with the highest percentage of speakers of languages other than English – New Mexico, where Spanish enjoyed considerable legal protection until the 1940s, California, and Texas – share borders with Mexico, and in each case Spanish is the most commonly spoken non-English language (see Bills, Hernández-Chavez, and Hudson 1995 for a discussion of the relationship between Spanish language maintenance and distance from the US–Mexico border). Spanish is also the most common minority language in eight of the nine remaining states with a higher than average percentage of speakers who use a home language other than

Table 14-2 *Population who speak languages other than English at home*

State	Population 5 years and older	Total non-English	Percent non-English	Most common non-English	Number most common non-English
USA Total	262,375,152	46,951,595	17.9	Spanish	28,101,052
California	31,416,629	12,401,756	39.5	Spanish	8,105,505
New Mexico	1,689,911	616,964	36.5	Spanish	485,681
Texas	19,241,518	6,010,753	31.2	Spanish	5,192,102
New York	17,749,110	4,962,921	28.0	Spanish	2,476,528
Hawai'i	1,134,351	302,125	26.6	Tagalog	60,967
Arizona	4,752,724	1,229,237	25.9	Spanish	927,395
New Jersey	7,856,268	2,001,690	25.5	Spanish	967,741
Florida	15,043,603	3,473,864	23.1	Spanish	2,476,528
Rhode Island	985,184	196,624	20.0	Spanish	79,443
Illinois	11,547,505	2,220,719	19.2	Spanish	1,253,676
Massachusetts	5,954,249	1,115,570	18.7	Spanish	370,011
Connecticut	3,184,514	583,913	18.3	Spanish	268,044

Source: US Bureau of the Census (2003b)

English: Arizona (19.5%), Connecticut (8.4%), Florida (16.5%), Illinois (10.9%), Massachusetts (6.2%), New Jersey (12.3%), New York (14%), and Rhode Island (8.1%). In the states with a higher than average percentage of speakers of languages other than English, only Tagalog, spoken by 5.4% of the residents of Hawai'i, has more speakers than Spanish within an individual state.

A further example of the extent of linguistic diversity can be seen in the number of languages spoken at home by 100,000 or more people. According to the 2000 census, there are twenty-nine such languages, ranging from Spanish, spoken by more than 28 million people 5 years of age and older, to Hungarian, spoken by 117,973 people 5 years and older. Of particular note is the fact that among these languages only Navajo is indigenous to North America, although Spanish was spoken by the non-indigenous population of the Southwest when the region was annexed by the USA.

Immigrant bilingualism and shift to English

In the USA, bilingualism in an immigrant language and English has normally been seen as a stage on the road to a desirable monolingual English norm (Crawford 1992). Indeed, up until the 1960s bilingualism was viewed as a disability in popular and in academic circles alike. The popular view of bilingualism and language diversity was summed up early in the twentieth century by Theodore Roosevelt, who said, "We have room for but one language here, and this is the English language; for we intend to see that the crucible turns our people out as Americans, and not as dwellers in a polyglot boardinghouse . . ." (cited by Portes and Rumbaut 1996: 206). The academic view that prevailed before the 1960s is typified by a psychologist who in the 1930s studied the language development of children of Chinese, Filipino, Japanese, Korean, and Portuguese immigrants to Hawaii, as well as children of native Hawaiians. On the basis of a comparison of fifty consecutive sentences from each child with similar samples from monolingual English-speaking children in Iowa, the psychologist concluded that bilingualism was responsible for a retardation in language development "so marked that, on most criteria, at the time of school entrance they [bilingual children] are at about the level of three-year-old children from a less polyglot environment" (Smith 1939: 271).

Those conclusions rested on unjustified assumptions and a faulty methodology (see Hakuta 1986: 59–65), and the "deficit view" of bilingualism they represent is no longer seriously entertained by researchers. Rather, beginning with pioneering work comparing bilingual and monolingual school children in Canada, researchers have explored the benefits of bilingualism for children's development (Peal and Lambert 1962, Hakuta, Ferdman, and Diaz 1987). Nevertheless, the view that language development is a zero-sum game in which maintenance of an immigrant language inevitably leads to problems in language development and even cognitive development has exerted considerable influence in popular and educational circles alike (Hakuta 1986, Valdés and Figueroa 1994).

A clear example of the continuing belief that maintaining a minority language causes low academic achievement may be found in a recent study of home language practices in Mexican-background families in Texas (Bayley, Schecter, and Torres-Ayala 1996). María and Esteban Gómez (not their real names),[1] the parents in one family studied, live on a south Texas ranch, where Esteban has worked for ten years. In order to maintain close family ties with their numerous relatives who live in the neighboring Mexican state of Coahuila, María and Esteban, who speak very little English, insisted that their three children speak only Spanish at home. From the point of view of minority language maintenance, the Gómezes' strategy proved successful. All three of their children were fluent in Spanish and the two older boys were fluent in English as well. The oldest child was a sixth-grade honor student, but the middle child, a fourth-grader, experienced considerable difficulty in school. As María Gómez reported (in Spanish), the first response of this boy's teachers was to blame his difficulties on the use of Spanish at home: "I've had problems with their teachers because the teachers tell me that they [the boys] have to forget about Spanish a bit so that they can progress more rapidly in their classes" (Bayley, Schecter, and Torres-Ayala 1996: 397).

Given the influence of mistaken ideas about the relationship between bilingualism and maintaining a minority language, on the one hand, and children's

---

[1] Data from the Gómez family, and from the Torres and Esparza families (not their real names) discussed below, were collected as part of the project on Family Language Environment and Bilingual Development, supported by grants from the US Department of Education and the Spencer Foundation to Robert Bayley and Sandra R. Schecter.

development on the other, even in areas such as south Texas, where most of the population is of Mexican origin, it is not surprising that full proficiency in immigrant languages is not usually retained for more than two or three generations. Members of the immigrant generation have usually been monolingual or dominant in the language of their country of origin, and the first US-born generation has typically shown the greatest degree of bilingualism, but with stronger literacy skills in English than in their parents' native language (Spener 1994, Wiley 1996). Members of the second US-born generation have often been monolingual in English or had only a limited understanding of their parents' language.

The impetus behind attempts to make English the official language of government and public life in the USA stems in part from the popular belief that the traditional pattern of language shift to English is no longer operating, particularly with immigrants from Mexico and other Spanish-speaking countries. However, despite the ethnic revival movements beginning in the 1970s and the best efforts of advocates of "maintenance bilingual education,"[2] empirical evidence suggests that the traditional pattern of intergenerational loss of immigrant languages continues even in areas of the country where the immigrant language would be expected to have the greatest chances of survival. Indeed, one study of Spanish language use concluded that, were it not for high levels of immigration, the number of speakers of the most common language other than English would decline rapidly (Veltman 1988).

That conclusion is supported by other studies, including a study of linguistic preferences of language minority groups that was conducted before the large-scale immigration of the 1980s and 1990s but still provided evidence that immigrants from Spanish-speaking countries and from Asia were switching to English at a very rapid rate (López 1982). Table 14-3 shows the language preferences of three Latin American and four Asian origin groups, grouped by age. Note that in each group, English was the preferred language or only language for the great majority of speakers between the ages of five and seventeen. Thus, although young Mexican-origin speakers showed less preference for English than did young Japanese- and Filipino-origin speakers (for whom a shift to English was nearly complete), 78 percent of the young speakers from the largest language minority group reported using only English or mainly English. Moreover, in every case, five to seventeen year olds reported much more use of English than speakers over eighteen. The difference is particularly striking with Cubans, among whom 73 percent of five to seventeen year olds reported using English mainly or exclusively, compared to a mere 26 percent of speakers eighteen and older.

A more narrowly focused study based on 1990 census data examined the numbers of people who claimed to use Spanish at home in five states with traditionally

---

[2] As the name suggests, the goal of maintenance bilingual education is to maintain and develop the minority language while assisting the child to acquire English. Although a number of maintenance bilingual programs exist, by far the most common model is transitional bilingual education, in which use of the minority language is continued for no more than three or at most four years, with the amount of minority language use decreasing each year until the child is transitioned into all-English classes.

Table 14-3 *Generation, nativity, and language use among selected ethnic groups, 1976*

Ethnicity	Age	Born in USA (%)	Language usually spoken (%)		
			Mother tongue only	Mother tongue mainly	English mainly or only
Hispanic					
Mexican	5–17	89	3	19	78
	18+	69	21	23	56
Cuban	5–17	42	1	26	73
	18+	3	33	41	26
Central, South					
American	5–17	60	7	19	74
	18+	7	26	29	45
Asian					
Japanese	5–17	90	1	2	97
	18+	68	8	9	83
Chinese	5–17	62	3	16	81
	18+	21	25	28	47
Filipino	5–17	59	0	5	95
	18+	17	6	25	69
Korean	5–17	31	0	26	74
	18+	5	32	20	48

Source: López (1982), as adapted by Portes and Rumbaut (1996: 215)

large Latino populations (Bills 1997). Table 14-4 shows the results by state and age group.

These 1990 census data are consistent with the general trends shown in other studies (López 1982, Veltman 1988), although the actual numbers are quite different. In Arizona, California, Colorado, New Mexico, and Texas, far more adults (aged eighteen and older) claimed to use at least some Spanish at home than did five to seventeen year olds (Bills 1997). That is, despite the impressive percentages of people claiming to speak Spanish in some states, the census provides yet another illustration of the gradual replacement of Spanish by English. Because the home is usually the last domain of an ethnic language to undergo shift (Bills 1997; cf. Fishman 1991), it seems reasonable to suppose that many of those who use Spanish at home use English in most of their interactions outside the home (a subject about which the 1990 census data do not provide much information). The census data also tell us nothing about the character of Spanish used at home, but recent work on language practices in Latino families reveals considerable variation in both the quantity and quality of Spanish used (Bayley, Schecter and Torres-Ayala 1996, Lambert and Taylor 1996, Vasquez, Pease-Alvarez, and Shannon 1994, Zentella 1997). Indeed, in some families, interactions in Spanish between parents and children, which are critical for maintaining the minority

Table 14-4 *Spanish home language claimants as a percentage of the Hispanic population*

	Total	Age 18+	Age 5–17
Arizona	79.6	87.1	62.4
California	81.7	84.9	73.3
Colorado	54.5	63.2	32.3
New Mexico	74.7	84.6	49.4
Texas	89.9	95.0	77.9
TOTAL	83.1	87.4	72.0

Source: US Bureau of the Census (1993), as adapted by Bills (1997: 157)

language (Hakuta and D'Andrea 1992, Hakuta and Pease-Alvarez 1994), were restricted to occasional endearments or to specific times set aside precisely to revive the minority language (Schecter and Bayley 1997).

The difficulty of minority language maintenance: an example

In addition to the large-scale statistical and demographic studies summarized above, recent studies of language practices in language minority families have highlighted the difficulties of maintaining languages other than English across generations, even when circumstances would seem to favor bilingual maintenance. The Torres family of San Antonio, Texas provides a convenient example of the obstacles faced by parents who wish to transmit a minority language to their children (for detailed accounts see Bayley, Schecter, and Torres-Ayala 1996; Schecter and Bayley 2002). José and Elena Torres and their three daughters, ages 10, 11, and 12, lived in an overwhelmingly Latino neighborhood on the south side of San Antonio. José and Elena acquired Spanish at home from their own parents, who had immigrated from northern Mexico as young adults, and both of them continued to use Spanish with their mothers. As for English, like many Mexican-Americans of their generation, the Torreses acquired it at school when use of Spanish on school grounds was a punishable offense (Hurtado and Rodríguez 1989). As a consequence, they never learned to read or write in Spanish. At home, José and Elena spoke both Spanish and English with one another. Outside the home, they accommodated to the language preferences of their interlocutors or to the demands of the situation.

In their daughters' formative years, José and Elena spoke only English with them in order to ease their transition to formal schooling and to spare them the difficulties they themselves had experienced as Spanish-speakers entering English-medium schools. As the girls grew older, however, the Torreses became increasingly concerned about their lack of Spanish proficiency, which they associated

with loss of cultural continuity and intergenerational communication. To address
their concerns, they set aside one day a week where Spanish was to be used
at home and they arranged for their daughters to spend more time with one of
their Spanish-speaking grandmothers. In addition, they regularly attended church
services conducted in Spanish. They sought assistance from the schools their
children attended, but none was available.

The following brief interaction between Elena and Marta, the middle child, was
recorded more than a year after the Torreses had begun their attempt to revive
Spanish at home. Although Marta had acquired considerable ability to understand
Spanish, her ability to speak it remained at a rudimentary level:

> MARTA: Mom, *ya hicimos* vacuum. (Mom, we finished vacuuming.)
> ELENA: ...*¿Ya barrites tu cuarto?* (Have you swept your room?)
> MARTA: *Sí. . . . Yo tieno, no yo tienes*. I don't know how you say 'have'.
>   Mom, how do you say 'have'? (Yes. . . . I have, no I have.)[3]
> ELENA: half? what? *medio* (half).
> MARTA: have, like you have to close the door.
> ELENA: *Tienes que*. (You have to.)

> (Bayley et al. 1996: 399)

To summarize, the preponderance of the evidence from large-scale surveys and
detailed studies of language minority communities and families suggests that the
traditional pattern of intergenerational shift to English remains unchanged. This
pattern is especially clear among populations of Asian language background. It
can also be seen among Latinos, even in the Southwest, where we might expect to
see the strongest maintenance of Spanish. As one researcher noted, "the appearance of language maintenance that so many see in the density of Hispanics and
Spanish speakers in the Southwest is attributable to one phenomenon: the continuing heavy immigration from south of the border" (Bills 1997: 157–58). For
minority languages whose speakers are fewer or more dispersed, the prospects
for maintenance are even less encouraging.

Acquisition of English

As shown in the previous section, speakers of immigrant languages are acquiring
English and in many cases they or their children are shifting to English as a sole
or dominant language. This section outlines the characteristics of those who are
less than fully proficient in English and explores the resources available to assist
them to acquire the dominant language, with special focus on adult learners.

---

[3] Neither *tieno* nor *tienes* is the correct first person singular form. *Tengo* is the correct form of this
very common verb. *Tieno* is not found in any Spanish dialect. *Tienes* is the second person singular
present tense form.

The scope of the problem

The previous sections have examined the extent of linguistic diversity in the USA, with emphasis on the number of persons who report speaking a home language other than English, as well as the overall shift of language minority populations to English. Such information, while it provides some guidance as to the potential need for English instruction, does not tell the full story. Proficiency in a language other than English certainly does not preclude proficiency in English, and many who speak a home language other than English do so not because they are unable to speak English but by choice. Indeed, according to the 2000 census, nearly 55 percent of adults who reported speaking a home language other than English reported that they spoke English "very well." (Self-reports of language proficiency are problematic, but a 1987 US Department of Education study showed that self-reports do correlate well with other measures of proficiency.)

Although a majority of those who reported speaking a home language other than English claimed to speak English "very well," a very substantial minority, 45 percent, speak English less than "very well," and projections indicate that this number will increase in the coming years. Many organizations have responded to the needs of adults with limited proficiency in English. English as a second language (ESL) classes are offered through federally funded programs for refugee resettlement, extended education departments of universities and community college districts, school district adult education programs, community and church organizations, and private companies that provide language training in the workplace. Indeed, the US Department of Education (1995b) reports that ESL is the fastest growing subject in adult education. Despite substantial growth in programs, however, the demand for ESL classes has been increasing every year, and numerous studies report shortages of available programs and long waiting lists in many places (see, e.g., Amastae 1990, Bliss 1990, Chisman 1989, US Department of Education 1995b).

Information about participation in ESL classes by the 12 million adults who reported speaking a primary home language other than English is contained in the 1995 National Household Education Survey (Brick et al. 1996), which aimed to be as inclusive as possible. To understand the nature of adult participation in ESL classes, the survey drew on a representative sample of all adults whose primary home language was other than English. About 1,304,000 adults (10.8 percent of the population that spoke a primary home language other than English) took ESL classes in 1994–95. In addition, approximately 3,382,000 people (28 percent of the relevant population) expressed some interest in taking ESL classes. Table 14-5 summarizes the characteristics of both participants and non-participants in ESL classes.

The greatest participation rate was by speakers aged sixteen to twenty-five. Nearly 19 percent of potential ESL students in this age group participated in ESL classes, compared with only 4 percent of potential students forty-six and older. Other factors associated with participation in ESL classes included education,

Table 14-5 *Percentage and number of the populations of interest* for ESL classes, by participation status and adult characteristics: 1994–95*

Characteristics	Number of adults (in thousands)	Participants (percent)	Nonparticipants		
			Number (in thousands)	% interested in taking ESL classes	% not interested in taking ESL classes
TOTAL	12,078	11	10,777	28	72
Age					
16 to 25 years	2,104	19	1,712	22	78
26 to 35 years	3,443	13	2,988	34	66
36 to 45 years	3,157	10	2,839	33	67
46 years and older	3,374	4	3,238	20	80
Education					
Less than high school diploma	4,947	8	4,571	31	69
High school diploma or equivalent	4,498	14	3,855	28	72
Some postsecondary education or more	2,633	11	2,351	22	78
How long lived in the United States					
2 years or less	973	31	668	41	59
3 to 5 years	1,354	27	987	34	66
6 to 9 years	1,878	9	1,703	39	61
10 to 24 years	4,202	9	3,832	33	67
25 years or more	1,731	3	1,680	15	85
Born in the United States	1,939	2	1,905	11	89
Self-reported ability to read English					
"very well"	2,630	5	2,513	9	91
"well"	3,340	12	2,948	25	75
"not well"	3,557	16	3,001	43	57
"not at all"	2,551	9	2,314	33	67

* Includes civilian, noninstitutionalized adults, age 16 or older, not enrolled in elementary or secondary school at the time of the interview, and whose primary language at home was any language other than English

Source: US Department of Education (1995a)

with persons with a high school diploma or equivalent participating at the highest rate, and length of residence in the USA. People who had been in the country for five years or less showed both the highest rates of participation, as well as a generally high level of interest. Note, however, that although participation declined sharply among speakers with more than five years of residence, dropping from 27 percent among people who had been in the country from three to five years to only 9 percent among people with six to twenty-four years of residence, interest remained high well beyond five years. Among speakers with six to nine years of residence, 39 percent expressed interest in such classes. Of those with ten to twenty-four years of residence, 33 percent expressed such interest. Finally, participation in ESL classes was related to self-reported English reading ability. Relatively few respondents who reported that they could read English "very well" participated in or were interested in ESL classes. They were unlikely to need further instruction in ESL (Kim, Collins, and McArthur 1997). Somewhat surprisingly, however, only 9 percent of the respondents who reported that they could not read English at all participated in ESL classes, although a substantial number of the non-participants in this group (33 percent) expressed interest in participation.

Barriers to participation in ESL classes

The very substantial number of participants in ESL classes, combined with the even larger number of potential students who expressed interest in such classes, is evidence that adults who are not fully proficient in English are keenly aware of the advantages of improving their proficiency. Still, the discrepancy between the number of participants and the number who expressed interest in ESL classes suggests that a variety of barriers prevent English language learners from achieving their goals. In some cases, options may be limited by the lack of trained teachers. One recent national study of opportunities available to limited English proficient students in public schools, for example, found that only 30 percent of teachers instructing students with limited proficiency in English had received any training for the task, and fewer than 3 percent had earned a degree in ESL or bilingual education (US Department of Education 1997). Given the relatively low priority accorded to adult education in many school districts, even fewer teachers engaged in adult education are likely to have had specific training in teaching English language learners.

Although the lack of availability of sufficient classes and trained teachers may limit participation in ESL classes, other problems beyond the purview of the educational system also inhibit adult participation. The main barriers to participation in ESL classes are summarized in table 14-6. Note that all the adults whose responses are reported were aware of available classes that they could have taken.

Time was a much greater barrier for employed adults than for those who were unemployed or not in the labor force. Moreover, participation in ESL classes is

Table 14-6 *Characteristics of adults[1] who reported a main barrier to attending ESL classes: 1994–95*

Characteristics of non-participants	Number[2] (thousands)	Main barriers to participation in ESL classes (%)			
		Time	Money/cost	Child-care or transport[3]	Other
Total	1,205	40.1	26.0	23.4	10.6
Age					
16 to 35 years	480	40.3	24.3	27.4	7.9
36 years and older	725	40.0	27.1	20.7	12.3
Sex					
Male	533	46.8	36.2	2.9	14.1
Female	672	34.8	17.9	39.6	7.8
Education					
Less than high school diploma	515	41.2	20.7	26.6	11.5
High school diploma or more	690	39.3	29.9	20.9	9.8
Labor force status					
Employed	637	53.2	24.5	12.0	10.3
Unemployed/not in the labor force	568	25.5	27.7	36.1	10.8
Household income					
$20,000 or less	618	35.4	27.6	28.1	8.9
$20,001 or more	588	45.0	24.3	18.4	12.3
Self-reported English reading ability					
"Very well" or "well"	396	52.6	21.1	18.9	7.4
"Not well" or "not at all"	809	34.0	28.4	25.5	12.1

[1] Includes civilian, non-institutionalized adults, aged sixteen or older, not enrolled in elementary or secondary school at the time of the interview, whose primary home language was other than English

[2] Includes nonparticipating adults who had an interest in taking ESL classes, knew of available classes they could have taken, and reported a major or minor barrier to participation: time, money/cost, child-care, transportation, and other main barrier

[3] Only adults who had a child or children under ten years old were asked about child-care

Source: US Department of Education (1995b), cited in Kim et al. (1997)

limited not only by the time available to potential students but by scheduling. More recent immigrants, particularly those from Central America, Mexico, and southeast Asia, tend to be concentrated in lower level occupations and to have had few educational opportunities in their own countries, including opportunities to learn English (Portes and Rumbaut 1996: 66–82). In addition to working at physically taxing jobs, immigrants in the lower economic brackets have very little control over their working conditions and hours. In such circumstances, adults who begin ESL classes may be forced to discontinue them when employers change their working hours.

Men and women reported important differences in barriers to participation in ESL classes. As table 14-6 also shows, lack of time constituted the main barrier for 46.8 percent of the male respondents, but only 2.9 percent of the men listed child-care or transportation as a barrier. For women the situation was quite different: although 34.8 percent listed time as a barrier, 39.6 percent listed child-care or transportation.

Taken together, the barriers to adult participation in ESL classes suggest that increases in the numbers of programs and qualified teachers, while important, will not be sufficient to address the problems of potential English-language learners. Rather, limited-English-speaking immigrants may require services that are beyond the usual purview of adult education. Among these is adequate childcare for immigrant mothers. Economic issues also play a role. Even though the cost of most adult programs is low, it is still a barrier for many potential learners.

Untutored English acquisition

When we examine the acquisition of English in formal educational settings, we may rely on large-scale surveys giving rates of participation in ESL classes and various standardized measures of proficiency. However, many who might benefit from ESL instruction do not participate in formal classes. Rather, they acquire English informally in their communities and workplaces, and large-scale studies of such acquisition are not generally available. In studying the informal acquisition of English, then, we must rely on different kinds of evidence. Fortunately, much of the literature on second-language acquisition and bilingualism focuses on detailed description and analysis of untutored second-language acquisition. To show how non-English-speaking immigrants acquire – and sometimes fail to acquire – English in untutored settings, this section summarizes two representative cases. One case, Schumann's (1978) study of an adult Costa Rican immigrant in the Northeast, has exerted considerable influence in the field of second-language acquisition. The second case, focusing on the simultaneous acquisition of English literacy by a Mexican immigrant mother and daughter, is based on recent research in northern California (Schecter and Bayley 2002).

The case of Alberto, a 33-year-old Costa Rican immigrant who participated in an early modern study of second language acquisition (Cazden et al. 1975), is one of the best known in the literature. In contrast to the other five participants in that study, Alberto demonstrated very little progress in English during ten months of observation. For example, unlike the other participants, he continued to use a very early form of negation, as in "I no use television" (Schumann 1978). Schumann explained Alberto's lack of progress as a result of social and psychological distance from the dominant North American culture. As a Latin American immigrant engaged in unskilled labor, Alberto was in a socially subordinate position to middle-class English speakers. Moreover, he was one of a small number of Spanish-speaking immigrants in a predominantly Portuguese-minority workplace. His life-style reflected his psychological distance from the English-speaking community, and he made little effort to become acquainted with English-speaking people, preferring instead to spend time with Spanish-speaking friends. He did not watch English-language television programs but preferred to listen to Spanish music. Finally, he did not attend English classes. Given his situation, it is not surprising that he made little progress in acquiring English.

The second case of untutored acquisition involves a more successful language-learning experience. Like Alberto, Teresa Esparza was a working-class Latin American immigrant. After a highly mobile childhood in Mexico, she immigrated to California as a young adult (for a fuller account, see Schecter and Bayley 2002). In Mexico she had completed six years of schooling. After immigrating, she settled in a largely working-class Mexican immigrant community approximately twenty miles south of San Francisco, where she eventually obtained a general equivalency high school diploma (GED) and completed a beauty course while working as a domestic and caring for her daughter Marcella. A single mother, Teresa, who at the time of Marcella's birth spoke virtually no English, radically modified her lifestyle to prepare her daughter for a school program that she felt would allow the child to obtain the social opportunities she herself had lacked.

Shortly after her daughter was born, Teresa decided that Marcella would attend an English-medium school. She regarded it as her responsibility to prepare her child for a school environment where she would have to compete with native speakers of English, but she faced a quandary. Her English proficiency fell far short of what was necessary to give Marcella a head start. So she devised an ingenious strategy to compensate for her own limited English and to prepare her daughter for school. Here is what Teresa reported. She began in Spanish:

> When Marcella was a baby, I didn't speak English, but I had cassettes and I bought books. I never read in Spanish. I had the cassettes and I used to lie down on the rug and put on the cassette as if I were reading with her . . . until I learned to read baby books, but I always read in English.

Teresa, who had achieved a generally high level of proficiency in English in the years since Marcella was a baby, concluded the narrative of her simultaneous language and literacy acquisition in English, "And I learned a lot that way." Marcella learned a lot as well. At the time she participated in the study, she was an 11-year-old honor student at a private Catholic English-medium school.

Numerous other cases might serve as well as those of Alberto and of Teresa and Marcella Esparza to illustrate the successes and failures of immigrants trying to acquire English in informal settings. These cases, however, are sufficient to illustrate two general principles: the debilitating effects of social and psychological distance, which are worsened by economic marginalization, and the lengths to which non-English-speaking immigrant parents will go to insure that their children succeed in English-medium schools.

Conclusion

This review of language use by language minority speakers leads to several conclusions. First, as a result of continuing large-scale immigration, the USA is becoming more linguistically diverse. Spanish remains by far the most widely spoken language other than English, but since 1990 Chinese, Vietnamese, Tagalog, Korean, and Russian have also shown remarkable gains. Despite very substantial increases in the number of speakers of minority languages, however, immigrant bilingualism has remained a transitory stage that seldom lasts beyond the second or third US-born generation. In the absence of major changes in educational policy, the extent of linguistic diversity in the USA is likely to continue to be a reflection of the number of immigrants rather than of deliberate attempts to foster bilingualism. Second, opportunities for non-native speakers of English to acquire the dominant language have increased substantially in recent years. Still, though, many non-native speakers of English find their efforts to acquire English hindered by a lack of suitable programs with well-trained teachers, by difficult working conditions, and by lack of time, transportation, and child-care. The lack of appropriate care for the children of many immigrant women, in particular, highlights the fact that men and women have unequal access to opportunities for learning English (cf. Norton 2000). Finally, immigrant parents often go to extraordinary lengths to insure that their children acquire the full English proficiency necessary for success in school. Too often, however, the efforts of both adults and children are hampered by a lack of teachers trained in second language learning and teaching, as well as by the belief among some teachers that full acquisition of English as a second language necessarily entails loss of the first language.

Suggestions for further reading and exploration

Sponsored by the National Research Council, August and Hakuta's (1997) report is essential reading for anyone who wishes to investigate the challenges and opportunities resulting from the increased linguistic diversity of the school-age population. The well organized summaries on topics ranging from assessment to second language acquisition are highly useful introductions to the more detailed discussion in the text. Although not focused specifically on the USA, Lightbown and Spada (1999) summarize current thinking about second-language acquisition in a highly readable text. Portes and Rumbaut (1996) provide an excellent overview of the social, economic, and educational conditions of immigrants in the USA, and the chapter treating "Language and Education" is a particularly useful review of bilingualism and patterns of English language acquisition among children and adults. Norton (2000) richly documents the barriers immigrant women face in their efforts to acquire English. Spener (1994) is a collection of highly readable papers on literacy practices in language minority communities; particularly useful chapters are those by Marcia Farr on literacy practices in Mexicano families and by Gail Weinstein-Shr on family literacy and second language learners. Schecter and Bayley (2002) offer a detailed account of language use in Mexican-American and Mexican immigrant families in California and Texas. Guerra (1998) closely examines literacy practices in Chicago's Mexican immigrant community.

References

Amastae, Jon. 1990. "Official English and the learning of English." In *Perspectives on Official English*, eds. Karen L. Adams and Daniel T. Brink. Berlin: Mouton de Gruyter. Pp. 199–208.

August, Diane and Kenji Hakuta, eds. 1997. *Improving Education for Language Minority Children*. Washington DC: National Academy Press.

Bayley, Robert, Sandra R. Schecter, and Buenaventura Torres-Ayala. 1996. "Strategies for Bilingual Maintenance: Case Studies of Mexican-Origin Families in Texas," *Linguistics and Education* 8: 389–408.

Bills, Garland B. 1997. "New Mexican Spanish: Demise of the Earliest European Variety in the United States," *American Speech* 72: 154–71.

Bills, Garland B., Eduardo Hernández-Chavez, and Alan Hudson. 1995. "The Geography of Language Shift: Distance from the Mexican Border and Spanish Language Claiming in the Southwestern US," *International Journal of the Sociology of Language* 114: 9–28.

Bliss, W. B. 1990. "Meeting the Demand for ESL Instruction: a Response to Demographics." In *Leadership for Literacy*, eds. F. P. Chisman and Associates. San Francisco: Jossey-Bass. Pp. 171–97.

Brick, J. M., J. Wernimont, and M. Montes. 1996. *The 1995 National Household Education Survey: Reinterview Results for the Adult Education Component*. NCES Working Paper 96-14. Washington DC: US Department of Education, National Center for Education Statistics.

Cazden, Courtney B., Herlinda Cancino, Ellen J. Rosansky, and John H. Schumann. 1975. *Second Language Acquisition Sequences in Children, Adolescents and Adults*. Final Report, National Institute of Education (Grant No. NE-6-00-3-0014).

Chisman, F. P. 1989. *Jump Start: the Federal Role in Adult Literacy Education*. Washington DC: Southport Press.

Crawford, James. 1992. *Hold Your Tongue: Bilingualism and the Politics of "English Only."* Reading MA: Addison Wesley.

Fishman, Joshua A. 1991. *Reversing Language Shift: Theoretical and Empirical Foundations of Assistance to Threatened Languages*. Clevedon: Multilingual Matters.

Guerra, Juan. 1998. *Close to Home: Oral and Literate Practices in a Transnational Mexicano Community*. New York: Teachers College Press.

Hakuta, Kenji. 1986. *Mirror of Language: the Debate on Bilingualism*. New York: Basic Books.

Hakuta, Kenji and Daniel D'Andrea. 1992. "Some Properties of Bilingual Maintenance and Loss in Mexican-Background High-School Students," *Applied Linguistics* 13: 72–99.

Hakuta, Kenji and Lucinda Pease-Alvarez. 1994. "Proficiency, Choice, and Attitudes in Bilingual Mexican-American Children." In *The Cross-Linguistic Study of Bilingual Development*, eds. Guus Extra and Ludo Verhoeven. Amsterdam: Royal Netherlands Academy of Arts and Sciences. Pp. 145–64.

Hakuta, Kenji, Bernardo Ferdman, and Rafael Diaz. 1987. "Bilingualism and Cognitive Development: Three Perspectives." In *Advances in Applied Psycholinguistics*, vol. 2: *Reading, Writing, and Language Learning*, ed. Sheldon Rosenberg. Cambridge: Cambridge University Press. Pp. 284–319.

Heath, Shirley Brice. 1981. "English in Our National Heritage." In *Language in the USA*, eds. Charles A. Ferguson and Shirley Brice Heath. Cambridge: Cambridge University Press. Pp. 6–20.

Hurtado, Aida and Raul Rodríguez. 1989. "Language as a Social Problem: the Repression of Spanish in South Texas," *Journal of Multilingual and Multicultural Development* 10: 401–19.

Kim, Kwang, Mary Collins, and Edith McArthur. 1997. *Participation of Adults in English as a Second Language Classes: 1994–1995*. NCES 97–319. Washington DC: US Department of Education, National Center for Education Statistics.

Lambert, Wallace E. and Douglas M. Taylor. 1996. "Language in the Lives of Ethnic Minorities: Cuban American Families in Miami," *Applied Linguistics* 17: 477–500.

Lightbown, Patsy and Nina Spada. 1999. *How Languages Are Learned*, 2nd edn. Oxford: Oxford University Press.

Lollock, Lisa. 2000. *The Foreign-Born Population of the United States: Population Characteristics*. Current Population Reports (P20-534). Washington DC: US Department of Commerce, Bureau of the Census.

López, David E. 1982. *Language Maintenance and Shift in the United States Today*, vols. 1–4. Los Alamitos CA: National Center for Bilingual Research.

Norton, Bonny. 2000. *Identity and Language Learning: Gender, Ethnicity, and Educational Change*. Harlow: Pearson Education.

Peal, Elizabeth and Wallace E. Lambert. 1962. "The Relationship of Bilingualism to Intelligence," *Psychological Monographs* 76: 1–23.

Portes, Alejandro and Rubén G. Rumbaut. 1996. *Immigrant America: a Portrait*, 2nd edn. Berkeley: University of California Press.

Schecter, Sandra R. and Robert Bayley. 1997. "Language Socialization Practices and Cultural Identity: Case Studies of Mexican-Descent Families in California and Texas," *TESOL Quarterly* 31: 513–41.

   2002. *Language as Cultural Practice: Mexicanos en el norte*. Mahwah NJ: Lawrence Erlbaum.

Schumann, John H. 1978. *The Pidginization Process: a Model for Second Language Acquisition*. Rowley MA: Newbury House.

Smith, Madorah. 1939. "Some Light on the Problem of Bilingualism as Found from a Study of the Progress in Mastery of English among Preschool Children of Non-American Ancestry in Hawaii," *Genetic Psychology Monographs* 21: 119–284.

Spener, David, ed. 1994. *Adult Biliteracy in the United States*. Arlington VA and McHenry IL: Center for Applied Linguistics and Delta Systems.

US Bureau of the Census. 1993. *1990 Census of Population: Social and Economic Characteristics, United States*. Washington DC: Department of Commerce.

   2003a. "File QT-P16: Language Spoken at Home: 2000." Washington DC: Department of Commerce.

   2003b. "Summary File 3 (SF3)." Washington DC: Department of Commerce. *http://www.census.gov/Press-Release/www/2002/sumfile3.html*

US Department of Education. 1987. *Numbers of Limited English Proficient Children: Nation, State, and Language-specific Estimates*. Washington DC: Office of Planning, Budget, and Evaluation.

   1995a. *National Household Education Survey* (Spring 1995). Washington DC: National Center for Education Statistics.

   1995b. *Teaching Adults with Limited English Skills: Progress and Challenges*. Washington DC: Office of Vocational and Adult Education, Adult Learning and Literacy Clearinghouse.

   1997. *1993–1994 Schools and Staffing Survey: a Profile of Policies and Practices for Limited English Proficient Students: Screening Methods, Program Support, and Teacher Training*. NCES 97-472. Washington DC: National Center for Education Statistics.

Valdés, Guadalupe and Richard A. Figueroa. 1994. *Bilingualism and Testing: a Special Case of Bias*. Norwood NJ: Ablex.

Vasquez, Olga, Lucinda Pease-Alvarez, and Sheila M. Shannon. 1994. *Pushing Boundaries: Language and Culture in a Mexicano Community*. New York: Cambridge University Press.

Veltman, Calvin. 1988. *The Future of the Spanish Language in the United States*. New York: Hispanic Policy Development Project.

Wiley, Terrence G. 1996. *Literacy and Language Diversity in the United States*. Arlington VA and McHenry IL: Center for Applied Linguistics and Delta Systems.

Wortham, Stanton. 1997. "Educational Success among Diaspora Latinos in New England." Paper presented to the American Anthropological Association, Washington DC.

Zentella, Ana Celia. 1997. *Growing Up Bilingual: Puerto Rican Children in New York*. Oxford: Blackwell.

PART 3

The sociolinguistic situation

15

Language ideology and language prejudice

ROSINA LIPPI-GREEN

Editors' introduction

This chapter is about an issue that has occupied Americans for centuries – and especially since the Civil Rights era of the 1960s. It is about prejudice (adverse pre-judgment) against people based on specific traits, like ethnicity or religion. The trait on which the chapter focuses is language, a discriminatory trait about which we are much less conscious and much less concerned. The chapter begins with a list of nine examples where people's intelligence, job effectiveness, or other personal and professional characteristics are unfairly evaluated on the basis of the varieties of English they speak.

In this chapter, Rosina Lippi-Green concentrates on the existence of a "standard language ideology" in the USA – "a bias toward an abstracted, idealized, non-varying *spoken* language" – and the various institutions (schools, the media, the courts) that promote it. She exposes some of the fallacies in this ideology (non-mainstream accents can be difficult if not impossible to change and they often do not impede communication per se) and the uneven, discriminatory ways in which it is used to effect language domination (not all ethnic or foreign groups are asked to change). But she also documents the different responses such domination elicits from the dominated (resistance versus acquiescence). The author also constructs a model of the language subordination process (including the uses it makes of authority, mystification, and misinformation) in order to expose and undermine it.

Although all linguists are to some extent aware of and critical of language prejudice, this chapter takes the radical position (like Sledd 1972) that the burden of change should rest on the discriminators alone. Alternatively, or additionally, some linguists encourage the dominated to keep their non-mainstream dialects for informal use but to become bidialectal, developing competence in a standard or mainstream variety for work, school, and other formal contexts in which it is preferred (see Alatis 1970).

Let's begin with the experiences of real people in everyday situations:

> A young woman comes to the United States from Uganda. After receiving a Master's Degree from the University of Wisconsin, Milwaukee, she accepts employment in that university's Office of Affirmative Action and Equal Opportunity. During the next four years three different supervisors are so satisfied with her performance that she is promoted to Administrative Program Specialist. Then a new Assistant Chancellor for Equal Opportunity, an African American woman, is hired. In the next few months, the new

supervisor makes numerous and documented demeaning and hostile remarks about the woman's Ugandan accent, excludes her from making oral presentations that she has been making successfully for four years, and restricts her responsibilities in other ways. After complaints and counter complaints to the Chancellor and to the federal Equal Employment Opportunity Commission, the new supervisor issues notice that the young woman's employment contract will not be renewed.   (*Kyomugisha v. Clowney*)

A woman phones into an Oprah Winfrey taping on "Black English" to make her opinion known: "I guess what I'd like to say is that what makes me feel that blacks tend to be ignorant is that they fail to see that the word is spelled A-S-K, not A-X. And when they say *aksed*, it gives the sentence an entirely different meaning. And that is what I feel holds blacks back."   (1989)

In 1992, 403 residents of Westfield, Massachusetts (a town of about 36,000 people and a broad ethnic mix), sign a petition and present it to the school board. The petition specifically urges that no teacher be assigned to first or second grade classrooms "who is not thoroughly proficient in the English language in terms of grammar, syntax and – most important – the accepted and standardized use of pronunciation."   (Associated Press 1992)

A professor originally from the south, later employed by a university in the midwest, relates this story of his first job search: "I got an interview with an extremely elite undergraduate college in the northeast. They conducted the first substantial part of the interview in [another language] and it went well. When they switched to a question in English, my first answer completely interrupted the interview . . . they broke out laughing for quite a while. I asked what was wrong and they said they 'never would have expected' me to have such an accent. They made a big deal about me having a [prestigious accent in the second language] and such a strong Southern accent. Of course, I had been aiming for bland standard English. After that, I got a number of questions about whether I'd 'be comfortable' at their institution. Subtle, but to me it was not ambiguous."   (Lippi-Green 1997)

In a Seattle bank, a Cambodian-American man with a long history of excellent work evaluations is repeatedly denied official promotion to a position he is already filling and performing well, but not being paid for. A managerial level employee tells him that he is not being promoted because he cannot speak "American."   (*Xieng v. Peoples National Bank*)

The novelist Orson Scott Card (2003) writes: "When I was at Brigham Young High School in Provo, Utah, the town of Lehi was seen as the ultimate hick town. Its major landmark was a grain elevator; its speech was the most extreme version of that hard-R rural Mormon accent that semi-sophisticated people like me delighted in scorning (unaware, of course, of our own less-than-elite accents)."

A doctoral candidate relates this story about her fieldwork: "The passenger in the seat next to mine asked about [the recording equipment], and I explained briefly about my research . . . He told me that he worked in sales for a large company in San Diego, and that it was his job to hire salesmen. He told me quite frankly that he would never hire anyone with a strong foreign accent, and especially not a Mexican accent. I asked him why. His only response was, 'That's smart business. I have to think of the customers. I wouldn't buy anything from a guy with a Mexican accent.'"   (Spicher 1992: 3–4)

The Internal Revenue Service removes an agent with a solid work history from working with clients "because of concern about the effect of her accent on the 'image' of the IRS, not any lack in either communication or technical abilities."   (*Park v. James A. Baker III, Secretary of the Treasury*)

A official elected to the state Assembly in California notes the multilingual commerce in his home town with considerable trepidation: ". . . you can go down and apply for a driver's license test entirely in Chinese. You can apply for welfare today entirely in Spanish. The supremacy of the English language is under attack."   (from a report on pending English-Only legislation in California, "CBS Evening News," October 1986)

These stories, and thousands of others just like them, provide evidence of what many people would acknowledge without dispute: we rely on language traits to judge others. This is not a cultural phenomenon particular to our place and time, but a human behavior that is characteristic of all language communities. Language is – among other things – a flexible and constantly flexing tool for the emblematic marking of social allegiances. We use variation in language to construct ourselves as social beings, to signal who we are, and who we are not – and cannot be. Speakers choose among sociolinguistic variants available (alternative pronunciations, expressions, grammatical structures), and their choices cluster together in ways that are obvious and interpretable to other speakers in the community. This process is a functional part of the way we communicate. It is not optional, but rather a basic design feature of spoken human language.

These sociolinguistic behaviors are specific to the spoken language alone; they do not transfer to the written language. Writing systems are a strategy developed in response to demands arising from social, technological, and economic change; the purpose of a writing system is to convey information over time and space – removed from its original context. We write things down because our memories are not capable of storing masses of information for ourselves or those who come after us or because we consider the message worthy of preserving beyond the limitations of memory.

The demands made on written language are considerable: we want it to span time and space, and we want it to do that in a social vacuum, without the aid of paralinguistic features (such as intonation and gestures) and often without shared context of any kind. Thus, the argument goes, written language needs to be free of excessive variation. This *lack* of variation – the variation that is an essential part of spoken human language – is the most distinctive characteristic of our (and most other) writing systems. The discussion in this chapter has to do exclusively with spoken language and particularly the way speakers use and interpret variation in spoken language.

Independent of issues of language effectiveness or communicative success, most people believe that there is such a thing as *good* language and *bad* language. Many assume that it is perfectly reasonable to judge others on the basis of language variety rather than on the content of what they have to say. Most would be surprised (if not shocked) at an employer or a teacher who turned away an individual on the basis of skin color; most would find nothing unusual or wrong with a teacher of Puerto Rican students who sees her students as a problem to be solved:

> These poor kids come to school speaking a hodge podge. They are all mixed up and don't know any language well. As a result, they can't even think clearly. That's why they don't learn. It's our job to teach them language – to make up for their deficiency. And, since their parents don't really know any language either, why should we waste time on Spanish? It is "good" English which has to be the focus.   (cited in Zentella 1996: 8–9)

And most people are very surprised, disquieted, and even angry to learn that this fund of commonsense knowledge about language on which they – and this teacher – depend so heavily is filled with inaccuracies, false assumptions, and simple mythology.

There is a great deal of evidence to indicate that what people believe they know about language is very different from the way language actually works. This phenomenon has been observed widely by linguists of many different theoretical orientations. One psycholinguist notes this:

> Most educated people already have opinions about language. They know that it is man's most important cultural invention, the quintessential example of his capacity to use symbols, and a biologically unprecedented event irrevo-cably separating him from other animals. They know that language pervades thought, with different languages causing their speakers to construe reality in different ways. They know that children learn to talk from role models and caregivers. They know that grammatical sophistication used to be nurtured in the schools, but sagging educational standards and the debasements of popular culture have led to a frightening decline in the ability of the average person to construct a grammatical sentence. They also know that English is a zany, logic-defying tongue . . . In the pages that follow, I will try to convince you that every one of these common opinions is wrong!   (Pinker 1994: 17–18)

What is of interest in this chapter, however, is how people use false assump-tions about language to justify judgments that have more to do with race, national origin, regional affiliation, ethnicity, and religion than with human language and communication. In public situations it has become unacceptable to reject individ-uals on the basis of the color of their skin, but some can and do reject individuals because of the variety of English they speak or the accent they speak it with. Somehow, many have come to believe that some types of English are "more

English" than others; that there is one perfect and appropriate kind of English that everyone should speak; that failure to speak it is an indication of stupidity, willfulness, or misguided social allegiance. Many hold this belief so firmly that they have convinced the very people who speak the stigmatized varieties of English to believe it too. Because these behaviors and beliefs are in themselves interesting and important, linguists have studied language ideologies, their origins, propagation, evolution, and effect.

In the most overly simplistic terms, ideology can be defined as a "belief system" or "body of ideas." On this basis, everything is ideological and everybody has multiple ideologies, as in an advertisement promoting the consumption of raw food: "This tape is a MUST for anybody who actively propagates the ideology of raw-foodism." Taken so broadly, ideology has little descriptive or analytical power. But there are other approaches, and in the examination of language in its social context, ideology provides a framework for what has been called *critical language studies*, where much of the work on language subordination (see below for more on language subordination) and the limiting of discourse takes place. For example, to understand arguments for standardization or for English only, we begin with the cultural conceptions that underlie such arguments (for example, "English has always been dominant; it must remain dominant"). To first understand how such arguments are linked to particular power structures and interests is to understand how and why they work.

Theorists provide dozens of possible definitions of ideology. In critical language studies ideology is taken as *the promotion of the needs and interests of a dominant group or class at the expense of marginalized groups, by means of disinformation and misrepresentation of those marginalized groups.* More specifically, when looking at the larger issues of language standardization, linguists often refer to a "standard language ideology," that is, a bias toward an abstracted, idealized, non-varying *spoken* language that is imposed and maintained by dominant institutions. Of course, *everyone* speaks a dialect, and a uniform language is an impossibility.

Ideology has been linked to language by many thinkers, but it was the French philosopher Michel Foucault who considered the way in which discourse is "controlled, selected, organised and redistributed" – what he called *disciplined*:

> . . . as history constantly teaches us, discourse is not simply that which translates struggles or systems of domination, but is the thing *for which and by which* there is struggle, discourse is the power which is to be seized. [Foucault 1984: 110; italics added]

In the simplest terms, the "disciplining" of discourse has to do with who is allowed to speak on a topic – and, thus, who is heard on that topic. A standard language ideology, which proposes that an idealized nation-state has one perfect, homogeneous language, becomes the means by which discourse is seized, and provides a rationalization for limiting access to discourse.

Authority that is associated with education is the most often cited and best established type of rationalization in this process. Thus, it might be argued that, in a culture like that of the USA, which obliges everyone to participate in the educational system, access to discourse is at least theoretically possible: marginalized groups can, by coming through the educational system, make themselves heard in their own languages. Foucault anticipates part of this argument by pointing out the fallacy of the assumption of education as an evenly distributed and power-neutral cultural resource: "Any system of education is a political way of maintaining or modifying the appropriation of discourses, along with the knowledges and powers which they carry" (123).

Of course, access to education itself is controlled and disciplined, in part on the basis of language variety and accent; the educational system may not be the beginning, but it is the heart of the standardization process. Asking children who speak non-mainstream languages to come to the schools in order to find validation for themselves, in order to be able to speak their own stories in their own voices, is an unlikely scenario.

Dominant institutions promote the notion of an overarching, homogeneous standard language. That language is primarily white, upper-middle class, and middle American; it is often claimed to be "unaccented." But of course it is accented, like all other language varieties. It just happens to be the accent of the mainstream. Whether the issues at hand are larger social or political ones or more subtle, whether the approach is coercion or consent, there are two sides to this process of standardization: first, devaluation of all that is not (or does not seek to be) politically, culturally, or socially mainstream; and second, validation of the social (and linguistic) values of the dominant institutions. The process of linguistic assimilation to an abstracted standard is portrayed as a natural one, necessary and positive for the greater social good.

In the USA at the beginning of the twenty-first century, the "dominant group or class" is a matter of both race and economics: the social and political power is predominantly white and upper-middle class. Some would claim it is also a matter of education, but education is an extension of economics and, arguably, of a developing class consciousness. Of course, individuals work together in institutions, and thus much of the work on language subordination focuses not on the behavior of individuals (what John said to Maria) but on how language ideologies become part and parcel of larger institutional practices. "Institution" is often used to refer to social relationships between individuals, as in "the *institution* of marriage." Here, *institution* can be defined simply as any organization that has social and structural importance and a specific set of goals important for continuing the established social structures of the community. Such institutions include the educational system, the news media, the entertainment industry, the business sector, the government and the legal system (which in large part exist to define and delineate social institutions), the military, and religious organizations.

The institutional approach relies on a simplistic model: language is communication; communication must be clear to be effective; to be clear, language must be unvarying, static, standardized. This model may seem reasonable on the surface, but because it rests on basic fallacies it is not reasonable. We know with certainty that spoken language is not homogeneous and can never be homogeneous, that communication is more complicated than the simple sharing of surface information, and most crucially that the goals we have developed for written language cannot apply to spoken language any more than our expectations for automobiles (speed and mileage) can be applied to the way we walk.

Given the serious and detrimental repercussions of speaking certain varieties of English and some foreign accents in the USA, you may wonder why the individuals described earlier don't just give up and assimilate linguistically: Why don't they just join the mainstream? This question is often asked but rarely examined very closely. Many people assume it is possible to substitute one accent for another. In fact, there is reason to believe that such a thing is impossible. Even more important is the fact that linguistic assimilation is not demanded of everybody. Because some people speak a distinctive regional or social variety of English that is *not* overtly stigmatized (e.g., the strong upper midwest English of radio entertainer Garrison Keillor or television newsbroadcaster Tom Brokaw or the Boston English of Senator Ted Kennedy), they are not asked to assimilate. Other individuals do speak a less favored or stigmatized variety of English but they possess other kinds of currency (social power, political power, or economic power) that offset the effect of their stigmatized speech. It is hard to imagine anyone insisting that political figures like US Secretary of State Henry Kissinger, Mexican president Vicente Fox, US president John F. Kennedy, United Nations Secretary General Kofi Annan (of Ghana), or Nobel Laureate Derek Walcott (of the Caribbean island nation of St. Lucia), or actors Antonio Banderas and Arnold Schwarzenegger attend classes for accent reduction or "better" English.

In the USA at the beginning of the twenty-first century, an Irish accent will rarely be overtly stigmatized, but Irish accents were often greeted negatively when immigration from Ireland was at a high point in the nineteenth century. Those varieties of English and non-native accents that are out of favor at any particular time reveal a great deal about the cultural and political climate of the moment. At the time of writing this, the accents that seem most stigmatized are associated with New York City and the deep South, as well as with immigrants from Asia, Africa, the Near East, and Central and South America. By contrast, none of the recent cases heard in US courts concerning alleged violations of Title VII of the Civil Rights Act (a topic to which we return below) involve speakers with French or Scottish or Norwegian accents, which all enjoy a certain social prestige at the moment.

Even if it were possible simply to exchange one variety of English for another, to adopt or drop a particular accent at will, then two questions would remain: first, would it make any difference, if the underlying animosity is not really about language, but about race, ethnicity or some other less-than-pleasing affiliation? And most relevant to the USA as it looks back on a century in which civil rights battles were fought and won at great cost, should it matter? Is it right to ask individuals to reject their own language? We do not – under US law *cannot* – ask a person to change religion, gender, or skin color, but we unhesitatingly demand of some people that they suppress or deny the most effective way they have of situating themselves socially in the world. Accent serves as the first point of gatekeeping because we are forbidden by law and social custom, and perhaps by a prevailing sense of what is morally and ethically right, from using race, ethnicity, homeland, or economics more directly.

What we don't understand clearly, what remains mysterious but is important to comprehend, is not so much the ways in which dominant groups deny non-dominant groups permission to be heard in their own voices, but more so *how and why those groups cooperate*. How do institutions manage to convince whole groups of human beings that they do not fully or adequately possess an appropriate human language? Even more mysteriously, why do those groups hand over this authority? One critic puts a more personal face on this question when he summarizes one way that ideology works:

> The study of ideology is among other things an inquiry into the ways in which people may come to invest in their own unhappiness. It is because being oppressed sometimes brings with it some slim bonuses that we are occasionally prepared to put up with it. The most efficient oppressor is the one who persuades his underlings to love, desire and identify with his power; and any practice of political emancipation thus involves that most difficult of all forms of liberation, freeing ourselves from ourselves.   [Eagleton 1991: xiii–xiiv]

When persons who speak languages that are devalued and stigmatized consent to the standard language ideology, they themselves become complicit in its propagation against themselves, their own interests and identities. Many are caught in a vacuum: when an individual cannot find any social acceptance for her language outside her own speech communities, she may come to denigrate her own language, even while she continues to use it.

Standard language ideology provides a web of commonsense arguments in which the speaker of a non-mainstream language can get tangled at every turn: at school, in radio and television news, at the movies, while reading novels, at work, people are told that the language that marks them as Mennonite, Hawai'ian, or Ugandan, for example, is ugly, unacceptable, incoherent, illogical. This is countered, daily, by experience: these same people do communicate, effectively, with those who are closest and most important to them, who mark their language similarly. They even manage to communicate with the people who are criticizing them, in spite of the complaints. The things being said about their home languages, about family and community make them uncomfortable and unhappy. The promises they hear about the rewards of assimilation may be very seductive:

money, success, recognition. They may think about trying to change the way they talk, pay some attention to grammatical points that have been criticized, but they can do little or nothing about accent.

This day-by-day, persistent devaluation of the social self has repercussions. While many accept this devalued notion of themselves and their language communities, others react with anger and personal resistance. If there is a group of people going through the same experience, consistent negative feedback might bring organized resistance. There are occasional signs of this: an accent reduction class scheduled in a South Carolina school that must close because of lack of student interest; a movement to validate Hawai'ian Creole in public forums; a group in Wisconsin that publicizes their commitment to African American Vernacular English and their wish to have it recognized for the functional language it is; individuals who file suit against employers who reject them on the basis of language traits linked to protected categories; teachers who stand up for the rights of bilingual students.

But the language mainstream does not let these small acts of resistance go unnoticed; its representatives strike back, and hard. The institutions that see themselves as protectors of the values of the nation-state wage an ongoing effort to validate their favored place in that state, in part on the basis of language. This resistance and counter-resistance that pits the empowered language mainstream against small groups or individuals who struggle for recognition is an ongoing process.

A model of the language subordination process

There have been many models of ideological processes, not all of them having to do directly with language. But the elements of subordination are surprisingly constant in the case of language. The first step is the seizing of authority, in which those who claim to have better or superior human language set themselves up as good models.

Of course, linguists also claim authority about language, but it is to a large extent authority based on training in observation, experimentation, and deduction. The announced goal of linguistics is descriptive rather than prescriptive, so that the claim "All living languages change" is not a matter of faith or opinion or aesthetics, but observable fact (which is not to say that all claims by linguists are equally supportable by fact).

Other parts of the subordination process include mystification (where some persons and institutions convince others that they alone understand what language is about and are the only possible resources and authorities) and misinformation. Misinformation about language is rampant. It can be found in any newspaper every day of the week and ranges from the truly trivial ("I am disturbed by the way young people these days misuse the word *like*") to the historically unfounded ("Shakespeare spoke the best English, and since then it's been all downhill") to the divisive and discriminatory ("If those people don't want to learn English the way it's supposed to be spoken, they should go back to where they came from!").

A great deal of misinformation and commonsense argumentation centers on communication, and this is also where most persons who discriminate on the basis of language will focus their rationalizations. "I've got nothing against [Taiwanese, Appalachians, Blacks]," the argument will go; "I just can't understand them. So maybe they can't do anything about their accent, but I can't help not understanding them either."

Communication seems to be a simple thing: one person talks and another listens; then they change roles. When the discussion focuses on accent, however, the characterization of communication becomes overly simplistic. The social space between two speakers is not neutral, in most cases. Think of the people you talked to today. Each time you begin an exchange, a complex series of calculations begins: Do I need to be formal with this person? Do I owe her respect? Does she owe me deference? What do I want from her, or she from me?

Or we might simply refuse to communicate. In an adversarial position, we may understand perfectly what our partners, parents, friends say to us, but still respond with "I simply cannot understand you." Magically, the listener is relieved of any responsibility in the communicative act, and the full burden is put directly on the speaker. "I can't understand you" may mean, in reality, "I dare you to make me understand you."

When native speakers of USA English are confronted by an accent that is foreign to them or with a variety of English they dislike, they must first decide whether or not they are going to accept their responsibility in the act of communication. What can be demonstrated again and again is this: members of the dominant language groups feel perfectly empowered to reject their portion of the burden and to demand that a person with an accent (that is, an accent that differs from their own accent) carry a disproportionate amount of the responsibility in the communicative act. On the other hand, even when there are real impediments to understanding – a bad telephone line, a crowded and noisy room – speakers make special efforts to understand those toward whom they are well disposed.

When speakers are confronted with a new person they want to talk to or must talk to, they make a quick series of social evaluations based on many external cues, one of them being the other person's language and accent. Those sociolinguistic cues are directly linked to homeland, the race and ethnicity and other factors – the entirety of the social self – of the other person. Based on our own personal histories, our own backgrounds and social selves (which together comprise a set of filters through which we hear the people we talk to), we will take a communicative stance. Most of the time, we will agree to carry our share of the burden. Sometimes, if we are especially positive about the configuration of social characteristics we see in the person, or if the purposes of communication are especially important to us, we will accept a higher-than-usual share of that burden.

Each of us would group the accents we come across in different configurations. For the majority of Americans, French and Swedish accents are positive ones, but not for all of us. Many have strong negative reactions to Korean accents, or to African American Vernacular English, but certainly not everyone does. In Hawai'i, where there is a long history of animus between people of Japanese and Filipino national origin, one person with a foreign accent may reject a different foreign accent or reject the creole that is spoken by so many in the islands. In black communities in the Bronx (in New York City) and elsewhere, there is a great deal of tension between African Americans and recent immigrants from Africa and the Caribbean. In other communities, some people may cringe or glower when they hear Spanish spoken on the street or spoken between sales clerk and customer, while others may smile broadly to hear Italian or Polish spoken in the same situations. The languages and language varieties we hear must pass through our language ideology filters. In extreme cases, we feel completely justified in rejecting the communicative burden – and, in so doing, the person in front of us.

The Civil Rights Act of 1964 (specifically Title VII of that law) provides recourse for workers who are discriminated against on the basis of race, color, religion, sex, or national origin. The scope of the law was broadened in 1980 to address trait-based discrimination (for example, language that is linked to national origin). The Equal Employment Opportunity Commission (abbreviated EEOC) is responsible for the overview and administration of Title VII. In its *Guidelines on Discrimination because of National Origin*, the EEOC currently defines national origin discrimination

> . . . broadly as including, but not limited to, the denial of equal employment opportunity because of an individual's, or his or her ancestor's place of origin; or because an individual has the *physical, cultural or linguistic characteristics* of a national origin group.   [Federal Register 1988: ¶1606.1; italics added]

The spirit of the law is clear: an employer may not reject a job candidate or fire or refuse to promote an employee because the employee externalizes in some way an allegiance to another culture. In the case of racial discrimination, the courts have determined that no personal preference (neither the employer's nor that of his customers) can excuse discrimination. Similarly, a qualified person may not be rejected on the basis of linguistic traits the employer or the employer's customers find aesthetically objectionable, as long as those linguistic traits are linked to a category protected by the Civil Rights Act, and that includes national origin. In contrast to racial discrimination, however, an employer has some latitude in matters of language: "An adverse employment decision may be predicated upon an individual's accent when – but only when – it interferes materially with job performance" (Civil Rights Act of 1964, §701 et seq., 42 U.S.C.A. §2000e et seq.).

Let's return now to the story we began with at the head of the chapter. Florence Kyomugisha lost her job at the University of Wisconsin in part because of alleged communication difficulties with her supervisor, Ms. Clowney. It is important to note that after its independence from Great Britain, Uganda adopted English as its official language. English is the language of government and commerce and the primary medium of education; official publications and most major newspapers appear in English, and English is often employed in radio and television broadcasts. Ms. Kyomugisha, a fluent speaker of Runyankole and Luganda, is also a native and fluent speaker of Ugandan English. As the chancellor of the university acknowledged in 1996, while Ms. Kyomugisha does not speak "Wisconsin English, she nevertheless speaks perfectly fine English" (*Kyomugisha v. Clowney*, complaint filed October 16, 1997).

In her complaint under Title VII of the Civil Rights Act, Ms. Kyomugisha claimed national origin discrimination linked to language traits. This is a subject her attorney explored during the deposition of her supervisor, Ms. Clowney, who is also an attorney. (A deposition is testimony taken under oath as part of the preparation for a trial.) The attorney uses the term *animus* to refer to prejudice or malevolent ill will.

> ATTORNEY: . . . You know about discriminatory animus from your professional preparation in the field of affirmative action and discrimination law; isn't that correct? . . . you were responsible for doing the investigations of discrimination at the university, and you need to know what the law is about that, correct?
>
> CLOWNEY: . . . Yes, sir.
>
> ATTORNEY: And you know about the sociology of discrimination, right?
>
> CLOWNEY: Yes.
>
> . . .
>
> ATTORNEY: And you would agree that the process of communication between two individuals involves a degree of burden sharing between the two individuals for purposes of making each other understood, correct?
>
> CLOWNEY: Sometimes. It depends on the nature of the two individuals. I would agree that the burden is more on an investigator to be understood in an university community than employees. The burden is more so on the professional than the nonprofessional.
>
> ATTORNEY: Now, I'm speaking of two people who speak with each other, who have divergent accents. You agree that you have an accent, correct?
>
> CLOWNEY: At times I might. I don't know if I do or not; you tell me.
>
> ATTORNEY: Well, isn't it true that all people have an accent of one kind or another?
>
> CLOWNEY: Not all people, some people. My mother is a schoolteacher and she doesn't necessarily have an accent.

ATTORNEY: Well, do you think somebody from another part of the country who speaks with a different intonation would say that that person in fact has an accent?

CLOWNEY: Possibly, yes.

. . .

ATTORNEY: And communication between two such people involves the acceptance of a certain responsibility for burden sharing between each other in order to effectuate communication; isn't that correct?

CLOWNEY: It can. It depends on the relationship between the two individuals.

ATTORNEY: One of the factors in that relationship that could make the communication difficult is when one individual refuses to accept burden, a burden in connection with effectuating comprehensibility; isn't that correct?

CLOWNEY: How about the burden on the other person to go and take courses and study and to be understood as well. What about – why should the burden – I also understand diversity, but why should the burden be on the recipient rather than, I mean, if you look at modern-day diversity studies, we'd be here all day. There's a double burden; there's a dual burden. I'll – I'll say there's a dual burden.

ATTORNEY: Isn't it true that in some conversations where one person has a racial animus of one type or a national origin animus of one type that person refuses to accept a burden, any burden for effectuating the communication . . . and thereby make – makes the allegation that the person is incomprehensible?

CLOWNEY: I'm not going to answer that. I'm not an expert on communications skills. I've written papers on communication skills and racial animus. I can't say that. You're – you're asking me to draw inferences here and I can't say that. There are people I know that are trained who don't have any kind of animus; and if they can't understand someone, they get frustrated, and then have nothing to do with race, sex, religion, whatever. But the bottom line is that, you know, it's – you have to listen a little bit carefully, but, you know.

. . .

ATTORNEY: Do you feel like you accepted your portion of the burden in trying to understand Florence's oral communications?

. . .

CLOWNEY: Yes.

ATTORNEY: . . . whether you feel that you accepted your portion of the
burden to comprehend what Florence was saying to you
when she was orally communicating with you?
CLOWNEY: Yes, I do.
ATTORNEY: Do you feel that you made a reasonable good faith effort
to understand Florence?
CLOWNEY: Yes, I do.
ATTORNEY: Is it your testimony that notwithstanding that effort that was
not enough and you still had oral communication problems
with Florence?
CLOWNEY: Yes, I do.

Subsequent to this deposition, the university decided to settle this case before
it came to trial, and Ms. Kyomugisha received compensatory damages, back
pay, and the attorney's costs she had incurred. The university's lawyers did not
disclose the reasons the university decided to offer a settlement, but from her
deposition there would seem to be some question about the true origin of Ms.
Clowney's communication difficulties with Ms. Kyomugisha. She asked, "How
about the burden on the other person to go and take courses and study and to
be understood as well . . . why should the burden be on the recipient . . . ?"
After Ms. Kyomugisha had worked successfully for four years with three other
supervisors, it would be difficult to justify a claim that her accent was a burden or barrier in any general sense. As Ms. Clowney herself seems to acknowledge, racial or national origin animus can raise a barrier of its own to successful
communication.
    Ms. Kyomugisha was knowledgeable about the law, and she had the strength
of will necessary to pursue her legal rights. She was successful, but many others
are not. Everyday in the USA, individuals are taught that the language they speak
marks them as less-than-good-enough. Some turn away from them, pretending
not to understand their language. The repercussions of such linguistic rejection
are vast, because

> . . . our identity is partly shaped by recognition or its absence, often by the
> misrecognition of others, and so a person or group of people can suffer real
> damage, real distortion, if the people or society around them mirror back
> to them a confining or demeaning or contemptible picture of themselves.
> [Taylor 1994: 25]

Linguists are interested in the process of language subordination – how it works,
why it works, and why we let it work. Standard language ideology is introduced
by the schools, vigorously promoted by the media, and further institutionalized by
the corporate sector. It is underscored and underwritten in subtle and not so subtle
ways by the judicial system. Thus, it is not surprising that many individuals do not
recognize the fact that, for spoken language, variation is systematic, structured,
and inherent, and that the *national standard* is an abstraction. What *is* surprising

and deeply disturbing is the way that many individuals who consider themselves democratic, even-handed, rational, and free of prejudice hold on tenaciously to a standard language ideology.

Suggestions for further reading and exploration

Lippi-Green (1987) exposes and indicts social institutions that instill language prejudice and discrimination, including how the spoken accents of animated Hollywood characters perpetuate stereotypes. Cameron (1995) is strong on political correctness, sexist language, and linguistic prescriptivism, but with examples drawn largely from Britain. Less accessible and more theoretical, Eagleton (1991) addresses ideologies from a Marxist point of view. Gee (1996) begins his excellent analysis of discourse and literacy from a moral perspective. McKay and Wong (1988) gathers in one place descriptions of contemporary language minorities in the USA, particularly Hispanic and Asian groups; some chapters offer a historical perspective and others address educational implications of language diversity. Herman and Chomsky (1988), relying on case studies, propose a propaganda model of the press and argue that the press is manipulated by government and corporations into playing a role in shaping events, rather than fairly reporting them. Fairclough (1992) gives good representation to analyses of critical language awareness and critical discourse analysis. Crawford (1992) documents the historical roots of US language policy (with pieces by Benjamin Franklin and Theodore Roosevelt, among many others), the official English movement and the issues surrounding it, and the symbolic implications of language conflict. Woolard and Schieffelin (1994) reviews and analyzes the literature on the subject of language ideology. Foucault (1984), in a classic treatment, addresses questions of who has the right to speak and be heard and the implications of the answers to those questions. Bourdieu (1991) is a classic treatment of the role of symbolic power in social life.

References

Alatis, James. 1970. "Linguistics and the Teaching of Standard English to Speakers of Other Languages or Dialects." In Alatis's *Report of the Twentieth Annual Round Table Meeting on Linguistics and Language Studies*. Washington DC: Georgetown University Press.

Associated Press. 1992. "Debate Over Teachers with Accents," *New York Times*. July 5, Sec. 1, p. 12.

Bourdieu, Pierre. 1991. *Language and Symbolic Power*. Ed. and intro. by J. B. Thompson. Trans. G. Raymond and M. Adamson. Cambridge MA: Harvard University Press.

Cameron, Deborah. 1995. *Verbal Hygiene*. London and New York: Routledge.

Card, Orson Scott. 2003. *http://www.hatrack.com/osc/reviews/restaurant/utah/gardenwall. shtml*

Crawford, James, ed. 1992. *Language Loyalties: a Source Book on the Official English Controversy*. Chicago: University of Chicago Press.

Eagleton, Terry. 1991. *Ideology: an Introduction*. London: Verso.

Fairclough, Norman, ed. 1992. *Critical Language Awareness*. London: Longman.

Foucault, Michel. 1984. "The Order of Discourse." In *Language and Politics*, ed. Michael Shapiro. New York: New York University Press. Pp. 108–38.

Gee, James Paul. 1990. *Social Linguistics and Literacies: Ideology in Discourse*. London and New York: Falmer.

Herman, E. S. and Noam Chomsky. 1988. *Manufacturing Consent: the Political Economy of the Mass Media*. New York: Pantheon.

Kyomugisha, Florence G. v. Charmaine P. Clowney and University of Wisconsin Milwaukee. Case No. 97C1089. Deposition taken July 7, 1998.

Lippi-Green, Rosina. 1997. *English with an Accent: Language, Ideology, and Discrimination in the United States*. London: Routledge.

McKay, Sandra Lee and Sau-ling Cynthia Wong, eds. 1988. *Language Diversity: Problem or Resource? A Social and Educational Perspective on Language Minorities in the United States*. Boston MA: Heinle.

Oprah Winfrey Show. November 19, 1987. No. W309. "Standard and 'Black English'." Produced by D. DiMaio; directed by J. McPharlin.

Park, Kee Y. v. James A. Baker III, Secretary of the Treasury, EEOC No. 05870646. 1988.

Pinker, Steven. 1994. *The Language Instinct*. New York: W. W. Morrow and Co.

Sledd, James. 1972. "Doublespeak: Dialectology in the Service of Big Brother," *College English* 33: 439–56.

Spicher, Lori Lea. 1992. "Language Attitude towards Speakers with a Mexican Accent: Ramifications in the Business Community of San Diego, California." Unpub. Ph.D. diss., University of Texas at Austin.

Taylor, Charles. 1994. *Multiculturalism: Examining the Politics of Recognition*. Princeton: Princeton University Press.

Woolard, Kathryn A. and Bambi B. Schieffelin. 1994. "Language Ideology," *Annual Reviews of Anthropology* 23: 55–82.

Xieng, Phanna K. et al v. Peoples National Bank of Washington. Washington State Supreme Court, opinion dated January 21, 1993. No. 59064–8.

Zentella, Ana Celia. 1996. "The 'Chiquitafication' of US Latinos and their Languages, OR Why We Need an Anthro*political* Linguistics." In *SALSA III. Proceedings of the Third Annual Symposium about Language and Society*, eds. R. Ide, R. Park, and Y. Sunaoski. Austin: University of Texas: *Texas Linguistic Forum* 36, 1–18.

16
Ebonics and its controversy

JOHN BAUGH

Editors' introduction

This chapter explores the origins and definitions of the term Ebonics, and the linguistic, educational and sociopolitical implications of the Oakland school board's 1996 resolution recognizing Ebonics as the primary language of its African American students. The controversy sparked by this resolution was both intense and international. It was one of the biggest linguistic brouhahas in the USA in the twentieth century.

   In this, as in other recent work (Baugh 1999), John Baugh emphasizes the links between the language of African Americans and their linguistic and educational legacies as slave descendants – people who, more so than other Americans, were not allowed to maintain their ancestral languages or have equal access to education and justice. As he notes, the African American linguists who first defined Ebonics in the 1970s saw it as a continuum, including "the communicative competence of the West African, Caribbean and US slave descendants of African origin" (Williams 1975: v). This international and multilingual connection was implicit in the Oakland school board's December 1996 resolution, but less so in their January 1997 revision, which portrayed it primarily as an American variety of English, in concert with the supportive resolution of the Linguistic Society of America. Baugh presents other definitions of Ebonics and discusses the reactions to and policy implications of recognizing the legitimacy of the vernacular of African Americans, including its potential role in developing fluency in standard English.

Orientation

Ebonics came to global attention on December 18, 1996. That was the day the Oakland, California school board passed a resolution declaring Ebonics to be the "predominantly primary language" of its 28,000 African American students. That linguistic assertion did more than label the speech of every African American student attending public schools in Oakland. It also set off a chain of political and research events that continue to reverberate in communities where people of African descent speak English. Some of these people are native English speakers, often residing in the Caribbean, Great Britain, or the United States. In other countries, such as Tanzania, South Africa, or Haiti, speakers of English who trace their ancestry to Black Africans may have learned English as a secondary language.

Strong emotional reactions to Ebonics occurred as its proponents attempted to embrace the term, while detractors were quick to denounce it. As is typically the case with any complex social phenomenon, the true story of Ebonics is not dichotomous. It does not fall neatly into racial categories, nor does it coincide with divisions in wealth, education, or residence. Ebonics continues to be greatly misunderstood, owing substantially to a plethora of definitions that have evolved among well-intended social scientists and educators who have tried to label the linguistic legacy of the African slave trade. Today few public figures dare speak of Ebonics, largely because of the scorn and ridicule heaped upon Oakland's educators who tried unsuccessfully to embrace the term.

This chapter does not presume familiarity with Ebonics, nor does it assume that readers are fully knowledgeable about the diversity of African American language, education, or culture. It does presume that readers know that African slaves and their descendants were historically deprived of access to schools and to equal justice under law. Oakland educators were keenly aware of these historical circumstances, but they were unprepared for the political, educational, financial, and emotional reactions that would greet their notorious linguistic resolution. Long before 1996, when Oakland's school board began their quest, the educational prospects of the vast majority of African Americans remained dim, and today they still lag far behind the vast majority of other US students.

One scholar who tried to strike a balance between linguistic evidence and the educational needs of African American students was John R. Rickford, who among other contributions was the primary author of a resolution on the Oakland Ebonics issue that the Linguistic Society of America (LSA) passed in January of 1997:

> Whereas there has been a great deal of discussion in the media and among the American public about the 18 December 1996 decision of the Oakland School Board to recognize the language variety spoken by many African American students and to take it into account in teaching Standard English, the Linguistic Society of America, as a society of scholars engaged in the scientific study of language, hereby resolves to make it known that:
>
> a. The variety known as "Ebonics," "African American Vernacular English" (AAVE), and "Vernacular Black English" and by other names is system-atic and rule-governed like all natural speech varieties. In fact, all human linguistic systems – spoken, signed, and written – are fundamentally reg-ular. The systematic and expressive nature of the grammar and pronuncia-tion patterns of the African American vernacular has been established by numerous scientific studies over the past thirty years. Characterizations of Ebonics as "slang," "mutant," "lazy," "defective," "ungrammatical," or "broken English" are incorrect and demeaning.
> b. The distinction between "languages" and "dialects" is usually made more on social and political grounds than on purely linguistic ones. For example, different varieties of Chinese are popularly regarded as "dialects," though their speakers cannot understand each other, but speakers of Swedish

and Norwegian, which are regarded as separate "languages," generally understand each other. What is important from a linguistic and educational point of view is not whether AAVE is called a "language" or a "dialect" but rather that its systematicity be recognized.

c. As affirmed in the LSA Statement of Language Rights (June 1996), there are individual and group benefits to maintaining vernacular speech varieties and there are scientific and human advantages to linguistic diversity. For those living in the United States there are also benefits in acquiring Standard English and resources should be made available to all that aspire to mastery of Standard English. The Oakland School Board's commitment to helping students master Standard English is commendable.

d. There is evidence from Sweden, the US, and other countries that speakers of other varieties can be aided in their learning of the standard variety by pedagogical approaches which recognize the legitimacy of the other varieties of a language. From this perspective, the Oakland School Board's decision to recognize the vernacular of African American students in teaching them Standard English is linguistically and pedagogically sound.

At a time when the vast majority of Americans took strong exception to Ebonics, Rickford and the LSA affirmed the linguistic integrity of vernacular African American English and elevated the Ebonics controversy from a domestic US dispute to one of global proportion. It was this multinational orientation that Oakland's educators did not fully articulate in their early resolution.

The birth of Ebonics

The term Ebonics was first introduced in 1973 at a conference on the psychological development of African American children. Two years later, Robert Williams published the conference proceedings as *Ebonics: the True Language of Black Folks*. In this book, Ebonics was defined for the very first time, as "the linguistic and paralinguistic features which on a concentric continuum represent the communicative competence of the West African, Caribbean, and United States slave descendants of African origin" (Williams 1975: v). The scholars at the 1973 meeting were all African Americans, and they spanned a broad range of disciplines including anthropology, communication, comparative cultures, education, speech pathology, and social psychology. Collectively they expressed concern over the term Black English, which was prevalent in professional linguistic circles after 1969. Linguists had previously used the term "nonstandard Negro English" for the speech of the majority of African Americans. Influenced by grassroots efforts within the African American community to affirm that "Black is Beautiful," scholars in linguistics and other fields began to replace "colored" and "Negro" with "Black" and "Afro-American" (see Baugh 1991, Smitherman 1991).

While these efforts were intended to demonstrate respect for African Americans, Williams and his colleagues took umbrage at the term *Black English*, not so much for its reference to blackness, but because the immediate juxtaposition of *Black* and *English* gave some scholars pause.

> Information about Black English has proliferated, creating a misunderstanding of the scope and function of the language. Ebonics as a designation for the language, usually referred to as Black English, attempts to remove some of the ambiguity created by connecting black with English.   (Asanti 1979: 363)

Under this interpretation, "Black" and "English" should not coexist as a sociolinguistic construct, and many educators in Oakland were sympathetic to this interpretation. One reason they embraced "Ebonics" is the fact that it provides African Americans with something that so many other Americans take for granted, namely, the ability to trace one's ancestral linguistic and cultural roots. Americans of British, German, Greek, Italian, or Mexican heritage, among many others, often know precisely which languages were spoken by their ancestors. Because slaves were never intended to be full participants in democracy, descendants of African slaves do not know their complete linguistic heritage. It is this historical discrepancy that Williams and his colleagues pondered as they combined "Ebony" with "phonics" to describe the linguistic consequences of the African slave trade in West Africa, the Caribbean, and the USA.

Inherent international implications

Although Williams and his colleagues lacked professional linguistic credentials, their desire to classify the linguistic legacy of the African slave trade helped to confirm the inherent multinational and multilingual foundations of Ebonics, beyond English. European slave traders did not know or speak African languages with anything resembling fluency, which resulted in pervasive human contact and language mixing among blacks and whites who were associated with the capture, transport, and sale of African captives throughout North and South America.

Because Ebonics was thrust upon politicians and the media through the Oakland school board resolution, government officials and journalists reacted to its contemporary interpretation with little historical reflection, which only served to shroud the issue in a domestic web of sensitive race relations. Vitriol toward Ebonics was so extensive that Black pundits were among the first to decry its existence. In a *New York Times* opinion piece called "The Last Train from Oakland: Will the Middle Class Flee the 'Ebonics' Fad?" Brent Staples (1997) asserted that "The Oakland, Calif. school board deserved the scorn that greeted its December edict declaring broken, inner-city English a distinct, 'genetically based' language system that merited a place in the classroom." He was not alone in this depiction, but his linguistic castigation failed to acknowledge the unique linguistic heritage of African slave descendants as compared with any other group of American immigrants.

In reply to Staples, I observed that "the typical European immigrant may have come to the United States in poverty, speaking a language other than English, (but) they were not enslaved captives who were isolated from other speakers of their native language, which was a practice employed by slave traders to prevent revolts. Nor were they denied statutory access to schools, literacy or judicial relief in the courts" (Baugh 2000: xiii). Longstanding misunderstanding of these historical details lies at the heart of lingering stereotypes about African American English (see chapter 5, this volume) and hip hop (see chapter 21), and of attitudes toward other American dialects (see chapters 15 and 26, Preston 2000).

Staples fell prey to the prevailing myth that linguistic behavior among African Americans is a matter of personal free will. The fact is that such linguistic behavior is a product of racially segregated historical circumstance. A-historical interpretations presume that any US citizen who desires to speak Standard English may do so through hard work, perseverance, and strength of personal will. The truth is that it is rare for those who are not native speakers of dominant language varieties to achieve native fluency in them (see chapter 15). Yet it is against this exacting degree of Standard English fluency that most Americans are judged throughout the country. The Ebonics controversy has added relevance to current debates about African slavery and its discriminatory consequences at the turn of the millennium.

Another reason that the unique linguistic heritage of African slaves was swept aside when Oakland brought Ebonics to global prominence involved confusion over how best to portray the linguistic behavior of African slave descendants. Some proponents of Ebonics believe African American students are entitled to the same educational funding as any other students for whom English is not native. Classifications of African American linguistic behavior as "a dialect of English" or "a language apart from English" have tremendous political, educational, and financial implications, to say nothing of the added entanglement of being exclusively pertinent to people who trace their family ancestry to former enslaved Africans.

Educational considerations

Because Ebonics was originally defined as being linguistically derivative of the African slave trade, it was an international construct that exceeded the resolutions framed by Oakland's school board. In 1996, when the original resolution was drafted, Oakland was one of very few cities with a majority African American population. Academic failure for any group was unacceptable, but, in a community where the African American population constituted a majority, longstanding academic failure exposed glaring educational flaws in need of immediate redress.

Oakland created an African American educational task force that included members who were actively involved with California's "Standard English

Proficiency Program for Speakers of Black Language," a program begun in 1981 in the wake of the Black English trial in Ann Arbor, Michigan (see Smitherman 1981, Labov 1982). The judge in the Ann Arbor case ruled that teachers' ignorance about and negative attitudes toward the vernacular variety of the African American students who were the plaintiffs in the case did indeed constitute a barrier to their attainment of equal educational opportunity.

Bolstered in part by knowledge of that legal decision, Oakland educators adopted strategies to embrace Ebonics as the language spoken by their African American students and in so doing they tried to help advance the standard English proficiency of Oakland's students. By choosing the term Ebonics, however, they did not engender sufficient support for their cause. Few people had ever heard of Ebonics before it was alleged to be the language of Oakland's African American students. The term proved to be highly controversial and evoked strong reactions among people from all races. Pundits and talk-show hosts were less concerned with the history of Ebonics or the special educational needs of African American students than with castigating Oakland's school board. It was under the glare of the global media spotlight that Ebonics reinvigorated serious linguistic dialogue about the consequences of Africa's slave trade.

Shifting definitions of Ebonics

Because so few people had ever heard of Ebonics before its Oakland appearance, there is little wonder that even fewer people realize that advocates and detractors of Ebonics often use different definitions for the same term. In fact, the Oakland Unified School district eventually revised their Ebonics resolution and dropped controversial references to "genetically based" language in favor of the concession that Ebonics was more than "a mere dialect of English." Their original resolution had claimed that Ebonics should not be considered related to English, whereas their revised resolution appears to endorse the opposite view. Of equal importance, the revised resolution brought Oakland's definition of Ebonics in line with the resolution of the Linguistic Society of America.

Recapping the major definitional trends, Williams offers the primordial account of Ebonics, previously described; it emphasizes the international foundations of Ebonics. A second definition was offered in the *Journal of Black Studies,* which is oriented exclusively toward the USA. Ebonics was defined as:

> a language (dialect) that is spoken by Black Americans living in low-income communities that has some specific characteristics observed in the phonological and grammatical system.   (Toliver-Weddington 1979: 364)

The third interpretation was an Afrocentric one. It concludes that Ebonics is unrelated to English, and it is this interpretation that had most influenced Oakland's educators.

> Ebonics is not "genetically" related to English, therefore, the term Ebonics is not a mere synonym for the more commonly used term "Black English." If anything the term is, in fact, an antonym for black English.   (Smith 1992: 41, drawing upon the work of Welmers 1973)

Whereas Williams was not explicit about the linguistic genealogy of Ebonics as the product of multilingual European and African contact, Smith (1992, 1998) was explicit in his claim that Ebonics is not English and should not be considered a dialect of English.

The fourth and broadest definition of Ebonics appeared shortly before the controversial Oakland resolution.

> In a practical sense we can say that to "ebonize" a language is to view the Ebony tree in the Ancient World (Africa) bearing fruit in the form of letters, syllables, and words of phonetic, morphological and syntactic value. Non-verbal communication patterns in African culture, for example, rhetorical style, body movement, expressions, gestures, are included in the process as well . . . I extend the term Ebonics to include all languages of African people on the continent and in the Diaspora that have created new languages based on their environmental circumstances.   (Blackshire-Belay 1996: 20)

This broad view reaffirms the international foundations that Williams introduced when he coined the term Ebonics, but in striking contrast to the scientific linguistics edict that a language can never be defined by the race of its speakers it goes beyond the linguistic consequences of African slavery. Whereas Williams defined Ebonics in terms of slavery, Blackshire-Belay's extension "to include all languages of African people on the continent and in the Diaspora" encompasses many different languages that should not be classified under a single linguistic term. Nevertheless, the similar linguistic plight of people of African descent should be acknowledged, and this much is consistent with the spirit of Blackshire-Belay's assertion.

The Oakland Ebonics resolutions

Toni Cook, an African American member of the Oakland school board in 1996, had noted dismal educational statistics for Oakland's Black students (see Rickford and Rickford 2000: 163). Faced with this daunting evidence, she embarked on a mission to improve the educational performance and graduation rates of African American students enrolled in Oakland's public schools. Recognizing the enormity of the task, she formed a strategic African American educational task force, which included local advocates of African American education, as well as consultants, scholars, and school officials.

After months of deliberations and encouraged by results of academic improvement at Prescott School, where teacher Carrie Secret had met with considerable success teaching African Americans and other students from diverse backgrounds, the task force was prepared to embrace Ebonics and its educational potential for teaching English. Carrie Secret was more than a nurturing teacher; she was also a staunch advocate of Ebonics, and she used the history of African American language as part of her inspirational pedagogy. Emboldened by the writings of Smith (1992), Oakland's African American educational task force wrote its controversial Ebonics resolutions. Rickford and Rickford (2000: 166–69) portray the resolution of December 18, 1996 in concert with the revised one of January 15, 1997. (Note that one date has been silently corrected in the passage below.)

> RESOLUTION (NO. 9697-0063) OF THE BOARD OF EDUCATION ADOPTING THE REPORT AND RECOMMENDATIONS OF THE AFRICAN AMERICAN TASK FORCE; A POLICY STATEMENT, AND DIRECTING THE SUPERINTENDENT OF SCHOOLS TO DEVISE A PROGRAM TO IMPROVE THE ENGLISH LANGUAGE ACQUISITION AND APPLICATION SKILLS OF AFRICAN AMERICAN STUDENTS
>
> [Clause numbers have been added here; italicized words were present in the original resolution of December 18, 1996, but deleted in the amended version of January 15, 1997; wording that was added at that time to replace or supplement the original wording appears in bold, in brackets; otherwise, in the words of the secretary of the Board of Education, this "is a full, true and correct copy of a resolution passed at a Regular Meeting of the Board of Education of the Oakland Unified School District held December 18, 1996."]

> 1. WHEREAS, numerous validated scholarly studies demonstrate that African American students as part of their culture and history as African people possess and utilize a language described in various scholarly approaches as "Ebonics" (literally "black sounds") or "Pan-African Communication Behaviors" or "African Language Systems"; and
> 2. WHEREAS, these studies have also demonstrated that African Language Systems *are genetically based* [**have origins in West and Niger-Congo languages**] and *not a dialect of English* [**are not merely dialects of English**]; and
> 3. WHEREAS, these studies demonstrate that such West and Niger-Congo African languages have been officially recognized and addressed in the mainstream public educational community as worthy of study, understanding *or* [**and**] applications of their principles, laws and structures for the benefit of African American students both in terms of positive appreciation of the language and these students' acquisition and mastery of English language skills; and
> 4. WHEREAS, such recognition by scholars has given rise over the past fifteen years to legislation passed by the State of California recognizing the unique language stature of descendants of slaves, with such legislation being prejudicially and unconstitutionally vetoed repeatedly by various California state governors; and
> 5. WHEREAS, judicial cases in states other than California have recognized the unique language stature of African American pupils, and such recognition by courts has resulted in court-mandated educational

programs which have substantially benefited African American children in the interest of vindicating their equal protection of the law rights under the Fourteenth Amendment to the United States Constitution; and

6. WHEREAS, the Federal Bilingual Education Act (20 U.S.C. 1402 *et. seq.*) mandates that local educational agencies "build their capacities to establish, implement and sustain programs of instruction for children and youth of limited English proficiency"; and

7. WHEREAS, the interests of the Oakland Unified School District in providing equal opportunities for all of its students dictate limited English proficient educational programs recognizing the English language acquisition and improvement skills of African American students are as fundamental as is application of bilingual education **[or second language learner]** principles for others whose primary languages are other than English **[Primary languages are the language patterns children bring to school]**; and

8. WHEREAS, the standardized tests and grade scores of African American students in reading and language arts skills measuring their applications of English skills are substantially below state and national norms and that such deficiencies will be remedied by application of a program featuring African Language Systems principles *in instructing African American children both in their primary language and in English* **[to move students from the language patterns they bring to school to English proficiency]**; and

9. WHEREAS, standardized tests and grade scores will be remedied by application of a program that teachers and *aides* **[instructional assistants]**, who are certified in the methodology of featuring African Language Systems principles *in instructing African American children both in their primary language and in English* **[used to transition students from the language patterns they bring to school to English]**. The certified teachers of these students will be provided incentives including, but not limited to salary differentials;

10. NOW, THEREFORE, BE IT RESOLVED that the Board of Education officially recognizes the existence and the cultural and historic bases of West and Niger-Congo African Language Systems, and each language as the predominantly primary language of **[many]** African American students; and

11. BE IT FURTHER RESOLVED that the Board of Education hereby adopts the report, recommendations and attached Policy Statement of the District's African American Task Force on language stature of African American speech; and

12. BE IT FURTHER RESOLVED that the Superintendent in conjunction with her staff shall immediately devise and implement the best possible academic program *for imparting instruction to African American students in their primary language* for the combined purposes of *maintaining the legitimacy and richness of such language* **[facilitating the acquisition and mastery of English language skills, while respecting and embracing the legitimacy and richness of the language patterns]** whether *it is* **[they are]** known as "Ebonics," "African Language Systems," "Pan African

Communication Behaviors" or other description, *and to facilitate their acquisition and mastery of English language skills;* and

13. BE IT FURTHER RESOLVED that the Board of Education hereby commits to earmark District general and special funding as is reasonably necessary and appropriate to enable the Superintendent and her staff to accomplish the foregoing; and

14. BE IT FURTHER RESOLVED that the Superintendent and her staff shall utilize the input of the entire Oakland educational community as well as state and federal scholarly and educational input in devising such a program; and

15. BE IT FURTHER RESOLVED that periodic reports on the progress of the creation and implementation of such an education program shall be made to the Board of Education at least once per month commencing at the Board meeting of December 18, 1996.

The national press pounced on the original Ebonics resolution, denouncing Oakland's educators and their explicit linguistic assertions as woefully misguided. The chorus of voices that decried Ebonics was racially diverse. Even such prominent African Americans as Maya Angelou, Kweisi Mfume, Bill Cosby, and others rejected Oakland's efforts as racially inflammatory and linguistically suspect. In this sea of emotional public turmoil, Rickford and Rickford (2000) offered the calm of alternative insights into Spoken Soul. Their observations were preceded by those of Perry and Delpit (1998), who provide a broad overview of Ebonics from various disciplinary and professional perspectives, including some of the most influential thoughts by scholars such as Geneva Smitherman, Mary Hoover, John Rickford, Carrie Secret, Wayne O'Neal, and Ernie Smith.

Of greatest linguistic and policy significance, the initial Oakland resolution set the stage for the prospect of bilingual education funding for African American students. This was a prospect that was most unwelcome for then-Secretary of Education Richard Riley, who responded to Oakland's assertions by declaring that bilingual education funds cannot be used for speakers of Black English. It was no accident that Secretary Riley chose to respond in a manner that inherently includes African Americans within the English-speaking population, for to concede otherwise would open the possibility that Black students would indeed demand the same bilingual education funds as others (see Smith 1998).

On January 15, 1997, the Oakland school board offered a revised resolution. It eliminated the controversial "genetic" reference (although there is no evidence that this term was ever intended to mean anything other than "historically related," as it does in the field of linguistics) and brought Oakland back within the limits of a definition consistent with the resolution of the Linguistic Society of America. The revised resolution did not claim that "Black English is the antonym of Ebonics" (see Smith 1998).

Stung by hostile reactions to their efforts by blacks and whites alike, Oakland educators eventually dropped all reference to Ebonics in their educational plans. Indeed, their web site now makes no reference to Ebonics whatsoever. In Oakland, as in many public school districts throughout the USA, every effort has been made to avoid calling special attention to the linguistic legacy of African slavery and its relation to the education of black children.

The continuing quest for greater Standard English fluency

Throughout my career I have stressed the existence of linguistic diversity among slave descendants. Some of us speak AAE, and do so with pride, while others who disassociate themselves from Black English and black culture embrace dominant linguistic norms with enthusiasm. Still others demonstrate considerable linguistic dexterity, conforming to contextually appropriate prevailing linguistic norms. As such it is misleading at best and misguided at worst to imply that any single language education policy or program will serve all American slave descendants of African origin or naturalized Americans who likewise trace their ancestry to the African continent.

As long ago as 1969, James Sledd argued that the politics of bidialectal education (that is, advocating that students learn how to shift between standard English and their home vernacular) were inherently racist because they called for unilateral linguistic conformation by blacks, while demanding nothing of middle-class white speakers whom black students were encouraged to emulate, that is, from a linguistic point of view. A decade later, other linguists argued strongly that schools educating students who speak AAE should treat their everyday speech (technically called the "vernacular") not as a product of linguistic pathology but as a legitimate linguistic system that differs from standard English (see Smitherman 1981).

In some cases the calls for bidialectal education have been explicit, while in others bidialectal goals have been implicit, or worse; African American students were openly criticized for speaking illogically or improperly. The ridicule and scorn that has been heaped upon vernacular African American speech since the inception of slavery has suggested that it is substantively inferior to standard American English, but nothing could be further from the truth (see Labov 1972).

Advances in linguistic understanding have resulted in a host of strategies to address the language arts education of African American students. Some approaches have proven to be far more productive than others, but most remain controversial regardless of their relative success. Fundamentally, American education fails to acknowledge the unique linguistic legacy of slave descendants in contrast to its policies and practices vis-à-vis every other immigrant group in the USA.

The historical devaluation of AAE set the political stage for the hostile reception of Ebonics, without the apparent linguistic discrimination that confronts the vast majority of AAE speakers ever being addressed (Lippi-Green 1997). Educators continue to struggle to motivate black students to learn (or acquire) mainstream linguistic norms – but with minimal success. It would be wrong, however, for educators to abandon their quest to help every student obtain greater fluency, if not mastery, of the dominant linguistic norms, even though many African American students equate adopting standard English with embracing white culture at the expense of their own African American identity and vernacular cultural loyalty (Ogbu 1992, Fordham and Ogbu 1986). The resulting paradox has yet to be resolved to anyone's complete educational satisfaction.

Conclusion

The Ebonics debate that began in Oakland was never fully resolved; in the wake of a hostile public reception, it was simply abandoned. However, the educational issues that inspired Oakland educators to take the risk that earned them considerable notoriety remain today. Far too many African American students continue to attend underfunded and overcrowded schools where they are more likely than their affluent peers to be taught by uncertified teachers who lack the skill or professional credentials to ensure that students are receiving an adequate education.

The Standard English proficiency goals of Oakland's Ebonics resolution remain worthy of our intellectual pursuit, and as one distinguished linguist (Labov 1997) portrayed the Ebonics debate before the US Senate,

> There are two major points of view taken by educators. One view is that any recognition of a nonstandard language as a legitimate means of expression will only confuse children, and reinforce their tendency to use it instead of Standard English. The other is that children learn most rapidly in their home language, and that they can benefit in both motivation and achievement by getting a head start in learning to read and write in this way. Both of these are honestly held and deserve a fair hearing.

Despite growing public trends supporting greater local educational control and educational philosophies that advocate greater school choice, Oakland's efforts to increase Standard English proficiency among students who are American slave descendants did not truly receive a fair hearing. Close inspection of the Ebonics controversy reveals well-intentioned educators who attempted to portray the linguistic legacy of slavery in ways that comply with federal educational regulations for other language minority students. It is my hope that fair-minded educators and policymakers will recognize the need to modify educational regulations to bolster academic prospects for the vast majority of African American students who lack proficiency in Standard English.

Acknowledgments

I would like to thank Edward Finegan, John R. Rickford, H. Samy Alim, and Charla Larrimore Baugh for helpful comments and suggestions on drafts of this paper. I would also like to thank Swarthmore College and Eugene M. Lang for their support and funding of my research immediately after the Ebonics controversy came to public attention. Since then I have benefited greatly from support by the US Department of Education, the Ford Foundation, and the National Science Foundation. Each seeks to advance literacy among students who speak African American English.

Suggestions for further reading and exploration

This volume contains many of the most recent and useful references pertaining to the Ebonics controversy. Corson (2001) considers Ebonics within a broader educational and linguistic context where matters of linguistic diversity touch upon other nonstandard varieties throughout the world. Similarly, Lippi-Green's (1997) studies of nonstandard dialects within the USA place AAE within a larger context that escaped media attention during the height of the Ebonics controversy.

Smitherman (2000) is a welcome alternative to the shrill voices of pundits who castigated Ebonics. Rickford (1997, 1999) places the Ebonics controversy within a larger linguistics context and does so with a different orientation from that found in most other works on this topic. He is particularly mindful of the linguistic heritage and circumstances surrounding AAE and provides a balanced survey of Ebonics within its political and educational context. Perhaps the most passionate advocate of Ebonics is Smith (1975), who introduces the concept as it pertains to his own life and that of his family and friends. Smith served as the primary linguistics advisor to Oakland's African American Educational Task force, and his beliefs are echoed by Secret (1998), who conveys her frustration with many linguistics experts who know little regarding the teaching of reading and even less about teaching African American children.

Arising from conferences held in the wake of the Ebonics controversy, Adger, Christian, and Taylor (1999) and Lanehart (2001) provide detailed and rational accounts of the academic, sociocultural, and historical factors relevant to African American language and education. The Center for Applied Linguistics *http://www.cal.org* and Rickford *http://www.stanford.edu/~rickford/* have produced major web sites pertaining to Ebonics and AAE. Additional web resources can be found through the Linguistic Society of America *http://www.lsadc.org*. Regrettably, because of the racially evocative nature of this subject, many racist web sites were created in the aftermath of the Ebonics controversy, and their hurtful content is antithetical to the spirit of this chapter; see Baugh (2000) and Rickford and Rickford (2000) for discussion.

References

Adger, Carolyn, Donna Christian, and Orlando Taylor, eds. 1999. *Making the Connection: Language and Academic Achievement among African American Students*. Washington DC: Center for Applied Linguistics.

Asanti, Molefi. 1979. "Editor's Statement: Ebonics (Black English): Implications for Education," *Journal of Black Studies* 9: 363.

Baugh, John. 1991. "Changing Terms of Self Reference among American Slave Descendants," *American Speech* 66: 133–46.

1999. *Out of the Mouths of Slaves: African American Language and Educational Malpractice*. Austin: University of Texas Press.

2000. *Beyond Ebonics: Linguistic Pride and Racial Prejudice*. New York: Oxford University Press.

Blackshire-Belay, Carol Aisha. 1996. "The Location of Ebonics within the Framework of the Africological Paradigm," *Journal of Black Studies* 27: 5–23.

Corson, David. 2001. *Language Diversity and Education*. Mahwah NJ: Lawrence Erlbaum.

Fordham, Signithia and John Ogbu. 1986. "Black Students' School Success: Coping with the Burden of 'Acting White'," *The Urban Review* 8: 176–206.

Labov, William. 1972. *Language in the Inner City: Studies in the Black English Vernacular*. Philadelphia: University of Pennsylvania Press.

1982. "Objectivity and Commitment in Linguistic Science: the Case of the Black English Trial in Ann Arbor," *Language in Society* 11: 165–201.

1997. Testimony before the US Senate: Senate Appropriation Committee's Subcommittee on Labor, Health and Human Services and Education, Chaired by Senator Arlen Specter. January 23.

Lanehart, Sonja, ed. 2001. *Sociocultural and Historical Contexts of African American English*. Philadelphia: John Benjamins.

Lippi-Green, Rosina. 1997. *English with an Accent: Language, Ideology, and Discrimination in the United States*. London: Routledge.

Ogbu, John. 1992. "Understanding Cultural Diversity and Learning," *Educational Researcher*, 21(8): 5–14.

Perry, Theresa and Lisa Delpit, eds. 1998. *The Real Ebonics Debate: Power, Language, and the Education of African American Children*. Boston MA: Beacon.

Preston, Dennis. 2000. "Some Plain Facts about Americans and their Language," *American Speech* 75: 398–401.

Rickford, John R. 1997. "Suite for Ebony and Phonics," *Discover* 18: 82–87.

1999. *African American Vernacular English: Features, Evolution, Educational Implications*. Oxford: Blackwell.

Rickford, John R. and Russell J. Rickford. 2000. *Spoken Soul*. New York: John Wiley.

Secret, Carrie. 1998. "Embracing Ebonics and Teaching Standard English: an Interview with Oakland Teacher Carrie Secret." In Perry and Delpit. Pp. 79–88.

Sledd, James. 1969. "Bi-Dialectalism: the Linguistics of White Supremacy," *English Journal* 58: 1307–15.

Smith, Ernie. 1975. "Ebonics: a Case History. In Williams. Pp. 77–85.

1992. "African American Language Behavior: a World of Difference." In *Reading the World: Multimedia and Multicultural Learning in Today's Classroom* (56th Yearbook of the Claremont Reading Conference), ed. Philip H. Dreywer. Claremont CA: Claremont Reading Conference. Pp. 38–53.

1998. "What Is Black English, What Is Ebonics?" In Perry and Delpit. Pp. 49–58.

Smitherman, Geneva. 1981. *Black English and the Education of Black Children and Youth*. Detroit: Wayne State University Press.

1991. "What is Africa to Me?: Language, Ideology, and African American," *American Speech* 66: 115–32.

2000. *Talkin that Talk: Language, Culture, and Education in African America*. London and New York: Routledge.

Staples, Brent. 1997. "The Last Train from Oakland," *New York Times*. January 24. A-30.

Toliver-Weddington, Gloria, ed. 1979. *Ebonics (Black English): Implications for Education*. *Journal of Black Studies* 9 (special issue).

Welmers, William E. 1973. *African Language Structures*. Berkeley: University of California Press.

Williams, Robert, ed. 1975. *Ebonics: the True Language of Black Folks*. St. Louis MO: Institute of Black Studies.

17

Language planning, language policy, and the English-Only Movement

TERRENCE G. WILEY

Editors' introduction

This chapter will capture the interest of many readers because of its detailed discussion of recent, controversial voter initiatives restricting bilingual education in California (Proposition 227) and Arizona (Proposition 203). But these developments are historically situated in the emergence of the English-Only Movement of the 1980s and its opposition, the English-Plus alternative. The English-Only Movement in turn is contextualized in a much older ideology of English monolingualism in the USA, in favor of which arguments including antighettoization and national unity have been amassed.

Terrence Wiley precedes and intersperses his discussion of English monolingualism and the current English-Only and English-Plus movements with a general introduction to language planning and policy. He distinguishes among corpus planning, status planning, and acquisition planning, and classifies language policies according to whether they are promotion oriented, expediency oriented, tolerance oriented, restriction oriented, or repression oriented.

Wiley reminds us that issues of language policy and planning ultimately involve the influence and control of social behavior, and he challenges what he sees as the "philistine logic of conquer or be conquered" underlying the ideology of monolingualism. He closes with a series of questions for us to consider, including the extent to which other languages can be allowed to coexist and even benefit US society as a whole at the same time that the influence of English expands. This and similar questions are not just about languages, but about their speakers, and their rights, statuses, advantages, and disadvantages.

At the beginning of the twenty-first century, one hears recurrent concerns about the official status of English in the USA and, simultaneously, about the preservation of languages other than English. These concerns echo those that held center stage at the outset of the twentieth century but had been raised even during the era of English colonization before the founding of the Republic. A historical review of language planning and policy formation and an analysis of their ideological underpinnings may be helpful in understanding current debates over language policy in the USA. This chapter represents a modest attempt at understanding the complexity of analyzing language planning and language policies (see Ricento and Hornberger 1996). Beginning with definitions that have relevance for both the USA and other countries, it discusses the ideological underpinnings of the dominant monolingual English ideology. It also presents a typology for positioning various language policies and provides contemporary and historical examples. It analyzes the official English movement of the late twentieth century and in conclusion raises language policy questions for the twenty-first century.

Defining language planning and language policy

Among many definitions of language planning is this useful one: "Language planning refers to deliberate efforts to influence the behavior of others with respect to the acquisition, structure, or functional allocation of their language codes" (Cooper 1989: 45). It is elastic enough to include among language planners official planning agencies of the government as well as those, such as major writers and publishers, who have the ability to influence linguistic behavior.

Language planning can also be seen as "the instrument of leaders who desire to change society; it implies a skepticism about the efficacy of 'natural' forces and aims at 'change' by means of rationally coordinated state actions" (Weinstein 1983: 37). It is frequently depicted as an attempt to *solve* language problems, but the historical record indicates that the attempt to plan language has often been a *source* of language problems, particularly when it results in a denial of language rights and linguistic access to social, educational, economic, and political benefits.

National languages typically undergo processes of standardization. Attempts to standardize, regularize, and codify languages fall under the technical name of *corpus planning*. Corpus planning may be undertaken by language academies that have the authority to officially define and delineate a language or through the efforts of popular writers and commercial publishers. Standardization of American English was accomplished largely through the efforts of influential commercial publishers such as Noah Webster. In the USA, proposals for a national language academy were rejected early on.

There are several probable reasons that the founders of the USA chose not to designate English as the official language (see Baron 1990, Heath 1976a, Kloss 1977/1998): (1) the dominance of English was self-evident, rendering an official policy unnecessary; (2) the founders respected linguistic diversity and minority rights; (3) hesitant to offend minorities who had supported the revolutionary cause, the founders opted for a tolerant approach.

Regardless of the original thinking of the founders, English has functioned *as if* it were the official language throughout the history of the USA, and it has often been designated as *official* for specific purposes. Thus, English has generally possessed the status of the official language, and this is functionally more important than its official designation (see Heath 1976b). This point seems to be missed by many who support official English policies.

National languages can be promoted through centralized official governmental planning or by the efforts of language strategists. *Official* language policies are imposed in deliberate attempts to *influence* language behavior by means of official codes. Again, despite some recommendations for a national language academy and the designation of English as an official language there has been insufficient support in the USA for such proposals (Baron 1990, Heath 1976b, Crawford 1992a).

Official versus implicit and covert policies

Official language policies are not the only ones that have significance. Thus, a distinction needs to be made among *official/overt*, *implicit*, and *covert/tacit* policies (Weinstein 1979, 1983, Schiffman 1996, Wiley 1996a, 2000). Much of the popular policy debate is focused on official or overt policies. However, *implicit* norms and expectations, such as those that are involved in *institutional practices* also influence, shape and control language behavior (Haas 1992). National languages, such as American English, are often promoted without official sanction through the creation of a broad-based ideological consensus. Throughout most of American history the dominance and status of English as the national language of the USA has been based on a consensus. Such a consensus had already emerged prior to the founding of the USA in the British colonies where the dominance and status of English had developed without centralized governmental planning. There was no call for the official designation of English during the colonial period because its dominant status was achieved through unofficial means (see Heath 1976b). Recent claims that the dominance and status of English are in jeopardy are even more outlandish than they were when Franklin voiced them two decades prior to the founding of the Republic. According to 1990 US Census data, among the 32 million people (over the age of five) who spoke languages other than English, only around 6 percent spoke no English at all. Overall, approximately 98 percent of the population claimed to have at least minimal facility in English.

Many *implicit* social and institutional practices (cf. Corson 1999) have the appearance of being policy even if they do not have official sanction. *Covert* or *tacit* policies are more insidious. They may be cloaked in lofty goals aimed at helping linguistic minority groups to assimilate, even as these groups are being systematically excluded and denied their linguistic human rights (Skutnabb-Kangas and Phillipson 1994). Linguistic minorities have always been keen to comprehend the implications of detrimental language policies, regardless of whether these policies have been official, implicit, or covert (Heath 1976b, Leibowitz 1971). For example, in the 1880s, Indian children were compelled to attend boarding schools for the express purpose of introducing them to English and the dominant culture and providing them with (marginal) job skills. But during daily school activities "there was an absolute prohibition on Native American children speaking their own languages, and those that did were humiliated, beaten, and had their mouths washed with lye soap"; and Indian children and their parents understood "the unswerving intent of officials to use the schools to destroy their cultures and languages" (Norgren and Nanda 1988: 186; see also Weinberg 1995).

Some have contended that the underlying purpose of language policies is *social control* in societal, political, and economic arenas (Leibowitz 1969, 1971, 1976), a point that has largely been understood by the language minorities targeted by punitive policies that are often veiled as being in their own best interests. Regardless of whether language planning is initiated by governmental language planners or results implicitly from the influence of language strategists or from accepted institutional practices, it has both social and political impact (Leibowitz 1969, 1971, 1976, Tollefson 1991, Wiley 1996a, b, 2000).

Although the United States federal government has never designated English an official language, English has historically been required for most of its operations. It is the language of courtrooms; it is required for federal grant applications; it is the decreed language of schooling; and it is a specific requirement for many jobs. English language and literacy requirements have served a gatekeeping function in immigration (McKay and Weinstein-Shr 1993), and they have provided legal sanction for discrimination in political and economic access (Leibowitz 1969). Historically, both language-minority immigrants and native English speakers deemed to be lacking English literacy skills were prohibited from voting. The gatekeeping function of language policies is often widely supported, even among those who are barred by them. Language and literacy policies that have become widely held are *hegemonic* (Collins 1991).

Dominance of the ideology of English monolingualism

As previously noted, efforts to plan or promote official policies have tended to be influenced by widely held beliefs shaped by an ideology of English monolingualism (Macías 1985, Wiley and Lukes 1996, Wiley 2000). In academic terms, ideology refers to the ability of dominant groups to "manufacture consent" or "gain consent for existing power relationships from those in subordinate positions" (Tollefson 1991: 11). In the USA, language diversity has also been discussed as if it were a consequence only of immigration; as if language diversity were *imported*. Immigration has certainly been a major source of language diversity in the USA, but it is not the only source. Historically, other major sources of language diversity include the incorporation of indigenous peoples through conquest and annexation and the involuntary immigration of enslaved Africans (Wiley and Lukes 1996). All too frequently, discussions of language policy in the USA ignore these additional sources of language diversity, leading some to ask quizzically "Don't you have to know English to be a United States citizen?" The answer is "yes" for those who immigrate, but "no" for those born or involuntarily here.

The ideology of English monolingualism has a long history, with antecedents dating from the colonial and early nationalist periods in the writings of influential individuals such as Benjamin Franklin and Noah Webster. It also appears in early nativist thought. Nativists attempted to establish the rights and privileges of whites born in the USA over those of immigrants. They attempted to prescribe the acquisition of English as an essential component of patriotism and *Americanization* and what it means to be "American." Neo-Nativists of the late nineteenth and early twentieth centuries eventually succeeded in making English a requirement for naturalization and citizenship. During the World War I era, nativist tenets regarding English were a major part of the agenda of the Americanization movement that sought to "Americanize" millions of recent immigrants (McClymer 1982). Its means became coercive and led to the widespread persecution of speakers of German and other languages (Wiley 1998a; see also Leibowitz 1971, Toth 1990, Tatalovich 1995).

The ideology of English monolingualism has remained consistent in its assumptions over time (Macías 1985, Wiley 2000). The major dogma of the ideology of English monolingualism parallels similar monolingual ideologies in countries where other languages are dominant and where immigration has also been a major source of language diversity. An analysis of monolingual ideologies in Spanish-dominant Argentina and Chile, Portuguese-dominant Brazil, and English-dominant USA identified four common arguments to justify the ideology of monolingualism (Kloss 1971; see also Wiley and Lukes, 1996).

One argument holds that immigrant minorities should surrender their languages as compensation for the privilege of immigrating into the receiving society. This expectation, though, is contrary to the historical fact that many language-minority immigrants have been allowed to maintain their native languages. In the USA, Germans and others were allowed to use their native languages in schools, churches, and the community with only occasional protestations or fear of reprisals until the World War I era (Toth 1990, Tatalovich 1995, Wiley 1998a). Many refugees came to this country to escape linguistic, religious, and ethnic persecution in their homelands and did not expect to have to surrender their ancestral languages as a condition of immigration.

Another argument assumes that because language-minority immigrants are likely to do better economically in their new country than they did in their countries of origin, they should waive any claims to linguistic minority rights and be required to shift to the dominant language. This argument fails to acknowledge benefits to the receiving society by the immigration of language minorities through the contribution of immigrant labor, technical expertise, and opportunities for economic expansion (Kloss 1971).

A third element of the monolingual ideology is the antighettoization argument, which contends that language maintenance and cultural maintenance lead to a self-imposed segregation from the dominant, mainstream society and its language and culture, and that this isolation results in a social and cultural lag for the minority group. In the USA, this argument is echoed by advocates of English-Only policies, who often claim that English should be promoted because it is an equal opportunity language (see Bennett 1995). Similar claims were made by proponents of California's Proposition 227, which was intended to severely restrict access to bilingual education (see chapter 18). However, the notion that language minorities deliberately isolate themselves distorts the historical experience of most immigrant groups. There have been rare instances in American history when language-minority groups sought a self-imposed isolation, for example among the Amish. Historically, unequal educational access, not self-imposed isolation, rendered many language-minority children functionally illiterate in both their native languages and in English (see Weinberg 1995, 1997).

Probably the most common argument for linguistic assimilation is national unity. For example, U.S. English, one of the major proponents of English-Only policies, distributed a flyer entitled "A Common Language Benefits Our Nation and Its People," which contended that a common language is of benefit to a nation "because Americans continue to be diverse in origin, ethnicity, religion, and culture" (cited in Donahue 1995: 114). This reasoning assumes that minority languages and ethnic, racial, and religious diversity pose a threat to national unity. According to one analyst, most of the positions taken by U.S. English "showed a suspicious thrust toward disinformation . . . [arguing] that Spanish causes racial tension and low economic achievement . . ." (Donahue 1995: 115). More than two decades prior to these outlandish claims, it had been observed that in most cases where language minorities were accused of lacking national loyalty their perceived disloyalty resulted from overt discrimination. "In other words: the majority, by dealing unfairly with the minority, created among it the very unrest, dissatisfaction and centrifugal tendency which in turn provided governmental authorities with arguments (sometimes not unwelcome) to bolster their restrictive policies" (Kloss 1971: 257). Given this alleged threat, the dominant society could require linguistic assimilation and a surrender of language-minority rights. Despite cogent rebuttals to these arguments, the national unity argument remains a persistent mantra of contemporary English-Only proponents.

Historically, linguistic assimilation into English has been the universal mandate and formula for language-minority groups because such groups are assumed to benefit from linguistic and cultural assimilation into the dominant language and culture of English speakers. The historical record shows, however, that a distinction must be made between *behavioral assimilation* and *structural incorporation* (Weiss 1982). Behavioral assimilation involves one's conforming to the outward trappings of another's linguistic and cultural norms. In other words, assimilation means that one would speak English and act like an Anglo-American. Structural incorporation requires social, political, and economic integration. It would mean that one acquires an equal footing in the economic and political system. Historically, the dominant English-Only ideology has prescribed *deculturation* for all linguistic minority groups. Deculturation results in losing one's ancestral language and culture through behavioral assimilation. Historically, the requirement of *behavioral assimilation* was applied about equally across all groups, but the expectation of *structural incorporation* was only selectively granted. Thus, the universal ideological prescription for English linguistic assimilation has been advanced as a singular means for achieving very different ends (Wiley 1998c, 2000).

Classifying language policies according to intents and consequences ▪

Some of the confusion that occurs in popular discussions of language policies results from dichotomizing choices regarding governmental recognition and support for languages, as if they involved only either–or choices between English and other languages. There remains some disagreement over the fundamental historical orientation of language policies in the USA. In the most comprehensive analysis of formal policy stances that can be taken by a state or by the federal government, Kloss (1998/1977) argued that *tolerance* has been the primary policy orientation throughout most of American history and that this orientation reflected the thinking of most of the founders (see also Heath 1976a, Crawford 1992a, 1995). Certainly, throughout much of American history, there was considerable tolerance toward European languages. However, this tradition of tolerance all but disappeared during the World War I era when an epidemic of anti-foreign-language sentiment and legislation was provoked in a climate of xenophobia, jingoism, and super-patriotism. German-speaking Americans, the largest linguistic minority of the period, were stigmatized, sometimes persecuted, and expected to use English (Toth 1990, Tatalovich 1995, Wiley 1998a, 2000).

In his classic *The American Bilingual Tradition*, Kloss (1998/1977) developed a useful schema to categorize various types of official language policies or language laws. Given that the definition of language policies can be expanded to include *official*, *implicit*, or *covert* policies, the major categories of Kloss's framework can be adapted and more broadly applied to encompass these categories (see Macías and Wiley 1998, Wiley 2000). The following schema, adapted from Kloss, allows for a classification of policies based on their intended purposes as well as their consequences. The emphasis is best placed on consequences because some consequences are unintended.

1. *Promotion-oriented policies* involve the use of governmental/state resources as part of an active governmental plan to further the official use of a language or languages. Much of the promotion of English has resulted from institutional practices that are conducted through the medium of English such as the government's printing and distribution of laws and records in English and its conducting nearly all governmental business in it.

2. *Expediency-oriented laws* or policies designate a weaker version of promotion-oriented policies but differ in purpose because they are not intended to enhance the use of a minority language. They allow the government to *accommodate* minority languages in the short term to facilitate educational and political access and to guarantee legal rights (e.g., by providing for court interpretation). Ironically, much of the controversy regarding bilingual education in recent years has been based on a confusion of expediency with promotion. Expediency provision for Title VII transitional bilingual education and bilingual ballots has often been attacked by English-Only advocates as if they were promotion-oriented in their intent.

3. *Tolerance-oriented* policies are characterized by the significant absence of state interference in the linguistic life of the language-minority communities. They leave language-minority communities

to their own devices to maintain their ancestral languages without any expectation of resources and support from the government. From the late 1600s until World War I, many German Americans experienced relative tolerance toward their language, the German-language press, and their efforts to educate their children using German-language and bilingual instruction (Toth 1990, Kloss 1998/1977, Wiley 1998a). Areas of the country with language-minority immigrant communities today often rely on privately funded and community-funded week-end schools in efforts to maintain or restore heritage languages. Even in periods of linguistic tolerance, however, efforts to promote their heritage language efforts have not generally achieved long-term success when language minorities have had sufficient opportunities for contact with the dominant society.

4. *Restriction-oriented* policies are those that make social, political, and economic benefits, rights, and opportunities conditional on knowing or using the dominant language. Language restrictions usually target communication in work-related or official domains. Despite evidence for tolerance-oriented policies (Kloss 1998/1977), there is also considerable evidence for restrictionism since the colonial period. Restriction-oriented policies were a major feature of territorial language policies during the period of US national expansion (Wiley 1998b, c, Wiley and Lukes 1996, Macías 2000). Historical examples of restrictive language policies have often been justified as leading to a greater good for those targeted by them. World War I era English-Only restrictions on education and Americanization efforts were rationalized on that basis (McClymer 1982). More recently, California's Proposition 227 and Arizona's Proposition 203 sought to severely limit access to bilingual education, and were similarly justified. The most widespread period of restrictionism occurred during the World War I era when most states passed restrictive and official English-Only policies (Kloss 1998/1977, Toth 1990, Tatalovich 1995, Wiley 1998a, b, c). Despite their noble sounding intentions to promote access to English, restrictive English-Only school policies have often had negative consequences for the acquisition of English literacy (Spring 1994, Weinberg 1995, Wiley 1996b).

5. *Repression-oriented* policies involve the self-conscious attempt to exterminate minority languages. There is a thin line between restrictive policies and repressive policies, and restrictive policies become repressive when they are linked to deculturation or linguistic genocide. Early examples include forbidding the enslaved Africans to use their native languages and the subsequent imposing of compulsory illiteracy and compulsory ignorance codes (see Day 1985, Hernández-Chávez 1994, Spring 1994, Weinberg 1995).

After the Civil War, the USA became more repressive in imposing English and Anglo culture on Indians. A policy of *coercive assimilation*, intended to expedite deculturation and pacification, was implemented during the 1880s when the Bureau of Indian Affairs instituted a system of English-Only boarding schools (Spicer 1962, 1980, Crawford 1995, Weinberg 1995, Wiley 1998b, c). Indian customs were to be destroyed. Indian deculturation was accompanied by patriotic indoctrination designed to instill allegiance to the USA. To achieve these ends and to diminish the authority of their families and tribal communities, Indian children were wrenched from their families at a young age (Spring 1994, Weinberg 1995, Wiley 1998c).

In the Midwest and other regions of the country during World War I and the early 1920s, the imposition of English-Only policies was accompanied by widespread persecution of German-speakers. Many cases were reported in which ministers were whipped, beaten, or tarred and feathered by mobs for preaching sermons in German; schools and churches were pillaged, and German books were burned (Luebke 1980). Some 5,000 German-speaking Mennonites fled the country to Canada (Wiley 1998a). The impact of restrictive language policies and widespread persecution on the ethnic identity of the German American population had instantaneous and longer-term effects. For example, a comparison of the 1910 (pre-war) and 1920 (post-war) US Censuses shows a surprising drop in the number of people claiming German birth – from some 2.3 million people in 1910 to less than 1.7 million in 1920 (Conzen 1980, Wiley 1998a). Table 17-1 provides highlights by historical period for the status of English and efforts to restrict the use of other languages.

The current English-Only Movement

Targeting immigrants and minority languages, especially Spanish, neo-nativism reemerged in the USA during the latter decades of the twentieth century. The 1970s witnessed a backlash to the federally funded Title VII Bilingual Education Act, passed in 1968 (Garcia 1997: 407). Several salvos with implications for language policy were fired by pundits who protested that federal bilingual education policies were tampering with the American melting pot. The influential education editor of the *Washington Post* wrote a book entitled *Language, Ethnicity, and the Schools: Policy Alternatives for Bilingual Education* (Epstein 1977), in which he attacked bilingual education programs for promoting "affirmative ethnicity" (see Crawford 1992a, 1995).

In 1981, Senator S. I. Hayakawa, a former university president, who had established a reputation as a hardliner against Vietnam War student protesters, introduced a constitutional amendment into the United States Senate that would make English the official language of the USA. Throughout the 1980s and 1990s various versions of the proposed amendment surfaced, and Hayakawa teamed with John

Table 17-1 *Historical highlights regarding the status of English and of efforts to restrict other languages*

---

1. British Colonial Period to 1789. English achieved unrivaled dominant status among European languages in the American colonies. Tolerance toward other European immigrant languages was differentially applied. English-Only practices were imposed on enslaved Africans, and, beginning in the late colonial period, compulsory English illiteracy/ignorance statutes were imposed on enslaved peoples in the southern colonies. During this period, American Indians were generally regarded as separate – albeit subordinate – nations with whom treaties could be negotiated; however, missionaries attempted to promote English among some eastern Indian nations, and as early as 1775, the Continental Congress allocated funds for Indian education with the intent of pacification.

2. 1789 to 1880. The USA sought territorial expansion in which many language-minority peoples were conquered or annexed. The federal government opted not to designate English as the official language and, despite some nativist stirrings, there was generally great tolerance for the use of European immigrant languages. Compulsory illiteracy laws for African Americans persisted in southern states until the end of the Civil War in 1865. Florida and the vast Louisiana Territory were incorporated, half of Mexico was conquered, and Alaska was purchased after the Civil War. Territorial language policies varied as the federal government exercised considerable central authority. English education remained a tactic for the economic destabilization and pacification of Native Americans where they were in contact with whites. Some Native Americans, most notably the Cherokee, ran their own schools and achieved impressive levels of native language literacy and biliteracy.

3. 1880 through the 1930s. Between 1880 and the end of the Spanish American War, the United States added Hawaii, the Philippines, and Puerto Rico to its empire with primacy placed on English and with attempts at language restrictionism, especially in Puerto Rico. On the US mainland, unprecedented levels of European immigration persisted until the early 1920s. English increasingly became the official language of schooling in most states. During and immediately following World War I, restrictions were placed on teaching German and other European languages other than English. For example, in many states it became illegal to teach foreign languages until the sixth or eighth grade. The Supreme Court (*Meyer v. Nebraska*) ruled against an English-Only restriction on the use of foreign languages in Nebraska schools, but the ruling also affirmed the state's right to mandate that English be the common and official language of instruction. Restrictions on the use of instruction in native languages persisted through the period, although some of the more stringent policies directed at Native Americans were relaxed during the 1930s.

4. World War II to present. Desegregation increasingly took center stage among social issues following the Second World War. During the mid to late 1960s language accommodations were seen as partial remedies for problems of equal educational opportunity and political access. Restrictive requirements were relaxed and some provisions made for the use of other languages, particularly in education and in voting and legal contexts. The *Lau v. Nichols* Supreme Court decision (see chapter 18) acknowledged that schools had to provide some proactive means of teaching English and making the curriculum comprehensive. The 1970s witnessed a mixed reaction to policies of linguistic accommodation. The trend since the 1980s has been toward official recognition and protection of English and restrictionism with minimal linguistic accommodation toward other languages.

For elaboration and discussion of specific case histories see Baron 1990; Crawford 1992a, b, 1995; Kloss 1977/1998; Huebner 1987; Sato 1985, 1991; Kawamoto 1993; Leibowitz 1971, 1976, 1980, 1982, 1984; Luebke 1980; Macías 2000; Schiffman 1996; Spicer 1962, 1980; Tamura 1993; Wiley 1998a, b, 2000.

Tanton, an ophthalmologist interested in environmentalism and population control, to found a high-profile organization named "U.S. English," which solicited endorsements from celebrities and amassed a war chest of millions of dollars to further its English-Only agenda. In addition to backing a federal constitutional amendment, U.S. English pursued an aggressive strategy among the states (Crawford 1992b, 1998) and within four years of its founding had succeeded in having its proposals contemplated in forty-eight states. Official English measures, many restricting the use of minority languages, were approved in twenty-three states, twenty-one of them during the '80s and '90s (Crawford 1998). By the late '90s, though, U.S. English had failed to achieve its goal of a constitutional amendment that would make English the official language of the USA.

In 1987, opponents of English-Only policies formed "English-Plus" and put forward an alternative constitutional amendment called the Cultural Rights Amendment. The English-Plus proposal aimed to preserve and promote linguistic diversity and cultural diversity. Wider criticism of English-Only policies has come from leaders of ethnic and immigrant groups, from ethnic-rights, minority-rights, and immigrant-rights groups, and from many professional educational organizations such as Teachers of English to Speakers of Other Languages, Linguistic Society of America, American Association for Applied Linguistics, and from teachers' unions such as the National Education Association (Crawford 1992a, 1995, Baker and Jones 1998). Common criticisms contend that the English-Only Movement and U.S. English:

1. ignore the civil rights traditions in the USA;
2. fail to promote the integration of language-minority children;
3. neglect the need for American business to communicate with foreign markets;
4. restrict the government's ability to reach all citizens;
5. attempt to disenfranchise minority citizens;
6. promote divisiveness and hostility toward those whose first language is not English.

(Baker and Jones: 291)

Charges of extremism have also been made against the English-Only Movement, and U.S. English has been accused of showing "a suspicious thrust toward disinformation . . . with . . . arguments that speaking Spanish causes racial tensions and low economic achievement" (Donahue 1995: 115). When a racially provocative internal memo Dr. Tanton had written in 1986 became public, he resigned his position from U.S. English (see Crawford 1992a, b, 1998). Still, Tatalovich (1995) downplays the extremist argument in analyzing the movement as a whole, and Crawford (2001) has noted this:

> I have been asked whether they can be linked to identifiable villains such as the Ku Klux Klan or the American Nazi Party. Such connections would certainly be convenient for opponents. If the English-Only campaign could be

exposed as an extremist conspiracy, mobilizing against it would be a simple matter. Already this theme has featured in counter-attacks. For the most part, however, it is a product of wishful thinking . . . Yet I have uncovered no evidence that groups promoting this campaign follow the leadership or share the ideology of racial extremists.

As Crawford (2001) further notes:

Reality must be faced: today's anti-bilingual current is a mainstream phenomenon . . . When Americans are asked simply, 'Should English be the official language?' the idea seems extremely popular. Variations on the proposal have received 60–90 percent approval in opinion polls and ballot boxes.

The issue of how such polling is conducted is a topic beyond the scope of this chapter. Suffice it to note that support for official English measures tends to be higher when the question is framed without reference to the restriction of other languages.

There is no doubt about the overwhelming support of the majority of people in the USA for English as the common language. Stated in more academic terms, support for the ideology of English monolingualism is hegemonic. Nevertheless, several questions remain: How deeply held is the ideology? Which sectors of the population are leading the charge? From a broad-based empirical study of these issues, Tatalovich (1995) posited five probable sources of the movement: racial hostility of the majority toward the minority; ethnic conflict among minorities toward one another; class antagonism by lower socioeconomic groups; politically partisan backlash; and anti-foreignism. He concluded that the first phase of the movement was dominated by elites and that the second stage involved more mass activism:

In sum there seems to be an elite–mass divergence across racial lines. White politicians are promoting official English even though the issue is not salient among whites in most states. Hispanic community and political leaders are strident in their hostility and quick to allege racist motives, despite the fact that views among their constituency are not monolithic. English Plus and English-Only may illustrate elite manipulation of the masses. Among African Americans, elites are simply misrepresenting the mass citizenry.   (Tatalovich 1995: 248–49)

The third phase shifts emphasis from the states back to the national scene where it is easily linked to the immigration issue, which is potentially more incendiary than it was during the first quarter of the twentieth century.

The questions remain: What function does the English-Only Movement have? Who benefits from it? Several answers have been offered:

Given the nature of wide publicity and exposure in the modern mass communication, ambitious individuals may wish merely to achieve notoriety for a given cause, without regard to the fairness, justice, ultimate tests of constitutionality, over even the immediate success of the cause. What matters is that

> to achieve leadership, one must first become widely known. In what seems
> to be an utterly cynical value, problems of truth and falsity can be dealt with
> not at the outset, but later, as a matter of process; indeed, truth may simply be
> a matter of what one can get the public to believe.   (Donahue 1995: 117)

For some states, the passage above appears almost prophetic because within a short period a private businessperson led two successful campaigns to restrict bilingual education in the states of California and Arizona (see discussion of Propositions 227 and 203 below). Obviously, language strategists, including individual politicians, pundits, and private individuals seeking notoriety have benefited, and the truth about the needs, contributions, and intentions of language minorities and about the efficacy of bilingual education have become early causalities in public debates over official-English legal measures that attempt to restrict bilingual education. Noting that the English-Only Movement emerges during a time of transfer of wealth from lower socioeconomic groups to the wealthy, Donahue (1995: 135–36) hypothesizes about the broader function of the English-Only Movement:

> Those who do not benefit from the transfer of wealth and power in the past
> two decades at least have in compensation a kind of emotional and intellectual
> recreation through their political opinions . . . Of course the long-term result
> is still a matter of misdirection and deception, and of masking or disguising
> what is going on in the upper reaches of American wealth.

A second hypothesis contends that to a great extent the official-English issue is a phony issue designed to "paralyze debate and to prevent the formation of alternative leadership in a democracy at a time when a two-decade old policy of resource reallocation proceeds unabated" (Donahue 1995: 137). The litmus test of language policies as forms of social policy, for Donahue, becomes the extent to which they are linked to opportunities for social mobility.

Recent developments: Propositions 227 and 203

In June of 1998, a controversial law called "English for the Children" (Proposition 227) was approved by 61 percent of California's voters. Two years later, a nearly identical, but slightly more stringent measure (Proposition 203) passed by nearly the same margin in Arizona. These measures were designed to have a major impact on the education of language-minority children. According to California law and Arizona law, if a sufficient number of registered voters petition, a proposed new law or proposition can be placed on the ballot for voter approval or rejection. In theory the initiative process is supposed to support a grassroots, or bottom–up, approach that allows citizens to further their own agendas without having to rely on the state legislative branch of government.

Although originally well intended, this process can be abused when voters are poorly informed about complex issues or when a majority is able to impose its will on minorities. These concerns were raised in 1986 when Proposition 63, which declared English to be the sole official language of California, was approved overwhelmingly. They were also raised in connection with Proposition 187, which attempted to limit benefits provided undocumented immigrants, and Proposition 209, which sought to end affirmative action programs intended to make competition between the majority and underrepresented minorities more equitable.

As it was presented to voters largely through the efforts of one of its authors, the rationale for California's Proposition 227 was based on five assumptions:

1. English is the language of opportunity because of its dominance in science, business, and technology;
2. immigrant language-minority parents are eager to have their children learn English;
3. given the importance of English, schools have a moral obligation to teach it;
4. for the preceding two decades, California schools have performed poorly in educating immigrant children, as indicated by their higher rates of dropping out of school;
5. young immigrant children acquire second languages easily.

Assuming all these assumptions to be correct, the argument concludes that "all children in California public schools shall be taught English as rapidly as possible" (cited from the text of the initiative).

Along with advocates of bilingual education, many language-minority parents have found little argument with the first three assumptions regarding the importance of English and the need to teach it. However, many have questioned the logic of posing the issue as an *either/or choice* between English and other languages. Moreover, although most language-minority parents enthusiastically want their children to learn English, when given an informed choice the majority also indicate that they desire their children to become bilingual (see Krashen 1996).

The fourth assumption that bilingual education causes high drop-out rates among language-minority children is dubious because only about 30 percent of California's 1.4 million language-minority students received any bilingual education prior to passage of Proposition 227, even though they were eligible. Had the cause of lower academic achievement for many language-minority children been investigated before the approval of 227, it would have been necessary to examine schools where no bilingual education was being offered because those schools constituted the majority.

The fifth assumption – that young immigrant children rapidly acquire second languages – is naive, unless we carefully examine the social and educational contexts of, and opportunities for, second language learning. The kinds of proficiencies in second language that we expect of students must also be specified.

Most children can quickly acquire some degree of oral competence in a second language if they have opportunities for frequent social contact with fluent speakers of the language. However, in some areas of California, language-minority children, especially Spanish-speaking ones, attend schools that have few native speakers of English. In schools where over 90 percent of the children are speakers of languages other than English, the position of English is analogous to that of a foreign language.

The assumption that any child can easily acquire a second language is also contradicted by the fact that many English-speaking monolingual children have difficulties mastering literacy skills in school. Often, the language expectations and demands of the schools are very different from those of the children's homes. Why then would we expect that language-minority children would find it easy to learn school English or use English to learn academic content? Experience and research make it clear that language-minority children face even greater obstacles in attaining school literacy in a second language when they do not have an opportunity to develop initial literacy in their home language and when they are required to compete with native speakers of the dominant language of schooling. Unfortunately, in the public debate regarding 227 and 203, many news writers gave more attention to the anecdotal opinions of pundits opposed to bilingual education than to the findings of educational researchers.

Since the passage of 227 and 203, several issues have posed major challenges for schools and parents. First, these measures impose English-Only instruction, which is normally 180 days of specially designed instruction in English. Second, they do not allow bilingual education, unless language-minority parents request a *waiver* from English-Only instruction and request bilingual education. Even if parents make such a request, there has been no guarantee that their children will receive it. To make matters more difficult, implementing these measures is complicated by the decentralized nature of education in the USA and California, where schools have considerable authority as to how they implement state policies. In addition, California schools do not have equal funding allocations. Instead, because a substantial portion of resources is derived locally, program quality for language-minority students varies greatly from locality to locality.

Preliminary reports regarding the implementation of 227 suggest considerable variation across California school districts because individual districts are developing their English programs for language-minority students and because districts vary in how well they inform parents of the right to request waivers from the English-Only programs. Some school districts, typically those that had good bilingual programs before 227, have managed to maintain bilingual programs because they successfully informed parents and had strong parental support. Other districts have dropped their bilingual programs and not made much effort to inform parents of their right to request waivers. In some cases, schools that had been offering dual immersion bilingual programs prior to 227 were exempted from 227's restrictions because of their special status as "Charter Schools." These schools are allowed to develop alternative education programs. (The impact of Arizona's Proposition 203 is just beginning to be documented.)

In California, for those schools that offer no bilingual programs, the first important question becomes one of what kind of developmental English language programs they have, or are developing. The second question raises the issue of what the relationship is between the developmental English programs and the required academic curriculum. From preliminary reports there appears to be considerable variation across districts in answer to both questions.

Conclusion: prospects and questions for the twenty-first century

Questions of language policy, such as were raised in the official English controversy, may be approached solely from a linguistic point of view. However, a principal argument in this chapter is that language policies, whether official, implicit, or covert, are used to influence and control social behavior. The ideology of English monolingualism presumes a contest between English and other languages in which it is assumed that only one language can prevail. Given that metaphors of social conflict dominate contemporary debates about language policy, it is impossible to avoid the social and political implications of policy prescriptions. The philistine logic of *conquer or be conquered* presents a false dichotomy that is an artifact of the ideology of monolingualism, which suppresses tendencies toward bilingualism and multilingualism. The metaphor of conflict precludes a longstanding missed opportunity in the USA, namely the development of a more widespread capacity for bilingualism (Wiley 1998c).

Given the unrivaled position and dominance that English has enjoyed historically and currently, the challenge for language planning and policy formation in the USA for the twenty-first century is not one of defending the position of English. Rather, given the expanding influence of English nationally and globally (Crystal 1997), the issues are these: To what extent can room be found for the co-existence of other languages? How are language minorities advantaged or disadvantaged by policy decisions involving language rights, accommodations, or restrictions? What losses to this society as a whole are incurred by the unprecedented intergenerational loss of languages other than English? How is the majority limited by lack of facility in languages other than English? What kinds of language policies would assist the monolingual English-speaking majority in benefiting from multilingualism? There is also room for questions from those interested in language policy simply because they love languages: What kinds of language policies would ensure that other languages in the USA can survive, given the unrivaled dominance of English? What policies would help to mitigate the rapidity of language loss?

Acknowledgments

The section entitled "Recent Developments: Propositions 227 and 203" is adapted with permission from Wiley (1999).

Suggestions for further reading and exploration

A growing body of research into literacy is of relevance to contemporary and historical contexts of language policy and planning. Baker and Jones (1998) is an encyclopedia on bilingualism with a number of useful articles discussing US language policy and the English-Only Movement. Corson (1999) offers a comprehensive view of school language policies. Crawford (1992a) provides a useful sampling of articles and documents on the Official English controversy, and Crawford (1992b) provides accessible coverage of local events through the 1980s. Crawford (1995) also addresses the political and policy context of the debate over bilingual education. Daniels (1989) provides a number of papers on the English-Only Movement, its dangers, and on options to respond to it. Dicker (1996) offers a useful and readable introduction for students new to the field.

Heath's historical analyses (1976a, b) provide background on the colonial and early national contexts of language policy formation in the USA. Kloss (1998/1977) remains the most thorough treatment of formal language policies in the USA. Because Kloss focused mostly on European groups and avoided focusing on connecting language policies to racial issues, his emphasis on a tradition of language tolerance needs to be read critically. The writings of Leibowitz (1969, 1971, 1976, 1980, 1982, 1984) provide important background on language policies and politics in the USA. Macías (1979) continues to provide valuable background on language rights.

Phillipson (1992) deals with the global spread of English and the contributing roles of Britain and the USA in promoting what he calls "linguistic imperialism." Schiffman (1996) offers an international and historical analysis that eschews ideological interpretations; it also provides a critique of Kloss. Skutnabb-Kangas and Phillipson (1994) deals with international language rights issues. Tatalovich (1995), Toth (1990), and Wiley (1998a) address historical language policy issues related to German in the USA, including the volatile World War I era. Tatalovich (1995) provides detailed findings from a major empirical study on the English-Only Movement. Tollefson (1991) looks at the impact of English-dominant policies on second language learners in US and international contexts and provides a critique of English language teaching policies.

James Crawford *http://ourworld.compuserve.com/homepages/JWCRAWFORD/* has compiled perhaps the best single-site web resource dealing with issues of language policy and politics in the USA, and it includes a good discussion of English-Plus. For perspectives favoring official English and English-Only policies, see the U.S. English site *http://www.us-english.org/* and the English First site *http://www.englishfirst.org/*. The Mexican American Legal Defense and Education Fund at *http://www.maldef.org/* has been one of the more proactive organizations promoting language rights.

References

Baker, Colin and Sylvia P. Jones. 1998. *The Encyclopedia of Bilingual Education and Bilingualism*. Clevedon: Multilingual Matters.

Baron, Dennis. 1990. *The English-Only Question: an Official Language for Americans?* New Haven CT: Yale University Press.

Bennett, David H. 1995. *The Party of Fear: the American Far Right from Nativism to the Militia Movement*, rev. edn. New York: Vintage Books.

Collins, James. 1991. "Hegemonic Practice: Literacy and Standard Language in Public Education." In *Rewriting Literacy: Culture and the Discourse of the Other*, eds. C. Mitchell and K. Weiler. New York: Bergin and Garvey. Pp. 229–53.

Conzen, Kathleen Neils. 1980. "Germans." In *Harvard Encyclopedia of American Ethnic Groups*, eds. Stephan Thernstorm, Ann Orlov, and Oscar Handlin. Cambridge, MA: Belknap Press. Pp. 404–25.

Cooper, Robert L. 1989. *Language Planning and Social Change*. Cambridge: Cambridge University Press.

Corson, David. 1999. *Language Policies in Schools. A Resource for Teachers and Administrators*. Mahwah NJ: Lawrence Erlbaum.

Crawford, James. 1992a. *Hold Your Tongue: Bilingualism and the Politics of "English Only."* Reading MA: Addison-Wesley.

1992b. *Language Loyalties: a Sourcebook on the Official English Controversy*. Chicago: University of Chicago Press.

1995. *Bilingual Education: History, Politics, Theory, and Practice*, 3rd edn. Los Angeles: Bilingual Education Services.

2001. Anatomy of the English-Only Movement. *http://ourworld.compuserve.com/homepages/JWCRAWFORD/anatomy.htm* (December 11, 2001).

Crystal, David. 1997. *English as a Global Language*. Cambridge: Cambridge University Press.

Day, Richard R. 1985. "The Ultimate Inequality: Linguistic Genocide." In *Language of Inequality*, eds. Nessa Wolfson and Joan Manes. Berlin: Mouton. Pp. 163–81.

Daniels, Harvey A., ed. 1989. *Not Only English: Affirming America's Multilingual Heritage*. Urbana: National Council of Teachers of English.

Dicker, Susan. 1995. "American Language Policy and Compensatory Opinion." In *Power and Inequality in Language Education*, ed. James Tollefson. Cambridge: Cambridge University Press. Pp. 112–41.

1996. *Language and Pluralism in America*. Clevedon: Multilingual Matters.

Donahue, Thomas S. 1995. "American Language Policy and Compensatory Opinion." In *Power and Inequality in Language Education*, ed. James W. Tollefson. Cambridge: Cambridge University Press.

Epstein, Noel. 1977. *Language, Ethnicity, and the Schools: Policy Alternatives for Bilingual Education*. Washington DC: Institute for Educational Leadership.

Fishman, Joshua A., ed. 1986. *The Question of an Official Language: Language Rights and the English Language Amendment. International Journal of the Sociology of Language*, Issue 60.

García, Ofelia. 1997. "Bilingual Education." In *The Handbook of Sociolinguistics*, ed. Florian Coulmas. Oxford: Blackwell. Pp. 405–20.

Haas, Michael. 1992. *Institutional Racism: the Case of Hawai'i*. Westport CT: Praeger.

Heath, Shirley Brice. 1976a. "A National Language Academy? Debate in the New Nation," *International Journal of the Sociology of Language* 11: 9–43.

1976b. "Colonial Language Status Achievement: Mexico, Peru, and the United States." In *Language and Sociology*, eds. A. Verdoodt and R. Kjolseth. Louvain: Peeters. Pp. 49–91.

Hernández-Chávez, Eduardo. 1994. "Language Policy in the United States: a History of Cultural Genocide." In Skutnabb-Kangas and Phillipson, eds. Pp. 141–58.

Huebner, Thom. 1987. "A Socio-Historical Approach to Literacy Development: a Comparative Case Study from the Pacific." In *Language, Literacy, and Culture: Issues of Society and Schooling*, ed. Judith A. Langer. Norwood NJ: Ablex. Pp. 179–96.

Kawamoto, K. Y. 1993. "Hegemony and Language Politics in Hawai'i," *World Englishes* 12: 93–207.

Kloss, Heinz. 1971. "Language Rights of Immigrant Groups," *International Migration Review* 5: 250–68.

1998/1977. *The American Bilingual Tradition*. Washington DC and McHenry IL: Center for Applied Linguistics and Delta Systems. [Reprint of Heinz Kloss. 1977. *The American Bilingual Tradition*. Rowley MA: Newbury House.]

Krashen, Stephen. 1996. *Under Attack: the Case Against Bilingual Education*. Mahwah NJ: Language Education Associates.

Leibowitz, Arnold H. 1969. "English Literacy: Legal Sanction for Discrimination," *Notre Dame Lawyer* 25(1): 7–66.

1971. "Educational Policy and Political Acceptance: the Imposition of English as the Language of Instruction in American Schools." ERIC No. ED 047 321.

1976. "Language and the Law – the Exercise of Political Power through the Official Designation of Language." In *Language and Politics*, eds. William M. O'Barr and Jean F. O'Barr. The Hague: Mouton. Pp. 449–66.

1980. *The Bilingual Education Act: a Legislative Analysis*. Rosslyn VA: National Clearinghouse on Bilingual Education.

1982. *Federal Recognition of the Rights of Minority Language Groups*. Rosslyn VA: National Clearinghouse on Bilingual Education.

1984. "The Official Character of Language in the United States: Literacy Requirements for Citizenship, and Entrance Requirements into American Life," *Aztlan* 15(1): 25–70.

Luebke, Frederick C. 1980. "Legal Restrictions on Foreign Languages in the Great Plains States, 1917–1923." In *Languages in Conflict: Linguistic Acculturation on the Great Plains*, ed. Paul Schach. Lincoln: University of Nebraska Press. Pp. 1–19.

Macías, Reynaldo F. 1979. "Choice of Language as a Human Right – Public Policy Implications in the United States." In *Bilingual Education and Public Policy in the United States. Ethnoperspectives in Bilingual Education Research*, vol. 1, ed. R. V. Padilla. Ypsilanti: Eastern Michigan University. Pp. 39–75.

1985. "Language and Ideology in the United States," *Social Education* (February): 97–100.

2000. "Language Politics and the Historiography of Spanish in the United States." In *Language in Action: New Studies of Language in Society. Essays in Honor of Roger W. Shuy*, eds. Joy K. Peyton, Peg Griffin, and Walt Wolfram. Cresskill NJ: Hampton Press. Pp. 52–83.

Macías, Reynaldo F. and Terrence G. Wiley. 1998. Introduction to the Second Edition. In "Introduction" Kloss 1998/1977. Pp. vii–xiv.

McClymer, John F. 1982. "The Americanization Movement and the Education of the Foreign-born Adult, 1914–1925." In *Education and the European Immigrant: 1840–1940*, ed. Bernard J. Weiss. Urbana: University of Illinois Press. Pp. 96–116.

McKay, Sandra Lee and G. Weinstein-Shr. 1993. "English Literacy in the US: National Policies, Personal Consequences," *TESOL Quarterly* 27(3): 399–419.

Norgren, Jill and Serena Nanda. 1988. *American Cultural Pluralism and the Law*. New York: Praeger.

Phillipson, Robert. 1992. *Linguistic Imperialism*. Oxford: Oxford University Press.

Ricento, Thomas and Barbara Burnaby, eds. 1998. *Language and Politics in the United States and Canada*. Mahwah NJ: Lawrence Erlbaum.

Ricento, Thomas and Nancy Hornberger. 1996. "Unpeeling the Onion: Language Policy and the ELT Professional," *TESOL Quarterly* 30(3): 401–27.

Sato, Charlene J. 1985. "Linguistic Inequality in Hawai'i: the Post-Creole Dilemma." In *Language of Inequality*, eds. Nessa Wolfson and Joan Manes. New York: Mouton. Pp. 255–72.

1991. "Language Attitudes and Sociolinguistic Variation in Hawai'i." In *English Around the World*, ed. Jenny Cheshire. Cambridge: Cambridge University Press. Pp. 647–63.
Schiffman, Harold F. 1996. *Linguistic Culture and Language Policy*. London: Routledge.
Skutnabb-Kangas, Tove and Robert Phillipson, eds. 1994. *Linguistic Human Rights: Overcoming Linguistic Discrimination*. Berlin: Mouton de Gruyter. Pp. 1–22.
Spicer, Edward H. 1962. *Cycles of Conquest: the Impact of Spain, Mexico, and the United States on the Indians of the Southwest, 1533–1960*. Tucson: University of Arizona Press.
1980. "American Indians, Federal Policy Toward." In *Harvard Encyclopedia of American Ethnic Groups*, eds. Stephan T. Thernstrom, Ann Orlov, and Oscar Handlin. Cambridge: Belknap Press of Harvard University Press. Pp. 114–22.
Spring, Joel. 1994. *Deculturalization and the Struggle for Equality: a Brief History of the Education of Dominated Cultures in the United States*. New York: McGraw-Hill.
Tamura, E. H. 1993. "The English-Only Effort, the Anti-Japanese Campaign, and Language Acquisition in the Education of Japanese Americans in Hawaii, 1915–1940," *History of Education Quarterly* 33(1): 37–58.
Tatalovich, Raymond. 1995. *Nativism Reborn? The Official English Language Movement and the American States*. Lexington: University of Kentucky Press.
Tollefson, James W. 1991. *Planning Language, Planning Inequality: Language Policy in the Community*. New York: Longman.
Toth, Carolyn R. 1990. *German–English Bilingual Schools in America. The Cincinnati Tradition in Historical Context*. New York: Peter Lang.
Weinberg, Meyer. 1995. *A Chance to Learn: a History of Race and Education in the United States*, 2nd edn. Long Beach: California State University, University Press.
1997. *Asian American Education: Historical Background and Current Realities*. Mahwah NJ: Lawrence Erlbaum.
Weinstein, Brian. 1979. "Language Strategists: Redefining Political Frontiers on the Basis of Linguistic Choices," *World Politics* 20: 344–64.
1983. *The Civic Tongue: Political Consequences of Language Choices*. New York: Longman.
Weiss, Brian., ed. 1982. *American Education and the European Immigrant, 1840–1940*. Urbana: University of Illinois Press.
Wiley, Terrence G. 1996a. "Language Planning and Language Policy." In *Sociolinguistics and Language Teaching*, eds. Sandra McKay and Nancy F. Hornberger. Cambridge: Cambridge University Press. Pp. 103–47.
1996b. *Literacy and Language Diversity in the United States*. Washington DC and McHenry IL: Center for Applied Linguistics and Delta Systems.
1998a. "The Imposition of World War I Era English-Only Policies and the Fate of German in North America." In Ricento and Burnaby, eds. Pp. 211–41.
1998b. "What Happens after English is Declared the Official Language of the United States? Lessons from Case Histories." In *Language Legislation and Linguistic Rights*, ed. Douglas Kibbee. Amsterdam: John Benjamins. Pp. 179–95.
1999. "Proposition 227: California Restricts the Educational Choices for Language Minority Children," *Bilingual Family Newsletter* 16(2): 1, 3. Clevedon: Multilingual Matters.
2000. "Continuity and Change in the Function of Language Ideologies in the United States." In *Ideology, Politics, and Language Policies: Focus on English*, ed. Thomas Ricento. Amsterdam: John Benjamins. Pp. 67–85.
Wiley, Terrence G. and Marguerite Lukes. 1996. "English-Only and Standard English Ideologies in the United States," *TESOL Quarterly* 3: 511–30.

18

Language in education

LILY WONG FILLMORE

Editors' introduction

This chapter should be read with chapter 17. Both discuss Proposition 227, the anti-bilingual education voter initiative that was approved by 61 percent of the California electorate in 1998, but in this chapter Lily Wong Fillmore comes at it from the focused perspective of the rise (and fall) of bilingual education, complementing the more general perspective of language planning and policy examined in the preceding chapter. Here, the time depth is also more restricted, since, despite early twentieth-century contestations of the assumption that schooling would be provided primarily if not entirely in English, bilingual education was not formally instituted at a federal level until 1968. It was in that year, partly in response to the example of Florida schools in which the children of Cuban immigrants were being successfully instructed in English and Spanish, that the Bilingual Education Act was passed. This chapter traces the developments leading up to this and to the subsequent Lau guidelines of 1975, which further ensured the provision of bilingual education for Limited English Proficient (LEP) students across the USA.

From the beginning there was ideological opposition to bilingual education, however. This chapter documents the increasing debate that would end in the passage of proposition 227 in California and identifies seven "challenges" or charges often raised against bilingual education (e.g., bilingual education programs "are educationally ineffective") along with counterarguments to each one. Lily Wong Fillmore also points out that hostility towards bilingual education came to be directed at Spanish-speaking immigrants in particular, and that its demise was anticipated to some extent by the 1994 voter approval of Proposition 187, which denied social services, health services, and other services to the children of undocumented immigrants in California. With more than 43 percent of all LEP students in the USA, California is an important bellwether state for the future of bilingual education and the preservation of immigrant language rights in the USA. Proposition 227 – the product of political expediency – was passed in California in 1998. To some extent it does not augur well for the future of bilingual education in the nation at large, but Wong Fillmore argues that to some extent Proposition 227 has not changed much. More pressing is the adoption of other California measures that demand higher curricular standards and better student performance at the same time that affirmative action has been set aside. These developments place additional strains on language minority students. Whether and how they survive, she argues, will depend on the ability of educators and ordinary citizens to liberalize their attitudes to linguistic and ethnic diversity, especially in our schools.

Conflict: community interests, American ideals and individual rights

In a society that is as diverse in linguistic, cultural, and national origins as the USA, it is inevitable that language would eventually become a source of conflict in education. How should American schools deal with the language needs of children who do not speak English or, more precisely, the variety of English used in school? What position should the society take towards family and community efforts to preserve the ethnic languages of native and immigrant students? What accommodations should the schools make for students who do not know English? Over the past several decades, these issues have become increasingly contentious, divisive, and political. This chapter examines these issues and considers what they reveal about American beliefs regarding language diversity and how our society has dealt with linguistic diversity in education.

The conflict over language in education may always have been an underlying issue, but it was not until the last quarter of the twentieth century that it surfaced as a topic of public debate and division. This chapter begins with an examination of the situations and events that led to a shift in how language is considered in education and then addresses questions that schools confront currently. The educational approach that brought public scrutiny to the language of schooling was bilingual education. When the US Congress passed the Bilingual Education Act of 1968, making funds available to states and local districts for the development of bilingual instructional programs, it recognized that language diversity was at the heart of a long-standing educational problem for the mostly English monolingual US school system.

The American schoolhouse has been the place where countless immigrants and American natives, speakers of a great many different languages, have been turned into English speakers, frequently at the cost of their ethnic languages and cultures. Until recently, however, little notice was given either to the problem this process presented to the schools or to how it affected the people who were being transformed. Certainly the need for the school to serve this purpose was never questioned. It was simply assumed that everyone who lived in the USA, irrespective of origin, would want to be transformed into English monolinguals, and that the schools were the appropriate place for children from diverse backgrounds to acquire the cultural and linguistic knowledge and skills required for participation in the larger society.

Until the 1960s, few groups contested the exclusive use of English in US public schools. This is not to say that minority groups were unconcerned about the retention of their ethnic languages. Historically, many groups have recognized that the continuation of cultural practices and traditions depended on the younger generations of the community learning and using those languages even as they were learning English. Immigrant groups wanting instruction for their children in their ethnic languages generally sought to establish such programs through church or religious organizations. A study of the use of ethnic languages in schools conducted in the 1960s found that, historically, most such efforts were church sponsored programs (Fishman and Nahirny 1966). According to the study, 81 percent of the ethnic day-school programs at the time were under religious sponsorship, an indication of the powerful role played by churches and religion in the maintenance of ethnic languages and cultures in the USA. The researchers estimated that there were approximately 2,000 church-sponsored schools operating in the USA that were providing some ethnic language instruction, and among the sponsoring religious groups were Roman Catholic, Eastern and Greek Orthodox, and various Protestant and Jewish groups.

The right of immigrant families to send their children to such schools did not go unchallenged, however. During the xenophobic period surrounding World War I, there were statutes passed in several states prohibiting the use of "foreign languages" in any school, whether public or private. In Nebraska, parochial school teacher Robert Meyer was found guilty of violating a 1919 law prohibiting the use of foreign languages in school before the eighth grade. His transgression? He taught a Bible story in German to a ten-year-old child. The conviction was later overturned by the US Supreme Court in a case known as *Meyer v. Nebraska*. The Court noted that the Fourteenth Amendment protects the rights of individuals to the pursuit of happiness, to acquire useful knowledge, to marry, establish a home and bring up children, and it also pointed out that parents had not only the duty to give their children a suitable education but also the "right of control" over that education (see Crawford 1992b).[1]

The Supreme Court's 1923 decision is an important one to consider as we examine the conditions leading to the present in which the use of languages other

---

[1] The ruling *Meyer v. Nebraska* reads:

> "The challenged statute forbids the teaching in school of any subject except in English; also the teaching of any other language until the pupil has attained and successfully passed the eighth grade, which is not usually accomplished before the age of 12. The Supreme Court of the state has held that 'the so-called ancient or dead languages' are not 'within the spirit or the purpose of the act.' Latin, Greek, Hebrew are not proscribed; but German, French, Spanish, Italian and every other alien speech are within the ban. Evidently, the Legislature has attempted materially to interfere with the calling of modern language teachers, with the opportunity of pupils to acquire knowledge, and with the power of parents to control the education of their own.
>
> It is said the purpose of the legislation was to promote civic development by inhibiting training and education of the immature in foreign tongues and ideals before they could learn English and acquire American ideals; and 'that the English language should be and become the mother tongue of all children reared in this state.' It is also affirmed that the foreign born population is very large, and that certain communities commonly use foreign words, follow foreign leaders, move in a foreign atmosphere, and that the children are thereby hindered from becoming citizens of the most type and the public safety is imperiled.
>
> That the state may do much, go very far, indeed, in order to improve the quality of its citizens, physically, mentally, and morally, is clear; but the individual has certain fundamental rights which must be respected. The protection of the Constitution extends to all, to those who speak other languages as well as to those born with English on the tongue. Perhaps it would be highly advantageous if all had ready understanding of our ordinary speech, but this cannot be coerced with methods which conflict with the Constitution – a desirable end cannot be promoted by prohibited means."   [262 U.S. 390, (1923)]

than English is being contested once again, this time in public schools. There had been a few scattered efforts to use languages other than English in the public schools prior to the 1960s (French in Louisiana, Spanish in New Mexico, German in Ohio and Wisconsin), but these early bilingual programs were limited and had not been regarded as a threat to the prevailing ideal of the American school as the place where polyglot immigrants and American natives were turned into monolingual English speakers.

The advent of federally sponsored bilingual education

For the most part, the use of ethnic languages was confined to private and parochial schools until the early 1960s when the Dade County schools in Florida were suddenly confronted with the problem of how to accommodate the region's many Spanish-monolingual children. They were the children of the hundreds of thousands of refugees who fled Cuba in the decade following the Castro revolution in 1959. These families were members of the upper class and professionals, who had the most to lose by remaining in Castro's Cuba after the revolution.

Ordinarily, non-English-speaking children coming into Florida's schools would have been placed in English-Only classrooms where they would have received short-term instructional help with English until they knew it well enough to get by on their own. The situation, however, was hardly ordinary. The numbers of Spanish-speaking immigrants enrolling in Dade County schools were staggering – so many in some schools that they outnumbered the English speakers. Then, too, many of the refugees did not plan to stay in the USA. They expected that Castro would be overthrown and they could then return home to Cuba. To school officials, it made sense to establish a bilingual program for these children, where they could be instructed both in Spanish and in English. Such an approach would allow the children to continue their schooling during their sojourn in Florida and also give them an opportunity to learn some English. The Dade County program was highly effective – the children thrived educationally in bilingual classes, and not only were they successfully incorporated into the American educational culture, but they also maintained the language and culture of their families and primary community. The success of the bilingual program was recognized by educators and researchers around the country as a model program (see Mackey and Beebe 1977).

The Florida experience convinced some policymakers and educators that bilingual education might be a solution for the vexing problem of under-achievement and school failure for many other Hispanic students who were limited in English proficiency (LEP). These children generally had difficulty making academic progress and dropped out of school at a much higher rate than English speakers did. Bilingual education might well be the answer for the many other Spanish-speaking children in the USA. This was in fact the major justification for the funding of the Bilingual Education Act. In his introduction of the legislation to Congress in 1967, Senator Ralph Yarborough of Texas noted that bilingual education offered a solution for the nearly 3.5 million Spanish speakers in the Southwestern states whose access to educational opportunities had been limited because English was the only language used in school:

> I am introducing today the Bilingual Education Act. Its declaration of policy reads as follows: In recognition of the special needs of the large numbers of students in the United States whose mother tongue is Spanish and to whom English is a foreign language, Congress hereby declares it to be the policy of the United States to provide financial assistance to local educational agencies to develop and carry out new and imaginative elementary and secondary school programs designed to meet these educational needs.

Title VII of the Elementary Secondary Education Act, as the Bilingual Education Act of 1968 was called, made it possible for schools to provide instruction for LEP students in languages they already understood, a constructive but nonetheless radical solution to a persistent educational problem, given the millions of children who came from homes where little English was spoken. The 1968 bill was based on the assumption that not knowing English constituted a deficiency and that the use of the home language in school would help compensate for that deficiency by giving LEP students access to the school's curriculum in language they understood. The use of English in such programs would enable LEP students to learn it as a second language, thus facilitating their eventual transition into the English monolingual school system.

There was little initial objection to bilingual instructional programs. Title VII provided federal funds to finance the development and establishment of bilingual programs. These early programs were not regarded as problematic by educators or by the public because states and local districts could choose whether or not to seek funding for them. The value of the Title VII programs funded under this act, however, was obvious to many members of the immigrant communities whose children could benefit from bilingual instruction.

In San Francisco, California, the school district was heavily impacted by the influx of many thousands of new immigrants and refugees from Asia, Southeast Asia, Mexico, and Central America during the early 1970s, and there were many more students needing bilingual education than the district could accommodate in its Title VII programs. San Francisco Unified School District (SFUSD) had received Title VII funding for Cantonese, Spanish, and Tagalog bilingual instruction, but these were small, experimental programs at a few schools and could serve only a small percentage of the children who spoke those languages and whose parents wanted them placed in the bilingual classrooms.

Lau v. Nichols, Lau Guidelines, and mandate for bilingual education

In 1973, a class action suit was brought against the SFUSD School Board on behalf of the many non-English-speaking Chinese children in the district who were not receiving any instructional support to help them overcome the linguistic barrier to school participation. This, the plaintiffs argued, was a violation of both the Equal Protection Clause of the Fourteenth Amendment and of §601 of the Civil Rights Act of 1964, which bans discrimination based "on the grounds of race, color, or of national origin" in "any program or activity receiving Federal financial assistance." The District Court initially ruled against the plaintiffs. The judge asserted that the non-English speaking Chinese children were attending the same schools, sharing the same classrooms, were taught by the same teachers, and were using the same textbooks as their English-speaking classmates, so there was no evidence that they were being discriminated against nor that they were being denied access to the programs provided by the school district.

After the ruling was upheld by the Court of Appeals, the case went to the US Supreme Court, which in 1974 reversed the judgment and ruled in favor of the plaintiffs in the landmark case, *Lau v. Nichols*, basing its ruling strictly on Title VI of the Civil Rights Act. The school district had agreed to comply with Title VI of the Civil Rights Act, which prohibits discrimination in services and programs when applying for federal funds to support its programs. The grounds on which discrimination was barred included language differences, which had earlier been defined as an indicator of national origins. Students could not be denied access to instructional services because they did not understand English. In the judgment of the Supreme Court, there was clear evidence of discrimination:

> It seems obvious that the Chinese-speaking minority receive fewer benefits than the English-speaking majority from respondents' school system which denies them a meaningful opportunity to participate in the educational program – all earmarks of the discrimination banned by the regulations. In 1970 HEW [the US Department of Health, Education, and Welfare] issued clarifying guidelines, 35 Fed. Reg. 11595, which include the following:
>
> "Where inability to speak and understand the English language excludes national origin-minority group children from effective participation in the educational program offered by a school district, the district must take affirmative steps to rectify the language deficiency in order to open its instructional programs to these students."

Attendance in school was mandatory by the compulsory education law, the Supreme Court declared, and the state's education code specifies that no student can graduate from high school without a demonstration of English proficiency. But how, it asked, were children to deal with subject matter taught exclusively in English if they did not know that language and were not provided instructional help in learning it? In the Court's opinion this was inherently discriminatory:

> Under these state-imposed standards there is no equality of treatment merely by providing students with the same facilities, textbooks, teachers, and curriculum; for students who do not understand English are effectively foreclosed from any meaningful education.

> Basic English skills are at the very core of what these public schools teach. Imposition of a requirement that, before a child can effectively participate in the educational program, he must already have acquired those basic skills is to make a mockery of public education. We know that those who do not understand English are certain to find their classroom experiences wholly incomprehensible and in no way meaningful.

This finding was important not only for the Chinese children in San Francisco's schools but for all LEP children throughout the USA. The Supreme Court directed the San Francisco Board of Education to rectify the problem that had led to the suit, and the remedy the Board found was bilingual education. The Office of Civil Rights assembled a task force to develop standards of compliance for school districts throughout the country with large enough concentrations of non-English speakers or LEP students to warrant attention. That task force found bilingual education to be the most appropriate educational remedy for children who did not understand English. LEP students should be provided instruction part of the time in their home languages, thus giving them access to the curricular content of school in language they already understood, and part of the time in English, providing them opportunities to learn it as a second language. The task force's document came to be known as the "Lau Guidelines" or "Remedies."

The debate over bilingual education

In the years after the Supreme Court's ruling in *Lau*, numerous states passed bilingual education legislation – thereby changing state education codes that had specified English as the sole language of instruction, and mandating bilingual education where it was feasible. These changes were lauded by educators and community members who saw bilingual education as perhaps the only pedagogically sound approach to educating students who did not already know the language of the school and society. They were as quickly denounced by others – including many educators and politicians – who viewed bilingual education as an abandonment of the ideal of the USA as a melting pot and who viewed the schools as the place where linguistic and cultural diversity were eliminated and immigrants transformed into English-speaking Americans. The heated debate over bilingual education and over language in education has not lessened in the quarter century since the *Lau* decision was handed down. Among the issues debated have been the following:

Challenge No.1: Bilingual programs make exclusive use of the students' primary languages in school. How are LEP students to learn English if they never hear it at school?

The response: The learning of English is an important goal but not the only educational goal for LEP students. LEP students must learn all of the content in the school's curriculum, just as native speakers of English must. If children were taught nothing but English until they knew it well enough to handle the curriculum in English, they would fall too far behind their age cohort ever to catch up in school. Research has shown that it ordinarily takes children from five to seven years to learn a new language (see especially Cummins 1981a, b, Collier 1987, Scarcella 1999). If during that period, they are not given access to the curriculum in language they understand, they are prevented from participating in school. That was the main point in the *Lau* decision. The charge that bilingual programs are conducted exclusively in the primary languages of the LEP students is absurd. If there is an imbalance in the use of language, it is invariably in the overuse of English.

Challenge No. 2: The programs are educationally ineffective. They are based on an "unproven" educational theory. LEP students perform no better in bilingual programs and in some cases perform worse than they would in English-Only programs.[2]

The response: The claims that bilingual education has been educationally ineffective are spurious and based on biased interpretations of the research data (see Crawford 1992a, Cummins 1992, 1996, Krashen 1996). There was a time when bilingual programs produced mixed results. During the early years of bilingual education, there were not enough teachers who were prepared or qualified to teach in such programs, and there was little in the way of instructional materials available in languages such as Spanish, Cantonese, and Vietnamese – but that situation has changed. In the past decade and a half, ample research evidence has showed that well-planned programs staffed by qualified and well-trained personnel get positive results (see Krashen and Biber 1988, Collier and Thomas 1989, Cummins 1989, 1996, Ramírez et al. 1991, Ramírez 1992, Krashen 1996, Gándara 1997, Greene 1998). The critics of bilingual education have systematically ignored that research and have even attempted to suppress evidence demonstrating its effectiveness.[3]

---

[2] See Baker and DeKanter's (1981) review of the evaluation studies of early bilingual education programs funded under ESEA Title VII. After setting up methodological criteria that excluded many studies from their review, the remaining ones did not support bilingual education. This was the first of many such examinations that have purportedly shown that bilingual education is ineffective.

[3] See, e.g., Willig's (1985) meta-analysis of the same studies that Baker and DeKanter had used to show that bilingual education was ineffective. Her reanalysis demonstrated the opposite effect. The most dramatic evidence comes from a large-scale longitudinal study funded by the US Department of Education, the design of which was heavily influenced by its project officer, Keith Baker. It was designed to compare the relative effectiveness of several program models: early exit (transitional) and late-exit (maintenance) bilingual programs, and a model that Baker believed was superior to any type of bilingual program – "structured English immersion," in which students are instructed entirely in English and are given help in learning English. The earliest reports for the study indicated that the students in both bilingual programs were outperforming those in the structured immersion programs. Nothing more was heard from the study thereafter until 1991, when the final report was released. That report, which Dolson and Mayer (1992) described as "carefully crafted" by its authors "in concert with directives from project officers from the US Department of Education," suggested that there were no great differences in final outcome from the three program types. Dolson and Mayer, two bilingual specialists from the California State Department of Education, in their review of the findings found that this was quite misleading. Looked at closely, the children in both

Challenge No. 3: Bilingual education is extremely expensive. It costs considerably more to educate LEP students in bilingual classrooms than it does in English-Only programs.

The response: Bilingual education adds little to the usual cost of educating students. It is less costly than alternative programs such as pull-out English as a second language (ESL) classes (where children are "pulled out" of regular classes for short periods of time and given instructional support by a special ESL teacher several times each week) and is much less expensive than compensatory or special education programs, where LEP students often end up when they are not provided instructional services that are more appropriate to their needs. A 1994 study (Parrish) comparing the added costs of various types of instructional support classes for LEP students found that bilingual programs in California that were judged to be effective added just $60 to the direct cost of educating students in that state, which was at that time in forty-sixth place among the fifty states in educational spending. In contrast compensatory education programs added $875 per student, and special education programs $2,402.[4]

Challenge No. 4: Bilingual education is little more than a jobs program for bilingual teachers and bilingual researchers (see, e.g., Porter 1990: 73).

The response: This is a strange and illogical allegation with no basis in reality. Is American education itself a jobs' program for teachers, school administrators, and educational researchers? A comparison of the student and teacher demographics of US schools reveals that, if anything, we ought to be troubled by the glaring mismatch in their backgrounds. Teachers are overwhelmingly white, middle class, and female. American students are not. Roughly a third of all students in US schools are minorities, while the proportion of teachers belonging to minority ethnic groups was just 13 percent (*Schools* 1996). While no one would argue that teachers and students must match in cultural, ethnic, or linguistic backgrounds, it is difficult to understand why anyone would object to teachers who have the skills and background to address the special needs of the students they are teaching. LEP students have special linguistic needs, and there are a great many students in US schools who require teachers who have special skills and training to work with them. At present, there are around 2.75 million school-age children who are limited in English proficiency in US schools. Only 29 percent of public school teachers who have LEP students in their classes are qualified to work with them (Issue 1996), and fewer still have the language background and qualifications to provide native language support for their students. In California, where LEP children are most heavily concentrated, the situation is somewhat better, but there has been a serious shortage of teachers who have the qualifications and preparation to work with children who do not speak English. The California State Department

bilingual conditions outperformed those in the structured immersion, but the longer the children were provided native language support, the better they did in school. There were differences that had been obscured by the bland statement of findings in the officially approved report.
[4] I am indebted to Patricia Gándara (1997) for bringing my attention to Parrish's study.

of Education estimates that at present there is a shortage of around 12,000 teachers, who are needed just to handle the large numbers of LEP students in the state (Gold 1996). The National Center for Educational Statistics estimates that by 2008–09 some 1.7 to 2.7 million new teachers will be needed (*Schools* 1999). Since the LEP population is not likely to decline in the next decade, one could hardly object to teachers with bilingual language skills who are also prepared to work with children who need language support.

Challenge No. 5: In some schools there are more than fifty languages spoken! How can the schools possibly provide bilingual education programs for all these groups?

The response: The linguistic situation is seldom as complicated as purported by critics who use this argument. A look at any list of languages reportedly spoken by the students in a given school will show that there is considerable confusion in how languages are identified by teachers and parents. One such list contained entries such as Filipino, Pilipino and Tagalog – all of which refer to the same language. Chinese, Mandarin, Putong-hua, Beijing dialect, Guo-yu, and Taiwanese often refer to the same language but are separately listed and counted. It may not always be possible to provide native language support in school for every child. The Lau guidelines specify that bilingual programs be provided where there are enough children from the same language background and at the same grade levels to make a bilingual program a viable option.

Challenge No. 6: Why should schools accommodate the linguistic needs of present-day immigrants when past immigrants had no need of such accommodations? In the past, immigrants accepted the necessity and responsibility of learning English, and they learned it quickly and well. These new immigrants expect the school to change and accommodate their needs.

The response: It may be true that in the past little accommodation was made in school for immigrants. As a result, many earlier immigrants failed in school, just as many will fail school now without bilingual education. The major difference was that until the 1940s and 1950s many people in the society did not finish high school, but they could still survive economically because the situation then was very different. Except for the years of the depression, there were job opportunities even for people with poor English language skills and little formal education, and many ways to earn a living in the USA. Present-day immigrants do not differ from past groups. What has changed is the economy. In the present situation, there are few jobs that can pay a living wage for people who do not have at least a high school education, and employers expect workers to have much higher levels of education than in the past. With stiff limits placed on social welfare these days, we expect every able-bodied person – especially immigrants – to support themselves with work. We expect immigrants to be self-sufficient and self-supporting, but how do they do it without some initial help? It's a matter of both fairness and economic self-interest that we should educate everyone as well as we can.

Challenge No. 7: Bilingual education allows immigrants to resist assimilation and avoid learning English. They want to live in the USA but are unwilling to be a part of the society. They are unwilling to change or give anything up as they must, if they are to become Americans. Why should the society promote and pay for the maintenance and continuation of immigrant languages and cultures?[5]

The response: There are no doubt a few immigrants who are not eager to learn English and who would prefer to remain isolated from the larger society. The overwhelming majority however – no matter what their origins are or the circumstances under which they have come to live in the USA – want nothing more than to learn English, to be accepted, and to become a part of the society. This is especially true of the young. Children want to participate in the social and the intellectual life of the schools they attend. They learn very quickly that English is the key to social acceptance and participation, and they are impatient to gain the linguistic and social knowledge needed to blend into the social scene. It can take as little as a year or two before children are putting aside their primary languages and speaking English exclusively whether or not they know it very well. What this can mean is that they lose their primary languages and have difficulty communicating with their own families and communities (see Fillmore 1991a, b, Olsen 1997). Bilingual education does not stop this process of language and cultural loss, but it can slow it enough so that young immigrants and their families can make a healthier adjustment to life in this society. It is true that many immigrant families would like their children to maintain their ethnic languages and cultures. Who would not want their children to remain close to their primary families and communities? Who would be happy to see their children become strangers who are unable to communicate with them and unable to participate in their own communities? If bilingual education makes it possible for immigrant children to retain their ethnic languages and cultures as they grow up and become English-speaking Americans, it can hardly be considered an undesirable outcome of schooling. The world of the twenty-first century will be a considerably smaller place than it has been in the past. The new global economy means that Americans will be conducting business across linguistic and national boundaries. The ability to speak languages other than English should be considered a resource to be developed rather than a costly and unnecessary burden for taxpayers! When critics complain that immigrant groups should not be expecting the society to bear the cost of supporting ethnic cultures through bilingual education, it is hard to know what part of the cost of educating children contributes to the society and what part supports their culture – immigrant or otherwise. In reality this is a complaint rooted in impatience. Americans are impatient with people who do not speak English, who appear not to be making as rapid an adjustment to life in this society as we think they should, or who need more than just a little help making that

---

[5] This is the so-called "affirmative ethnicity" complaint, first discussed in 1981 by Noel Epstein, a journalist with the *Washington Post*. As an education writer, Epstein took a look at bilingual education and decided it was an ethnic plot to get the government to support the maintenance of ethnic cultures and languages, rather than a pedagogical approach that would ease the transition of LEP students into the US school system.

adjustment. We are not comfortable around people who speak languages we do not understand – and it is a fact that not many Americans are able to speak any language but English. That is where the angst over language choice in education comes from. This has always been the case.

Immigration and the focus on Hispanics

This hostile debate over bilingual education – its justification, appropriateness, necessity, cost, effectiveness, benefits, fairness, and true goals – began in the mid-1970s, with virtually no let-up in polemics since then. In the media, the courts, state legislative chambers, congress, and virtually every public venue, the opposing sides of the bilingual education debate have clashed over this pedagogical approach. From the beginning, the hostility towards bilingual education was directed at one group in particular – Spanish speakers – despite the fact that bilingual education served children from all language backgrounds (see Crawford 1992a). Why? Spanish speakers are by far the largest language minority group in the USA. Children from Spanish-speaking families comprise 80 percent of the LEP students in American schools. Without a doubt, another reason is that Latinos have been the staunchest and most vocal supporters of bilingual education. There has often been a strong anti-immigrant sentiment in our society – whenever there are large enough numbers of newcomers to call attention to themselves by being different from the American norm in appearance, behavior, and speech, people tend to get nervous and fearful about their intentions and influence. With the large influx of Spanish-speaking immigrants from Mexico, the Caribbean, and Central America in the 1970s and 1980s, there has been a great increase in the number of Latino residents in many parts of the country. (See chapters 10 and 11 in this volume.) Underlying the debate against bilingual education has been a frequently expressed belief that the USA is being "overrun" by "illegal aliens" – people who have immigrated illegally, who take advantage of services provided by the society but are unwilling to assimilate into it. In California, this belief led to the passage of a public referendum denying social, health, and educational services to undocumented immigrants in 1994, and it also made it illegal for employers to hire them. Among the arguments presented by supporters of Proposition 187, as the referendum was designated, was that services like social welfare, medical care, and bilingual education were "magnets" drawing illegal aliens to California and that these aliens were swamping the state and its services. California voters passed that referendum by 59 percent to 41 percent, a vote that reveals how deeply Americans are divided not only on the issue of immigration but also towards people they view as dependent on the society. Many Hispanics saw Proposition 187 as an anti-Hispanic movement, having little to do with the legal status of immigrants. It was about the growing numbers of Latino immigrants especially in the southern part of the state, numbers that could eventually translate into political power. The legality of this referendum was challenged by civil rights organizations, and it was eventually overturned, with a federal judge ruling in 1997 that it was unconstitutional.

Language in education: conflict in California

At the heart of the controversy in California over immigration was the rapidly growing number of LEP students in the public school system, students who required special linguistic services. As shown in table 18-1, California has many foreign-born residents – both old and new immigrants. It is the most frequent destination of most new immigrants. 25 percent of its residents are foreign born, comprising a third of the total foreign population in the USA. Table 18-1 also shows the large proportion of LEP students in California schools. One of every four students is limited in English, totaling 1.4 million students who do not speak English. In fact, California has 43 percent of all LEP students in the USA, more than the next four states (Texas, Illinois, New York, Florida) combined. In Los Angeles Unified School District, 50 percent of the students are LEP, and 97 percent of those speak Spanish.

Table 18-1 *US and California immigrant and student population, 1997*

1997 population	USA	California
Total population	267.6 million	32.3 million
Foreign born immigrants	25.8 million	8+ million
% Foreign born immigrants	9.6%	25%
Total student population	26.5 million	5.6 million
LEP students	3.3 million	1.4 million
% LEP students	12.5%	25%

Source: US Census Bureau and California State Department of Education

Statewide, 80 percent of the LEP students speak Spanish as their primary language. Others speak various Asian and South Asian languages (Mandarin, Cantonese, Korean, Vietnamese, Hmong, Laotian, Khmer, Tagalog and other languages of the Philippines) and others. California had provided bilingual education programs for some but not all of these groups since 1976, when the state legislature amended its bilingual education provision, which had permitted school districts to establish bilingual instructional programs for LEP students but did not mandate them. After the Lau decision, the legislature passed the Chacon–Moscone Bilingual Education Act of 1976, which mandated bilingual programs in California schools wherever ten or more non-English speakers, or fifteen or more limited English speakers, from the same language background could be found at the same grade level. That Act required school districts to conduct a language census each year and to test the language proficiency of those students who came from homes where a language other than English was spoken, as did the Lau Guidelines.

For the next ten years, bilingual education developed and expanded in California, along with the LEP population. And it soon became a hot issue in the schools, the legislature, and the press. In fact, bilingual education became controversial as soon as school districts were required to adopt it. Before *Lau* and the 1976 California Bilingual Education Act, local school districts could disregard the language needs of LEP students. It was not possible to do so after 1976. Monitoring compliance with the legislation, the state exerted pressure on districts to adopt bilingual education as required by law. Bilingual programs were established throughout the state. Some districts became committed to the approach once teachers and administrators saw what a difference primary language support made to their LEP students. Others adopted it only under duress and did as little as required to make the programs work. Still other districts and educators did everything they could to subvert the effort. Bilingual programs in some schools were staffed mostly by teachers who did not believe in bilingual education or lacked the language skills to teach bilingually. A single "bilingual class" in such a school might be composed of students whose primary languages were as diverse as Vietnamese, Khmer, Laotian, Mien, Cantonese, and Thai – children who spoke six or seven unrelated first languages. Under such conditions, bilingual instruction was impossible. All teachers could do was to teach in English. These classes were "bilingual," as required by law, but they were bilingual in name only (see Fillmore 1992a).

Ironically, as bilingual educators became more skilled at their craft, the approach became more controversial. There were numerous attempts in the state legislature during the 1980s to weaken the mandate for bilingual education as the 1976 law came up for renewal. The state legislature renewed the law, but the governor opposed bilingual education and vetoed the bill. In fact, he did so on several different occasions. The final veto was in 1987, when anti-immigrant and anti-bilingual movements were gaining support throughout the country, particularly in places like California with large immigrant populations. A year earlier, California voters had passed Proposition 63, the Official English referendum, by a 73 percent vote. (See table 18-2 for a summary of Proposition 63 and other relevant California propositions.) The bilingual education law was "sunsetted" after 1987, but that did not mean that school districts could dismantle their bilingual programs. The Lau Guidelines still required schools to provide language support for LEP students, and the Office of Civil Rights continued to use those guidelines in monitoring compliance with the Equal Educational Opportunities Act. However, school districts in California had greater discretion to provide alternative programs, particularly after a district court judge ruled in 1989 against the plaintiffs in *Teresa P. v. Berkeley Unified School District*, a case brought against the district on the grounds that it had failed to provide enough qualified and trained bilingual teachers for its LEP students. The ruling, which hinged on whether bilingual instruction was more effective than ESL, was that the plaintiffs had not demonstrated the superiority of bilingual instruction. It allowed Berkeley to continue its practice of providing instruction for children largely in English, with ESL support. It also encouraged other school districts to adopt the same approach, further weakening bilingual education in California. By 1997, slightly less than 30 percent of students in California who qualified for some form of linguistic support in school were receiving assistance that could be described as bilingual education. The bilingual programs that remained, however, were mostly well conceived and properly implemented, and they were having positive results.[6]

It is this fact that makes California's Proposition 227 especially puzzling. Why, when bilingual education was hardly a pedagogical issue in California anymore, should it become a major political issue? What was the motivation behind the drive to put on the June 1998 ballot a draconian referendum that would eliminate bilingual education as a pedagogical approach for LEP students in that state?

The answer to both questions is politics. Ron Unz, a Silicon Valley software entrepreneur, had ambitions to be governor of California and had earlier attempted to run for the governorship. Running against incumbent Governor Pete Wilson in the 1994 primaries, Unz declared himself opposed to Proposition 187, which Wilson strongly supported. Illegal immigration was not as great a problem as bilingual education and affirmative action, he declared in his 1994 campaign (Wallace 1994). Unz had little chance of winning the Republican primary against Wilson, although he did receive 34 percent of the primary election votes.

It was not a bad showing for someone whose name was virtually unknown to the voters of California, but Unz had failed to see how much support Proposition 187 had from California voters. It was the second anti-immigrant, anti-diversity voter initiative to garner support from California voters, each measure a part of a conservative agenda to check the political power of California's growing minority population. The first such measure was the "English-Only initiative" in 1986. For his next race, Unz would have to gain better name recognition, and for that he needed to position himself on the right side of an issue that would attract the conservative vote in California. In 1996, the anti-affirmative action initiative,

---

[6] See, e.g., Parrish 1994, Gándara 1997, Collier 1992, Ramírez et al. 1991, Ramírez 1992. Ironically, the most striking evidence for the success of bilingual education came out one month after the vote on Proposition 227, in July, 1998, when the state of California released its first annual comparative test data from the Standardized Testing and Reporting program. The *San Francisco Chronicle* reported the following: "The results appeared on the state's new Standardized Testing and Reporting (STAR) exam, a multiple-choice test that uses a 99-point scale. Third-graders who had graduated from bilingual classrooms in San Francisco, for example, scored 40 percentage points higher in math than their native English-speaking counterparts. On the language portion, bilingual fourth-graders scored 25 points higher than the natives. And in reading, eighth-grade bilingual graduates outscored the natives by nine points – although their reading scores slipped behind in later grades. Similar but less impressive differences showed up in San José. There, for example, fourth-grade bilingual graduates scored 19 points higher than natives in spelling. In the seventh grade, they outscored the natives by 7 points in math." ("Bilingual Surprise in State Testing: Many Native English Speakers Outscored in S. F., San José." N. Asimov, staff writer, San Francisco Chronicle, July 7, 1998).

Table 18-2 *A decade of anti-immigrant, anti-diversity voter initiatives in California*

1986 – Proposition 63: Makes English the only official language in California and prohibits the use of other languages in public documents and in public meetings.

1994 – Proposition 187: Abolishes health, welfare, social and educational services for undocumented immigrants.

1996 – Proposition 209: Abolishes affirmative action programs for women and minorities in jobs and in education.

1998 – Proposition 227: Eliminates bilingual education for LEP students; limits LEP students to one school year of instructional support to learn English; allows teachers, school administrators and school board members to be sued if they are found not to be in compliance with 227.

Proposition 209, was passed by California voters, ending consideration of gender, race, and ethnicity in hiring and admissions decisions in the state. Proposition 209 was another voter referendum that Pete Wilson had ardently supported. Unz was left with one hot issue: bilingual education.

In 1997, Unz positioned himself as the arch-foe of bilingual education by funding a drive to put an anti-bilingual education initiative on California's ballot. Joining forces with a first-grade teacher who was running for the state school superintendency on an anti-bilingual education platform, Unz wrote the "English Language Education for Immigrant Children Initiative." This referendum did more than end bilingual education. It also limits LEP children to one year of instructional support to learn English, and it dictates the type of instructional support schools can provide such students. The prescribed program is "sheltered English immersion" – the approach that has the support of other anti-bilingual critics but is neither well described nor supported by research as the authors of 227 claimed. The initiative attempts to forestall legal challenges on the grounds that it denies parents the right to have any control over their children's education, a major issue in the *Meyer v. Nebraska* case as discussed above. It allows parents, after children have been in English-Only classes for thirty days, to apply for a waiver of the required placement, provided the school principal and instructional staff agree that a given child has "physical, emotional, psychological, or educational needs" that necessitate such an exemption. In the end, however, it allows parents or children's guardians and members of the public to sue school board members and public school teachers and administrators who they believe are not implementing 227 fully. Strangely, the voters of California did not even question the peculiarity of this initiative being on the ballot: it was a vote, of all things, on a pedagogical approach. Never before in the history of education had pedagogy been put to a public vote. This referendum also weakens and invalidates the important principle of local control of schools. School boards are elected by communities to decide how best to educate students at the local level. Proposition 227 dictates how language minority students will be instructed, and it puts school board members in jeopardy of being taken to court if they do not implement its provisions to the letter. Further, it nullifies the professional judgment of teachers – they too can be sued if they use children's primary languages in school even if they believe it is in their students' best interest to do so.

The opponents of the measure argued that 227 imposes one untested method for teaching English on every local district in California; it also negates the right of school boards, teachers, and parents to make pedagogical decisions for the children in their care. Children who do not know the language of instruction are at an educational disadvantage. It takes time to learn English well enough to deal with its use as a medium of instruction – far more time than the one year allowed under 227. And while English is crucial, it is not the only goal of schooling for LEP students. They must also learn everything else in the curriculum as well. Before the adoption of bilingual education in California in 1976, children were sometimes given instructional support for learning English, but little help in dealing with the rest of the curriculum. The curriculum was provided only in English, and students had to know that language well in order to get anything out of school. The high drop-out and academic failure rates – as high as 50 percent for some groups in the pre-bilingual education period – showed how great a barrier language differences can be to getting an education.

But when they were raised during the debate on 227, these issues were not as persuasive to voters as the arguments made by supporters of the initiative. The "Arguments in Favor of Proposition 227" given in the election materials recite the familiar litany of complaints: bilingual education does not work; "bilingual education actually means monolingual SPANISH-ONLY [caps in original] education for the first 4 to 7 years of school"; it fails to teach children to read and write in English; children are not being moved into mainstream classes fast enough; Latino children receive "the lowest test scores and have the highest drop-out rates of any immigrant group" despite bilingual education; there are 140 languages spoken by immigrant students in California schools – how are all of these languages to be accommodated?

Opponents of the referendum fought valiantly (see Crawford 1997), but in the end 227 prevailed. By a 61 percent to 39 percent vote, California voters passed it in 1998, revealing not only how little the public understood the pedagogical issues, but also how conflicted Americans are about their diversity and how unwilling to change their institutions and practices to accommodate diversity. In a state where over half the residents are foreign-born immigrants or US-born children of immigrants, why would 61 percent of the voters want to end a pedagogical approach that gave non-English-speaking students access to the curriculum of the school in language they understood while they were in the process of learning English?

Immediately after the election, a coalition of civil rights organizations requested that the state be enjoined from putting 227 into effect at the beginning of the coming school term, arguing that implementation of 227 would constitute a violation of the state's responsibility under the provisions of the Equal Educational Opportunity Act of 1974. They also argued that sixty days – the period allowed between the passage of 227 and its implementation – was not enough time for districts to gear up for change and would result in chaos in the schools. The federal judge who had been assigned the case turned down the request and wrote in his ruling that the test for such an injunction was whether irreparable harm was likely to result from the implementation of 227. He dismissed virtually all the arguments made by the civil rights groups involved in the suit, noting that the claim that 227 would cause irreparable harm if implemented was "speculative" – 227 had not yet caused actual harm to anyone.

How has 227 affected the education of children in California? Some educational researchers say it has not changed things much.[7] School districts that were committed to bilingual education before 227 have maintained their programs by informing parents of their right to request waivers for their children from placement into English-Only programs; districts that had little commitment to bilingual education closed their programs as soon as it was possible to do so, and have done little to inform parents about the possibility of waivers. Two large urban districts with effective programs, San Francisco and San José, found legal support for continuing bilingual education in spite of 227. San Francisco is still operating under the consent decree in *Lau*, while San José is obligated to continue its bilingual programs under a consent decree on school desegregation. For the most part however, bilingual education is no longer provided for LEP students in California. It remains to be seen how long it will be before there is evidence that 227 is harmful to LEP students in California. In the meanwhile, Unz and his supporters are attempting to pass similar laws and initiatives in other states.

The curtailment of bilingual education as an instructional approach comes at an especially trying time for language minority students in California. It is but one of several major changes in educational policy that are likely to affect educational and subsequent economic opportunities for immigrants and other language minorities. The adoption of new and higher curricular standards has been a nationwide reform, and it has been a necessary change. A critical self-examination of the status of US education by participants at the 1989 Education Summit led to the adoption of the Goals 2000 Educate America Act of 1994 in the hope that such a change would help close the achievement gap between Americans and students in other societies, especially in areas such as reading, writing, math, and science. There has also been the adoption of new benchmark assessments to measure the effectiveness of improvements in programs of instruction that

---

[7] This is the preliminary finding of a study conducted by Gene Garcia and Tom Stritikus, as reported at the Linguistic Minority Research Institute Conference in May 1999 in Sacramento, CA.

states and local districts have adopted: are students learning what they should be learning in school? The termination of social promotion is another important change: students who do not learn what they are expected to learn at each grade level will not be promoted to the next in many states. A fourth important change has been the adoption of high school exit examinations by twenty-three states at last count. Students must pass tests on English language and literacy and on mathematics before they can graduate from high school in states that have adopted this requirement. And the clincher – the change in California that may predict the future in other places too – the abandonment of affirmative action in higher education admissions and in consideration of jobs.

Conclusion

How will language minority students fare under these changes? Can LEP students deal with the newly adopted higher curricular standards and expectations in reading and writing, math and science, without instructional support in language they understand? Can they learn the English needed to deal with the school's curriculum at each grade level with as little help as 227 allows them? How much English can they acquire in a year?[8] Will LEP students be able to pass the high school graduation examination that California recently adopted? What chance have they of going to college, or getting a job with the education they will be getting from the public schools, if affirmative action no longer exists?

The answer to these questions will depend on the ability of educators to find solutions to the problem of language differences in school that do not threaten the fundamental beliefs of people in our society about matters of language and culture. It is fair to say that while the USA has a diverse linguistic heritage, it is not a linguistically diverse society by choice. As a society, we value just one language – and while English is unchallenged as the language of discourse in all spheres of public life, we are militant whenever we perceive any threat to its primacy. For many Americans, English is not just a language, it is synonymous with being American. It has the force of an ideology for some: English symbolizes the willing acceptance of what it means to be an American, and the necessary abandonment of other loyalties, belief systems, and languages. We do tend to judge people according to whether or not they agree with this

---

[8] A study conducted by students and faculty from the University of California at Berkeley and San Francisco State University in 1998 (Declaration by L. W. Fillmore submitted in support of the request for an injunction in the case of 227) found that 61 percent of a sample of 238 children selected randomly from those who entered school the previous fall with no English at all remained virtually free of English, despite having been in "sheltered English immersion" programs for a year; another 32 percent had learned enough that they could no longer be regarded as non-English speakers, but they were still so limited in English proficiency that they could not have survived in school with no further instructional assistance. Thus 93 percent of the children after a year of submersion in English could be expected to have difficulty dealing with an all-English curriculum if they were entirely on their own.

ideology. Why else are so many members of our society so hostile toward the use of languages other than English in school? Why are people so adamant that non-English-speaking children be required to function in English as soon as they enter school?

The problem is that in the public mind the use of languages other than English in school means that speakers of those languages do not have to change or learn English. People fear that the use of children's home languages at school will allow them to keep using those languages and not become fully Americanized. Many millions of immigrants and indigenous peoples have encountered these sentiments in the American schoolhouse. They enter school speaking many different languages, but few of those languages survive the experience. Language shift and loss has long been a problem for both immigrants and American natives alike. In the past, it took at least a generation or two for an immigrant language to be lost. At the beginning of the twenty-first century, the process has become greatly accelerated. Many first generation immigrants are losing their ethnic languages well before they have mastered English (see Fillmore 1991a, b, 1992b). Indigenous languages that have managed to survive against all odds in the past are fighting a valiant battle just to stave off further erosion (see Benjamin et al. 1998). The loss of immigrant and indigenous languages is more than the loss of valuable linguistic resources and of cultural and linguistic diversity in our society.[9] Too often it also means the breakdown of family relations, particularly where parents do not speak or understand English, and it means the weakening of bonds within communities where participation in community practices requires knowledge and use of the ethnic language. The loss of community and family cohesion and intimacy added to the cost in human resources of not educating students well – the high rate of school failure among language minority students – tally up to a hefty tariff for the society to pay for its insistence on English-Only. Americans might well consider the real cost of how we deal with language diversity in our society's schools.

Suggestions for further reading and exploration

The footnotes and references within the chapter point to sources of additional information, and perhaps the most convenient of these are the books by Crawford (1989, 1992a, 1992b), Cummins (1989, 1996), Krashen (1996), and Olsen (1997).

---

[9] See especially Hale et al. (1992), where Krauss notes that 90 percent of the indigenous languages of North America have become extinct and that most of the few that remain are spoken only by a small number of elderly people. He points out that of the twenty Native languages in Alaska only two (Central Yup'ik and the Siberian Yup'ik of St. Lawrence Island) are still being learned by children. Recently, I visited a village along the Kuskokwim River where slightly less than 20 percent of the children entering kindergarten were able to speak any Yup'ik, as compared to ten years ago, when 90 percent of the children were fluent in Yup'ik when they entered school!

References

Baker, Keith A. and A. DeKanter. 1981. *Effectiveness of Bilingual Education: a Review of the Literature*. Washington DC: Office of Planning, Budget and Evaluation, US Department of Education.

Benjamin, Rebecca, Regis Pecos, Mary Eunice Romero, and Lily Wong Fillmore. 1998. "Reclaiming Communities and Languages," *Journal of Sociology and Social Welfare* 25: 81–104.

Collier, Virginia P. 1987. "Age and Rate of Acquisition of Second Language for Academic Purposes," *TESOL Quarterly* 21: 617–41.

    1992. "A Synthesis of Studies Examining Long-term Language Minority Student Data on Academic Achievement," *Bilingual Research Journal* 16: 187–212.

Collier, Virginia P. and Wayne P. Thomas. 1989. "How Quickly Can Immigrants Become Proficient in School English?" *Journal of Educational Issues of Language Minority Students* 5: 26–38.

Crawford, James. 1989. *Bilingual Education: History, Politics, Theory, and Practice*. Trenton NJ: Crane.

    1992a. *Hold your Tongue: Bilingualism and the Politics of 'English Only.'* Reading MA: Addison-Wesley.

    1992b. *Language Loyalties: a Source Book on the Official English Controversy*. Chicago: University of Chicago Press.

    1997. "The Campaign against Proposition 227: a Post Mortem," *Bilingual Research Journal* 21(1).

Cummins, Jim. 1981a. "The Role of Primary Language Development in Promoting Educational Success for Language Minority Students." In *Schooling and Language Minority Students: a Theoretical Framework*, ed. California State Department of Education. Los Angeles: Evaluation, Dissemination and Assessment Center, California State University.

    1981b. "Age on Arrival and Immigrant Second Language Learning in Canada: a Reassessment," *Applied Linguistics* 2: 132–49.

    1989. *Empowering Minority Students*. Ontario: California Association for Bilingual Education.

    1996. *Negotiating Identities: Education for Empowerment in a Diverse Society*. Ontario: California Association for Bilingual Education.

Dolson, David P. and Jan Mayer. 1992. "Longitudinal Study of Three Program Models for Language-Minority Students: a Critical Examination of Reported Findings," *Bilingual Research Journal* 16 (1&2): 105–57.

Epstein, Noel. 1977. *Language, Ethnicity, and the Schools: Policy Alternatives for Bilingual-Bicultural Education*. Washington DC: George Washington University, Institute for Educational Leadership.

Fillmore, Lily Wong. 1991a. "Language and Cultural Issues in Early Education." In *The Care and Education of America's Young Children: Obstacles and Opportunities. The 90th Yearbook of the National Society for the Study of Education*, ed. S. L. Kagan. Chicago: University of Chicago Press.

    1991b. "When Learning a Second Language Means Losing the First (For the No Cost Research Group)," *Early Childhood Research Quarterly* 6: 323–46.

    1992a. "Against our Best Interest: The Attempt to Sabotage Bilingual Education." In Crawford 1992b.

    1992b. "Learning a Language from Learners." In *Text and Context: Cross Disciplinary Perspectives on Language Study*, eds. Claire Kramsch and Sally McConnell-Ginet. Lexington MA: Heath.

Fillmore, Lily Wong, P. Ammon, B. McLaughlin and M. S. Ammon. 1985. *Final Report: Learning English through Bilingual Instruction*. Prepared for National Institute of Education. Berkeley: University of California. (NIE-400-80-0030)

Fishman, Joshua A. and Vladimir C. Nahirny. 1966. "The Ethnic Group School and Mother Tongue Maintenance." In *Language Loyalty in the United States: The Maintenance and Perpetuation of Non-English Mother Tongues by American Ethnic and Religious*

Groups, eds. J. A. Fishman, V. C. Nahirny, J. E. Hofman, and R. G. Hayden. The Hague: Mouton.

Gándara, Patricia. 1997. *Review of the Research on Instruction of Limited English Proficient Students: A Report to the California Legislature from The UC Linguistic Minority Research Institute Education Policy Center.* Davis: University of California.

Gold, Norman. 1996. *Teacher Supply, Demand and Shortages.* Sacramento: California Department of Education.

Greene, J. P. 1998. *A Meta-Analysis of the Effectiveness of Bilingual Education.* Austin TX: Tomas Rivera Policy Institute, Public Policy Clinic of the Department of Government, University of Texas at Austin, and Program on Education Policy and Governance at Harvard University.

Hale, Kenneth, Michael Krauss, Lucille J. Watahomigie, Akira Y. Yamamoto, Colette Craig, LaVerne Masayesva Jeanne, and Nora C. England. 1992. "Endangered Languages," *Language* 68: 1–42.

Issue Brief: Are Limited English Proficient (LEP) Students Being Taught by Teachers with LEP Training? 1996. US Department of Education: OERI, National Center for Education Statistics. December. IB-7-96.

Krashen, Steven. 1996. *Under Attack: the Case Against Bilingual Education.* Culver City CA: Language Education Associates.

Krashen, Steven and Douglas Biber. 1988. *On Course: Bilingual Education Success in California.* Ontario: California Association for Bilingual Education.

Mackey, William Francis and Von Nieda Beebe. 1977. *Bilingual Schools for a Bicultural Community: Miami's Adaptation to the Cuban Refugees.* Rowley MA: Newbury House.

Olsen, Laurie. 1997. *Made in America: Immigrant Students in Our Public Schools.* New York: New Press.

Parrish, Thomas B. 1994. "A Cost Analysis of Alternative Instructional Models for Limited English Proficient Students in California," *Journal of Education Finance* 19: 256–78.

Porter, Rosalie Pedalino. 1990. *Forked Tongue: the Politics of Bilingual Education.* New York: Basic Books.

Ramírez, J. David. 1992. "Executive Summary of the Final Report: Longitudinal Study of Structured English Immersion Strategy, Early-Exit and Late-Exit Transitional Bilingual Education Programs for Language-Minority Children." (Vols. 1 and 2) *Bilingual Research Journal* 16(192): 1–62.

Ramírez, J. D., D. Pasta, S. Yuen, D. Ramey, and D. Billings. 1991. *Final Report: Longitudinal Study of Structured English Immersion Strategy, Early-Exit and Late-Exit Bilingual Education Programs for Language Minority Children.* (Vol. 2) Prepared for US Department of Education. San Mateo CA: Aguirre International. No. 300-87-0156.

Reed, John and Roberto R. Ramírez. 1997. "The Hispanic Population in the United States: March 1997." (Update Current Population Report P20–511)'. Washington DC: US Bureau of the Census.

Scarcella, Robin. 1999. "Balancing Approaches to English Language Instruction." Unpub. paper presented at the California Reading and Literature Conference, Sacramento.

Schools and Staffing in the United States: a Statistical Profile, 1993–1994. 1996. US Department of Education: OERI, National Center for Educational Statistics, July 1996. NCES 96–124.

Schools and Staffing Surveys. 1999. US Department of Education: OERI, National Center for Educational Statistics. August.

Wallace, A. 1994. "Unlikely Path Led to Wilson Foe's Far-right Challenge," *Los Angeles Times*, May 8, 1994.

Willig, A. 1985. "A Meta-analysis of Selected Studies on the Effectiveness of Bilingual Education," *Review of Educational Research* 55: 269–317.

Yarborough, Ralph. 1967. "Speech to Congress Introducing the Bilingual Education Act, January 17, 1967." Reproduced in Crawford 1992b.

19

Adolescent language

PENELOPE ECKERT

Editors' introduction

Adolescence is defined by *Webster's Third New International Dictionary* as "the period . . . from puberty to maturity," and it is, as Penelope Eckert notes, a time in which the construction and marking of identity through style are prominent, particularly in secondary schools. Language is a key resource in the process. Among the features associated with adolescent language in the USA are the use of words like *dweeb* and *hella*, the ending of statements with a rising (instead of a falling) intonation, and the use of *be like* and *be all* to report interactions (as in *he's like* (shake head); *I'm all – 'what?!'*). Contrary to adult stereotypes and complaints, these adolescent usages are not evidence of inarticulateness or vagueness, Eckert argues. Instead, they are innovations that serve discourse functions and mark identity, just like their adult counterparts such as *software* or the use of *okay* with rising intonation (*We need to prepare a presentation, okay?*).

Moreover, what is striking about adolescent language is not its uniformity and conformity, but its diversity and its connection with ideology, as adolescents choose to adopt or avoid various linguistic resources depending on their ethnicity, gender, orientation to school, and other factors. Eckert discusses several examples, including the use of African American Vernacular English among immigrant adolescents in Northern California who identify with street culture rather than school, and the shunning of double negation by "jocks" in suburban Detroit schools (particularly jock girls), in contrast with its more frequent adoption by "burnouts" (among whom gender differences are less pronounced). Again, differences among adolescent Latina gang members in California (*Norteños* and *Sureños*) are marked by differences in the relative use of Spanish (vs. English) and other features like "creaky" voice. What unites these diverse examples is that they represent the common attempts of adolescents to construct their own identities and their own worlds, but in very different ways, at a life stage where noting and marking difference are paramount.

We often hear the adult lament that adolescents are irresponsible, sloppy, imprecise, faddish, profane and overly flamboyant speakers of English. Some worry that they may even *hurt* the language, as though they were tagging the lexicon with graffiti or kicking up the grammar with their Doc Martens.

Adolescents have a special place in American ideology, and it stands to reason that their language would be the object of ideological construction as well. This projection of social stereotypes onto ways of speaking is a common process around the world. Iconization, as this projection has been called (Gal and Irvine

1995), involves stereotyping both the speakers and their speech patterns and viewing the patterns as unfolding naturally from the speakers. It is traditional to view adolescents in our society as sloppy (they leave their clothes on the floor), rebellious (they don't do what they're told), and irresponsible (they forget their pencils). This view of adolescents is visited on their language, which is judged sloppy in its imprecision, rebellious in its supposed use of slang and profanity, and irresponsible in its greater use of non-standard grammar. Apparently, adults put their clothes away, do what they're told, and always have writing instruments handy. It remains an empirical issue whether any of the popular characterizations of adolescent language are valid. What is more interesting is the sheer existence of such characterizations. Why does our society focus so much on adolescents, their behavior and their language?

Adolescence is not a natural life stage. It is peculiar to industrialized nations, where people approaching adulthood are segregated from the adult world and confined to schools where they are expected to interact and identify primarily with those their own age. In many ways adolescents' position in society is similar to that of the aged. One could say that they are an institutionalized population, and much of their care is left to professionals who have come to constitute a major industry in our society. The rest of adult society, "mere amateurs," look upon adolescents as mysterious – and somewhat horrifying. Parents quake as their children approach adolescence; they read self-help books; they may even seek professional advice. One would think that adults had never been adolescents themselves, and this alienation from our own developmental past is one of the most intriguing social-psychological phenomena in our society.

Adolescents are people who are becoming adult, but they are systematically denied adult roles. Society confines them for long hours to institutions of secondary education, where they are crowded into a small space with hundreds or thousands of age mates and virtually isolated from the adult sphere. Unable to make their mark in the world of adults, they must make for themselves a world in which they *can* make a mark. That world, commonly referred to as "teen culture," is a response to the opportunities and constraints of the institution that houses it. In some sense, high schools are "holding tanks" for people who aren't yet "ready" to go out into the adult world. With its close quarters and its isolation, the secondary school serves as a social hothouse, nourishing both friendship and conflict, conformity and differentiation. Groups, cliques, and categories form and re-form, and all kinds of styles emerge as students lay claim to resources, and work to make meaning of their existence and their activities. Adults tend to point to the resulting flamboyance and self-conscious stylistic elaboration as evidence of immaturity. Some professionals are fond of saying that adolescents are "trying on" identities. But is this adolescent identity work qualitatively different from adult activity?

Adults like to think of themselves as having stable identities and as not being swayed by fads and opinion – in short, of not being subject to "peer pressure." When businessmen all wear the same suit, tie, white shirt and shoes day after day; when politicians suddenly have to have a red tie; and when we see hordes of people flocking to designers who offer not just an interesting piece of clothing but an entire look – a self that is embodied in shoes, clothing, furniture, bed linens, and other paraphernalia – we're looking at the adult version of Doc Martens, rock concert tees, and bedroom walls covered with posters. When I hear adults say that they've bought a particular designer car because it's safer, I think of a high school boy in California who told me he's only wearing his wild colored shorts because he likes them.

Because the world of teens is set aside from the adult world, not productively engaged in its government or its economy, its pursuits are viewed as trivial. But how else could it be? Adolescents aren't allowed to save the world. Instead, they are expected to participate in a special world that adults create for them – a kind of a practice world. In the midst of this practice world, when they manage to create something for themselves, adults trivialize it. And when they reject this practice world and insist on acting in the adult world, adults may feel threatened.

Any generalizations about adolescent use of language will have to be directly related to similarities in the situations in which adolescents use language similarities that set them off from other age groups. I believe that the relevant similarity is the struggle to define themselves in relation to the world, including both struggling to gain access to the adult world, and struggling to construct a worthy adolescent alternative to the adult world.

Making a world for themselves

Adolescence is brought into being in discourse, our institutions, our practices. Adolescents constitute an important consumer market, to be exploited by every industry that trades in material for identity: cosmetics, clothing, media, self-help, and paraphernalia of all sorts. So the category "adolescence" has clear utility for many powerful forces in our society. These industries do not simply cater to adolescents; they create adolescence as well, selling adolescence itself to adolescents and to younger children who are moving toward adolescence. The adolescent life stage is so mythologized in US culture that younger children look forward to it with a mixture of anticipation and anxiety. Kids do not all feel equally prepared for this new environment, and status differences begin already in elementary school around this preparedness. "Popular" groups take form, providing their members with a vaster network and hence information, protection, and support in a new environment, and fast change and construction of style – including linguistic style – becomes a crucial part of activity.

Because the school is society's official institution for adolescents, many issues about adolescent identity and civil status have to do with relations to the school. Society rewards people who stay in school and cooperate with its institutional arrangements. It stigmatizes and punishes those who marginalize themselves in school, or who leave school altogether. The kind of social order that arises among adolescents in the high school is related to the structure and practices of the school. The American secondary school is unique in the world by virtue of its comprehensiveness. In most countries, separate schools serve those who are bound for further education and those who are bound directly for the workplace. The public school system in the USA is comprehensive in the sense that the same schools house both of these populations. But, furthermore, while schools in most countries focus on academic or vocational training, American public schools attempt to be comprehensive civic and social institutions as well through elaborated extracurricular programs. Together, these two kinds of comprehensiveness bring a diverse student body into competition for recognition and resources.

The American high school's vast extracurricular sphere is designed to engage students in varied pursuits: limited self-government, music, art, drama, athletics, journalism, social events, and more. It is this comprehensiveness that makes it a potential total institution (Goffman 1961) – an institution that encompasses people's lives. For some, this offers an opportunity to prepare an institutional dossier for college admissions. For others, particularly those who do not intend to go to college but intend to seek employment locally, it is an unwelcome alternative to engagement in the world outside of school. Ultimately, the issue is whether to base one's activities and social networks in the institution, or in the larger community. Those who pursue an institutional life in school gain access to school resources and develop institutionally based status, while those who do not are increasingly marginalized and consequently increasingly alienated with respect to the institution. There are many reasons why one might choose to reject the institutional life, from feeling that one is already excluded on the basis of, for example, race, class, or interests, to feeling that the extracurricular sphere is infantilizing. Whatever the reasons, people of conflicting orientations are nonetheless thrown into competition for resources (such as space and freedom) day after day. Energetic processes of differentiation are an inevitable result, and stylistic production is key to differentiation.

Adding passion to the process of differentiation is the place of adolescence in social development. And by this I mean not so much the development of the individual but the development of the age cohort and the relations among individuals within this cohort. During childhood and elementary school, adults provide norms, sanctions and rewards for behavior. Children relate directly to adults – whether parents or teachers – as figures of authority. As they approach adolescence, the age cohort appropriates much of this authority. Adulthood is not simply an individual state of mind, but a social order, and adolescence represents the transition from childhood into that social order. The adolescent social order is transitional not only from dependence on adults, but from an identity based in the family. This is a scary move for most people, and there are significant differences within the age cohort in the speed and willingness with which people move away from their families and engage on new terms with their peers. This move brings greater freedom and new opportunities on the one hand, and makes new social demands on the other. The adolescent social order, then, is not just a game that people may opt in or out of; it is the dominant discourse and everyone must deal with it in some way.

The combination of anxiety, close quarters, and ideological conflict makes the high school a very passionate milieu. And the social categories that form in this milieu tend to be intense in their efforts to distinguish themselves from others through activity ranging from the elaboration of styles to claiming territories to physical violence. The elaboration of styles is fundamental identity work, and public high schools foster strikingly diverse stylistic landscapes. These styles affect just about every manipulable resource – clothing, makeup, hair styles, jewelry and other bodily adornment, posture, motion, possessions, food consumption, and on and on. And, finally, language.

The power of age

We tend to notice styles that are unlike our own – we come to see some ways of talking, acting, and looking as "normal," unremarkable, and others as "different." The world is full of people who think they don't have an accent – that everyone else, or certainly every other region, has an accent, but that their own way of speaking is normal or neutral. But the fact is that everyone has an accent – after all, we all have to pronounce the phonemes of our language some way or another. Some people, however, are in a position to define their own way of pronouncing those phonemes as "normal." Indeed, part of what constitutes power in society is the ability to define normality – to get others to view one's own style as unremarkable, as not a style at all. This domination of others by making them complicit in their oppression (rather than by imposing brute force) has been called *hegemony* (Gramsci 1971). In any community, most middle-aged adults speak somewhat differently from most adolescents. And these differences are not viewed neutrally, but are evaluated in favor of the adults. But what is the real nature of these differences and what is their origin?

Language is not a static resource. We mold it to suit our purposes – to emphasize, to elaborate, even to bring new things into being. Speakers – communities of speakers – in the course of mutual engagement in shared enterprise, create innovations in the areas they are engaged in. They develop new ways of doing things, and new ways of talking about what they are doing – ways that suit their purposes as a group. And the fate of these innovations will depend on the status of the innovators. If the innovators are viewed as doing important things, their innovations will be judged useful; if they are viewed as doing trivial or harmful or dirty things, their innovations will be judged trivial, or harmful, or dirty. Depending on the community and the endeavor, lexical innovations, for example, might be called "technical terminology," "jargon," or "slang." So what are adolescents and adults doing with language that is different?

Engaged in a fierce negotiation of the social landscape, social values, differences, tolerances, and meanings, adolescents are continually making new distinctions and evaluations of behavior. In the course of this endeavor they come up with new terms for evaluation and social types (*dweeb*, *homie*) as well as for emphasis (*totally*, or *hella*, as in *She's hella cool*). Middle-class adults, on the other hand, engaged in the negotiation of other space, come up with words like *software*, *Hispanic*, *throughput*. The main difference between these new coinages is in the situations in which they emerge – the landscape that the innovators are negotiating, and the social work that the innovations accomplish. The linguistic and social processes are the same. Lexical innovations mark new distinctions. When a community takes up a new word, it recognizes, ratifies and expands the importance of that new distinction. If the innovating community has sufficient power and influence, that innovation will spread well beyond it. Kids who use words such as *dweeb*, *homie*, and *hella* may well at some point come to refer to themselves or others as *Hispanic* – or at least check a box on a form that says *Hispanic*. The chances that the people who coined the term *Hispanic* will use the term *dweeb*, *homie*, or *hella* are fairly small.

I have seen any number of media pieces on adolescents' use of *like*, as in *I'm **like** just standing there, you know, and she **like** comes up to me and **like** pushes me like that, you know?* and on rising intonation (which is heard as question intonation) in clearly affirmative sentences such as *my name is Penny Eckert(?)*. These innovations are touted as evidence of adolescent inarticulateness, sloppiness, vagueness, unwillingness to commit – you name it. By contrast, all kinds of innovations come from adult quarters and barely attract public attention. Particularly trendy these days is the spate of nouns used as verbs (technically called denominalized verbs), as in *that should **impact** the market*, *please **access** the mail file*, and *let's **team***, and *I recently **accessed** my hotel's **messaging** service*. These snappy turns of phrase seem to suggest that we are dealing with people of action. I am willing to bet that if it were adolescents introducing these forms, we would see a considerable negative public reaction, with claims that adolescents were unwilling to go to the trouble of using the longer forms *have an impact on, gain access to, work as a team*. While I have seen many articles on the evils of *like*, I have yet to see one on the use of *okay* with a rising intonation, as in *We need to prepare a presentation, **okay(?)**, and that will make it absolutely clear, **okay(?)**, that we're the only people who can do this kind of work. **Okay(?)***. Like *like* and rising intonation, *okay* is not just a random insertion; it serves to help organize the discourse – to highlight certain things, to guide the listener's interpretation of the finer points of the speaker's intent. But *okay* isn't used by teenagers; it's used by business people, as a way of asserting their authority, and it is hardly noticed.

Consider a couple of crutches for the inarticulate that have become popular among adults in recent years: ***What we have here is a situation where** the market is extremely unpredictable* and ***What it is, is that** the market is extremely unpredictable*. One might say that both of these devices allow the speaker to hold the floor without saying *uh*, while figuring out what to say or how to say it. (One might also say that both of these devices also reify what follows, elevating it in importance by setting it apart as a thing, a situation, something of note sitting on its little verbal pedestal.) One could dwell on the fact that these devices point to the inarticulateness of the average middle-aged person. Or one might say that they are evidence of speakers' fluency since the speaker does indeed maintain the floor without a pause. Which evaluation one chooses depends entirely on one's attitude toward the speakers.

Just a few years ago, people were laughing about kids using *go* (as in *she goes* or *I go*) as a quotative. What is interesting about *go* is that an entire interaction can be reported in which action and speech are treated equivalently because, of course, *he goes* doesn't just mean 'he says.' You can say, *he goes* and shrug or make a face. This makes for a very lively narration. More recently, attention has been drawn to the new quotative use of *be like* and *be all*, as in *she's like, "go away"*; *he's like* (shake head); *I'm all – "what?!"*; *She's all "yeah right."* One difference between *go* and *be like* or *be all* is the nuance in reporting. *He goes* reports one of a sequence of actions. *He's like* invites the listener to interpret the slant on the events being reported.

What *like*, rising intonation, *I'm like*, *I'm all*, and *she goes* have in common is their ability to dramatize a narration – and narration is a genre central to adolescent discourse. Narration is a difficult skill to learn, and the ability to tell competent narratives and have an audience actually attend to these narratives is an important sign of growing up and of social entitlement. Preadolescents engage intensely in narration, and as they move towards an adolescent peer controlled social order, narration becomes an important resource for the construction of this order. In a population that is continually negotiating identity and the social order, narrative is used to go over events in the negotiation of norms, values, and beliefs. Narrative is a means of holding people accountable and of putting actions on the table for consideration and evaluation. It is central to working out the peer social order.

Linguists are frequently confronted with popular beliefs about language that count certain speakers as "irresponsible," certain speech varieties as "ungrammatical," and certain speech practices as "illogical." These judgments are systematically passed on language spoken by the poor, by minorities, by women, and by children. From a linguist's point of view, none of these judgments have value. Rather, such beliefs are commonly based on selective observation and on biased judgment of what those observations mean. Adolescents are just going about their business, trying to make the best of a marginalized position in society – and using language to do so. While adults may be concerned about the linguistic products, they should be more concerned with the marginalization that provides the conditions for adolescent linguistic production.

Linguistic movers and shakers

So far I have been defending adolescents against common attacks on the way they speak. But in doing this I run the risk of reifying the notion of "adolescent language." Before I do so any further, I would like to emphasize that while one might be able to point to certain linguistic features that are currently being used primarily by adolescents (such as certain expressions like *hella* and the quotative *be all*), these are relatively fleeting and have already spread well beyond the age group in which they appear to have originated. At the same time, not all adolescents use them. Like middle-aged people, adolescents do not all speak alike.

With the focus on adolescence as a unified life stage comes an assumption that adolescents constitute a homogeneous category. Social scientists talk of "teen culture" or "youth culture," and people of all sorts generalize about the beliefs and behavior of "teenagers." But adolescents are as diverse as any other age group. First of all, they do not constitute a unified place in the path to adult status. While they all have in common their subjection to the national discourse of adolescence, they vary hugely in the extent to which they fit into this discourse and the ways in which they deal with this subjection. For example, the mythologized "typical" adolescent is fancy free, with no responsibilities such as contributing financially to their families or caring for children or elders. But, in fact, this model of adolescence does not apply to many people in the adolescent age group, for many of them have considerable family responsibilities. Nonetheless, it is the standard against which all are compared – and it marginalizes those who have such responsibilities. And while adolescents are all subject to the societal norm that they stay in school until they graduate, they differ in their ability and willingness to stay in school, and those who do stay in school differ widely in their orientation to the institution. Differences in orientation to adolescence and to the school institution that defines adolescence are fundamental to adolescent life, and language is a prime resource for signaling and maintaining these differences.

One of the important properties of language is its potential to convey social meaning somewhat independently of the sentences that are being uttered. As we use language to convey content, our choice of linguistic resources simultaneously signals who we are, what we're like, where we're from, what we qualify for, who we hang out with. The resources among which we choose may be words, pronunciations, grammatical constructions, prosody, idioms, etc. Different speakers combine such resources in distinctive ways, and if these combinations come to be associated with particular people or groups of people, one could say that they constitute styles. Style in language, as in dress, home decoration, and demeanor, is one of our most important assets. It represents who we are and how we align ourselves with respect to other styles. Our style can gain us entrée, elicit trust, attract people and resources. And just as easily, it can exclude us and frighten or alienate others.

When we speak, we draw on a multitude of resources – not just any resources, but those that are available through exposure to people and places. We all have a way of speaking that is centered in a dialect, depending on where we're from and who (or whom!) we hung out with when we were young. But we also may modify that dialect – for instance if we move away or if we dis-identify with the locality. In addition to our native dialect, we may draw on pronunciations associated with other regions, countries, ethnic groups, or specific localities, and sometimes even small groups develop their own special pronunciations. These linguistic resources are structured, and not random.

The term *vernacular* has many uses and is somewhat controversial in sociolinguistics. In this chapter it refers to language that is the most closely associated with locally based communities – and the product of life in those communities. It exists in opposition to the *standard* – the language variety embraced by and required for use in globalizing institutions (financial, business, governmental, and educational institutions). The success and credibility of these institutions depends, to some extent, on their ability to appear to transcend the local – to serve the interests of the more general population. As a consequence, the language they endorse is devoid of obvious local or ethnic features. Standard language is a powerful tool of membership, or at least of commitment to gaining membership, in the halls and homes of global power. Vernaculars, by contrast, emphasize local and regional difference and must be learned in the neighborhood, in locally based families and social networks; consequently, they are tied up with local flavor and membership. Those whose loyalties and aspirations are tied to this local milieu are most likely to embrace the vernacular, as part of a construction and an expression of local identity and solidarity. And those who orient more towards globalizing institutions are more likely to embrace the standard. The high school is the globalizing institution that dominates the life of most adolescents, and adolescents' adoption of more standard or more vernacular speech is related, among other things, to their orientation to that institution.

African American Vernacular English (AAVE) is a very important vernacular resource for many adolescents in the USA. For example, white kids in Northern California use AAVE features as a way of laying claim to coolness (Bucholtz 1999). Immigrant teenagers in urban areas often adopt AAVE as their dialect of English, not simply as a matter of exposure but also often as an act of identity. A study of the development of English among a group of adolescents in Northern California shows that as they moved into American adolescence, those who became school-oriented developed standard English, while the speech of those who moved into the street culture showed more AAVE features (Kuwahara 1998). The relation between the use of AAVE features and engagement in local street culture is reflected among native speakers of AAVE as well. Preadolescent African American boys in a friendship network in a New York housing project show a relation between the use of features of AAVE and the speaker's place in the peer network (Labov 1972). While members of the group as a whole prided themselves on their engagement in street life, some members were more engaged in school than others. The boys more engaged in school were somewhat peripheral in the group, and their peripheral status showed up in their language use. In particular, their speech showed far fewer occurrences of zero copula, as in *he bad* (an AAVE feature) and of more general non-standard features such as non-agreement between subject and verb (*he don't*) than did the speech of their peers more centrally engaged in the peer group.

White regional vernaculars play a similar role. My work in predominantly white high schools in the Detroit suburban area showed a repeated opposition between two class-based categories: the "jocks" and the "burnouts." The jocks (who in an earlier era in the same school were called *soshes*, short for socialites) constitute a middle-class, school-oriented culture. Planning to continue to college after graduation, they base their social lives in the school and in its extracurricular sphere, intertwining their public institutional roles with their identities and their social networks. On the other hand, the burnouts (who in an earlier era were called *greasers*) are mostly bound for the local work force and reject the school as their social base. Preferring to function on their own terms in the urban area, they find the school's practices and activities infantilizing. Differences of this sort cannot be neutral in an environment where the jocks' way of life is the institutional norm, and where their activities give them institutional status and freedoms denied to others. The opposition between the jocks and the burnouts, therefore, can be an extremely bitter one, and is manifested not only in interpersonal and intergroup conflict, but in stylistic manifestations of every sort. The linguistic styles of the jocks and burnouts reflect their orientations to the globalizing institution of the school, on the one hand, and to the local urban area on the other.

The linguistic variable that most clearly reflects the different stances of jocks and burnouts toward the school and everything it represents is negation. Negation is a powerful sociolinguistic variable throughout the English-speaking world. Negative concord, commonly referred to as double negation or multiple negation (as in *I didn't do nothing*), is strongly non-standard, and generally evaluated as reflecting lack of education. But this grammatical strategy is as much a device for expressing attitude toward educational institutions and the values associated with them, as a reflection of one's actual academic background. While there are speakers whose native dialect requires negative concord, and who have not mastered the simple negatives of standard English, far more speakers know both forms and alternate between them. Given their attitude toward school, it is not surprising that the burnouts use more negative concord than the jocks. Overall, the burnouts in my study use negative concord 42 percent of the time, while the jocks use it 13 percent of the time. This differential use is not a matter of grammatical knowledge: there are no burnouts who make exclusive use of negative concord.

But the difference between jocks and burnouts with respect to negation does not apply across the board. As shown in table 19-1, jock girls are the most standard users of negation, while jock boys use negative concord one-fifth of the time. Both burnout girls and burnout boys, on the other hand, use negative concord almost half the time. This difference points to the important fact that gender is inseparable from other aspects of social identity. If we assume that the use of linguistic features is a way of constructing differences between groups, then the difference between jocks and burnouts is far greater among the girls than among

Table 19-1 *Percentage use of negative concord by jock and burnout girls and boys*

Jock girls	Jock boys	Burnout girls	Burnout boys
2	19	40	45

the boys. And, indeed, the consequences for a jock girl of looking, acting, or talking like a burnout are far greater than for a jock boy doing the same thing. Jock girls are expected to maintain a squeaky-clean image, while burnout girls pride themselves in their disregard for institutional authority and their claim on adult prerogatives (such as controlled substances, sexual activity, and mobility). Because norms of masculinity dictate autonomy, jock boys must maintain a clean-cut image without appearing to be under adult or institutional domination. As a result, the difference between jock and burnout boys, in language as in dress and general behavior, is never as great as that between jock and burnout girls.

Negative concord has similar social significance around the USA. By contrast, features of pronunciation are more regionally specific. In the Detroit area, several vowels have distinctive local and regional pronunciations, and particularly characterize the dialect of white speakers. Of these, three are clearly new pronunciations, showing up only in the speech of the younger generation. They are:

raising of the nucleus in /ay/, so that, for example, *buy* and *rice* sound like *boy* and *Royce*;
backing of /ɛ/ so that, for example, *flesh* and *dell* sound like *flush* and *dull*;
backing of /ʌ/ so that, for example, *but* and *fun* sound like *bought* and *fawn*.

The innovative variants of /ay/, /ɛ/, and /ʌ/ occur more in the speech not only of young Whites, but particularly those living closer to urban Detroit. This reflects the fact that these are actually sound changes in progress, which tend to spread outward from urban centers. While the use of negative concord is associated with education and attitudes towards normative institutions, vowels such as these have a different social significance. As sound changes traveling outward from the city, they have the potential to carry urban significance – to be associated with urban life, and the street smarts and relative autonomy of urban kids. In keeping with this, within schools throughout the suburban area, it is the burnouts who lead their classmates in the use of these innovations. The pattern shown in table 19-2, based on speakers in one high school, is repeated in schools across the urban area.

The category differences in table 19-2 are statistically significant, but it is important to note that they are far less pronounced than the difference in use of negative concord shown in table 19-1. This suggests that the differences in pronunciation are not quite as socially salient as the prominent and well-ensconced negative pattern.

The equivalent of jocks and the burnouts are hegemonic categories in white-dominated schools across the country. While the jocks and the burnouts (or their

Table 19-2 *Percentage use of innovative vowel variants by jock and burnout girls and boys*

Variable	Jock girls	Jock boys	Burnout girls	Burnout boys
ay	1	1	4	2
ɛ	23	27	31	33
ʌ	40	40	51	49

equivalents) are working to distinguish themselves from each other, other categories arise – among other things, in opposition to the hegemony of the jock–burnout split. In a Northern California school, a group of girls who embraced a *geek* identity distanced themselves from their peers' concerns with coolness and from what they viewed as demeaning norms of femininity (Bucholtz 1996). They prided themselves on their intelligence and freedom from peer-imposed constraints, and they based their common practice in intellectual pursuits. They did well in school but considered their intellectual achievement to be independent of the school, priding themselves in catching their teachers' errors. Their linguistic style was an important resource for the construction of their more general joint intellectual persona, and two aspects of their linguistic style are particularly salient. Living in Northern California, their peers – particularly their "cool" peers – make high stylistic use of current California sound changes – the fronting of back vowels /u/ as in *dude* (pronounced [dɪud] or [dyd], and /o/ as in *no* (pronounced [nɛw]). These girls use these changes, which seem to convey "cool California," far less than their peers, preferring to move away from that cool image through the use of more conservative pronunciations of both vowels. Another linguistic feature they exploit is the release of /t/ between vowels and at the ends of words. Generally in American English, /t/ is pronounced the same as /d/ when it occurs between two vowels as in *butter* or *at a*. At the ends of words before a pause, as in *you nut* or *what's that?*, the /t/ is generally not released at all. In British English, on the other hand, /t/ in both of these environments is generally released or aspirated: [bʌtʰ], [nʌtʰ]. This aspirated pronunciation of /t/ serves as an important stylistic resource for the geek girls' style. By aspirating many of their occurrences of /t/, they mark themselves as "articulate," in keeping with the American stereotype of the British and their speech. The geeks are quite consciously using conservative and prestige features of English to construct a distinctive style – not so much to claim social status within the adolescent cohort as to disassociate themselves from the adolescent status system altogether, and what they clearly see as trivial adolescent concerns.

In immigrant groups, adolescents play an important role in negotiating their community's transition to life in the new community. Immigrant children divide their lives between the home culture and the Anglo-American school culture. In both cases, they are primarily under the control of adults. But as they move toward adolescence and begin to develop a peer-based culture, the negotiation of home and school cultures is appropriated into the social norms and arrangements of the age group. Issues such as immigrant status, and ethnic and national orientation, become issues of identity and status among adolescents. A study of adolescent Latinas in California's Silicon Valley noted ways in which styles of English, on the one hand, and choices between English and Spanish, on the other, served as resources for constructing and disputing Latina identities (Mendoza-Denton 1996a). Immigration history and class, among other things, are important terms of difference in a community that is seen as monolithic from the outside. Of particular importance was the differentiation between opposed gangs, the Norteños and the Sureños. These gangs are not based on territory as is common with gangs, but on ideologies with respect to orientations towards Mexico and the USA. The Norteños emphasize their American, *Chicano*, identities, while the Sureños consider themselves *Mexicano*, emphasizing their ties to Mexico. Extensive ethnographic work with girls affiliating with either of these gangs showed that the two were set apart by subtle and not-so-subtle differences in the use of stylistic resources (Mendoza-Denton 1996a). Most striking – and not surprising – is the issue of language choice: the Sureñas making greater use of Spanish in their peer interactions than the Norteñas.

In addition, there were interesting linguistic dynamics in the development of styles of English. While linguists tend to focus on the use of the linguistic system strictly defined, Mendoza-Denton (1996b) draws explicit connections between linguistic and bodily style. She shows how a Chicana gang style is constructed through the combination of speech patterns and material resources such as makeup and dress. But she also connects speech to the body through an examination of voice quality, focusing on the girls' strategic use of "creaky" voice. This style is constructed in distinct opposition to the hegemonic Anglo culture and to the Anglo styles that dominate the high school, as well as to the styles of more assimilated Latinas.

Conclusion: raging hormones or not?

Adolescence is not a natural life stage. Despite all the popular talk about puberty and "raging hormones," adolescence is a purely social construction – and much of the flamboyant and frantic behavior attributed to hormones can be directly attributed to the situations that adolescents find themselves in. Placed in the transition between childhood and adulthood, but isolated both from children and adults, adolescents have to construct their own world for this life stage. It is no wonder that they should have passionate disagreements about what that world should be, what they should be doing with their time, and how they should act. And it is no wonder that they should use stylistic resources of all sorts to vivify these disagreements. While people often talk about adolescent speech as if it were a single style, this is anything but true. Adolescents do not all talk alike. On the contrary, speech differences among them are probably far greater than among members of any other age group – and it is this production of difference that defines adolescents linguistically. What unifies adolescents is not their similarities, but their joint participation in a life stage that brings out difference.

Suggestions for further reading and exploration

Bucholtz (1996), a sketch of a group of high school girls who claim "nerd" identities, describes their use of linguistic resources in the construction of a female nerd style. Bucholtz (1999) portrays a complex set of dynamics in a white boy's use of features of African American Vernacular English. Eckert (1989), an ethnographic account of the social order in a Detroit suburban high school, focuses on the opposition between the class-based social categories – the *jocks* and the *burnouts*. Mendoza-Denton (1996b) analyzes the construction of gang style in language and bodily adornment.

References

Bucholtz, Mary. 1996. "Geek the Girl: Language, Femininity, and Female Nerds." In *Gender and Belief Systems*, eds. N. Warner, J. Ahlers, L. Bilmes, M. Oliver, S. Wertheim, and M. Chen. Berkeley CA: Berkeley Women and Language Group. Pp. 119–31.
    1999. "You Da Man: Narrating the Racial Other in the Production of White Masculinity," *Journal of Sociolinguistics* 3: 443–60.
Eckert, Penelope. 1989. *Jocks and Burnouts: Social Categories and Identity in the High School*. New York: Teachers College Press, Columbia University.
Gal, Susan and Judith T. Irvine. 1995. "The Boundaries of Languages and Disciplines: How Ideologies Construct Difference," *Social Research*, 62(4): 967–1001.
Goffman, Erving. 1961. *Asylums: Essays on the Social Situation of Mental Patients and other Inmates*. New York: Anchor.
Gramsci, A. 1971. *Selections from the Prison Notebooks*. London: Lawrence and Wishart.
Kuwahara, Yuri L. 1998. "Interactions of Identity: Inner-city Immigrant and Refugee Youths, Language Use, and Schooling." Unpublished Ph.D. dissertation, Stanford University.
Labov, William. 1972. "The Linguistic Consequences of Being a Lame." In William Labov, *Language in the Inner City*. Philadelphia: University of Pennsylvania Press. Pp. 255–92.
Mendoza-Denton, Norma. 1996a. "Language Attitudes and Gang Affiliation among California Latina Girls." In *Gender and Belief Systems*, eds. N. Warner, J. Ahlers, L. Bilmes, M. Oliver, S. Wertheim, and M. Chen Berkeley. CA: Berkeley Women and Language Group. Pp. 478–86.
    "Muy Macha: Gender and Ideology in Gang Girls' Discourse about Makeup," *Ethnos* 6: 91–2.

20

Slang

CONNIE EBLE

Editors' introduction

This chapter deals with slang – a subject of perennial interest to college students and to many other age groups. As Connie Eble notes, slang words and expressions cannot be reliably distinguished from other vocabulary items by how they sound or how they are constructed. (Like other vocabulary innovations, they may draw on old words or parts of words, and make use of metaphor, irony, and metonymy.) Instead, slang is usually deliberately chosen over more conventional vocabulary to send a social signal – to mark informality, irreverence, or defiance; to add humor; or to mark one's inclusion in, admiration for, or identification with a social group, often a non-mainstream group. Slang is, as she suggests, vocabulary with attitude.

Slang is most commonly created and used by youth (see chapter 19 on language and adolescence) and it is often ephemeral in nature, like fashions in clothes or cars. But some slang terms persist for long periods, like *bull* 'empty talk,' while others, over time, become general American colloquialisms, like *buck* 'dollar' (which dates from 1856). Slang is most commonly used to describe types of people, relationships, social activities, and behavior (e.g., inebriation, which boasts more slang terms, in the USA, than any other concept), and judgments of acceptance or rejection.

Two important elements in American slang are non-mainstream cultures and music, and from both perspectives the ethnic group that has made the most significant contributions to slang in recent times is African Americans. Through African American musicians, entertainers, and sports figures, as well as the mass media, slang words like *nitty-gritty*, *gig*, *cool*, *diss*, *homeboy*, and *word* have spread from the African American community to young people in particular and the American public more generally. (On rap and hip hop, see chapter 21.) Sharing in-vogue slang words like these provides a measure of psychological security while allowing individuals to adopt and explore more daring social personas.

Language is subject to fashion – just as automobiles, clothing, food, architecture, home furnishings, and other indicators of status are. What is in or out of fashion changes constantly. For example, in the late 1990s the Jeep (now a registered trademark of DaimlerChrysler) became a status symbol. However, the jeep (whose name is probably from the abbreviation *g.p.*, for *general purpose*) began as a no-frills, all-purpose vehicle used by the military during World War II. After the war, the jeep had no glamorous associations to make it a desirable or prestigious purchase for private citizens. It was not then a fashionable car. A half century later, though, a thoroughly contemporary Jeep came into style in the United States as one of the class of luxurious and expensive *sports utility vehicles* so much in favor in suburbia today. The wartime workhorse turned into a prized thoroughbred, and early models are now collectors' items. The fashion value of items can go down also. Thrift shops throughout the United States are museums of various fashions that have swept the nation: macramé hanging baskets, shag carpets, fondue pots, polyester leisure suits, cabbage patch dolls, teenage mutant ninja turtles, Ataris, Nintendos, and many others. At one point each of these items was perceived nationally as new, interesting, progressive, or fun, and their owners enjoyed the feeling of being up-to-date and in-the-know. Sometimes the outmoded can even emerge into fashion for a second or third life, as happened at the end of the 1990s with extremely short skirts, very high thin heels on women's shoes, swing dancing, and other *retro* styles.

Words and phrases can be items of fashion too, giving their users pleasure and assurance. The use of trendy vocabulary can be just as important to status or image as can preferences in hairstyles, clothing, music, or possessions. Americans at the beginning of the twenty-first century who characterize 'something excellent' as *tubular* or 'something repulsive' as *grody to the max* reveal themselves to be behind the times, stuck culturally in the era of Valley Girl chic of the mid 1980s. A decade later in the late 1990s, under the influence of urban African American music and styles, *phat* and *da bomb* became favored terms for 'excellent' among adolescents and young adults, and *skanky* and *ghetto* meant 'unappealing.' Ever-changing fashionable vocabulary of this sort is usually a deliberate alternative to more stable neutral terms that are already available to speakers. For instance, *tubular* or *phat* can be paraphrased with words from the general vocabulary like *excellent* or *exceptionally good*. Yet, in totality of meaning, *tubular* and *phat* are not equivalent to *excellent* and *exceptionally good*. *Tubular* and *phat* send social signals that their conventional counterparts do not. Their use can show what group or what trend in the larger culture a speaker is identifying with or can convey an attitude of extreme casualness, flippancy, or irreverence. Deliberate alternative vocabulary that sends social signals is called *slang*.

No one can distinguish slang from other words or phrases that constitute the ordinary, general vocabulary of a language either by what slang sounds like or by how it is constructed. As a matter of fact, slang almost always arises from recycling words and parts of words that are already in the language and assigning them additional meanings – which is exactly how the non-slang vocabulary grows too. Here are some examples of slang that most Americans would recognize. *Magic bullet* 'something that cures or prevents disease or a problem' is a compound of two readily recognizable English words. The slang words *megatravel* and *megabooks* are formed by adding the trendy prefix *mega-* (meaning 'large quantities of') to standard words. *Freaky* 'frightening' and *peachy* 'wonderful' both add the ordinary adjective-forming suffix *-y* to the nouns *freak* and *peach*, which have different meanings as slang. Little words like *out*, *off*, and *up* are often added to a word to create a slang expression, like the verbs *pig out* 'eat voraciously,' *kick off* 'begin,' and *pick up on* 'notice.' Slang words are often the result of shortening, as in *bro* from *brother* or *OD* from *overdose*. Some words do not change form at all when they function as slang but do evoke a new meaning. For example, the verb *fry* in slang means 'electrocute'; the noun *lettuce* designates 'paper money'; and the adjective *cool* means 'pleasant, desirable.' In evoking new meanings without changing the shape of the word, slang often relies on the same processes of indirect reference that poetry does, making use of figures of speech like metaphor (*porcelain god* for 'toilet'), irony (*bad* for 'good'), and metonymy (*wheels* for 'car').

Slang vocabulary rarely refers to meanings that the ordinary vocabulary does not have words to express. Nor do slang items develop as alternatives to the entire expanse of meaning covered by the standard vocabulary of English. For example, abstractions like *oligarchy*, technical terms like *calibrate*, physical phenomena like *gravity,* and countless words from specialized subject areas do not inspire slang equivalents. Slang tends to refer to types of people, relationships between people, social activities and behavior, and judgments of acceptance or rejection. Common slang meanings are represented by items such as *dipstick* 'stupid person,' *goldbricker* 'shirker,' *big enchilada* 'important person,' *numero uno* 'self,' *fuzz* 'police,' *fink out* 'withdraw support,' *gross out* 'disgust,' and *rip off* 'steal.' Historically, in English the single meaning with the greatest number of slang synonyms has been 'impaired by drinking alcohol.' Standard English vocabulary expresses this meaning with at least three words: ordinary and neutral *drunk* and less frequent and more formal *intoxicated* and *inebriated*. However, slang synonyms for this condition number in the thousands, for example, *blitzed, juiced, looped, polluted, smashed, soused, tanked,* and *wasted*. A speaker who chooses a slang expression for this condition conveys emotional or attitudinal meaning in addition to simple denotation.

The social and psychological complexities encoded in slang vocabulary make the term *slang* difficult to define precisely. For purposes of study, slang must be distinguished from other subsets of the vocabulary such as *dialect words* or *regionalisms, jargon, profanity* or *obscenity, colloquialism,* and *cant* or *argot* – even though slang can share some characteristics with each of these and can overlap them.

Slang is not geographically restricted vocabulary. For example, in southern parts of the USA people across the social spectrum wear *toboggans* 'knit caps' in winter; they *mash* 'press' buttons on elevators and remote controls; they have *hissy fits* 'bouts of temper or agitation'; and they complain that a child's room is a *hoorah's nest* 'untidy mess.' These uses are not slang; they are dialect or regional terms. Yet some slang items can be associated with a particular region, for example, *guy* with North America and *bloke* with Britain.

Jargon is, strictly speaking, the vocabulary needed to do a job or to pursue a specialized interest, for example, *phonology, syntax,* and *semantics* for the study of language or *iambic pentameter, free verse,* and *villanelle* for the study of poetry. Of course, in addition to jargon people who work together or have a common interest can develop a slang vocabulary, which usually conveys feelings and attitudes and unity of spirit. Americans who devote their weekends to reenacting Civil War encampments and battles, for instance, have a term for those who lack commitment to absolute historic authenticity. They are called *farbs* (perhaps from *barf* 'vomit' spelled approximately backwards). The synthetic fabrics of their long underwear are *farby*, and their general *farbiness* is not admired by the painstakingly accurate reenactors who call themselves *hardcores*. Civil War reenactors are careful to use precise jargon for armaments and maneuvers, but in their casual interactions they reinforce their solidarity by using slang vocabulary that changes and develops from one weekend to the next.

The taboo subjects of a culture customarily give rise to vocabulary that the general society judges profane or obscene. In the United States, as in many other parts of the world, sex and bodily elimination have traditionally been uncomfortable topics for conversation, and many words and expressions that refer to these topics are objectionable in public settings. Yet only some of these expressions are slang, for example, *slampiece* 'sexual partner' and *dump a load* 'defecate.' Moreover, most American slang expressions – particularly those items sustained by the national popular culture – are not obscene, though they may certainly be inappropriate in some contexts for reasons of insensitivity rather than obscenity. Slang *croak* or *buy the farm* instead of standard *die* would probably not be said in offering condolences to a grieving friend.

Colloquialisms belong to the spoken part of language and are seldom written except in direct quotation of speech. Because slang is largely spoken rather than written, it is usually colloquial. But not all colloquial expressions are slang. Sayings like *poor as Job's turkey* and *scarcer than hen's teeth* and the nationally used *shut up* for 'be quiet' or *That's incredible!* qualify as colloquialisms. Yet they are not slang.

Cant and argot refer to the specialized and sometimes secret vocabulary of underworld groups whose activities often skirt the borders of what is lawful. The group-identifying vocabulary of thieves, con-artists, prisoners, drug addicts, and other marginalized segments of society has always been a major source of slang and colloquial vocabulary in English. The argot of the racetrack, for instance, is responsible for a number of words that now apply more generally than to horse racing: a *piker* is an 'unimportant or inconsequential participant,' a *ringer* an 'illegal substitution,' and a *shoo-in* an 'easy win.'

The compiling and publication of lists and dictionaries of English slang has gone on steadily for over two hundred years. However, only in the past twenty years has the analysis of slang been undertaken as a part of the expanding inquiry into the intersection of language and social factors. In a pioneering article in 1978, two linguists explored the inadequacy of the definition of the term *slang*. They showed that slang is a category of vocabulary that is identifiable by its effects rather than by its form or meanings. Slang is like an inside joke and depends on the consciousness of shared knowledge between speaker and hearer. Fundamentally, slang arises from the social rather than from the ideational functions of language (Dumas and Lighter 1978).

Despite the difficulty of defining the term, slang does have some consistent characteristics. Slang is ephemeral, entering the lexical choices of its users and falling into disuse at a more rapid rate than the vocabulary as a whole. Slang is used in informal situations where spontaneous rather than planned language is the norm. Slang identifies its users with a group or an attitude. Slang projects at least a nuance of irreverence or defiance toward what is proper.

Most slang is created, used briefly by a small number of speakers, and forgotten before it is ever recorded in a list of slang expressions or noticed by a dictionary maker. Among themselves, for example, suitemates in a college residence hall might use the name of an overly anxious parent to refer to 'nervous agitation,' as in "Don't be so marianna – you're gonna ace that test." At the end of the semester the suitemates go in different directions, interact with different people, and no longer think to use *marianna* in this way. The life cycle of one slang word has thus been completed. Thousands of other slang words may enjoy longer and more widespread use, sometimes retaining the flavor of slang but sometimes moving into the colloquial and less formal ranges of standard usage. The American *buck* for 'dollar,' first attested as slang in 1856, is probably now more accurately classified as a colloquialism. On the other hand, *bull* 'empty talk' and its vulgar equivalent *bullshit* have been in use for a century and are judged by dictionary makers still to convey the nuances of slang. Like fashion, many items of slang exhibit peaks of popularity. As an expression of enthusiastic approval, *the cat's pajamas* is associated with the roaring 1920s, *groovy* with the drug culture of the late 1960s, and *awesome* with the surfing and Valley Girl image emanating from California in the 1980s. Also like fashion, old slang can reemerge with renewed vigor. The adjective *hot* 'sexually attractive' is abundantly documented from the 1920s as used by males to refer to females. Its popularity soared again in the more gender-egalitarian 1990s, but then just as likely used by females to refer to males and giving rise to *hottie* for 'good-looking male; boyfriend.' Commonly, one slang term yields to another. For instance, for commenting negatively, *the pits* lost ground to *sucks*: "This weather is the pits" vs. "This weather sucks." As with fashion, value is associated with the newest version.

The injection of slang decreases the formality or dignity of speech or writing. In general, styles of language use that are comparatively formal are deemed suitable and sometimes necessary for serious and important occasions. As a result, vocabulary that conveys little about the speaker or the speaker's attitude toward the subject matter or audience has been the norm in impersonal public contexts, and slang is avoided. Compare "The Secretary of State appeared *uninformed* about the border dispute" with "The Secretary of State appeared *clueless* (*out to lunch, an airhead, spacey*) about the border dispute." However, the ability of slang momentarily to disrupt the serious tone particularly of spoken pronouncements can make it a useful means of adding humor, easing tension or establishing rapport with an audience. In one case of this kind, a government official had been diagnosed with cancer and was undergoing treatment for the dreaded disease. At the end of a press conference about public policy, a reporter, voicing the concern of everyone present, asked about the official's health. The official diffused the tension with the answer: "Chemotherapy sucks."

Because in the USA today most forms of social interaction, including language, have been moving in the direction of informality, the criterion of informality as a defining characteristic of slang is probably limited. Laborers' denim overalls have become expensive designer fashions. Baseball caps are seen everywhere out of doors, and most wearers do not feel compelled to remove them indoors. Few restaurants enforce a coat-and-tie dress code for men or a no-pants policy for women. Widows no longer observe a prolonged period of mourning by wearing black. Many offices have designated Friday as "dress down day" when employees eagerly wear jeans, tennis shoes, and tee-shirts to work. Conventions and colors of table settings are more varied and creative. Receiving lines at wedding receptions have been replaced by the happy couples circulating among the guests, and at large banquets the head table with its diners awkwardly facing the entire assembly is disappearing. Many college professors invite students to call them by their first names, and twenty-something Americans are not uncomfortable using first names with people of their grandparents' generation.

Language use reflects this more comfortable approach to social interaction. Rarely in spoken American English is formal discourse more appropriate than informal. Even in discussions of the most pressing problems facing the United States conducted in highly structured formats, informal vocabulary occurs frequently. The weekly program *Washington Week in Review* features four prominent journalists interpreting the important events of the preceding week for the public television audience. The subject matter is important and serious, and the panelists have expert knowledge. Yet the interchange between participants gives the impression of casual friendliness, and informal vocabulary peppers the discussion. For example, commenting on the coming congressional election, one said, "California is the odd-man-out in this election" (David Broder on October 16, 1998). Another described the State of the Union address as "a speech to the nation and Congress that said, 'I ain't going nowhere'" (Mara Liason on January 22, 1999). When formality is called for, as on ceremonial occasions such as inaugurating public officials or burying them, speakers usually read from a prepared written text.

In the *Random House Historical Dictionary of American Slang*, the editor traces the escalation of informality in America to the tremendous explosion in mass communication that took place around the beginning of the twentieth century. Improved technology allowed the print media for the first time to reach a national and multi-class audience. Between the Civil War and World War I, the number of daily newspapers in the United States increased over ten times, many carrying the new vernacular art form of the 1890s, the comic strip (Lighter 1994: xxvi–xxvii). Soon phonograph records, movies, radio, and television quickly expanded the means of disseminating a national popular culture, making the national spread of slang and other ephemeral vocabulary possible. By the 1990s the alliance of technology and marketing made the fashionable vocabulary of the United States a sign of being in-the-know throughout the world. Slang is the distinctive vocabulary of groups or of people who wish to identify with a popular or avant-garde style.

It has been well documented in English-speaking contexts since the eighteenth century that social groups are breeding grounds for an idiosyncratic vocabulary to enhance their solidarity (Lighter 1994, Bailey 1996). Groups that operate on the periphery of society – thieves, drug addicts, musicians and nightclub performers, con-artists, carnival workers, prisoners, and enlisted personnel in the military, to name a few – seem particularly adept at creating slang. Some of these groups are indeed on the edges of respectable society and engage in activities that are immoral if not illegal. Others – like low-ranking military personnel – feel isolated from society because they lack freedom and ordinary access to the channels of power. Most groups that are known for creative and colorful slang lead lives in which the printed word, mastery of the written forms of English, and formal education are not important. By contrast, their oral language is often rich, complex, and powerful, and they live by using it effectively. Rap music is a recent and commercially successful product of one marginal group's cultivation of language as a social weapon, the group being young African Americans from urban ghettos.

The group-identifying functions of slang are indisputable, perhaps because they are so obvious and have been experienced by nearly everyone. Speakers use slang when they want to be creative, clear, and acceptable to a select group. Slang can serve to include and slang can serve to exclude. Knowing and keeping up with constantly changing in-group vocabulary is often an unstated requirement of group membership, and failure to talk the talk can result in discomfort or estrangement. In addition, a group's slang often provides users with automatic linguistic responses that assign others to either an in crowd or an out crowd. For example, in 1998 undergraduate students at the University of North Carolina in Chapel Hill had at least sixteen nouns to label someone negatively: *bama*, *busta*, *chode*, *donut*, *dork*, *geek*, *gimp*, *goober*, *gromit*, *herb*, *loser*, *muppet*, *sherm*, *tool*, *wienie*, and *zero*. Among the same speakers, a positive experience could be *all that*, *bad*, *blaze*, *da bomb*, *bout it*, *cool*, *dope*, *groovy*, *hype*, *kickass*, *neat*, *phat*, *radical*, *rocking*, *the shit*, *slamming*, *smoking*, *sweet*, and *tight*.

Some slang indicates knowledge of contemporary currents in popular and widespread culture rather than affiliation with a particular group. If expressions like *channel surf* 'use a remote control device to sample television programs quickly,' *chick flick* 'film that appeals to females,' *go postal* 'lose control, act insane,' and *senior moment* 'temporary loss of thought or memory' can be considered slang at all, they are a kind of national slang and say little or nothing about group identification. This kind of vocabulary has been called *secondary slang* (as opposed to the *primary slang* of groups) and one lexicographer predicts that in the future it will be the major type of slang in the United States (Chapman 1986: xii). Words and expressions that become part of secondary slang may well be acquired from groups, but usually via television, films, music, and the like rather than through personal interaction with members of the originating group. For example, the terms *high five* and *raise the roof* and their accompanying gestures now serve as 'signs of affirmation, exhilaration, or victory' to all ages and classes throughout the United States. But they were originally innovated and made popular by African American sports figures and performers. Another item of secondary slang from African American sources spread by the mass media is *attitude* 'uncooperative, resentful, hostile, or condescending state of mind.'

Slang is vocabulary with *attitude*. It opposes established authority. Groups that have historically developed colorful slang usually have little political power or may have reason to hide what they know or what they do from people in authority. They stand outside the publicly sanctioned structures of power – a relationship that inspires *attitude* rather than cooperation. The attitude projected by slang can range from downright subversion to slight irreverence. Regardless of the degree of opposition, however, as one commentator observed during the roaring twenties, "the spirit of slang is that of open hostility to the reputable" (McKnight 1923: 46). Incarcerated criminals offer an example of the subversive end of the continuum. Prisoners wield their language like a weapon, sometimes for contest and display – using it to release pent-up aggression, to express fear and terror, to retaliate against their treatment, and to gain authority among fellow prisoners. For many other groups that cultivate slang and for those who use secondary slang, the irreverence is ordinarily targeted at social customs, and the opposition to authority consists of breaches of good taste. For instances, *brain fart* for 'mental error' is indelicate, and *asshole* for 'incompetent or unlikable person' is vulgar. Even an innocuous expression like *couch potato* for 'someone who lies around doing nothing except perhaps watching television' carries a tinge of irreverence – toward the work ethic that is widely honored as the basis of the success of the USA.

Informal and colloquial vocabulary, including slang, is thriving as the USA enters the era of the *global village* made possible by the end of the Cold War and by the rapid development of the information superhighway. American slang today shows both continuity with the past and those elements of fresh appeal that are required by fashion. Aside from the primary slang of counter-cultural groups in which age is often not a factor, slang is associated with youth or with an effort to project a youthful image. Adolescents and young adults don't attempt to be *cool* by imitating the behavior, styles, or vocabulary of the middle-aged and elderly. The direction of imitation is the opposite. Although older people may be the models and arbiters of *standard* language use, young people are the primary purveyors of slang.

The phrase *youth culture* did not emerge until 1962 (Lighter 1994: xxxviii), but the first signs of youth culture and its linguistic manifestations appeared in the 1920s (Dalzell 1996). The Great Depression of the early 1930s took young people off the farms and out of the workplace and put them together in high schools, thus creating a generation we now refer to as *teenagers* (Dalzell 1996: 26).

In chronologically cataloging the slang of successive generations of middle-class American youth, *Flappers 2 Rappers* describes the crucial role of mass communication in making a national youth culture possible.

Many patterns and consistencies are apparent in thousands of slang expressions from across the decades, and two particularly noteworthy ones are the importance of non-mainstream cultures and the importance of music (Dalzell 1996). These are indeed the two salient factors at work in current American slang, where the music and styles of African Americans dominate.

The group that has had the greatest impact on American slang in general has been African Americans. According to the *New Dictionary of American Slang*, "Close analysis would probably show that, what with the prominence of black people in the armed forces, in music, in the entertainment world, and in street and ghetto life, the black influence on American slang has been more pervasive in recent times than that of any other ethnic group in history" (Chapman 1986: xi). Some 435 slang items in the dictionary are associated with African Americans (Eble 1996: 80–83). Many of these have been adopted into general informal use, and their users may be unaware of their African American origins, for example, *bug* 'pester,' *the nitty-gritty* 'harsh reality,' *ripoff* 'theft,' and *do one's own thing* 'follow one's own inclination.' For a period of five years ending in 1998, one linguist tracked the occurrence of sixty-nine verbal expressions associated with African Americans in the *Daily Press*, a mainstream newspaper of the Virginia Peninsula (Lee 1999). Although she found instances of the items in articles of local, national, and international scope, as well as in syndicated columns and stories from wire services, they clustered in editorials and comic strips and in portions of the newspaper dedicated to celebrities, sports, and entertainment. That is, African American expressions were more typical in those parts of the newspaper that pertain to culture and personal opinion than to newsworthy events. The items of highest frequency were *cool*, *gig*, and *hip* – now a part of at least the recognition vocabulary of all generations and all segments of American society. Americans in general have a largely unconscious and superficial knowledge of vocabulary of African American origin, but young adults in mainstream America have knowingly and eagerly adopted that vocabulary. A study of college slang at one American university during the period 1972–93 showed that seven of the forty terms most frequently identified as slang entered the student vocabulary from African American usage: *jam* 'have a good time, perform well,' *diss* 'criticize, belittle,' *bad* 'good,' *homeboy/homey* 'person from one's hometown, friend,' *dude* 'male,' *word/word up* 'I agree,' and *fox/foxy* 'attractive female, attractive' (Eble 1996: 84).

Vocabulary from non-mainstream cultures often strikes mainstreamers as novel, rich, and imaginative. It suggests a way of life with greater fun and excitement than the well-regulated lives of most. Adopting the vocabulary of a non-mainstream culture is a way of sharing vicariously in the plusses of that culture without having to experience the minuses associated with it. Users of selective vocabulary drawn from other than mainstream cultures are, in the words of one dictionary maker, "*pretending*, momentarily, in a little shtick of personal guerilla theater, to be a member of a street gang, or a criminal, or a gambler, or a drug user, or a professional football player, and so forth – and hence to express one's contempt, superiority, and cleverness by borrowing someone else's verbal dress" (Chapman 1986: xii). In the USA at the beginning of the twenty-first century, it is the hip-hop scene developed by African Americans that is the alluring non-mainstream culture.

The power of music to form connections among people separated by distance, class, ethnicity, opportunity, and even language cannot be disputed. Conservative older generations in democratic societies as well as totalitarian governments have recognized the ideological potential of music and have sought to censor it. When advances in technology made the transmission of music easier, quicker, and less expensive, music became a defining, and often defiant, characteristic of non-mainstream cultures. Today rap music is the primary vehicle of the incipient international youth culture spreading across the planet. The elder statesman of the verbal art form, Chuck D. of *Public Enemy*, writes, "I've been to 40 countries, and I testify that this grass-roots transformation of culture has spread over the planet like a worldwide religion for those 25 and under" (Chuck D. 1999: 66). There is even a twenty-five-page scholarly study written in German analyzing "the appropriation and the re-coding of American hip-hop culture in Italy" (Scholz 1998: 257). (For more on the topic of hip hop, see chapter 21 of this volume.)

Like other items of fashion, slang is a human strategy for keeping in balance the unique, isolated self and the social self. A distinct vocabulary shared with others can bolster psychological security, helping people to both enjoy and endure life together. A fashionable vocabulary gives people a way to adopt another self – a more daring and exciting social self – whose day-to-day life is governed in large part by interaction with others and by the expectations of the culture.

Suggestions for further reading and exploration

The name most associated with slang and other kinds of non-mainstream vocabulary of the English-speaking world is Eric Partridge. In numerous revisions and reprintings, his books *A Dictionary of Slang and Unconventional English* (1984) and *A Dictionary of the Underworld, British and American* (1968) represent the best-known collections of English slang of the twentieth century.

Three major dictionaries of American slang have been published in the past forty years. *Dictionary of American Slang* by Wentworth and Flexner (1960) included many words of everyday American life that had never been printed in a dictionary before, as well as appendices of word lists organized by word-building processes, users, and subject matter. Flexner's explanation of the nature and use of slang ("Preface to the *Dictionary of American Slang*" [reprinted in Chapman 1986: xvii–xxviii]) has still not been surpassed. A completely revised dictionary based on Wentworth and Flexner was published in 1986 with the title *New Dictionary of American Slang* (Chapman 1986). It has now been revised and the original title reinstated (Chapman 1995). Among the innovations of these most recent revisions are typographic marks called *impact symbols* that warn readers of the relative offensiveness of a slang expression. The multi-volume *Random House Historical Dictionary of American Slang* (Lighter 1994 and 1997, with further volumes to come) is the most ambitious project of American slang lexicography. It is the work of a single scholar, who began collecting slang as a teenager, and the first volume contains an excellent essay on the history of slang in America. Dalzell (1996) traces the development of the slang of middle-class American youth, and *Cool: the Signs and Meanings of Adolescence* (Danesi 1994) illustrates the role of talk among high school students in Toronto in the early 1990s. *Slang U!* (Munro 1989) shows the in-group vocabulary in use among students at UCLA during a single academic year.

The world wide web has brought the collecting of words into a new era for professional and amateur dictionary makers alike. The publishers Merriam-Webster *http://www.m-w.com* and Random House *http://www.randomhouse.com* maintain free user-friendly websites about words. Customarily they feature "new words" and a "word of the day," many of which are slang. Word lovers surfing the web need not be content with the sites of commercial publishers, however. *World Wide Words http://www.quinion.com/words/* contains articles about the origin, usage, and meaning of various words, as well as lists and citations of brand new words, mostly from British sources. Webpages devoted to slang are as ephemeral as slang itself, with new ones being spun and others turning into cobweb sites every day.

References

Bailey, Richard W. 1996. *Nineteenth-Century English*. Ann Arbor: University of Michigan Press.

Chapman, Robert L., ed. 1986. *New Dictionary of American Slang*. New York: Harper and Row.

  1995. *Dictionary of American Slang*, 3rd edn. New York: HarperCollins.

Chuck D. 1999. "The Sound of Our Young World," *Time* (February 28). P. 66.

Dalzell, Tom. 1996. *Flappers 2 Rappers: American Youth Slang*. Springfield MA: Merriam-Webster.

Danesi, Marcell. 1994. *Cool: the Signs and Meanings of Adolescence*. Toronto: University of Toronto Press.

Dumas, Bethany K. and Jonathan Lighter. 1978. "Is *Slang* a Word for Linguists?" *American Speech* 53: 5–17.

Eble, Connie. 1996. *Slang and Sociability: In-Group Language Among College Students*. Chapel Hill, NC: University of North Carolina Press.

Lee, Margaret G. 1999. "Out of the Hood and into the News: Borrowed Black Verbal Expressions in a Mainstream Newspaper," *American Speech* 74: 369–88.

Lighter, Jonathan. 1994. *Random House Historical Dictionary of American Slang*. Vol. 1, A-G. New York: Random House.

  1997. *Random House Historical Dictionary of American Slang*. Vol. 2, H-O. New York: Random House.

McKnight, George H. 1923. *English Words and their Background*. New York: Appleton and Co.

Munro, Pamela. 1989. *Slang U!* New York: Harmony House.

Partridge, Eric. 1968. *A Dictionary of the Underworld, British and American*, 3rd edn. London: Macmillan

    1984. *A Dictionary of Slang and Unconventional English*. Ed. Paul Beale. 8th edn. London: Macmillan.

Scholz, Arno. 1998. "[rep] oder [rap]? Aneignung und Umkodierung der Hip-Hop-Kultur in Italien." In *Jugendsprache langue des jeunes youth language*, eds. Jannis K. Androutsopoulos and Arno Scholz. Frankfurt am Main: Peter Lang. Pp. 233–57.

Wentworth, Harold and Stuart Berg Flexner, eds. 1960. *Dictionary of American Slang*. New York: Crowell.

21 Hip Hop Nation Language

H. SAMY ALIM

Editors' introduction

This chapter is a good example of how rapidly American English can change, for it deals with a phenomenon that had scarcely begun when the first edition of *Language in the USA* was published in 1980. "Rapper's Delight," the first hip hop song, was recorded in 1979. Between then and now, rapping ("the aesthetic placement of verbal rhymes over musical beats") and other elements of hip hop have come to dominate popular music and youth culture, not only in the USA but all over the world, including Africa, Europe, and Asia. Among the five other hip hop elements identified in this chapter are DJing (record spinning) and breakdancing (streetdancing). Like rappin, all had their roots in the streets, party and concert halls, and other performance venues of African America. Although African Americans still predominate on the American hip hop scene, performers now come from other ethnic groups too (e.g., Eminem, who is white, and Fat Joe, who is Puerto Rican).

Pointing to the frequency with which it comes up in song and album titles and in his own interviews with writers and hip hop artists, H. Samy Alim argues that language – especially Hip Hop Nation Language (HHNL) – is central to the Hip Hop Nation (the "borderless" composite of hip hop communities worldwide). He identifies ten tenets of HHNL, including its rootedness in African American language and discursive practices, its regional variability, its synergistic combination of speech, music, and literature, and its links with surrounding sociopolitical circumstances, like police brutality and the disproportionate incarceration of the African American hip hop generation.

Much of the distinctiveness of HHNL comes from its inventiveness with vocabulary, and Alim provides several rich examples of this, from "Puffy" Combs' popularizing of *benjamins* for '$100 bills' to E-40's coinage of new slang terms like *What's crackulatin* for 'What's happenin.' But although Alim agrees with previous researchers that the grammar of HHNL is essentially that of African American Language (AAL), the correspondence is not complete. For instance, hip hop lyrics provide examples of invariant *be* before noun phrases (e.g., "Dr. Dre be the name") – an environment in which most conversation-based AAVE studies did not note it – and there is some question about whether its meaning is "habitual" in the usual sense. Hip hop artists sometimes exploit regional pronunciation features to mark their distinctiveness. Finally, HHNL richly exploits other discourse and discursive features of AAL, such as call and response, multilayered totalizing expression, and signifyin.

Hip hop culture and its investigation in the street

> The Black Language is constructed of – alright let me take it all the way back
> to the slave days and use something that's physical. All the slavemasters gave
> our people straight chittlins and greens, you feel me, stuff that they wasn't
> eating. But we made it into a delicacy. Same thing with the language. It's
> the *exact* same formula. How our people can take the *worst*, or take our bad
> condition, and be able to turn it into something that we can benefit off of.
> Just like the drums. They didn't want the slaves playing drums because we
> was talkin through the drums. "What the hell did my slaves do? Oh, no, cut
> that! Take them drums!" you feel me? So through the music, that's kinda
> like going on now with the rap thang. It's *ghetto* music. People talkin about
> they issues and crime and, you feel me? "Don't push me cuz I'm close to the
> eeedge!" [Rappin Grandmaster Flash and the Furious Five's "The Message"]
> You feel me? He talkin about, "Man, I'm so fed up with you people in this
> society, man." So this is the voice of the ghetto. The rap come from the voice
> of the ghetto . . . Hip hop and the streets damn near is one, you might as well
> say that . . . Straight from the streets.   [Interview with rapper JT the Bigga
> Figga, cited partially in Alim 2000]

Hip hop culture is sometimes defined as having four major elements: MCing
(rappin), DJing (spinnin), breakdancing (streetdancing), and graffiti art (writing).
To these, KRS-One adds knowledge as a fifth element, and Afrika Bambaata, a
founder of the Hip Hop Cultural Movement, adds overstanding. Even with six
elements, this definition of a culture is quite limited in scope, and it is useful to
distinguish between the terms hip hop and rap. Rappin, one aspect of hip hop
culture, consists of the aesthetic placement of verbal rhymes over musical beats,
and it is this element that has predominated in hip hop cultural activity in recent
years. Thus, language is perhaps the most useful means with which to read the
various cultural activities of the Hip Hop Nation (HHN). This chapter provides
a sociolinguistic profile of language use within the HHN in the sociocultural
context of the streets. The chapter also examines the varied and rich hip hop
cultural modes of discourse.

Sociolinguists have always been interested in analyzing language and language
use within varying contexts. Given a healthy respect for vernacular languages
among sociolinguists, and given the richly varied and diverse speech acts and
communicative practices of the HHN, it is surprising that until the late 1990s no
American sociolinguist had written about hip hop culture in any major academic
journal. It was a Belgian student of African history and linguistics at the University of Ghent who first collected data about hip hop culture in the Lower East Side
of New York City in 1986–87. In his quest to learn about the social and cultural
context of rap performances, Remes (1991) produced one of the earliest sociolinguistic studies of rappin in a hip hop community (the borderless HHN comprises
numerous hip hop communities around the world). His pioneering study provided a brief account of the origin of rap, identified several "Black English"

linguistic features found in rap, and highlighted the communicative practices of call-and-response and verbal battling. Only in 1997 did sociolinguist Geneva Smitherman publish her pioneering analysis of the communicative practices of the HHN (Smitherman 1997, presented before an audience in South Africa in 1995).

Since then sociolinguists have presented papers at professional conferences and published in academic journals. In 2001 at the thirtieth anniversary meeting of New Ways of Analyzing Variation (or NWAV) Conference, the major gathering of sociolinguists, several scholars participated in a panel called "The Sociolinguistics of Hip Hop: New Ways of Analyzing Hip Hop Nation Language." To paraphrase the poet–dramatist Amiri Baraka, a leading figure of the Black Arts Movement of the 1960s and 1970s, African American linguists are now celebrating hip hop culture and beginning to see that the "Hip Hop Nation is Like Ourselves."

To be fair, at least since 1964, there has been considerable scholarship on language use within what are now called hip hop communities. It started with investigations "deep down in the jungle" in the streets of South Philly ("it's like a jungle sometimes it makes me wonder how I keep from goin under"[1]) that recorded "black talkin in the streets" of America (Abrahams 1964, 1970, 1976) and the analysis of "language behavior" of Blacks in Oakland (Mitchell-Kernan 1971) to the analysis of the narrative syntax and ritual insults of Harlem teenagers "in the inner city" (Labov 1972) to the critical examination of "the power of the rap" in the "Black Idiom" of the Black Arts Movement rappers and poets (Smitherman 1973, 1977) and an elucidation of the "language and culture of black teenagers" who skillfully "ran down some lines" in South Central Los Angeles (Folb 1980). In myriad ways, then, scholars had prepared the field for the extraordinary linguistic phenomenon that was about to leave an indelible mark on the language of parts of the English-speaking world. This linguistic phenomenon is, of course, hip hop culture. Most of the works cited above were published before the advent of the first hip hop recording in 1979, the Sugar Hill Gang's "Rapper's Delight." By describing the linguistic patterns and practices of African Americans in the "inner cities," these scholars were studying the linguistic forebears of the HHN. Some of the remaining sections of this chapter will show that language use within the HHN is intricately linked to language use within other African American institutions, such as churches and mosques, as well as to the everyday linguistic practices of Black folk in their communities from the hood to the amen corner.

The work of these pioneering scholars and others demonstrated the creativity, ingenuity, and verbal virtuosity of Africans in America by examining language use at the very loci of linguistic-cultural activity. What is the locus of the linguistic-cultural activity known as hip hop? "The street is hardcore and it is the rhythmic

---

[1] Grandmaster Flash and the Furious Five released "The Message" in 1982 and it became one of the first major hip hop records to document street life and street consciousness. The line, "It's like a jungle sometimes it makes me wonder how I keep from goin under" is perhaps one of the most frequently quoted hip hop choruses to this day. In the epigraph to this chapter, we see JT the Bigga Figga rappin another part of the chorus, "Don't push me cuz I'm close to the eeedge!"

locus of the Hip Hop world" (Spady 1991: 406, 407). Foregrounding the streets as the site, sound, and soul of hiphopological activity allows one to gain a more thorough understanding of the origins and sociocultural context of hip hop culture, which is critical to understanding language use within this Nation. Rapper Busta Rhymes, often introduced on stage as being "straight from the muthafuckin street," defends the introduction with his characteristic tenacity:

> What do you mean what it mean?! It's straight and plain, plain and simple. Hip hop is street music! It ain't come from nobody's house! You know what I'm saying? It's something that we all gathered in the street to do. As far as the founders of the hip hop thing, you know what I'm saying, the hip hop way of life, it was established in the street. It wasn't established in people's houses, in people's homes, you know what I'm saying? People came from their homes to celebrate the culture of hip hop in the parks, in the streets, on the street corners, you know what I'm saying?   (Spady, Lee, and Alim 1999: 183)

"Rap artists affirm that one has to come from the streets, or understand the urban black street tradition, in order to properly interpret and perform rap music," according to one ethnomusicologist (Keyes 1991). In the new millennium, the streets continue to be a driving force in hip hop culture. On "Streets Done Raised Us" (2001), rappers Drag-On and Baby Madison extend the notion that the streets are the center of hip hop cultural activity because for many young Black hip hop artists the streets are the locus of life itself. And as if to make certain of no misunderstanding, the L.O.X. proudly proclaim *We Are the Streets* – equating self and street (2000).

Answering calls for Black linguists to set the standards for linguistic research on the language of Black Americans (Labov 1972, Hymes 1981), Baugh (1983: 36) went straight "to the people" in a variety of social contexts where "black street speech breathes." He writes: "It is one thing to recognize the need to gather data from representative consultants, but it is another matter altogether to get the job done." The "code of the streets" (Anderson 1999) does not look fondly upon someone carrying a tape recorder and asking too many questions, particularly in a cultural environment where people avoid "puttin their business out in the street" at all costs.

The hip hop saturated streets of America today are quite different from the streets of yesteryear. The changing nature of the city streets in the last decade of the twentieth century has been captured by Spady (1991: 407): "Changing. Those streets of yesteryear are no more. Now it is crack-filled and gang-banged. Loose and cracked. Yet most of our people walk straight through these streets night and day. Risking lives. But this is a risqué world . . . The street is hardcore and it is the locus of the Hip Hop world." What do we mean by hip hop saturated streets? In urban areas across the nation, it is clear that young hip hop heads exist in a state of hiphopness – their experience is saturated with the sights, sounds, smells, and stares of what it means to be a hip hop being. It is the "dynamic and constant sense of being alive in a hip hop, rap conscious, reality based world," Spady (1993: 95–96) explains. He writes:

> Hip hop is preeminently a cultural free space. Its transformatory and eman- cipatory powers are evident each time you see a young blood locked to the music being transmitted through the earphone. They exist in a community of expressive rebellion, in states of **always always**, altering what has tradition- ally been the culture of the ruling class.

The streets are saturated on multiple levels. An illuminating study of the "New Black Poetry" of the 1960s and 1970s uses the term "saturation" to mean both "the communication of Blackness in a given situation" and "a sense of fidelity to the observed and intuited truth of the Black Experience" (Henderson 1973: 62). In the hip hop saturated streets of America, we are speaking of the communication of the hip hop mode of being (Spady and Alim 1999) and the sense of fidelity to the absolute truth of existing in a state of hiphopness. A close examination of the hip hop saturated streets of America reveals that the street is not just a physical space – it is a site of creativity, culture, cognition, and consciousness. When Jigga (Jay-Z) said "the streets is watchin," and Beans (Beanie Sigel) turned it into "the streets is not only watchin, but they talkin now," they extended the notion of the streets into a living, breathing organism, with ears to hear, eyes to see, and a mouth to speak. Examination of hip hop culture and language must begin in the streets.

Hip Hop Nation Language [HHNL]

My own research on Hip Hop Nation Language and hip hop culture in general has led to the streets, homes, cars, jeeps, clubs, stadiums, backstage, performances, hotels, religious centers, conferences and ciphers (highly competitive lyrical cir- cles of rhymers) where hip hop lives – up inside the "actual lived experiences in the corrugated spaces that one finds reflected in the lyrical content of rap songs" (Spady, Dupres, and Lee 1995). The centrality of language to the HHN is evident in such song and album titles as the "New Rap Language" (Treacherous Three 1980), "Wordplay" (Bahamadia 1996), "Gangsta Vocabulary" (DJ Pooh 1997), "Project Talk" (Bobby Digital 1998), "Slang Editorial" (Cappadonna 1998), *Real Talk 2000* (Three-X-Krazy 2000), "Ebonics" (Big L 2000), *Country Grammar* (Nelly 2000), and *Project English* (Juvenile 2001). In numerous ethnographic interviews, I have found that language is a favorite topic of discussion in the HHN, and its members are willing to discuss it with great fervor – and to defend its use.

What do we mean by "Nation Language"? In exploring the development of nation language in Anglophone Caribbean poetry, Caribbean historian, poet, and literary and music critic Kamau Brathwaite (1984: 13) writes: "Nation language is the language which is influenced very strongly by the African model, the

African aspect of our New World/Caribbean heritage. English it may be in terms of some of its lexical features. But in its contours, its rhythm and timbre, its sound explosions, it is not English."

Concerned with the literature of the Caribbean and the sociopolitical matrix within which it is created, Brathwaite used the term "nation language" in contrast to "dialect." Familiar with the pejorative meanings of the term "dialect" in the folk linguistics of the people, he writes that while nation language can be considered both English and African at the same time, it is an English which is like a "howl, or a shout, or a machine-gun or the wind or a wave." Then he likened it to the blues. Surely, nation language is like hip hop (as rapper Raekwon spits his "machine-gun-rap" (1999)). HHNL is, like Brathwaite's description, new in one sense and ancient in another. It comprises elements of orality, total expression, and conversational modes (Brathwaite 1984).

Rapper Mystikal, known for having a unique, highly energetic rhyming style highlighted with lyrical sound explosions, provides a perfect example of Nation Language when he raps: "You know what time it is, nigga, and you know who the fuck this is/ DAANNN-JAH!!! [Danger] DAANNN-JAH!!! [Danger]/Get on the FLO' [floor]!/ The nigga right, yeaaahhHHH!"[2] (2000). Mystikal starts out speaking to his listener in a low, threatening growl, asserting his individuality ("you know who the fuck this is"), and then explodes as if sounding an alarm, letting everyone know that they have entered a dangerous verbal zone! "Get on the FLO'!" has a dual function – simultaneously warning listeners to lie down before the upcoming lyrical "DAANNN-JAH!" and directing them to get on the dance floor. When rapper Ludacris (2001) commands his listeners to "ROOOLLLL OUT!" and raps: "Oink, Oink, PIG! PIG! Do away with the POORRK-uh/ Only silverwuurrr [silverware] I need's a steak knife and FOORRK-uh!" he stresses his words emphatically, compelling one to do as he says. In that brief example, he is in conversation with African American Muslim and Christian communities currently dialoguing about the eating of swine flesh (which Muslims consider unholy).

When we speak of "language," we are defining the term in a sense that is congruent with the HHN's "linguistic culture" (Schiffman 1996), and HHNL can be situated in the broader context of African American speech:

> There is no single register of African American speech. And it's not words and intonations, it's a whole attitude about speech that has historical rooting. It's not a phenomenon that you can isolate and reduce to linguistic characteristics. It has to do with the way a culture conceives of the people inside of that culture. It has to do with a whole complicated protocol of silences and speech, and how you use speech in ways other than directly to communicate information. And it has to do with, certainly, the experiences that the people in the speech situation bring into the encounter. What's fascinating to me about African

---

[2] The transcription of HHNL into print often leaves a lot to be desired. I have attempted to reconstruct the verbal agility of these hip hop artists on the printed page, but, as Brathwaite (1984) admits, it is best for the reader to listen along to the music whenever possible (see discography).

> American speech is its spontaneity, the requirement that you not only have a
> repertoire of vocabulary or syntactical devices/constructions, but you come
> prepared to do something in an attempt to meet the person on a level that
> both uses the language, mocks the language, and recreates the language.
> (Wideman 1976: 34)

On her single recording "Spontaneity" (1996), Philadelphia rapper Bahamadia
validates Wideman's assertion. She raps about her "verbal expansion" in a stream
of consciousness style: "Rip here be dizz like everybody's on it cause eternal
verbal expansion keeps enhancin brain child's ability to like surpass a swarm
of booty-ass-no-grass-roots-havin-ass MC's." The verbal architect constructs her
rhymes by consciously stretching the limitations of the "standard" language. In
describing her lyrical influences, she cites rappers Kool Keith of the Ultramagnetic
MCs, De La Soul, and Organized Konfusion as "masters at what they do in that
they explore the English language and they try to push the boundaries and go
against the grains of it, you know what I mean?" (Spady and Alim 1999: xviii).

"It's a very active exchange," says Wideman (1976: 34). "But at the same
time as I say that, the silences and the refusal to speak is just as much a part, in
another way, of African American speech." Rapper Fearless of the group Nemesis
exemplifies the point: envisioning rappers, including himself, among the great
orators and leaders in the Black community, he says:

> I always looked up to great orators like Martin Luther King, Malcolm X.
> Anybody who could ever stand up and persuade a group of young men or a
> nation . . . Just the way they were able to articulate. The way they emphasized
> their words. And the way they would use pauses. They would actually use
> *silence* powerfully . . . Just the way they made words cause feelings in you,
> you know what I'm saying? Just perpetuate thought within people, you know.
> (Spady and Alim 1999: xviii)

So "language" in HHNL obviously refers not only to the syntactic constructions of the language but also to the many discursive and communicative practices, the attitudes toward language, understanding the role of language in both
binding/bonding community and seizing/smothering linguistic opponents, and
language as concept (meaning clothes, facial expressions, body movements, and
overall communication).

In addition to the above, HHNL can be characterized by ten tenets.

(1) HHNL is rooted in African American Language (AAL) and com-
     municative practices (Spady 1991, Smitherman 1997, Yasin 1999).
     Linguistically, it is "the newest chapter in the African American book
     of folklore" (Rickford and Rickford 2000). It is a vehicle driven by
     the culture creators of hip hop, themselves organic members of the
     broader African American community. Thus HHNL both reflects and
     expands the African American Oral Tradition.

(2) HHNL is just one of the many language varieties used by African Americans.

(3) HHNL is widely spoken across the country, and used/borrowed and adapted/transformed by various ethnic groups inside and outside of the United States.

(4) HHNL is a language with its own grammar, lexicon, and phonology as well as unique communicative style and discursive modes. When an early hip hop group, The Treacherous Three, rhymed about a "New Rap Language" in 1980, they were well aware of the uniqueness of the language they were rappin in.

(5) HHNL is best viewed as the synergistic combination of speech, music, and literature. Yancy (1991) speaks of rap as *musical literature* (or rhythmic-praxis discourse)." Henderson (1973) asserts that the Black poetry of the 1960s and 1970s is most distinctly Black when it derives its form from Black speech and Black music. HHNL is simultaneously the spoken, poetic, lyrical, and musical expression of the HHN.

(6) HHNL includes attitudes about language and language use (see Pharcyde dialogue below).

(7) HHNL is central to the identity and the act of envisioning an entity known as the HHN.

(8) HHNL exhibits regional variation (Morgan 2001a). For example, most members of the HHN recognize Master P's signature phrase, *Ya heeeaaard may?* ('You heard me?') as characteristic of a southern variety of HHNL. Even within regions, HHNL exhibits individual variation based on life experiences. For example, because California rapper Xzibit grew up in the hip hop saturated streets of Detroit, New Mexico and California, his HHNL is a syncretization of all these Hip Hop Nation Language varieties.

(9) The fundamental aspect of HHNL – and, to some, perhaps the most astonishing aspect – is that it is central to the lifeworlds of the members of the HHN and suitable and functional for all of their communicative needs.

(10) HHNL is inextricably linked with the sociopolitical circumstances that engulf the HHN. How does excessive police presence and brutality shift the discourse of the HHN? How do disproportionate incarceration rates and urban gentrification impact this community's language? As Spady (1993) writes: "Hip Hop culture [and language] mediates the corrosive discourse of the dominating society while at the same time it functions as a subterranean subversion . . . Volume is turned up to tune out the decadence of the dominant culture."

Rappers are insightful examiners of the sociopolitical matrix within which HHNL operates. Discussing the role of HHNL in hip hop lyrics, Houston's Scarface concludes that HHNL functions as a communal "code of communication" for the HHN:

It's a code of communication, too ... Because we can understand each other when we're rapping. You know, if I'm saying, [in a nasal, mocking voice] "Well, my friend, I saw this guy who shot this other guy and ..." I break that shit down for you and you say, "Goddamn, man! Them muthafuckas is going crazy out where this dude's from." You know what I'm saying? It's just totally different. It's just a code of communication to me. I'm letting my partner know what's going on. And anything White America can't control they call "gangsters." *Shit!* I get real. Politicians is gangsters, goddamn. The presidents is the gangsters because they have the power to change everything. That's a gangster to me. That's my definition of gangster.   (Spady, Lee, and Alim 1999: 301)

Members of Tha Pharcyde actively debated the concept of HHNL:

BOOTY BROWN: There's more than just one definition for words! We talk in slang. We always talk basically in slang. We don't use the English dictionary for every sentence and every phrase that we talk!

PHARCYDE: No, there's a lot of words out of the words that you just said which all ...

BOOTY BROWN: Yeah, but the way I'm talking is not the English language ...We're not using that definition ... We're making our own ... Just like they use any other word as a slang, *my brotha*! Anything. I'm not really your brother. Me and your blood aren't the same, but I'm your brother because we're brothas. That's slang ... We make up our *own* words. I mean, it depends whose definition you glorify, okay? That's what I'm saying. Whose definition are you glorifying? Because if you go by my definition of "Black," then I can say "a Black person." But if you go by the *Webster Dictionary's* ... You have your own definition. It's your definition.

(Spady, Lee, and Alim 1999: xix)

Sociolinguistically, so much is happening in the first exchange above. The HHN continues to "flip the script" (reverse the power of the dominant culture). Scarface is reacting to the media's labeling of reality-based rap lyrics as "gangster." By redefining gangster, he effectively turns the tables on what he believes is an oppressive state. If the presidents have the power to change everything, why ain't a damn thing changed?

In Tha Pharcyde conversation, when the *brotha* says the way he is talking is not the English language, he is talking about much more than slang. He asks point-edly, "Whose definition are you glorifying?" By making up your own words, he attests, you are freeing yourself from linguistic colonization (Wa Thiongo 1992). In an effort to combat the capitalistic comodification of hip hop culture, and to "unite and establish the common identity of the HHN," KRS-One refined the definition of hip hop terms and produced a document known as "The Refinitions"

(2000) – putting the power of redefinition to action. KRS defines the language of hip hop culture as "street language" and proposes that "Hiphoppas" speak an Advanced Street Language, which includes "the correct pronunciation of one's native and national language as it pertains to life in the inner-city." KRS is reversing "standard" notions of correctness and appropriateness, realizing that the HHN has distinct values and aesthetics that differ from the majority culture. Clearly, members of the HHN would agree that the use of AAL stems "from a somewhat disseminated rejection of the life-styles, social patterns, and thinking in general of the Euro-American sensibility," as the writer of the first AAL dictionary outside of the Gullah area put it (Major 1970: 10).

The relationship between HHNL and AAL: lexicon, syntax, and phonology

> "Dangerous dialect/ Dangerous dialect/ I elect . . . to impress America." That's it, that's what it was about . . . Dangerous dialect, dangerous wording, you know what I mean? "I elect," that I pick, you know. "To impress America." That's what I pick to impress America, that dangerous dialect, you know. (San Quinn, 2000, Alim and Spady, unpublished interview)

The relationship between HHNL and AAL is a familial one. Since hip hop's culture creators are members of the broader African American community, the language that they use most often when communicating with each other is AAL. HHNL can be seen as the *submerged area* (Brathwaite 1984: 13) of AAL that is used within the HHN, particularly during hip hop centered cultural activities, but also during other playful, creative, artistic, and intimate settings. This conception of HHNL is broad enough to include the language of rap lyrics, album interludes, hip hop stage performances, and hip hop conversational discourse. African Americans are on the cutting edge of the sociolinguistic situation in the USA (as evidenced by abundant recent sociolinguistic research on the topic). HHNL, thus, is the cutting edge of the cutting edge.

A revised edition of the lexicon of "Black Talk" (Smitherman 1994, 2000) begins with a chapter entitled, "From Dead Presidents to the Benjamins." The term *dead presidents* (meaning 'money' and referring to American notes with images of dead presidents) has been in use in the African American community since the 1930s. In the late 1990s, hip hop group dead prez both shortened the term and made explicit its multivariate meanings (within the revolutionary context of their rhymes and philosophy, they are surely hinting at assassination – a form of verbal subversion). The *benjamins* is a term from the late 1990s popularized by rapper Sean "Puffy" Combs (P. Diddy).

While several scholars and writers have produced work on the lexicon of AAL (Turner 1949, Major 1970, 1994, Anderson 1994, Smitherman 1994, 2000, Stavsky, Mozeson and Mozeson 1995, Dillard 1977, Holloway and Vass 1997), it is important to note that hip hop artists, as street linguists and lexicographers, have published several dictionaries of their own. Old school legend Fab Five Freddy (Braithwaite 1992, 1995) documented the "fresh fly flavor" of the words and phrases of the hip hop generation (in English and German). Atlanta's Goodie Mob and several other artists have published glossaries on the inside flaps of their album covers. Of course, as lexicographers hip hop artists are only continuing the tradition of Black musicians, for many jazz and bebop artists compiled their own glossaries, most notable among them Cab Calloway (1944), Babs Gonzales, and Dan Burley.

Vallejo rapper E-40 discusses the genesis of *E-40's Dictionary Book of Slang, vol. 1* (2003):

> I feel that I *am* the ghetto. The majority of street slang . . . "It's all good." "Feel me." "Fo' shiiiiiziiie," all that shit come from 40. "What's up, folks?" As a matter of fact, I'm writing my own dictionary book of slang right now . . . It's a street demand [for it]. Everywhere I go people be like, "Dude, you need to put out a dictionary. Let them know where all that shit come from," you know what I mean?   (Spady, Lee, and Alim 1999: 290)

E-40 is credited with developing a highly individualized repertoire of slang words and phrases. If he were to say something like, "What's crackulatin, pimpin? I was choppin it up wit my playa-potna last night on my communicator – then we got to marinatin, you underdig – and I come to find out that the homie had so much fedi that he was tycoonin, I mean, pimpin on some real boss-status, you smell me?" not very many people would understand him. ("crackulatin" = happening, an extended form of "crackin"; "pimpin" is sometimes used as a noun to refer to a person, like, "homie"; "choppin it up" = making conversation; "playa-potna" = partner, friend; "communicator" = cell phone; "marinatin" = a conversation where participants are reasoning on a subject; "underdig" = understand; "fedi" = money; "tycoonin" = being a successful entrepreneur; "pimpin" = being financially wealthy; "boss-status" = managing things like a CEO; "you smell me?" = you feel me? or, you understand me?)

In HHNL, *pimp* refers not only to someone who solicits clients for a prostitute; it has several other meanings. One could be *pimpin a Lex* ('driving a Lexus while looking flashy'), suffering from *record company pimpin* ('the means by which record companies take advantage of young Black artists lacking knowledge of the music industry') or engaging in *parking lot pimpin* ('hanging around the parking lot after large gatherings'). As we also saw above, *pimpin* can also refer generally to an individual, or specifically to one who sports a flashy lifestyle. The word *politickin* can refer to the act of speaking about political subjects relevant to the Black community, simply holding a conversation, or trying to develop a relationship with a female. One might catch *frostbite* or get *goosebumps* from all of the *ice* they got on [*ice* = 'diamonds']. In the HHN, *rocks* can be a girl's best friend ('diamonds') or a community's silent killer ('crack cocaine'), while *to rock* can mean 'to liven up a party,' 'to wear a fashionable article of clothing,' or 'to have sexual intercourse.'

Given the fluidity of HHNL, speakers take a lot of pride in being the originators and innovators of terms that are consumed by large numbers of speakers. Rappers, as members of distinct communities, also take pride in regional lexicon. For instance, the term *jawn* emerged in the Philadelphia hip hop community. *Jawn* is what can be called a context-dependent substitute noun – a noun that substitutes for any other noun, with its definition so fluid that its meaning depends entirely upon context. For instance, you can say, *Oh, that's da jawn!* for *da bomb!* if you think something is superb; "Did you see that *jawn*?" for 'female' when an attractive female walks by; "I like that new Beanie *jawn*" for 'song,' when the song is played on the radio, and so on. Recently, Philadelphia's Roots have handed out T-shirts with "JAWN" written on the front, advocating the use of the distinctive Philly hip hop term. Placed in a broader context, the meaning of the distinct lexicon of HHNL can be nicely summed up: "Slick lexicon is hip-hop's Magna Carta, establishing the rights of its disciples to speak loudly but privately, to tell America about herself in a language that leaves her puzzled" (Rickford and Rickford 2000: 86).

Several scholars have written that the syntax of HHNL is essentially the same as that of AAL (Remes 1991, Smitherman 1997, 2000, Morgan 1999, Spady and Alim 1999, Yasin 1999, Rickford and Rickford 2000, Morgan 2001b). This is true. We must also examine the syntax of HHNL closely enough to elucidate how the language users are behaving both within and beyond the boundaries of AAL syntax. What is happening syntactically when Method Man gets on the air and proclaims, "Broadcasting live from the Apocalypse, it be I, John Blazzzazzziiinnnyyyyy!" (KMEL 2001b)? What is happening when Jubwa of Soul Plantation writes in his autobiography: "Jubwa be the dope mc, freestylin' to the beat deep cover" (cited in Alim 2001). An important question is, How does HHNL confirm our knowledge of AAL syntax – and how does it challenge that knowledge?

Probably the most oft-studied feature of AAL is *habitual* or *invariant be* (see chapter 5, this volume). Early studies of AAL syntax (Labov 1968, Wolfram 1969, Fasold 1972) noted the uniqueness of this feature and were in agreement that it was used for recurring actions (*We be clubbin on Saturdays*) and could not be used in finite contexts (*She be the teacher*). Building upon this research, we see that HHNL provides numerous examples of what I call *be₃* or the "equative copula" in AAL (Alim 2001b). Some examples of this construction (Noun Phrase *be* Noun Phrase) follow:

I be the truth. – Philadelphia's Beanie Sigel
Dr. Dre be the name. – Compton's Dr. Dre
This beat be the beat for the street. – New York's Busta Rhymes
Brooklyn be the place where I served them thangs. – New York's Jay-Z
I be that insane nigga from the psycho ward. – Staten Island's Method Man

These are but a few of countless examples in the corpus of hip hop lyrics, but this equative copula construction can also be found in everyday conversation, as in these examples:

We be them Bay boys. – Bay Area's Mac Mall in a conversation with James G.
   Spady
It [marijuana] be that good stuff. – Caller on the local Bay Area radio station
You know we be some baaad brothas. – Philadelphia speaker in conversation

It is possible that speakers of AAL have begun using this form only recently and that AAL has thus changed. Alternatively, the form may always have been present in the language but escaped the notice of investigators. Certainly it is present in the writings of Black Arts Movement poets of the 1960s and 1970s, most notably in Sonia Sanchez's *We Be Word Sorcerers*. We also find the form being cited in one linguistic study of Black street speech (*They be the real troublemakers*; *Leo be the one to tell it like it is*) (Baugh 1983). It is possible that members of the HHN, with their extraordinary linguistic consciousness and their emphasis on stretching the limits of language, have made this form much more acceptable by using it frequently (Alim, in press).

The HHN's linguistic consciousness refers to HHNL speakers' conscious use of language to construct identity. Addressing the divergence of AAL from standard English, Smitherman and Baugh (2002: 20) write:

> Graffiti writers of Hip Hop Culture were probably the coiners of the term "phat" (meaning excellent, great, superb) . . . although "phat" is spelled in obvious contrast to "fat," the former confirms that those who use it know that "ph" is pronounced like "f." In other words, those who first wrote "phat" diverged from standard English as a direct result of their awareness of standard English: the divergence was not by chance linguistic error. There is no singular explanation to account for linguistic divergence, but Hip Hop Culture suggests that matters of personal identity play a significant role.

This conscious linguistic behavior deals with matters of spelling and phonemic awareness. (See Morgan 2001a and Olivo 2001 on "spelling ideology.") One case – one of the more controversial uses of language in hip hop culture – is the term *nigga*. The HHN realized that this word had various positive in-group meanings and pejorative out-group meanings, and thus felt the need to reflect the culturally specific meanings with a new spelling (*nigger* becomes "nigga"). A *nigga* is your 'main man,' or 'one of your close companions,' your 'homie.' Recently the term has been generalized to refer to any male (one may even hear something like, "No, I was talkin about Johnny, you know, the white nigga with the hair") although it usually refers to a Black male. Demonstrating hip hop's affinity for acronyms, Tupac Shakur transformed the racial slur into the ultimate positive ideal for young Black males – **N**ever **I**gnorant **G**etting **G**oals **A**ccomplished.

As with the highlighting of regional vocabulary, HHNL speakers intention-ally highlight regional differences in pronunciation by processes such as vowel lengthening and syllabic stress (Morgan 2001b). When Bay Area rappers JT the Bigga Figga and Mac Mall announced the resurgence of the Bay Area to the national hip hop scene with "Game Recognize Game" (1993), they did so using a distinctive feature of Bay Area pronunciation. The Bay Area anthem's chorus repeated this line three times: "Game recognize game in the Bay, man (mane)." *Man* was pronounced "mane" to accentuate this Bay Area pronunciation feature. Also, as fellow Bay Area rapper B-Legit rhymes about slang, he does so using the same feature to stress his Bay Area linguistic origins: "You can tell from my slang I'm from the Bay, mane" (2000).

When Nelly and the St. Lunatics "busted" onto the hip hop scene, they were among the first rappers to represent St. Louis, Missouri on a national scale. Language was an essential part of establishing their identity in a fiercely competitive world of hip hop culture. For example, in a single by the St. Lunatics featuring Nelly they emphasize every word that rhymes with "urrrr" to highlight a well-known (and sometimes stigmatized) aspect of southern/midwest pronunciation (here → *hurrrr*; care → *currrr*; there → *thurrrr*; air → *hurrrr* and so on). By intentionally highlighting linguistic features associated with their city (and other southern cities), they established their tenacity through language as if to say, "We have arrived."

Nelly and the St. Lunatics are conscious not only of their pronunciation, but also of their syntax. On his platinum single "Country Grammar" (2000), Nelly proclaims, "My gramma bees Ebonics." Clearly, HHNL speakers vary their grammar consciously. An analysis of copula variation in the speech and the lyrics of hip hop artists concluded that higher levels of copula absence in the artists' lyrics represented the construction of a street conscious identity – where the speaker makes a linguistic-cultural connection to the streets, the locus of the hip hop world (Alim 2002). John Rickford has suggested (in a conference comment made in 2001) that the use of creole syntactic and phonological features by many rappers supports the ability of HHNL speakers to manipulate their grammar consciously. Like San Quinn (see opening quote in this section) HHNL speakers elect dialects to demonstrate their high degree of linguistic consciousness and in order to construct a street-conscious identity.

Hip hop cultural modes of discourse and discursive practices

Keyes (1984: 145) applied Smitherman's (1977) Black modes of discourse to HHNL. Working in hip hop's gestation period, she wrote that "Smitherman schematized four broad categories of black discourse: narrative sequencing, call-response, signification/dozens, and tonal semantics. All of these categories are strategically used in rap music." We know that rappin in and of itself is not entirely new – rather, it is the most modern/postmodern instantiation of the linguistic-cultural practices of Africans in America. Rappers are, after all, "postmodern African griots" (a class of musicians–entertainers who preserved African history through oral narratives) (Smitherman 1997). This section will demonstrate how the strategic use of the Black modes of discourse is manifested in HHNL and how the new ways in which these modes are practiced generate correspondingly new modes of discourse. This section is based on various forms of HHNL data – rap lyrics, hip hop performances and hip hop conversational discourse.

Call and Response

Here is perhaps the most lucid definition of call and response:

> As a communicative strategy this call and response is the manifestation of the cultural dynamic which finds audience and listener or leader and background to be a unified whole. Shot through with action and interaction, Black communicative performance is concentric in quality – the "audience" becoming both observers and participants in the speech event. As Black American culture stresses commonality and group experientiality, the audience's linguistic and paralinguistic responses are necessary to co-sign the power of the speaker's rap or call.   (Daniel and Smitherman 1976, cited in Spady 2000: 59)

The quintessential example of the HHN's use of call and response grows out of the funk performances and is still heard at nearly every hip hop performance today. "[Rapper] Say 'Hoooo!' [Audience] 'Hoooooooo!' [Rapper] Say 'Ho! Ho!' [Audience] 'Ho! Ho!' [Rapper] 'Somebody screeeaaaaammm!' [Audience] 'AAAHHHHHHHHHHHHHH!!!'" Anyone who has ever attended a hip hop performance can bear witness to this foundational call and response mechanism.

A description of a hip hop performance by Philadelphia's Roots paints a picture of a scene where lead MC Black Thought senses that there is a communicative schism developing between him and his Swiss audience (Jackson et al. 2001: 25). The rapper says, "Hold it, hold it, hold it!" and stops the music abruptly. What follows is an "impromptu instruction" in the call and response mode of Black discourse: "Y'all can't get the second part no matter what the fuck I say, right . . . I wonder if it's what I'm saying . . . A-yo! We gonna try this shit one more time because I like this part of the show." Providing more explicit instruction, Thought slows it down a bit: "Aight, Aight this is how I'm gonna break it down. I'm gonna be like "ahh," then everybody gonna be like "ahhh." Then – I don't know what I'm gonna say second but y'all gotta listen close cause then y'all gotta repeat that shit – that's the fun of the game!" Thought is not only providing instruction but he is also administering a challenge to his European audience: either *git sicwiddit* [get sick with it] *or git hitwiddit* [get hit with it]*!* (in this context meaning, 'Become active participants in this activity or get caught off guard looking culturally ignorant!')

Call and response mechanisms are so pervasive in HHNL that talented MCs (rappers, Masters of Ceremonies) have taken this mode to new heights. Mos Def describes one of the elements that made Slick Rick a legendary rapper:

> Slick Rick is one of the greatest MC's ever born because he has so many
> different facilities that he would use. Style. Vocal texture. The way he would
> even record. Like, he was doing call and response with himself! He would
> leave four bars open, and then do another character, you understand what I'm
> saying?   (Alim 2000, unpublished interview)

The individualized uses of call and response in the hip hop cultural mode of
discourse deserve more attention. Also, as is evident from Mos Def's comments,
HHNL speakers can be cognizant of the fact that they are operating within and
expanding upon the African American Oral Tradition. The linguistic and communicative consciousness of the HHN also needs to be explored.

Multilayered totalizing expression

Beyond the explicit instruction, one can witness the multilayered nature of the call
and response mode at hip hop performances where both performer and audience
are fully conversant with hip hop cultural modes of discourse. At the first Spit-
kicker Tour (2000) in San Francisco's Maritime Hall, I observed this multilayered,
multitextual mode. Here's an excerpt from my fieldnotes:

> Maaan, all performers are on stage at once – [DJ] Hi-Tek, Talib [Kweli],
> Common, Biz [Markie], De La [Soul], Pharoahe [Monch] – and they just
> kickin it in a fun-loving communal-type hip hop atmosphere! Common
> and Biz are exchanging lines from his classic hit . . . The DJ from De La
> starts cuttin up the music and before you know it, Common is center stage
> freestylin. The DJ switches the pace of the music, forcing Common to switch
> up the pace of his freestyle [improvisational rap], and the crowd's lovin it!
> 'Ooooooohhhhh!' . . . Hi-Tek and Maseo are circling each other on stage
> giving a series of hi-fives timed to the beat, smilin and laughin all along, as
> the crowd laughs on with them. Common, seizing the energy of the moment,
> says, "This is hip hop music, y'all!" Then he shouts, "It ain't nuthin like hip
> hop music!" and holds the microphone out to the crowd. "It ain't nuthin like
> hip hop music!" they roar back, and the hall is transformed into a old school
> house party frenzy . . . Gotta love this hip hop music.

What is striking about this description is that there are multiple levels of call
and multiple levels of response, occurring simultaneously and synergistically, to
create something even beyond "total expression" (Brathwaite 1984: 18). This
is a *multilayered totalizing expression* that completes the cipher (the process of
constantly making things whole). We witness a call and response on the oral/aural,
physical (body), and spiritual/metaphysical level. My final note ("Gotta love this
hip hop music") captures a moment of realization that meaning resides in what I've
just witnessed – in the creation of a continuum beyond audience and performer.
We hear varied calls made by the DJ and responded to by a freestylin MC; by
the two MC's exchanging lines and by their impromptu leading of the audience
in celebration of hip hop; by the physical reaction of performers to each other

and the audience (who were also slappin hands with the performers); and by the spirited and spiritual response created during the climax of the performance. Like Common says, "Find heaven in this music and God / Find heaven in this music and God / Find heaven in this music and God" (cited in Jackson et al. 2001).

Signifyin and bustin (bussin)

Scholars have studied signification or signifyin – or, in more contemporary, semantically similar Black terms, *bustin, crackin*, and *dissin* (Abrahams 1964, Kochman 1969, Mitchell-Kernan 1971, 1972, Smitherman 1973, 1977). Signifyin has been described as a means to encode messages or meanings in natural conversations, usually involving an element of indirection (Mitchell-Kernan 1972). Ironically noting the difficulty in pin-pointing a dictionary definition for the speech act, Rickford and Rickford (2000: 82) cite Mitchell-Kernan's (1972: 82) attempt:

> The black concept of *signifying* incorporates essentially a folk notion that dictionary entries for words are not always sufficient for interpreting meanings or messages, or that meaning goes beyond such interpretations. Complimentary remarks may be delivered in a left-handed fashion. A particular utterance may be an insult in one context and not in another. What pretends to be informative may intend to be persuasive. Superficially, self-abasing remarks are frequently self-praise.

In Scarface's comments and Tha Pharcyde dialogue given earlier, we see evidence of this folk notion that "standard" dictionaries are insufficient to interpret Black language and life. But looking more closely at Tha Pharcyde dialogue, we witness an extremely sly (skillful and indirect) signification in hip hop conversational discourse. In the dialogue, Booty Brown is advocating the Black folk notion described by Kernan above. He implies that his partner is glorifying a Eurocentric meaning-making system over a meaning-making system that is African derived. This does not become clear until Brown chooses his examples – carefully and cleverly. "Just like they use any other word as a slang, *my brotha!*" He emphasizes the "slang phrase" *my brotha*, as it is usually used as a sign of cultural unity and familial bond between African American males (females will use *my sista* in a similar way).

Then he proceeds to ask the direct question, "Whose definition are you glorifying?" which is, in fact, a statement. Finally, as if to *really* lay it on thick (add insult to injury), he chooses to use the word *Black* to show that *Webster's Dictionary* is inadequate. The heat is diffused when "P" says, "I'm sayin, I'm sayin, that's what I'M sayin!" and they – and others around them – break into laughter. This dialogue is an example of how language is used to remind, scold, shame, or otherwise bring the other into a commonly shared ethic through signification.

We see an example of signifyin in Rapper Bushwick Bill's (of Houston's Geto Boys) description of the ever-changing, fluid and flexible nature of "street slang" and the dangers of not "keepin your ear to the street" (being aware of what's happening around you at all times). In this case, Bushwick is referring to the rapidly evolving street terminology for law enforcement officials. Bushwick takes us deep into the locus of hip hop linguistic-cultural activity:

> You lose flavor. You lose the slang. You lose the basic everyday kickin it, you know, knowing what's going on at all times, you know what I'm saying? Knowing the new names for "5–0s". They ain't even 5–0s no more. They call them "po-pos". That means everything changes. And they call them "one-time", you know what I'm saying? But you got to be in there to know that the police might know these words already. So they got to change up their dialect so that way it sounds like Pig Latin to the police.   (Spady, Lee, and Alim 1999: 308)

Bushwick's comment refers us directly to tenet (10) above. He is describing the changing nature of the various terms for *police* in the streets – from *5–0s* to *po-pos* to *one time*. At one time, bloods referred to the *one-time* as *black and whites* (Folb 1980). The socio-political contexts of many depressed and oppressed Black neighborhoods necessitate these speedy lexical transformations.

Even though the police are not present in the dialogue above, Bushwick signifies on them with a clever one-liner that also serves to buttress his point. After runnin down all of the various terms (which have gone out of vogue as quickly as the police comprehended them), he concludes, "So they got to change up their dialect so that way it sounds like Pig Latin to the police." *Pig Latin* is chosen here, rather than Greek, Chinese, Swahili, or other unfamiliar languages, to echo the fact that at one time police officers were called *pigs*. Bushwick is not only signifyin on the police, but he is also demonstrating yet another term for 'police' that has gone out of fashion! In addition, he is referencing an old form of Afroamericanized Pig Latin that employs innuendo, wordplay, letter and syllabic shifting, rhyming and coded language designed to communicate with those in the know.

Like call and response, signifyin is ubiquitous in hip hop lyrics. In an example of male–female urban verbal play, in "Minute Man" (2001) with Missy Elliot and Ludacris, Jay-Z signifies on female R&B group Destiny's Child. Some insider knowledge is required to fully understand this speech act. Earlier that year, Destiny's Child had released "Independent Women," in which they asked a series of questions of men who dogged ('treated poorly') females. For example, they introduced each question with the word *question* and then proceeded, "How you like them diamonds that I bought?" (to demonstrate to such men that they had their own income). Given that one of Jay-Z's many personas is the *playa-pimp*-type ('one who uses women for sex and money'), he rhymes to the listeners (including Destiny's Child): "I'm not tryin to give you love and affection / I'm tryin to give you 60 seconds of affection / I'm tryin to give you cash, fare and directions / Get your independent-ass outta here, Question!" The signification doesn't become clear until the last line or, really, the last word, when Jay-Z borrows the word *question* from their song (saying it in such a way as to match their rate of speech, tone and pronunciation). The only thing left to do is say, "Oooohhhhhh!"

We also witnessed signification in the call and response section of the Black Thought performance described above. As Jackson (2001) notes, Thought appears to be signifyin on the audience by highlighting their lack of familiarity with Black cultural modes of discourse: "I wonder if it's what I'm saying . . . A-yo!" The Roots have been known to signify on audiences that are not as culturally responsive as they would like them to be. During a 1999 concert at Stanford University, they stopped the music and began singing theme songs from 1980s television shows like "Diff'rent Strokes" and "Facts of Life," snapping their fingers and singing in a corny (not cool) way. The largely white, middle-class audience of college students sang along and snapped their fingers – apparently oblivious to the insult. After the show, the band's drummer and official spokesman, Ahmir, said: "Like if the crowd ain't responding, we've done shows where we've stopped the show, turned the equipment around, and played for the wall, you know" (Alim 1999). In this sense, the Roots remove any hint of indirection and blatantly *bust on* the unresponsive audience.

The examples above make clear that HHNL speakers readily incorporate *signifyin* and *bustin* into their repertoire. Whether hip hop heads are performing, writing rhymes, or just "conversatin," these strategies are skillfully employed. Other hip hop cultural modes of discourse and discursive practices, which fall out of the purview of this chapter, are tonal semantics and poetics, narrative sequencing and flow, battling and entering the cipher. Linguistic scholars of the hip hop generations (we are now more than one) are needed to uncover the complexity and creativity of HHNL speakers. In order to *represent* – reflect any semblance of hip hop cultural reality – these scholars will need to be in direct conversation with the culture creators of a very widely misunderstood Nation.

Acknowledgments

It is my pleasure to acknowledge the assistance and encouragement of John Baugh, Mary Bucholtz, Austin Jackson, Marcyliena Morgan, Geneva Smitherman, James G. Spady, and Arthur Spears in the preparation of this chapter. I would also like to thank Ed Finegan for his scrupulous reading of the manuscript and for his insight and many helpful suggestions, and John Rickford for his support and careful review of an early draft of the manuscript. The chapter has been greatly improved by their efforts as editors. Lastly, much props to my students in Linguistics 74: "The Language of Hip Hop Culture"; they have challenged me to represent to the fullest.

Suggestions for further reading and exploration

For a thorough understanding of the philosophies and aesthetic values of hip hop's culture creators, the Umum Hip Hop Trilogy is an excellent source. Its three volumes (Spady and Eure 1991, Spady et al. 1995, Spady et al. 1999) offer extensive hip hop conversational discourse with such members of the HHN as Ice Cube, Busta Rhymes, Chuck D, Kurupt, Common, Eve, Bahamadia, Grandmaster Flash, and others. These volumes also provide primary source material for scholars of language use within the HHN. For early works on hip hop culture, see Hager (1984), Toop (1984, 1994, 1999), Nelson and Gonzales (1991), Rose (1994), and Potter (1995).

For updates on what's happening in the HHN, the most informative website is Davey D's Hip Hop Corner (www.daveyd.com). Useful hip hop periodicals include *Murder Dog*, *The Source*, *XXL*, *Vibe* and *Blaze*. One might gain the most insight by "reading" the hip hop saturated streets of America.

References

Abrahams, Roger. 1964. *Deep Down in the Jungle: Negro Narrative Folklore from the Streets of Philadelphia*. Chicago: Aldine Publishing Co.

1970. "Rapping and Capping: Black Talk as Art." In *In Black America*, ed. John Szwed. New York: Basic Books.

1976. *Talking Black*. Rowley, MA: Newbury House.

Alim, H. Samy. 1999. "The Roots Rock Memorial Auditorium." "Intermission" section of *The Stanford Daily*, Stanford University.

2000. "360 Degreez of Black Art Comin at You: Sista Sonia Sanchez and the Dimensions of a Black Arts Continuum." In *360 Degreez of Sonia Sanchez: Hip Hop, Narrativity, Iqhawe and Public Spaces of Being*, ed. James G. Spady. Special issue of *BMa: the Sonia Sanchez Literary Review*, 6.1, Fall.

ed. 2001a. *Hip Hop Culture: Language, Literature, Literacy and the Lives of Black Youth*. Special issue of *The Black Arts Quarterly*. Committee on Black Performing Arts: Stanford University.

2001b. "I Be the Truth: Divergence, Recreolization, and the 'New' Equative Copula in African American Language." Paper presented at NWAV 30, Raleigh, North Carolina, October.

2002. "Street Conscious Copula Variation in the Hip Hop Nation," *American Speech* 77: 288–304.

2003a. "On some serious next millenium rap ishhh: Pharoahe Monch, Hip Hop poetics, and the internal rhymes of Internal Affairs," *Journal of English Linguistics* 31(1), 60–84.

2003b. " 'We are the streets': African American Language and the strategic construction of a street conscious identity." In Makoni, S., G. Smitherman, A. Ball, and A. Spears (eds.). *Black Linguistics: Language, Society, and Politics in Africa and the Americas*. New York: Routledge.

In Press. *'You know my Steez': an Ethnographic and Sociolinguistic Study of Styleshifting in a Black American Speech*.

Anderson, Elijah. 1999. *Code of the Street: Decency, Violence, and the Moral Life of the Inner City*. New York: W. W. Norton.

Anderson, Monica. 1994. *Black English Vernacular (From "Ain't" to "Yo Mama": the Words Politically Correct Americans Should Know)*. Highland City FL: Rainbow Books.

Baugh, John. 1983. *Black Street Speech: Its History, Structure, and Survival*. Austin TX: University of Texas Press.

1991. "The Politicization of Changing Terms of Self-Reference Among American Slave Descendants," *American Speech* 66: 133–46.

Braithwaite, Fred. (Fab Five Freddy). 1992. *Fresh Fly Flavor: Words and Phrases of the Hip-Hop Generation*. Stamford CT: Longmeadow Press.

Braithwaite, Fred. 1995. *Hip Hop Slang: English-Deutsch*. Frankfurt am Main, Eichborn.

Brathwaite, Kamau. 1984. *History of the Voice: the Development of Nation Language in Anglophone Caribbean Poetry*. London: New Beacon Books.

Calloway, Cab. 1944. *Hepster's Dictionary: Language of Jive*. Republished as an appendix to Calloway's autobiography, *Of Minnie the Moocher and Me*. 1976. New York: Thomas Y. Crowell.

Daniel, Jack and Geneva Smitherman. 1976. "How I Got Over: Communication Dynamics in the Black Community," *Quarterly Journal of Speech* 62 (February): 26–39.

Dillard, J. L. 1977. *Lexicon of Black English*. New York: Seabury.

Fasold, Ralph. 1972. *Tense Marking in Black English: a Linguistic and Social Analysis*. Washington DC: Center for Applied Linguistics.

Folb, Edith. 1980. *Runnin' Down Some Lines: the Language and Culture of Black Teenagers*. Cambridge: Harvard University Press.

Hager, Steven. 1984. *Hip Hop: the Illustrated History of Breakdancing, Rap Music, and Graffiti*. New York: St. Martin's Press.

Henderson, Stephen. 1973. *Understanding the New Black Poetry: Black Speech and Black Music as Poetic References*. New York: William Morrow.

Holloway, Joseph E. and Winifred K. Vass. 1997. *The African Heritage of American English*. Bloomington: University of Indiana Press.

Hymes, Dell. 1981. "Foreword." In *Language in the U.S.A.*, eds. Charles A. Ferguson and Shirley B. Heath. New York: Cambridge University Press.

Jackson, Austin, Tony Michel, David Sheridan, and Bryan Stumpf. 2001. "Making Connections in the Contact Zones: Towards a Critical Praxis of Rap Music and Hip Hop Culture." In *Hip Hop Culture: Language, Literature, Literacy and the Lives of Black Youth*, ed. H. Samy Alim. Special issue of *The Black Arts Quarterly*. Committee on Black Performing Arts: Stanford University.

JT the Bigga Figga, Personal interview with H. Samy Alim, November, 2000.

Keyes, Cheryl. 1984. "Verbal Art Performance in Rap Music: the Conversation of the 80s," *Folklore Forum* 17(2): 143–52.

   1991. "Rappin' to the Beat: Rap Music as Street Culture Among African Americans." Unpublished Ph.D. diss., Indiana University.

Kochman, Thomas. 1969. "'Rapping' in the Black Ghetto," *Trans-Action* (February): 26–34.

KRS-One. 2000. "The First Overstanding: Refinitions." The Temple of Hip Hop Kulture.

Labov, William. 1972. *Language in the Inner City: Studies in the Black English Vernacular*. Philadelphia: University of Pennsylvania Press.

Labov, William, Paul Cohen, Clarence Robins, and John Lewis. 1968. *A Study of the Non-standard English of Negro and Puerto Rican Speakers in New York City*. Report on Co-operative Research Project 3288. New York: Columbia University.

Major, Clarence. 1970 [1994]. *Juba to Jive: a Dictionary of African American Slang*. New York and London: Penguin.

Mitchell-Kernan, Claudia. 1971. *Language Behavior in a Black Urban Community*. University of California, Berkeley: Language Behavior Research Laboratory.

   1972. "Signifying and Marking: Two Afro-American Speech Acts." In *Directions in Sociolinguistics*, eds. John J. Gumperz and Dell Hymes. New York: Holt, Rinehart and Winston. Pp. 161–79.

Morgan, Aswan. 1999. "Why They Say What Dey Be Sayin': an Examination of Hip-Hop Content and Language." Paper submitted for LING 073, *Introduction to African American Vernacular English*. Stanford University.

Morgan, Marcyliena. 2001a. "Reading Dialect and Grammatical Shout-Outs in Hip Hop." Paper presented at the Linguistic Society of America Convention. Washington DC, January.

   2001b. "'Nuthin' But a G Thang': Grammar and Language Ideology in Hip Hop Identity." In *Sociocultural and Historical Contexts of African American Vernacular English*, ed. Sonja L. Lanehard. Amsterdam: John Benjamins. Pp. 187–210.

Mos Def, Personal interview with H. Samy Alim. October 2000.

Nelson, Havelock and Michael Gonzales. 1991. *Bring the Noise: a Guide to Rap Music and Hip Hop Culture*. New York: Harmony Books.

Olivo, Warren. 2001. "Phat Lines: Spelling Conventions in Rap Music," *Written Language and Literacy* 4(1): 67–85.

Potter, Russell. 1995. *Spectacular Vernaculars: Hip-Hop and the Politics of Postmodernism*. Albany: State University of New York Press.

Remes, Pieter. 1991. "Rapping: a Sociolinguistic Study of Oral Tradition in Black Urban Communities in the United States," *Journal of the Anthropological Society of Oxford*, 22(2), 129–49.

Rickford, John and Russell Rickford. 2000. *Spoken Soul: the Story of Black English*. New York: John Wiley.

Rose, Tricia. 1994. *Black Noise: Rap Music and Black Culture in Contemporary America*. Middletown CT: Wesleyan University Press.

San Quinn, Personal interview with H. Samy Alim and James G. Spady, November 2000.

Schiffman, Harold. 1996. *Linguistic Culture and Language Policy*. London and New York: Routledge.

Smitherman, Geneva 1973. "The Power of the Rap: the Black Idiom and the New Black Poetry," *Twentieth Century Literature: a Scholarly and Critical Journal* 19: 259–74.

    1977 (1986). *Talkin and Testifyin: the Language of Black America*, Houghton Mifflin; reissued, with revisions, Detroit: Wayne State University Press.

    1991. "'What is African to Me?': Language, Ideology and *African American*," *American Speech* 66(2): 115–32.

    1994 [2000]. *Black Talk: Words and Phrases from the Hood to the Amen Corner*. Boston and New York: Houghton Mifflin.

    1997. "'The Chain Remain the Same': Communicative Practices in the Hip-Hop Nation," *Journal of Black Studies*, September.

    2000. *Talkin That Talk: Language, Culture and Education in African America*. London and New York: Routledge.

Smitherman, Geneva and John Baugh. 2002. "The Shot Heard from Ann Arbor: Language Research and Public Policy in African America." *Howard Journal of Communication* 13: 5–24.

Spady, James G. 1993. "'IMA PUT MY THING DOWN': Afro-American Expressive Culture and the Hip Hop Community," *TYANABA: Revue de la Société d'Anthropologie*, December.

    2000. "The Centrality of Black Language in the Discourse Strategies and Poetic Force of Sonia Sanchez and Rap Artists." In *360 Degreez of Sonia Sanchez: Hip Hop, Narrativity, Iqhawe and Public Spaces of Being*, ed. James Spady. Special issue of *BMa: the Sonia Sanchez Literary Review*, 6.1, Fall.

Spady, James G., and H. Samy Alim. 1999. "Street Conscious Rap: Modes of Being." In *Street Conscious Rap*. Philadelphia: Black History Museum/Umum Loh Publishers.

Spady, James G., and Joseph D. Eure, eds. 1991. *Nation Conscious Rap: the Hip Hop Vision*. New York/Philadelphia: PC International Press/Black History Museum.

Spady, James G., Stefan Dupres, and Charles G. Lee. 1995. *Twisted Tales in the Hip Hop Streets of Philly*. Philadelphia: Black History Museum/Umum Loh Publishers.

Spady, James G., Charles G. Lee, and H. Samy Alim. 1999. *Street Conscious Rap*. Philadelphia: Black History Museum/Umum Loh Publishers.

Stavsky, Lois, Isaac Mozeson, and Dani Reyes Mozeson. 1995. *A 2 Z: the Book of Rap and Hip-Hop Slang*. New York: Boulevard Books.

Toop, David. 1984 (1994, 1999). *Rap Attack: from African Jive to New York Hip Hop*. London: Pluto Press.

Turner, Lorenzo. 1949. *Africanisms in the Gullah Dialect*. Chicago: University of Chicago Press.

Wa Thiongo, Ngugi. 1992. *Moving the Center: the Struggle for Cultural Freedom*. London: Heinemann.

Wideman, John. 1976. "Frame and Dialect: the Evolution of the Black Voice in American Literature," *American Poetry Review* 5(5): 34–37.

Wolfram, Walter. 1969. *A Sociolinguistic Description of Detroit Negro Speech*. Washington, DC: Center for Applied Linguistics.

Yancy, George. 1991. "Rapese." Cited in Spady and Eure, eds.

Yasin, Jon. 1999. "Rap in the African-American Music Tradition: Cultural Assertion and Continuity." In *Race and Ideology: Language, Symbolism, and Popular Culture*, ed. Arthur Spears. Detroit: Wayne State University Press.

Discography

B-Legit. 2000. *Hempin Ain't Easy*. Koch International.
Bahamadia. 1996. *Kollage*. EMI Records.
Big L. 2000. *The Big Picture*. Priority Records.
Cappadonna. 1998. *The Pillage*. Sony Records.
DJ Pooh. 1997. *Bad Newz Travels Fast*. Da Bomb/Big Beat/Atlantic Records.
Drag-On and Baby Madison. 2001. *Live from Lenox Ave*. Vacant Lot/Priority Records.
Grandmaster Flash and the Furious Five. 1982. *The Message*. Sugarhill Records.
JT the Bigga Figga. 1993. *Playaz N the Game*. Get Low Recordz.
Juvenile. 2001. *Project English*. Universal Records.
L.O.X. 2000. *We Are the Streets*. Ruff Ryders Records.
Ludacris. 2001. *Word of Mouf*. Universal Records.
Missy Elliot f/ Jay-Z and Ludacris. 2001. *Miss E . . . So Addictive*. Elektra/Asylum.
Mystikal. 2000. *Let's Get Ready*. Jive Records.
Nelly. 2000. *Country Grammar*. Universal Records.
Raekwon. 1999. *Immobilarity*. Sony.
Rza. 1998. *Rza as Bobby Digital in Stereo*. V2/BMG Records.
Three X Krazy. 2000. *Real Talk 2000*. DU BA Records.
Treacherous Three (Kool Moe Dee, LA Sunshine, Special K and DJ Easy Lee). 1980. "New Rap Language." Enjoy Records.

22

Language, gender, and sexuality

MARY BUCHOLTZ

Editors' introduction

A chapter called "Language, Gender, and Sexuality" could hardly have appeared in the first *Language in the USA* because the field of language and gender studies was too young in 1980. Mary Bucholtz here contextualizes her discussion of the subject within the historical, intellectual, and political forces at play in recent decades, and she illustrates how fluid both language use and scholarly understanding of it can be. For decades, many sociolinguists had established correlations between linguistic features such as pronunciations and grammatical forms with fixed social categories like socioeconomic status, sex, and ethnicity. A notable development in the late twentieth century was the rise of feminist studies, gender studies, and studies of sexuality in language and literature. This chapter analyzes language variation from these latter perspectives.

Beginning with "the fundamental insight of feminism" that "the personal is political," Bucholtz describes analyses of women's language in the 1970s and the unprecedented move to replace sexist nouns like *fireman* and *stewardess* and sexist pronouns like *he* (meaning 'he and she') with nongendered expressions (*firefighter*, *flight attendant*, *he and she*, *s/he*). Less well known is the notion of indexes – how "identities form around practices and . . . practices develop around identities." The chapter shows that temporary identities (interaction-specific identities, Bucholtz calls them) such as ring maker or hopscotch player can take precedence over broader identities such as girl, African American, or Latina.

Even more important is the fluid nature of identity and of the role of language, including performed language, in creating identity. Performance and performance language can enact an identity that "may or may not conform to the identity of the performer by others." In other words, identity may be deliberately chosen and performed. Calling some findings of correlational sociolinguistics into question, Bucholtz observes that "studies of the relationship between gender and sexuality bring performance to the forefront because they emphasize the fluidity of categories often believed to be fixed, and they challenge traditional assumptions of what it means to be female or male, feminine or masculine. By suggesting that gender and sex are not natural and inevitable but socially constructed, studies of the performance of these dimensions of identity raise questions about the fixedness of all social categories."

Despite a long tradition of folk beliefs in the USA and elsewhere about how women speak, the scholarly study of language and gender is a relatively recent phenomenon. Developing in response to the emergence of feminism as a political movement, this young and vibrant field changes rapidly as a result of debates and developments both within language and gender studies and within feminist scholarship more generally. It is not surprising that feminism has had such a powerful impact on the formation of language and gender studies, for the fundamental insight of feminism – "The personal is political" – is nowhere more evident than in how language is used by, to, and about women. But there is no single variety of feminism: feminist thinkers disagree on a number of fundamental issues. And although language and gender studies have traditionally focused on research *on* women *by* women from a feminist perspective, men too are increasingly involved in the field both as researchers and as study participants; it is important to keep in mind that men too may be feminists. Moreover, gender is related to but distinct from sexuality, and thus the study of language and sexuality is both a branch of language and gender studies and a subfield in its own right.

For these reasons, the following discussion is not simply a summary of "what we know" about language, gender, and sexuality, but an overview of the historical, intellectual, and political issues that have given rise to different strands of research. I have tried to highlight rather than gloss over these issues in order to show that like all of sociolinguistics the linguistic study of gender and sexuality is embedded in ongoing debates and that these issues, far from being settled, are still open for discussion and further research.

Early language and gender studies: language and sexism

For most Americans, questions about how language interacts with gender are most prominent in their English classes in high school and college in which as part of their instruction in writing they are taught to avoid sexist language. Whereas only a generation ago, masculine forms such as *he* and *chairman* were considered to encompass female referents as well, student writers today are encouraged to use gender-neutral and gender-inclusive nouns and pronouns and to treat women and men in a parallel fashion. Writing handbooks recommend, for example, that compounds with -*man* be replaced by nongendered forms (*police officer* for *policeman*, *firefighter* for *fireman*, etc.) and that *humanity* and *humankind* substitute for *man* and *mankind*. They further urge writers to refer to women and men of equivalent status equivalently: women should not be referred to by first name or by a title such as *Mrs.* (or *Ms.*) when men are referred to by last name alone or as *Dr.*

The promotion of nonsexist language represents perhaps the greatest impact of language and gender scholarship on the American public. But while Americans have generally been eager to be told where to put their prepositions (not at the end of the sentence) and how to protect their infinitives from adverbial interlopers (no split infinitives), guidelines for nonsexist language have not met with the same warm welcome. Such guidelines were slow to catch on and gained ground only with a great deal of resistance from opponents. In fact, the Linguistic Society of America itself adopted guidelines for nonsexist writing as late as 1992, and then only over strong objections from some members of the association, who maintained that the guidelines were prescriptivist in intent and thus counter to the linguistic principle of descriptivism. (For more discussion of language ideologies such as prescriptivism, see chapter 15 by Lippi-Green in this volume.) If linguists have had difficulty coming to agreement over this issue, then feminists have found it an even more challenging task to convince nonlinguists of the importance of nonsexist language.

The use of the masculine pronoun *he* has been a particular source of controversy. Advocates of traditional prescriptive grammar argue that *he*, *his*, and *him* can function in certain contexts as *epicene* pronouns (that is, as pronouns that include both genders). And members of the general public, uneasy about abandoning the prescriptive principles drilled into them in school, are equally skeptical about what at first seemed to many to be a faddish and politically motivated practice. Because the nonsexist language movement grew out of the women's liberation movement of the 1970s, it was viewed with suspicion by those who disagreed with the aims of feminism. It is all the more remarkable, then, that nonsexist language guidelines have been so successful, taking hold not only in high school and college writing handbooks but in the professional publication manuals of a number of fields. In part this success has to do with greater acceptance of certain feminist principles (if not the label *feminism* itself) by most Americans. But some part of the success of gender-inclusive pronouns – such as *she or he* (or *he or she*), *she/he*, and *s/he* – can be attributed to the fact that, unlike other nonsexist language practices, these pronominal forms are limited almost entirely to written and formal contexts of language use. Because they do not occur in everyday speech they do not require an extensive revision of pre-existing linguistic habits. And because they are used only in situations in which language is carefully planned and often edited, they can be consciously learned and used, for learning the linguistic practices associated with formal contexts already involves the mastery of explicit rules, unlike the mostly unconscious acquisition of spoken language. Moreover, some nonsexist alternatives (such as *s/he*) are unpronounceable, and therefore written discourse is more conducive to their use.

The issue of nonsexist pronouns does not arise for ordinary spoken English because most speakers of American English use *they* rather than *he* as the epicene or indefinite pronoun, as in *Somebody left their book on the desk*. But in formal writing the use of *they* to refer to a single person is generally considered "incorrect" from a prescriptive standpoint. Prescriptivists hold that the use of epicene *they* replaces grammatical correctness with political correctness. But some feminists (women and men alike) are proponents of the use of indefinite *they* even in written formal contexts; they point out that the form has a long and respectable history and is found in earlier stages of the English language, along with *he or she*. Epicene *he*, by contrast, entered the language quite late and only took hold by Parliamentary fiat: during the prescriptive grammar craze of the eighteenth century in England a grammarian named John Kirby proposed that *he* should, from that time forward, be understood as including female referents as well. A century later, Parliament banned the official use of *he or she* in favor of *he* (Bodine 1975).

Since few modern-day Americans hold themselves accountable to the laws of the British Parliament, this appeal to history has done a great deal to rebut the objections of prescriptivists and descriptivists alike. But feminist scholars relied on other kinds of research to strengthen their argument as well. Studies of readers showed that those who encountered epicene masculine forms in texts tended to envision male rather than female referents (Martyna 1983). And close analysis of texts revealed that so-called epicene masculine forms in fact often referred to males exclusively: "In practice, the sexist assumption that man is a species of males becomes the fact. Erich Fromm certainly seemed to think so when he wrote that man's 'vital interests' were 'life, food, access to females, etc.' Loren Eisley implied it when he wrote of man that 'his back aches, he ruptures easily, his women have difficulties in childbirth . . .'" (Graham 1975: 62). Some feminists attempted to introduce entirely new epicene pronouns, such as *co*, but they did not catch on. Such efforts to change fixed elements of the linguistic system were often viewed by nonfeminists as ludicrous; even the use of generic *she* as a counterbalance to the overwhelming use of generic *he* was found objectionable, on the grounds that the pronoun called too much attention to itself. Yet many feminists would argue that it is one of the great virtues of these innovative pronominal systems that they require language users to think about linguistic choices – and the social consequences of those choices.

At the same time that battles were being waged over pronouns in the 1970s, feminist scholars were scrutinizing other elements of English for evidence of sexism and misogyny. A set of feminist lexical studies demonstrated that the English lexicon treats women and men differently. For example, over time words for women become more negative or trivialized in their meaning while equivalent terms for men do not shift in meaning: *governess* versus *governor*; *lady* versus *lord*; *courtesan* versus *courtier*, etc. Moreover, English has far more negative terms for women than for men, and insult terms for women, but not for men, most often involve sexual promiscuity (Schulz 1975). In a widely read book that cleared the way for the new field of language and gender studies, Robin Lakoff described the features of a speech style she called "women's language," which she argued was culturally imposed on women and put them in a communicative double bind: to sound helpless and ladylike or to sound powerful and unladylike. Among the characteristics of "women's language" proposed by Lakoff are:

(1)   . . . a large stock of words related to [women's] specific interests, generally relegated to them as "women's work": magenta, shirr, dart (in sewing), and so on. . . .

(2)   "Empty" adjectives like divine, charming, cute. . . .

(3)   Question intonation where we might expect declaratives: for instance tag questions ("It's so hot, isn't it?") and rising intonation in statement contexts ("What's your name, dear?" "Mary Smith?").

(4)   The use of hedges of various kinds. Women's speech seems in general to contain more instances of "well," "y'know," "kinda," and so forth: words that convey the sense that the speaker is uncertain about what he (or she) is saying . . .

(5)   . . . the use of intensive "so" . . .

(6)   Hypercorrect grammar: women are not supposed to talk rough. . . .

(7)   Superpolite forms. . . .
(8)   Women don't tell jokes. . . .
(9)   Women speak in italics . . .

(1975: 53–56)

It is important to note that Lakoff does not suggest that all women use "women's language" (which might more aptly be called "ladies' language") but that they choose not to use it at their peril. Many scholars have sought to disprove or modify Lakoff's claims, but her larger claim – that women's experience of sexism constrains (but does not determine) their use of language – is widely accepted by feminists.

The feminist work of the 1970s was invaluable for bringing the issue of sexism in language to public attention for the first time. Scholars persuasively described how language systematically participates in sexism by allotting different acceptable linguistic behavior to women and men, by denigrating women through insulting and trivializing labels, by engulfing women's experience in a purportedly generic but actually male perspective. But these studies did not look at how individual women resisted linguistic sexism or turned a seemingly sexist system to their own ends. To ask such questions would have been premature at a time when few people would even admit that language could contribute to sexism, or that sexism itself should be eliminated. Today, however, most people in the USA would argue that women and men should be treated – both linguistically and otherwise – as equals. As a result, it has become necessary to move beyond the concerns of the 1970s and to turn to the questions asked in later phases of feminism.

The struggle to eradicate sexist linguistic practices is by no means over, despite the feminist victory with regard to nonsexist pronouns. Although nonsexist language is promoted as policy, it is less often accepted as practice. Some of the worst offenders are linguists themselves, as shown in an analysis of example sentences in linguistics textbooks, such as:

> Susie was appointed secretary to the president of the company.
> The man is hitting the woman with a stick.
> Margie wears clothes which are attractive to men.
>
> (cited by Macaulay and Brice 1997)

And some commentators on the nonsexist language debate choose to focus less on the successes of the movement than on its apparent failure with regard to innovative pronominal systems. Yet new nonsexist systems of gender reference were successfully employed in feminist science fiction of the 1970s to introduce the reader to worlds where the possibilities of gender are different from those of our own society, as in June Arnold's use of the pronoun *na* in her speculative feminist novel *The Cook and the Carpenter* (1973):

> A hand covered Leslie's nose and mouth, pushing into nan face; one deputy easily dragged na to the car; another followed by the side, whacking Leslie's body wherever nan stick could land.   (cited in Livia 1999: 338–39)

The subversive effects of the new pronoun *na* are shared by other reworkings of sexist language. Recent studies of women's language have shown that although the existence of a set of gendered linguistic practices undeniably restricts both women's and men's expressive repertoires, as an ideological system it is vulnerable to subversion, creative adaptation, and outright rejection. Indeed, one of the primary audiences of Lakoff's book is male-to-female transsexuals, who use it as a guide in their transition to their new gender (Bucholtz and Hall 1995). And phone sex workers use this apparently "powerless" linguistic style to gain economic power (as well as the power to control callers' sexual fantasies) (Hall 1995). Admittedly, such uses do not challenge the pre-existing gender system but only exploit it for new purposes. However, the elements of "women's language" described by Lakoff can become a critique of racism, poverty, and gender constraints, when they are employed by some African American drag queens in performance (Barrett 1999). So-called "women's languages" in US languages other than English are similarly flexible in practice, despite linguists' tendency to view certain Native American linguistic structures as rigidly gender-specific (and hence Native American languages as different and exotic) (Trechter 1999). In Lakhota, for example, there is a language ideology that "Men say *yo* and women say *ye*," where *yo* and *ye* express an imperative or emphatic force. These and other such markers in Lakhota are not entirely restricted by gender (both women and men say *ye*) and are susceptible to the same sorts of creative extensions and adaptations that we find with "women's language" in American English. Speakers may also opt out of gender constraints altogether, as shown by the linguistic and social practices of high school girls who describe themselves and are viewed by other students as "nerds" (Bucholtz 1998, 1999). Unlike popular girls, nerd girls do not dress, act, or talk according to the constraints of dominant ideologies of femininity. However, in rejecting this gender ideology they pay the price of social marginalization. It is important to keep in mind that all linguistic choices may have associated costs. Such examples demonstrate that even when linguistic norms, and the linguistic system itself, impose limitations on speakers, language users do not need to accept this situation passively, although they cannot entirely escape the effects of social structures.

Difference and dominance

In the late 1970s and the 1980s, feminist scholarship shifted from considering how women were oppressed by sexist cultural practices, both linguistic and non-linguistic, to a recognition and even a celebration of women's own practices. In language and gender studies, the focus on women's ways of speaking was partly an effort to validate the dimensions of women's language use that men often denigrated, ranging from gossip to the characteristics of "women's language" described by Lakoff. Researchers argued that gossip promotes social cohesion among women, that "women's language" does not mark women as powerless but instead enables them to be effective and adept conversational partners – in short, that women were worth listening to.

But this approach, despite its importance as a corrective measure to more pessimistic views of women's speech, had two limitations owing to its emphasis on the distinctiveness of women's practice. First, it invited the inference that all women adhered to the same practices, and second, it implied that the social behavior of women and men is entirely different. This emphasis on difference between genders and the accompanying deemphasis on differences within genders has been labeled *essentialism* for its suggestion that these gender patterns emerge from deep-seated cultural essences of femininity and masculinity, and the strand of feminism that promotes this view has been called *cultural feminism* because of its assumption that women and men belong to different cultures. Sociolinguists who hold the cultural view maintain that gender-based "cultures" and hence language patterns develop through the sex-segregated play practices of children, in which girls learn to be cooperative and group-oriented and boys learn to be competitive and individual-oriented (Maltz and Borker 1982).

Perhaps the most well-known proponent of the culture-based view of gender in linguistics is Deborah Tannen, who extended her earlier research on cross-cultural miscommunication to include cross-sex miscommunication under the rubric of "cross-cultural" (Tannen 1990). In its concern with interaction between the genders, Tannen's work connected with a tradition of language and gender scholarship from the 1970s and early 1980s that examined women's and men's linguistic behavior in conversation. These researchers found, for example, that men interrupted women more often than the reverse (West and Zimmerman 1983) and that women performed most of the conversational "shitwork" in interactions among married couples: asking questions, giving feedback, and so on (Fishman 1983). But where these earlier studies were interpreted as supporting the thesis of men's *dominance* over women, Tannen's work argued for men's *difference* from women. She noted that many heterosexual couples fail to communicate successfully in spite of their good intentions, and proposed that this was because each gender brought different cultural expectations to the task of conversation. Thus Tannen suggests that in the following exchange miscommunication arises when culturally based gender styles clash: the woman tries to connect with the man while the man tries to assert that his experience is unique:

> HE: I'm really tired. I didn't sleep well last night.
> SHE: I didn't sleep well either. I never do.
> HE: Why are you trying to belittle me?
> SHE: I'm not! I'm just trying to show that I understand!
>
> (Tannen 1990: 51)

Tannen's work has been widely criticized by language and gender scholars for many reasons, but perhaps most of all for discounting the role of male dominance in interaction. Such critics point out that any "no-fault" account of cross-sex interaction ends up penalizing women, both because women are the ones who are expected to adjust (they note that Tannen's readership is mostly female) and because setting aside issues of gender inequality undoes feminism's key principle by making the personal apolitical. Yet despite such objections, the fact that Tannen's book achieved bestseller status and made her a frequent guest on talk shows and self-help programs attests to the resonance of her ideas, especially among white middle-class heterosexual women. It is important to acknowledge this fact, but it is equally important to acknowledge that other groups may not see themselves in a culture-based analysis. Indeed, both difference and dominance perspectives focus narrowly on the behavior of white middle-class heterosexuals, and both approaches' broad claims about "women" and "men" do not account for the linguistic behavior of those who do not fit this profile.

Women in their speech communities

The objection that not all women act in the ways that cultural feminists describe was first issued by some women of color and lesbians (and especially by lesbians of color), who found their own experiences excluded from the cultural feminist account. The development of multicultural feminism had a strong if somewhat belated impact on language and gender studies. Several early studies described a variety of speech communities that differed in important ways from the white, heterosexual, middle-class speakers who figured centrally in most language and gender analyses. These studies did not emphasize dramatic differences between female and male speech community members but neither did they marginalize or subordinate women's participation in community interaction. The work of Mitchell-Kernan (1972), for example, documented the everyday interactions of African American women and men and corrected a number of oversights with respect to African American women's speech practices. Where early work on the African American linguistic practice of *signifying* erroneously portrayed it as an almost exclusively male activity devoted to the public and ritual insulting of one's opponent, Mitchell-Kernan showed that women participated in a conversational form of signifying that, though private and nonritualized, shared basic elements of the more widely studied public style of signifying. Like its more public form, conversational signifying uses allusions to cultural knowledge rather than direct statements for its effect, as shown in the following example:

> The relevant background information is that the husband is a member of the class of individuals who do not wear suits to work.

> WIFE: Where are you going?
> HUSBAND: I'm going to work.
> WIFE: (You're wearing) a suit, tie and white shirt? You didn't tell me you got a promotion.
> (Mitchell-Kernan 1972: 169)

Linguistic resources such as conversational signifying reveal as much about culture as they do about gender. In fact, some speakers have access to linguistic resources that are unavailable to members of other speech communities, and these may be exploited for the expression of cultural background, gender, and other dimensions of identity. Thus, Mexican American women who are bilingual in Spanish and English have been found to follow their conversational partner's lead in *codeswitching* (see chapters 10 by Zentella and 11 by Silva-Corvalán in this volume) more often with men than with women (Valdés-Fallis 1978). And gender-related social patterns may also affect women's access to and attitudes toward linguistic resources. In one Puerto Rican neighborhood in New York, women more often than men had a strong belief in the importance of Spanish as a part of Puerto Rican identity, and girls tended to be more fluent Spanish speakers than boys (Zentella 1997). Both of these gender differences can be attributed to women's and girls' greater participation in roles that involved the use of Spanish: girls had family obligations that kept them closer to home, while boys' friendship networks often led them outside the Spanish-speaking block where they lived. But both girls and boys had access to a wide range of linguistic resources, including Standard Puerto Rican Spanish, Nonstandard Puerto Rican Spanish, Puerto Rican English, African American Vernacular English, and Standard New York City Spanish. Thus any temptation to view these girls (and boys) as linguistically impoverished is immediately refuted by the evidence (see also chapter 10 by Zentella in this volume); on the contrary, such speakers have access to a much wider array of linguistic resources for the construction of identity, including gender identity, than monolingual and monodialectal speakers (see chapters 7 by Fishman and 14 by Bayley in this volume).

More recent scholarship on the linguistic practices of women of color likewise challenges stereotypes about the behavior of women as an undifferentiated group. Some white cultural feminist psychologists have extolled "women's ways of knowing" (Belenky et al. 1986), but it is clear that women of different cultural backgrounds can view the same events very differently. For example, the value placed upon indirect communication such as signifying in many African American speech communities can lead African American women and European American women to make different assumptions about intention and responsibility. Such issues arise in interpreting the following story, developed by a researcher to test black and white views of responsibility:

Regina's Story

I was talking to some close women friends of mine, and another friend of mine that they hadn't met, Margaret, joined us. Well, I've known Margaret for years but this was the first time that my other friends had really socialized with her. Anyway, all of my friends live in Black neighborhoods. Margaret and I happen to live in white neighborhoods. Anyway, at some point in the conversation Margaret started talking about how much she loved living outside the ghetto and away from Black people and how much better it was and how she felt that she had moved up in life, living high on the hill away from Black folk. I couldn't believe it, but I didn't say anything. Well, a little later on, Margaret had already gone home, and I asked my friends if we were all still going to the movies like we planned. They all just looked at me. Then one of them said, "The way *you* talk, we don't know if we want to go to the movies with you." Well, I really couldn't believe that they'd get an attitude over that. (Morgan 1991: 431)

The researcher found that white women were more likely than black women to believe that Regina's friends got an attitude because they thought she agreed with Margaret, while black women were evenly split between this interpretation and the interpretation that Regina's friends got an attitude because she didn't speak up. The African American women recognized a wider range of possible intentions behind the statement made by Regina's friend, and also believed that even if her friends didn't actually believe that she agreed with Margaret, she should have been aware that she could be held responsible for Margaret's statements. In other words, the African American women, but not the European American women, saw the inherent ambiguity in Regina's friend's statement, and as a result they understood the interaction differently. The value placed on the ability to infer meaning from purposefully ambiguous statements is part of what has been called the *counterlanguage* of African Americans, a system of communication that allows for multiple levels of meaning, only some of which are available to outsiders. This counterlanguage, which finds parallels in African discourse, emerged from African Americans' need to communicate with one another in hostile, white-dominated environments from the time of slavery onward (Morgan 1991). While avoiding the danger of imposing a new culturally specific stereotype on African American women, Morgan (1991) demonstrates that a view of "women" as a homogeneous group is inadequate to describe the experiences of many women, such as those who must confront a legacy of slavery and racism.

In contrast to cultural feminism, multicultural feminism emphasizes the particular practices of women and girls of color, which may or may not differ from the practices of white women and girls or those of men and boys of color. Thus, as cultural feminism would predict, a study of African American girls and boys at play found gender differences in the language used to accomplish particular tasks, as in the following examples:

The boys are making slingshots

(1) MALCOLM: All right. Gimme some rubber bands.
(2) MALCOLM: PLIERS! I WANT THE PLIERS!
                    (Goodwin 1991: 103; simplified transcription)

The girls are making rings out of soda bottles

(1) MARTHA: Let's go around Subs and Suds.
    BEA: Let's ask her "Do you have any bottles."
(2) BEA: We could go around lookin for more bottles.

                              (Goodwin 1991: 110, 111)

While the boys influenced one another's behavior using imperatives and other direct means that emphasized the differences among them, the girls underplayed differences by using suggestions. But in other contexts, girls were as able as boys to use direct linguistic forms and to create hierarchies, as during social conflicts:

> KERRY: GET OUTA MY STREET GIRL! HEY GIRL GET OUTA MY
> STREET!
>
> (Goodwin 1991: 118; simplified transcription)

or while playing house:

> MARTHA: BRENDA PLAY RIGHT.
> THAT'S WHY NOBODY WANT YOU FOR A CHILD.
>
> (Goodwin 1991: 131)

The range of girls' interactional abilities makes clear that interactional styles are not specific to a particular gender but to the activity that speakers are engaged in carrying out.

Other girls' games, such as hopscotch and jump rope, also challenge the frequent claim that boys are concerned with rules and girls are concerned with feelings. Latina and African American girls strenuously and vociferously monitor one another's play for possible rule violations, as the following interchange during a hopscotch game in Los Angeles demonstrates:

> Marta jumps with one foot outside grid
>
> ROXANA: Out.
> CARLA: (simultaneously) Out!
> ROXANA: Out.
> MARTA: AY! (throws up hands smiling, turning head)
> GLORIA: (simultaneously) HAH HAH!
> CARLA: Pisaste la raya! ('You stepped on the line.') (stepping multiple
>   times on the line where violation occurred)
> GLORIA: (claps hands three times excitedly while laughing)
>
> (Goodwin 1999; simplified transcription)

Such interactions among Latina girls contradict the stereotyped claims of some white feminists that Latinas are passive or suffer from low self-esteem. Likewise, adult Latinas may assert themselves by using *caló*, a special vocabulary associated primarily with men, despite gendered language ideologies that women should not use this lexicon (Galindo 1992).

Language and sexuality

While multicultural feminism has worked to correct the bias toward studies of white women, lesbian feminism and, more recently, queer theory have encouraged researchers to pay greater attention to lesbians and gay men. Although these two groups have many experiences in common and belong to a larger "queer" category, along with bisexuals and transgendered individuals, they must be studied separately (as well as together) in order to understand each group's linguistic practices on their own terms. Indeed, just as the issue of "women's language" preoccupied early researchers of language and gender, so too a central question in language and sexuality studies has been whether lesbians and gay men each have a recognizably distinctive speech style or "accent." While there has been some study of this issue (Gaudio 1994; Moonwomon [1985] 1997), methodological difficulties and inconclusive findings make it problematic to state that there is a uniquely "gay" or "lesbian" style of speaking.

It is likely, in fact, that neither lesbians nor gay men have a distinctive linguistic system but instead may draw on patterns of language use that index these identities. These patterns result in part from contact with a vast array of linguistic communities and their resources, as shown by representations of lesbian speech in comics such as "Hothead Paisan" (Queen 1997). Resources for lesbian speech include a number of stereotypes, including stereotypes of women's language, as described by Lakoff; stereotypes of nonstandard varieties (see chapter 4 by Wolfram in this volume); stereotypes of gay male language; and stereotypes of lesbian language. In the following exchange, the comic's heroine, Hothead, tells another lesbian character, Alice, that violence is preferable to education in dealing with rapists:

HOTHEAD:	Oh, right! Tell me how to educate a serial rapist! You get what you put out, an' those motherfuckers deserve everything they get!!! . . . An' education is too fuckin' slow! The way I operate . . . it's eat my dust!!! The problem is gone!
ALICE (TO ROZ):	Shall I respond to the infant child?
ROZ:	Oh, do!
ALICE (TO HOTHEAD):	Don't you sit there and sass me about what works and what doesn't! Your arrogant little butt can't see the forest for the trees!
	(cited in Queen 1997: 252)

Here Hothead and Alice use language very differently from each other, and Alice uses language differently depending on her addressee. It is clear that lesbians, even in fictional representations such as comics, do not face a simple dichotomy: "Either we speak like women or we speak like men" (Queen 1997: 254). Yet because both lesbians and gay men are still marginalized within language and gender studies (as the field's name suggests) and because the field of language and sexuality is still young, there is still a great deal we do not know about the relationship between language and sexual identity.

Like African Americans, lesbians and gay men have historically been and continue to be in danger of violence and hostility from members of the dominant social group. Just as the threat of danger led to the development of a counterlanguage among African Americans, a similar indirect speech style has developed in which lesbians and gay men can identify themselves to one another without making themselves vulnerable to potentially homophobic and hostile straight overhearers. Such "gay implicature" (Liang 1999) is exemplified in the following interchange:

> In a department store (S = gay male sales clerk; C = gay male customer)
> S: Can I help you find something?
> C: No thanks, I am just looking.
> [*Pause. S continues to fold and arrange the merchandise. C continues to browse; both look discreetly at each other; ten seconds pass*]
> C: What are you asking for these? [*Points to one set of grey sweatshirts*]
> S: Oh. I'm afraid they're not on sale today. But that colored shirt would look nice on you. [*Points to a pile of lavender sweatshirts, which are on sale*]
> C: Yeah, I know. I own a few of them already. [*Grins*]
> S: [*Grins back; no verbal comment*]
> C: Thanks for your help. [*C walks off*]
>
> (Leap 1996: 13)

In this example, signals of a gay identity – such as the clerk's comments on the customer's appearance, his selection of a lavender shirt, a color that is associated with gay men and lesbians, and the customer's indication that he has understood this coded reference – are embedded in an interaction that appears unremarkable to many straight observers. The existence of gay implicature, like African Americans' counterlanguage, indicates that traditional theories of gender-based dominance must be revised to account for men whose identities place them partly or wholly outside the dominant group.

Identity in practice and performance

Studies of women of color and of lesbians and gay men have shown the importance of moving away from broad, even universal, categories like gender as the sole explanation for speech patterns and toward other dimensions of identity that enrich and complicate language and gender analyses. But if it is not enough to invoke gender to account for linguistic behavior, then neither is it enough to invoke gender plus race or ethnicity, or gender plus ethnicity plus sexuality. Recent work argues that invoking categories is itself dangerously deterministic, in that it implies that membership in a particular category necessarily results in a predictable linguistic behavior. Instead, scholars have called for greater attention to speakers' *agency*, their ability to use language strategically to achieve goals in spite of the constraints of cultural ideologies. This emphasis on agency replaces earlier views of identity, including gender identity, as *assigned* and *fixed* with a view of identity as *achieved* and *fluid*.

Studies of identity from an agency-centered perspective are of two kinds: those that consider identity primarily as a *practice* and those that understand it primarily as a *performance*. These two perspectives are compatible but each offers a different analytic emphasis. The focus on practice is a reminder that identities are created in activities, not assigned by membership in particular social categories, like "woman," "bisexual," "Asian American." Women as a group do not form a community of practice because they do not all engage in the same practices in the same ways, and, as already suggested, viewing all women as a single group blinds us to the vast differences among women.

Identities form around practices and, conversely, practices develop around identities. This process of forging and making use of links between social practices (including linguistic practices) and social categories is known as *indexing* (Ochs 1992). The following example illustrates how indexing works. The speaker is a teenage girl who is reporting her past exploits with her best friend:

> . . . we used to tell our moms that we'd – uh – she'd be sleeping at my house, I'd be sleeping at hers. We'd go out and pull a all-nighter, you know (laughter). I'd come home the next day, "Where were you?" "Jane's." "No you weren't." Because her mom and my mom are like really close – since we got in so much trouble they know each other really good.   (Eckert and McConnell-Ginet 1995: 503)

The speaker pronounces the word *all-nighter* as *all-noiter*, which is characteristic of a change in pronunciation in Michigan, where this example was recorded. But not all teenagers in Michigan use this pronunciation. By using it in the context of an interview with an adult researcher and particularly in the context of the word *all-nighter*, which evokes wild partying, the speaker – a "Burned-Out Burnout" girl – creates an association between the new pronunciation and the kind of person who uses it: someone who likes to party and doesn't accommodate herself to adult authority. The form comes to index, or point to, this sort of identity, so that similar associations are evoked each time the form is used. As a consequence, the new pronunciation becomes a resource for claiming an identity as a Burnout girl, a girl who rejects the college-prep culture of the high school in favor of the world beyond school (see also chapter 19 by Eckert in this volume).

Instead of classifying individuals first and then examining how their language "reflects" this preordained identity, a practice approach looks at how individuals use language and what sort of identity this constructs for them as a result. Interaction-specific identities, such as "ring maker" or "hopscotch player," may then take precedence over broader identities like "girl," "African American," or "Latina." Or the most salient identities in a given interaction or setting may be local and specific: "Burnout," "Jock," "nerd." In these instances gender works in connection with other aspects of the self. Thus "Burnout" girls speak differently not only from "Jock" or mainstream girls, but also from "Burnout" boys (Eckert and McConnell-Ginet 1995).

Practice is a doubly useful concept for language and gender studies because it has a double meaning: practice is also the prelude to performance. If practice emphasizes the dailiness of social activity, performance highlights deliberateness. In the sense of this term within gender studies, performance is the enactment of an identity that may or may not conform to the identity assigned to the performer by others. Performance may have a degree of drama and spectacle, and certainly performance always connotes an element of display, but many everyday performances are relatively unremarkable.

Studies of the relationship between gender and sexuality bring performance to the forefront because they emphasize the fluidity of categories often believed to be fixed, and they challenge traditional assumptions of what it means to be female or male, feminine or masculine. By suggesting that gender and sex are not natural and inevitable but socially constructed, studies of the performance of these dimensions of identity raise questions about the fixedness of all social categories. A study of African American drag queens who, as noted above, used elements of Lakoff's "women's language," effectively illustrates this point (Barrett 1999). Naive analysts might interpret such use as an indication that these black men want to be women, or even that they want to be white, since "women's language" is an ideology about how white middle-class women speak. Instead, however, African American drag queens use "women's language" to critique the gender and racial ideologies underlying (white) "women's language." They do so by highlighting the disjunctions in their performance of a race and gender not their own, as in the following example, from an African American drag queen in a predominantly black gay bar:

> Oh, hi, how are you doing?
> White people. *Love* it.
> I . . I'm not being racial 'cause I'm white.
> I just have a <obscured> I can afford more suntan.   (Barrett 1994: 9)

Here the drag queen's claim to whiteness is clearly false, just as her claim to femaleness is clearly false. But her claims also invoke ideologies of race and gender, of who counts and cannot count as a member of certain categories and what benefits and privileges are granted to members (such as the cultural desirability of dark white skin but not dark black skin).

This study of drag queens raises important questions not only about gender and sexuality but about race as well, and especially about the relative invisibility of whiteness as a racial category. Identities like whiteness, masculinity, and heterosexuality are *unmarked*: that is, they are taken as unnoticed "norms" or "defaults" from which other categories supposedly deviate. Recent research has begun to look at unmarked categories as performances – social constructions – in their own right. Researchers often focus on groups that seem different from an assumed norm; by contrast, studies of unmarked categories turn attention instead to the group that constitutes the norm. Such studies demonstrate that identities that seem normal and natural are as performed and constructed as every other social identity; meanwhile, the lessons of early feminist research offer reminders that even normative categories are not monolithic. Thus there is no single masculinity any more than there is a single femininity, although a dominant ideology of masculinity often shapes men's performances of their gender identities. Even members of a single fraternity may show very different orientations to masculinity in their language use, taking up powerful masculine identities based on knowledge, experience, or even an oppositional stance to the fraternity's institutional trappings (Kiesling 1997).

Like masculinity, heterosexuality is not given in advance but is achieved in practice. The following is a performance of heterosexuality via homophobia by several male college students who are talking about a classmate:

> ED: he's I mean he's like a real artsy fartsy fag he's like (indecipherable) he's so gay he's got this like really high voice and wire rim glasses and he sits next to the ugliest-ass bitch in the history of the world and
>
> BRYAN: (overlapping) and they're all hitting on her too, like four guys hitting on her
>
> ED: (overlapping) I know it's like four homos hitting on her
>   (Cameron 1997: 56; simplified transcription)

This interaction looks more like a stereotypical "women's" conversation, with an emphasis on gossip and a high degree of overlapping cooperative and supportive talk. Despite the claims of cultural feminism, then, both "women's talk" and "women's language" extend well beyond the bounds of women's identities. While African American drag queens use a linguistic practice that indexes femininity and thus perform a gay, gender-transgressive identity, for the European American college-age men in the example above, no indexing of femininity is intended; in fact, such strategies of "women's talk" become resources for performing a normative homophobic masculine identity. The use of language in the construction of identity thus becomes a much more complex problem than simply mapping linguistic behavior onto given social categories. Understanding such uses of language constitutes one of the most pressing questions of current studies of language, gender, and sexuality.

Conclusion

This chapter has described the trajectory of language and gender studies from its initial concern with linguistic sexism to its more recent focus on intragender variation and women's and men's agentive linguistic practices, as well as the development of language and sexuality as a related subfield. Despite their many real differences, what all these approaches have in common is a concern with how the interrelationship of language and identity is bound to issues of power. Some critics have objected that earlier feminist efforts to change language use were misplaced, that changing words does not change the world. But scholars of language, gender, and sexuality have shown repeatedly that language does indeed construct social realities in multiple ways. Language mediates our experience of the world; it shapes our understanding and creates our identities through the linguistic choices we make both consciously and unconsciously. In so doing, it limits us in some ways and empowers us in others. Thus the study of language, gender, and sexuality is always also the study of the politics of language. From this perspective, early feminist linguists do not seem so far from the mark. Words are our world, and therefore changing language – the language that we use, the language that is used to and about us – to correspond with the world we want to inhabit is a crucial and realistic political act.

Suggestions for further reading and exploration

Because most of the volumes suggested here do not focus exclusively on the USA, they provide valuable comparative data for those whose primary interest is language and gender in the USA. A useful point of entry for the study of language and gender is Lakoff (1975), which lays out a wide range of theoretical and empirical questions that other scholars have been responding to ever since its publication (see Lakoff forthcoming). Because of the importance of feminist theory to language and gender studies, it is advisable to consult Cameron (1992) early and often.

There are several overviews of the field of language and gender, including Eckert and McConnell-Ginet (2003) and Talbot (1998), while many edited volumes provide a wealth of studies on particular communities and contexts: Benor et al. (2002), Bergvall, Bing, and Freed (1996), Bucholtz, Liang, and Sutton (1999), Hall and Bucholtz (1995), Kotthoff and Wodak (1997), McIlvenny (2002), Mills (1995), and Wodak (1997). Most of these collections range widely, but there are differences: for example, Mills (1995) has substantial sections on gender in written language and in educational contexts; both Hall and Bucholtz (1995) and Bucholtz, Liang, and Sutton (1999) have several chapters on communities of color; Kotthoff and Wodak (1997) is highly international in scope.

For revisitations and updates on the sexist language debate, see Pauwels (1998) and Romaine (1999) and Livia (2001). Frank and Treichler (1989) offers both theoretical and practical perspectives on gender, language, and professional writing. Leap (1996) focuses on gay men's English, while Leap (1995) and Livia and Hall (1997) treat a variety of relationships between language and gay, lesbian, bisexual, and transgendered identities. From a somewhat different perspective, Harvey and Shalom (1997) explore language, sex, and intimacy. Johnson and Meinhof (1997) establishes language and masculinity studies as a new subfield of language and gender studies. Cameron and Kulick (2003) provide an overview of language and sexuality; see Bucholtz and Hall (forthcoming) and contributions to Campbell-Kibler et al. (2002) for other perspectives.

References

Barrett, Rusty. 1994. "'She is *Not* White Woman': the Appropriation of White Women's Language by African American Drag Queens." In *Cultural Performances: Proceedings of the Third Berkeley Women and Language Conference*, eds. Mary Bucholtz, A. C. Liang, Laurel A. Sutton, and Caitlin Hines. Berkeley: Berkeley Women and Language Group. Pp. 1–14.

    1999. "Indexing Polyphonous Identity in the Speech of African American Drag Queens." In Bucholtz et al. Pp. 313–31.

Belenky, Mary Field, Blythe McVicker Cuncley, Nancy Rule Goldberger, Jill Mattuck Tarule 1986. *Women's Ways of Knowing*. New York: Basic Books.

Benor, Sarah, Mary Rose, Devyani Sharma, Julie Sweetland and Qing Zhang, eds. 2002. *Gendered Practices in Language*. Stanford, CA: CSLI Publications.

Bergvall, Victoria L., Janet M. Bing, and Alice F. Freed, eds. 1996. *Rethinking Language and Gender Research: Theory and Practice*. London: Longman.

Bodine, Ann. 1975. "Androcentrism in Prescriptive Grammar: Singular *They*, Sex-indefinite *He* and *He or She*," *Language in Society* 4: 129–46.

Bucholtz, Mary. 1998. "Geek the Girl: Language, Femininity, and Female Nerds." In *Gender and Belief Systems: Proceedings of the Fourth Berkeley Women and Language Conference*, eds. Natasha Warner, Jocelyn Ahlers, Leela Bilmes, Monica Oliver, Suzanne Wertheim, and Mel Chen. Berkeley: Berkeley Women and Language Group. Pp. 119–31.

    1999. "'Why Be Normal?': Language and Identity Practices in a Community of Nerd Girls," *Language in Society* 28(2): 203–23. [Special issue: Communities of Practice in Language and Gender Research. Ed. Janet Holmes.]

Bucholtz, Mary and Kira Hall. 1995. "Introduction: Twenty Years after *Language and Woman's Place*." In Hall and Bucholtz. Pp. 1–22.

    (Forthcoming). Theorizing identity in language and sexuality, *Language in Society*.

Bucholtz, Mary, A. C. Liang, and Laurel A. Sutton, eds. 1999. *Reinventing Identities*. New York: Oxford University Press.

Cameron, Deborah. 1992. *Feminism and Linguistic Theory,* 2nd edn. New York: St. Martin's Press.

    1997. "Performing Gender Identity: Young Men's Talk and the Construction of Heterosexual Masculinity." In Johnson and Meinhof. Pp. 47–64.

Campbell-Kibler, Kathryn, Robert J. Podesva, Sarah J. Roberts, and Andrew Wong, eds. 2002. *Language and Sexuality: Contesting Meaning in Theory and Practice*. Stanford, CA: CSLI Publications.

Eckert, Penelope and Sally McConnell-Ginet. 1995. "Constructing Meaning, Constructing Selves: Snapshots of Language, Gender, and Class from Belten High." In Hall and Bucholtz. Pp. 469–507.

    2003. *Language and Gender*. Cambridge: Cambridge University Press.

Fishman, Pamela. 1983. "Interaction: The Work Women Do." In Thorne, Kramarae, and Henley. Pp. 103–18.

Frank, Francine Wattman and Paula A. Treichler. 1989. *Language, Gender, and Professional Writing*. New York: Modern Language Association.

Galindo, D. Letticia. 1992. "Dispelling the Male-only Myth: Chicanas and Caló," *Bilingual Review/Revista Bilingüe* 17: 3–35.

Gaudio, Rudolf P. 1994. "Sounding Gay: Pitch Properties in the Speech of Gay and Straight Men," *American Speech* 69: 30–57.

Goodwin, Marjorie Harness. 1990. *He-Said-She-Said: Talk as Social Organization among Black Children*. Bloomington: Indiana University Press.

    1999. "Constructing Opposition Within Girls' Games." In Bucholtz, Liang, and Sutton. Pp. 388–409.

Graham, Alma. 1975. "The Making of a Non-sexist Dictionary." In Thorne and Henley. Pp. 57–63.

Hall, Kira. 1995. "Lip Service on the Fantasy Lines." In Hall and Bucholtz. Pp. 183–216.

Hall, Kira and Mary Bucholtz, eds. 1995. *Gender Articulated: Language and the Socially Constructed Self*. New York: Routledge.

Harvey, Keith and Celia Shalom, eds. 1997. *Language and Desire*. London: Routledge.

Johnson, Sally, and Ulrike Hanna Meinhof, eds. 1997. *Language and Masculinity*. Oxford: Blackwell.

Kiesling, Scott. 1997. "Power and the Language of Men." In Johnson and Meinhof. Pp. 65–85.

Kotthoff, Helga and Ruth Wodak, eds. 1997. *Communicating Language and Gender in Context*. Amsterdam: John Benjamins.

Lakoff, Robin. 1975. *Language and Woman's Place*. New York: Harper and Row.
   Forthcoming. *Language and Woman's Place: Text and Commentaries*. Ed. Mary Bucholtz. Revised and expanded edn. New York: Oxford University Press.

Leap, William L. 1996. *Word's Out: Gay Men's English*. Minneapolis: University of Minnesota Press.

Leap, William, ed. 1995. *Beyond the Lavender Lexicon*. Amsterdam: Gordon and Breach.

Liang, A. C. 1999. "Conversationally Implicating Lesbian and Gay Identity." In Bucholtz, Liang, and Sutton. Pp. 293–310.

Livia, Anna. 1999. "'She Sired Six Children': Feminist Experiments with Linguistic Gender." In Bucholtz, Liang, and Sutton. Pp. 332–47.
   2001. *Pronoun envy: Literary Uses of Linguistic Gender*. Oxford: Oxford University Press.

Livia, Anna and Kira Hall, eds. 1997. *Queerly Phrased: Language, Gender, and Sexuality*. New York: Oxford University Press.

Macaulay, Monica and Colleen Brice. 1997. "Don't Touch My Projectile: Gender Bias and Stereotyping in Syntactic Examples," *Language* 73: 798–825.

Maltz, Daniel N. and Ruth A. Borker. 1982. "A Cultural Approach to Male–Female Miscommunication." In *Language and Social Identity*, ed. John J. Gumperz. Cambridge: Cambridge University Press. Pp. 196–216.

Martyna, Wendy. 1983. "Beyond the He/Man Approach: the Case for Nonsexist Language." In Thorne, Kramarae, and Henley. Pp. 25–37.

McIlvenny, Paul, ed. 2002. *Talking Gender and Sexuality*. Amsterdam: John Benjamins.

Mills, Sara, ed. 1995. *Language and Gender: Interdisciplinary Perspectives*. London: Longman.

Mitchell-Kernan, Claudia. [1972] 1986. "Signifying and Marking: Two Afro-American Speech Acts." In *Directions in Sociolinguistics: the Ethnography of Communication*, eds. John J. Gumperz and Dell Hymes. Oxford: Blackwell. Pp. 161–79.

Moonwomon, Birch. [1985] 1997. "Toward the Study of Lesbian Speech." In Livia and Hall. Pp. 202–13.

Morgan, Marcyliena H. 1991. "Indirectness and Interpretation in African American Women's Discourse," *Pragmatics* 1: 421–51.

Ochs, Elinor. 1992. "Indexing Gender." In *Rethinking Context: Language as an Interactive Phenomenon*, eds. Alessandro Duranti and Charles Goodwin. Cambridge: Cambridge University Press. Pp. 335–58.

Pauwels, Anne. 1998. *Women Changing Language*. London: Longman.

Queen, Robin M. 1997. "'I Don't Speak Spritch': Locating Lesbian Language." In Livia and Hall. Pp. 233–56.

Romaine, Suzanne. 1999. *Communicating Gender*. Mahwah NJ: Lawrence Erlbaum.

Schulz, Muriel. 1975. "The Semantic Derogation of Women." In Thorne and Henley. Pp. 64–75.

Talbot, Mary. 1998. *Language and Gender*. Cambridge: Polity.

Tannen, Deborah. 1990. *You Just Don't Understand: Women and Men in Conversation*. New York: William Morrow.

Tannen, Deborah, ed. 1993. *Gender and Conversational Interaction*. New York: Oxford University Press.

Thorne, Barrie and Nancy Henley, eds. 1975. *Language and Sex: Difference and Dominance*. Rowley MA: Newbury House.

Thorne, Barrie, Cheris Kramarae, and Nancy Henley, eds. 1983. *Language, Gender, and Society*. Cambridge MA: Newbury House.

Trechter, Sara. 1999. "Contextualizing the Exotic Few: Gender Dichotomies in Lakhota." In Bucholtz, Liang, and Sutton. Pp. 101–19.

Valdés-Fallis, Guadalupe. 1978. "Code-switching among Bilingual Mexican-American Women: towards an Understanding of Sex-related Language Alternation," *International Journal of the Sociology of Language* 17: 65–72.

West, Candace and Don H. Zimmerman. 1983. "Small Insults: a Study of Interruptions in Cross-sex Conversations Between Unacquainted Persons." In Thorne, Kramarae, and Henley. Pp. 103–18.

Wodak, Ruth, ed. 1997. *Gender and Discourse*. New York: Sage.

Zentella, Ana Celia. 1997. *Growing Up Bilingual: Puerto Rican Children in New York*. Malden MA: Blackwell.

23

Linguistic identity and community in American literature

JAMES PETERSON

Editors' introduction

Of the characters in a literary text, this chapter asks how we know who we are reading – how is a character's social identity represented and conveyed in a literary work? To answer the question, James Peterson proposes four analytical tools: the author's identity; stereotypes; situational contexts; and orthographic practices. With a warning against the dangers of essentialism, he notes that critically acclaimed representations of ethnicity, gender, and sexual orientation have typically been produced by authors with first-hand knowledge of those identities – from Ralph Ellison and James Baldwin to Toni Morrison and Alice Walker; from Sherman Alexie to Amy Tan, and from Richard Rodriguez to Sandra Cisneros. Similar to author identity in its transparency is situational context – the setting of the activities of fictional characters – whether living on Indian reservations or playing the dozens on the streets of Detroit. A third device is stereotypical representation, which writers may use to upend the oppressive effects of stereotyping, subverting the negative import of those effects. Lastly – and most obviously linguistic – is orthography, the characteristics of spelling, punctuation, and other devices of written linguistic representation by which authors endeavor to indicate social identity.

In this chapter you will see how Peterson applies these analytical tools to the representation of identity in the works of Native American writer Sherman Alexie, Latin novelists Esmeralda Santiago and Piri Thomas, and African American authors from Charles Chesnutt in the nineteenth century to Ellison, Richard Wright, and Zora Neale Hurston, among others, in the twentieth century.

Many of the ways in which writers present and represent social identity in American literature are not directly related to traditional linguistic analyses, but all depend on language, of course. The question we might ask of any novel or poem or play is how we know the identity of the characters in the text: who are we reading? This question has many possible answers, but for the student of literature and linguistics the answers can be limited to four modes for analyzing the social identity of a character. Whether or not the representation is authentic to the ethnicity, social class, or sexual orientation characteristics of "real-life" persons or community haunts the discussion in this chapter. The four modes here explained and exemplified address some of these concerns, while offering an economical means of analyzing social identity in American literature and the roles that language plays in constituting that identity.

Ethnic identity in literature is the primary focus of this chapter. How are Native American, Latino/Latina American, and African American identities linguistically presented and represented in American literature? Throughout the discussion, gender, class, and sexual orientation will be incidentally subsumed within the analyses of ethnicity, but the same analytical tools illustrated here will be helpful in ferreting out other types of identity in literature.

1. Author's identity

Linguistics, particularly sociolinguistics, grapples with inside-outside dynamics with respect to collecting and confirming accurate linguistic data from communities. While we would not want to be essentialist in our thinking, it is worthy of note that critically acclaimed representations of ethnic identities and gender identities in American literature have generally been written by authors whose ethnic or sexual identities correspond to those of their principal characters (for more on essentialism, see chapter 22). Consider Alice Walker (b. 1944) and Nobel Prize winner Toni Morrison (b. 1931), as well as Ralph Ellison (1914–94) and James Baldwin (1924–87) for African American and lesbian and gay literature. Witness Sherman Alexie (b. 1966) for Native American and working poor literature, Amy Tan (b. 1952) and Frank Chin (b. 1940) for women and men's Asian American literature, and Esmeralda Santiago (b. 1940), Richard Rodriguez (b. 1944), and Sandra Cisneros (b. 1954) for Latina/Latino American literature. The abilities of these authors and others to provide cogent sociolinguistic situations and representations of their ethnic backgrounds, as well as their gender and their sexual orientation can be credited to their insider knowledge and personal experiences. The identity of an author does not ensure an authentic rendering of character, of course, but the history of American literature suggests that misrepresentation and over-determined linguistic techniques (think of Twain's Huck Finn) have been resoundingly *counter-represented* in the works of the aforementioned non-white or non-heterosexual or non-middle-class authors and many of their contemporaries. These counter representations develop comparable ethnic and linguistic portraits of traditionally biased characterizations. In short, they proffer a competing frame of reference for nonstandard-speaking characters in American literature.

2. Stereotypes

Many times authors like those named above, authors who have often charged themselves as protectors of their particular cultures, utilize the very same stereotypes that have been propagated as tools of oppression against them and their constituents. Of course, they often turn these stereotypes on their heads or otherwise subvert them so that they reflect the ignorance of the American mainstream or the strength of the culture in question. (Below, we will exemplify this with Piri Thomas and Charles Chesnutt.) Stereotypes operate on many linguistic levels, including discourse, and you may note that the discursive relationships – who can speak, and when – in texts like Chesnutt's *The Conjure Woman* or Thomas's *Down These Mean Streets* are informed by stereotypical ethnic situations and often have corresponding oppressive/power relations.

3. Situational contexts

Situational contexts form the pragmatic milieu for sociolinguistic variation. If a book is about slavery, we can expect many of the main characters to be black or southern and to speak African American Vernacular English or Southern American English. If a novel is about life on an Indian reservation, we can expect Native Americans as main characters. There are much more subtle instances of situational contexts. Certain discursive situations (or speech events, as ethnographers call them) lend themselves to specific identities. Children playing "the dozens" are most likely African American children. In any number of Asian or Latina/Latino American texts there are situations where a character is confronted with English as a second language. These moments are cast as linguistic epiphanies for characters across the spectrum of American multicultural literatures (for example, Esmeralda Santiago's *Almost a Woman*). In certain situations, readers can readily discern the nuances of identity from the linguistic contextual information.

4. The politics of orthography

Sociolinguistic representations in literature reveal the hegemonic relationship between standard English spellings and the vernaculars that have distinctive linguistic systems but must conform to the standard orthography for standard American English. Politics also underscores the narrative interface between social biases like racism or sexism and the plot, with its characters and their ways of speaking. When speech is represented in literature through misspellings and the use of apostrophes and other diacritical marks (consider *dey be chillin'*), the vernacular is always visually incorrect. This style of representing sociolinguistic variation is a kind of eye dialect – a term linguists have traditionally used to describe techniques for representing in print the speech of characters who speak vernaculars of American English. This is often the most subtle, but probably the most linguistically productive, approach for analyzing the literary representation of identity. As described particularly in chapters 4 and 5 of this book, vernaculars of American English are as systematic and rule-governed as standard American English. In order to portray these vernaculars, authors regularly scramble standard spelling into what appears to be gibberish and looks and reads like a form of language derived from standard American English and subordinate to it.

There are other, less visible ways of conveying vernacular language in literature. Some rely on stereotypes and situational contexts (numbers 2 and 3 above), others on insider knowledge of the vocabulary and sociolinguistic conventions of the vernacular in question (like the dozens in the works of Richard Wright and Zora

Neale Hurston). They also rely on a thorough knowledge of the more subtle (that is, less visible) features of the vernacular such as copula deletion, regularization of verb patterns, and distinct vocabulary features, all of which we will illustrate.

These four modes of arriving at social identifications in literature function as an analytical model for applying general linguistic concepts not only in literary analysis, but also in critical thinking about race, gender, class, sexual orientation, and other aspects of culture as represented in literature. Literary representations of identity provide critical opportunities for readers to apply linguistic and socio-linguistic concepts to their own thinking and writing on race, gender, class, and sexual orientation. A reader may need to employ only a single technique to recognize the identity of a fictional character. But, beyond the identifying function, these modes reveal the continuous re-creation of identity throughout a text. They present the evolution of identity within the same narrative, for example by code-switching within a few sentences or a paragraph (as in our example below, when in his thoughts Piri Thomas uses a Spanish word to refer to a social worker – thereby representing one of his own identities – but then offers a standard-English reply to the worker, suggesting another identity).

Although these categories appear simple, each of them veils cultural and linguistic nuances. The sections that follow aim to create a general context for various multicultural subsets of American literature. Passages, concepts, and characters from popular texts within these subsets will demonstrate ways in which authors can linguistically key readers into the social identities of their characters.

Autobiography, grammar, and vocabulary in Native American literary identity

In the novel *Indian Killer*, Sherman Alexie creates exemplary fictional and auto-biographical contexts for hashing out many of the issues related to the literary representation of identity. Alexie is the son of a Coeur d'Alene Indian father and a Spokane Indian mother, and his life reads like an American myth. Born with water on the brain and not expected to live, by the age of three he was literate and by the age of five nourishing his mind on Steinbeck's novels. He chose to attend high school in Reardan, Washington, fifty miles outside his own speech community on the Spokane Indian Reservation in Wellpinit, and he excelled athletically and academically. I rehearse his biography only to establish a context for reading his fiction and the world it recreates and for making deductions regarding his use of language and vernacular speech in that fiction.

Indian Killer is a murder mystery that chronicles protagonist John Smith's journey from identity crisis (born Indian and raised white) toward redemption (he is the killer of the title). The linguistic cues originate in the title of the novel and are fleshed out in a scene involving "a stormy Indian activist" named Marie and her professor of Native American literature, Dr. Clarence Mather. The fiery exchange between them ultimately leads Professor Mather to suggest that Marie withdraw from the class. The classroom atmosphere is already tense as Marie cynically suggests that her white classmates are skipping the class because of a media-inflamed fear of the deadly Indian Killer: "Just like white people, worried that some killer Indian was going to storm a university classroom" (Alexie 1996: 246). After rudely interrupting Mather's lecture, Marie boldly questions his authenticity as a scholar. He is not a Native American and from Marie's perspective does not proffer an authentic representation of Indian culture in "Intro to Native American Literature." When one volatile classroom discussion shifts to the Indian Killer, Marie explodes.

> "I mean, calling him the Indian Killer doesn't make any sense, does it? If it was an Indian doing the killing, then wouldn't he be called the Killer Indian? I mean Custer was an Indian killer, not a killer Indian."   (Alexie 1996: 247)

Marie's syntactic re-interpretation of the title – and, by implication, of the general theme of the entire book – highlights the linguistic underpinnings of the divide between Seattle's Native American and white populations with respect to the enigmatic Indian Killer.

The notion that racial prejudice can be reinforced by discrete grammatical structures is a reminder that Native American (Vernacular) English retains linguistic residue from various Native American languages. Consider the structure of the ritualized greeting interrogative: *Which tribe you are?* Spoken by numerous characters in Sherman Alexie's work, this question initiates contact between Native Americans who mark their greeting discourse with syntax that harkens back to the history about which they are inquiring. The most common employment of eye dialect in Alexie's work is the tag *enit*, which represents a form of consonant cluster reduction in the phrase *isn't it*, which is short usually for *isn't it true* or possibly *ain't it*. In general, though, Alexie and other Native American authors do not use eye dialect to capture the vernacular language of their characters. Still, the linguistic cues to identity are plentiful. In greeting rituals, Native American characters refer to each other as *cousin*, regardless of their actual relationship, and this vocabulary choice to mark ethnic identity is telltale. There are other examples in Alexie's work and in the entire corpus of Native American literary works. But *Indian Killer* posits itself as a linguistic text (one chapter carries the title "Deconstruction"), and so it is not surprising that it exemplifies many of the nuances and markers of Native American speech communities as they function and interact with the standard American-English-speaking community.

Representing Latino/Latina American identity in stereotypes, vocabulary, and codeswitching

Each type of American literature entails a unique combination of historical and cultural issues that complicates the critical process of integrating sociolinguistics into the interpretive process. Latino/Latina American literature exemplifies these complications fully. Because there are no "Latino" people and no single Latin nation, the descriptor "Latino American" in *Latino American literature* represents a pan-ethnic identity that would include Mexicans, Puerto Ricans, Cubans, Colombians, and others who are writing about or from a Latino/Latina American experience. Much as chapter 13 makes the point about the term *Asian American*, describing the varied Latino/Latina population with a single term is problematical. "Although loosely united by a common heritage as native Spanish speakers from the Americas or their descendants, the numerous Latino groups in the United States are ethnically, racially, and socioeconomically heterogeneous; each Latino subgroup represents a distinct cultural and geographic area of the Americas" (Augenbraum and Olmos 2000).

Each group also represents a distinct (geo)political and linguistic relationship to the USA. Scholars pinpoint 1848 as the birth of Chicano or Mexican American literature because in that year Mexico ceded the southwest territories to USA domination (Martinez and Lomell 1985). Chicano literature was thus born as Mexicans were forced geographically and linguistically to become Americans. Likewise, US Puerto Rican literature is defined against Puerto Rico's colonial relationship to the USA. And the complexities abound as Puerto Rican writers grapple with island (that is, Caribbean) and Nuyorican (US Puerto Ricans, who in early migration periods were concentrated in New York City) distinctions that challenge their ethnic authenticity.

Within this mixture of political circumstances can be found explanations for the sociolinguistic strategies employed by Latino American authors. Certainly, the Latino names of authors such as Sandra Cisneros and Esmeralda Santiago provide autobiographical cues for how to interpret uses of language within a given narrative. In Latino American literature in general, the use of Spanish (and Spanglish) words and phrases clues readers into the ethnicity of characters, as with Piri Thomas's use of *maricon*, which we will discuss further below.

Maybe the most common employment of eye dialect among Latino American literary characters is the use of *ee* for the *i* vowel in spellings like *leetle seesters* ('little sisters') or *hospeetal*. This visual dialect highlights the Spanish vowel system. More significantly, though, it represents characteristic pronunciation features of some American English vernaculars and positions certain characters outside mainstream communities speaking standard American English. The fact that Latino American literature (like Asian American literature) has a vibrant national language outside American English creates linguistic and literary space for authors to play with the politics of orthography. When a misspelling can be directly attributable to an acknowledged independent language (rather than being a "measly" vernacular or dialect), a reader's experience with those nonstandard-speaking characters has a greater propensity for linguistic respect and understanding. Our sociolinguistic biases seem to favor languages with their own nations. A rudimentary introduction will instruct students of Spanish that the long *e* vowel is far more common than the short *i* vowel. Moreover, this long *e* vowel is often orthographically rendered as the letter 'i' in Spanish languages. Thus, the eye-dialectal mistake is understood as circumstantial (a consequence of second-language acquisition) rather than being an indication of intelligence or a lack of it.

In her memoir, *Almost a Woman*, Esmeralda Santiago (1998: 17) writes about her confusing experiences with learning American English.

> In school, I listened for words that sounded like those I'd read the night before. But spoken English, unlike Spanish, wasn't pronounced as written. *Water* became "waddah," *work* was "woik," and wordsranintoeachother in a torrent of confusing sounds that bore no resemblance to the neatly organized letters on the pages of books.

What is striking about the examples in this passage is that Santiago's ability to learn standard English is impeded by vernacular features of American English, some of which are peculiar to the Northeast: the loss of /r/ at the end of words (*water*) and when it occurs before consonants (as in *work*), the characteristic New York City pronunciation of *work* as "woik," as well as the more generally American pronunciation of intervocalic /t/ almost like /d/ in *water*. This autobiographical episode speaks to the false hierarchical status of standard American English, which, in reality, is an aggregate of vernaculars that vary from region to region, as well as by ethnicity, socioeconomic status, and age. Standard American English is more of a sociopolitical ideal than a linguistic reality, as Santiago ultimately figures out. "We invented words if we didn't know the translation for what we were trying to say, until we had our own language . . ." (17).

When Santiago must learn "The Star-Spangled Banner," her own linguistic instincts take over. We can focus our interpretation of the following with an understanding that Santiago uses this literary opportunity to highlight both the linguistic irony in learning to speak English and, from her Puerto Rican viewpoint, the mystification inherent in the process. Her mishearing and misspeaking of "The Star-Spangled Banner" subtly (and not so subtly) reveal the oppressive undercurrents in her American experience.

> Ojo se. Can. Juice. Y
> Bye de don surly lie
> Whassoprowow we hell
> Add debt why lie lass gleam in.
> Whosebrods tripe sand by Stars?
> True de perro los Ay
> Order am parts we wash
> Wha soga lang tree streem in.

The fact that *lie* and *hell* have become part of Santiago's "Star-Spangled Banner" suggests the dire nature of her situation and all the miscues that nonnative speakers must come to grips with in order to become full-fledged linguistic members of mainstream American society. As the national anthem, "The Star-Spangled Banner" is the song that allegedly represents the USA and its important ideals. Yet for Santiago, who is forced to learn it before she has completely grasped American English, it has become an anti-anthem. The nonsense – the hell and lies of racism and linguistic oppression – are what she most immediately associates with her American experience. Santiago's vehicle for expressing these sentiments is a common stereotype that exploits the difficulties nonnative speakers face in acquiring standard American English.

Reminiscent of other traditional stereotypes directed at Latino Americans are the autobiographical accounts of Piri Thomas in *Down these Mean Streets*. On welfare, Thomas's family masked their thoughts and feelings in order to survive economically while navigating a mainstream set of social stigmas directed at them. During an exchange with a social worker when Thomas was a young boy, he thinks to himself, "Damn . . . don't beg that maricon, don't get on your knees no more, Momma." But what he says to the worker is altogether different: "My mother says she needs sheets, blankets, a mattress, shoes for the kids, coats and a pair of pants for me." He then quickly says to his mother (in Spanish, but written in English) "Can I tell him I need some gloves too?" Note the contrasts among the vernacular thinking (a double negative in *don't get on your knees no more* and the disparaging Spanish-language term *maricon*, meaning 'faggot, queer'), the standard pronunciations (*My mother says* . . .), and the spoken Spanish orthographically represented as standard American English. Thomas thinks in the vernacular but speaks standard English or in Spanish when he engages in economic discourse. The standard English orthography in the question directed to his mother (and spoken in Spanish so that the social worker could not understand it) suggests that he uses a standard Spanish to ask it.

The strategies that emerge from autobiographical narratives like those of Piri Thomas are akin to what has been described as claiming the "power of the image." The signal difference is that language and linguistic expectations along racial or gender lines become the object of power. As a young boy, Thomas uses his bilingual code-switching abilities and his ability to codeswitch between vernacular and standard varieties in concert with subtle strategies performed by his mother (in her exchange with the officer, she presents herself as a feeble old woman, which in fact she is not), all strategically designed to achieve a desired economic result. Language can thus represent not only social identity but also strategic identity – an identity role-played for those in superordinate positions of power. As critic Karla Holloway (1995: 34) puts it, "knowing what others may imagine they see when they look at us is necessary and critical information. Without this awareness, we behave as if our bodies and our color do not provoke a certain stereotype and initiate a particular response. And we turn over to others, who do not have our best interests at heart, the power of the image." Stereotypes function the same way with respect to language attitudes and mainstream opinions regarding nonstandard speakers.

Representing African American literary identity by situational context and orthography

Applying the four analytical concepts described earlier in this chapter to the interpretation of African American literature presents some of the most fruitful analyses for understanding the myriad relationships among identity, linguistics, and literature. After mainstream American literature, African American literature provides the largest corpus of texts from which to make assessments and draw conclusions about representing identity in American literature. African American literature and literary representations of the speech of black people date back to the dawn of American literature. From the very start, however, the speech of slaves and later of ex-slaves, as expressed even by well-intentioned authors, has been orthographically contorted into what appears to be ignorant approximations of standard English.

In *Huckleberry Finn*, Huck's sidekick, Jim, provides a prototypical example.

> "Goodness gracious, is dat you Huck? En you ain' dead – you ain' drownded – you's back ag'in? . . . Lemme look at you chile, lemme feel o' you. No, you ain' dead! You's back ag'in, 'live en soun', jis de same old Huck."   (Twain, BEP version: 73)

Orthography overindulged (as in this example) is the least subtle way of conveying identity in literature, and it is sometimes the most offensive. Traditionally, Twain has been praised as a dialectologist, a southern scholar who traveled the south thoroughly in order to represent the speech of his characters accurately. This may be true, but it is useful to bear in mind that literature limits the authenticity of vernacular speech in at least two ways. First, you cannot hear it. Second, vernaculars cannot be adequately represented using standard orthography.

By contrast with Twain and others, African American authors have made orthographic transitions away from eye dialect toward a textually invisible vernacular. If orthography is a way of representing language using letters and diacritics, then traditional literary attempts to represent African American Vernacular English tend to destabilize standard English orthography and limit the reader's understanding of the vernacular by representing it as orthographic approximations to standard English – an approximation highlighted by the use of apostrophes, for example. Note how, in the excerpt below from Chesnutt's *The Conjure Woman* (1899), the use of apostrophes does not highlight the character of the vernacular but its difference from standard English:

> De nex' mawnin' de man wuz foun' dead. Dey wuz a great 'miration made 'bout it, but Dan did'n say nuffin, en none er de yuther niggers had n' seed de fight, so dey wa'n't nuffin done 'bout it, en de cunjuh man come en tuk his son en kyared 'im 'way en buried 'im.   (1969: 172)

There is a spectrum of representations of African American Vernacular English in literature, ranging from Harriet Beecher Stowe (1811–96) and Charles

Chesnutt (1858–1932) in the nineteenth century to Jean Toomer (1894–1967) and Gloria Naylor (b. 1950) in the twentieth. It is Richard Wright (1908–60), though, who demonstrates in *Uncle Tom's Children* a politically profound orthographic transition away from the earlier representation exhibited by Chesnutt. Here there are no diacritics that invite comparison with other vernaculars or with standard English orthography.

> The white folks ain never gimme a chance! They ain never give no black man a chance! There ain nothin in yo whole life yuh kin keep from em! They take yo lan! They take yo freedom! They take yo women! N then they take yo life!
> (Wright 1993 [1938]: 152)

Note that Wright does not use the excessive apostrophes characteristic of Chesnutt's orthography. With Wright's representation of African American Vernacular English, the vernacular begins, orthographically, to stand on its own, as it stands on its own in conversational interaction. Showing "less" orthographically can reveal *more* of the systematic and stylistically beautiful elements of African American Vernacular English. Compare Wright's *em* with Chesnutt's *'im*, his *lan* and *nothin* with Chesnutt's *nex'* and *foun'* and *mawnin'*. Of course, in some respects, both Wright and Chesnutt treat the vernacular the same: Wright's *yuh*, *yo*, *kin* resemble Chesnutt's *nuffin* and *gimme*.

In addition to orthographical innovation, Wright also employs distinctive ritualistic features of African American Vernacular English such as the dozens. "Big Boy Leaves Home," his first short story, begins with several black boys playing the dozens.

> "Yo Mama don wear no drawers,
> Ah seena when she pulled em off,
> N she washed 'em in alcohol,
> N she hung 'em out in the hall . . ."
>   (1993 [1938]: 17)

In the words of Smitherman (2000), the dozens is "a verbal ritual of talking negatively about someone's mother . . . by coming up with outlandish, highly exaggerated, often sexually loaded, humorous 'insults'. . . . The term . . . is believed to have originated during enslavement, wherein slave auctioneers sold defective 'merchandise,' e.g., sick slaves or older slaves, in lots of a dozen; thus a slave who was part of a dozens group was 'inferior'." Through the figurative language of African American Vernacular English in African American literature (including the dozens, sermons, and rapping), readers can begin to understand a more comprehensive, systematic approach to identifying black speakers without the visible orthographic approximations found, for example, in the excerpts from Chesnutt's *The Conjure Woman* and Twain's *Huck Finn*.

Variations in orthographic strategies for representing black speech in literature highlight political subtleties in how authors portray characters and, by extension, how readers perceive the real-life speech communities these characters represent.

An excerpt from Ralph Ellison's *Invisible Man* (1952: 65) demonstrates how some of the less visible orthographic strategies play themselves out in literature.

> "When I see Matty Lou stretched out there I think she's dead. Ain't no color in her face and she ain't hardly breathin'. She gray in the face. I tries to help her but I can't do no good and Kate won't speak to me nor look at me even; and I thinks maybe she plans to try to kill me agin, but she don't. I'm in such a daze I just sits there the whole time while she bundles up the younguns and takes 'em down the road to Will Nichols'. I can see but I caint do nothin'."

Although Ellison relies on apostrophes in his orthography (*'em, nothin'*), he also displays significant vernacular verbal regularization in this speech (*I tries, I thinks, I just sits*), as well as deleted copulas (*She gray in the face*). These features of African American Vernacular English are orthographically "invisible" in that they are not represented by "errors" in the standard spelling. They can thus convey the style and language of the vernacular without making African American Vernacular English seem orthographically derivative or inferior. Essential to the African American writer's work, this is *underground signifying*. Beneath the surface of standard orthography lurks the linguistic structure and vernacular dexterity of African American Vernacular English. In this sense, "underground" describes the encoded or hidden vernacular features versus the more obvious – and misleading – representations of eye dialect.

Analyzing orthography and various individual vernacular features is not the only way of reading linguistic identity in African American literature. Zora Neale Hurston's oeuvre provides an exceptional opportunity for appreciating the relationships among literature, linguistics, and identity. Hurston (1903–60) was a student of Franz Boas, a firm believer in an anthropological approach to language analysis and regarded by some as the father of American linguistics; he led the field toward thoroughly empirical goals (Harris 1993: 19–20). Hurston's life work was dedicated to collecting and representing the vernacular culture of southern black people, particularly from speech communities in her home state of Florida. More importantly, she undertakes to represent the verbal virtuosity of black women. Sociolinguists who studied black speech after Hurston had published her most famous novel, *Their Eyes Were Watching God* (1937), attributed much of the quantifiable data on African American Vernacular English to male speakers. Not only does Hurston present understudied female informants in her anthropological work, but in *Their Eyes Were Watching God* she also creates characters who advance a womanist agenda (long before the term *feminism* came into vogue) through vernacular speech, often in speaking situations dominated by males. In order fully to appreciate the worldview that Hurston affects through language and speech community, you must read the novel. Its protagonist Janie is "powerful, articulate, self reliant, and radically different from any woman character [that black women readers] had ever before encountered in literature" (Washington 1998: xi). Her narrative is actually told by her friend Phoeby, and one literary critic has argued that "Janie's voice at the end of the novel is a communal one, that when she tells Phoeby to tell her story ('You can tell 'em what Ah say if you wants to. Dat's just de same as me 'cause mah tongue is in mah friend's mouf') she is choosing a collective rather than an individual voice, demonstrating her closeness to the collective spirit of the African American Oral tradition" (Michael Awkward; quoted in Washington 1998: xiv). The words *mah tongue is in mah friend's mouf* also speak directly to a bond between Phoeby and Janie. In Phoeby's mouth, Janie's life story is safe from misrepresentation.

Janie's journey toward her full-fledged identity begins in puberty and ends in tragedy. Along the way, she marries a politically ambitious dominating husband named Joe Starks. After years in an economically stable relationship, Janie's capacity for holding her tongue in verbally abusive interactions with Joe utterly diminishes. In a store that the couple owns and operates, several dozens-like exchanges with Joe in front of an audience of their (mostly men) friends involving "some good natured laughter at the expense of women" bring Janie to her boiling point (Hurston 1998 [1937]: 78–79).

> "Naw, Ah ain't no young gal no mo' but den Ah ain't no old woman neither. Ah reckon Ah looks mah age too. But Ah'm uh woman every inch of me, and Ah know it. Dat's uh whole lot more'n you kin say. *You* big-bellies round here and put out a lot of brag, but 'tain't nothin' to it but yo' big voice. Humph! Talkin' 'bout me lookin' old! When you pull down yo' britches, you look lak de change uh life."

Within weeks of this exchange (just four pages later in the novel), Joe Starks becomes fatally ill, and the narrative implies that he does not recover from having been verbally put in his place in front of his own speech community. After Joe's death, Janie takes over the store and eventually moves into the next phase of her development as a woman: a relationship in which she finds some spiritual and sexual satisfaction.

Among the most extraordinary moments in American literature with respect to linguistics and the identity of speech communities is one that occurs in Chesnutt's *The Conjure Woman* (1899). Above, we saw examples of the eye dialect Chesnutt used to depict the speech of his main character Julius, who recounts various tales of a surreal way of life that features root work and conjuring amongst slaves in Lumberton, North Carolina. Lumberton is a tri-dialectal community, including southern vernacular varieties of speech from Native Americans (the Lumbee), African Americans, and southern white Americans. But that's not what is most striking about the use of language in *The Conjure Woman*.

Chesnutt is deliberate in distinguishing Julius's speech community from that of the northern white couple who take up residence on his former master's plantation. The couple speaks standard American English. Julius speaks African American Vernacular English, and he tells his stories – explains his reality – in the vernacular. Most of his folktale-like narratives involve a metamorphosis or transformation. One woman turns her illegal husband (illegal because by law slaves could not marry) into a tree in an attempt to keep him close to her. The conjure woman turns another character into a humming bird so that he might find a loved one. In another tale, a conjure man turns a slave into a donkey. In general, the northern, white business-minded husband does not believe the surreal aspects of these vernacular narratives. His wife, however, is somewhat more sympathetic to the fantastic tales.

One day, before Julius is able to bend the wife's ear, her husband begins to read to her from a philosophy text.

> The difficulty of dealing with transformations so many-sided as those which all existences have undergone, or are undergoing, is such as to make a complete and deductive interpretation almost hopeless. So to grasp the total process of redistribution of matter and motion as to see simultaneously its several necessary results in their actual interdependence is scarcely possible. There is, however, a mode of rendering the process as a whole tolerably comprehensible. Though the genesis of the rearrangement of every evolving aggregate is in itself one, it presents to our intelligence –   (Chesnutt 1969: 163–64)

At this point, the husband is interrupted by his wife, who refers to his philosophy as nonsense. The husband thinks to himself: "I had never been able to interest my wife in the study of philosophy, even when presented in the simplest and most lucid form" (164).

We can think of this episode as a complex case of sociolinguistic irony. The wife believes the philosophical passage is nonsense, but a close reading shows that this philosophy is grappling with a (standard English) scientific explanation of the fantastic reality that Julius has so vividly described (in the vernacular) to the couple since they moved south. The irony is further complicated by the fact that the husband critiques his wife as though he completely understood the philosophy he is reading. Yet he makes no connection between "transformations" or "redistribution of matter" and the tales of metamorphosis that Julius tells. To the husband this *philosophy* is completely legitimate, but Julius's world is inauthentic fantasy. In reality, the only "thing" that separates these two worldviews is variation in language.

We can push the envelope of this interpretation a bit further by introducing the notion of linguistic transformations. In the 1950s and 1960s, transformational-generative grammar shifted some subfields of linguistic inquiry away from empiricism and closer to cognition. Grammar developed into an abstract formula whereby linguistic structure accounted for meaning. Transformations were viewed as cognitive functions that transformed underlying phrase markers (say, noun phrases or verb phrases) into grammatical sentences (see Harris 1993: 47). But such transformations are absent from the linguistic processes of the husband and wife in *The Conjure Woman*: the surface sentences of the philosophical passage are incomprehensible to them both.

Chesnutt's sense of transformation and its inherent function in language and in the realities created and shaped by language are fleshed out in the narratives of Julius, as well as in this peculiar philosophical passage where transformation gets a standard overhaul, but, still, speakers of standard American English cannot grasp the totality of its meaning.

Conclusion

We have examined four modes of representing ethnic identity in literature and thus four ways of analyzing literary representation of social identity more generally. In Native American literature, we exemplified how autobiography, grammar, and vocabulary represent identity. We saw literary representations of Latino/Latina American identity in stereotypes, vocabulary, and codeswitching. We exemplified how African American identity may be represented by situational context and by orthography. Analysis of sociolinguistic identity presents several possible interpretive approaches to American literature.

Acknowledgments

I thank Marcela Poveda for her invaluable research assistance and ability to select passages for this chapter.

Suggestions for further reading and exploration

The principles discussed in this chapter are exemplified in Alexie's *Indian Killer* (1996), Chesnutt's *The Conjure Woman* (1969), Ellison's *Invisible Man* (1995), Hurston's *Their Eyes Were Watching God* (1998), Wright's *Uncle Tom's Children* (1993), Santiago's *When I was Puerto Rican* (1994) and *Almost a Woman* (1998), and Thomas's *Down These Mean Streets* (1967). Twain's *Adventures of Huckleberry Finn* (1999) is of course a classic. Among helpful analysis of ethnic identity in literature are Holloway (1995) and Martinez and Lomell (1985). In addition to the suggestions for further reading made by the author, the editors would add Hagedorn (1993), a rich collection of Asian American fiction written by dozens of authors, Kudaka (1995), which contains pieces of general and linguistic interest by scores of Asian American authors, and Leong (2000), containing several short stories by a single author. Helpful analysis can be found in Wong (1993) and Eng and Hom (1998). We also recommend Rodriguez (1993), a coming of age tale set among gangs in East Los Angeles and winner of the Carl Sandburg Literary Arts Award for Nonfiction. Among work by Native Americans, we would recommend Welch (1986, 1990) and for nonfiction Welch (1994). Toni Morrison was awarded the Nobel Prize for *Sula* (1973), which deserves attention for its representation of language.

References

Alexie, Sherman. 1996. *Indian Killer*. New York: Warner Books.
Augenbraum, Harold and Margarite Fernández Olmos, eds. 2000. *U.S. Latino Literature: a Critical Guide for Students and Teachers*. Westport CT: Greenwood.
Chesnutt, Charles. 1969 [1899]. *The Conjure Woman*. Ann Arbor: University of Michigan Press.

Ellison, Ralph. 1995 [1952]. *Invisible Man*. New York: Random House/Vintage.

Eng, David L. and Alice Y. Hom, eds. 1998. *Q&A: Queer in Asian America*. Philadelphia: Temple University Press.

Hagedorn, Jessica, ed. 1993. *Charlie Chan is Dead: an Anthology of Contemporary Asian American Fiction*. New York: Penguin.

Harris, Randy Allen. 1993. *The Linguistic Wars*. New York: Oxford University Press.

Holloway, Karla F. C. 1995. *Codes of Conduct: Race, Ethics, and the Color of our Character*. New Brunswick NJ: Rutgers University Press.

Hurston, Zora Neale. 1998 [1937]. *Their Eyes Were Watching God*. New York: Harper Perennial.

Kudaka, Geraldine. 1995. *On a Bed of Rice: an Asian American Erotic Feast*. New York: Anchor.

Leong, Russell Charles. 2000. *Phoenix Eyes and Other Stories*. Seattle: University of Washington Press.

Martinez, Julio and Francisco Lomell, eds. 1985. *Chicano Literature: a Reference Guide*. London: Greenwood.

Rodriguez, Luis J. 1993. *Always Running: La Vida Loca: Gang Days in L.A*. New York: Touchstone.

Santiago, Esmerelda. 1994. *When I was Puerto Rican*. New York: Vintage.
    1998. *Almost a Woman*. Reading MA: Perseus.

Smitherman, Geneva. 2000. *Black Talk: Words and Phrases from the Hood to the Amen Corner*, rev. edn. Boston: Houghton Mifflin.

Thomas, Piri. 1967. *Down these Mean Streets*. New York: Knopf.

Twain, Mark. 1999. *Adventures of Huckleberry Finn*. New York: Norton.

Washington, Mary Helen. 1998. "Foreword." *Their Eyes Were Watching God*: a Novel by Zora Neale Hurston with a Foreword by Mary Helen Washington and an Afterword by Henry Louis Gates, Jr. New York: HarperPerennial.

Welch, James. 1986 [1974]. *Winter in the Blood*. New York: Penguin.
    1990. *The Indian Lawyer*. New York: Penguin.

Welch, James, with Paul Steklar. 1994. *Killing Custer: the Battle of the Little Bighorn and the Fate of the Plains Indians*. New York: Penguin.

Wong, Sau-ling Cynthia. 1993. *Reading Asian American Literature: From Necessity to Extravagance*. Princeton: Princeton University Press.

Wright, Richard. 1993 [1938]. *Uncle Tom's Children*. New York: HarperPerennial Edition.

24

The language of doctors and patients

CYNTHIA HAGSTROM

Editors' introduction

The late twentieth century witnessed a surge in interest in the professional language of law and medicine. Concern about the gap between expert language – in law, for example – and the abilities of clients to understand specialized "legal" language that could significantly impact their lives prompted legislation designed to ensure comprehensible consumer contracts such as insurance policies, automobile rental agreements, and apartment leases. Another enterprise in which language is critical to success is the interaction between doctors and patients, although it has not been the subject of legislation to the same degree. This chapter outlines three stages in the history of medical practice – from a time when neither doctors nor patients understood much about sickness to one in which scientific understanding and advanced diagnostic and therapeutic technologies have enhanced the practice of medicine but brought dissatisfaction and frustration to patients and some doctors over their medical encounters. Examining interaction in office visits, Cynthia Hagstrom exemplifies open-ended and closed-ended questions directed by doctors to their patients, and she suggests how different question types can affect replies and hinder or enhance the shared objectives of doctor and patient. You will see how the "voice of the life-world" and the "voice of medicine" can lead to misunderstanding and poorer medical outcomes.

The chapter also analyzes conversational asymmetry. Socially and culturally, as a consequence of physicians' technical knowledge and the institutional asymmetry of a patient seeking a doctor's expertise and guidance, doctors exercise greater power and control in interaction with patients. The asymmetry can be underscored by recognizing that doctors ask questions of patients and touch them in ways that would be alarming (or antic) the other way around. Among the linguistic factors that maintain the asymmetry are depersonalized language (not "*your* leg" but "*the* leg") and asymmetrical terms of address (title plus family name for "Dr. Smith" vs. first name for patient "Chris"), and even humor. Doctors ask questions of patients and interrupt them more frequently than the other way around. The sex of doctor and of patient can also affect interactional style – and the medical outcome. Successful doctor–patient interaction is an essential element in effective medical encounters. Looking to the future, Hagstrom sees a more consumerist view of medicine and a continuation of the "Patient Bill of Rights" movement, with a better balance in communication between doctor and patient – and better medical outcomes. Reading this chapter may be an exercise in good health all by itself.

Language and medicine

> I recently found myself in a situation that to most doctors is more terrifying than a malpractice lawsuit – being a patient myself . . . The health-care system has traditionally been controlling and dehumanizing, and it is up to patients, at least in part, to make it more respectful, collaborative, and understanding of the needs of people and their families.   (Zeev E. Neuwirth, MD, *New York Times*, 22 June, 1999)

> Our trail leads us to an energetic, caring woman about our age who runs a thriving practice of her own while raising four young children on the side. She applauds our careful consumerism. "Medicine is all about how you feel," she agrees. "If you don't feel good about your doctor, your doctor probably isn't going to help you feel good about your health."   (Doug Adrianson, Editor, Ventura County Edition, *Los Angeles Times Magazine*, 1 February, 1998)

Everyone has opinions about how medical talk should be conducted, and the two fragments above from newspaper articles about contemporary medical care express common assumptions about the roles of patients and doctors – that patients should be good consumers of medicine, question their doctors, and expect sympathy and respect. Doctors today are expected to talk to patients in a way that demonstrates sensitivity to their needs and to collaborate with patients to make them "feel good." Of course, talk is the essential tool to accomplish these goals.

Medical communication has been extensively researched, and studies in the fields of medical education, communication, anthropology, linguistics, sociology, and psychology have made important contributions to our understanding. It's fair to say that these researchers would generally agree that talk is the central ingredient in medical encounters, but there are differences of opinion as to how to evaluate medical talk. When an area of investigation is at the intersection of several disciplines, each discipline applies its own methods of analysis. Some have characterized these different methods as a focus on "cure" versus "care," a medico-biological orientation versus a socio-relational orientation. In either approach, talk is crucial. The "cure" (medico-biological) studies are concerned with how information about the patient's condition gets transferred between doctor and patient, and talk is viewed merely as a transmission channel to gather information about a patient or to persuade the patient to take the appropriate action. The "cure" studies tend to be results-oriented with goals such as the satisfaction of the patient, how quickly the patient recovered from the illness (outcome), or how well patients followed the treatment plan (compliance).

The socio-relational approach is concerned with observing how education, gender, ethnic origin, socioeconomic status, and power affect the delivery of healthcare. Socio-relational approaches have shown that doctors and patients often manipulate talk to mirror the perceived role, or the position or power of the speaker. The "cure" and "care" orientations are based on different conceptions of physician and patient: patient as object, with a body to be repaired (medico-biological) or doctor and patient as a team negotiating solutions to the patient's health concerns (socio-relational).

Another way of distinguishing approaches to medical communication is quantitative versus qualitative studies. Quantitative approaches emphasize the scientific method and tend to connect observations to numbers. Qualitative approaches seldom abstract away from their observations by assigning numerical values. Qualitative studies often focus on individual cases and rely on interviews and direct records from verbatim transcripts of audio and video recordings. In a method called Conversation Analysis researchers have examined how the medical encounter unfolds turn by turn. Valuable insights into power and control have been gained from these close analyses. Of course, the situation is more complicated than this. Both quantitative and qualitative methods are often applied to the same study, and they can complement each other in pursuit of greater understanding (Roter and Frankel 1992).

A brief history of medical communication

To understand the evolution of talk in medicine it is helpful to understand the social history of medicine. The history of "modern" medicine can be divided into three periods (Shorter 1985): the traditional period (1750–1850), the modern period (1880–1950), and the post-modern period (1960 to the present). The time gaps between each period are transitional phases when some of the previous attitudes remain as the next period is emerging.

During the traditional period doctor training was by apprenticeship. There was limited ability to treat disease. The common view was that disease resulted from excess or from corrupt putrefaction that should be drained or cut out of the body. That is, patients were thought to cause their own disease either by neglect or by overindulgence. Cures entailed removing the foul humors. From the patient's perspective, diseases seemed random. There was great tolerance for terrible symptoms because little could be done. Patients relied on magical remedies, treated themselves and often argued with their doctors about treatment. Doctors had little formal training, and their main power over patients was in their ability to administer strong drugs. Patients did not believe that physicians had much special knowledge, and they viewed doctors as a last resort.

During the modern period (1880–1950) scientific techniques developed that enabled doctors to diagnose more diseases and even cure them. The invention of tools such as the stethoscope, microscope, blood pressure cuff, and electrocardiogram, as well as the identification of bacteria as a cause of disease produced a revolution in medical practice. Scientific experiments that showed the direct connection between drugs (like aspirin, quinine, insulin) and their palliative effect led to a mechanical approach in treating patients. Essentially patients presented their bodies as objects to be repaired, and healing came from taking the correct drug and following the doctor's orders. Medical education became formal, and doctors obtained specialized knowledge of disease and treatment methods in medical schools. Medical education and the resulting successful treatment led to the social elevation of doctors in the community. Treatments based on scientific principles were believed to be beyond the understanding of most ordinary patients, and a paternalistic mode of interaction between doctor and patient became the norm. "Put yourself in the hands of the expert, do what the doctor orders, do not question decisions – and you will get better."

The post-modern period from 1960 onwards has seen a further shift in attitudes. Once doctors had the ability to cure major illnesses and make accurate predictions about prognosis, the attention of patients shifted to health problems of lesser magnitude. Today patients' expectations about doctors' abilities to treat any illness have increased, and they have become more and more consumerist in their approach to healthcare. They shop around for the "best" treatment in terms of both cure and care. Meanwhile today's doctors are confronted with cost pressures and time demands to accomplish cures and as a consequence they become irritated by trivial or imaginary complaints. Because modern medical training focuses on the scientific method, doctors are pressured to have selective attention and to exclude non-observable or untestable symptoms. This in turn leads to patients who are willing to criticize physicians or take charge of their own care because it seems the doctor isn't listening. In some ways the behavior of the postmodern patient is becoming more like traditional patient behavior questioning their doctor's decision. Many patients select their caregivers for their ability to spend time, listen, and take their concerns seriously. These general shifts in attitudes toward treatment have important implications for the talk that occurs in the interaction between doctor and patient.

The role of talk in medical encounters

In medical encounters, talk is used to obtain and convey information, to influence or control situations. By labeling the structures of the events taking place, talk is used to define them. For example we can say that a doctor's speaking style is doctor-centered or patient-centered. Medical talk has been studied quantitatively (using large samples of talk) and qualitatively (looking at a single case or just a few cases) (Ong et al. 1995).

The structure of medical encounters: two points of view

The organization of a medical encounter is familiar because it is so consistent. We could say that medical encounters are like any multi-step service encounter. I realize I have a health problem that I cannot remedy myself. I make an appointment with my doctor. I appear at the doctor's office at the appointed time. I complete some forms regarding payment for services. I see a nurse who does a preliminary exam (weight, blood pressure) and asks me a few questions. Then I go to an examining room and wait for the doctor. When the doctor comes in to examine me s/he has a copy of my record. I tell the doctor what my concerns are, s/he reads my record, asks me questions, examines me, makes a diagnosis and recommends treatment that may include medications, further tests, referral to another doctor. Then the encounter ends. I fill my prescription, arrange for the tests, or make a new appointment. This procedure is repeated thousands of times every day in US clinics. Throughout these events talk is used to obtain information, to describe conditions, to indicate understanding, to give directions and explain the situation. In spite of what appears to be a shared experience, the doctor and the patient may expect different things from the encounter and perceive the talk in different ways.

A detailed study of more than 2000 medical encounters in Britain (Byrne and Long 1976) has led to the classification of six phases in a consultation, and these provide the operating framework that doctors use with patients.

(1) Relating to the patient
(2) Discovering the reason for the visit
(3) Verbal and/or physical examination
(4) Consideration of patient's condition
(5) Detailing treatment or further investigation
(6) Termination

A striking thing about each of the six phases as they are presented here is that they assume the doctor is the agent who controls the events. Returning to my "service encounter" above, we can see that the activities are more or less the same as the six phases but with a decidedly opposite point of view. In the service encounter I am the agent obtaining the service. The goal of the British study was to identify the systematic "process" within the consultation as well as individual components. This structure is called an "ideal," but actual encounters often have variations prompted by time constraints or the degree to which patient and doctor know one another, and so forth. For example the doctor may omit a physical examination with a returning patient who is refilling medications. Also, the order of the consultation is subject to some changes because many patients do not state their main concern in phase 2 but wait even as late as phase 6 to bring it up. These late-breaking revelations are seen as a time management problem for the doctor, since it is the doctor who controls the encounter.

Talk as a channel in medical encounters: information transfer and patient satisfaction

Medico-biological studies of doctor–patient communication are often concerned with information transfer, and talk is viewed merely as the means to accomplish that transfer. *What's the most effective way to tell a patient a negative prognosis? How does questioning style influence satisfaction? What are the reasons that*

patients don't comply with treatment advice? Does detailed explanation influence
a patient's compliance?

Studies that view talk as a tool to accomplish some goal are correlational studies, including surveys of doctors' and patients' attitudes. For example, the cause
of low patient satisfaction is most often correlated with communication difficulties in the doctor–patient interaction. Patients say their doctor did not hear them
and doctors say the patient did not understand. The failure to transfer information has been correlated with compliance with doctors' instructions, satisfaction
with services, and even speed of recovery from surgery (Waitzkin 1985). Patients
often say their doctors don't tell them enough. One survey of patient satisfaction
showed that doctors underestimated patients' desire for information 65 percent
of the time and estimated correctly only 29 percent of the time. One interesting
finding about sharing information was that in encounters with working-class, less
educated patients, the patients asked fewer questions and the doctors provided
less information. The researchers attributed the low number of patient questions
to patients' belief that doctors did not want them to ask questions. The most
common reason given by physicians for not offering information was based on
the observation that the less educated patients frequently used medical vocabulary incorrectly, leading physicians to conclude that medical terminology was too
difficult to understand. With this "competence gap" it is easy to imagine a cycli-
cal scenario in which the physician offers less information, an absence that the
patient misinterprets as a lack of personal interest by the physician in the patient.
The patient comes to believe that the doctor is in a hurry and not interested in
the patient. Fearing that "foolish" questions would waste the doctor's valuable
time, the patient does not ask. The physician believes that the patient does not
ask questions because of the competence gap.

In reality, when they were asked about preferences for sharing information,
working-class patients were just as eager for information as other patients in spite
of their demonstrated reluctance to pursue the information. This research suggests an explanation based on social class. Patients view doctors as superior and
unapproachable because of demonstrated medical expertise and social distance
deriving from social class positions.

One outcome of inadequate information transfer is reduced satisfaction. In
a study of 800 visits to pediatric clinics, 24 percent of the mothers who were
interviewed after the visit stated that they were moderately to highly dissatisfied
with the doctor's performance (Korsch and Negrete 1972). They cited information
sharing as the cause of their dissatisfaction. Nearly one fifth of the mothers stated
that the physician had never discussed what was wrong with their child and nearly
half of the mothers expressed disappointment that the cause of their child's illness
was never explained.

In addition, the correlation between expressed satisfaction with doctor behavior
and patient compliance with instructions seems to be a strong one. For doctors,
compliance means taking medications as directed and following the treatment

plan. When compliance with doctor's instructions was considered, 38 percent of patients complied only in part and 11 percent did not comply at all (Korsch and Negrete 1972). In other words, nearly half the mothers did not follow the treatment recommendations, and that failure to follow the doctor's prescription underlines just how important successful communication is.

Correlational studies connect attitudes reflected through talk. They rely on some kind of coding system to connect the features being correlated. A typical system would be to have independent raters listen to tapes or examine transcripts of medical encounters and code the utterances by doctor and patient into mutually exclusive attitudinal categories. One of the most common coding schemes is derived from Interaction Process Analysis. All utterances are classified into three behavioral categories – positive affect (friendliness, strong agreement, simple attention, tension release), negative affect (shows antagonism, disagrees, shows tension), or neutral affect (introductory phrases, gives information, gives instructions, asks for instructions, seeks opinion, gives opinion, seeks information). The coding systems use "units of sense" but leave it to the coder to identify the unit and classify it. These psychological categories are defined by our understanding of language. For example, in extract 1 below you could imagine coding line 4 as "introductory phrase" or "gives information" or even "gives opinion." All three are *neutral affect* categories. On the other hand, line 4 could also be coded "disagrees," which is a *negative affect* category. Studies of talk as a channel do not rely on the language itself but on what the language means to the coder. (In the transcription, square brackets mark overlapping speech.)

Extract 1 [DPC64BH]
((Opening of the conversation))
1   Doctor: So.
2   Patient: So everything's- just fine
3   Doctor: You look terrific.
4   Patient: My wife don't think so.
5   Doctor: No? Why- what does she think the problem [is]
6   Patient: [She] says my eyes
7   don't look good ([   ])
8   Doctor: [What] do you think.
9   Patient: My knees are- uh I'm healthy healthy as can be.
10 Doctor: Prime-a health.
11 Patient: As far as health. As far as my- I work seven days a week.

The strengths of coding systems are their ability to make generalizations about emotional tone. The coding schemes have yielded strong correlations with other measures of patient satisfaction and compliance. But the system does not allow a statement to be coded as two categories simultaneously even though the speakers may have had more than one thing in mind. Correlational studies are a valuable way to discover the broader uses of medical talk, but to understand all facets we should also look at specific details.

Doctor-centered talk and patient-centered talk

The recent shift to a less paternalistic and more consumer-oriented view of medicine has resulted in a closer look at physicians' language use. The focus on patient satisfaction has led to attention to observations about physician interview style. The two extremes are called doctor-centered talk and patient-centered talk.

In doctor-centered talk the perspective taken is the doctor's point of view with his or her focus on hypothesis testing to discover the medico-biological basis for the patient's problem. In doctor-centered talk, doctors ask closed-ended questions, give directions, and announce decisions. There are few references to what patients say or to the motivations for patient behavior aside from the goal of receiving treatment or medication.

With some more experienced doctors, doctor-centered style is believed to be a "frozen" pattern. During medical training doctors develop a style that stresses the collection of medical facts and the time limitations for the average visit. Implicit in the doctor-centered approaches is the sense of causation. Doctors *cause* actions. Doctors often have a restricted definition of the scope of medicine and do not wish to explore psychosocial care.

By contrast, the goal of patient-centered talk is to maximize collaboration between the doctor and patient. Patient-centered behaviors are described as information-giving, counseling, asking open-ended questions, supplying interpretation of symptoms and tests, paraphrasing to assure comprehension, requesting opinion, confirming comprehension, offering reassurance, making statements of concern, agreement and approval.

Just as physicians have a style for consultations, so patients carry a style to the medical encounters. A "communication gap" that occurs in doctor-centered talk has been called the "voice of the lifeworld" versus the "voice of medicine" (Mischler 1984). There is a potential clash between the way some patients present symptoms from the point of view of their personal life experience and the way doctors gather information in the objective world of medicine. These two general categories ("voice of the life-world" and "voice of medicine") are ways of speaking about experience. The voice of medicine is concerned with facts that are testable and relevant to a medical condition. The voice of the lifeworld is concerned with social reality and may not be viewed by doctors as relevant to a medical condition. (Again, square brackets mark overlapping speech; length of pauses in seconds are indicated within parentheses.)

Extract 2
((The doctor is asking the patient about the history of her severe abdominal pains.))
1 Doctor: How-how soon after you eat it?
2 Patient: (1.5) Well (0.5) probably an hour (0.4) maybe [less
3 Doctor: [About an hour?
4 Patient: Maybe less

5   (1.3) I've cheated and I've been drinking which I shouldn't have done.
6 Doctor: (1.8) Does drinking make it worse?

                              (adapted from Mischler 1984: 106)

The doctor asks questions in the voice of medicine (lines 1 and 6). The patient responds to his questions with factual replies ("Probably an hour, maybe less" in line 2 and "Maybe less" in line 4). Then, after a 1.3-second pause (line 5), the patient adds in the voice of the lifeworld, "I've cheated and I've been drinking which I shouldn't have done." Completely ignoring his patient's shift to the lifeworld, the doctor continues in the voice of medicine, "Does drinking make it worse?" (line 6). It's not difficult to imagine that this patient's real reason for coming to the doctor had more to do with her reasons for drinking than with the physical illness it caused. The lengthy pauses in the utterances of both the doctor (1.8 seconds in line 6) and the patient (1.3 seconds in line 5) give evidence that they recognize the breakdown, though they are at a loss for alternative ways of dealing with the problem (Mischler 1984: 106–08). Both the patient and the doctor come away less than satisfied because of misunderstanding, miscommunication, and failure to address the real problem embedded in the lifeworld utterance.

Talk as the object of study in medical encounters: linguistic details

Both quantitative and qualitative studies examine details within medical talk. Investigators have quantified different forms of talk: total questions, types of questions, length of turns, number of interruptions, use of technical jargon, use of depersonalizing language (*the pregnancy* vs. *your pregnancy*), formality of address (*Mr. Smith* vs. *Bill*), and frequency of laughter. Looking at many of the same language structures, qualitative studies have tried to explain their occurrence in specific contexts.

Questions and answers

Questions and answers constitute a significant part of a medical encounter. Question behavior is related to power because whoever asks a question holds the addressee accountable for an answer; in this sense, the questioner can be said to control the conversation. Studies of questioning behavior in medical encounters show fairly strong patterns, and in one study of twenty-one medical encounters in which 773 questions were asked, patients initiated fewer than 9 percent of them (West 1984).

There are two kinds of questions, called open-ended and closed-ended (Roter and Hall 1992). Closed-ended questions can usually be answered with a single word like "yes" or "no." Closed-ended questions have been associated with scientific objectivity, which limits emotional components. They are often used for hypothesis testing because they restrict the range of possible answers available to the patient, as in this example:

> DOCTOR: Are your leg symptoms worse after standing for several minutes?
> PATIENT: No.

By contrast, open-ended questions typically begin with *what*, *why*, or another WH-word, as in this example:

> DOCTOR: Tell me about your leg pain. What seems to be the problem?

Open-ended questions allow patients greater latitude in their answers and afford them an opportunity to exercise greater control over their response. Open-ended questions can elicit vital information about symptoms that might not have been discovered by using the more restrictive closed-ended questions.

A reconsideration of the conversation opening in extract 1 (repeated below) and a second opening (extract 3) provides examples of the sort of detailed analysis that can be done. (The equal sign (=) indicates latched, closely connected speech, and square brackets mark overlapping speech.)

Extract 1 [DPC64BH] ((repeated))
((Opening of the conversation))

1	Doctor:	So.
2	Patient:	So everything's- just fine
3	Doctor:	You look terrific.
4	Patient:	My wife don't think so.
5 →	Doctor:	No? Why- what does she think the problem [is]
6	Patient:	[She] says my eyes
7		don't look good ([ ])
8 →	Doctor:	[What] do you think.
9	Patient:	My knees are- uh I'm healthy healthy as can be.
10	Doctor:	Prime a health.
11	Patient:	As far as health. As far as my- I work seven days a week.

Extract 3 [DPC2KIM]
((Opening of the conversation))

1	Doctor:	Have a seat.
		((11 lines of discussion about being recorded omitted))
13	Patient:	Well [ah yes
14	Doctor:	Well [yes well
15 →	Doctor:	How have things been going since we last [spoke?
16	Patient:	[Well we were a
17		little bit early I think I think we expected a little
18		bit too much from the cortisone=
19 →	Doctor:	=Did things=
20	Patient:	=Yeah I think we lost its effectiveness.
21	Doctor:	Tell me what happened.

These conversation openings have a familiar ring to them. Even without speaker labels you can probably recognize whose lines are the doctor's and whose are the patient's. Some features that tell us this is a medical encounter include the way that Doctor seems to be in charge. Doctor asks the questions, Patient answers. Both conversations move rather quickly from preliminaries ("So everything's fine" "Have a seat") to specific health concerns ("my knees" in extract 1 and the effectiveness of the cortisone in extract 3). The medical term *cortisone* also alerts us to the likely location of the conversation, a medical clinic. In spite of the different content of the two conversations, we can attribute our instant recognition that this is a medical encounter (and not, say, an ordinary conversation) to our familiarity with the situation. We have all been patients.

The doctor is asking the "reason for the visit" question (lines 5 and 8 in extract 1; and line 15 in extract 3). If we look more closely at the replies of the patients we begin to see that these patients sound somewhat hesitant. In line 9 of extract 1, the patient begins to say, "my knees are –", but he falters, cuts himself off (that's what the dash represents), and then returns to opening pleasantries ("I'm healthy healthy as can be"). He seems reluctant to complain even though, like all of us, he knows that doctors expect patients to have complaints. In lines 16–18 of extract 3, the patient appears to have a clear idea about his problem, but despite his seeming confidence about the reason for his condition, he speaks hesitantly ("a little bit early, I think I think, a little bit too much"). It appears that he is being careful not to tread on the doctor's professional turf by making a diagnosis. This patient's answer, while much more detailed and complete than the patient's answer in extract 1, seems nearly as mitigated. Notice also that in extract 1 and extract 3 the questions are open-ended but the patients chose very different ways to respond. The first patient truncated the reply, while the second one gave a detailed account.

Asymmetry in medical talk: claims to knowledge and power

What is going on in extracts 1 and 3 concerns claims to knowledge and power. Control, and how speakers claim power in conversations, has been thoroughly researched. Investigators have learned that, in medical communication, imbalances of power and control in the doctor–patient interaction come from three sources: institutional asymmetry, situated authority (i.e. the patient comes to the doctor for help), and medical authority based on technical knowledge and professional prestige (West 1984, Ainsworth-Vaughn 1998).

Authority is conferred on physicians by the role they play in the institution. A doctor is a stranger who may ask very personal questions about daily habits (for example about sexual behavior) and then does an examination in which s/he physically touches the patient. These procedures are part of an institutionalized medical encounter. Imagine for a moment what would happen if a patient asked the physician the same personal questions about his or her daily habits and family. By virtue of the institution s/he represents, the doctor has a right to ask these questions; the patient does not.

Studies have focused on different kinds of knowledge or having the right to knowledge. For example, the doctor as a representative of the institution is the expert whom the patient consults for advice. The patient is in a one down position, knowing less than the doctor. Also as part of the institution the physician sees the patient as one of possibly many with the same condition. Thus the doctor has a larger context in which to judge the patient's condition. Further the physician has access to knowledge about the infrastructure of the medical institution itself. In general, patients do not have much information about the function of the medical institution. The doctor is a "guide" who tells the patient what tests should be done or which specialists should be consulted.

Another sort of asymmetry concerns the status of knowledge: How you came to know what you know. What is the source of your knowledge? The objective observations of a physical exam and medical tests performed with impersonal equipment generally have higher status as a way of knowing. Related to direct observation is the way of describing that knowledge. The patient's observation of a sore throat becomes more official when labeled a "strep" infection after being observed and tested by the physician.

Expressions of power in doctor–patient encounters are numerous. *Talking with Patients* (Cassell 1985: 1) begins with a story about the author's grandmother (during the "modern" period) who went to a specialist about a skin cancer on her face. When she asked the doctor a question, he responded by slapping her face and saying, "I ask the questions here. I'll do the talking!" As shocking as it is to imagine being slapped by one's doctor for asking a question, the doctor's sentiment about who has the right to ask questions is an ongoing concern in medical talk. The right to ask a question is seen as one expression of power.

Managing social distance: what is appropriate?

Traditional variables in sociological research – age, socioeconomic status, gender, and race – are used to explore communication problems that arise in the doctor–patient setting. Most often these problems are related to managing asymmetry, reducing or preserving social distance.

Age and mental ability are often discussed with respect to the amount of communicative "work" done in a doctor–patient encounter. Physicians often take more control when they deal with patients who are deemed less able, such as the old and the young. It has been noted by many (e.g. Caporael and Culbertson 1986, Greene et al. 1987) that elder addressees are often infantilized or patronized. The physician talks down to them by using first names, by oversimplifying, or by joking. Patients in these categories often reinforce the asymmetry through their talk. In one study of teenagers, four of the five asked no questions (West 1984). Perhaps, as West suggests, adolescent patients are unwilling to ask questions because of the age asymmetry. With terms of address, patients frequently addressed doctors using titles or did not address them by name at all. Doctors, on the other hand, frequently used first names with patients especially if the patient was an ethnic minority or young.

Other means of creating or reducing social distance are through the use of depersonalized language and through humor. Laughter is not very common in doctor–patient interaction. Studies have shown that patients are far more likely to invite laughter than physicians and, when invited, physicians were less likely to accept. One explanation for this asymmetry is that if the goal of laughter is to reduce social distance doctors might decline because it is unprofessional. It could be seen as a challenge to medical authority.

The choice of using depersonalized forms when speaking about a patient's body may be a means of maintaining social distance. Depersonalized forms are a way to show objectivity. For example, a doctor might report the results of an x-ray by saying "the bone in the left leg is not broken." This is contrasted with "your leg is not broken." In the first example the doctor has reported an observation without reference to the person, in the second case the owner of the leg is personalized by saying "your."

Turn-taking, interruption, and conversational control

There is a strong relationship between interruption and conversational dominance.

In a study of openings in medical encounters (Frankel 1990), after only eighteen seconds of giving their "reasons for the visit," patients were interrupted by the physician, even though, when they were allowed to continue, none of the patients spoke for more than ninety seconds.

Findings on interruptions in medical encounters are consistent with other research on gender (e.g. Zimmerman and West 1975), which shows that males interrupt more than females. One study (West 1984) found that male doctors interrupt their patients more than female doctors and that male patients interrupt female doctors more than female patients do; interestingly, both male patients and female patients interrupt female physicians considerably more than they interrupt male physicians.

Asymmetries at the most local level in conversation are concerned with how speakers take turns or control the floor. Speakers can manage the social organization in turn-taking with questions, repairs of misunderstandings and clarifications and through acknowledgment strategies. In ordinary conversation speakers take turns on a more or less equal basis. The control of the conversation in medical encounters is somewhat different.

In a study of twenty-one encounters with patients ranging from age 16 to 82, the eighteen doctors initiated more than 90 percent of the 773 questions, and in four interviews the patient asked no questions at all (West 1984). Ratios ranged from no questions asked by patients to 50 percent by the doctor and 50 percent by the patient. Another study found that the gender of physician and patient affected question behavior. With a female physician, both male and female patients asked almost the same number of questions as the doctor. When the doctor was male, though, both male and female patients asked only about half as many questions.

It is not sufficient merely to count questions, however (Ainsworth-Vaughn 1998). The definition of "question" is important when doing calculations of control of the floor because some utterances may be genuine questions while others may be quasi-questions such as mishearings or requests for clarifications. Roughly, a question is forward looking – it looks toward an answer. By contrast, the answer looks back to the question, and an "acceptable" answer is one that is appropriate for the question. Quasi-questions, on the other hand, are backward looking. For instance, in extract 4 you can see that the physician's question in line 4 merely requests a repetition of line 3, which the patient obligingly repeats as line 6.

Extract 4 ((simplified transcription))
((conversation about blood pressure))
1 Physician: . . .'bout one fifty over ninety [Uh-]
2 Patient: [How] in the
3   world could she have gotten that?
4 Physician: Pardon me?
5   (.2)
6 Patient: How in the world could she have gotten that?

(West 1984: 80–81)

Neither the request in line 4 nor the repetition in line 6 should count as a question/answer sequence; instead they would be counted as quasi-questions (mishearing or clarification). Generally, quasi-questions are equally common for doctors and patients because they are necessary for successful information exchange. They are not related to control of the floor.

Getting down to specific parts of the medical encounter we find different patterns of talk. Using Conversation Analysis (CA), some investigators have looked at the details of how speakers present themselves in the different parts of the medical encounter. In extract 5 we see a fragment of the history-taking in a medical interview. In lines 19–22 the patient is suggesting a possible explanation for her back pain.

Extract 5
((Conversation about history of back pain))
18 DrA: 'Bout how often does that come.
19 Pt2:   Uh (1.0) This can (1.5) m- be like at least
20   once or twice a week. And I've been trying to see if
21   I've been you know, lifting something or doing
22   something. ((deep breath))
23   (1.5)
24 DrA: How long does it last when you
25   [get it.]
26 Pt2:   [Ah m] (.) maybe a day or two.

        Gill (1994) Dr.A with Patient 2 ((simplified transcription))

Lines 18 and 24 are both medical interview questions. The patient responds to the first question (lines 19–20) and then offers up her own possible explanation (lines 20–22) ("And I've been trying to see if I've been . . . lifting something or doing something"). The doctor, pursuing further details of the history, appears to ignore the patient's explanation. By ignoring the patient's remark about possible causes the doctor remains in control of the encounter.

Other CA researchers such as Heath have noted that patients are incredibly passive during the diagnosis phase of encounters. Frequently the diagnosis given by the doctor was not acknowledged at all or only with minimal *yeah*, or *uh-huh*.

Extract 6 ((simplified transcription))
((ear examination findings and treatment))

```
1    Doctor:   er Yes (0.3) this one's blocked
2              (.) the other one's not.
3              (1.2)
4    Doctor:   Well when would you like to have them done
5              (.) next week some time?
6    Patient:  Yes: (.) yes please.
7              (1.2)
8    Doctor:   If you'd like, to (.) call at um (0.5)
9              reception (0.5) the girls (0.2) on your way
10             out (.) the girls will (0.7) sort out the
11             appointment for you.
```

(Heath 1992: 239)

Extract 6 occurs in the diagnosis and treatment phase of the encounter. One would expect the patient to be very involved and interested in the doctor's findings (lines 1–2). The 1.2-second pause at line 3 would have been an opportunity for the patient to acknowledge the diagnosis. When the patient remains silent the doctor moves immediately to treatment (line 4). The patient agrees (line 6) with the doctor's implicit decision about "having them done" and about the appropriate time (next week, line 5). Then the doctor closes the encounter, sending the patient to reception to make an appointment (lines 8–10). Patients' reluctance to say anything about the diagnosis may reflect acquiescence to the superiority of the medical knowledge of doctors.

Singling out one feature such as the gender of physician or patient or observing question-initiating strategies does not give a complete picture of power dynamics but such studies are useful to index perceived power relationships within doctor–patient encounters (Ainsworth-Vaughn 1998). Patients can and do claim power in encounters with their physicians and physicians can and do conduct themselves in ways that acknowledge and facilitate the patients' claims to power. For instance patients who are undergoing treatment for cancer and other illnesses which involve consultations with the same doctor over a long period of time are much more likely to collaborate with their doctor on planning and implementing treatment (Roberts 1999). An increasing number of studies show how power in medical encounters can be negotiated.

The future of medical communication

The rules for medical communication in the USA continue to change. Most of the changes have been related to shifts in decision-making power, a shift to an increasingly consumerist model. This trend is notable in a number of areas of everyday life. Many common medications are sold directly to consumers today (like Advil™ and Tagamet™), which only a few years ago were sold by prescription only. Drug companies now advertise products in evening prime time that are still "prescription only" with the admonition "Ask your doctor if Xenical™ is right for you." These advertisements typically conclude with a lengthy disclaimer list of side effects. Such an advertising strategy is proposing that patients should be more active in decision-making about their medications.

Recently there has been a "Patient Bill of Rights" movement including the right to choose your provider and the right to a second opinion. Many patients come to the doctor with information obtained from the Internet. And finally there is the issue at the center of so much current political debate: the availability of health care and who decides which medical procedures will be paid for. The bureaucratic intervention of managed care has altered medical decision-making most of all. Doctors have found themselves in the difficult position of having to justify their treatments to insurance companies on the basis of time and cost. At the same time they face increasing demands from their patients.

We can see that the concern about how patients and doctors communicate is a complicated topic. Doctors with good communication practices are rewarded with satisfied patients, positive health outcomes, and perhaps fewer malpractice lawsuits. Medical training is long and difficult. Medical schools are devoting more time to the socio-emotional components of medical practice even as they have an increasingly sophisticated medico-biological curriculum to cover. As patients we value the knowledge doctors have. We rely on physicians to have our best interests in mind. We expect a high level of expertise yet we want to be able to have a say in the decisions that are made about our bodies. On the other hand patients don't always want to make their own health decisions. This means that doctors must not only be able to communicate their medical knowledge to us but they must also be able to take into account what we as patients want from them.

Suggestions for further reading and exploration

Most discussions of doctor–patient communication begin with reference to the classic sociological work of Parsons (1951) in which he describes the conventional roles of doctors and patients in Western medicine. Roter and Hall (1992) provides a more recent overview of doctor–patient communication, primarily from the perspective of the physician. Other studies consider how doctors manage the frame of medical talk. Tannen and Wallat (1993) explores how a pediatrician's presentation style shifts when she is talking to the patient, the patient's mother, or other health professionals. Maynard (2003) examines the conversational intricacies of reporting bad news to patients. Cicourel (1992) describes the role context plays in how physicians speak to medical students, peers, and medical experts from other departments. Lipkin et al. (1996) offers a detailed description of how clinical interaction skills are taught in medical schools. Still other recent studies explore medical communication from the perspective of the patient. Kleinman (1988) contains case studies of what being ill means to patients in Western society and in China. The sociolinguistic papers in Fisher and Todd (1993) focus on how patients talk with their doctors and how treatment is negotiated. Labov and Fanshel (1977) is a detailed discourse analysis of a single case of psychoanalytic talk.

References

Ainsworth-Vaughn, Nancy. 1998. *Claiming Power in Doctor–Patient Talk*. New York: Oxford University Press.

Byrne, P. and B. Long. 1976. *Doctors Talking to Patients*. London: Her Majesty's Stationery Office.

Caporael, Linnda and Glen Culbertson. 1986. "Verbal Response Modes of Baby Talk and Other Speech at Institutions for the Aged," *Language and Communication* 6(1/2): 99–112.

Cassell, Eric. 1985. *Talking with Patients*. Cambridge MA: MIT Press.

Cicourel, Aaron. 1992. "The Interpretation of Communicative Contexts: Examples from Medical Encounters." In *Rethinking Context*, eds. Alessandro Duranti and Charles Goodwin. New York: Cambridge University Press. Pp. 291–310.

Fisher, Sue and Alexandra Dundas Todd, eds. 1993. *The Social Organization of Doctor–Patient Communication*. 2nd edn. Norwood NJ: Ablex.

Frankel, R. 1990. "Talking in Interviews: a Dispreference for Patient-Initiated Questions in Physician–Patient Encounters." In *Interactional Competence*, eds. George Psathas, G. Coulter, and R. Frankel. Washington DC: University Press of America. Pp. 231–62.

Gill, Virginia. 1994. "How Patients Explain, How Doctors Respond: Lay Explanation in Medical Interaction." Paper presented at the American Sociological Association meeting. Los Angeles.

Greene, M., S. Hoffman, R. Charon, and R. Adelman. 1987. "Psychosocial Concerns in the Medical Encounter: a Comparison of the Interactions of Doctors with their Old and Young Patients," *The Gerontologist* 7(2): 164–68.

Heath, Christian. 1992. "The Delivery and Reception of Diagnosis in the General-Practice Consultation." In *Talk at Work*, eds. Paul Drew and John Heritage. Cambridge: Cambridge University Press. Pp. 235–67.

Kleinman, Arthur. 1988. *The Illness Narratives: Suffering, Healing and the Human Condition*. New York: Basic Books.

Korsch, Barbara M. and V. F. Negrete. 1972. "Doctor–Patient Communication," *Scientific American* 227: 66–74.

Labov, William and David Fanshel. 1977. *Therapeutic Discourse. Psychotherapy as Conversation*. New York: Academic Press.

Lipkin, Mack, Jr., Samuel M. Putnam, and Aaron Lazare, eds. 1996. *The Medical Interview: Clinical Care, Education, and Research*. New York: Springer-Verlag.

Maynard, Douglas. 1991. "On the Interactional and Institutional Bases of Asymmetry in Clinical Discourse," *American Journal of Sociology* 92(2): 448–95.

2003. *Bad News, Good News: Conversational Order in Everyday Talk and Clinical Settings*. Chicago: University of Chicago Press.

Mischler, Elliot G. 1984. *The Discourse of Medicine: Dialectics of Medical Interviews*. Norwood NJ: Ablex.

Ong L. M. L., J. C. J. M. deHaes, A. M. Hoos, and F. B. Lammes. 1995. "Doctor–Patient Communication: a Review of the Literature," *Social Science & Medicine* 40(7): 903–18.

Parsons, Talcott. 1951. "Social Structure and Dynamic Process: the Case of Modern Medical Practice." In Parsons, *The Social System*. New York: Free Press. Pp. 438–79.

Roberts, Felicia. 1999. *Talking about Treatment: Recommendations for Breast Cancer Adjuvant Therapy*. New York: Oxford University Press.

Roter, Debra and Richard Frankel. 1992. "Quantitative and Qualitative Approaches to the Evaluation of the Medical Dialogue," *Social Science & Medicine* 34(10): 1097–103.

Roter, Debra L. and Judith A. Hall. 1992. *Doctors Talking with Patients, Patients Talking with Doctors*. Westport CT: Auburn.

Shorter, Edward. 1985. *Bedside Manner: the Troubled History of Doctors and Patients*. New York: Viking.

Shuy, Roger. 1998. *Bureaucratic Language in Government and Business*. Washington DC: Georgetown University Press.

Tannen, Deborah and Cynthia Wallat. 1993. "Interactive Frames and Knowledge Schemas in Interaction: Examples from a Medical Examination Interview." In *Framing in Discourse*, ed. Deborah Tannen. New York: Oxford University Press. Pp. 57–76.

Waitzkin, Howard. 1985. "Information Giving in Medical Care," *Journal of Health and Social Behavior* 26: 81–101.

West, Candace. 1984. *Routine Complications, Troubles with Talk between Doctors and Patients*. Bloomington: Indiana University Press.

Zimmerman, Don. H. and Candace West. 1975. "Sex Roles, Interruptions and Silences in Conversation." In *Language and Sex: Difference and Dominance*, eds. Barrie Thorne and Nancy Henley. Rowley, MA: pp. 105–51.

25

The language of cyberspace

DENISE E. MURRAY

Editors' introduction

Like a few chapters in this volume, this one could not have appeared in the earlier edition of *Language in the USA*. When Denise E. Murray started her research into the language of cyberspace in 1984, the World Wide Web did not exist. Now many people, especially younger ones, can hardly imagine life without "the web." In just a couple of decades, computer-mediated communication (CMC) has developed characteristic uses and characteristic linguistic features, as well as a "netiquette" of e-interaction. So prevalent and so important has computer-mediated language become – and of such excitement to so many people (though not to everyone) – that a book treating language in the USA but lacking a chapter on this topic would disappoint many student readers and their teachers.

The basic question this chapter asks is what effects the new form of communication has had on language and language use, and Murray tackles the question from three perspectives: Which new communicative situations does CMC enable and foster? Which metaphors do we use in our discussions about CMC and its venues – and what effect do those metaphors have on our perceptions and judgments about CMC? What is the place – now and in the future – of English in cyberspace? While the discussion of how CMC has affected English and other languages will interest many of you because of your familiarity or fascination with CMC, the processes influencing the formation of new words and practices in CMC are subject to the same general principles that influence language use and language change in other domains and that are discussed in the other chapters of this volume. Still, there is much that is unique to the virtual world and much that makes its language use distinctive.

Among the interesting matters addressed here are the ways in which CMC is more writing-like than speech and more speech-like than writing. Another fascinating part of the discussion concerns how the metaphors we use as part of our computer-mediated communication influence our perceptions – and affect our judgments and assessments. Our metaphors have anthropomorphized computers, making them appear more human-like and less machine-like. The chapter also raises important questions about the distribution of this extraordinary resource across users – and its accessibility to current non-users.

In 1984, when I first began research into the language of cyberspace, the World Wide Web did not exist, the Internet was not a household world, and whenever I said I was studying e-mail I needed to explain in great detail just what it was. Now the World Wide Web, e-mail, and surfing the net are commonplace terms in the USA. What effect has this new form of communication had on language and language use? We examine this effect from three perspectives: computer-mediated communication as a new site for using language, the use of metaphor to describe the new technology, and the place of English in cyberspace. This chapter focuses primarily on the first perspective and discusses the other two; still, other aspects of computer technology are also of interest to linguists and others – for example, the analysis of language for the purposes of artificial intelligence (AI) and language translation programs, but we will not examine them in this chapter.

Computer-mediated communication (CMC) includes many uses of computer technology for communication. Some researchers (e.g., Herring 1996a, Hiltz and Wellman 1997, Jones 1998) include e-mail, bulletin boards, computer conferences, Internet Relay Chat, listservs, chat rooms, and World Wide Web homepages as forms of CMC. Others (e.g., Warschauer 1999) restrict CMC to those forms through which people send messages to individuals or groups; they place hypermedia and its most familiar implementation, the World Wide Web, into a different category. In this chapter, I expand the broader and more common definition – ". . . CMC is communication that takes place between human beings via the instrumentality of computers" (Herring 1996a: 1) – to include only those uses of the computer that are transparent but modify communication to include only text-based modes. I do this to reflect current CMC. Once we begin using voice-activated CMC, we'll need to research language use and refine our terminology. This definition includes the World Wide Web, but excludes text (such as this book) that is produced on a computer, but delivered via print. CMC can be either synchronous, that is, occurring in real time, or asynchronous, where a reader reads the message at a later time. Chat rooms are an archetypal example of synchronous CMC and e-mail of asynchronous CMC. Even the so-called synchronous modes can be considered asynchronous because of the time delay in typing a message and its being sent electronically, even when no breakdowns in communications networks occur (Murray 1991). In a chat room, for example, the sender types the message, which appears on his/her screen as it's being typed, but does not appear on recipients' screens until the sender hits the enter key. In the meantime, one or more of the recipients may have sent their own message, causing an overlap. Participation in a chat room conversation has more immediacy and is more dynamic than e-mail interactions, but it is neither as extensive nor as interactive as telephone or face-to-face communication.

Although CMC use has only recently become ubiquitous, appearing in cartoon strips, general newspaper articles, talk-back shows, and in legal cases, its use dates back to the 1970s. That use was largely in businesses and other proprietary organizations for internal communications or among researchers whose work was supported by federal grants. This communication system has grown to where an estimated 350 million (Ipsos-Reid 2001) to 429 million people (Nielsen//Netratings 2001) access the Internet in some way using computer chip technology, leading many writers to comment on the potential for interconnectedness. But is this potential realized? "In fact, the world could be said to be growing less and less connected, if only because the gap between the few of us who babble about the wiring of the planet and the billions who do not grows ever more alarming" (Iyer 1997: 28). Even if people are on-line, we have limited accurate measurement of their on-line use – for communication, for surfing the Web for information. Collecting data on usage is fraught with methodological peril. Some data available on-line reports regular use, other reports mere connectedness, some reports per house-hold, others per user, making comparisons and accurate statements extremely difficult. In countries like the USA with technological infrastructure, CMC is still not universal, its distribution and use mirroring wider socio-economic patterns, whether within or across countries. Access to CMC varies widely, with limited access in poor urban and rural areas, among minority-group families, among those older than eighteen, and among the less well educated. The 2000 Census reports that 63 percent of homes with residents aged 18–49 use the Internet, compared with 37 percent of households aged 50 and over (Digital Divide Network 2001). Yet there are anecdotal and small study reports that indicate that the number of older users is increasing. On a trip in 2001 to Australia's outback, I was stranded in a small town because of flooded roads. The town had an Internet Centre, one of a dozen such funded by the Australian government to bring greater access to new communications technology to people in remote areas. The manager of the project said her greatest users were older folk who wanted to keep in contact with family members spread all over the country. They were using this relatively cheap medium instead of the more conventional telephone or letter writing. Such stories are often reported, but the only firm statistical data we can rely on are from Census, large-scale government funded research, and market research companies. And these all indicate that more young people are on-line than older people.

In 1995, surveys of Internet users found that 65 percent were affluent and 67 percent were male (Castells 1996). The most comprehensive series of studies, undertaken by the US Department of Commerce has shown changes over time. The most recent study, reporting data for Fall 2000 found that 41.5 percent of all US homes had Internet access. An earlier gender divide seems to have disap-peared, with men (44.6 percent) and women (44.2 percent) equally likely to be on-line, although Usenet users are still predominantly male. So the gender gap may not be one of how many people are on-line, but in terms of what types of CMC males and females engage in. Divides other than gender remain: the affluent were still most likely to be on-line (86.3 percent); Blacks and Hispanics are mostly not on-line; nor are people with disabilities, those living in inner cities, single-parent families, or those fifty years of age and older. These data also show that the major use of the Internet in the USA is for e-mail. By 2000, 98 percent of schools in the USA had Internet access, but only 77 percent of classrooms are wired. This percentage is lower in schools with high poverty rates or with a large number of minority students and higher in affluent, white schools. Just because a school is on-line or a classroom wired does not ensure student access. The ratio of students to computer has decreased steadily over the last few years down to seven students per computer in 2000 (the Department's target is one for every five students). But again, this ratio is vastly different for poor and minority schools. Even in schools wired to the Internet, only about 4 percent have a computer for every five students (US Department of Education 1996). When we move outside the USA, we find that while the number of Internet sites has increased and e-mail use is increasing, access is limited, often for lack of infrastructure, or because of unreliable power or a limited number of telephone lines. In 1997, the USA accounted for 60.5 percent of the world's Internet host computers (Network Wizard 1997). In 2001, the USA has more computers than the rest of the world combined (Digital Divide Network 2001). According to the Nielsen//Netrating, in 2001, 41 percent of these 429 million global users are from the USA and Canada; and 429 million means less than 6 percent of the world's population has access to the Internet. While 6 percent is a threefold increase from 1999 estimates, it still represents a miniscule section of the world's population. So while this chapter examines the effects of new technology on language and its use, it is important to remember *whose* language and *whose* use we are referring to.

The second perspective concerns the language we use to talk about cyberspace. As with any new field or technology, the formation of new words obeys general linguistic principles. Words already in use have been redefined for the new technology (e.g., *virtual*, *lurking*, *flaming*). Some of this narrowing of meaning has then been broadened as the words have re-entered other semantic fields with the additional cyber meaning. *Virtual* is an excellent example. In 1969 a Random House dictionary defines it as "being such in force or effect, though not actually or expressly such" and to illustrate cites "reduced to virtual poverty." The word became used in the technical term *virtual memory* to refer to the ability of the computer to use hard-disk space to simulate high-speed storage. From this, it replaced the word *simulated* in many computer applications. Thus, IBM developed a mainframe operating system called *VM* for 'virtual machine.' Other extensions include *virtual reality*, *virtual community*. From this we now find its use in non-computer language to mean 'simulated' or 'the opposite of real.' So we hear someone talk about a *virtual* policy, referring to an unexpressed policy, one that has never been articulated but everyone knows. Words have also been created for cyberspace through blending (*netiquette* from *net* and *etiquette*, *emoticons* from *emotion* and *icons*), through compounding (*database*, *wordprocessor*), through backformation (*net* from *network*) and other well-established word-formation processes. *Cyberspace* itself is an interesting example of several of these processes. The term *cybernetics* was coined in the 1940s by Norbert Weiner to encompass the field of control and communication theory, both human and machine. Weiner's work was primarily with trying to understand life mechanisms and actions and build machines that could imitate such human actions. The term was created from the Greek word for 'governor.' Through the process of back formation, *cyber* became used adjectivally (e.g., *cyber chat*, *cyber punks*, *cyber marriage*). Having been around the longest, *cyber* + *space* has become compounded. I have also noticed others, mostly proprietary names that have become compounded (e.g., *Cybersitter*, a software product for filtering out adult material from the Internet to protect children; *CyberAtlas*, which provides Internet statistics and market research for the Web). These uses of *cyber* are designed to invoke ideas of computer technology + another concept, especially when a short adjectival form is required. We will not pursue this linguistic perspective further because in this respect CMC does not demonstrate any new linguistic principles. Instead, we explore the use of metaphor to describe cyberspace because these metaphors demonstrate how we make computers seem more human – we anthropomorphize the computer – as though the potential for artificial intelligence were already realized, and we thus reveal society's attitudes to the technology.

The third perspective, the role of English as the language of cyberspace – whether on the Internet or in publications in the various disciplines that support the technology – raises questions of great interest to linguists. If English dominates cyberspace, which variety is privileged? What will happen to other Englishes and other languages? How does the use of privileged varieties of English affect access to CMC?

Computer-mediated communication

Like the introduction of the telephone, the introduction of computer technology has created a new site for discourse, and just as telephone conversation came to differ from face-to-face conversation, researchers are now asking in what ways the language of CMC is similar to or different from the language of face-to-face conversations, telephone conversations, and written texts. For which functions is computer-mediated communication used?

The language of CMC

Users of CMC immediately note its similarity to spoken language, even though it appears as written text on a screen. CMC demonstrates that text is no longer located only on a page and that the space for writing is not permanent. Some have claimed that CMC has diminished the importance of the written word, which has dominated communication for the past three hundred years and empowered those who are literate while disempowering those who are not. Thus, as one commentator notes, "The historical divide between speech and writing has been overcome with the interactional and reflective aspects of language merged in a single medium" (Warschauer 1999: 7). Others, however, see it differently, and the book title *Page to Screen* (Snyder 1998) suggests that CMC is merely written text appearing on a computer screen. How oral or written *is* CMC text?

CMC as genre or register

A number of models for examining language variation across media have been used to categorize the characteristics of spoken language compared with written language. One model identifies six dimensions in terms of their communication function, and one of those dimensions is "involved versus informational" (Biber 1988). A highly "involved" text is characterized by frequent occurrences of linguistic features such as the verbs *feel* and *believe*, hedges (*kind of, sort of*), first-person and second-person pronouns (*I, us, you*), and certain others. More "informational" texts exhibit longer words, more frequent occurrences of nouns and prepositional phrases, and specific other linguistic features. Other dimensions in this model are narrativity, explicitness, persuasion, abstraction, and elaboration. The model shows that oral and written language are not dichotomous, as some early research had suggested. Instead, some spoken genres (e.g., formal lectures) have more features in common with written language than with other oral genres (e.g., cocktail party conversations), whereas certain written genres (e.g., personal letters) are more speech-like than some spoken genres. Research on CMC has shown that, while some CMC displays features more commonly associated with oral language, it also has features more commonly associated with written language (see Herring 1996a). Trying to categorize CMC as either oral or written seems not particularly useful. Rather, a more fruitful approach is to identify how the language of CMC varies based on changes in the context (Murray 1991). Aspects of the context that affect language use include field (including topic, organization of topic, and focus), speaker/hearer relationships (including knowledge of audience and role relations), and setting (including space and time).

Can CMC currently be described as a separate genre or register? Registers are intuitively recognizable (and linguistically demonstrable) kinds of language that arise in particular communication situations, and genres are conventionalized, recurrent message types that have specific features of form, content and use in a community (Ferguson 1994). Following this definition, sportscasts would be a genre and so would mystery novels. The language used in sportscasts would be the register of sportscasting and the language of scientific texts would be a scientific register. Given that CMC includes a variety of different forms of messages via computers, it cannot be a genre. But could some specific types of CMC qualify as genres? E-mail, for example, has distinctive features of form – a header consisting of sender, recipient, subject; text; optional closing or signature. But the content varies depending on the topic – the same e-mail might be about a business matter and a personal matter.

The notion of community is also fluid in CMC. Many people refer to virtual communities, which have been defined as "social aggregations that emerge from the Net when enough people carry on those public discussions long enough, with sufficient human feeling, to form webs of personal relationships in cyberspace" (Rheingold 1993: 5). But most people who use CMC use it within already existing communities so that on-line communication is only one medium among several, including face-to-face, telephone, and written communication. Whether virtual communities have the characteristics of other human communities is still being debated. Human face-to-face communities are characterized by shared values and space, where people feel connected by common bonds – of family, religious affiliation, hobbies, and so on; where people have strong bonds of trust and mutual obligation, necessitated by the social and environmental context. What we do know about on-line communities is that they may have lurkers (those who read but don't otherwise participate), may have few guidelines of behavior, may allow for anonymity or creation of a virtual self or multiple selves, may include breaking contact without explanation, and may pull people away from their other off-line communities as they spend more time interacting on-line (see Smith and Kollock 1999 for a sociological discussion of the ambivalence of virtual communities). The social effects of on-line communities continue to be an important area for research and oversight – "Armed with knowledge, guided by a clear, human-centered vision, governed by a commitment to civil discourse, we the citizens hold the key levers at a pivotal time. What happens next is largely up to us" (Rheingold 1993: 300). So if CMC and even specific modes of CMC do not consist of conventionalized, recurrent message types that have specific features of form, content, and use in a community, we cannot claim that CMC or its submodes such as e-mail are genres.

But does CMC satisfy Ferguson's definition of register (intuitively recognizable and linguistically demonstrable kinds of language that result from particular communication situations)? Some scholars have identified CMC as a simplified register, that is, one that uses simplified vocabulary and grammar (Ferrara et al. 1991, Murray 1991). Simplified registers result from particular aspects of the context, such as a speaker's perception that the listener is not competent in the language. For example, caretaker talk is a simplified register used in some cultures when talking to children; foreigner talk is a simplified register used when talking to non-native speakers. Other simplified registers result from restrictions in time, as with note-taking, or in space, as with newspaper headlines. CMC exhibits some features of simplified registers. Abbreviations as a time-saving strategy are becoming conventionalized, such as *BTW* for "by the way," *IMHO* for "in my humble opinion," or *ROFL* for "rolling on the floor laughing." Grammar is simplified, with an almost telegraphic style often being employed. Typos and other surface errors are ignored. Symbols such as multiple question marks????? or exclamation marks!!!!! or emoticons (for example, :> [to represent a sad/disappointed emotion]) are used to represent emotional meaning since non-linguistic cues (like facial expressions) and paralinguistic cues (like intonation) are absent. Because CMC is still evolving technically and in its distribution, conventions are not firmly established. Yet many conventions begun two decades ago by computer professionals are still being acquired by novice users.

Conversation analysts have investigated the structure of conversations, identifying components such as openings, closings, turn-taking, and adjacency pairs (e.g., greeting–greeting; compliment–acknowledgment) as mechanisms for the orderly organization of spoken interactions. In what ways does CMC follow the conventions of conversation? Face-to-face conversations and telephone conversations open with self-identification, greetings, and often a summons, which are usually paired, that is, the listener responds. In other genres – letters and lectures, for example – a salutation begins the speech event. In these more monologic speech events, the salutation is not paired. Similarly, these genres have a closing that might include pre-closing elements like *okay* and terminals such as *bye*, which are also usually paired ("bye"/ "bye"). In CMC, openings and closings are optional, largely because computer software programs automatically supply identification of sender and recipient. But in Internet Relay Chat (IRC), senders address their intended recipient by name because IRC involves one-to-many interactions (sometimes called *multilogues*) and carries no other cues to identify the person to whom a question or statement is directed (Werry 1996). In face-to-face conversation and telephone conversations, turn-taking is conventionalized within a community; for example, one person speaks at a time, or the current speaker can select the next speaker or continue to speak. In asynchronous CMC, turn-taking is constrained by time delays and often by the particular software application – the e-mail or contribution to a discussion list arrives after the sender has typed it and it has made its way through the network(s). Thus, the overlaps and interruptions that mark telephone and face-to-face conversations are not possible in real time, but neither are CMC conversations linear and orderly. In synchronous CMC, overlaps occur but do not appear on the screen as "speaking at the same time"; rather, they appear as several messages arriving one after the other, but perhaps all of them in response to an earlier question. The receiver then decides which message to respond to, unlike in face-to-face conversations, where, if two people begin to answer or talk at the same time, one will quickly concede the floor to the other. (For more details of turn-taking in CMC, see Murray 1989, Werry 1996, Davis and Brewer 1997.) CMC, then, has a variety of forms, the structure of which is still developing.

The functions of CMC

For what purposes do people use CMC? Is it added to current individual repertoires? Does it supplant other media? Does its apparent normlessness matter? Many scholars have predicted and some have found that because CMC lacks cues like intonation that are normally present in telephone and face-to-face conversations and lacks the established conventions for written language (e.g., salutations in letters), its use would lead to more equality of communication – in particular, that inequalities resulting from gender, race, age or other signals of power would not operate. The limited research on the issue of power and CMC has produced mixed results. Two instructors found that as instructors they dominated e-space as much as they dominated conversations in regular classrooms (Hawisher and Selfe 1998). Gender equity has not been realized in CMC; rather, CMC reflects the patterns found in other types of discourse (Adams 1996). Males tend to prefer an ethic of agonistic debate or competition and freedom from rules (an adversarial dimension), while females tend to prefer an ethic of politeness and consideration (what has been called an attenuated dimension) (Herring 1996b). However, some researchers found that females viewed CMC more favorably than males – perhaps because they can speak without male interruptions (Allen 1995, Hiltz and Johnson 1990). A male discourse style dominates the current Internet, which can be seen not only in discourse practices, the most extreme of which is flaming or personal put-downs. Additionally, the rules of netiquette reflect this male style dominance – though authored by a woman; if women prefer a more collaborative approach, one might expect a woman writing about netiquette to say that flaming should be banned, rather than that it should be accommodated. If the gender of the author is not stated, the reader might think the author is male and trying to impose his preferred style on others. A recent volume on netiquette (Shea 1994) claims flaming is part of tradition and should be accommodated. Interestingly, while flaming is well documented, some CMC investigations (Davis and Brewer 1997, Ferrara, Brunner, and Whittemore 1991, Murray 1991) have not found incidents of flaming. It seems that if politeness norms already exist in a particular community, as in one corporation studied, they become reflected in CMC (Murray 1991). "All interaction, including CMC, is simultaneously situated in multiple external contexts. Rather than disappearing when one logs on, the preexisting speech communities in which interactants operate provide social understandings and practices through and against which interaction in a new computer-mediated context develops" (Baym 1988: 40). When such norms do not exist, they are created anew by the community itself and in some such CMC communities a male adversarial style becomes the norm. A meta-analysis of a decade of research on how CMC supports group decision-making shows that while such groups focus more on their task, participation is more equal, decisions are of higher quality, and participants believe more strongly in the rightness of the final group decisions, it takes them longer to reach decisions and there is less likely to be consensus (McLeod 1992). Within the various domains of CMC, some differences emerge. Hiltz and Wellman (1997), for example, have found that while CMC supports instrumental relationships, it can also support more social community-building. They note a difference between computer-supported cooperative work groups and virtual communities that have developed through mutual interests, such as MUDs (Multiple User Dimension/Durgeon/Dialoge – an interactive virtual game played on the Internet by several people at the same time) or newsgroups. In the former, people focus on the task at hand and mostly have limited emotional, social exchanges. In the latter, emotional support and a sense of belonging are in fact aims of the communication. So, while the potential exists for CMC to be less hierarchical and more inclusive, the nature of the language itself often exhibits the same gendered, hierarchical characteristics as do other registers; and so, rather than providing opportunities for new social relationships to develop, instead contributes to the maintenance of the power status quo.

People may choose from among the many media of communication from their available repertoire, depending on the characteristics of the particular context. One study found that when someone wanted to start discussing personnel matters they switched from e-mail to a face-to-face conversation (Murray 1991). Another

(Kress 1998: 54) takes a similar stance, arguing that if we take the social situation (the context) as our starting point, we find that people use informal language in e-mail when the person they're writing to is a close friend or there is some other relationship of solidarity. He goes on to say that we can, of course, just as in face-to-face situations, choose informal language precisely to create a sense of solidarity.

When a move to a different medium is not possible, people use the CMC appropriate for their own personal context, and they manipulate the linguistic features to suit this context. For example, in Internet Relay Chat (IRC), a highly interactive chat channel, the "communication . . . is shaped at many different levels by the drive to reproduce or simulate the discursive style of face-to-face spoken language" (Werry 1996: 61). It remains to be seen whether these tendencies to choose particular media and particular language for specific contexts will develop over time into accepted conventions that might constitute genres – not for CMC as a whole, but for individual types of CMC (e.g., IRC) – just as over time business letters and other types of letters have developed distinctive genre characteristics.

Metaphors

The metaphors we use constantly in our everyday language shape our understanding and view of the world (Lakoff and Johnson 1980, Lawler 1995). Many of the terms and metaphors used to describe the new technology lead us to ignore the social context in which the technology is introduced and to anthropomorphize the technology – to make it more human-like. The new metaphors present a positive, progressive, stance: computer technology is *a revolution*; it is *transformative* and *liberating*; it will make us *more productive* and will create *a global village*. What they hide is the historical fact that the introduction of any new technology, from the stylus to the printed book to the spinning jenny, is not socially or morally neutral. The new technology enters an already existing social and cultural context, and that context determines how it will be used. Thus, any changes brought about by the computer are likely to reflect current values. As a result, many computer metaphors focus on productivity, and computer technology is most often introduced into an organization because it will lead to greater productivity of workers – whether in an office or on a factory floor. If, however, we ask questions about public policy and social ethics, rather than about how much data a computer can store or process, we find the same tensions that exist in societies at large – tensions among competing needs for privacy, security, freedom, access, and control (for details on these aspects of cyberspace, see Murray 1993).

One prevailing metaphor is that of the Information Superhighway. Newspapers, politicians, scholars, and grocery store clerks are all fascinated by the notion of unlimited access to information and communications. However, this metaphor also invokes ethical issues – who will build and who will get paid for building the highway? Who will pay for its construction? Who will have access to it? Will it be a toll road or a freeway? Will travel be restricted, controlled? What will the rules of the road be like? Who will police it? What, if any, on-ramps will there be?

The use of the highway metaphor also makes information technology appear benign. By choosing a known, accepted metaphor, we can gloss over some of the essential characteristics of information technology, characteristics that have the potential for both good and bad. Computer technology is highly complex, as all of us know. Most people choose not to become experts, preferring instead to use the technology much as they use a refrigerator or automobile. When it doesn't work, the thing to do is call in a specialist to fix it. If we take this approach with computer technology, we leave ourselves in the hands of an emerging profession that to date has only limited self-regulatory practices. Indeed, this emerging profession has long admired hackers, those computer programmers who delight in knowing all there is to know about computer software and hardware – whether their own or others'. Over time, some programming experts used their knowledge to cause malicious damage. We see released onto the market programs that have known bugs and hardware with known faults (often cynically called "design features" by insiders). While organizations such as Computer Professionals for Social Responsibility strive for ethical behavior, not only on the part of practitioners, but also on the part of user communities such as governments, there is neither a code of ethical practice nor a professional regulatory association as in law and medicine. So, if we choose to view the technology like a toaster or a car, we run the risk of breakdowns and malfunctions for which the makers/designers/ producers are not responsible. In fact, many software programs specifically state that the company is not responsible for its not working! The Internet was once a community of tightly knit academics and scientists with a shared social consensus and informal rules of conduct. Now that it has burgeoned into a world of 20 million people, the same destructive and deviant behavior found in the real world can be found in the virtual one. Most professional computer organizations such as the Association of Computing Machinery have developed ethical standards that they ask their members to adhere to. But unlike medicine, with its disciplinary hearings and the possibility of de-certification, there is no unified code of enforceable ethics in computing.

Interestingly, like all other metaphors, this highway metaphor also limits our thinking. Had we thought of telephone technology only as a voice superhighway, describing how voices travel through wires from one place to another, we would not, perhaps, have so readily understood the psychological and emotional roles that phones have come to play in our lives – how they save time and provide peace of mind (Stefik 1997). From such understandings have been developed cellular phones and answering machines and voice mail, all of which are not so much superhighways of voice, but pacifiers, security blankets, and time savers.

Metaphors abound in talk about computers. One metaphor used to great advantage by software developers is that of the computer as desktop. Apart from the fact that this metaphor is one of the workplace and, thus, of productivity, rather than of games, say, or communication, the question is: whose desktop, whose workplace? Is it the person who always has a clean desk and neatly files away all papers, and reads and answers mail as it comes in? Or the desktop of the worker who has piles of papers – on the desk, on the floor, on top of filing cabinets – with files in the filing cabinet that are either not labeled or not filed alphabetically. Both people can usually find what they're looking for. For the first person, it's a question of, "Now, what heading did I file that memo under." For the second person it's more likely to be "Well, yes, I remember I was reading it a couple of days ago and I put it in the pile over there, and yes, I remember, it was thick . . . ," etc. As human beings we have different ways of organizing information for different tasks and also according to our own ways of processing information. This is referred to as density, some people preferring information to feel dense, to have post-it notes and other information resources visible. Others prefer their information less dense, with fewer high-level nodes. So does the desktop metaphor work for all people? Clearly not.

Hypertext is built on a metaphor of branching trees and webs – the World Wide Web being its most famous application. The underlying assumption is that human beings process information by linking and that hypertext in some way maps a natural human way of dealing with information. Yet human beings use linear processing of information, as some psycholinguists have shown. Additionally, the cognitive architecture of the hypertext is imposed on the reader by an author. The author makes the links and paths that he or she thinks are salient. The reader may see *different* words or ideas as needing exploration. For example, if this chapter were part of a hypertext, some readers might have begun branching at Interactive Relay Chat and embarked on an ongoing voyage leading to joining an IRC and participating in the conversation. Others might have wanted to explore the notion of turn-taking in face-to-face conversation and chosen to link to scholarly articles on the subject. But those possibilities exist only if links are provided. In exercising my authority as author of the chapter (notice where the word *authority* comes from), I may not have provided links to either. So the web may entangle us – we as readers may be the fly, not the spider. If you have tried to navigate the Web, you will have experienced moving along so many branches that you no longer know where you are. Even the provision for going back in most browsers can lead to a dead end. This has important implications for the design and use of such systems in business or education. The hypertext and desktop metaphors raise the question of adaptation – either we have to adapt ourselves to the design of the computer or we have to adapt the computer to our own strategies. Our own adapting lies within our control, but adapting the computer is the province of the computer industry, unless educators and others make their needs known.

Another group of metaphors involves the use of terms that usually describe human activities, feelings, appearance, and so on in order to describe how computers work. Computer programmers say "a program runs," network managers talk about computers "seeing or talking to each other." Computer professionals ascribe other human traits to computers – a computer can be "anemic" or "deprived" and "lack intelligence." Such metaphors lead us to anthropomorphize the computer more than other machines.

This examination demonstrates that the metaphors we use reflect the values of current society (e.g., productivity and work) and also mask some of the issues society needs to discuss and resolve. It is vital for each of us to uncover the metaphors and determine how we want this new medium of communication to work. Such discussions are even more important when we recognize the dominance of English (mostly Standard American English) in cyberspace and consequently the dominance of American middle-class cultural and ethical values.

The dominance of English as the language of cyber technology

Computer technology has reinforced the already existing trend of English as the language of international business, communication, entertainment, and scholarship (Kachru and Nelson 1996, Pennycook 1994). In 1997, 83 percent of Web pages were in English (Cyberspeech 1997). English dominates communication using and about the technology both because the Internet and much of the technology originated in the USA and because English is the language of international communication. Much of the early work that led to the digital computer originated with English speakers – the Analytical Engine originated with Charles Babbage of England and the Universal Machine with Alan Turing, also English. Commercial implementation of the original idea and subsequent advances in the technology occurred mostly in the USA. The Internet, for example, was an outgrowth of Arpanet, the network developed by the US Department of Defense to connect the department with several universities so that researchers could access each other's work and share information via electronic messaging.

Because the technology was largely developed in English, the character system (ASCII-American Standard Code for Information Exchange) used to represent written language in cyberspace privileges the Roman alphabet and makes it extraordinarily difficult to represent other writing scripts. Even languages that use the Roman alphabet with diacritic marks are more difficult to represent. In most wordprocessors, for example, to add an accent to a letter requires several moves. Most e-mail systems either strip these accents or represent them with one of the standard ASCII code symbols. Thus the é in José (which took five moves to produce) may become a "?" so we find Jose? or Jos?e when we receive the e-mail.

Language death is of concern to linguists. As one has written, "To lose a language is to lose a unique view of the world that is shared by no other" (Crystal 1997: 44). Will the expansion of CMC threaten the world's languages because of the dominance of English? Is it inevitable that the Internet and other cyber technologies will advantage speakers of English and disadvantage those who do not speak English? Many claim quite the opposite – that the technology will in fact give voice to the unheard. Native American tribes, Canadian heritage language groups, and Australian aborigines are going on-line in their mother tongue. There is certainly a growing number of examples of uses of languages other than English. Many indigenous groups use the Internet to promote their development and rights, but when not in English these are often in the local language of wider communication, not the indigenous language. For example, using Spanish as the medium of communication, the Ashaninka in Peru have created a communications network among many indigenous communities. Yet others argue that having one world language (English) will help foster world peace. None of these predictions is inevitable. What we do have is the potential for exclusion and the potential for inclusion. If we agree that linguistic diversity is a human societal asset (see chapter 7 by Fishman in this volume), then linguists, members of organizations working on replacing ASCII, and groups speaking languages other than standard English need to develop language policies that exploit the potential of the communication medium for everyone.

Conclusion

The language of cyberspace can be examined from many perspectives – from how words for computer technology are borrowed for general language use to whether the language and interactional patterns of CMC are gendered. Since CMC is a new discourse site, its characteristics are not yet conventionalized. We are seeing language change dynamically and quickly, compared with many language changes in the past. This chapter has focused on only three areas and only briefly discussed each. One exciting, but at the same time most frustrating, aspect of the language of cyberspace is that by the time this book is published the landscape will have already changed. The technology will have created new sites of language use, the language itself will have changed, and our knowledge about that language will have changed. Despite all that change, the underlying issues of power, access, and inclusiveness will remain. These issues present a challenge, but also an opportunity, for language study.

Acknowledgments

The discussion of metaphor is adapted from a plenary talk made by the author at the 1997 TESOL Convention in Orlando, Florida. The talk was also adapted for publication in *TESOL Matters* (August/September 1998).

Suggestions for further readings and exploration

Murray (1991) is the first in-depth linguistic examination of CMC and ranges from issues of literacy to the conversational features of CMC to the structure of CMC. Ferrara, Brunner, and Whittemore (1991) presents results from an empirical study of CMC and is among the most quoted articles concerning the register of CMC. Herring (1996a) is an edited volume presenting the most thorough collection of papers examining CMC's linguistic properties; all chapters describe empirical studies and thus provide factual information, rather than the speculative information that characterizes much of the literature on CMC. Davis and Brewer (1997) is primarily a report of using computer conferencing for class discussion over a period of four years between students at two campuses in South Carolina; its theoretical base is from linguistics and rhetorical studies, and the early chapters provide an excellent overview of the linguistics of CMC. Warschauer (1999) reports on a study of the challenges of using CMC with linguistically diverse learners and how they engage in new literacy practices in their computer-mediated classes; although the focus is primarily pedagogic, the author uses linguistic knowledge and principles to examine the data. Written for both educators and researchers but with a particular focus on pedagogical implications, Snyder (1998) is a collection of papers that relate literacy practices to the use of new technologies. Ess (1996) is an edited volume that claims to be about philosophy, but several chapters discuss the language of CMC from a variety of perspectives that were not discussed in this chapter – phenomenology, semiotics, Frankfurt schools, and critical theory. Jones (1998) is a collection of crossdisciplinary papers that focus on the community formation of CMC; some papers are empirical, others descriptive, still others theoretical. Rheingold (1993), the standard text on how CMC is creating and changing communities, is highly readable and contains useful descriptions of a variety of CMC uses not explored in this chapter (e.g., MUDs and MOOs). Smith and Kollock (1999) provides an excellent collection of balanced sociology essays that explore the opposing views of CMC as community creating or as community destroying. For a history of computers themselves, see Augarten (1984); for a history of the Internet, see Hafner and Lyon (1996); for a comprehensive treatment of Internet language, see Crystal (2001).

References

Adams, Carol J. 1996. " 'This is not our fathers' pornography': Sex, Lies, and Computers." In Ess. Pp. 147–70.

Allen, Brenda J. 1995. "Gender and Computer-mediated Communication," *Sex Roles: a Journal of Research* 32(7/8): 557–64.

Augarten, Stan. 1984. *Bit by Bit: an Illustrated History of Computers*. New York: Ticknor and Fields.

Baym, Nancy K. 1998. "The Emergence of On-line Community." In Jones. Pp. 35–68.

Biber, Douglas. 1988. *Variation across Speech and Writing*. Cambridge: Cambridge University Press.

Castells, Manuel. 1996. *The Rise of the Network Society*. Malden MA: Blackwell.

Crystal, David. 1997. "Vanishing Languages," *Civilization* (Feb./March): 40–45.
    2001. *Language and the Internet*. Cambridge: Cambridge University Press.
    1997. "Cyberspeech," *Time* (June 23): 23.
Davis, Boyd H. and Jeutonne P. Brewer. 1997. *Electronic Discourse: Linguistic Individuals in Virtual Space*. Albany: State University of New York Press.
Digital Divide Network 2001. Digital divide basics fact sheet. *http://digitaldividenetwork. org/content/stories/index.cfm?key=168*.
Ess, Charles, ed. 1996. *Philosophical Perspectives on Computer-Mediated Communication*. Albany: State University of New York Press.
Ferguson, Charles A. 1994. "Dialect, Register, and Genre: Working Assumptions about Conventionalization." In *Sociolinguistic Perspectives on Register*, eds. Douglas Biber and Edward Finegan. New York: Oxford University Press. Pp. 15–30.
Ferrara, Kathleen, Hans Brunner, and Greg Whittemore. 1991. "Interactive Written Discourse as an Emergent Register," *Written Communication* 8: 8–34.
Hafner, Katie and Matthew Lyon. 1996. *Where Wizards Stay Up Late: the Origins of the Internet*. New York: Simon & Schuster.
Hawisher, Gail E. and Cynthia L. Selfe. 1998. "Reflections on Computers and Composition Studies at the Century's End." In Snyder. Pp. 3–19.
Herring, Susan. 1996b. "Posting in a Different Voice: Gender and Ethics in Computer-mediated Communication." In Ess. Pp. 115–45.
Herring, Susan C., ed. 1996a. *Computer-Mediated Communication: Linguistic, Social and Cross-Cultural Perspectives*. Amsterdam: Benjamins.
Hilz, Starr Roxanne and Kenneth Johnson. 1990. "User Satisfaction with Computer-Mediated Communication Systems," *Management Science* 36: 739–64.
Hilz, Starr Roxanne and Barry Wellman. 1997. "Asynchronous Learning Networks as a Virtual Classroom," *Communication of the ACM* 40(9): 44–50.
Ipsos-Reid. 2001. Has the World Wide Web hit its high-water mark? *http://www.ipsosreid.com/ media/content/displaypr.cfm?id_to_ view=1154*.
Iyer, Pico. 1997. "The Haiti Test: Proving the World *Isn't* Small – Except in Our Minds," *The Nation* 28: 30–31.
Jones, Steven G., ed. 1998. *Cybersociety 2.0: Revisiting Computer-Mediated Communication and Community*. Thousand Oaks CA: Sage.
Kachru, Braj B. and Cecil L. Nelson. 1996. "World Englishes." In *Sociolinguistics and Language Teaching*, eds. Sandra Lee McKay and Nancy H. Hornberger. Cambridge: Cambridge University Press. Pp. 71–102.
Kress, Gunther. 1998. "Visual and Verbal Modes of Representation in Electronically Mediated Communication: The Potentials of New Forms of Text." In Snyder. Pp. 53–79.
Lakoff, George and Mark Johnson. 1980. *Metaphors We Live By*. Chicago: University of Chicago Press.
Lawler, John M. 1995. "Metaphors We Compute By." A Lecture Delivered to Staff of the Informational Technology Division, University of Michigan *http://www.ling.lsa.umich.edu/ jlawler/meta4compute.html*.
Mabrito, Mark. 1995. "The E-mail Discussion Group: an Opportunity for Discourse Analysis," *Business Communication Quarterly* 58(2): 10–12.
McLeod, Poppy Lauretta. 1992. "An Assessment of the Experimental Literature on Electronic Support of Group Work: Results of a Meta-Analysis," *Human-Computer Interaction* 7: 257–80.
Murray, Denise E. 1989. "When the Medium Determines Turns: Turn-taking in Computer Conversation." In *Working with Language*, ed. Hywel Coleman. The Hague: Mouton. Pp. 210–22.
    1991. *Conversation for Action: the Computer Terminal as Medium of Communication*. Amsterdam: Benjamins.
    1993. *Knowledge Machines: Language and Information in a Technological Society*. London: Longman.
National Center for Education Statistics. 2000. "Internet Access in U.S. Public Schools and Classrooms: 1994–2000." *http://www.ed.gov/Technology/*.

Network Wizards. 1997. Internet domain survey. *http://www.nw.com/zone/WWW/top.html*

Nielsen//Netratings. 2001. 429 million people worldwide have internet access. *http://www.nielsen-netratings.com/news.jsp?thetype=dateandtheyear= 2001andthemonth=5*

Pennycook, Alastair. 1994. *The Cultural Politics of English as a World Language*. New York: Longman.

Rheingold, Howard. 1993. *The Virtual Community: Homesteading on the Electronic Frontier*. Reading MA: Addison-Wesley.

Shea, Virginia. 1994. *Netiquette*. San Francisco: Albion.

Smith, Marc A. and Peter Kollock, eds. 1999. *Communities in Cyberspace*. London: Routledge.

Snyder, Ilana, ed. 1998. *Page to Screen: Taking Literacy into the Electronic Era*. London: Routledge.

Stefik, Mark. 1997. *Internet Dreams: Archetypes, Myths and Metaphors*. Cambridge MA: MIT Press.

The Random House Dictionary of the English Language. 1969. New York: Random House.

US Department of Commerce. 2000. "Falling through the Net: Toward Digital Inclusion." *http://www.ntia.doc.gov/ntiahome/fttn00/contents00.html*.

US Department of Education. 1996. "Getting America's Students Ready for the Twenty-First Century: Meeting the Technology Literacy Challenge." A Report to the Nation on Technology and Education. *http://www.ed.gov/Technology/Plan/NatTechPlan/inex.html*.

Warschauer, Mark. 1999. *Electronic Literacies: Language, Culture, and Power in Online Education*. Mahwah NJ: Erlbaum.

Werry, Christopher C. 1996. "Linguistic and Interactional Features of Internet Relay Chat." In Herring. Pp. 47–63.

26

Language attitudes to speech

DENNIS R. PRESTON

Editors' introduction

Some people recognize they speak with an accent, but many others believe their speech carries no accent. The speech of *other* groups may be accented, but the speech of our own friends and neighbors we tend to perceive as accent*less*. To a great extent, accents mark the speech of *others*, of outsiders to our own group, but not of "us." From the perspective of outsiders, of course, it is not their speech but *ours* that carries the accent! Accents are salient triggers in our judgments of people. We favor and disfavor people – like and dislike them – partly because of the way they speak. In this chapter, Dennis Preston recounts his investigation of language attitudes among college students in the Midwest and William Labov's earlier investigation in New York City.

Respondents college students in Michigan identified fourteen dialect areas of the USA, the most important being the South, the North, the Northeast, and the Southwest. In characterizing these dialects, respondents college students used polar terms like *slow* or *fast*, *polite* or *rude*, *smart* or *dumb*, *good* or *bad*, and *educated* or *uneducated*. As in earlier investigations, these judgments about language cluster into a set related to *standardness* and another set related to *friendliness*. The respondents gave high marks to their own Northern dialect on the characteristics related to "standardness," but they rated the Southern accent more "friendly." Preston interprets this as a group dividing its "symbolic linguistic capital," apportioning a significant amount to their own dialect for one set of characteristics (in the case of the Michiganders, for standardness) but not for the other (friendliness). By contrast, the dialect of the South was ranked low for standardness but high for friendliness. New York City English was disparaged by college students in Michigan and Alabama, and the chapter rehearses findings from the mid 1960s in which New York City respondents who were asked to judge the job suitability of tape-recorded speakers imposed severe penalties on speakers who dropped /r/ from words like *beer* and *cart*.

Language attitudes are a significant part of how we assess one another. Understanding folk attitudes toward ways of speaking contributes to our knowledge of how speech can influence educational success, housing opportunities, and job opportunities, as well as other critically important matters for maintaining equality in a democratic society.

> Beneath that deceptive North Carolina drawl, there's a crisp intelligence.
>
> Of Charles Kuralt, on his retirement, in the *Lansing* (Michigan) *State Journal*

> "What's a Michigan accent? I always thought that people from Michigan and other Midwestern states are known for a lack of accent."
>
> A columnist in the *Detroit Free Press*

In most of this book, discussions of the varieties of language in the USA are based on the ways people talk. In this chapter, we investigate not how people talk but the attitudes we have to those different ways of talking. If you think about it, you'll probably have to admit that you do not have the same attitude to a message delivered by a speaker from Alabama as you do to one delivered by a speaker from New York City; nor do you respond in the same way to men's and women's speech, or to higher-status versus lower-status speech, or to European American versus African American English, or to Spanish versus English, but we focus here on the different attitudes we have toward regional varieties (or "dialects") of US English.

It is likely that language is only a carrier of the attitudes we have toward the speakers of different varieties. If we like people from Maine, it is probably true that we will have a positive attitude towards their speech; if we dislike Californians, we will probably have a negative attitude towards theirs.

This commonsense reasoning, however, leaves a number of questions unanswered. Here are three important ones that I will deal with.

(1)   Where do people in the USA believe dialect distinctions exist? For example, maybe we like people from Wyoming and dislike people from Montana, but do we believe that Montana and Wyoming are different dialect areas?

(2)   What does it mean to have a positive or negative attitude to a dialect? Are there different kinds of attitudes? If so, what are they and how are they distributed in US English?

(3)   Which linguistic features allow us to distinguish among dialect areas (and play the biggest role in triggering our attitudes)?

In language attitude research, it is important to determine which regionally or socially distributed varieties of a language are thought to be distinct. Where do people believe linguistically distinct places are? That is, what mental maps of regional speech areas do they have?

Suppose we played authentic examples of Midwestern US speech for judges and they consistently rated them positively. It would be misleading to say they had positive attitudes toward Midwestern speech because we do not know if the Midwest is a linguistically distinct area in their mental (dialect) maps. What we can say is that the judges had generally positive attitudes to those particular voices (which happened to be Midwestern), but we do not know if they could have identified such voices correctly as Midwestern ones.

How can we devise research that avoids this problem? Following the lead of cultural geographers, we could simply ask respondents to draw maps of where they believe varieties are different. Figure 26-1 is a typical example of such a hand-drawn map from a young Michigander.

Although we may profit from an investigation of these individual maps (for example, by looking at the labels assigned various regions), their usefulness for general language attitude studies depends on the degree to which generalizations may be drawn from large numbers of such maps. This can be done with computer

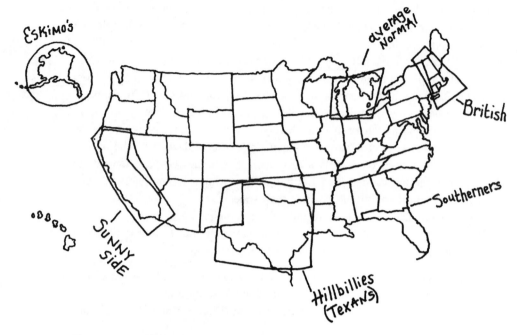

Figure 26-1 *A Michigan hand-drawn map*

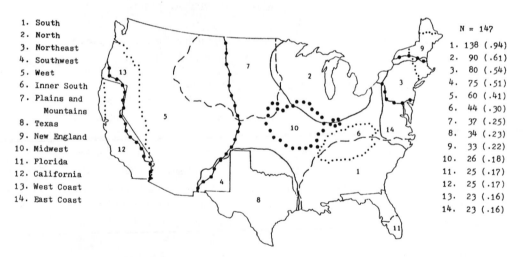

Figure 26-2 *Computer-assisted generalizations of hand-drawn maps showing where southeastern Michigan respondents believe speech regions exist in the USA*

assistance by first copying the boundary of each region from each respondent's map and then drawing an outline of each region based on the most general agreement among all the respondents for both the identity and shape of each region. Figure 26-2 shows a composite mental map of US regional speech areas derived from the hand-drawn maps of 147 southeastern Michigan respondents (from a variety of status and age groups, male and female).

We now have an answer to the first question above (at least for southeastern Michigan respondents). We know that the South, the North, the Northeast, the Southwest, and so on are (with decreasing importance) real dialect areas for these respondents, and we have a pretty good idea of where they believe these dialect areas are.

Now we can begin to fashion an answer to the second question above. What characteristics would be relevant to an investigation of attitudes to these speech areas? Again, the best method is to go to the respondents themselves. Characteristics for judging were elicited by showing a large number of Michigan respondents a simplified version of figure 26-2 and asking them to mention any characteristics of the speech of those regions that came to mind. The most frequently mentioned items were arranged into the following pairs.

slow – fast	formal – casual	educated – uneducated
smart – dumb	polite – rude	snobbish – down-to-earth
nasal – not nasal	normal – abnormal	friendly – unfriendly
drawl – no drawl	twang – no twang	bad English – good English

It was important, of course, that the Michigan map was shown to Michigan respondents and that the characteristics elicited were to be used by Michigan judges. Respondents from other areas have different mental maps and might list other characteristics.

The judges (eighty-five young, European American southern Michigan residents who were undergraduate students at Michigan State University) were shown a simplified version of figure 26-2 and given the following instructions:

> This map shows where many people from southern Michigan believe speech differences are in the U.S. We will give you a list of descriptive words that local people have told us could be used to describe the speech of these various regions. Please think about twelve of these regions, and check off how each pair of words applies to the speech there.
>
> For example, imagine that we gave you the pair "ugly" and "beautiful"

ugly ____ ____ ____ ____ ____ ____ beautiful
        a   b   c   d   e   f

> You would use the scale as follows:
> If you very strongly agree that the speech of a region is "ugly," select "a."
> If you strongly agree that the speech of a region is "ugly," select "b."
> If you agree that the speech of a region is "ugly," select "c."
> If you agree that the speech of a region is "beautiful," select "d."
> If you strongly agree that the speech of a region is "beautiful," select "e."
>
> If you very strongly agree that the speech of a region is "beautiful," select "f."

The next step in this research is to determine whether or not the number of paired items used in evaluating the regional dialects can be reduced – an attempt to refine the answer to question 2 above. This is normally carried out by means of

Table 26-1 *The two factor groups from the ratings of all areas*

Factor Group 1		Factor Group 2	
Smart	.76	Polite	.74
Educated	.75	Friendly	.74
Normal	.65	Down-to-earth	.62
Good English	.63	(Normal)	(.27)
No drawl	.62	(Casual)	(.27
No twang	.57		
Casual [Formal]	−.49		
Fast	.43		
Down-to-earth [Snobbish]	−.32		

Note: Parenthesized factors indicate items that are within the 0.25–0.29 range; "−" prefixes indicate negative loadings and should be interpreted as loadings of the opposite value (given in brackets)

a factor analysis, a statistical procedure that allows us to group together those characteristics that were rated so similarly that there is no important difference among them. The results of such an analysis for all areas rated are shown in table 26.1.

Two groups of paired items emerged from this statistical procedure. The first (which I will call "Standard") contains those characteristics that we associate with education and the formal attributes of the society. Note, however, that the last three items in this group ("Formal," "Fast," and "Snobbish") are not necessarily positive traits. The second group (which I will call "Friendly") contains very different sorts of characteristics (including two that are negative in Group 1 but positive here – "Down-to-earth" and "Casual").

These two groups will not surprise those who have looked at any previous studies of language attitudes. As researchers have noted, the two main dimensions of evaluation for language varieties are most often those of *social status* ("Standard" above) and *group solidarity* ("Friendly" above).

A full analysis of these data would go on to consider how each of the rated regions fared with regard to these two groups, but even a sample of two particularly important areas (for these respondents and doubtless others) will provide good insight into the mechanisms at work here.

Let's look at the respondent ratings of areas 1 and 2 from figure 26-2. Region 1 is the US "South," and figure 26-2 shows that it was outlined by 94 percent (138) of the 147 respondents who drew hand-drawn maps. For these southeastern Michigan respondents, the South is clearly the most important regional speech area in the USA. Although one might note anecdotal or popular culture characterizations of why that might be so, a look at figure 26-3 will provide an even more dramatic explanation.

I asked southeastern Michigan respondents to rate the fifty states (and Washington, D.C. and New York City) for "correctness," and it is clear that

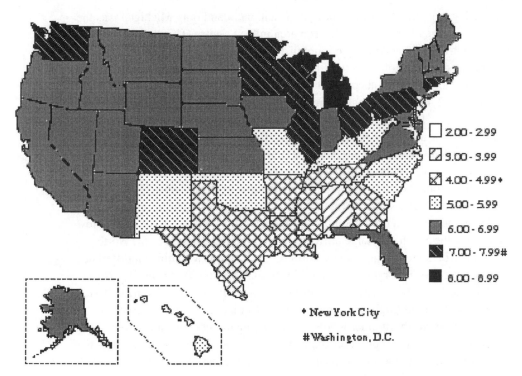

☐ 2.00 - 2.99

▨ 3.00 - 3.99

⊠ 4.00 - 4.99♦

⠿ 5.00 - 5.99

▤ 6.00 - 6.99

◤ 7.00 - 7.99#

■ 8.00 - 8.99

♦ New York City

Washington, D.C.

Figure 26-3 *Means of ratings for language "correctness" by Michigan respondents for US English (on a scale of 1 to 10, where 1 = least and 10 = most correct)*

the South fares worst. On a one-to-ten scale (with one being "least correct"), Alabama is the only state that reaches a mean score in the 3.00–3.99 range, and, with the exception of New York City and New Jersey, the surrounding southern states (Texas, Arkansas, Louisiana, Mississippi, Tennessee, and Georgia) are the only other areas rated in the 4.00–4.99 range. In short, the importance of southern speech would appear to lie in its distinctiveness along one particular dimension – it is incorrect English. If that were not thought to be so, why would the Michigan journalist who wrote the lines at the beginning of this chapter have felt compelled to say that Charles Kuralt's "crisp intelligence" was somehow hidden "beneath [his] North Carolina drawl"?

The second most frequently rated region (by 90 out of 147 respondents or 61 percent) is the local one, called "North" in figure 26-2, but more accurately "North Central" or "Great Lakes." At first, one might be tempted to assert that the local area is always important, but a closer look at figure 26-3 will show that these southeastern Michigan raters may have something else in mind when they single out their home area. It is only Michigan that scores in the heady 8.00–8.99 range for language "correctness." In short, perception of language correctness (in the positive direction) determines the second most important area for these respondents. Look back at figure 26-1; this respondent was not unique among the Michigan respondents in identifying Michigan – and only Michigan – as the uniquely "normal" or "correct" speech area in the country. This belief may help explain why the other Michigan journalist cited at the beginning of this chapter was puzzled to find reference to a Michigan accent. How could anyone believe that such "normal" speech could constitute an "accent"!

Table 26-2 shows the mean scores for the individual attributes for the North and the South. Perhaps the most notable fact is that the rank orders are nearly opposites. "Casual" is lowest rated for the North but highest for the South. "Drawl" is lowest rated (meaning "speaks with a drawl") for the South but highest rated (meaning "speaks without a drawl") for the North. In factor group terms, the scores for Group 2 (and "–1" loadings) are the lowest-ranked ones for the North; these same characteristics ("Casual," "Friendly," "Down-to-earth," and "Polite") are the highest ranked for the South. Similarly, Group 1 characteristics are all low ranked for the South; the same attributes are all highest ranked for the North.

These scores are not just ordered differently. There is a significant difference between the attribute ratings for the North and the South, except for "Nasal" and "Polite." For those attributes in group 1 ("No Drawl," "No Twang," "Fast," "Educated," "Good English," "Smart," and "Normal"), the means scores are all higher for the North. In other words, these Michigan raters consider themselves superior to the South for every attribute of the "Standard" factor group. This is not very surprising, considering the results from earlier research on "correct" English shown in figure 26-3 (and well-known folk and popular culture attitudes).

For those attributes in group 2 (or –1), the mean score is higher for the South for "Casual," "Friendly," and "Down-to-earth." There is no significant difference for "Polite" (as noted above), and the North leads the South in group 2 attributes only for "Normal," but it is important to note that "Normal" is to be found in both groups. These data suggest that, at least for these eighty-five young Michiganders, the "Friendly" attributes (except for "Polite") are more highly associated with southern speech than with speech from the local area.

A few other statistical facts confirm and add to the results reported so far. Note (in table 26-2) that no attribute rating for the North falls below 3.5 (the median value of the six-point scale), while all of the group 1 ("Standard") attributes are rated below that score for the South. Even more dramatically, statistical tests of the mean scores for North and South independently show that there is no significant break between any two adjacent mean scores for ratings of the attributes for the North. On the other hand, there *is* such a significant difference for the South between the group 2 (and –1) attributes and the group 1 attributes, as shown by the "*" in table 26-2. In other words, there is a continuum of relatively positive scores for the North and a sharp break between the two groups for the South.

Since many of the hand-drawn maps of US dialect areas by Michigan respondents label the local area "standard," "normal (as in figure 26-1)," "correct," and "good English," there is obviously no dissatisfaction with the local variety as a representative of "correct English." What, though, is the source of the preference for the southern varieties along the "friendly" dimensions? Perhaps a group has

Table 26-2 *Mean scores of individual factors for North and South*

Mean scores (ordered) South				Mean scores North			
Factor	Mean	Attribute	Rank	Rank	Factor	Mean	Attribute
−1 and 2	4.66	Casual	1	12	−1 and 2	3.53	Casual
2	4.58	Friendly	2	9.5	2	4.00	Friendly
2 and −1	4.54	Down-to-earth	3	6	2 and −1	4.19	Down-to-earth
2	4.20	Polite	4	9.5	2	4.00	Polite
Ø	4.09	Not nasal	5	11	Ø	3.94	Not nasal
		*					
1 and 2	‡3.22	Normal [Abnormal]	6	3	1 and 2	4.94	Normal
1	‡3.04	Smart [Dumb]	7	4	1	4.53	Smart
1	#‡2.96	No twang [Twang]	8	2	1	5.07	No twang
1	‡2.86	Good English [Bad Eng.]	9	5	1	4.41	Good English
1	‡2.72	Educated [Uneducated]	10	8	1	4.09	Educated
1	#‡2.42	Fast [Slow]	11	7	1	4.12	Fast
1	‡2.22	No drawl [Drawl]	12	1	1	5.11	No drawl

"*" marks the only significant (0.05) break between adjacent means scores; "‡" marks values below 3.5 (shown in brackets here); "#" indicates the only mean scores where there were significant differences for gender; in both cases women ranked the South lower – assuming "twang" and "slow" are negative

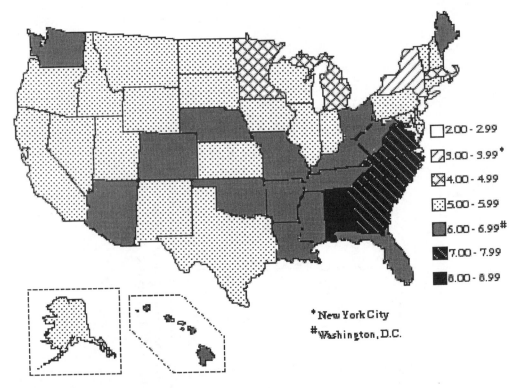

Figure 26-4 *Means of ratings for language "pleasantness" by AL respondents for US English (on a scale of 1 to 10, where 1 = least and 10 = most pleasant)*

a tendency to use up what might be called the "symbolic linguistic capital" of its variety in one way or the other (but not both). Speakers of majority varieties have a tendency to spend the symbolic capital of their variety on a "Standard" dimension. Speakers of minority varieties usually spend their symbolic capital on the "Friendly" dimension.

Perhaps many northerners (here, southeastern Michiganders) have spent all their symbolic linguistic capital on the standardness of local English. As such, it has come to represent the norms of schools, media, and public interaction and has, thus, become less suitable for interpersonal value. These young Michiganders, therefore, assign an alternate kind of prestige to a variety they imagine would have more value than theirs for interpersonal and casual interaction, precisely the sorts of dimensions associated with group 2.

If this is true, can we show it in a pattern of ratings from southern judges? Unfortunately, I do not have responses to a set of labels (as in the Michigan study), but I will show you how undergraduate students at Auburn University (Alabama) rated areas for "pleasantness."

I hope figure 26-4 reminds you of figure 26-3 in reverse. Recall, however, that it is a rating of language "pleasantness" (group 2 characteristics), not language "correctness" (group 1 characteristics). Alabamians find their state as uniquely *pleasant* as Michiganders found theirs *correct*. These southerners have used up their linguistic capital on those aspects of their language that symbolize local rather than national norms, private rather than public values, family and friends rather than unknowns. (The Michigan map of "pleasantness" (which is not shown) looks a good deal more like the Alabama map of "correctness," completing the pattern of preferences I have outlined so far.)

In summary then, both the mental maps of and attitudinal responses to regional varieties of US English are dominated by the notions of "correctness" (the more powerful) and "pleasantness." Further, a great deal of folk belief and language ideology stems from these facts. Speakers of "correct" dialects do not believe they speak dialects, and educational and even legal repercussions arise from personal and institutional devaluing of "incorrect" varieties. On the other hand, speakers of prejudiced-against varieties (like prejudiced groups in general) derive solidarity from their distinct cultural behaviors – in this case, linguistic ones.

I would like to tell you that we also know a great deal about which specific linguistic features of regional varieties play the most important role in triggering attitudes, but too little work of this sort has been done. You'll have to settle for one example.

You have already seen that New York City (NYC) English is a prejudiced-against variety by both Michigan and Alabama speakers for both "correct" and "pleasant" dimensions. Aware of the low regard in which their variety is held, New Yorkers have, as a rule, severe "linguistic insecurity." Work done in the 1960s shows that they are also sensitive to some linguistic features that they most strongly associate with their "bad" speech.

The pronunciation of "r" (after vowels) in NYC is the "prestige" or "correct" form. Higher-status speakers and all speakers when they are more careful of their speech are more likely to pronounce such words as *car*, *here*, and *door* with a final "r" sound. In fact, New Yorkers never completely delete "r"; they produce a little "uh" sound in its place ("cah-uh," "hih-uh," "doh-uh"), but this is the less prestigious pronunciation.

In a clever experiment, the linguist William Labov asked NYC judges to listen to passages containing such sentences as "He *darted* out about *four* feet *before* a car and got hit *hard*" and "We didn't have the *heart* to play ball *or cards* all *morning*." He got the same female respondents to read these passages several times and obtained samples in which they always used "r" and others in which they deleted "r" only once (one in the word *hard* in the first passage and another in *cards* in the second). He called these passages the "consistent r" and "inconsistent r" samples. He then played both samples of each woman's performances interspersed with other voice samples and asked NYC residents from different social status groups to pretend they were personnel managers who were to judge the voice samples they heard for "occupational suitability" along a seven-point scale:

> TV personality – executive secretary – receptionist – switchboard operator – salesgirl – factory worker – none of these

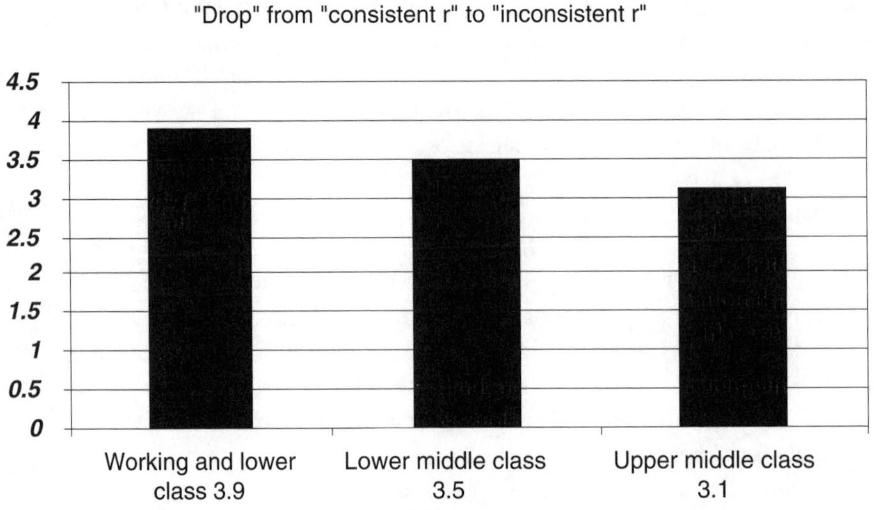

"Drop" from "consistent r" to "inconsistent r"

Figure 26-5 *Three social status group judgments of lower "occupational suitability" of "inconsistent r" production*

The judges in every social status group rated the "inconsistent r" performances dramatically lower on the occupational suitability scale. Figure 26-5 shows the average drop in ratings along the occupational suitability scale between the "consistent r" and "inconsistent r" performances. For example, if a lower-class or working-class judge said that a "consistent r" performance was that of an "executive secretary," then he or she was likely to rate the "inconsistent r" presentation as that of a "factory worker" (four steps down the scale). It's interesting to note that upper-middle-class judges rated the two performances less dramatically different (only three steps down the scale for the "inconsistent r" performance), but we cannot concern ourselves here with why that is so.

As these ratings show, New Yorkers are sensitive to even "mild" use of "r"-deletion, and they rate speakers three to four full categories down on the occupational scale when they fail to realize even just a single one of four or five instances of this feature. Such tests could be developed for a large range of linguistic features of US English. Of course, they should test the sensitivity of out-group as well as in-group respondents (expecting that different features and different degrees of sensitivity might emerge).

Finally, although the research tradition is not as long or as active, particularly in the USA, some attitude researchers have collected and analyzed overt folk comment about language. When asked how New Yorkers speak, for example, a southern Indiana respondent replied with a little folk poetry (showing that sensitivity to NYC "r" is not an exclusively in-group phenomenon):

T'ree little boids, sitting on a coib
Eating doity woims and saying doity woids.

Other comments are more detailed and revealing. In the following exchange, Michiganders D, G, and S assure the fieldworker (H) that they (just like national newscasters) are speakers of "standard" English:

> H: Northern English is standard English?
> D: Yeah, yeah.
> G: That's right. What you hear around here.
> S: Yeah, standard.
> D: Because that's what you hear on the TV. If you listen to the news-cast of the national news, they sound like we do; they sound sort of Midwestern, like we do.

And, not surprisingly, Michiganders know where English that is not so standard is spoken:

> G: Because of TV though I think there's kind of a standard English that's evolving.
> D: Yeah.
> G: And the kind of thing you hear on TV is something that's broadcast across the country, so most people are aware of that, but there are definite accents in the South.

We could analyze more complex (and rewarding) conversations about social and regional varieties of US English to show not only relatively static folk belief and attitudes but also how these beliefs and attitudes are used in argument and persuasion. Such investigations are particularly important in showing what deep-seated presuppositions about language we all have.

In many of these conversations (and revealed in the analysis of them as well) there is nothing to contradict the patterns of attitudes towards varieties already discussed here. Correctness dominates in US concerns for regional variation, and those regions that fare worst in our national assessment of correctness (the South and NYC) loom largest in our identification of regional distinctiveness.

Suggestions for further reading

The classic work on the statistical treatment of language attitudes by means of attribute rating scales is Lambert et al. (1960), and the first important work to treat regional and social varieties of a single language was Tucker and Lambert (1969). More recent work (and interpretations) is summarized in Ryan, Giles, and Sebastian (1982). A good introduction to the social geographer's interest in mental maps is Gould and White (1974). These mapping and rating procedures are applied to language variation data in Preston (1989), and a more recent summary of such work for US varieties can be found in Preston (1996).

The classic study of English in New York City is Labov (1966), which contains a variety of quantitative and qualitative approaches to the study of attitudes.

A special issue of the *Journal of Language and Social Psychology* (Milroy and Preston 1999) is devoted to a study of the influence of specific linguistic variables on perception and attitude. Conversational data on US varieties are treated extensively in Niedzielski and Preston (1999).

References

Gould, Peter and Rodney White. 1974. *Mental Maps*. Harmondsworth, Middlesex: Penguin.

Labov, William. 1966. *The Social Stratification of English in New York City*. Arlington, VA: Center for Applied Linguistics.

Lambert, Wallace E., R. C. Hodgsen, R. C. Gardner, and Samuel Fillenbaum. 1960. "Evaluational Reaction to Spoken Language," *Journal of Abnormal and Social Psychology* 60: 44–51.

Milroy, Lesley and Dennis R. Preston, eds. 1999. Special issue of *Journal of Language and Social Psychology*, March.

Niedzielski, Nancy and Dennis R. Preston. 1999. *Folk Linguistics*. Berlin: Mouton de Gruyter.

Preston, Dennis R. 1989. *Perceptual Dialectology*. Dordrecht: Foris.

1996. "Where the Worst English is Spoken." In *Focus on the USA*, ed. Edgar Schneider. Amsterdam and Philadelphia: Benjamins. Pp. 297–360.

Ryan, Ellen Bouchard, Howard Giles, and Richard J. Sebastian. 1982. "An Integrated Perspective for the Study of Attitudes toward Language Variation." In *Attitudes Towards Language Variation*, eds. Ellen Bouchard Ryan and Howard Giles. London: Arnold, 1–19.

Tucker, G. Richard and Wallace E. Lambert. 1969. "White and Negro Listeners' Reactions to Various American-English Dialects," *Social Forces* 47: 463–68.

Index